COSMETOLOGY FUNDAMENTALS
A DESIGNER'S APPROACH®

© 2009, 2010, 2013 Pivot Point International, Inc.

ISBN 978-1-937964-35-1 (Volume 1)
ISBN 978-1-937964-49-8 (2 Volume Set)

3rd Edition
7th Printing, June 2016
Printed in Hong Kong

Cosmetology Fundamentals, A Designer's Approach is published with the same core theory concepts required for cosmetology licensure that are contained in *Salon Fundamentals® Cosmetology, A Resource for Your Cosmetology Career*. *Cosmetology Fundamentals*, in conjunction with Pivot Point's *A Designer's Approach* library, meets and exceeds the compliance requirements for cosmetology licensure.

This publication is protected under U.S. and worldwide copyright laws and may not be copied, reproduced, stored in a retrieval system, transmitted, broadcast or quoted in whole or in part in any form, or by any means: electronically or mechanically, printed, photocopied, recorded, scanned or otherwise, nor may derivative works be created from it without written permission from Pivot Point International, Inc. More detailed information on copyright can be found at: pivot-point.com/copyright.html.

Trademark: Pivot Point, the Pivot Point Logo, the P Design, and *A Designer's Approach* are trademarks or registered trademarks of Pivot Point International, Inc., in the United States and other countries, and may not be used without written permission.

Pivot Point International, Inc.
World Headquarters
8725 W. Higgins Road, Suite 700
Chicago, IL 60631 USA

847-866-0500
pivot-point.com

SCAN THIS CODE
TO LOG IN TO *ARTIST ACCESS*
DA.ARTIST-ACCESS.COM

UNIT 1 THEORY ESSENTIALS

UNIT 2 HAIR SERVICES

UNIT 3 NAIL AND SKIN SERVICES

UNIT 1
THEORY ESSENTIALS

CHAPTER 1, PROFESSIONAL DEVELOPMENT 21

1.1 HEALTHY BODY AND MIND 23
REST AND RELAXATION 23
EXERCISE 23
NUTRITION 24
HYGIENE 25
IMAGE 26
ERGONOMICS 29

1.2 EFFECTIVE COMMUNICATION 32
NONVERBAL COMMUNICATION 32
VERBAL COMMUNICATION 33

1.3 HUMAN RELATIONS 36
PERSONALITY 36
TEAMWORK 40
ETHICS 40

CHAPTER 2, SALON ECOLOGY 43

2.1 MICROBIOLOGY 45
BACTERIA 45
GROWTH OF BACTERIA 47
VIRUSES 47
EXTERNAL PARASITES 48
INFECTION 48
IMMUNITY 49

2.2 INFECTION CONTROL 50
SANITATION 51
DISINFECTION 53
STERILIZATION 56
INFECTION CONTROL GUIDELINES 57

2.3 FIRST AID 58
BLEEDING AND WOUNDS 58
BURNS 58
CHOKING 59
FAINTING 59
EYE INJURY 60

CHAPTER 3, ANATOMY AND PHYSIOLOGY 61

3.1 BUILDING BLOCKS OF THE HUMAN BODY 63
CELLS 64

TISSUES 6
ORGANS 6
BODY SYSTEMS 6

3.2 BASIC BODY SYSTEMS 6
THE SKELETAL SYSTEM 6
THE MUSCULAR SYSTEM 7
THE CIRCULATORY SYSTEM 7
THE NERVOUS SYSTEM 7
THE DIGESTIVE SYSTEM 8
THE EXCRETORY SYSTEM 8
THE RESPIRATORY SYSTEM 8
THE ENDOCRINE SYSTEM 8
THE REPRODUCTIVE SYSTEM 8
THE INTEGUMENTARY SYSTEM 8

CHAPTER 4, ELECTRICITY 8

4.1 PRINCIPLES OF ELECTRICITY 8
VOCABULARY OF ELECTRICITY 8
ELECTRIC CURRENT 9
SAFETY MEASURES 9

4.2 ELECTRICITY IN COSMETOLOGY 9
EFFECTS OF ELECTRIC CURRENT 9
ELECTROTHERAPY 9
LIGHT THERAPY 10

CHAPTER 5, CHEMISTRY 10

5.1 MATTER 10
ELEMENTS 1
CHEMICAL BONDS 1

5.2 THE pH SCALE 1

5.3 CHEMISTRY OF COSMETICS 1
COSMETIC CLASSIFICATIONS 1
SHAMPOOS 1
RINSES AND CONDITIONERS 12
PERMS 12
RELAXERS 12
CURL REFORMATION 12
HAIR COLOR 12
PRODUCT INFORMATION 13

CHAPTER 6, SALON BUSINESS 137

6.1 THE SALON INDUSTRY 139
WHAT YOU NEED TO KNOW 139
YOUR PROFESSIONAL GOALS 140

6.2 JOB SEARCH 140
RESUMÉS 141
JOB INTERVIEWS 142
EVALUATING THE SALON 144

6.3 PROFESSIONAL RELATIONSHIPS 146
NETWORKING 147
BUILDING A CLIENTELE 147
THE DESIGNER-CLIENT RELATIONSHIP 148
THE DESIGNER-STAFF RELATIONSHIP 150
PERFORMANCE REVIEW 151

6.4 SALON OWNERSHIP 151
SELF-APPRAISAL 151
TYPES OF SALON OWNERSHIP 153
REQUIREMENTS OF A SALON 154
GETTING THE RIGHT ADVICE 154
SPACE REQUIREMENTS AND FLOOR PLANS 155
BORROWING MONEY 156
RENTAL AGREEMENTS 157
TYPES OF INSURANCE 157
TAXES 158
EXPENSES AND INCOME 158
SALON PHILOSOPHY, POLICIES AND PROCEDURES 160
SALON OPERATION 161

6.5 SALON RETAILING 166
SELLING 166
PROFESSIONAL PRODUCTS 168
CLOSING THE SALE 170
BUYER TYPES 171
FOLLOW-UP 173
EFFECTIVE DISPLAYS 174

UNIT 2
HAIR SERVICES

CHAPTER 7, TRICHOLOGY 177

7.1 HAIR THEORY 179
HAIR BULB FORMATION 179

HAIR GROWTH 180
HAIR STRUCTURE AND BEHAVIOR 182
NATURAL HAIR COLOR 184

7.2 HAIR CARE 185
HAIR EVALUATION 185
COMMON HAIR CONDITIONS 187
COMMON SCALP CONDITIONS 189
HAIR LOSS 189

7.3 DRAPING, SHAMPOOING AND SCALP MASSAGE . . . 195
DRAPING THEORY 195
SHAMPOOING AND CONDITIONING THEORY 196
SCALP MASSAGE THEORY 198
DRAPING, SHAMPOOING AND
SCALP MASSAGE ESSENTIALS 200
INFECTION CONTROL AND SAFETY 203
01 BASIC DRAPING, SHAMPOOING AND CONDITIONING . . . 203
02 BASIC SCALP MASSAGE 210

CHAPTER 8, DESIGN DECISIONS 215

8.1 DESIGN COMPOSITION 217
SEE AND THINK AS A DESIGNER 219
DESIGN ELEMENTS 221
DESIGN PRINCIPLES 232
BALANCE 235
CREATE AND ADAPT AS A DESIGNER 235

8.2 DESIGN ADAPTABILITY 236
PROPORTION 237
HAIR 251
CLOTHING 255
LIFESTYLE 257

8.3 CLIENT COMMUNICATION 258
THE FOUR SERVICE ESSENTIALS 258
CONTRIBUTORS TO EFFECTIVE COMMUNICATION 260

CHAPTER 9, SCULPTURE 267

9.1 SCULPTING THEORY 269
HAIR SCULPTURE ANALYSIS 270
FOUR BASIC FORMS 272
COMBINATION FORMS 275

9.2 SCULPTING TOOLS 277
SHEARS 278
TAPER SHEARS 280
RAZORS 282
CLIPPERS 284
COMBS 285

COSMETOLOGY FUNDAMENTALS

| 9.3 | **SCULPTING SKILLS** | 285 |

PIVOT POINT'S SEVEN SCULPTING PROCEDURES 286
TEXTURIZING TECHNIQUES 293
SHORT HAIR TECHNIQUES 297
SCULPTING CONSIDERATIONS 302
SCULPTING ESSENTIALS 305
INFECTION CONTROL AND SAFETY 307
SCULPTING SERVICE ESSENTIALS 307
SCULPTING PROCEDURE OVERVIEW 308

CHAPTER 10, HAIR DESIGN 311

10.1 HAIR DESIGN THEORY 313

HAIR DESIGN ANALYSIS 315
TOOLS FOR HAIR DESIGNING 320
SETTING 323
BASE CONTROL 329
FINISHING 333
HAIR DESIGN ESSENTIALS 335
INFECTION CONTROL AND SAFETY 337
HAIR DESIGN SERVICE ESSENTIALS 339

10.2 WET DESIGN TECHNIQUES 340

FINGERWAVES 340
PINCURLS 341
SKIP WAVES 345
ROLLERS 346
WET DESIGN PROCEDURE OVERVIEW 349

10.3 THERMAL DESIGN TECHNIQUES 351

AIR FORMING 352
HAIR PRESSING 354
THERMAL IRONS 355
THERMAL DESIGN PROCEDURE OVERVIEW 360

10.4 LONG HAIR DESIGN THEORY 361

LONG HAIR DESIGN ANALYSIS 362
CLIENT CONSIDERATIONS 365
LONG HAIR DESIGNING 366
LONG HAIR DESIGN ESSENTIALS 370
INFECTION CONTROL AND SAFETY 371
LONG HAIR DESIGN SERVICE ESSENTIALS 372

10.5 LONG HAIR DESIGN TECHNIQUES 373

TWISTS 373
KNOTS 374
OVERLAPS 375
BRAIDS 376
LOOPS 377

ROLLS 378
LONG HAIR DESIGN PROCEDURE OVERVIEW 378

CHAPTER 11, WIGS AND HAIR ADDITIONS 381

11.1 WIGS AND HAIRPIECES 383

HISTORY 383
COMPOSITION, COLORS AND CONSTRUCTION 386
WIG AND HAIRPIECE ESSENTIALS 388
INFECTION CONTROL AND SAFETY 389
WIG AND HAIR ADDITION SERVICE ESSENTIALS 389
WIG SERVICES 390
HAIRPIECES 394

11.2 HAIR ADDITIONS 403

HAIR ADDITION METHODS 404

CHAPTER 12, TEXTURE 411

12.1 PERMING THEORY 413

HISTORY OF PERMING 414
PHYSICAL PHASE OF PERMING 417
CHEMICAL PHASE OF PERMING 420
PERM ESSENTIALS 430
INFECTION CONTROL AND SAFETY 433
PERM SERVICE ESSENTIALS 434
PERM PROCEDURE OVERVIEW 436
PERM PROBLEMS AND SOLUTIONS 438

12.2 RELAXING THEORY 441

HISTORY OF RELAXING 442
BASIC RELAXING THEORY 444
ADVANCED RELAXING THEORY 450
RELAXER ESSENTIALS 455
INFECTION CONTROL AND SAFETY 459
RELAXER SERVICE ESSENTIALS 460
PRODUCT OVERVIEW 461
RELAXER PROCEDURES OVERVIEW 462
RELAXER PROBLEMS AND SOLUTIONS 465

CHAPTER 13, COLOR 469

13.1 COLOR THEORY 471

WHAT IS COLOR? 472
THE LAW OF COLOR 474
CHARACTERISTICS OF COLOR 477

13.2 IDENTIFYING EXISTING HAIR COLOR 481

MELANIN 482
GRAY HAIR 483
IDENTIFYING NATURAL LEVEL AND TONE 484

IDENTIFYING ARTIFICIAL LEVEL AND TONE 485
ADDITIONAL CONSIDERATIONS 487

13.3 CHANGING EXISTING HAIR COLOR 488
COLOR CHEMISTRY 489
DESIGNING COLOR 503
HAIR COLOR ESSENTIALS 511
INFECTION CONTROL AND SAFETY 515
COLOR SERVICE ESSENTIALS 519
PRODUCT OVERVIEW 522
COLOR PROCEDURES OVERVIEW 523
HAIR COLOR PROBLEMS AND SOLUTIONS 531

UNIT 3 NAIL AND SKIN SERVICES

CHAPTER 14, THE STUDY OF NAILS 537

14.1 NAIL THEORY 539
NAIL STRUCTURE 539
NAIL GROWTH 540
NAIL DISEASES, DISORDERS AND CONDITIONS 540

14.2 NATURAL NAIL CARE 546
NAIL SHAPES 547
NAIL ESSENTIALS 547
INFECTION CONTROL AND SAFETY 550
NATURAL NAIL CARE SERVICE ESSENTIALS 551
01 BASIC MANICURE 552
02 MALE MANICURE 556
PEDICURE ESSENTIALS 556
03 BASIC PEDICURE 557
SPECIAL NAIL SERVICES 560

14.3 ARTIFICIAL NAIL CARE 562
ARTIFICIAL NAIL ESSENTIALS 562
INFECTION CONTROL AND SAFETY 563
04 NAIL TIPS 564
05 TIPS WITH ACRYLIC OVERLAY 567
06 SCULPTURED NAILS 569
ADDITIONAL ARTIFICIAL NAIL SERVICES 573

CHAPTER 15, THE STUDY OF SKIN 575

15.1 SKIN THEORY 577
FUNCTIONS OF THE SKIN 577
COMPOSITION OF THE SKIN 578
TYPES OF SKIN 582
SKIN DISEASES AND DISORDERS 584

15.2 SKIN CARE 590
MASSAGE 591
FACIAL MASKS 593
SKIN CARE ESSENTIALS 593
INFECTION CONTROL AND SAFETY 595
SKIN CARE SERVICE ESSENTIALS 596
01 BASIC FACIAL 597

15.3 HAIR REMOVAL 604
HAIR REMOVAL ESSENTIALS 604
INFECTION CONTROL AND SAFETY 605
HAIR REMOVAL SERVICE ESSENTIALS 606
TEMPORARY HAIR REMOVAL 606
02 BASIC WAXING 609
PERMANENT HAIR REMOVAL 612

15.4 MAKEUP 614
FACIAL SHAPES 614
COLOR THEORY 616
MAKEUP ESSENTIALS 617
INFECTION CONTROL AND SAFETY 619
MAKEUP SERVICE ESSENTIALS 619
MAKEUP TECHNIQUES AND PRODUCTS 620
03 BASIC MAKEUP APPLICATION 635

TODAY'S HAIR DESIGNER

The 21st century holds promise and unlimited opportunities for you, the professional cosmetologist. New techniques, new products and new opportunities appear every day. The numbers of people who visit beauty salons and the amount of money spent on beauty services are constantly increasing. If you are innovative and ambitious, there is no limit to your career potential.

No other industry has such a constant demand for qualified, creative, well-trained graduates. None offers such bright opportunities for an individual to start a personal business and work toward financial independence. Your artistic skills and training give you the potential for changing people's lives by making them look good and feel beautiful.

BUILDING YOUR CAREER

The professional salon business has grown into a very sophisticated industry. Salon owners and hair designers serve a new breed of consumer, one who makes knowledgeable demands and expects the salon to offer a full range of services and retail products. Salon professionals must be highly educated and highly skilled in order to meet these demands.

Personal commitment is a key ingredient in achieving professional success. Invest in yourself. Learn everything you can in school. Take an active part in school activities. Take advantage of extra classes and seminars. After graduation, continue to invest in your education by attending seminars, shows and workshops. There is no limit to the success you can achieve if you are willing to invest the time and energy success demands.

You made your first professional investment when you enrolled in this cosmetology school. You can, and should, make another investment in your professional success even while you're in school…begin to "network."

In networking, a professional creates communication opportunities with other professionals in the same or a related field. Through networking, you can develop contacts that can be instrumental in your climb to success.

The ideal vehicles for networking in the professional salon business are the outstanding professional associations that serve the industry. Some have student memberships available, and that means you can begin networking even now.

PROFESSIONAL ORGANIZATIONS

(CAF) COSMETOLOGY ADVANCEMENT FOUNDATION

The Cosmetology Advancement Foundation's mission is to develop a unified approach to issues and trends affecting the salon industry and to seek opportunities for contributing to the industry's image, growth and development. To achieve its mission CAF subscribes to the values of dedication to education, continuous communications, commitment to teamwork, trust and professionalism among all industry associations, organizations and their members. CAF has led an all-industry task force in developing technical and non-technical skill standards for entry-level cosmetologists.

(PBA/NCA) PROFESSIONAL BEAUTY ASSOCIATION/NATIONAL COSMETOLOGY ASSOCIATION

PBA/NCA is the largest nonprofit trade association whose mission is to provide resources, education, ideas and advocacy to enhance the power and performance of the professional beauty community. This organization meets the diverse needs of its members and provides a powerful network in the professional beauty industry. Members include all licensed cosmetologists, barbers, electrologists and estheticians and non-licensed related professionals (educators, distributors and manufacturers). The group maintains a national executive office, state associations, and local or regional affiliates.

PBA/NCA has expanded the ABBIES awards, raises money through sponsorship of the Beauty Ball & Charity Gala and with European partners continues to sponsor the Cosmoprof North America trade show.

PBA/NCA sponsors international and national competitions. The goal of these competitions is to prepare the participant to perform excellent salon work while building self-confidence and stage presence. The winner represents the United States in HairWorld championship competitions, held every two years.

Students may compete to become members of the Student Hairstyling Team. For a student interested in developing skills needed to become a guest artist or an educator, this competition is an excellent training ground. After graduation, competitions are open to all licensed professionals and could be a personal opportunity for you. The PBA/NCA web address is probeauty.org.

INTERCOIFFURE

Intercoiffure is an organization that consists of 260 salons in the USA/Canada and 2,000 internationally. It is a nonprofit organization of elite salon, spa and school owners. The Intercoiffure members share educational and business ideas, customers and staff with each other around the world. The Intercoiffure web address is intercoiffure.com.

(NACCAS) NATIONAL ACCREDITING COMMISSION OF COSMETOLOGY ARTS & SCIENCES

The National Accrediting Commission of Cosmetology Arts and Sciences (NACCAS) is an autonomous, independent accrediting commission constituted as a nonprofit Delaware corporation, with its main offices located in Alexandria, Virginia. The Commission's origins date back to 1969, when two accrediting agencies in the field merged to form the Cosmetology Accrediting Commission (CAC). CAC changed its name to "NACCAS" in 1981.

NACCAS is recognized by the U.S. Department of Education as a national agency for the institutional accreditation of postsecondary schools and departments of cosmetology arts and sciences, including specialized schools. It presently accredits approximately 1,500 institutions that serve over 120,000 students. These schools offer more than 20 courses an programs of study that fall under NACCAS' scope of accreditation.

(AACS) AMERICAN ASSOCIATION OF COSMETOLOGY SCHOOLS

The purpose of the association is to keep members abreast of changes in federal and state laws and regulations, to provide the membership with educational services, to promote the welfare of cosmetology education in the United States, and to establish a unity of spirit and understanding among institutions and their instructional staff in pursuing the goals and resolving the problems related to postsecondary cosmetology education. The AACS web address is beautyschools.org.

(ACCSC) ACCREDITING COMMISSION OF CAREER SCHOOLS AND COLLEGES

ACCSC is a private, nonprofit, independent accrediting agency whose goal is maintaining educational quality in the career schools and colleges it accredits by striving to assure academic excellence and ethical practices. ACCSC is dedicated to the more than 360,000 students who annually pursue career education at its accredited institutions. The ACCSC web address is accsc.org.

(CCA) CAREER COLLEGE ASSOCIATION

The Career College Association (CCA) is a voluntary membership organization made up of private, postsecondary schools and colleges that provide career-specific educational programs. The association's primary objectives are to foster public policies that ensure equitable access for students to quality career and skill education; to assist member institutions in coping with a complex federal regulatory scheme; and to help member institutions achieve the highest possible standards of educational quality. The CCA web address is career.org.

(NIC) NATIONAL-INTERSTATE COUNCIL OF STATE BOARDS OF COSMETOLOGY

NIC is a not-for-profit organization whose membership consists of state board members of a 50 states, the District of Columbia, Guam and Puerto Rico. NIC provides for an interchange of ideas, promotes professionalism, encourages standardization of regulations and provides national examinations for licensure in cosmetology and related fields. The NIC web address is nictesting.org.

CAREER OPPORTUNITIES

A licensed cosmetologist has completed a local, government-regulated number of hours of study (usually from 1,000 to 2,100) and has successfully passed a written and/or practical exam.

The licensed cosmetologist is in daily contact with clients, performing all the services learned in cosmetology school. Your knowledge, image and all of your professional skills, from sculpting to communication, will be key components in determining your income.

While most licensed cosmetologists are employed in salons, those who want something different and, perhaps, a bit outside of the "routine," might explore more imaginative alternatives, including signing on as a ship's stylist for a passenger cruise line. A **cruise ship stylist** has no living expenses, can see at least a portion of the world and has a clientele in constant turnover as one cruise ends and the next begins. The licensed cosmetologist can also work as a **photo stylist**, working with photographers, modeling agencies or magazine departments to prepare those being photographed. Additional entry-level career opportunities include working in hospital hair-care service areas, theater groups or with major movie studios.

The cosmetology profession offers many opportunities beyond the entry-level position. Most of these jobs require experience, advanced training or a degree of some kind. Here is a sampling of those opportunities:

A **colorist** is someone who specializes in hair color services and is generally hired by a salon with a color department. Clients then go to another salon professional for additional services. Most colorists take advanced training courses and/or attend color seminars in order to keep up with the latest coloring techniques and hair color trends. Color is also uniquely lucrative. Many color services command substantial fees.

COSMETOLOGY FUNDAMENTALS

A **guest artist** or **platform stylist** is self-employed and contracted by a professional beauty product manufacturer or by schools that offer continuing education courses in the beauty field. Guest artists train licensed cosmetologists by teaching them about products, techniques, the newest trends and product sales. The position requires long-distance travel and extensive weekend work.

A **salon coordinator** is often an experienced cosmetologist acting as a director for the activities of a large salon. He or she is responsible for booking and scheduling appointments, greeting customers, public relations, retailing, inventory control, bookkeeping, recordkeeping and client retention.

A **salon manager** is often a highly skilled hair designer who also has the ability to deal with clients. Training in advertising, marketing, purchasing, client relations, budgeting, employee management techniques and finance or accounting is helpful.

A **salon owner** may, or may not, be a licensed cosmetologist. It's desirable for the salon owner to have had some business management experience before investing in a salon. The owner is responsible for all salon operations, physical and financial.

An **instructor** is someone with proven design skills, advanced training in products and techniques and specialized training in vocational education. Most area regulating agencies require instructors to be licensed. Some require a specific number of years of salon experience, others 400 to 2,500 hours of training and others a written and practical licensure examination. Instructing is an excellent training ground for future managers, owners, guest artists and manufacturer representatives.

A **manufacturer's representative** or **field technician** is usually a licensed cosmetologist with 2-5 years of successful salon experience. This position requires travel in a specific area of the country during which the representative holds in-salon or in-school workshops and classes on a variety of subjects.

A **distributor** or **sales consultant** may or may not be a licensed cosmetologist. This position involves selling products to salon owners and managers within a specific geographic territory and providing training for cosmetologists.

A **school owner** or **director** is usually a licensed cosmetologist with experience as a hair designer, salon manager, salon owner, instructor, manufacturer's representative or state board examiner. School owners don't necessarily need to be licensed cosmetologists so long as they have a business degree or experience and have a passion for this industry.

A **manufacturer's spokesperson** is often a cosmetologist with a business or marketing degree. The opportunity to market new products for national distribution can be challenging and profitable.

A **test salon cosmetologist or product analyst** is usually a licensed cosmetologist with specialized skills in a select type of product, such as perms, colors, relaxers or cosmetics. This person is responsible for the final product that cosmetologists use and sell in salons.

An **education manager or trainer** may have a business or personnel management degree and/or may be a licensed cosmetologist with a good deal of experience similar to a long-term instructor's or school owner's. This person trains and manages manufacturers' representatives, chain salon staff, chain school staff or distributor staff for a company region or territory.

A **sales, marketing, or management consultant** is employed by a chain salon, distributor or manufacturer to "supplement" the company's existing educational staff. This consultant may not have any industry experience, but may have a personal reputation for helping companies overcome problems.

Chain salon employees are employed by chain salons. These chain salons make up a very large and growing segment of the salon industry and offer many opportunities for cosmetologists that include positions as salon coordinators, assistant and salon managers, district and area directors, local and company-wide technical educators, retail supervisors, product testing supervisors, warehouse managers and more.

The position of **trade publication publisher, writer or editor** requires that individuals have a journalism background combined with knowledge of the cosmetology profession. Trade publications include magazines, newsletters and textbooks.

OVERVIEW

Cosmetology is the art and science of beauty care.

The *Cosmetology Fundamentals, A Designer's Approach®* program is your official introduction into the cosmetology industry and the exciting career that will reward you personally, professionally and financially. As you read this coursebook, you'll be learning a lot of new information and practicing many new skills. Your classmates will be sharing this experience with you while your instructors support and encourage you every step of the way. Most of the time, this learning process will be exciting and inspiring. This is only natural when learning new things. To make the road easier, there are some built-in features at the beginning and end of every chapter, as well as throughout each chapter, that will help you clarify, understand and remember what you are learning.

A DESIGNER'S APPROACH®

COSMETOLOGY FUNDAMENTALS   **SCULPTURE**   **HAIR DESIGN**   **COLOR**   **TEXTURE**   **SALON SUCCESS**

A Designer's Approach consists of 6 core disciplines: *Cosmetology Fundamentals, Sculpture Hair Design, Color, Texture* and *Salon Success*, which are color-coded for easy recognition. The entire library is designed to deliver licensure-based education as well as salon-relevant training, while promoting mindful learning and future success in the salon. *A Designer's Approach* focuses on visualizing and creating hair designs that are as unique as each individual client. It includes:

- Theory that gives you the thought process you'll need to guide your design decisions
- Procedures and techniques that will help you produce predictable results
- Language that allows you to think and communicate clearly with your clients and other designers

LEARNING STRATEGIES WITHIN *COSMETOLOGY FUNDAMENTALS*

This program has been specifically designed using state-of-the-art educational methods to make your learning process engaging as well as systematic and effective. To help you make the most of your time with your coursebook, a brief description of these learning strategies is provided here so you can become familiar with them before diving into the chapters.

First, take a look at the icon to the left. This icon will appear throughout your coursebook to help guide you through this program and help you make the most out of *Artist Access*, your online resource for all the coursebooks, video segments and other activities and learning resources.

This icon indicates that there are additional learning resources for the topic the icon is positioned with on *Artist Access*. These resources can be found by logging in to artist-access.com and navigating to the particular program and topic. These resources can range from answer keys for Brainworks activities, to supplemental workshop exercises and deeper content on some concepts presented in your coursebook.

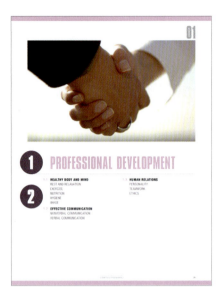

The chapter overview is located on the first two opening pages of the chapter and provides a preview of the chapter in a concise, easy-to-read format. It contains seven elements that will orient you to the chapter so you are prepared and keyed-in to the important learning concepts.

CHAPTER TITLE (1)
This is the overriding theme of the chapter.

ADVANCE ORGANIZER (2)
A "mini-outline" of the chapter headings and subheadings that identifies the main content points and provides an overall view of the chapter in its entirety.

SIGNATURE COLOR (3)
Each title in the *A Designer's Approach* library is easily identifiable by its signature color. Shades of purple you see on the pages as graphic treatments and titles help identify *Cosmetology Fundamentals*.

CENTRAL MESSAGE (4)
A statement that highlights the critical value of the chapter.

LEARNING GOALS (5)
Learning outcomes that pinpoint exactly what you will learn as a result of working with the material in the chapter and preview how you will be evaluated.

CONNECTING THEORY TO REAL-WORLD PRACTICE (6)
A chart that summarizes how the information in the chapter will benefit you in professional settings.

INTROVIEW (7)
An introduction to the chapter that not only previews the content, but also relates the content to you in a personal way. The introview answers questions such as, "Why is this information important to me?" "Why should I care about this?" "How will I be better off in the future as a result of understanding this subject?"

Large **CHAPTER NUMBERS (8)** appear in the upper right corner of every two-page spread to quickly help you locate the specific chapter you are looking for.

Material contained in **SIDEBARS (9)** provides examples and additional information that make the content clearer and more relevant to real-life salon settings.

Information within the chapters is presented in ways that make it easy for you to spot and remember what's important. Pay particular attention to information in:
- Bold print
- Bulleted and numbered lists
- Charts, tables, sidebars, shaded boxes, callouts, "Alerts"

Some of the chapters in Units 2 and 3 of this coursebook contain overviews of procedures that you will be performing in the salon. Shorter procedure overviews are presented in one bulleted list with the heading, **GUIDELINES (1)**. The lengthier procedure overviews, **WORKSHOPS (2)** are divided into three sections:
- PREPARATION —Steps to be done before beginning the service
- PROCEDURE —Actual steps for performing the service
- COMPLETION —Final steps to be done at the end of the service

The steps in the procedure overviews are based on the **RUBRICS (3)** found either in the study guide (for Chapters 7, 14 and 15) or within their respective program titles. Rubrics are self-assessment tools that help gauge your level of performance. These are designed to compare your skill and technique to industry standards. At the end of each chapter there are three elements that will help you put the entire chapter into perspective.

CONNECTING THEORY TO REAL-WORLD PRACTICE (4) is a similar chart to the one presented at the beginning of the chapter. Here, however, the personal, professional and client-centered benefits are linked to each of the chapter's main headings, giving you an even more specific view of the relationship between the theory you have learned and how it will apply to you and your career.

IN OTHER WORDS (5) summarizes the content with a brief statement at the end of every chapter.

LESSONS LEARNED (6) provides a list of statements that recaps the chapter's critical messages and learning objectives. These are "words of wisdom" that you can take with you throughout your career.

The *Cosmetology Fundamentals* study guide is a companion to this coursebook that serves as your personal learning notebook. The study guide will help you direct your thinking, manage and remember the information presented in each chapter and make the most of your own learning style and natural intelligence.

Now that you know how to use the features of this coursebook to help you learn the fundamentals of the salon industry, you're ready to begin your cosmetology education with confidence. The best place to begin is with a clear understanding of what it takes to be successful in any career: *Chapter 1, Professional Development*.

ACKNOWLEDGEMENTS

Cosmetology Fundamentals is designed to provide cosmetology education to meet the requirements of government agencies and the Skills Standards set for entry-level cosmetologists. An undertaking of such magnitude requires the expertise and cooperation of many people. Pivot Point International wishes to take this opportunity to acknowledge with gratitude and respect some of those many contributors.

Thank you to the models, outside consultants, individual and chain salons, industry manufacturers, Pivot Point's Educational Advisory Board and the dedicated Core Development Team that made this course possible.

In addition, we give special thanks to the North American Regulating agencies whose careful work protects our clients and thereby enhances the high quality of our work. These regulatory agencies include the Occupational Safety and Health Administration (OSHA), the Environmental Protection Agency (EPA) and the U.S. Equal Employment Opportunity Commission (EEOC), which enforces the Americans with Disabilities Act (ADA). The *Cosmetology Fundamentals* program makes extensive use of their policies and procedures.

Following is a listing of the many individuals and organizations that made this program possible.

EXECUTIVE MANAGEMENT

Melanie Kopeikin
President

Guy Harrington
Vice President, Domestic Sales and Field Education

Jan Laan
Vice President, International Business Development

Judie Maginn
*Vice President, Global Marketing and
Business Development*

Robert Passage
Chairman and CEO

Judy Rambert
Vice President, Education and Research

Robert Sieh
Senior Vice President, Finance and Operations

PRODUCTION

John Bernin
Digital Media Manager

Eileen Dubelbeis
Program Development Coordinator

Jennifer Eckstein
Marketing Manager

Brian Fallon
Educational Content Supervisor

Janet Fisher
Senior Director, Instructional Support

Marilyn Geary
Developmental Editor

Deidre Glover
Editorial Associate

Sabine Held-Perez
Senior Director, Program Development

Melissa Holmes
Program Development Associate

Amy Howard
Program Development Coordinator

Steve Janssen
Pivot Point International

Joanna Jakubowicz
Graphic Design Associate

Debbie Mack
Pivot Point International

Matt McCarthy
Production Manager

Vic Piccolotto
Program Development Associate

Denise Podlin
Illustrator

Benjamin Polk
Editorial Associate

Francis Pugh
Pivot Point International

Tina Rayyan
Production Director

Markel Richards
Program Development Associate

Rick Russell
Graphic Design Associate

Maureen Spurr
Editorial Manager

Vasiliki Stavrakis
Education and Research Director

Jane Wegner
Educational Research

Csaba Zongor
Graphic Design Associate

CONSULTANTS AND CONTRIBUTORS

Olivia Barr
Hair Specialist

Ron Barris
Headstart Hair for Men

Dr. Keith Brown
Color Specialist/Chemist, Clairol

Gerri Cevetillo
Infection Control Specialist, Ultronics

Gloria DiSanza
Color Specialist, Clairol

Dianna Kenneally
Senior Scientist/P&G Beauty

Mary Lee Krantz
Fantastic Sams

Theresa Lewis
Nail Specialist, OPI

Lori Neopolitan
Makeup Specialist

RoseAnn Perea
Supercuts

Robert Richards
Fashion Illustration

Sue Sansom
Salon Ecology Expert

Kim Schottler
Great Clips, Inc.

Clif St. Germain
Educational Consultant

Cheryl Tricoci
Mario Tricoci Hair Salon and Day Spa

Michael Hill, Larry Walthers, Aurie Gosnell, Peggy Moon, Kitty Pierre
(National Interstate Council)

American Hairlines

Celebrity Signatures International

Chicago Hair Goods

Cornrows & Co.

Garland Drake International

Great Lengths

Hairologi

Surfacine Development, LLC

01

PROFESSIONAL DEVELOPMENT

1.1 **HEALTHY BODY AND MIND**
REST AND RELAXATION
EXERCISE
NUTRITION
HYGIENE
IMAGE
ERGONOMICS

1.2 **EFFECTIVE COMMUNICATION**
NONVERBAL COMMUNICATION
VERBAL COMMUNICATION

1.3 **HUMAN RELATIONS**
PERSONALITY
TEAMWORK
ETHICS

THE FOUNDATION FOR SUCCESS AS A SALON PROFESSIONAL COMES FROM A COMMITMENT TO DEVELOPING A HEALTHY BODY AND MIND, EFFECTIVE COMMUNICATION SKILLS AND POSITIVE RELATIONSHIPS

FOLLOWING THIS LESSON
YOU WILL BE ABLE TO:

Establish routines to maintain a healthy body and mind

Explain the elements of effective communication

Develop and maintain positive human relations

CONNECTING THEORY TO REAL-WORLD PRACTICE

APPROACHING PROFESSIONAL DEVELOPMENT AS A PRACTICAL SCIENCE WILL HELP YOU:

| **PERSONAL CONNECTION:** | **INDUSTRY CONNECTION:** | **CLIENT CONNECTION:** |
IMPROVE YOURSELF	BECOME A PROFESSIONAL	SERVE THE GUEST
Make the most of your potential by developing productive attitudes that will support you in any endeavor	Showcase your talents to their best advantage so you can make the most of career opportunities	Create immediate connections with new guests that grow into long-lasting bonds

Cosmetology is the art and science of beauty care. Cosmetology professionals are people who openly express the value of their chosen field in the way they work, communicate and conduct themselves. Putting the two together, cosmetology professional, also known as a salon professional, is someone who believes in the value of bringing beauty to the lives of others and works hard to achieve the highest standards of beauty care and professional behavior.

1.1 HEALTHY BODY AND MIND

Establishing routines to maintain a healthy body and mind is the first step toward professional development. Dedication to each of these areas will help ensure that you are on the right track.

REST AND RELAXATION

Sufficient rest and relaxation are as necessary as work for a healthy, happy life. Sleep helps relieve the frustrations and tensions that are a result of everyday activities. Most people need six to eight hours of sleep or they become fatigued and cannot function properly. Rest and relaxation are necessary to prevent fatigue.

Being able to relax and "get away from it all" are also very important for a healthy body and mind. Reading a good book, listening to music, watching TV or going for a walk can all provide a relaxing change of pace, allowing you to return to work refreshed.

EXERCISE

A regular exercise program will help you feel better, look better and work better. Your muscles, heart muscles included, need to be in their best possible condition. Exercise is a proven method through which you can keep your muscles toned and equip your body to better cope with the stressful situations in your business and personal life. Exercise also helps stimulate the blood circulation in your body and encourages proper functioning of organs.

Take the time to set up an exercise program you will enjoy, such as a brisk daily walk, bicycling or hiking on the weekend, or yoga to keep your body toned and in shape. Just getting out a few times a week to enjoy the fresh air will help. Remember, you have chosen a profession that is very physical, and the better conditioning you give your body, the greater the chances of your success and health. Round out your exercise program by remembering to exercise your mind also. Reading is the best form of exercise for the mind.

Worry and fear are two emotions that can be injurious to mental health. Sometimes you may tend to get caught up in these two emotions and fail to exercise your choice to take charge of your life by controlling your thoughts and emotions.

NUTRITION

A balanced diet is essential for your personal and professional well-being, and may help prevent certain diseases. A typical day in the salon can be demanding and your diet may be one of the most important factors for your success.

Almost all foods contain mixtures of the three energy nutrients:
- Carbohydrates
- Fats
- Proteins

The energy they contain is measured in calories. The body uses this energy in several ways: to heat itself, to build its structures and to move its parts during exercise and activities. The energy may also be stored in body fat for later use. In addition to the energy nutrients, other essential nutrients are vitamins, minerals and water.

You may have heard the term **RDA - Recommended Dietary Allowances**. The U.S. government established the RDA as the appropriate nutrient intakes for people in this country in an attempt to help them select an adequate diet from the array of available foods.

RDA Guidelines for Daily Average
Based on % of calories:

Carbohydrates – 60% (complex)
Fat – 30% (10% or less saturated)
Protein – 10%

CALORIES BURNED DURING EXERCISE AND ACTIVITIES

ACTIVITY (1 HOUR)	140 LB PERSON	195 LB PERSON
Aerobics, general	381	531
Basketball game	508	708
Bicycling, 10 mph, leisure	254	354
Cleaning house, general	222	310
Gardening, general	318	443
Horseback riding, walking	159	221
Jogging	445	620
Judo, karate, kick boxing, tae kwon do	636	885
Mowing lawn	350	487
Rope jumping, moderate	636	885
Running, 6 mph (10 minute mile)	636	885
Tennis, singles	508	708

Data is based on research from Medicine and Science in Sports and Exercise, the "Official Journal of the American College of Sports Medicine."

01

HYGIENE

Hygiene is the science that deals with healthful living. The practice of public hygiene is important because it helps to preserve the health of the community. Impure air from poor ventilation, inadequate lighting, improper disinfection practices and improper storage or use of food are the primary health hazards against which health officials expect you to protect clients. Your job as a professional is to protect and serve the public.

Your individual system for maintaining your cleanliness and health is your personal hygiene. In your work, you will constantly be very close to your clients. Scents that wouldn't ordinarily even be noticed or soil that wouldn't normally be detected can, therefore, offend. Establishing and maintaining a personal hygiene routine is essential if you expect your clients to enjoy your company and want to come back.

Though you might like to believe otherwise, all bodies produce odors. **Regular bathing using soap for cleanliness, followed by the application of a deodorant, plays a major role in preventing unpleasant body odors.** Avoid excessive use of perfume or cologne. More and more clients have sensitivities to some fragrances. Soiled clothing accumulates odors. No article of clothing should be worn more than a few times before it's washed or your clothing will produce odors that offend no matter how often you bathe.

Few people consider the cleanliness of the inside of their shoes. Yet unclean shoes and the length of time you wear them in a day can create foot odor if not checked. A little talc or foot deodorant can often be of help.

The food you eat and the state of your health affect the condition of your breath. Most of you know that eating too much garlic results in unpleasant body smells from perspiration... and **bad breath, referred to as halitosis (hal-eh-TOH-siss).** Did you know, as well, that a sore throat often produces unpleasant odors from your mouth? Brush your teeth as often as you can each day, certainly after every meal, and use mouthwash.

Consider all potential hygiene problems and establish a personal hygiene plan that addresses them daily. Your personal hygiene contributes to or detracts from your success.

CHECKLIST FOR
PERSONAL HYGIENE PLAN:

☐ Regular Bathing
☐ Deodorant
☐ Mouthwash
☐ Perfume or Cologne
☐ Clean Clothing

Oral hygiene refers to maintaining healthy teeth and keeping the breath fresh.

IMAGE

The salon business is a service business; therefore, close attention to personal grooming is a priority. Care of your hair, skin, hands, feet and clothing needs to be of the utmost importance. Follow the basic guidelines listed in this section to help ensure your professional image.

HAIR CARE

The most beautiful hair is clean and healthy hair. As a salon professional, of course, the condition of your hair is of particular importance. A daily hair-care program is essential for the salon professional you are studying to become.

Your own hair design communicates your professional expertise. Your hair design should be fashionable yet include any necessary modification that will allow it to better suit your face.

The way you wear color in your hair will help or hinder your efforts to introduce color to your clients. Fashion colors can be fun and flattering. However, if the fashion colors of the season are shades that are not flattering to you, don't wear them. Your ability to call attention to your personal use of hair color to flatter your complexion, "broaden" a narrow forehead or "narrow" a too-wide jaw will be a far greater help to you in encouraging your clients to try color than if you simply follow the current color fashion trends.

SKIN CARE AND MAKEUP

The proper care of your skin isn't limited to the products you put on it. **Healthy, glowing skin is equally dependent on good nutrition, exercise and rest.** As a salon professional, you will need to keep your skin looking its best. Research the variety of skin care products now available and find the regimen best suited for your skin type. It will become increasingly apparent to you how personal skin care knowledge will be an advantage when recommending skin care products for your future clients.

Cosmetics can enhance attractive facial features and help balance proportions that aren't quite right. Just as one can contour a face with creative hair color techniques, one can contour facial features with the careful use of cosmetics.

When fashion trends change, the popular makeup look usually changes, too. In your profession, it's as important to update your use of cosmetics as it is to wear a hair design that reflects the correct fashion look.

CONTOUR TIPS

1 An overly wide jaw can be visually narrowed by applying darker contour creme on the outer areas of the jawline.

2 Narrow foreheads can be visually broadened by applying lighter cosmetic shades along the hairline.

3 Small lips can be made to appear larger by creating a lipstick line just outside the natural lip line.

4 Large lips can be minimized by applying the lipstick line just inside the natural line of the lips.

It's important that you learn to modify current cosmetic trends into looks that are flattering for you. **The basics of makeup application never change:**
- Foundation should match your skin tone.
- Contouring with light colors always broadens.
- Contouring with dark colors always narrows.

Cosmetic shades change. So does the fashionable use of makeup...from obvious and dramatic to light and natural. Master the basic techniques and then you will be able to learn how to apply makeup to suit any fashion trend in the manner that will complement you best.

HANDS

Your hands will touch many people during the course of your career, so they need to be smooth, soft, immaculately clean and well manicured. Maintaining attractively manicured, well-cared-for hands is particularly challenging for a salon professional. The services you'll perform will often require the use of chemicals: perm solution and hair color, to name only two. **Wear protective gloves whenever performing chemical services.** Use moisturizing lotions frequently. Keep your nails attractively manicured. Avoid wearing rings that can chafe or irritate. Take the best care of your hands that you can.

FEET

A great deal of your time as a salon professional will be spent standing on your feet. You will need to take proper care of your feet, practice good posture and wear good-fitting, low, broad-heeled shoes. Make sure your feet are thoroughly dry after bathing to prevent fungus infections like athlete's foot.

To keep your feet at their best, schedule regular pedicures that will include cleansing, removal of callused skin, massage and toenail trims. If you develop bunions, corns or ingrown toenails, etc., see a podiatrist (foot doctor).

TIP

 DRESS WELL

 **MAKE MONEY**

Some people think they can't dress well until they make enough money. What they don't understand is that to make more money, you need to dress like those who do.

CLOTHING

Your clothing should be freshly washed, or cleaned, and pressed. No unsightly rings around the collar or the armpit can be accepted. Shoulder fit should be loose enough to allow easy movement. No article of clothing should be uncomfortably or unflatteringly tight. **Shoes look best when clean and polished.**

DRESS FOR SUCCESS

Your clothing should be selected to incorporate current trends into a statement consistent with your personal sense of style. You're in an age of fashion that shows a variety of designer looks for any given season. Some will be more popular than others, but if the one that's popular doesn't look good on you, go on to something else. Exercise good sense by taking into consideration your height and silhouette when selecting fashions.

Many schools and salons have a dress code for their employees or students. Follow it with careful consideration of your personal sense of style and fashion, and you'll look like the professional you aspire to be.

POSTURE

The need for good posture goes beyond just standing correctly. **Good posture enhances your physical well-being.** As a professional designer you'll be on your feet every day. As you shampoo and style your clients, you'll bend and stretch and stoop. As you restock inventory *it may be necessary for you to lift boxes as heavy as 50 pounds.* Maintaining good posture and moving properly will:

- Protect you from muscle strain and potential injury
- **Reduce physical fatigue**
- Present an attractive image

DOs & DON'Ts FOR GOOD POSTURE

DO	DON'T
Do use the height adjustments provided on styling chairs. Styling chairs are designed to raise and lower so you can work on your client's hair without stooping over or reaching up.	Don't slump over a shampoo bowl; bend forward at the waist holding your shoulders straight.
Do keep your head up, your chin level, your shoulders relaxed but straight and your abdomen held flat when standing.	Don't bend at the waist when lifting objects from the floor. Bend at the knees to lower your whole body.
Do keep your feet and knees together, feet on the floor, when sitting, and sit well back in the chair.	Don't, when standing, place more of your weight on one leg than the other. Choose positions that distribute your weight evenly.

ERGONOMICS

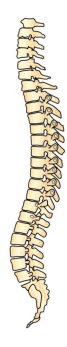

As a salon professional you will be spending long hours standing, bending, reaching and repeating the same motions. Any repeated activities can cause fatigue and pain in various parts of the body, sometimes even serious injury. Some aches, pains and injuries develop slowly over a long period of time. In many cases, health challenges can be prevented through improved posture, better work habits and proper equipment. A science called **ergonomics** looks at how you do your work; what body movements, positions, tools and equipment you should use; and the effect all these things have on you and your client's health and comfort. This growing science is continually developing new tools and equipment to support these health issues, while facilitating longer productivity in your salon career.

You need to be aware of the recommendations for preventing problems with the hand, wrist, shoulder, neck, back, foot and leg. The science of ergonomics provides ideas for designing the space we work in and the equipment we use so they are easier on the human body. Developing the right habits at the beginning of your training is the best way to get started in the right direction.

NECK AND BACK

Your spine runs from the top of your neck down to your lower back. It is made up of many bones called vertebrae, one below another. Between each pair of vertebrae are joints and discs that give your neck and back flexibility, so they can move.

Discs are flexible because they have a substance like jelly inside. Both joints and discs can be hurt if you strain or squeeze them. Prolonged bending or twisting of your body can cause pain in your neck, back, arms or legs, especially if a disc ruptures (the jelly inside leaks out).

NECK AND BACK STRAIN CAN OCCUR IF YOU:
- Bend forward when performing a service.
- Twist your body to get closer to a client or to reach for something.
- Reach overhead for supplies.
- Arch (lean) backward because you've been standing for a long time.
- Stand for a long time in high-heeled shoes.

RECOMMENDATIONS TO PREVENT NECK AND BACK PROBLEMS INCLUDE:
- Work with your back straight. Bend at the hips instead of the waist (a straight-back bend).
- Use a free-standing sink for shampooing so you can reach the client's hair without twisting. (These are sometimes called back-wash systems.)
- Adjust the height of the client's chair.
- Tilt the client's head to a position that is comfortable for you.
- Work with the client standing up if the hair is very long.
- Use a chair with a tilted seat when doing manicures or sit on a wedge-shaped cushion that tilts your body forward.
- Bend your knees slightly and pull in your abdominal muscles when you have to reach up. Called a pelvic tilt, this motion keeps you from arching backward.
- When you stand for long periods of time, place one foot on a stool or on a rung under the client's chair.
- Avoid high-heeled shoes.
- Stand on a footstool when you reach for supplies on a high shelf.

LOW, BROAD-HEELED SHOES

FOOT AND LEG

If you stand for a long time, your feet and ankles may swell and you have more risk of getting varicose veins (swollen veins). Also, if any part of your foot is under pressure, you can get calluses or skin irritation at the pressure point.

FOOT AND LEG PROBLEMS CAN OCCUR IF YOU:
- Stand for long periods, especially on a hard floor.
- Wear high-heeled shoes, especially if the toes are pointed.
- Wear shoes with poor arch support or hard soles.
- Wear shoes that don't fit well.

RECOMMENDATIONS TO PREVENT FOOT AND LEG PROBLEMS INCLUDE:
- Don't stand for long periods of time without sitting. Change positions frequently. Use a stool or movable seat if necessary to rest your feet while you work on a client.
- Raise your feet on a stool when you take a break.
- Wear comfortable, rubber-soled shoes with good arch support.
- Use shock-absorbing inserts inside your shoes.
- Wear low, broad-heeled shoes; avoid shoes with high heels or pointed toes. They increase pressure on the toes and jam them into the front of the shoe.
- Use a cushioned floor mat to reduce the fatigue of standing on a hard floor.
- Use support hose to reduce leg swelling.
- Hydraulic chairs for clients should adjust up and down at least five inches.

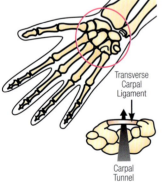

HANDS AND WRISTS

Most of the muscles that move your hand and fingers are actually in your forearm. These muscles are connected to the hand and fingers by tendons, which are like cords passing through your wrist. **Tendonitis** occurs when the tendons get inflamed.

The carpal tunnel is a tunnel in the wrist, surrounded by bone and tissue. A nerve and several tendons pass through this tunnel. If you have tendonitis, the tendons swell and the nerve in the tunnel gets pinched. This condition, called **Carpal Tunnel Syndrome**, can make your hand numb and weak.

THE MAIN CAUSES OF TENDONITIS AND CARPAL TUNNEL SYNDROME ARE:
- Bending your wrist a lot.
- Pinching or gripping with force.
- Repeating a motion over and over.

YOU MAY BEND YOUR WRIST A LOT OR USE FORCEFUL PINCHING OR GRIPPING MOTIONS WHEN YOU:
- Cut hair, hold a hair dryer or use a round brush, curlers or curling iron.
- Cut with shears that don't fit your hand.
- Cut with shears that are dull or not lubricated properly.
- Massage a client.
- Curl with a hot iron.
- Use a comb that doesn't glide smoothly.

USE PALM-TO-PALM TECHNIQUE

RECOMMENDATIONS TO PREVENT HAND AND WRIST PROBLEMS INCLUDE:

- Adjust the height of the chair. Lower it to work on the crown of the head and raise it to work below ear level. To avoid bending your wrist, the chair should go up and down at least five inches.
- Swivel the chair so you don't have to reach over or across the client.
- Tilt the client's head so you don't have to bend your arm, hand and wrist as much.
- Use sharp shears that fit your hand and that are correctly adjusted and lubricated. You'll be able to make fewer cuts, and you won't need to apply as much force for each cut you make.
- Twirl the handle of your round brush between your thumb and index finger, instead of continually bending your wrist.
- Use procedural techniques that help you keep your wrists straight.
- Manicure stations should have arm rests for the client and salon professional.

SHOULDERS

Your shoulder has muscles and tendons. If you strain your shoulder, you can get muscle aches, tendonitis or **bursitis,** which is an inflammation of the fluid-filled sac (bursa) that lies between a tendon and skin or a tendon and bone. It's easy to strain your shoulder if you often hold your arm stretched away from your body or if you often hold your arm up, with your elbow above shoulder height.

YOU MAY STRAIN YOUR SHOULDER WHEN YOU:

- Reach up to cut, dry or curl the crown of the head.
- Reach across the client's body to shampoo or dry hair.
- Reach across a table to manicure.
- Reach for shears and combs on the counter.
- Reach for supplies on a high shelf.
- Hold heavy clippers, especially if your arm is stretched out or raised.

RECOMMENDATIONS TO PREVENT SHOULDER PROBLEMS INCLUDE:

- Adjust the height of the chair when you work on a client so your arms are close to your sides.
- Swivel the chair and get as close to the client as possible.
- Tilt the client's head to a position that is comfortable for you.
- Hold your tools so you don't have to raise your arms.
- Have the client extend a hand toward you when you're doing nails; don't reach for a hand.
- Use an armrest when you do a manicure or support your arms on folded towels.

Adapted from Health and Safety for Hair Care and Beauty Professionals, Labor Occupational Health Program, University of California at Berkeley.

1.2 EFFECTIVE COMMUNICATION

Throughout your career there will be one element that will propel you toward your goals of success faster than anything else. That element is your ability to communicate effectively.

Every time you exchange ideas, thoughts or feelings with someone, you are communicating. Therefore, your communication skills are every bit as important to your success as your technical skills.

COMMUNICATION

1. The act of communicating
2. Exchange of thoughts, information, etc., by conversation or writing
3. A message; news
4. A means of communication; connection
5. [pl.] System, as by telephone, for communicating

NONVERBAL COMMUNICATION

POSITIVE BODY LANGUAGE

NEGATIVE BODY LANGUAGE

In nonverbal communication, sometimes called "body language," messages are exchanged without speaking. Appearance, posture, poise, touch, facial expression, eye contact, gestures and silence often "speak more loudly than words." For example, a smile is a universal sign of approval. One who stands straight, shoulders squared, head held high and extends a hand to greet communicates self-confidence. Bowed shoulders and sloping body posture convey uncertainty.

Eye contact tells your client or anyone with whom you are talking, that he or she has your full attention. Simple eye contact can validate and reassure. It is a universal sign of acknowledgement.

In preliminary client conversations, or on any occasion when you're communicating face-to-face, leaning slightly forward conveys the unspoken message that the speaker has your complete attention and intense interest. A slightly forward lean communicates that you are interested in what is being said. A backward lean is an unspoken message that you are doubtful or uninterested.

Become aware of the subtle ways posture can communicate your feelings about you and those around you. Be sure your posture conveys confidence and your movements indicate interest in what your client is saying.

01

BODY LANGUAGE

List the messages that you feel the following body language sends:

Arms folded across the chest _____

Nodding head up and down _____

Shaking a pointed finger in someone's face _____

Shaking head back and forth _____

Can you think of other body language messages? Create a list here.

LANGUAGE   MESSAGE

VERBAL COMMUNICATION

How you speak is as important as what you're saying. A well-modulated voice gains greater positive attention than a voice that is unnecessarily and often unattractively high or shrill. A listener may well "tune out" an irritating voice and then miss the information being shared. Listen to your own voice in various situations. A voice that can carry very harmonious tones in normal conversation may become shrill during excitement. Be certain your voice always reflects the personal image you want to project.

Verbal communication (how you speak) can also influence the meaning of what you say. **The tone or inflection of your voice, level and rate of speech all play an important role in verbal communication.**

GRAMMAR

Your language, used correctly, can clearly and beautifully communicate all your thoughts and needs. Used incorrectly, however, the beauty of the language may be marred. Worse still, your level of communication can be impaired.

The use of poor grammar can begin accidentally, as you copy poor speech patterns used by those around you. It can also begin intentionally, when you choose to use it to imitate certain peers or to create particular effects. In either case, once the use of poor grammar has begun, it can become habitual and, therefore, difficult to recognize and correct.

The use of double negatives, certain slang words or words whose true meanings aren't quite appropriate to one's messages can all detract from the thought you are attempting to communicate. The listener can be confused by such communication and left with a completely incorrect understanding of the intended message. *No professional can afford to misuse language.*

TWO-WAY COMMUNICATION

Your success in providing your clients with exactly the service they desire depends on *how well you are able to understand and interpret their initial request.*

The best way to do this is, first, encourage them to give you enough information so that you perfectly understand their desires. Be a good listener and ask questions, if necessary. *Second, practice reflective listening by repeating back to them in your own words what they just told you.* For example:

"Mrs. Jones, if I understand you correctly, today you would like me to give you more fullness on the top and shorten the back and sides. To do this I will layer the top and cut about one inch from the sides and back to achieve the look you want..."

When you have finished your explanation, always ask if the client understands and is comfortable with what you will be doing. Encourage questions. It is important that you are able to communicate comfortably and that you and your client understand each other. Here are several points that will help your communication skills become more effective:

PRESENT A PLEASANT GREETING
- Always greet a client by using the last name (Mrs. Brown, Mr. Smith, Ms. Johnson) unless the client offers permission for a first-name basis and it is acceptable in the school and/or salon.
- Use a pleasant tone of voice that projects your eagerness to offer your services.

USE TACT
- **Tact** is learning to say the proper thing to a person without giving offense. This skill requires sensitivity.
- Tact is a very important communication skill to use in building an honest professional relationship with your clients.
- It is your responsibility to communicate honestly with the client, without offending.
- Deciding whether your ideas or feelings should be expressed in public or private is considered being discreet.

- For example, a client may insist on a certain hair color, which you know will not be flattering. It is your responsibility to tactfully suggest otherwise:

"Mrs. Jones, I have just returned from a training seminar where I took a special class on coloring and studied color as it relates to the natural tones of the complexion. If we make you a 'cool brown,' I believe it will tend to wash out your face and make your complexion a bit sallow. But if we weave some subtle warm blond highlights…"

EXPRESS YOUR IDEAS CLEARLY
- Think an idea through completely before you talk about it.
- Many good ideas fail because they are not thought through before they are expressed.

DEFINE THE PURPOSE OF YOUR COMMUNICATION
Before you begin to express your idea, determine the purpose of your communication. Is it to:
- Gain information?
- Change an attitude?
- Seek support?
- Motivate?

KNOW THE IMPORTANCE OF YOUR IDEAS
Be certain that the communication is valuable to others. When speaking:
- Consider the listener's needs and desires.
- Ask yourself…How will the listener benefit by what I'm saying?
- Be prepared to show visual representation of the ideas being suggested to the client by using style books, color charts, photographs, etc.

BE AWARE OF YOUR ENVIRONMENT
- Be sure the timing is right for your communication.
- Decide whether your ideas or feelings should be expressed in public or private.
- Decide who should be the recipient of your communication.

WATCH YOUR OVERTONES
- An overtone occurs when your tone of voice, inflection, expressions and reactions do not match your words. Example: You say, "I'm so happy to see you today," but you are not smiling or extending your hand in greeting.
- Be sure you are communicating the idea you want to convey.

CONSULT WITH OTHERS WHEN NECESSARY
- Be certain you have all the facts and information available.
- If you're in doubt, consult with others to gain new insights, ideas, opinions…and support.

BE A GOOD LISTENER
- Concentrate on understanding others first.
- **Listening is the important key to good communication.**
- The most successful businesspeople and the best communicators are those who have learned to listen.

AVOID DISCUSSING THE FOLLOWING TOPICS WITH CLIENTS:
- Religion
- Politics
- Personal problems
- Other clients' behavior
- Staff or competitor's workmanship
- Information given to you in confidence

To be sure you succeeded in communicating, take the time to ask questions. Encourage others to express their opinions. Your success in communicating your thoughts is strongly related to how well you communicate your professionalism. Everything you say and do should convey that you're a professional.

The **topics** you select to discuss with your clients **should be chosen with care. Avoid controversial topics.** Too many salon professionals rely on the weather, current movies and famous personalities to provide topics to discuss with clients. As a true salon professional, you'll want to focus your conversation on your client's lifestyle and salon-related needs and then completely focus on your client's hair care needs. A client's very active life, for example, would probably be well served with a short, easy-to-care-for design. You'll use particular products on each client for particular reasons. Explain what you're using and why. If you ensure that each client is satisfied, your success will be guaranteed.

BE SURE EACH CLIENT RECEIVES YOUR FULL ATTENTION

1.3 HUMAN RELATIONS

The psychology of **getting along with others** is referred to as **human relations**. Many factors influence good human relations in the workplace, including personality, teamwork and your professional code of ethics. Long hours of standing, high customer expectations and the need to increase the pace of work, may tend to cause added stress. Be cautious that this stress does not negatively reflect in how you deal with people.

PERSONALITY

Personality is defined as the outward reflection of your inner feelings, thoughts, attitudes and values. Your personality is the sum total of the emotional and behavioral characteristics that make you unique. Your individual personality consists of combinations of thousands of different human characteristics, such as emotions, attitudes, skills, beliefs, values and goals. All your many experiences influence the development of your personality, as well. These personality characteristics are not quickly changed, but can be modified over time.

PERSONALITY ATTRIBUTES

A pleasing personality is a tremendous asset to a salon professional and includes personal attributes such as:

- A good sense of humor
- A considerate nature
- A positive attitude
- Emotional control
- Vitality
- Flexibility
- Friendliness
- Good manners

Select three of the words or phrases above and describe something that you have done or something that happened to you in the last three days that involved those personal attributes.

CHOSEN WORD OR PHRASE
Good manners

ACTION
I opened the door for an elderly client yesterday.

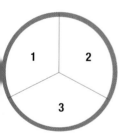

Fill in the blanks provided below for the pie chart with your 3 best personality attributes. You can use those personality attributes listed in the graphic above as a reference or create your own descriptive words.

1.
2.
3.

ATTITUDES

An **"attitude"** is the specific and identifiable emotion and/or reaction one experiences and projects in dealing with the demands of life. Because your attitude is projected, it can have an effect on those around you. **A negative attitude, obviously, can have a negative impact on others.** Conversely, projecting a positive attitude can have an uplifting effect on the people with whom you come in contact.

People are born with very few attitudes; attitudes, like habits, are "learned." Therefore, attitudes, like habits, can be "unlearned," changed and modified. Although attitudes are primarily learned, as parts of your personality they are very resistant to immediate change. "Positive" and "negative" are the two adjectives most often used to describe attitudes. Other descriptions include (but aren't limited to): enthusiastic, caring, confident, defensive, aggressive, fearful.

All of us have attitudes. Some are so ingrained that we've come to accept them as unchangeable parts of our personalities. Too often, on questioning someone who constantly complains, for example, you'll hear, "Oh, don't mind me. That's just the way I am." Not true. It's the way that person has, consciously or unconsciously, chosen to be.

Attitudes, like habits, can be changed. It is not easy but is quite often the key to having your life run more smoothly.

Attitudes can be changed. Because an attitude can be so deeply ingrained that it has become a way of life no longer even noticed—let alone examined—changing that attitude can be very hard to do. You must remember that an attitude is projected…it touches and affects others. Allowing yourself to project negativity in any form because "it's just the way I am" is grossly unfair to everyone around you. In the long run, you will suffer most.

Some self-assessment and management may be necessary merely to identify ingrained emotions as reactions that fall under any of the "negative" descriptions. Once identified, they can be changed. The process of such change can require frequent re-evaluation and continual focus. However, consider the rewards. Not only will you be happier within yourself, but other people will find greater pleasure in knowing you and spending time with you.

An attractive personality, including a positive attitude, is one of your greatest assets in life. The total effect you have on other people is the charm revealed in your speech, appearance, behavior and manner.

CHECK YOUR ATTITUDE!

How would your best friend describe your attitude?

How would your closest living relative describe your attitude?

How would your instructor describe your attitude?

How would you describe your attitude?

As a salon professional, your potential success will be enhanced if your peers and clients feel good in your presence. If you develop and nurture a positive attitude, not only will you have the ability to make your clients look good, you'll be able to make them feel good, too.

01

HABITS

Some people bite their nails, others bite their lips. Some people drum their fingers, others tap their feet. The only thing all these actions have in common is that the people performing them are probably not aware of doing so. These actions are very likely all habits.

Habits are "learned" and reinforced through events in your environment, which strengthen the habit. Like attitudes, habits become ingrained and are difficult to change. Most habits are harmless, inoffensive actions that others barely notice. *But some habits are annoying and unattractive.*

You're entering a service business and can't allow yourself to keep those habits that others may find annoying. Unattractive habits will limit your potential for success.

Make a well-considered list of all your habits. Review each item on your list. Is each habit consistent with the personal image you want to present to others? If not, begin a program of change now.

LIST OF HABITS	
GOOD	NEED CHANGE

CHANGING HABITS

Have you changed a habit in the past? If so, list the efforts you put forth to make the change occur.

_____
_____
_____

If you want to change a habit you currently have, can you apply these same efforts?

_____
_____

Having a positive attitude and practicing good habits will serve as fundamental principles in developing effective human relationships. Additional tips that will help along the way to your success include:

MAINTAIN ATTENDANCE AND PUNCTUALITY
- Manage your personal and professional schedule to avoid conflicts with time.
- Arrive at work on time. (Fifteen minutes prior to starting time is preferred by most employers.)

CONNECT WITH YOUR CLIENT
Be sensitive to the mood of your client. Some clients need and want the appointment time to be quiet and relaxing; others will want to talk and visit. Be a respectful listener and keep your conversation within the realm of your client's needs. **Never gossip or tell off-color stories.**

EXTEND COURTESY
- **Courtesy is the key to success**. Your thoughtfulness of others will go a long way in allowing clients to feel comfortable and relaxed with you.

TEAMWORK

The emotional atmosphere of a salon has unique importance. The existence of a harmonious salon environment depends heavily on teamwork.

As an individual member of a team, you can bring certain valuable characteristics to it that will have a positive influence on the group. Your behavior, skills and abilities are important to the success of the group. Strong, positive, professional relationships and team spirit will not be built overnight. You can begin by establishing a rapport with each person and continuing to work toward good communication, understanding and teamwork every day. The people you work with can become your friends as well as your professional associates.

Keeping your workstation clean, with all your tools in place, is usually set forth by a regulating agency, but also adds visually to the overall atmosphere you'll be trying to create. Placing and storing salon tools after use avoids the potential frustration that can occur when another co-worker needs the tool and it's not where it belongs. Respecting confidences shared by peers or clients is essential for an atmosphere of trust and sharing to exist. These are only a few of the many things a good team player will learn to do to help maintain the salon staff as a productive, happy team. **The key words for teamwork are consideration and cooperation**. If you're considerate and cooperative, you'll add to your team's success.

ETHICS

Over the years your parents and teachers may have taught you to live by the "Golden Rule": "Do unto others as you would have them do unto you." The Golden Rule may have been your first introduction to a code of ethical conduct. As you grow older, you begin defining and learning what is good or bad, right or wrong, according to the rules of society. **As your personality develops, you establish your own personal system of moral principles and values, which become known as your personal ethics.**

Your personal ethics, how you live your life and demonstrate your positive values and beliefs, such as honesty and fairness, carry over into your profession as you apply them to your working environment and relationships. **Professional ethics** deal with proper conduct in relationships with your employer, co-workers and clients.

Most professions have associations that establish a "Code of Professional Ethics" for their individual members. It is important for you to familiarize yourself with the Cosmetology Code of Ethics in your area. Adherence to a professional code of ethics reflects your personal integrity. These codes are designed not only to protect the public and guarantee that they will be treated honestly and fairly, but also to help you build confidence and increase your clientele.

Some of the responsibilities and work ethics that will help you gain respect and build solid professional relationships with your clients and co-workers are listed on the sample "Professional Code of Ethics."

PROFESSIONAL CODE OF ETHICS

- Show respect for the feelings and rights of others. Remember the Golden Rule.
- Be fair and courteous to your co-workers. Don't attempt to win clients away from your fellow professionals.
- Be fair and courteous to your clients. Be consistent in pricing your services. Don't show favoritism to certain clients.
- Always be eager to learn new methods and techniques. Attend educational programs that provide updated information or help you to improve your skills.
- Represent yourself, your services and products honestly to the public. Do not advertise a service that you cannot perform.
- Set a good example of good conduct and good behavior. Always cherish a good reputation. It will carry you a long way.
- Be loyal to your employer and co-workers. A successful salon will aid in your success.
- Keep your word and fulfill your obligations. Never break the confidence entrusted to you by a client or co-worker.
- Practice only the highest standards of infection control as provided by your regulating agency laws. Keep your work area and tools spotlessly clean.
- Believe in and be proud of your profession, just as you believe in yourself

---

COMMITMENT TO EXCELLENCE

Invest in yourself. Learn everything you can in school. Take an active part in school activities. Take advantage of advanced education and seminars. After graduation, continue to invest in your education by attending seminars, shows and workshops. Keep pace with what's happening in the industry. Become known for your willingness to share your knowledge and your enthusiasm for the salon industry. There is no limit to the success you can achieve if you are willing to invest the time and energy success demands of the true professional.

CONNECTING THEORY TO REAL-WORLD PRACTICE

PROFESSIONAL DEVELOPMENT	PERSONAL CONNECTION: IMPROVE YOURSELF	INDUSTRY CONNECTION: BECOME A PROFESSIONAL	CLIENT CONNECTION: SERVE THE GUEST
HEALTHY BODY AND MIND	Promote strength, independence	Increase productivity, ability to learn	Instill trust, confidence
EFFECTIVE COMMUNICATION	Express your true meaning and intent	Build career-enhancing skills and contacts	Demonstrate sincerity, dedication
HUMAN RELATIONS	Raise self-esteem, mutual respect	Create a harmonious work environment	Encourage rapport, loyalty

IN OTHER WORDS

Professional development is a commitment you make to yourself. Your ongoing dedication to professional development will elevate your physical and mental health, your professional status and your relationships with clients and co-workers.

LESSONS LEARNED

- Establishing routines to maintain a healthy body and mind puts you on the right track toward attaining your professional goals.

- Effective communication reflects your professionalism and includes both verbal and nonverbal messages.

- Positive human relations are influenced by personality, teamwork and ethical conduct.

02

SALON ECOLOGY

2.1 MICROBIOLOGY
BACTERIA
GROWTH OF BACTERIA
VIRUSES
EXTERNAL PARASITES
INFECTION
IMMUNITY

2.2 INFECTION CONTROL
SANITATION
DISINFECTION
STERILIZATION
INFECTION CONTROL GUIDELINES

2.3 FIRST AID
BLEEDING AND WOUNDS
BURNS
CHOKING
FAINTING
EYE INJURY

A HEALTHY AND SAFE
SALON DEPENDS
ON THE SALON
PROFESSIONAL KNOWING
THE CAUSES OF DISEASE,
WAYS TO CONTROL
INFECTION AND BASIC
SAFETY PROCEDURES

FOLLOWING THIS LESSON
YOU WILL BE ABLE TO:

Recognize the structure and function of bacteria and viruses by their:

- Types
- Classifications
- Growth and reproduction patterns
- Relationship to the spread of infection

Identify the infection control procedures and precautions used in schools and salons

List simple safety procedures and first-aid applications for minor burns, cuts, choking, eye injury and fainting

CONNECTING THEORY
TO REAL-WORLD PRACTICE

IMPLEMENTING TECHNIQUES THAT PREVENT OR MINIMIZE DISEASE AND INJURY WILL HELP YOU:

PERSONAL CONNECTION:	**INDUSTRY CONNECTION:**	**CLIENT CONNECTION:**
IMPROVE YOURSELF	BECOME A PROFESSIONAL	SERVE THE GUEST
Be proactive in keeping yourself and the people you care about as healthy as possible	Exemplify the responsibility and high standards expected of a licensed professional for ensuring a safe and healthy workplace	Maintain the health and safety of clients using scientifically and medically sound procedures

Ecology is the science of living beings in relationship to their environment. **Salon ecology** involves how to keep the special environment of the salon in balance to guarantee everyone's well-being.

SALON ECOLOGY

2.1 MICROBIOLOGY

02

Microbiology might seem like a big word to describe the study of small organisms. Yet that's exactly what microbiology is, the study (ology) of small (micro) living (bio) organisms called microbes, such as bacteria.

A basic knowledge of microbiology is important to you as a salon professional so that you can prevent the spread of disease through proper disinfection within the salon. It is your responsibility to protect your client's health and your own by taking the steps necessary to ensure that potentially infectious organisms aren't transmitted from one client to another—or to yourself and other co-workers—via the use of contaminated (dirty) tools and implements.

BACTERIA

Bacteria, sometimes called germs or microbes, are one-celled micro-organisms. The study of bacteria is referred to as **bacteriology**. While there are thousands of different kinds of **bacteria**, they can generally be classified into two types:
1. Nonpathogenic: non-disease producing bacteria
2. Pathogenic: disease-producing bacteria

NONPATHOGENIC BACTERIA

Nonpathogenic bacteria are harmless and can be very beneficial. Some bacteria have medical applications. Other bacteria, like some found in certain dairy products (such as yogurt), have health-enhancing properties. Still other bacteria cause the decay of refuse or vegetation and thereby improve the fertility of soil. **Saprophytes (SAP-ro-fights)** are nonpathogenic bacteria that live on dead matter and do not produce disease. Approximately 70% of all bacteria are nonpathogenic and many live on the surface of the skin.

PATHOGENIC BACTERIA

Pathogenic bacteria live everywhere in your environment and even exist inside your body. There are several different types of pathogenic bacteria that are harmful because they cause infection and disease, and some produce toxins. These infectious bacteria can be easily spread in the salon by using unsanitary implements or via dirty hands and fingernails.

When a disease spreads from one person to another via contact, it is referred to as contagious or communicable. Examples are the common cold, hepatitis and measles.

COSMETOLOGY FUNDAMENTALS

45

Bacteria are single cells with one of three basic shapes. Remember that you won't be identifying them with a microscope in the salon. You need mainly to prevent their growth and spread. Listed below by shape and kind are the more common pathogenic bacteria that you might encounter.

1. **Cocci** (**KOK**-si) are spherical (round)-shaped bacterial cells, which appear singularly or in groups.

   To remember, think C = circle and Cocci. There are three groups of Cocci:

   a. **Staphylococci** (staf-i-lo-**KOK**-si) are pus-forming bacterial cells that form grape-like bunches or clusters and are present in abscesses, pustules and boils.

   b. **Streptococci** (strep-to-**KOK**-si) are also pus-forming bacterial cells that form in long chains and can cause septicemia (sometimes called blood poisoning), strep throat, rheumatic fever and other serious infections.

   c. **Diplococci** (dip-lo-**KOK**-si) are bacterial cells that grow in pairs and are the cause of certain infections, including pneumonia. *Diplo means double.*

2. **Bacilli** (ba-**SIL**-i) are the most common form of bacterial cells. Bacilli are bar- or rod-shaped cells that can produce a variety of diseases including tetanus, bacterial influenza, typhoid fever, tuberculosis and diphtheria. *To remember, think B = bar and Bacilli.*

3. **Spirilla** (speye-**RIL**-a) are spiraled, coiled, corkscrew-shaped bacterial cells that cause highly contagious diseases such as syphilis, cholera and lyme disease. *To remember, think S = spiral and Spirilla.*

Bacteria can cause infections by invading the body through a break in the skin or through any of the body's natural openings (nose, mouth, etc.). An infection occurs when an insufficient number of antibodies are produced by the body's defense (immune) system to "fight" harmful bacteria.

GROWTH OF BACTERIA

Bacteria go through a growth cycle that consists of two stages: an active stage and an inactive stage.

ACTIVE STAGE

During the **active stage**, bacteria reproduce and grow rapidly. This reproduction usually takes place in dark, damp or dirty areas where a food source is available. As the bacteria absorb food, each cell grows in size and divides, creating two new cells. This activity is called mitosis. The process of cell division in bacteria is similar to the budding process in plants. Under favorable conditions, bacteria reproduce quickly, with as many as sixteen million offspring developing in twelve hours.

Over 1,500 of some types of bacteria will fit on the head of a pin.

INACTIVE STAGE

Bacteria are not always active; when conditions are unfavorable, the cells die or become inactive. Some bacteria, such as anthrax and tetanus, also have a normal **inactive or dormant stage**. When the environment makes the bacteria's survival difficult, some bacteria enter this inactive stage by creating spherical spores that are not harmed by disinfectants, cold or heat. Spore formation and other means by which bacteria can resist disinfection are factors to be considered when keeping the salon sanitary. Some bacteria can survive for a long time in extreme heat or cold. When conditions again become favorable for the bacteria's growth, the bacteria return to the active stage.

MOVEMENT OF BACTERIA

Because of their tiny size, bacteria can travel easily from place to place through air or water, from you to your client and vice versa. Bacilli and spirilla have the ability to move by themselves by using hair-like projections called **flagella** (flah-**JEL**-ah) or **cilia** (**SIL**-ee-a), which extend from the sides of the cell. A wave-like motion of these projections can easily propel the cell through a liquid.

VIRUSES

Viruses are sub-microscopic particles (much smaller than bacteria) that cause familiar diseases like the common cold, which is caused by a filterable virus. Other familiar diseases caused by viruses include respiratory and gastrointestinal infections, chicken pox, mumps, measles, small pox, yellow fever, rabies, hepatitis and polio.

Human Hepatitis B (HBV) is a highly infectious disease that infects the liver. Personal service workers (PSWs), such as nurses, doctors, teachers and salon professionals, are asked to take precautions against HBV, which is a vaccine-preventable disease. Because these professionals work with the public, inoculation is often recommended. Check with your local health agency or doctor to determine if you are a candidate for this inoculation.

Acquired Immunodeficiency Syndrome (AIDS) is a disease caused by HIV (Human Immunodeficiency Virus). HIV interferes with the body's natural immune system and causes the immune system to break down. Scientists have gained a great deal of knowledge about HIV and how it is spread and how to prevent it. HIV is spread when body fluids from an infected individual are absorbed into the blood stream of an uninfected individual. The fluids from the infected person must contain sufficient amounts of the virus. Fluids known to contain sufficient amounts of HIV are blood, semen, vaginal fluids and breast milk. Body fluids must enter the uninfected person for that person to be infected. Infectious fluids can enter through sexual intercourse, sharing needles or syringes, childbirth, cuts or sores (that are exposed to the infectious materials) and other instances where the body fluid of one individual enters the body of another.

Adapted from "AIDS - The War Within," Museum of Science and Industry, Chicago, IL

EXTERNAL PARASITES

TINEA CAPITIS (RINGWORM)

External parasites (PAR-ah-sights) are organisms that live on or obtain their nutrients from another organism called a host. External parasites generally cause harm to the host. Parasitic fungi are molds and yeasts that produce such contagious diseases as ringworm (tinea capitis) honeycomb ringworm (favus) and nail fungus, and noncontagious conditions such as dandruff and seborrheic dermatitis. Parasitic mites are insects that cause contagious diseases, such as itch mites (scabies) and head lice (pediculosis capitis). Professionals prevent the spread of contagions (fungi, bacteria, and mites) through proper disinfection procedures.

A mosquito is an example of an external parasite that lives on the blood of a host.

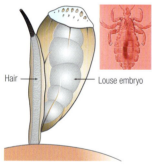

MAGNIFIED VIEW OF HEAD LICE AND EGG, OR NIT

HEAD LICE

Head lice are transmitted directly from one person to another, or by contact with articles that have come in contact with an infested person (such as combs and brushes, etc.). The presence of head lice is usually accompanied by head scratching, redness or small bite marks on the scalp. Close inspection of the hair and scalp with a fine-tooth comb, a strong light, and a magnifying glass will sometimes reveal the tiny, grayish adult lice. But you are more likely to see their eggs, called nits, which are whitish, oval specks attached to the hair shafts about ¼" (.6 cm) from the skin. The infestation is very easy to control, if detected, by using a pediculicide (lice-killing) shampoo.

INFECTION

An **infection** occurs when disease-causing (pathogenic) bacteria or viruses enter the body and multiply to the point of interfering with the body's normal state. A **contagious infection** or **communicable disease** is one that can be transmitted from one person to another, usually through touch or through the air. Micro-organisms that are spread to a new person frequently cause no infection unless they actually enter the body. **Bloodborne pathogens** are disease-causing bacteria or viruses that are carried through the blood or body fluids.

Common means of spreading infection in a salon include:
- Open sores
- Unclean hands and implements
- Coughing or sneezing
- Common use of drinking cups and towels
- Use of same implements on infected areas and noninfected areas
- Unsanitary salon conditions

Infections can be controlled by personal hygiene, public awareness and by practicing infection control procedures in the salon. If you have a contagious disease, it is important that you practice infection control procedures in order not to spread the infection. Check with your area's regulating agency for specific guidelines on dealing with contagious disease and refer a client with a contagious disease to a physician.

There are two basic classes of infection:

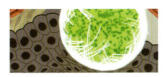

1. **A local infection** is located in a small, confined area. This is often indicated by a pus-filled boil, pimple or inflamed area. *To remember, think local = little.*

2. **A general (or systemic) infection** occurs when the circulatory system carries bacteria and their toxins to all parts of the body. *To remember, think general = giant.*

It is possible for a person to carry disease-producing bacteria or viruses with no recognizable symptoms of the disease. Such a person is called an "asymptomatic" carrier. For this reason, the same infection control procedures should be used with all clients. This practice is called "universal precautions." An example of a universal precaution is disinfecting salon equipment and implements.

IMMUNITY

Immunity is the ability of the body to destroy infectious agents that enter the body. To remember, think immunity gives you ammunition to fight disease. The body has remarkable defense mechanisms that fight infections in two basic ways:

1. **Active immunity** results when exposure to a disease organism triggers the immune system to produce antibodies to that disease. Exposure to the disease organism can occur through infection with the actual disease (resulting in natural immunity), or introduction of a killed or weakened form of the disease organism through vaccination (vaccine-induced immunity), such as polio or flu. Either way, if an immune person comes into contact with that disease in the future, their immune system will recognize it and immediately produce the antibodies needed to fight it. Active immunity is long-lasting, and sometimes life-long.

2. **Passive immunity** is provided when a person is given antibodies to a disease rather than producing them through his or her own immune system. A newborn baby acquires passive immunity from its mother through the placenta. A person can also get passive immunity through antibody-containing blood products such as immune globulin, which may be given when immediate protection from a specific disease is needed (such as rabies). This is the major advantage to passive immunity; protection is immediate, whereas active immunity takes time (usually several weeks) to develop. However, passive immunity lasts only for a few weeks or months. Only active immunity is long-lasting.

Adapted from cdc.gov

2.2 INFECTION CONTROL

Infection control is the term used to describe efforts to prevent the spread of disease and kill certain or all microbes. Infection control is divided into three main categories.

ALERT!

Many items in the salon come into contact with more than one person and can carry contagious microbes. Be proactive and take steps to prevent cross-contamination.

THREE CATEGORIES

- SANITATION
- DISINFECTION
- STERILIZATION

Beauty and Barber Shop, Instruments and Tools:
Thoroughly pre-clean. Completely immerse brushes, combs, scissors, clipper blades, razors, tweezers, manicure and other shop tools for 10 minutes (or as required by local authorities). Wipe dry before use. Fresh solution should be prepared daily or more often when the solution becomes diluted or soiled .

*Virucidal: For Complete Instructions For Hepatitis B Virus (HBV) and Human Immunodeficiency Virus (HIV-1) DISINFECTION Refer To Enclosed Hang Tag .

Statement of Practical Treatment: In case of contact, immediately flush eyes or skin with plenty of water for at least 15 minutes. For eye contacts, call a physician. If swallowed, drink egg whites, gelatin solution or if these are not available, drink large quantities of water. Avoid alcohol. Call a physician immediately.

Note to Physician: Probable mucosal damage may contra-indicate the use of gastric lavage.

Sanitation standards apply to removing dirt to aid in preventing the growth of microbes. Disinfection standards require that all tools and implements, including those that have come in contact with blood or body fluids, must be free from a broad spectrum of microbes. Sterilization standards mean that all microbes must be killed or destroyed.

Very important also to the area of infection control is the term **efficacy**, which means "ability to produce results" or "effectiveness." In relation to disinfectant products, standards have been established that require efficacy labels on all disinfectants to inform the user about what the product is "effective in fighting against." An example might be a disinfectant that states "effective against human Hepatitis B Virus and HIV-1." You will be required to use products based on the efficacy label.

Reading the manufacturer's directions is another important step in ensuring infection control practices. You will notice that methods will vary from product to product. Times for immersion (soaking) in a disinfectant, storage practices and application methods will be different for each product. The only way you can be sure that a product will do what you want it to is to **follow the directions**. It cannot be repeated often enough that two steps are necessary for effective infection control: **read the label and follow the directions**.

SANITATION

Sanitation is a term that means the process of removing dirt to aid in preventing the growth of microbes. Sanitation is the first level of infection control. It is important to note that **sanitation methods clean and reduce microbes on the surface, but do not kill microbes.**

An antiseptic is a product that can be applied to the skin to reduce microbes. Prior to a pedicure, manicure or other skin care procedure, apply an antiseptic to clean the skin. You may also use liquid soap as a manicure or pedicure soak to further reduce microbes on your client's skin before you begin your service. Remember, some of that bacteria might be good (nonpathogenic) and some may be harmful (pathogenic). Because you will not be breaking the skin, it is not necessary to use a product stronger than an antiseptic.

Infection control practices for sanitation of the school or salon require shared responsibilities from everyone on the team in order to provide a healthy environment. Review the infection control Sanitation Guidelines chart to gain knowledge in the steps taken to prevent the growth of microbes. Remember, preventing the growth of microbes and killing microbes are two different functions. Sanitation practices do not kill microbes, but do help in the prevention of the growth of microbes.

BASICS OF HAND WASHING

1. Moisten hands with warm water and liquid soap.
2. Spend at least 20 seconds working up a good lather. Pay particular attention to the fingers and the spaces between them and the fingernails.
3. Rinse hands well in warm water. Position hands and fingertips downward so the rinse progresses from wrist to fingertips.
4. Dry hands well to remove any remaining micro-organisms. A single-use paper towel or hands free air blowers are the most effective and do not carry the risk of cross-contamination posed by communal cloth towels.

SANITATION GUIDELINES

- Provide well-lit work areas.
- Provide hot and cold running water.
- Sanitize shampoo bowls before and after each use.
- Clean and remove hair and debris from all implements before disinfecting.
- Wash your hands with liquid soap and warm water immediately before serving each client. Liquid soap is recommended since bar soaps can harbor and transmit microbes.
- Remove all hair clippings after each service to prevent accumulation.
- Provide clean restrooms that are well stocked with tissue and paper towels. Never use restroom areas for storage of chemicals.
- Provide disposable drinking cups. Clean sinks and water fountains regularly.
- Keep salon free from insects and rodents.
- Never use the salon for cooking or living quarters.

SANITATION GUIDELINES (CONT'D)

- Empty waste receptacles daily.
- Wear clean, freshly laundered clothing.
- Use freshly laundered or disposable towels on each client. Never allow the protective cape to touch the client's neck.
- Never place tools, combs, rollers or bobby pins, etc., in your mouth or pockets.
- Properly launder all client gowns and headbands before reusing.
- Store soiled towels in a covered receptacle until laundered.
- Launder towels/linens after each use with an approved disinfectant so they don't accumulate and present a safety hazard (due to chemicals that may be present).
- Avoid touching your face, mouth or eyes during services.
- Never allow pets or animals in service area except for service animals as identified in the Americans With Disabilities Act.
- Allow smoking only in designated areas.
- Dispense all semi-fluids and powders with a shaker, dispenser pump, spray-type container, spatula or disposable applicator.

Rules of infection control are developed by area regulating agencies to protect the consumer. These rules require salons and cosmetology schools to keep the working areas, styling implements and all equipment in a sanitary condition. To do so, salons employ infection control methods to meet the required guidelines.

VENTILATION

It is important that the salon be sufficiently ventilated so that the air does not have a stale, musty odor or contain the odor of sprays, bleaches and various chemical solutions. The average room temperature should be about 70° Fahrenheit (21° Celsius).

The following guidelines provide an overview of various ventilation and sanitation practices for a healthy environment:
- Air conditioners permit changes in the quality and quantity of air as they cool, dehumidify (remove moisture) and cleanse pollutants from the air. Remember to change air filters as needed.
- Forced-air furnaces heat the air and cleanse it, to a degree. Remember to change air filters as needed.
- Exhaust fans help circulate the air but do not clean it.
- Air should be mechanically supplied through vents and air returns and/or supplied by opening windows and doors and using blower fans to circulate the fresh air.
- Provide local exhaust ventilation for areas in which chemicals are mixed or artificial nails are applied. Always keep all bottles capped when not in use.

- For localized exhaust systems in chemical mixing areas, manicure areas or perm areas, etc., make sure the fan in the unit is powerful enough to draw or blow the chemical vapor or dust away in an attempt to improve the safety of the salon professional and client.

DISINFECTION

Disinfection is the second level of infection control. **Disinfection** standards require products to destroy or kill bacteria and a broad spectrum of viruses on nonporous surfaces. These standards apply to all tools and implements used by the salon professional. Note that disinfection products are toxic.

Disinfectants are chemical products used to destroy or kill bacteria and some viruses (except bacterial spores). Bactericidals (kill harmful bacteria), tuberculocidals (kill tuberculosis), fungicidals (destroy fungus), viricidals (kill viruses) and pseudomonacidals (kill pseudomonas) are all categories of disinfectant products designed to kill specific organisms. The disinfecting chemicals used to kill these microbes are very strong and work well to disinfect styling implements but could be harmful to your skin. Follow manufacturer's directions regarding their use.

The Occupational Safety and Health Administration (OSHA) is the regulating agency under the Department of Labor that enforces safety and health standards in the workplace. OSHA Standards require that employees be informed of the dangers of the materials used in the workplace and the exposure they might have to toxic substances. **Material Safety Data Sheets (MSDS) and labeling of products are two important regulations that this group has put in place to assist in safe operations.** A Material Safety Data Sheet is designed to provide the key information on a specific product regarding ingredients, associated hazards, combustion levels, storage requirements, etc. Remember that for your protection and safety, it is your right as an employee to know what is contained in the product being used. OSHA Standards are important to the industry and help ensure general safety, especially in regard to mixing, storing, labeling and disposing of chemicals.

The Environmental Protection Agency (EPA) approves the efficacy of products used for infection control. This means that a manufacturer submits a product to this agency for verification of effectiveness against the organisms listed on the label. Once that determination has been made, an EPA registration number is given to the product along with approval of the efficacy claims on the label, stating what the product will destroy or be effective against. This registered number ensures the product is both safe and effective.

Broad spectrum disinfectants are a group of disinfectants that kill bacteria, viruses, fungi and pseudomonas. These products are effective and quick-acting. The label on a broad spectrum disinfectant will have an EPA-registered number along with an efficacy label stating that the product is an effective bactericidal, virucidal, fungicidal and pseudomonacidal.

ALERT!

MRSA (Methicillin-resistant Staphylococcus aureus) is a highly contagious bacterium that enters the skin through open wounds and can cause extremely serious staph infections. MRSA may initially appear as pimples or boils and is resistant to most antibiotics. Proper disinfection procedures using broad spectrum disinfectants are required to reduce exposure and protect consumers.

Always follow the manufacturer's directions, wear gloves and safety glasses when mixing disinfectants.

ALERT!

The 2001 OSHA (Occupational Safety and Health Administration) Bloodborne Pathogens Standard requires the use of an EPA registered disinfectant with an efficacy against HIV and HBV or tuberculocidal. This requirement applies to implements that accidentally come into contact with blood or body fluids.

The disinfectant may also be effective against HIV and HBV or tuberculocidal. Many regulating agencies have adopted this efficacy label for disinfection of all tools and implements. Check your area's rules and regulations for required usage.

The most important thing for you to know is that the efficacy label will tell you what the disinfectant is effective against. You will be guided by your area's rules as to what efficacy standard you need to use. One standard may guide you for disinfection of all tools and implements that **have not** come in contact with blood or body fluids, and another standard may guide you for disinfection of all tools and implements that **have** come in contact with blood or body fluids. A broad spectrum disinfectant with an efficacy label that reads "effective against HIV and Human Hepatitis B Virus or tuberculocidal" will meet both requirements.

Chemical disinfecting agents are available in varied forms, including liquid, capsule and powder. When choosing one from your beauty supply vendor, consider the following:
- Is it nonirritating to the skin?
- Is it in compliance with your area's regulating agency or Health Department?
- Is it economical and easy to purchase?
- Is it easy to use?
- Does it work quickly?
- Is it noncorrosive (harmless to metal or plastic implements)?
- What type of container is recommended for storage and usage?

Read the directions carefully and follow recommended safety precautions. Always note and follow specific immersion times. Preclean implements before disinfecting.

It is important to remember that disinfecting methods do not work instantly, but require some time to destroy microbes. Procedures and timing will vary, based on the product you are using. To familiarize you with a procedure used during general disinfection, an outline for disinfecting a brush or comb is listed on the next page.

NOTE: Many regulating agencies are very specific in their rules pertaining to precleaning metal instruments thoroughly with soap and water before immersing in any disinfectant solution. Precleaning instruments eliminates any minute particles that could cling and cause infection.

BRUSH OR COMB DISINFECTION PROCEDURE

1. Remove all hair from the brush or comb.
2. Wash the brush or comb thoroughly with soap and water to remove any dirt, grease or oil.
3. Rinse the brush or comb thoroughly and pat dry to avoid dilution when immersed in disinfectant.
4. Immerse the brush or comb completely in disinfecting solution. Follow timing instructions from manufacturer.
5. Remove the brush or comb with forceps, tongs or gloved hands. Follow manufacturer's directions for rinsing and drying.
6. Store in a disinfected, dry, covered container or cabinet (referred to as a dry sanitizer) until needed.

Prior to using a disinfectant, ultrasonic cleaners can be used. Ultrasonic cleaners use high-frequency sound waves to create a cleansing action that cleans areas on implements or tools that are difficult to reach with a brush. Hand cleaning is eliminated through the use of ultrasonic cleaners.

DISINFECTION GUIDELINES AND PROCEDURES

WET DISINFECTANT CONTAINER

DISCARD OR DISINFECT

An easy way to remember if you need to use sanitation or disinfection procedures is to tell yourself, "Implements that come in contact with the client must be discarded or disinfected." The following is an overview of the primary infection control procedures used for disinfection in the cosmetology environment:

- Disinfect combs and brushes after each use.
- Change chemical solutions in disinfectant containers regularly as recommended by manufacturer.
- Disinfect unplugged electrical appliances by spraying or wiping with a regulatory agency-approved solution. This includes parts of tools such as the guards on hair clippers.
- Wash, rinse, dry and disinfect by complete immersion, all cosmetology, nail care, esthetic and electrolysis tools and metal implements after each use in an approved, disinfectant solution mixed and used in accordance with the manufacturer's directions. In most cases, an EPA-registered, broad spectrum bactericidal, virucidal, fungicidal and pseudomonacidal disinfectant (which are effective against HIV, HBV or tuberculocidal) is used to ensure safety even in the case of exposure to blood or body fluids.
- Discard emery boards, cosmetic sponges and orangewood sticks after each use or give to the client, unless the manufacturer has specified that the product used can be disinfected (based on your area's requirements). **Implements must be nonporous to be disinfected. Regulatory agencies state proper disposal guidelines for nonporous items. The guiding principle here is discard or disinfect.**
- Store all disinfected tools in a disinfected, dry, covered container or cabinet.
- Dispose of sharp objects (razor blades, insulin needles, etc.) in a sealable, rigid container (puncture-proof) strong enough to protect you, the client and others from accidental puncture wounds that could happen during the disposal process.

- Ensure that all disinfecting products are labeled properly.
- Label and properly store prepared commercial disinfecting products, such as household bleach, to clean shampoo bowls, sinks, floors, working surfaces and bathroom fixtures. Even though your floor may be cleaned daily, never pick up and use an implement, cape, towel or anything that you have dropped. **Always continue your services with clean, disinfected materials and implements.**

DISINFECTION PRECAUTIONS

Decontaminated means free from dirt, oil and/or microbes.

Since the use of chemical disinfecting agents can be dangerous, they must be used cautiously to prevent mistakes and accidents. When using these chemical agents, work in a well-ventilated area, keep a first-aid kit on hand and always remember to take the following precautions:

- Tightly cover and label all containers; store in a cool, dry area (air, light and heat can weaken their effectiveness). Purchase chemicals in small quantities; always follow manufacturer's instructions.
- Avoid inhaling or spilling chemical solutions; avoid contact with skin or eyes; wipe up all spills at once; wear gloves and safety glasses; wash hands with liquid soap and water after handling all chemicals.
- Refer to Material Safety Data Sheet for proper handling if spills occur and for procedures if contact with eyes and skin occurs.

BLOOD SPILL PROCEDURE

If a blood spill should occur, use the following steps:

1. Stop the service; wash your hands; cover your hands with protective gloves when dealing with an injured party.
2. Apply antiseptic and/or liquid or spray styptic product to the injured party. If you are injured, stop the service and clean the injured area; apply antiseptic and/or liquid or spray styptic product.*
3. Dress or cover the injury with appropriate dressing.
4. Cover injured area with finger guard or glove as appropriate.
5. Clean and disinfect implements and workstation with a broad spectrum disinfectant.
6. Double-bag all blood-soiled (contaminated) articles and label the bag as hazardous waste or as directed by your area's regulating agency; remove your gloves and clean your hands with a liquid soap.
7. Return to client and continue the service.

*Do not allow containers, brushes, nozzles or styptic containers to touch the skin or come in contact with the wound.

STERILIZATION

Sterilization is the most effective level of infection control. **Sterilization** procedures kill or destroy all microbes. **You will be guided by your area's regulating agency for standards regarding cosmetology services and sterilization procedures.** Usually sterilization does not apply to cosmetology services because you are not puncturing or invading the skin when performing these services.

The amount of blood or body fluid that might be present during an offered service is a prime factor when regulators decide if sterilization procedures are required. Sterilization procedures are normally required for electrolysis and some esthetics services. For example, needles used by electrologists and lancets used by estheticians to invade (puncture) the skin must be sterilized, or they must be designed to be disposable. Sterilization standards require the use of a liquid sterilant and/or moist or dry heat, calibrated to various temperatures, to produce a surface free from all living organisms, even bacterial spores. Specific calibrations and timeframes are normally required for sterilization procedures. In addition, periodic checks by manufacturer representatives or approved technicians are assigned to ensure that procedures and equipment are being used in the proper way. Sterilization methods are costly, time-consuming and require a high degree of quality control to ensure results.

INFECTION CONTROL GUIDELINES

	LEVEL OF INFECTION CONTROL	ITEMS	PROCEDURE
STERILIZATION KILLS ALL MICROBES	HIGH	• Tools and implements that are used to puncture or invade the skin	• Use a liquid sterilant and/or moist or dry heat, calibrated to various temperatures to produce a microbe-free result on nonporous substances.
DISINFECTION KILLS CERTAIN BACTERIA	MEDIUM	• Tools and implements that **have** come in contact with blood or body fluids	• Use antibacterial, EPA-registered disinfectant effective against HIV and human Hepatitis B Virus or tuberculocidal mixed and immersed according to manufacturer's directions or as required by your area's regulating agency.
		• Tools and implements that **have not** come in contact with blood or body fluids	• Use broad-spectrum, EPA-registered bactericidal, virucidal, fungicidal, pseudomonacidal disinfectant, mixed and immersed according to manufacturer's directions or as required by your area's regulating agency.
SANITATION REMOVES DIRT	LOW	• Countertops, sinks, floors toilets, towels, linens	• Use EPA-registered cleaning product. Efficacy label will state "appropriate for floors, countertops, sinks, toilets, towels wand/or linens."
		• Your hands before each service	• Use liquid soap. Avoid bar soaps.
		• Your hands and client's hands and/or feet prior to manicuring or pedicuring service	• Use antiseptic designed for hands and/or feet.

2.3 FIRST AID

Most states have enacted **Good Samaritan Laws** to encourage people to help others in emergency situations. These laws give legal protection to people who provide emergency care to ill or injured persons. They require that the "Good Samaritan" use common sense and a reasonable level of skill not to exceed the scope of the individual's training in emergency situations. As a licensed professional, you are in contact with many people during the course of your career. Being prepared will help make the most of a serious situation. Following are some basic first-aid techniques that can be used in the workplace or at home:

BLEEDING AND WOUNDS

1. Place a clean cloth or gauze and gloved hand over the wound. Apply firm steady pressure for at least 5 minutes.
2. Call 9-1-1 or other emergency personnel if bleeding is severe.
3. Elevate an injured arm or leg above the level of the victim's heart if practical.
4. When bleeding stops, secure the cloth with a bandage. **Do not** lift the cloth completely from the wound to check if bleeding has stopped. Instead, visually inspect the flow of blood through the cloth. Be sure the bandage is not too tight. It may cut off circulation.
5. Never use a tourniquet unless you cannot control the bleeding. Tourniquets may result in subsequent medical amputation.
6. Have emergency personnel check the victim for shock if necessary.

COVER WOUND, **APPLY** PRESSURE

ELEVATE INJURED LIMB ABOVE HEART

WHEN BLEEDING STOPS, **APPLY** BANDAGE

NEVER USE A TOURNIQUET

BURNS

CHEMICAL BURNS

1. Rinse away all traces of chemicals while moving away any contaminated clothing from burn area.
2. Cover the burn loosely with a clean, dry cloth.
3. Refer person to medical attention if necessary.

HEAT OR ELECTRICAL BURNS

1. If the skin is not broken, immerse the burned area in cool (not ice) water or gently apply a cool compress until pain is relieved. Bandage with a clean, dry cloth.
2. Do not break a blister if one forms. Do not apply ointments or creams.
3. If skin is broken or if burns are severe:
   - Call 9-1-1 or other emergency personnel.
   - Do not clean the wound or remove embedded clothing.
   - Cover the burn loosely with a clean, dry cloth.

CHOKING

1. Determine if the victim can speak or cough forcibly and is getting sufficient air. Do not interfere with the victim's attempts to cough the obstruction from the throat. If victim cannot speak or is not getting sufficient air, have someone call 9-1-1 while you perform abdominal thrusts.
2. Stand behind the victim and wrap your arms around the stomach.
3. Make a thumbless fist with one hand and place that fist just above the navel and well below the ribs, with the thumb and forefinger side toward the victim.
4. Perform an upward thrust by grasping this fist with the other hand and pulling it quickly toward you with an inward and slightly upward movement. Repeat if necessary.

NOTE: These instructions are for choking victims over one year of age. There are specific guidelines for treatment of infant choking that are not outlined in this text.

DETERMINE IF VICTIM CAN TALK OR COUGH

WRAP YOUR ARMS AROUND VICTIM FROM BEHIND AND MAKE A THUMBLESS FIST

PERFORM AN UPWARD THRUST

FAINTING

1. Lay the victim down on back and make sure he or she has plenty of fresh air.
2. Reassure the victim and apply a cold compress to the face.
3. If the victim vomits, roll him or her on side and keep the windpipe clear.

NOTE: Fainting victims regain consciousness almost immediately. If this does not happen, the victim could be in serious danger and you should call 9-1-1 as soon as possible.

Material Safety Data Sheets

A separate Material Safety Data Sheet (MSDS) for potentially hazardous products used in the salon should be kept readily available in a file in case of an emergency. The MSDS provides information on the contents, including potential hazards, which may be helpful if an allergic reaction or injury occurs related to the product's usage.

EYE INJURY

CHEMICAL

1. Hold the eyelids apart and flush the eyeball with lukewarm water for at least 15 to 30 minutes. Be careful not to let runoff water flow into the other eye.
2. Place a gauze pad or cloth over both eyes and secure with a bandage.
3. Get to an eye specialist or emergency room immediately.

CUT, SCRATCH OR EMBEDDED OBJECT

1. Place a gauze pad or cloth over both eyes and secure with a bandage.
2. Do not try to remove an embedded object.
3. Get to an eye specialist or emergency room immediately.

The safety, protection and welfare of the clients you serve is the reason you are licensed as a professional. Remember that your health and safety are important issues as well. Make sure you know the procedures necessary for a clean, healthy, safe environment.

CONNECTING THEORY TO REAL-WORLD PRACTICE

SALON ECOLOGY	PERSONAL CONNECTION: IMPROVE YOURSELF	INDUSTRY CONNECTION: BECOME A PROFESSIONAL	CLIENT CONNECTION: SERVE THE GUEST
MICROBIOLOGY	Understand what causes disease and how it spreads	Lead by example in health awareness and disease prevention	Exemplify total client care through a healthy environment
INFECTION CONTROL	Maintain your health for peak performance	Uphold responsibility for preventing the spread of disease	Protect clients from preventable disease
FIRST AID	Know what to do in a safety emergency	Embody the role of a "Good Samaritan"	Take decisive action to minimize possible injuries

IN OTHER WORDS

Your attention to salon ecology will enable you to protect the safety and well-being of your clients by preventing unnecessary infections and performing first-aid procedures when needed.

LESSONS LEARNED

- A basic knowledge of microbiology provides the foundation for preventing the spread of disease through proper disinfection in the salon.

- Infection control involves the steps you take to prevent the spread of disease and kill certain or all microbes.

- First-aid safety precautions allow a salon professional to help people in emergency situations.

03

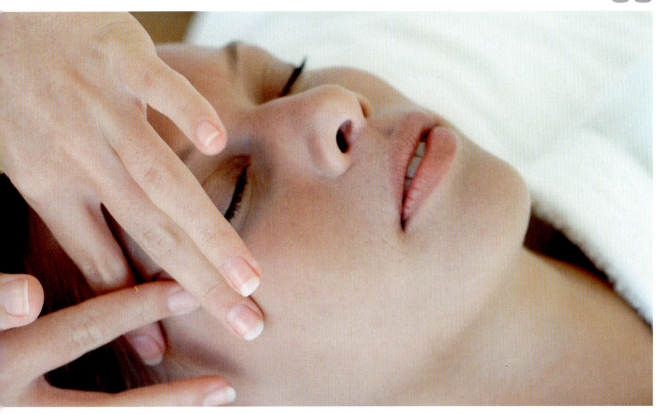

ANATOMY AND PHYSIOLOGY

3.1 BUILDING BLOCKS OF THE HUMAN BODY
CELLS
TISSUES
ORGANS
BODY SYSTEMS

3.2 BASIC BODY SYSTEMS
THE SKELETAL SYSTEM
THE MUSCULAR SYSTEM
THE CIRCULATORY SYSTEM
THE NERVOUS SYSTEM
THE DIGESTIVE SYSTEM
THE EXCRETORY SYSTEM
THE RESPIRATORY SYSTEM
THE ENDOCRINE SYSTEM
THE REPRODUCTIVE SYSTEM
THE INTEGUMENTARY SYSTEM

KNOWLEDGE OF THE
HUMAN BODY AND
ITS SYSTEMS IS THE
FOUNDATION FOR
PROVIDING QUALITY
SALON SERVICES THAT
RESPECT AND CARE
FOR THE WHOLE CLIENT

FOLLOWING THIS LESSON
YOU WILL BE ABLE TO:

Explain the relationship and function of cells, tissues and primary organs within the human body

Identify the structure, function and primary cosmetological significance, where appropriate, of 8 body systems

CONNECTING THEORY TO REAL-WORLD PRACTICE

UNDERSTANDING THE HUMAN BODY'S STRUCTURAL BUILDING BLOCKS AND HOW THEY FUNCTION, WILL HELP YOU:

PERSONAL CONNECTION:	**INDUSTRY CONNECTION:**	**CLIENT CONNECTION:**
IMPROVE YOURSELF	BECOME A PROFESSIONAL	SERVE THE GUEST
Be more aware of why the body acts and responds the way it does and the power you have to affect it	Excel at design, sculpture and massage services that involve familiarity with muscles, circulation and bone structure	Produce results that have immediate and long-lasting positive effects on how clients look and feel

Understanding anatomy and physiology—the parts of the body and how they work—will allow you to provide the be care to your clients while delivering the salon services that help them look and feel their best.

3.1 BUILDING BLOCKS OF THE HUMAN BODY

Salon professionals, like doctors and nurses, are licensed to touch a client. Whether you are shampooing, massaging, styling or working on nails or skin, you have the privilege of bringing relaxation, well-being and personal enhancement to others.

Of particular interest to the salon professionals are the muscles, nerves, circulatory system and bones of the head, face, neck, arms and hands. An understanding of muscles, circulatory system and nerves will help you develop beneficial facial and massage techniques. Knowledge of the bones of the skull is essential for the design of flattering hairstyles and for the proper application of cosmetics. The major groups of muscles, nerves and bones will receive the greatest focus in this chapter. However, you will also review other fundamental structures and functions of the human body to have a broader context for understanding the importance of touch within your profession.

The study of the human body can be conveniently divided into two general categories: **Anatomy, the study of the organs and systems of the body, and physiology, the study of the functions these organs and systems perform. The study of structures that can be seen with the naked eye is called gross anatomy. The study of structures too small to be seen except through a microscope is called histology or microscopic anatomy.**

To understand anatomy and physiology you must first be aware of the building blocks of the human body, which are:
- Cells
- Tissues
- Organs
- Systems

CELLS

Your knowledge of muscles, nerves, bones and all bodily systems needs to start at the level of the single cell. **Cells are the basic units of living matter (life).** Cells are composed of **protoplasm** (PRO-to-plazm), a gel-like substance containing water, salt and nutrients obtained from food. Cells vary in size, shape, structure and function, but they have certain characteristics in common. A cell contains three basic parts:

1. The nucleus (NU-kle-us), or control center, of cell activities
2. The cytoplasm (SI-to-plazm), or production department of the cell, where most of the cell's activities take place
3. The cell membrane, or outer surface of the cell, which encloses the protoplasm

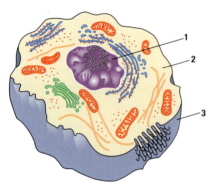

The nucleus is located in the cytoplasm, and both are surrounded by the cell membrane. Cells with common properties or functions combine to form the various tissues of the body.

In order to grow and remain healthy, cells need adequate supplies of food, oxygen, water, proper temperature and the ability to eliminate waste products. If these criteria are not present, cell growth will be impaired. The chemical process in which cells receive nutrients (food) for cell growth and reproduction is known as metabolism (me-TAB-e-lism). There are two phases of metabolism:

1. **Anabolism** (ah-NAB-oh-lizm), the process of building up larger molecules from smaller ones. During this phase, the body stores water, food and oxygen for the times when they are needed by the body.
2. **Catabolism** (kah-TAB-oh-lizm), the process of breaking down larger molecules or substances into smaller ones. This phase causes a release of energy within the cell, necessary for the performance of specific body functions, including muscular movements and digestion.

TISSUES

Groups of cells of the same kind make up tissues. There are five primary types of tissue in the human body:
1. **Epithelial** (ep-i-THE-le-el) tissue that covers and protects body surfaces and internal organs
2. **Connective tissue** that supports, protects and holds the body together
3. **Nerve tissue** that coordinates body functions in addition to carrying messages to and from the brain and spinal cord
4. **Muscular tissue** that contracts, when stimulated, to produce motion
5. **Liquid tissue** that carries food, waste products and hormones

ORGANS

Organs are separate body structures that perform specific functions. They are composed of two or more different tissues. Organs of primary importance include:

1. The **brain**, which controls all body functions

2. The **eyes**, which control vision

3. The **heart**, which circulates the blood

4. The **lungs**, which supply the blood with oxygen

5. The **stomach** and **intestines**, which digest food

6. The **liver**, which removes the toxic byproducts of digestion

7. The **kidneys**, which eliminate water and waste products

8. The **skin**, the body's largest organ, which forms the external protective layer of the body

BODY SYSTEMS

A system is a group of body structures and/or organs that, together, perform one or more vital functions for the body. Of the 10 body systems, you will study eight in this chapter. The reproductive system is mentioned briefly and in *Chapter 15, The Study of Skin*, you will study the integumentary system.

> **SKELETAL** – Provides framework of the body
> **MUSCULAR** – Moves the body
> **CIRCULATORY** – Circulates blood through the body
> **NERVOUS** – Sends and receives body messages
> **DIGESTIVE** – Supplies food to the body
> **EXCRETORY** – Eliminates waste from the body
> **RESPIRATORY** – Controls breathing of the body
> **ENDOCRINE** – Controls growth and general health and reproduction of the body
> **REPRODUCTIVE** – Allows living organisms to procreate others of its kind
> **INTEGUMENTARY** – Controls the sebaceous (oil) and sudoriferous (sweat) glands

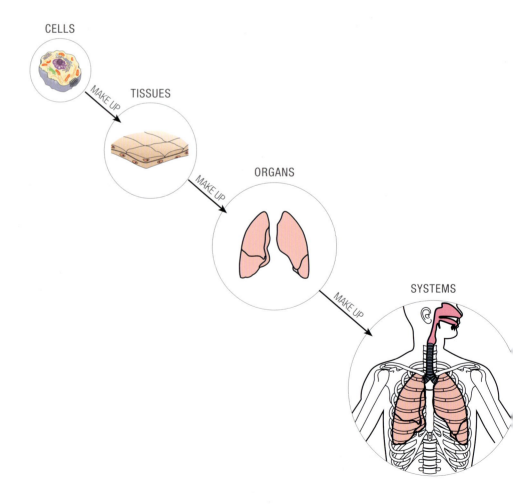

03

3.2 BASIC BODY SYSTEMS

THE SKELETAL SYSTEM

The physical foundation of the body, the skeletal system, is composed of **206** bones of different shapes and sizes, each attached to others at movable joints such as elbows and knees or immovable joints found in the pelvis and skull. A **joint** is the point at which two or more bones are joined together.

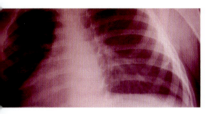

Osteology (as-te-AL-e-je) is the study of bone. The term "os" is the technical term for bone. Bones are described as either long, flat, or irregular in shape. **Long bones** are found in the arms and legs. **Flat bones** are plate-shaped and located in the skull. Irregular bones are found in the wrist, ankle and spinal column (the back). **Bone** is composed of $2/3$ mineral matter and $1/3$ organic matter and produces red and white blood cells and stores calcium. You might have thought of bone as the hardest part of the body but in reality, tooth enamel is the hardest substance of the body.

The functions of the skeletal system include:
1. Supporting the body by giving it shape and strength
2. Surrounding and protecting internal organs
3. Providing a frame to which muscles can attach
4. Allowing body movement

THE SKULL
The skull is the skeleton of the head that encloses and protects the brain and primary sensory organs. Bones of the skull are divided into two groups: the eight bones of the cranium and the 14 bones of the facial skeleton.

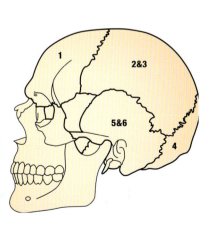

THE CRANIUM
Of the eight bones that compose the cranium, only 6 are affected by scalp massage.
1. The **frontal** is the bone that extends from the top of the eyes to the top of the head and forms the forehead.
2-3. The **parietal** (pah-RI-e-tal) are the two bones that form the crown and upper sides of the head.
4. The **occipital** (ak-SIP-et-al) is the bone that forms the back of the skull, indenting above the nape area.
5-6. The **temporal** (TEM-poh-ral) are the two bones located on either side of the head, directly above the ears and below the parietal bones.

These bones will frequently be referred to when directions are given for sculpting and designing techniques.

COSMETOLOGY FUNDAMENTALS

67

The remaining 2 bones of the cranium have no part in either massage or styling techniques and are not labeled on the illustration on the previous page.
- The **sphenoid** (**SFE**-noid) is located behind the eyes and nose and connects all the bones of the cranium.
- The **ethmoid** (**ETH**-moid) is the spongy bone between the eyes that forms part of the nasal cavity.

FACIAL SKELETON

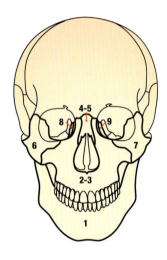

Of the 14 bones that compose the facial skeleton, only 9 are involved in facial massage.
1. The **mandible** (**MAN**-di-bl) is the lower jaw and the largest bone of the facial skeleton.
2-3. The **maxillae** (mak-**SIL**-e) are the 2 bones of the upper jaw.
4-5. The **nasal** (**NA**-zel) are the 2 bones which join to form the bridge of the nose.
6-7. The **zygomatic** (zi-go-**MAT**-ik) or **malar** (**MA**-ler) are the 2 bones that form the upper cheek and the bottom of the eye socket.
8-9. The **lacrimal** (**LAK**-ri-mal) are the smallest 2 bones of the facial skeleton and form the front part of the inner, bottom wall of the eye socket.

The remaining 5 bones of the facial skeleton are unaffected by facial massage and are not shown on the illustration.
- The **turbinal** (**TUR**-bi-nal) are the 2 spongy bones that form the sides of the nasal cavity.
- The **vomer** (**VO**-mer) or Nasal System is the bone in the center of the nose that divides the nasal cavity.
- The **palatine** (**PAL**-ah-tin) are the 2 bones that form the roof of the mouth and the floor of the eye sockets.

The shape and size of all bones of the skull and their relationship to one another will help you determine the most flattering use of makeup and hair designs for individual clients.

NECK BONES

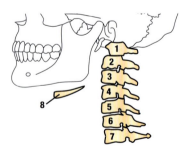

1-7. The **cervical vertebrae** (**SUR**-vi-kel **VURT**-e-bray), the seven bones that form the top part of the spinal column, are often manipulated in extended scalp massage.
8. The **hyoid** (**HI**-oid) bone is the u-shaped bone at the base of the tongue that supports the muscles of the tongue.

03

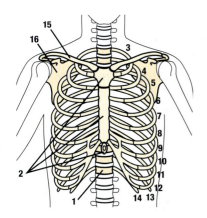

BACK, CHEST AND SHOULDER BONES

The chest, or **thorax** (tho-raks), is the bony cage composed of the spine, or **thoracic** (tho-RAS-ik) vertebrae (1), and the **sternum** (2) and 12 **ribs** (3-14). It encloses and protects the heart, lungs and other internal organs. The bone that forms the area from the throat to the shoulder is known as the **clavicle** (klav-i-kel) (15) or collarbone. The large, flat bone extending from the middle of the back upward to the joint where it attaches to the clavicle is called the **scapula** (SKAP-yu-lah) (16).

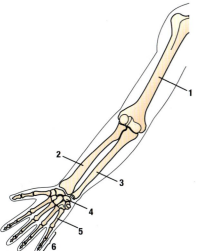

ARM, WRIST AND HAND BONES

1. The **humerus** (HU-mur-us), the largest bone of the upper arm, extends from the elbow to the shoulder.
2. The **radius** (RAD-e-us) is the small bone on the thumb side of the lower arm or forearm.
3. The **ulna** (UL-nah) is the bone located on the little finger side of the lower arm.
4. The **carpals** (KAR-pels) are the 8 small bones held together by ligaments to form the wrist or carpus.
5. The **metacarpals** (met-ah-KAR-pels) are the 5 long, thin bones that form the palm of the hand.
6. The **phalanges** (fah-LAN-jes) are the 14 bones that form the digits or fingers. Each finger has 3 phalanges, while the thumb has only 2.

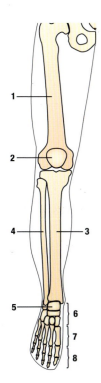

LEG, ANKLE AND FOOT BONES

Four bones make up the leg:
1. The **femur** (FEE-mur) is the thigh bone or longest bone in the body.
2. The **patella** (pah-TEL-lah), or kneecap, sits over the front of the knee joint.
3. The **tibia** (TIB-ee-ah), or shinbone, is the inner and larger of the two lower leg bones, extending from the knee to the ankle.
4. The **fibula** (FIB-u-lah) is the outer and narrower of the two lower leg bones, extending from the knee to the ankle.

Three bones make up the ankle:
5. The **talus** (TA-lus), or anklebone, sits above the heel bone and forms the lower part of the ankle joint. The talus, tibia and fibula form the ankle joint.

Twenty-six bones make up the foot:
6. The **tarsals** (TAHR-suls) are seven bones that makeup the mid foot and rear foot, including talus, calcaneus (heel), navicular, three cuneiform bones, and the cuboid.
7. The **metatarsals** (met-ah-TAHR-sul) are five long, slender bones (one for each digit) that connect the phalanges to the tarsals.
8. The **phalanges** (fuh-LAN-jeez) are 14 bones that form the digits; three phalanges in each toe and two in the big toe.

COSMETOLOGY FUNDAMENTALS

69

THE MUSCULAR SYSTEM

Myology (mi-OL-o-je) is the study of the structure, function and diseases of the muscles. There are more than 500 large and small muscles in the body, composing approximately 40% of the body's weight. **Muscles** are fibrous tissues that contract, when stimulated by messages carried by the nervous system, to produce movement.

The functions of the muscular system include:
1. Support of the skeleton
2. Production of body movements
3. Contouring of the body
4. Involvement in the functions of other body systems (e.g., digestive, circulatory and nervous systems)

VOLUNTARY OR STRIATED

INVOLUNTARY OR NON-STRIATED

There are 2 types of muscle tissues:
1. The **voluntary** or **striated** (STRI-at-ed) muscles respond to commands regulated by will.
2. The **involuntary** or **non-striated** muscles respond automatically to control various body functions including the functions of internal organs.

The same muscles may function both voluntarily and involuntarily. For example, eye muscles respond to a conscious command to blink, but they also blink automatically to maintain eye moisture. **The salon professional is primarily concerned with the voluntary muscles of the head, face, neck, arms and hands.**

The cardiac (heart) muscle is the muscle of the heart itself and is the only muscle of its type in the human body. This rugged muscle functions involuntarily.

SPECIAL TERMINOLOGY

The following common terms will be used to describe what a muscle does or where it is located.

ANTERIOR (an-TER-e-er) – in front of
POSTERIOR (pos-TER-e-er) – behind or in back of

SUPERIORIS (su-per-e-OR-es) – located above or is larger
INFERIORIS (in-FIR-e-or-es) – located below or is smaller

LEVATOR (le-VA-ter) – lifts up
DEPRESSOR (de-PRES-er) – draws down or depresses

DILATOR (DI-la-ter) – opens, enlarges or expands

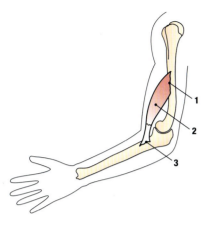

The three parts of the muscle are:
1. The **origin** is the nonmoving (fixed) portion of the muscle attached to bones or other fixed muscle. The term skeletal muscles refers to muscles attached to bone.
2. The **belly** is the term applied to the midsection of the muscle, between the two attached sections.
3. The **insertion** is the portion of the muscle joined to movable attachments: bones, movable muscles or skin.

Muscles produce movement through contraction (tightening) and expansion (relaxing). When a contraction occurs, one of the muscle attachments moves (insertion) while the other remains fixed (origin). All muscles (except those of the face) are attached at both ends either by bone or another muscle. Facial muscles are only attached at one end.

Stimulation of muscular tissue can be achieved by using the following methods:
1. Massage
2. Electric Current (high-frequency and faradic current)
3. Light Rays (infrared rays and ultraviolet rays)
4. Heat Rays (heating lamps and heating caps)
5. Moist Heat (steamers, warm steam towels)
6. Nerve Impulses (through nervous system)
7. Chemicals (certain acids and salts)

SCALP AND FACE MUSCLES

The scalp and face muscles are of primary interest as you perform scalp and neck massages and facials. The salon professional will also often employ general massage techniques to the scalp and neck just before or during a shampoo. Muscles affected by massage are generally manipulated from the insertion attachment to the origin attachment. The professional who performs facials must know the position of the muscles in the face. Light facial massage, used when applying certain facial treatment products, should follow the muscle line.

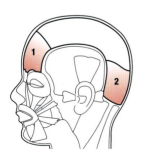

SCALP MUSCLES

The **epicranium** (ep-i-KRA-ne-um) consists of all of the structures above the cranium, including muscle, skin and aponeuroses. The **epicranius** (ep-i-KRA-ne-us) or **occipitofrontalis** (ok-SIP-ih-to-fron-TA-les) is a broad muscle formed by two muscles joined by the **aponeurosis** (ap-o-noo-ROH-sis) tendon:
1. The **frontalis** (frun-TA-les) muscle extends from the forehead to the top of the skull. It raises eyebrows or draws the scalp forward.
2. The **occipitalis** (ok-sip-i-TAL-is) muscle is located at the nape of the neck and draws the scalp back.

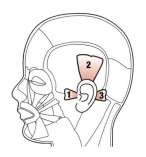

EAR MUSCLES

The three muscles of the ear are stationary and have no recognized function.
1. The **auricularis** (aw-rik-ya-**LA**-ris) **anterior** muscle is located in front of the ear.
2. The **auricularis superior** muscle is located above the ear.
3. The **auricularis posterior** muscle is located behind the ear.

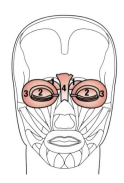

EYE AND NOSE MUSCLES

1. The **corrugator** (**KOR**-e-gat-er), located between the eyebrows, controls the eyebrows, drawing them in and downward.
2. The **levator palpebrae** (pol-pe-bra) **superioris,** located above the eyelids, functions to raise the eyelid.
3. The **orbicularis oculi** (or-bik-ye-**LAR**-es **AK**-yu-le) circles the eye socket and functions to close the eyelid.
4. The **procerus** (pro-**SER**-us), located between the eyebrows across the bridge of the nose, draws brows down and wrinkles the area across the bridge of the nose.

Four muscles located inside the nose, called the **nasalis, posterior dilator naris, anterior dilator naris, and depressor septi,** control contraction and expansion of the nostrils.

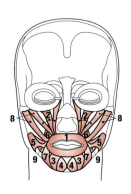

MOUTH MUSCLES

1. The **orbicularis oris** (or-bik-ye-**LAR**-es **O**-ris) circles the mouth and is responsible for contracting, puckering and wrinkling the lips, as in kissing or whistling.
2. The **quadratus labii superioris** (kwod-**RA**-tus **LA**-be) (also known as the Levator Labii Superioris) consists of 3 parts. It is located above the upper lip, raises both the nostrils and the upper lip, as in expressing distaste.
3. The **quadratus labii inferioris** (also known as the Depressor Labii Inferioris), located below the lower lip, pulls the lower lip down or to the side, as in expressing sarcasm.

4. The **mentalis** (men-**TAL**-us), located at the tip of the chin, pushes the lower lip up and/or wrinkles the chin, as in expressing doubt.
5. The **risorius** (re-**SOR**-e-us), located at the corner of the mouth, draws the mouth up and out, as in grinning.
6. The **caninus** (kay-**NEYE**-nus) (also known as the Levator Anguli Oris), located above the corners of the mouth, raises the angle of the mouth, as in snarling.
7. The **triangularis** (tri-an-gu-**LAR**-us) (also known as the Depressor Anguli), located below the corners of the mouth, draws the corners of the mouth down, as in expressing depression.
8. The **zygomaticus** (zi-go-**MAT**-ik-us), located outside the corners of the mouth, draws the mouth up and back, as in laughing and consists of zygomaticus major and minor.
9. The **buccinator** (**BUK**-si-na-ter), located between the jaws and cheek, is responsible for compressing the cheek to release air outwardly, as in blowing.

MASTICATION MUSCLES

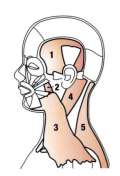

1. The **temporalis** (tem-po-**RA**-lis) is located above and in front of the ear and performs both opening and closing the jaw, as in chewing (mastication).
2. The **masseter** (**MAS**-se-ter) covers the hinge of the jaw and aids in closing the jaw, as in chewing (mastication).

NECK AND BACK MUSCLES

Refer to both diagrams for clarification.

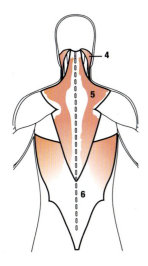

3. The **platysma** (plah-**TIZ**-mah) extends from the tip of the chin to the shoulders and chest and depresses the lower jaw and lip, as in expressing sadness.
4. The **sternocleido mastoideus** (stur-no-**KLI**-do mas-**TOID**-e-us) extends along the side of the neck from the ear to the collarbone and causes the head to move from side to side and up and down, as in nodding "yes" or "no".
5. The **trapezius** (trah-**PE**-ze-us) is a flat, triangular muscle covering the upper and back part of the neck and shoulders. It aids in drawing the head back and elevating the shoulder blades.
6. The **latissimus dorsi** (lah **TIS**-i-mus **DOR**-se) is a flat, triangular muscle that covers the lumbar (lower back) region and lower half of the thoracic region. This muscle aids in swinging of the arms.

SHOULDER, CHEST AND ARM MUSCLES

1. The **pectoralis** (pek-to-RAL-us) **major** (**1a**) and **pectoralis minor** (**1b**) extend across the front of the chest. These muscles assist in swinging the arms.
2. The **serratus anterior** (ser-RA-tus an-TER-e-er) is located under the arm. This muscle helps in lifting the arm and in breathing.

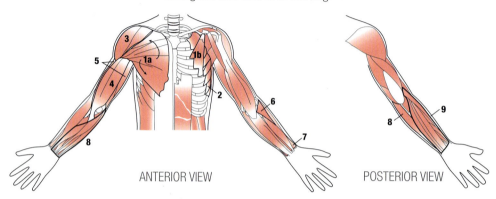

ANTERIOR VIEW   POSTERIOR VIEW

3. The **deltoid** (DEL-toid) covers the shoulder. This triangle-shaped muscle lifts the arm or turns it.
4. The **bicep** (BI-cep) is the primary muscle in the front of the upper arm. This muscle raises the forearm, bends the elbow and turns the palm of the hand down.
5. The **tricep** (TRI-cep) extends the length of the upper arm to the forearm. This muscle controls forward movement of the forearm.
6. The **supinator** (SU-pi-nat-or) runs parallel to the ulna. This muscle turns the palm of the hand up.
7. The **pronator** (PRO-nat-or) runs across the front of the lower part of the radius and the ulna. This muscle turns the palm of the hand downward and inward.
8. The **flexor** (FLEX-er) is located mid-forearm, on the inside of the arm. This muscle bends the wrist and closes the fingers.
9. The **extensor** (eks-TEN-sor) is located mid-forearm, on the outside of the arm. This muscle straightens the fingers and wrist.

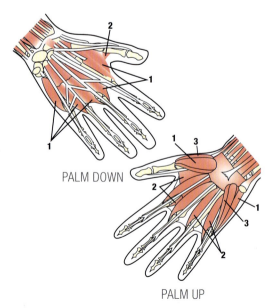

PALM DOWN

PALM UP

HAND MUSCLES

A number of small muscles stretch over the fingers, connect the joints and provide dexterity. **Abductor** (ab-DUK-tor) muscles (**1**) separate the fingers while **adductor** (ah-DUK-tor) muscles (**2**) draw them together. The **opponens** muscles (**3**) are located in the palm (palmor view) of the hand and cause the thumb to move toward the fingers, giving the ability to grasp or make a fist.

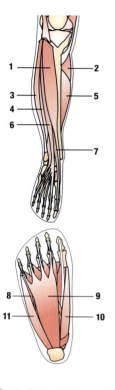

LEG AND FOOT MUSCLES

1. The **tibialis anterior** (tib-ee-**AHL**-is an-**TEHR**-ee-ohr) covers the front of the shin and bends the foot upward and inward.
2. The **gastrocnemius** (gas-truc-**NEEM**-e-us) is at the back of the leg attached to the lower rear surface of the heel and pulls the foot down.
3. The **peroneus longus** (per-oh-**NEE**-us **LONG**-us) originates in the upper two-thirds of the outer fibula and causes the foot to invert and turn outward.
4. The **peroneus brevis** (per-oh-**NEE**-us **BREV**-us) originates in the lower third of the fibula and bends the foot down and out.
5. The **soleus** (SO-lee-us) originates in the upper portion of the fibula from just below the knee to the heel and bends the foot down.
6. The **extensor digitorum longus** (eck-**STEN**-sur dij-it-**TOHR**-um **LONG**-us) is located on the outside of the lower leg and bends the foot up and extends the toes.
7. The **extensor hallucis longus** (eck-**STEN**-sur ha-**LU**-sis **LONG**-us) is located between the tibialis interior and extensor digitorum longus and extends the big toe and flexes the foot.

Four muscles of the foot

8. The **flexor digiti minimi brevis** (**FLEK**-sur dij-it-ty **MIN**-eh-mee **BREV**-us) flexes the joint of the small toe.
9. The **flexor digitorum brevis** (**FLEK**-sur dij-ut-**TOHR**-um **BREV**-us) lies in the middle of the sole of the foot; flexes toe digits 2 through 4.
10. The **abductor hallucis** (ab-**DUK**-tohr ha-**LU**-sis) moves the big toe away from the other toes.
11. The **abductor digiti minimi** (ab-**DUK**-tohr dij-it-ty **MIN**-eh-mee) moves the smallest toe away from the other toes.

THE CIRCULATORY SYSTEM

The **circulatory** or **vascular system** controls the circulation of blood and lymph through the body. As a salon professional, you will use massage treatments that will directly influence or stimulate this very important body system. The circulatory system is divided into two, interrelated subsystems called:

- The **cardiovascular** or **blood-vascular system**, which is responsible for the circulation of blood, includes the heart, arteries, veins and capillaries.
- The **lymph-vascular system**, which is responsible for the circulation of lymph through lymph glands, nodes and vessels.

The cardiovascular system, using **arteries**, **veins** and **capillaries** as blood-carrying vessels, combines with the lymph system to maintain steady circulation of the blood. **Lymph** is a byproduct of the blood system and, after traveling through the lymph glands and vessels, moves back into the normal bloodstream. Lymph filters the blood by removing toxins (poisons). The main function of lymph is to reach the parts of the body not reached by blood.

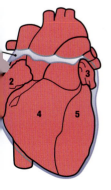

THE CARDIOVASCULAR SYSTEM
THE HEART

The heart, a cone-shaped, muscular organ located in the chest cavity, is normally about the size of a closed fist. The rugged muscle of this organ, entirely encased in a membrane called the **pericardium** (per-i-**KAR**-de-um) (**1**), contracts and relaxes to force blood to move through the circulatory system. The interior of the heart contains four chambers: The upper chambers consist of the **right atrium** (**AY**-tree-um) (**2**) and the **left atrium** (**3**). The lower chambers consist of the **right ventricle** (**VEN**-tri-kel) (**4**) and the **left ventricle** (**5**). The average resting heart rate is 60-100 beats per minute, according to impulses received from the sympathetic nervous system and the **vagus** (10th cranial nerve), which regulate the heartbeat.

THE BLOOD

Blood is the sticky, salty fluid that circulates through the body bringing nourishment and oxygen to all body parts and carrying toxins and waste products to the liver and kidneys to be eliminated. On the average, an adult has 8 to 10 pints of blood flowing through the circulatory system. The blood is made up of red and white corpuscles, platelets and plasma. These three components are referred to as the blood cells and compose the semisolid part of the blood. Additional details regarding these blood cells are listed below:

1. **Red blood cells (RBC) are also called erythrocytes** (e-**RITH**-ro-sitz) or **red corpuscles.** These cells carry oxygen and contain a protein called hemoglobin. **Hemoglobin** (**HE**-mo-glo-bin) attracts oxygen molecules through a process known as **oxygenation** (ok-si-je-**NA**-shun). The blood appears bright red in color when oxygen is being carried. As the red blood cell moves through the body, it releases oxygen molecules and collects molecules of carbon dioxide. When oxygen is low, the blood appears deep scarlet red.

2. **White blood cells (WBC) are also called leukocytes** (**LOO**-ko-sitz) or **white corpuscles.** These cells fight bacteria and other foreign substances and increase in number when infection invades the body.

3. **Blood platelets** (**PLAT**-letz) or **thrombocytes** (**THROM**-bo-sitz) **are responsible for the clotting of blood,** starting the process of coagulation (clotting) when they are exposed to air or rough surfaces (bruised skin).

4. **Plasma is the fluid part of the blood** in which red and white blood cells and blood platelets are suspended, to be carried throughout the body by this liquid's flow. Plasma is about 90% water.

BLOOD VESSELS

Blood vessels are any vessels through which blood circulates through the body. There are 3 types of blood vessels:

Arteries are tubular, elastic, thick-walled branching vessels that carry pure blood from the heart through the body. Because arteries carry pure blood (blood containing oxygen), the color of the blood is bright red.

Veins are tubular, elastic, thin-walled branching vessels that carry the blood from the capillaries to the heart.

Varicose veins are bulges that might form if veins stretch and lose their elasticity. Salon professionals may experience varicose veins due to long periods of standing. Preventive measures such as support hose and appropriate size shoes are recommended practices.

Veins contain cup-like valves to prevent back flow. Impure blood (blood containing carbon dioxide) is carried by the veins (dark red in color) back from capillaries to the heart. Veins are positioned closer to the outer surface of the body than arteries.

Capillaries are small vessels that take nutrients and oxygen from the arteries to the cells and take waste products from the cells to the veins.

BLOOD FLOW THROUGH THE HEART

The entire process of blood traveling from the heart throughout the body and back to the heart is referred to as **systemic** or **general circulation.** The right and the left atrium are also known as the right and the left auricle.

- Oxygen-poor blood enters the right auricle through the **superior vena cava.**
- From the right auricle, blood is pumped through the **tricuspid** (tri-**KUS**-pid) valve into the right ventricle.
- From the right ventricle, blood is pumped into the **pulmonary** (**PUL**-mo-ner-e) **artery.**
- Blood travels through the pulmonary artery to the lungs where it is oxygenated (combined with oxygen). This phase of the circulation of blood is referred to as **pulmonary circulation.**
- From the lungs the newly oxygenated blood returns to the heart via the pulmonary vein and enters the heart's left auricle.
- Blood is pumped from the left auricle to the left ventricle by the bicuspid valve or mitral valve.
- From the left ventricle, blood pumps through the valve into the aorta.
- Blood then flows from the aorta to arterioles, capillaries, venules and veins as it circulates through the body, only to return to the superior vena cava and begin the circulatory process once again.

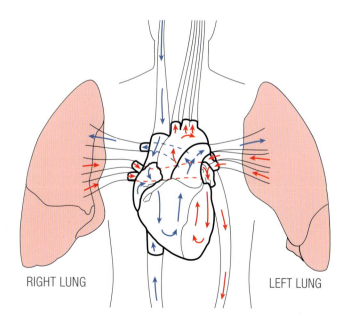

RIGHT LUNG   LEFT LUNG

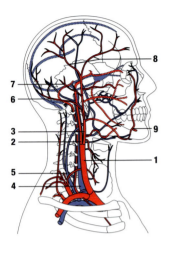

ARTERIES AND VEINS OF THE FACE, HEAD AND NECK
Blood is supplied to the head, face and neck by the **common carotid** (kah-ROT-id) **arteries** (CCA) (**1**) located on either side of the neck. These arteries split into the **internal carotid artery (ICA)** (**2**) and the **external carotid artery (ECA)** (**3**). The internal carotid artery supplies blood to the brain, eyes, and forehead. The **external carotid** branches into smaller arteries, supplying blood to the skin and muscles of the head. All blood from the head, face and neck returns through two veins, the **internal** (IJV) (**4**) and **external jugular** (EJV) (**5**) (JUG-u-lur) **veins**.

The external carotid artery branches into smaller arteries.
6. The **occipital** (ak-SIP-et-el) supplies blood to the back of the head, up to the crown.
7. The **posterior auricular** (pos-TER-e-or aw-RIK-u-lur) supplies blood to the scalp above and behind the ears.
8. The **superficial temporal** (su-pur-FI-shul TEM-po-ral) supplies the sides and top of the head with blood and branches farther into five smaller arteries that supply more precise locations.
9. The **external maxillary** (EKS-tur-nal MAK-si-ler-e) (facial artery) supplies blood to the lower portion of the face, including the mouth and nose. Like the superficial temporal artery, the external maxillary breaks down into smaller branches with more specific destinations, includ the **submental artery**, which supplies blood to the chin and lower lip; the **inferior labial**, whi supplies blood to the lower lip; the **angular artery**, which supplies blood to the sides of the nose; the **superior labial**, which supplies blood to the upper lip and septum; the **frontal arte** which supplies blood to the forehead; the **parietal artery**, which supplies blood to the crow and sides of the head; the **middle temporal**, which supplies blood to the temples; the **transverse artery**, which supplies blood to the masseter; the **anterior auricular**, which supp blood to the anterior part of the ear.

The **internal carotid artery** also separates into smaller branches, including the important **supra orbital artery** which supplies blood to parts of the forehead and eyes.

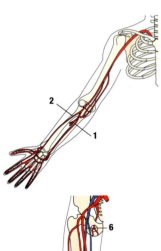

ARTERIES OF THE HAND AND ARM
The **ulnar** (UL-nur) **artery** (**1**) supplies blood to the little finger side of the forearm and the small arteries in the hand. The **radial** (RAY-dee-ul) **artery** (**2**) supplies blood to the thumb side of the a and hand.

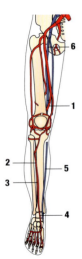

ARTERIES OF THE LOWER LEG AND FOOT
The **popliteal** (pop-lih-TEE-ul) **artery** (**1**) supplies blood to the knee joint and muscles in the thig and calf. The **anterior tibial** (an-TEER-ee-ur TIB-ee-al) **artery** (**2**) supplies blood just below the k and passes down between the tibia and fibula to branch off into smaller arteries into the skin ar muscles in the lower leg. The **posterior tibial** (poh-STEER-ee-ur TIB-ee-al) **artery** (**3**) supplies bl beneath the calf muscle to the skin, muscles and other tissues of the lower leg. The **dorsalis ped** (DOR-sul-is PEED-is) **artery** (**4**) carries blood to the upper surface of the foot.

Blood is transported from veins in the foot to the **saphenous** (SA-FEEN-us) **vein** (**5**) located in the calf and then transported via the **femoral** (FEM-er-uhl) **vein** (**6**) to the heart and lungs for oxygenation.

ANATOMY AND PHYSIOLOGY

THE LYMPH-VASCULAR SYSTEM

The **lymph-vascular system** (also referred to as the **lymphatic system**) is the second subsystem of circulation. **Lymph** is a colorless liquid produced as a byproduct in the process through which plasma passes nourishment to capillaries and cells. Lymph also nourishes the parts of the body not reached by blood, such as the far extremities.

Lymph travels through lymph nodes or glands that filter out toxic substances, like bacteria, and adds antibodies to the fluid. Swollen or tender lymph nodes indicate infection in the body.

There are over 100 lymph nodes in the body that act as barriers to infection from one part of the body to another. As the lymph nodes take on this protective task, they may swell and cause pain. The lymph nodes most often affected in this way are in the neck and under the arms. Many other circumstances may be causing the swelling, but a doctor should be consulted at the first sign of any swelling in these areas.

The lymphatic system picks up leaked fluid and plasma proteins and returns them to the cardiovascular system.

THE NERVOUS SYSTEM

The study of the nervous system is called **Neurology.** The nervous system coordinates and controls the overall operation of the human body.

The nervous system is divided into 3 subsystems:
1. The central or cerebrospinal nervous system
2. The peripheral nervous system
3. The autonomic or sympathetic nervous system

Primary components of the nervous system include the brain, spinal cord and nerves.
The components of the nervous system, operating in harmony, receive and interpret stimuli and send messages away from the nerve cell to the appropriate tissues, muscles and organs.

THE CENTRAL NERVOUS SYSTEM

The central or cerebrospinal nervous system is composed of the brain, spinal cord and spinal and cranial nerves. The central nervous system is responsible for all voluntary body action.

THE BRAIN

The brain controls all 3 subsystems of the nervous system. For that reason, it is referred to as the command center. The brain is the largest of the nerve tissues and is located in the cranium. **The average human brain weighs between 44 and 48 ounces.** Anatomically, the brain can be conveniently divided into 4 parts.

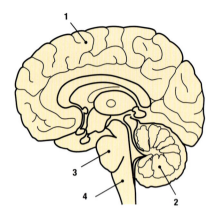

1. The **cerebrum** (se-RE-brum), responsible for mental activity, is located in the upper, front portion of the cranium.
2. The **cerebellum** (ser-e-BEL-um), responsible for the control and coordination of muscle movement, is located in the occipital area directly below the cerebrum.
3. The **pons** connects other parts of the brain to the spinal column and is located below the cerebrum and directly in front of the cerebellum.
4. The **medulla oblongata** (me-DOOL-ah ob-long-GA-ta) also connects parts of the brain to the spinal column and is located just below the pons.

THE SPINAL CORD

The spinal cord, composed of long nerve fibers, originates in the base of the brain and extends to the base of the spine. The spinal cord holds 31 pairs of spinal nerves that branch out to muscles, internal organs and skin.

THE PERIPHERAL NERVOUS SYSTEM

The **peripheral** (pe-RIF-ur-al) nervous system is composed of sensory and motor nerves that extend from the brain and spinal cord to other parts of the body. This network of nerve cells carries messages to and from the central nervous system.

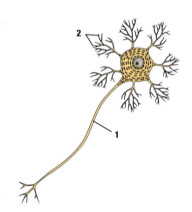

NERVE CELLS

Like other cells, the **nerve cell** or **neuron** (NU-ron) has a nucleus, **cytoplasm** (SI-to-plazm) and membrane. Nerve cells, however, differ in appearance from other cells due to the long and short threadlike fibers, called **axons** (AK-sonz) (1) that extend from them. At the end of each axon is a **nerve terminal** (synapse). These terminals may connect the neuron to muscles, organs or other nerve cells. They are responsible for sending messages away from the nerve cell in the form of nerve impulses. The short fibers are called **dendrites** (DEN-dritz) (2). These structures receive the messages sent to the nerve cell.

The dendrite system is similar to over a million interstate highways traveling back and forth from nerve cell to nerve cell. Certain activities, such as harmful narcotic drugs or a prolonged lack of oxygen, can close the highways down, never to open again.

TYPES OF NERVES

Nerves or nerve tissues perform two basic functions. Sensory or **afferent nerves** carry messages to the brain and spinal cord. These are the nerves that determine our sense of smell, sight, touch, hearing and taste. Nerve cells called **receptors** are located in the papillary layer of the dermis. Receptors react and send sensory messages. These cells react to outside stimulation by sending a sensory message to the brain.

Motor or **efferent nerves** carry messages from the brain to the muscles. When the brain sends a message, motor nerves receive the message and cause a muscle to contract or expand.

Sensory and motor nerves can work together or independently. For example, if you want to close this book, the brain simply sends a message to the **motor** nerves of your hand. This is a conscious decision. You are in control of your hand movement. However, remember the last time you accidentally touched a hot curling iron? Your **sensory** nerves sent a rapid message to your brain transmitting the sensation you experienced. Your brain immediately responded by sensing "pain" and by sending impulses back to **motor** nerves to move your hand away. This interaction of sensory and motor nerves is called a **reflex action**.

Many large nerves perform both sensory and motor functions. These are called **mixed nerves**. Large nerves have many branches. One branch of the **trifacial nerve**, for instance, may be helping you chew, while another branch is sensing an "itch" in your eyebrow.

FACE, HEAD AND NECK NERVES

Two of the 12 pairs of cranial nerves exert primary control in the areas of the face, head and neck: the **trifacial** (**trigeminal** or **5th cranial**) nerve and the **facial** (**7th cranial**) nerve.

THE TRIFACIAL NERVE

The largest of the cranial nerves, the trifacial (5th cranial) nerve is the mixed nerve primarily responsible for transmitting facial sensations to the brain and for controlling the muscle movements of chewing (mastication). The trifacial nerve divides into 3 main branches.

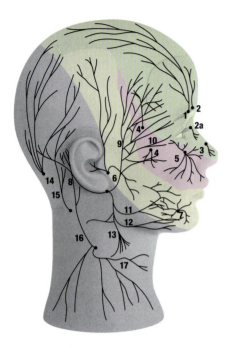

The **ophthalmic** (of-**THAL**-mik) branch is the main nerve branch to the top $^1/_3$ of the face, which further divides into:
1. The **supraorbital** nerve: extending to the skin of the upper eyelid, eyebrow, forehead and scalp
2. The **supratrochlear** nerve: extending to the skin of the upper side of the nose and between the eyes. The **infratrochlear** nerve (**2a**) emerges on the skin of the upper eyelid and side of the nose.
3. The **nasal** nerve: extending to the tip and lower side of the nose

The **maxillary** (**MAK**-si-ler-e) branch is the main nerve branch to the middle $^1/_3$ of the face, which further divides into:
4. The **zygomatic** (zi-go-**MAT**-ik) nerve: extending to the side of the forehead, temple and upper part of the cheek
5. The **infraorbital** nerve: extending to the lower eyelid, side of the nose, upper lip and mouth

The **mandibular** (man-**DIB**-u-lur) branch is the main nerve branch to the lower $^1/_3$ of the face and further divides into:
6. The **auriculo temporal** (aw-**RIK**-u-lo **TEM**-po-ral) nerve: extending to the ear and to the area from the top of the head to the temple
7. The **mental** nerve: extending to the lower lip and chin

THE FACIAL NERVE

The facial (7th cranial) nerve emerges from the brain at the lower part of the ear and is the primary motor nerve of the face. Of its many branches, 6 are of particular importance.
8. The **posterior auricular** (pos-**TER**-e-er aw-**RIK**-u-lur) branch extends to the muscles behind and below the ear.
9. The **temporal** (**TEM**-po-ral) branch extends to the muscles of the temple, the side of the forehead, the eyebrow, eyelid and upper cheek.
10. The **zygomatic** (zi-go-**MAT**-ik) branch extends to the upper muscles of the cheek.
11. The **buccal** (**BUK**-al) branch extends to the muscles of the mouth.
12. The **marginal mandibular** (mahr-**JUH**-nl man-**DIB**-u-lur) branch extends to the muscles of the chin and lower lip.
13. The **cervical** (**SUR**-vi-kal) branch extends to the muscles on the side of the neck.

Other cervical nerves originate in the spinal cord with branches into the scalp and neck.
14. The **greater occipital** (ak-**SIP**-et-el) nerve extends up the back of the scalp to the top of the head.
15. The **lesser occipital** nerve extends into the muscles at the back of the skull.
16. The **greater auricular** (aw-**RIK**-u-lur) nerve extends into the side of the neck and external ear.
17. The **cervical** (**SUR**-vi-kal) **cutaneous** (ku-**TA**-ne-us) nerve extends into the side and front of the neck to the breastbone.

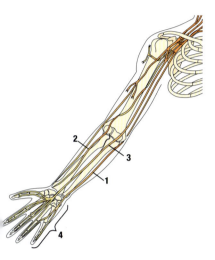

ARM AND HAND NERVES

All 4 of the primary nerves found in the arm and/or hand are mixed nerves; they transmit sensations to the brain and carry impulses from the brain to the muscles.

1. The **ulnar** nerve extends down the little finger side of the arm into the palm of the hand.
2. The **radial** nerve extends down the thumb side of the arm into the back of the hand.
3. The **median** nerve extends down the mid-forearm into the hand.
4. The **digital** nerve extends into the fingers of the hand.

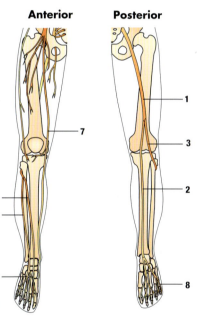

LOWER LEG AND FOOT NERVES

The **sciatic** nerve (sy-AT-ik NURV) (**1**) begins in the lower back and runs through the buttock and down the lower limb. The **tibial** nerve (TIB-ee-al NURV) (**2**) passes behind the knee and the common **peroneal** nerve (KAHM-un per-oh-NEE al NURV) (**3**) runs alongside the sciatic nerve from the femur to the buttocks, then ventures further down on its own along the knee and behind the fibula. The nerve then splits inside the neck of the fibula into two parts: the **deep peroneal** nerve (**4**) also known as the **anterior tibial** nerve, and the **superficial peroneal** (**5**) nerve. The superficial nerve simply sits closer to the skin than the deep nerve and becomes the **dorsal** nerve (DOOR-sal NURV) (**6**). The **saphenous** nerve (sa-FEEN-us NURV) (**7**) begins in the thigh and the **sural** nerve (SUR-ul NURV) (**8**) runs down the back of the leg to the outside of the foot and little toe.

NERVES AND MASSAGE

The nerves of the face, head, neck, hands and feet, listed above and on the preceding pages, may be stimulated during facials and/or scalp massage. During massage services, manipulations can stimulate sensitive nerve tissues resulting in nerve impulses that expand and contract corresponding muscles. Through this process, tight muscles can be relaxed; fatigued muscles can be soothed.

THE AUTONOMIC NERVOUS SYSTEM

The **autonomic** (aw-to-NOM-ik) or **sympathetic** nervous system is physically part of the central nervous system. The same nerve tissues are involved but perform different functions. **The autonomic system is responsible for all involuntary body functions.** It operates the respiratory, digestive, circulatory, excretory, endocrine and reproductive systems.

THE DIGESTIVE SYSTEM

The digestive system breaks food down into simpler chemical compounds that can be easily absorbed by cells or, if not absorbed, eliminated from the body in waste products. The digestive process begins as soon as food is ingested, when **enzymes** (EN-zimz) secreted by the **salivary** (SAL-i-ver-e) glands (**1**) start breaking down the food. Food travels down the **pharynx** (FAR-ingks) (**2**) and through the **esophagus** (e-SOF-ah-gus) (**3**) into the stomach (**4**) propelled by a twisting and turning motion of the esophagus called **peristalsis** (per-i-STAL-sis). In the **stomach, hydrochloric** (hi-dro-KLO-rik) acids and several other enzymes further break down food. One of these other enzymes called pepsin is responsible for the breakdown of protein into **polypeptide** (pol-e-PEP-tide) molecules and free amino acids, which are of particular importance to the production of hair, skin and nails.

As partially digested food passes from the stomach into the **small intestine** (**5**), the assimilation of nutrients begins. Nutrients are absorbed by the **villi** (VIL-i), which are finger-like projections of the intestine walls, and transported through the circulatory system to the tissues and cells of the body.

Undigested food passes into the **large intestine** (**6**), or colon, which stores the waste for eventual elimination through the anal canal. This entire process of digestion takes about 9 hours to complete. **Happiness and relaxation promote good digestion.** Good digestion helps keep all other bodily functions on track.

As a reminder, the digestive system, also known as the gastrointestinal system includes,
1. Salivary glands
2. Pharynx
3. Esophagus
4. Stomach
5. Small intestine
6. Large intestine

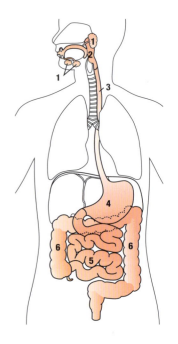

THE EXCRETORY SYSTEM

The excretory system eliminates solid, liquid and gaseous waste products from the body. Organs of the excretory system include:
- The **skin** covers nearly 20 square feet of body surface and is the body's largest organ. The skin releases water, carbon dioxide and other waste through the sweat glands.
- The **liver** converts and neutralizes ammonia from the circulatory system to **urea** (u-RE-ah). Urea is then carried, through the bloodstream, to the kidneys for excretion.
- The **kidneys** receive urea from the liver and then pass the urea through small tubelike structures known as **nephrons** (NEF-ronz) (**1**). Nephrons filter out waste products and water, allowing usable nutrients to be reabsorbed into the blood. Excreted waste products travel through the **ureter** (U-re-tur) and bladder and are eliminated from the body in urine.

THE RESPIRATORY SYSTEM

The respiratory system is made up of organs and tissues that help you breathe.
The primary functions of the respiratory system are:
- The intake of oxygen to be absorbed into the blood
- The exhalation of oxygen's toxic byproduct, carbon dioxide

Both of these functions take place every time you take a breath.

While it is possible to breathe through both the mouth and the nose, breathing through the nose is the healthier option. The nose contains mucus membranes, to filter out dust and dirt, and warms the inhaled air as it travels through the nasal passages.

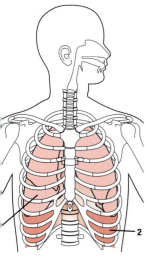

Primary respiratory system organs include:
1. The **lungs** are spongy organs composed of cells into which air enters when you inhale. These cells process oxygen for absorption into the blood and release carbon dioxide as you exhale.
2. The **diaphragm** is a muscular organ that separates the chest cavity from the abdomen. The diaphragm expands and contracts automatically, forcing air into and out of the lungs.

THE ENDOCRINE SYSTEM

The endocrine system is composed of a group of specialized ductless glands that regulate and control the growth, reproduction and health of the body. These glands manufacture chemical substances called hormones and secrete them directly into the blood stream.

The endocrine system is a carefully balanced mechanism that directly affects hair growth, skin conditions and energy levels. Nutrition plays a key role in the proper regulation of this system. Signs of fatigue or changes in hair growth may signal the need for medical attention.

COSMETOLOGY FUNDAMENTALS

THE REPRODUCTIVE SYSTEM

The **reproductive system** is responsible for the process by which a living organism procreates others of its kind.

THE INTEGUMENTARY SYSTEM

The skin and its layers make up the **integumentary system** of the body. The two primary glands of the integumentary system are the sebaceous (si-BAY-shus) (oil) and the sudoriferous (soo-dohr-IF-er-us) (sweat) glands. These glands are referred to as duct glands because both secrete into canal-like structures (ducts) that deposit their contents on the surface of the skin.

CONNECTING THEORY TO REAL-WORLD PRACTICE

ANATOMY AND PHYSIOLOGY	PERSONAL CONNECTION: IMPROVE YOURSELF	INDUSTRY CONNECTION: BECOME A PROFESSIONAL	CLIENT CONNECTION: SERVE THE GUEST
BUILDING BLOCKS OF THE HUMAN BODY	Increase awareness of how the human body operates at its most basic levels	Elevate professional stature through advanced understanding of the human body	Add value to clients' perception of your knowledge and concern for their well-being
BASIC BODY SYSTEMS	Understand the importance and inter-connectedness of the major body structures	Make decisions that reveal their significance and impact with respect to people's physical well-being	Perform services and client care that consistently meet expectations and reflect best practices

IN OTHER WORDS

Cosmetology is one of the few professions with licensure that allows you to touch an individual. This means you have a responsibility to understand the human body and how it functions in order to make the best possible judgments when recommending and delivering services to your clients.

LESSONS LEARNED

- The building blocks of the human body include cells that make up tissues, tissues that make up organs and organs that make up systems.

- The skeletal system supports the body, surrounds and protects internal organs, provides a frame to which muscles can attach and allows body movement.

- The muscular system supports the skeleton, produces body movements, contours the body and aids in the functions of other body systems.

- The circulatory system controls the circulation of blood and lymph through the body.

- The nervous system coordinates and controls the overall operation of the human body by receiving and interpreting stimuli and sending messages away from the nerve cells to the appropriate tissues, muscles and organs.

04

ELECTRICITY

4.1 PRINCIPLES OF ELECTRICITY
VOCABULARY OF ELECTRICITY
ELECTRIC CURRENT
SAFETY MEASURES

4.2 ELECTRICITY IN COSMETOLOGY
EFFECTS OF ELECTRIC CURRENT
ELECTROTHERAPY
LIGHT THERAPY

USING ELECTRICITY SAFELY HELPS ENSURE THE WELL-BEING OF BOTH THE SALON PROFESSIONAL AND THE CLIENT

FOLLOWING THIS LESSON
YOU WILL BE ABLE TO:

Define the 10 major terms used in electricity

Describe the safety measures to be followed when using electrical appliances

Explain the three kinds of effects that can be created by electric current

List the effects that can be created by special electric current (modalities) used during electrotherapy and light therapy treatments

CONNECTING THEORY TO REAL-WORLD PRACTICE
UNDERSTANDING HOW ELECTRICITY WORKS AND IS APPLIED IN THE SALON WILL HELP YOU:

PERSONAL CONNECTION: IMPROVE YOURSELF	**INDUSTRY CONNECTION:** BECOME A PROFESSIONAL	**CLIENT CONNECTION:** SERVE THE GUEST
Use electricity skillfully, efficiently and safely in all facets of your life	Deliver state-of-the-industry services proficiently and confidently	Produce a variety of specialized, client-enhancing results safely and comfortably

It's nearly impossible to imagine a modern salon without electricity. The discussion in this chapter will help you safely and efficiently use appliances and deliver forms of therapy that rely on electricity.

04

4.1 PRINCIPLES OF ELECTRICITY

Electricity is a powerful and important form of energy. Anyone who has ever watched lightning in a stormy sky has seen its power. Anyone who has felt an electric shock knows what that power feels like. The power of electrical energy is essential in modern life. No salon could function without it. Of course, as a salon professional you aren't expected to develop the knowledge and skills of an electrician, just an understanding of electricity's basic principles and its important uses in your future work.

VOCABULARY OF ELECTRICITY

Familiarity with some of the key terms used in this chapter will help you jump start your understanding of electricity. Keep this list handy as you move through this chapter.

TOP 10 ELECTRICITY TERMS

1. **Electricity** is a form of energy that produces light, heat, magnetic and chemical changes.
2. **Electric current** is the movement of electricity along a path called a conductor.
3. **Load** is the technical name for any electrically powered appliance.
4. **Conductor** is a material that allows electricity to flow through it easily.
5. **Insulator** is a material that does not allow the flow of electric current.
6. **Amp** is a unit of electric strength.
7. **Volt** is a unit of electric pressure.
8. **Ohm** is a unit of electric resistance.
9. **Watt** is a measure of how much electrical energy is being used.
10. **Electrotherapy** is the application of electrical currents during treatments to the skin.

ELECTRICITY AND ELECTRIC CURRENT

Electricity is a form of energy that produces light, heat, magnetic and chemical changes. Most of the electricity you use daily consists of a flow of tiny, negatively charged particles called **electrons**. That flow of electrons is called an **electric current**, which moves along a path called a **conductor**.

LOADS, CONDUCTORS AND INSULATORS

A salon is full of **loads** (electrically powered appliances) just waiting to be activated by the flow of electric current. Think of all the blow dryers, curling irons and clippers that need electrical energy to work.

The materials that best transport electricity are called conductors. The best conductors are silver and copper. However, other metals, carbon, graphite and water containing ions allow current to flow as well. Since the human body is composed of 60% water, it too, can be a conductor.

The purpose of a conductor is to transport current in a circuit to a load. This conductor is safely contained in an **insulator, which is a material that does not allow a current to pass through it.** Insulators protect you from electric current and allow you to handle electricity safely. Examples of insulating materials include silk, plastic, rubber, wood, glass, paper, air, brick, cloth and certain liquids such as alcohol, oil and pure distilled water. Most currents in the salon are carried by copper wire (conductors) insulated with varying amounts of rubber. You know this combination of conductor and insulator as a cord. *Cords on appliances should be kept straight and free of knots, kinks, and tangles to prevent breaks.* **A break in any electrical cord can put you or your client in contact with an active current, causing electric shock.**

Amp = strength
Volt = pressure
Ohm = resistance
Watt = electricity used

AMP

An amp or ampere is a unit of electric *strength.* The amp rating indicates the number of electrons flowing on a line. Your house has a power box with a certain number of amps coming to it that enables you to use all the appliances in the house. The conductors (wires) in your home have the ability to carry a limited number of amps at a time. Circuits will have 10, 20, 30 or larger "amp ratings." When buying or remodeling an older building, you may have to have new powerlines laid to run the appliances in the building. Through the years, additional uses for electricity, such as the microwave, clothes dryer, computer, etc., have increased the amp requirements for the modern home. One ampere equals 1,000 milliamperes.

VOLT

A volt, also called voltage, is a unit of electric *pressure.* In simple terms, a volt measures how hard the electrons are being forced or pushed by the source. AC generators force or push 110 or 220 volts in a circuit. Large motors, such as those found in clothes dryers and air conditioners, may require the higher electrical pressure of 220 volts to operate properly. The 220-volt sockets look different from standard wall sockets, in that the prongs that plug into the wall are generally round and pointed into the shape of a "v" at the end. This precaution reduces the danger of someone attempting to plug a 220-volt appliance into a 110-volt wall socket. The cord carrying 220-volt current is also much thicker and there is a higher cost to install lines that carry higher voltage currents.

OHM

An ohm is a unit of electric *resistance*. A German physicist named Georg Ohm discovered that every conductor has a specific rate at which it will allow electrons to move through it. **The measure of how difficult it is to push electrons through a conductor is called impedance or resistance. The resistance to the motion of the electrons through a conductor is the ohm's rating.** The manufacturer of an appliance determines the current needed to power the machine, then installs a conducting wire with an ohm's rating allowing the desired flow.

WATT

A watt is a measure of how much electrical energy is being used. One watt is a small amount of energy. A blow dryer can use 1,000 watts per second. A light bulb can use 25, 60, or 100 watts per second. You can use thousands of watts in a short period of time. To deal with these large numbers, the power company describes watt use in larger terms: 1,000 watts equal one **kilowatt.** With many appliances on at one time, thousands of kilowatts can be used in a short time. The power company defines how fast energy is used in hourly terms.

A hertz rating provides the number of cycles, per second, a generator alternates the current from the source. One hertz unit indicates a frequency equal to one cycle per second.

If you turned on a 500-watt dryer and let it run for 8 hours, you would have used 4,000 (500 x 8 = 4,000) watt hours (or 4 kilowatt hours) of power. You pay the electric company so many cents per kilowatt hour used. Energy conservation is important to the salon. When not in use, appliances should be turned off and stored safely.

The nameplate of an appliance tells the frequency-Hertz (Hz needed), volts needed (110 or 220 V), and the watts this appliance consumes per second (100W, 200W, etc.). It may also have a UL or Underwriter's Laboratory designation. A UL rating means the appliance has been certified to operate safely under the conditions the instructions specify. Look for these ratings on your tools.

ELECTRIC CURRENT

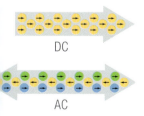

DC

AC

Electrical current exists in 2 forms:
1. DC, or direct current, in which electrons move at an even rate and flow in only one direction.
2. AC, or alternating current, in which electrons flow first in one direction and then in the other.

Special instruments can be used to change alternating current (AC) to direct current (DC) or direct current to alternating current. A converter changes direct current to alternating current. A rectifier changes alternating current to direct current. In cosmetology, certain currents (as explained later in this chapter) are used to produce certain effects on the skin.

LIGHT UP YOUR CREATIVITY

Here is an activity to help you remember the meaning of the terms you have read about so far. Draw a picture of the following "electric" words. Refer to pages 90-91. A sample is provided to jump start your creativity.

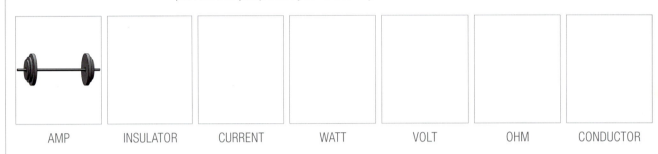

AMP   INSULATOR   CURRENT   WATT   VOLT   OHM   CONDUCTOR

SOURCES OF ELECTRIC CURRENT

Electrons cannot move through a conductor without help. A **source** provides the force to move the electrons in the conducting material. Two common sources of electric current are batteries and generators. A **battery** has a positive terminal (+) and a negative terminal (-) and produces **direct current** only. The negatively charged electrons are both attracted to the positive terminal and repelled by the negative terminal of the source. This means the electrons flow toward the positive terminal in a circuit.

A **generator** is the power source most often used in a salon. Generators produce **alternating current.** When you want to turn on a dryer, you plug it into a wall socket. The wall socket itself is not the source of current. The source is the **generator,** a machine that uses mechanical energy to produce a flow of electrons. A separate form of energy—nuclear, hydroelectric, solar, thermal or wind—propels the generator, usually from a source located many miles away. Engineers have devised ways for these sources of energy to force generators to mechanically pump huge numbers of electrons into power lines that bring electricity to our homes and businesses.

The generator has two terminals (one positive and one negative). During the operation of the generator, these terminals mechanically alternate their charges, producing an **alternating current.** They switch (or cycle) from positive to negative and back. The number of times this cycling occurs per second is called the **frequency.** A generator is built to "cycle" at a specific rate. The rate of cycling, or frequency, is measured in cycles per second.

In the United States, generators are built at a frequency of 60 cycles per second or 60 hertz (60 Hz). The nameplate of an appliance will indicate the frequency of the source into which the appliance must be plugged to operate safely.

Appliances from other countries have different hertz (hz) or cycle ratings and cannot be operated in the U.S. without an adapter. The same is true of appliances made for the U.S. but taken out of the country.

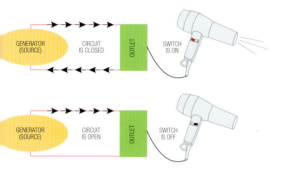

CLOSED VS. OPEN CIRCUIT

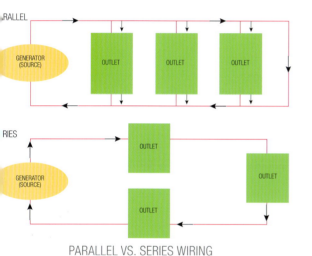

PARALLEL VS. SERIES WIRING

HOW ELECTRIC CURRENT IS PRODUCED

Two conditions must exist for electric current to be produced. First, as you just read, there must be a source. Second, there must be a closed path, called a **circuit**, through which the electrons travel. A **closed path** is a path on which the electrons leave the source and operate an appliance. When this path is broken, it is called an **open circuit**. If you plug in a blow dryer, turn it on and air begins to flow, you have an example of a closed or completed circuit. When you turn the switch off, the circuit breaks and is now an open circuit.

There are two ways circuits can be connected to power loads. **Parallel wiring** allows the user to power several loads at different times or at once. With parallel wiring, a blow dryer, curling iron and blow comb can be plugged into the same circuit. Each can be run alone or all three can be run at once. **Series wiring** forces the user to have all loads running at the same time, since the circuit travels from one load to the next. An example of this would be many connected strings of Christmas tree lights. If one string of lights is malfunctioning, the electric current cannot flow to the next string. The malfunction causes an open circuit, and none of the strings work. In the salon, only parallel wiring should be installed.

OVERLOAD AND SHORT CIRCUIT

When a building is constructed, an electrician normally wires it with a certain number of circuits (each capable of carrying 20 or 30 amps). When you turn on an appliance, such as a blow dryer, the appliance causes current to flow on the line to meet its power needs. A problem can occur when too many appliances are put on one circuit and are operated all at the same time. More current flows than the line is designed to carry. This situation is called an **overload**. Although there are safety devices to detect overloading, they can fail. If they do, the lines of the circuit will heat up and may burn.

In general, it takes 1 amp on the circuit to operate every 100 watts of an appliance. So, to operate a 1,000-watt blow dryer, a 10-amp circuit is required. If you operated a 1,000-watt dryer

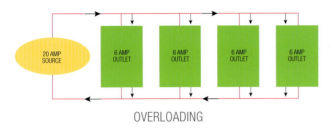

OVERLOADING

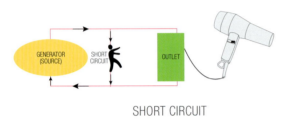

SHORT CIRCUIT

on a 5-amp circuit, it would overload. **Fires can occur when an extension cord with multiple plugs is used to attach 4 or 5 appliances to one wall socket.** If all the appliances are turned on, that extension cord (if not rated for the amp flowing) can melt and burn in seconds. It is essential to hire a qualified electrician to install adequate wiring. The number of amps demanded by each appliance (dryers, air conditioner, washer) during a normal working day must be determined to safely predict the number of amps needed by the salon.

A second problem that frequently occurs in the salon is called a short circuit. A **short circuit** can occur any time a "foreign conductor" comes in contact with a wire carrying current to load (appliance). A classic short circuit occurs when someone tries to plug in an appliance and gets a finger between the wall socket and the plug. The finger becomes the foreign conductor and receives the electrical current instead of the appliance for which the current was intended.

ALERT!
Electric shock can be fatal.

Dropping an appliance into water will cause the current to flow through the water, which in this case is a foreign conductor. **If you tried to retrieve the appliance while still on, you would be electrocuted.** With dry hands, remove the plug from the wall socket first.

Short circuits occur commonly in thermal styling tool cords. Twisting and bending of cords can eventually break the copper wires. If you touch the break, you'll get an electrical shock.

SAFETY MEASURES

Because of the possibility of overloads and short circuits, safety devices are installed in many appliances and buildings. Two of these devices, fuses and circuit breakers, connect directly to the circuits in the power box, the carefully insulated location where the electric current enters a building from a generator or power plant. From the power box, many circuits continue throughout the building.

FUSE

A **fuse** is a device that contains a fine metal wire that allows current to flow through it. If an overload occurs (too much current flowing), the fuse will heat up and the wire will melt, breaking the circuit and cutting the flow of electricity. Fuses cannot be reused. A new fuse of the same amp rating (10, 20, or 30) must be installed.

Installing a new fuse:
1. Turn off all appliances operating on that circuit.
2. Go to the power box and turn off the main power handle on the side of the box.
3. Remove the burned-out fuse and replace it with a new one.
4. Close the box and switch on the main power handle.

If your salon still has fuses, it's a good idea to have extra fuses on hand. Remember, too many appliances on one circuit caused the problem. Change your appliance use or switch to a different circuit.

CIRCUIT BREAKER

A **circuit breaker** is simply a reusable device that breaks the flow of current when an overload occurs. It contains two pieces of metal that make contact with each other. Like a fuse, these pieces of metal conduct electric current unless too much current flows on the line. If the flow is too high, there is a heat-sensing device that causes the two pieces to separate, and the circuit is broken. In order to restore power when circuit breakers are being used:
1. Turn off appliances.
2. Go to the power box and open it.
3. Find a row of switches that look just like wall light switches.
4. Look for a switch that has a color marker (red or yellow) showing. Turn this switch completely to the "off" position, then immediately to the "on" position. This resets the breaker. The circuit is now operating.

It would be wise to become familiar with the power box in your salon. Know where it is and how to safely operate it. Each circuit should be clearly labeled, and you should have a flashlight available in case it is dark when a circuit breaks.

GROUNDING WIRE

Another safety device is called a three-wire system. Wall sockets contain three holes for plugging in an appliance. Two of the holes are long and rectangular. Some appliances use only these two. The third hole is circular. This circular opening is connected to a wire that runs directly into the ground below the building. If this **grounding wire** did not exist, your body would receive the excess flow of electric current. This grounding wire is designed to protect you when operating certain kinds of appliances. Some appliances have conducting mechanisms inside that could accidentally come in contact with the outside case, for example, a hooded dryer, vacuum cleaner or hair clipper. The manufacturer installs a special wire for conducting high and sudden flows of electric current out of the appliance, into the cord and to the plug. Any appliance requiring this protection has a three-prong plug.

SHOCK

Human contact with an electric current causes a shock. If someone comes in contact with an electric current, it is most important to break the circuit carrying the power. You can:

1. Knock the person out of the circuit by using an **insulator** like a broom, a plastic brush or a plastic garbage pail.
2. Unplug the appliance. Be careful to use an insulator to keep yourself out of the circuit.
3. Rush to the power box and turn off all the circuit breakers.

A *local shock* passes through a small part of the body, causing burns and muscle contractions. Immerse the burn in cool water immediately and, if severe, take the person to a hospital or physician.

A *general shock* passes through the nervous system. Again, break the circuit before touching the person. This type of shock causes the heart to stop, the breathing to cease and the muscles to convulse. Emergency help should be called. Dial 9-1-1. Start CPR (cardiopulmonary resuscitation). CPR is the only procedure that can save the victim's life. Don't stop CPR until an emergency team arrives.

If a fire results from an overload of an electric circuit and an appliance melts and burns, **do not put water on it.** Turn off the circuit. Smother the fire with a rug, a heavy towel, or a powder, such as cornstarch or laundry detergent, or a fire extinguisher.

KNOW YOUR EQUIPMENT

There are three types of electrically powered equipment typically used in the salon:

- **THERMAL EQUIPMENT** is used to generate heat. Curling irons, heat lamps, color machines, manicure heaters, facial steamers and scalp steamers are thermal appliances. Facial steamers and scalp steamers produce moist heat at a constant temperature.
- **MECHANICAL EQUIPMENT** has a motor. Clippers and massagers are mechanical appliances.
- **COMBINATION EQUIPMENT** generates heat and produces a flow of air. Hooded dryers, blow dryers and blow combs fall into this category.

4.2 ELECTRICITY IN COSMETOLOGY

Now that you understand the principles of electricity, you can take a look at how it is used in the salon.

EFFECTS OF ELECTRIC CURRENT

Three kinds of effects can be created by electric current during cosmetology services. They are **heating** effects, **mechanical** or **magnetic** effects and **electrochemical** effects.

HEATING EFFECTS

Every conductor has some resistance to the flow of current through it. The more resistance, the more "drag or friction" in the line. The result is increased heat. A curling iron, a light bulb and a blow dryer all create heating effects because they contain special conductors (heating elements) that heat up when current flows through them. A low setting simply cuts the amount of current allowed to pass through the special conductor. This fact explains why a blow dryer can have a "cold" setting. This setting stops all flow of current to the heating element but still allows current to flow to the blower.

MECHANICAL OR MAGNETIC EFFECTS

As you've learned, electrical generators push alternating current through the conductor. Alternating current flows first one direction and then the other. Manufacturers of mechanical equipment—clippers, massagers, electrodes, etc.,—design motors with magnetic fields with positive and negative polarity. When the current travels through the conductor and into the magnetic field of the motor, a push-pull effect is created as the negative and positive charges interact. This push-pull effect causes the motor to turn, creating a mechanical motion like the rotating blades of a fan.

ELECTROCHEMICAL EFFECTS

Electrochemical effects are created when electric current travels through a water-based solution (a liquid conductor) in order to produce relaxing or stimulating results.

ELECTROTHERAPY

Electrotherapy is the application of special currents (or modalities) that have certain effects on the skin. It is important to know what they are promoted to do so you are familiar with their potential in the salon.

ALERT!
A person with any potentially restrictive medical condition should always consult a physician before receiving electrotherapy treatment.

There are four types of current you should know: Galvanic, Faradic, Sinusoidal and Tesla.

In order to be safely used in **Galvanic**, **Faradic**, **Sinusoidal** and **Tesla Current** electrotherapy electric current must be reduced from the 120 volts of electric power carried through a wire-conductor to a level safely handled by the human body. This reduction of power is accomplished by a portable appliance known as a wall plate. The wall plate is available in various sizes and styles and plugs into the stationary wall outlet. The current conductors to be used in electrotherapy applications are plugged into and operated through the wall plate allowing voltage regulations as necessary for a particular treatment or current. A current conductor called an **electrode** is used to bring the current from the appliance to the client's skin. The most common electrodes are:

1. A comb electrode (for use on the scalp)
2. A rake electrode (for use on the scalp)
3. A wrist electrode (for the salon professional)
4. A carbon electrode (for the patron to hold)
5. A massage roller electrode (for application to the client by the salon professional)

An electrode, like those listed above, is the only safe contact point through which the current can pass to the client.

RAKE ELECTRODE

GALVANIC CURRENT

Galvanic Current has an electrochemical effect and is the oldest form of electrotherapy in the salon. **Galvanic Current is a direct current (DC) of low voltage and high amperage.** Because Galvanic Current is a direct current and generally only alternating current is available in the salon, a special appliance is necessary to convert the salon's alternating current to the direct current.

Galvanic Current has chemical effects that are caused by passing the current through particular acid or alkaline solutions and/or by passing the current through body tissues and fluids.

All electrotherapy applicators have both a negatively charged electrode (called a **cathode**) and a positively charged electrode (called an **anode**). The cathode is usually black in color or displays a large "N" or negative sign (-). The anode, usually colored red, displays a large "P" or a positive sign (+).

If the electrodes are not visibly marked as negative or positive, test for polarity. You can determine polarity by separating the tips and submerging the tips only into a glass of water. Salt water is best but tap water will do. Keep tips from touching each other. Slowly turn up the Galvanic Current using the wall plate's regulator. The negative electrode will create more and smaller bubbles than will the positive electrode.

Phoresis is sometimes referred to as "bleaching the skin."

The process of forcing an acid (+) or alkali (-) into the skin by applying current to the chemical is called **phoresis** and is probably the most typical application of Galvanic Current. **Anaphoresis** uses a negative pole (cathode) or electrode to force negatively charged (alkaline) solutions into the skin without breaking the skin. **Cataphoresis** uses a positive pole (anode) or electrode to force positively charged (acidic) solutions into the skin without breaking the skin.

ANAPHORESIS

The **negative pole of Galvanic Current** is believed to have the following temporary effects on the area of the body to which it is applied:

1. Produces an alkaline reaction, which can force alkaline solutions to penetrate the skin.
2. Increases the blood flow by expanding the vessels to aid circulation.
3. Softens tissues.
4. Stimulates nerves.

CATAPHORESIS

The **positive pole of Galvanic Current** is believed to have temporary effects opposite to those produced by the negative pole, including:

1. Produces an acidic reaction, which can force acidic solutions to penetrate the skin.
2. Slows the blood flow by contracting the vessels to decrease redness or inflammation when applied to simple blemishes on the skin.
3. Hardens tissues, closing pores after facial treatment.
4. Soothes nerves.

GALVANIC CURRENT ELECTROTHERAPY

- The salon professional applies the active **electrode** to the client. The active electrode is connected to either the positive or negative pole, depending on the therapeutic reaction desired.
- The client holds the inactive electrode, which is connected to the opposite pole.
- Both the active and inactive electrodes should be wrapped lightly in moist cotton. While the comfort level for the current will vary from one client to the next, never use more than one milliampere of current.

ALERT!
Do not use the Galvanic Current over an area that has many broken capillaries.

A Galvanic Current machine is also used for a process called iontophoresis (eye-on-to-fo-**REE**-sis). **Iontophoresis** introduces water-soluble treatment products into the skin. Desincrustation is a treatment in which sebum is broken down or blackheads are liquefied, as in deep-pore cleansing.

FARADIC CURRENT

Faradic Current is an alternating current (AC), interrupted to produce a mechanical, non-chemical reaction. Faradic Current stimulates nerve and muscle tissue. Benefits believed to be derived from the application of Faradic Current include:

1. Improved blood circulation
2. Improved muscle tone
3. Stimulation of hair growth
4. Increased glandular activity

Used chiefly to cause muscle contractions during scalp and facial massage, Faradic Current can be soothing and relaxing and is believed to help preserve muscle tone.

The most frequently used application of the Faradic Current is the **indirect method** of Faradic Current electrotherapy. In the indirect method, the salon professional usually wears a wrist band with a moistened electrode. The second electrode is wrapped in moist cotton and either held by the client or, better, attached to the client's lower neck between the shoulders. The salon professional's fingers are then placed on the client's face before the current is turned on to prevent shock. When the current reaches the desired level, a facial massage is given, with particular focus on motor points. The current is gradually decreased and finally turned off completely before the salon professional's fingers are removed.

The **direct method** of application, used less often for Faradic Current electrotherapy, places both electrodes on the client's skin, **being certain that they never touch.** The current is turned on and slowly increased only after the electrodes are in place. In this application, the current travels through the motor nerves between the two electrodes, causing muscle stimulation.

SINUSOIDAL CURRENT

Sinusoidal Current is an alternating current (AC) with a mechanical effect, much like the Faradic Current that produces muscle contractions. (Machines that cause muscle contraction are illegal in some areas. Be sure to read your area's rules and regulations.) Sinusoidal Current electrotherapy is performed by using the indirect method application.

Some users believe Sinusoidal Current to be superior to Faradic Current because Sinusoidal Current penetrates more deeply and can provide greater stimulation to the treated area. For this reason, it is most often preferred to Faradic Current for middle-aged and older clients. Treatments using Sinusoidal Current generally last no longer than 30 minutes.

ALERT!

Sinusoidal Current electrotherapy should not be used on unhealthy and/or broken skin.

DIRECT

INDIRECT

TESLA CURRENT

Tesla, High Frequency Current, known as the "violet-ray," is an alternating current which can be adjusted to different voltages to produce heat. Because the Tesla is a high oscillation current, its use does not produce muscle contractions. Use of the Tesla Current can result in relaxation or stimulation, depending on method of application.

There are three methods for using the Tesla Current:
1. When using **direct application** of the Tesla High Frequency Current, the salon professional applies the electrode directly to the client's scalp or face.
2. When using **indirect application,** the salon professional hands the glass electrode to the client before activating the current to avoid the electrical shock that could result in passing an active current from one person to another. The client then holds the activated electrode while the salon professional manually stimulates the area being treated. The current is turned off before the client returns the electrode to the salon professional after the treatment.
3. In **general electrification**, the salon professional hands the electrode to the client before activating the current. The power is switched on and a generalized tingling or vibration effect is experienced by the client.

To create soothing or relaxing effects, the electrode must be kept in direct contact with the areas being treated. To stimulate an area through rapid vibration, during a direct application, a towel is placed over the skin and the electrode is applied over the towel. The slight separation of the electrode from the skin creates a mild, stimulating sensation.

Benefits believed to be derived through application of the High Frequency or Tesla Current include:
1. Improved blood circulation
2. Increased rate of metabolism
3. Increased sebaceous (oil glands) glandular activity

COSMETOLOGY USES FOR TESLA CURRENT

DRY SKIN FACIAL TREATMENT.– INDIRECT APPLICATION

1. Cleanse client's face.
2. Have the client hold the glass rod electrode.
3. Place the tips of your fingers against skin on client's face before turning on the High Frequency current.
4. Turn on the current, slowly increasing strength. Perform usual facial massage manipulations, being careful not to lift fingers from client's skin.
5. Massage according to manufacturer's directions, in most cases for no more than 7 minutes per treatment. Your fingertips may tingle slightly during contact. This is normal.
6. Turn off current before removing your fingers from client's face to avoid shock.
7. Complete facial treatment.

MILD ACNE AND/OR BLACKHEAD FACIAL TREATMENT – DIRECT APPLICATION

1. Cleanse client's face.
2. Apply the facial electrode directly to the skin and turn on current.
3. Move the electrode gently across skin, in small circular rotations, while slowly increasing strength of the current.
4. Repeat until entire face has been covered at least once, but do not exceed a total of 5 minutes for the entire treatment.
5. Turn the current down slowly until it's turned off completely.
6. Remove the electrode from your client's skin and proceed with the rest of the facial.

DRY SCALP – INDIRECT APPLICATION

1. Apply moisturizing scalp treatment cream.
2. Have client hold glass rod electrode.
3. After putting your hand on the client's scalp, turn on the current.
4. Perform normal scalp massage, being careful not to break contact with the client, while gradually increasing current.
5. Time treatment according to manufacturer's directions, massaging entire scalp.
6. Turn off the current, maintaining contact with client.
7. Complete scalp treatment.

SCALP TREATMENT – DIRECT APPLICATION

1. Apply moisturizing scalp treatment cream.
2. Apply scalp electrode (rake) to scalp and turn on current.
3. Using push-pull movements, manipulate rake electrode over entire scalp while slowly increasing strength of current.
4. Continue treatment for approximately 5 minutes.
5. Turn off current.
6. Remove electrode rake from scalp and complete scalp treatment.

04

> **ELECTROTHERAPY PRECAUTIONS**
>
> **GENERAL**
> - Always read the manufacturer's directions and follow them carefully.
> - Electrodes should never touch each other.
>
> **GALVANIC/FARADIC/SINUSOIDAL**
> - Never take the current over one milliampere.
> - Make sure the current is off before beginning indirect application and before breaking contact with client at the end of the treatment.
> - Sinusoidal electrotherapy treatment should never exceed 30 minutes.
>
> **TESLA HIGH FREQUENCY**
> - Begin each treatment with a mild current, increasing strength slowly.
> - Keep client out of contact with metal during treatment.
> - Limit treatment duration to approximately 5 minutes.
> - If you use cream during scalp or other high frequency treatments, be sure the cream contains no alcohol. Alcohol-based creams may be flammable and could be ignited by a spark.
> - Turn the current on only after the client is holding the electrode. Turn the current off before removing the electrode from client's contact.

HEAT ENERGY

Heat always moves from a hotter body to a cooler body and can be transferred from one object to another in one of three ways:

1. Conduction – the transfer of heat via direct contact
2. Convection – the transfer of heat via liquid or gas
3. Radiation – the transfer of heat through a vacuum (empty space)

EFFECTS OF HEAT

Mild heat relaxes the muscles, causes blood circulation to increase and helps salon professionals perform many hair and skin care services. Intense heat destroys cells and tissues. You can observe this chemical breakdown of the skin (called pyrolysis) when you are burned and a blister forms.

SHORT WAVELENGTH

LONG WAVELENGTH

LIGHT THERAPY

Light therapy is the production of beneficial effects such as reducing acne through treatments using light rays or waves. Radiation is the transfer of heat energy through an empty air space (a vacuum). Heat energy is simply movement of electrons. When heat energy is transferred by radiation, these electrons move in wave-like patterns. These waves of electrons are called electromagnetic radiation. The waves can be long or short. They are measured from the crest of one wave to the crest of the next.

This measurement is a wavelength. The range of all the wavelengths that can be produced by radiant energy is called the electromagnetic spectrum. The shorter the wavelength, the more energy the wave is carrying. X-rays have a short wavelength.

TV and radio broadcasts are examples of long wavelengths of radiant energy. Heat lamps used in chemical services have long wavelengths as well.

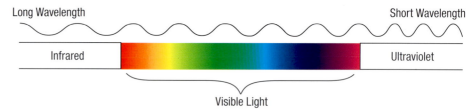

Laser, light-emitting diode (LED), and intense pulse light are used in medical devices to treat a variety of skin conditions. Laser is an acronym for light amplification simulation emission of radiation. For example, laser devices can remove blood vessels, tattoos or wrinkles without destroying skin tissue. Light-emitting diode devices are primarily used to reduce acne (blue light), increase circulation (red light), reduce inflammation (yellow light) or reduce hyperpigmentation (green light). Intense pulse light devices are used to treat spider veins and rosacea. Be sure to follow regulatory guidelines.

VISIBLE LIGHT

The portion of the electromagnetic spectrum humans can see is called visible light. This range of wavelengths produces visible color. When these waves hit an object, they are either absorbed or reflected. Our eyes pick up the reflected waves and interpret them as color.

White light is referred to as combination light. This visible light can be broken into its individual wavelengths by a prism. A prism is a three-sided glass object. If white light (sunlight or light from a light bulb) passes through a prism, the wavelengths are separated and become visible to the eye as seven colors: Red, orange, yellow, green, blue, indigo and violet. Raindrops can act as prisms by breaking up white light into those seven colors to create a rainbow. **The wavelengths that produce red are the longest waves of the visible spectrum.** The wavelengths that produce violet are the shortest.

Two kinds of light in the salon produce "white light": fluorescent light and incandescent light.

FLUORESCENT LIGHT

Fluorescent light is an economical and long-lasting light source. However, depending on its design, fluorescent light can create "blue" tones or "cool" casts in the objects it lights. In the salon, fluorescent light can create hair coloring problems unless natural sunlight is available, or the fluorescent bulbs are balanced for daylight.

INCANDESCENT LIGHT

To balance the tones of light in the salon, a second source of light can be used. This source is called incandescent light. This kind of light is provided by an ordinary light bulb. Normally this light produces redder tones or warmer casts in the objects it lights. Although more expensive to operate and replace than fluorescent light, incandescent light creates the closest substitute for natural sunlight.

Salon owners need to plan a balance of incandescent and fluorescent lighting in the salon design. Balanced lighting systems can have a pleasant psychological effect on staff and clients. Fluorescent light can be irritating to some people, while incandescent light can create excessive heat. Lighting should be comfortable to work under and easy to adjust.

INVISIBLE LIGHT

Salon professionals use invisible light to produce physical effects in the skin. Since this range of light is not visible to the human eye, you can be overexposed to invisible light in natural sunlight without knowing it.

Eighty percent of sunlight is composed of invisible rays beyond red, which are called infrared. Eight percent of natural sunlight is composed of invisible rays beyond violet, which are called ultraviolet.

Small doses of infrared or ultraviolet light can produce beneficial effects. Using either ultraviolet or infrared light to treat the skin is called light therapy.

INFRARED LIGHT

Just as infrared rays produce pure heat rays, any infrared light produces heat. Heat lamps or infrared bulbs can be purchased for use in processing chemical services. Take care to position the lamps according to the manufacturer's instructions.

Benefits of using infrared light during a facial include:
1. Increased circulation
2. Increased skin gland secretions
3. Relaxation of muscles
4. Stimulation of cell and tissue activity

Exposure times range from 5 to 15 minutes. The light must be placed at least 30 inches from the client's face. Eye pads or protective eye forms must be used to cover the client's eyes.

ULTRAVIOLET LIGHT

Ultraviolet rays, also known as actinic rays, have a shorter wavelength and can be more damaging than infrared rays. Ultraviolet light, or UV, produces both positive and negative effects on the skin, depending on the exposure time. Small doses of UV light can tan the skin and may help the body produce Vitamin D. UV light is germicidal and can kill bacteria that cause skin infections. It can also produce harmful chemical effects on the skin. Skin can be sunburned, eyes can be damaged, and hair can be photochemically damaged by UV rays. Studies prove overexposure to UV light can result in skin cancer. Conversely, it is believed that ultraviolet rays may promote healing and are used in the treatment of acne.

ALERT!

Both client and salon professional need to wear protective eyewear during infrared or UV light therapy treatments.

During facials or scalp massage, UV light can be used effectively. The skin or scalp should be cleansed before using ultraviolet light on the client. The client's eyes should be covered with protective eyewear, such as cotton eye pads, goggles, etc. The salon professional should wear protective eyewear also. For germicidal treatments, place the lamp at least 12 inches from the area to be treated. This distance allows the strong "short waves" to penetrate intensely. Expose the skin initially for 1 minute. Check for reactions. 1 to 5 minutes of total exposure time is often recommended.

For larger areas, like the scalp, place the lamp 20 to 30 inches from the area. Exposure can be up to 10 or 15 minutes. This exposure time would include the normal scalp massage.

The current trend of tanning beds or booths in salons poses serious questions related to client health and well-being. Dry, leathery skin, peeling, itching, wrinkling, sagging, permanent discoloration and possible skin cancers are all reactions to long exposure. **When using ultraviolet rays, you and your client should wear protective eyewear.**

CONNECTING THEORY
TO REAL-WORLD PRACTICE

ELECTRICITY	PERSONAL CONNECTION: IMPROVE YOURSELF	INDUSTRY CONNECTION: BECOME A PROFESSIONAL	CLIENT CONNECTION: SERVE THE GUEST
PRINCIPLES OF ELECTRICITY	Build expertise, self-reliance by understanding how electricity works	Improve safety, efficiency of salon operations	Deliver a safe, seamless, comfortable guest experience
ELECTRICITY IN COSMETOLOGY	Expand your personal skill set and career options	Model proficiency in a broad range of in-demand services	Provide a variety of services to safely enhance clients' health and appearance

IN OTHER WORDS

Understanding the basics of electricity will enable you to serve your clients more efficiently and safely, especially when working with electrotherapy and specialized electrical appliances.

LESSONS LEARNED

- Using electricity safely ensures the well-being of the salon professional and the client.

- Electric current may result in heat, mechanical or magnetic and electrochemical effects.

- Electric currents used during electrotherapy and light therapy treatments include Galvanic Current to produce chemical effects, Faradic and Sinusoidal Currents to produce mechanical, non-chemical reactions and Tesla Current to produce heat.

CHEMISTRY

5.1 MATTER
ELEMENTS
CHEMICAL BONDS

5.2 THE pH SCALE

5.3 CHEMISTRY OF COSMETICS
COSMETIC CLASSIFICATIONS
SHAMPOOS
RINSES AND CONDITIONERS
PERMS
RELAXERS
CURL REFORMATION
HAIR COLOR
PRODUCT INFORMATION

UNDERSTANDING
THE PRINCIPLES OF
CHEMISTRY HELPS IN
MARKETING PRODUCTS,
IN MAKING SOUND
DECISIONS ABOUT
WHICH PRODUCTS TO
USE, AND IN GUARDING
CLIENTS' SAFETY

FOLLOWING THIS LESSON
YOU WILL BE ABLE TO:

Describe matter, the five elements of hair and the structure
and behavior of atoms and bonds

Describe the pH scale and values associated with water, acid
and alkalines

Identify the precautions necessary for various classifications
of chemicals when working with professional products
and cosmetics

CONNECTING THEORY
TO REAL-WORLD PRACTICE
APPROACHING CHEMISTRY AS A PRACTICAL SCIENCE WILL HELP YOU:

| **PERSONAL CONNECTION:** | **INDUSTRY CONNECTION:** | **CLIENT CONNECTION:** |
IMPROVE YOURSELF	BECOME A PROFESSIONAL	SERVE THE GUEST
Be confident in your ability to understand the composition of hair and to make sense of product labels	Draw on scientific underpinnings that elevate your work to higher levels	Apply products and treatments that complement the chemical characteristics of clients' hair, skin and nails

Are all shampoos and conditioners pretty much the same? What is the difference between permanent and temporary
hair color? The answers to these questions, and many others that you will face every day in the salon, depend on an
understanding of chemistry.

5.1 MATTER

Matter is anything that occupies space. Look around. Matter is everywhere. Nails, hair and skin are matter. Water and even oxygen are matter. All of these things occupy physical space. **Chemistry is the scientific study of matter and the physical and chemical changes of matter.**

Chemists are scientists who study matter, its properties and changes. Chemists study properties or characteristics such as color, odor, weight (density) and hardness or softness that define a substance. Chemists teach that matter exists in three basic forms:

- **Solids** – matter with definite weight, volume and shape
- **Liquids** – matter with definite weight and volume but no definite shape
- **Gases** – matter with definite weight but indefinite volume and shape

For example, hair is a solid because it has definite weight, volume and shape. Conditioners, perm solutions and most shampoos are liquids. They have weight and volume but no definite shape which explains why liquids take the shape of the solid container into which they are poured. Oxygen is a colorless, odorless gas. It has weight, even though it may not seem to, but no definite volume or shape.

Matter can be changed from one of these forms (solid, liquid or gas) to another in two ways:

- **Physical Change** – a change in the physical characteristics of a substance without creating a new substance.
- **Chemical Change** – a change in a substance that creates a new substance with chemical characteristics different from those of the original substance.

An example of a physical change in matter would be when water freezes and becomes ice. It is still water, but now it's a solid instead of a liquid.

An example of a chemical change occurs when hydrogen combines with oxygen to form a new substance, water.

Some matter is living and some is not. It is the presence of the element carbon that distinguishes living matter from nonliving matter. Chemistry has a special division for each kind of matter:

- **Organic chemistry** deals with all matter that is now living or was alive at one time, with carbon present, such as plants and animals.
- **Inorganic chemistry** studies all matter that is not alive, has never been alive and does not contain carbon, such as rocks, water and minerals.

ELEMENTS

All matter, whether solid, liquid or gas, whether living or nonliving, is made up of elements. **Elements** are basic substances that cannot be broken down into simpler substances.

As of this printing, there are 118 known elements. Those above the 92nd element are synthetic and do not occur naturally. Five of these elements, because they form the basis of hair, nails and skin, are important for the salon professional to know. These elements are carbon, oxygen, hydrogen, nitrogen and sulfur. Look at this chart to notice a few more things about elements:

All matter is composed of atoms, which make up elements.

Hair is comprised of two solids (carbon and sulfur) and three gases (hydrogen, nitrogen and oxygen).

ATOMIC NO.	ELEMENT	SYMBOL	CATEGORY
1	Hydrogen	H	Gas
2	Helium	He	Gas
3	Lithium	Li	Solid
6	Carbon	C	Solid
7	Nitrogen	N	Gas
8	Oxygen	O	Gas
13	Aluminum	Al	Solid
16	Sulfur	S	Solid
80	Mercury	Hg	Liquid

On this chart, the left-hand column shows each element's **atomic number**. You'll read more about this number in the next few pages. Even more important to you and your work are the letters after each element's name. These letters, called symbols, are a kind of scientific shorthand, like a nickname, that makes it easier for you to identify the elements. You will see these symbols used throughout this book, in other professional literature and on some product labels. **Oxygen is the most abundant element in the earth's crust and the second most abundant element in the earth's atmosphere.** To remember the elements found in hair, use this acronym: COHNS (carbon, oxygen, hydrogen, nitrogen and sulfur).

ATOMS

Atoms are the smallest complete unit of an element. Each element consists of a certain kind of atom different from the atoms of any other element.

Atoms have three main parts: protons, neutrons and electrons. Protons and neutrons are packed together tightly to form a dense core, or nucleus, at the center of the atom. Electrons move about this nucleus on orbiting paths or shells at nearly the speed of light.

Protons have a positive electrical charge (+) and identify the atom as, for example, a hydrogen atom or an oxygen atom, etc.

Neutrons have no electrical charge. They are neutral, hence their name, neutron. The neutron determines the weight of the atom.

Electrons have a negative electrical charge (-). Under certain circumstances, they make it possible for atoms to unite with other atoms to form bonds.

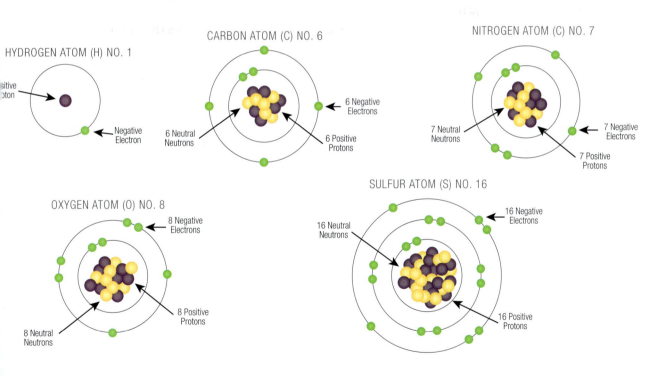

Above is a diagram of the atomic structure of the five elements important to you as a salon professional. Notice how different one atom is from another in terms of number of protons, neutrons and electrons.

The atomic number indicates how many protons are in a single atom of a particular element. For example, the atomic number of hydrogen is 1, which means it has only 1 proton and 1 electron. **Hydrogen is the simplest atomic structure.** Carbon has an atomic number of 6, which means it has 6 protons, 6 neutrons and 6 electrons. Nitrogen has 7, oxygen 8 and sulfur 16.

The chemical behavior of an atom depends mostly on the number of electrons in its outermost orbiting path or shell. Some atoms by their very structure are not missing any electrons in their outer shell. These atoms are considered stable and are electrically neutra

If the outer shell of the atom is missing electrons, however, the atom is considered unstable or reactive. Unstable atoms seek other atoms with which they can share electrons to complete their outer shell. When they combine, they make more complex units, known as molecules.

MOLECULES

When unstable atoms combine chemically by sharing electrons, they form molecules. **A molecule is two or more atoms joined together by a chemical bond**. If the atoms that combine are different, for example, an atom of hydrogen and an atom of oxygen, the resulting molecule is a compound. Different atoms joined together as molecules become the smallest parts of a compound.

When two hydrogen atoms, each with one electron, combine with one oxygen atom and its eight electrons, the result is a water molecule of the compound H_2O. This is an example of two gases—hydrogen and oxygen—uniting and becoming a liquid.

CHEMICAL BONDS

You are now familiar with the diagrams of the atoms of the five elements of hair—carbon, oxygen, hydrogen, nitrogen and sulfur. These atoms combine chemically to create compound that eventually create the protein of hair. To see how they join to form hair, you'll need to lea a little about chemical bonds, starting with amino acids.

With an element, the atoms are the same. With a compound, the atoms are different.

AMINO ACIDS

Amino acids are compounds consisting of carbon, oxygen, hydrogen and nitrogen. There are 22 common amino acids. These amino acids join together in chains to become proteins, which provide the chemicals the body needs for growth and repairing tissues.

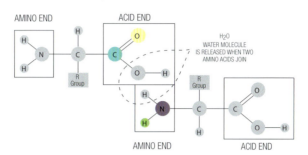

Although amino acids create all proteins, each protein is different because of the way it is put together. **Hair is a form of protein called keratin.** Keratin in hair contains 19 of 22 common amino acids. In fact, **hair is made of 97% keratin protein and 3% trace minerals.**

The chain, or the order in which the amino acids link together, makes each type of protein one of a kind. Also, the number of amino acids in the chain is important. For example, the 19 amino acids found in hair must all be present or the structure won't be hair.

PEPTIDE BONDS (END BONDS)

The amino acids that create protein are linked together end to end by a peptide bond, also known as an end bond. The **peptide bond** is the backbone of all protein molecules. When two amino acids are positioned end to end, the acid end of one amino acid attaches to the amino end of another amino acid. **The peptide bond forms when these two ends join.** The polypeptide bond ("poly" means many) connects thousands of amino acids lengthwise to form a chain.

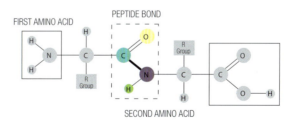

In other words, **hair is the linking together of protein groups.** You, as a designer, will be altering these links. You need to know how your techniques and tools will affect your client's hair. **It's very important not to disturb peptide bonds.** For instance, if you put a sodium hydroxide relaxer under a hair dryer, **the combination of the alkaline chemicals and heat could break these critical peptide bonds and destroy the protein structure.** If they are broken, the protein chains separate into small fragments or revert to groups of amino acids that no longer have the characteristics of hair.

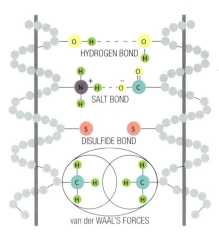

SIDE BONDS

When amino acids combine to form the keratin protein of hair, they take on a spiraling configuration. When these long, spiraling protein chains are placed next to each other, they can be linked together by four side bonds. The four bonds holding protein chains together behave differently and they each serve a different purpose in building hair. The four side bonds created are:

1. The Hydrogen Bond
2. The Salt Bond
3. The Disulfide Bond
4. van der Waal's Forces

When giving chemical services, you are affecting all these bonds. In order to minimize damage to the hair, it is important to understand how the four side bonds work.

The first bond is the **hydrogen bond**, which works on the principle that unlike charges attract. Hydrogen bonding takes place when the hydrogen atom in one molecule is attracted to an atom of another molecule that has many negative electrons. **Hair has many hydrogen bonds, which are individually very weak and can easily be broken by heat or water.** Although the attraction in these hydrogen bonds is weak, there are so many of them in the protein of hair that they tend to organize the protein chains and give hair its shape. **About 35% of the hair's strength is due to the millions of hydrogen bonds in its structure.**

A second type of bond between protein chains is the **salt bond**. This bond is also a result of the attraction of unlike charges. The negative charge in one amino acid grouping attracts the positive charge in another amino acid grouping. Salt bonds also help to organize the protein chains. They account for another 35% of the hair's resistance to change and, like hydrogen bonds, are not particularly strong.

Since both **hydrogen and salt bonds can be weakened by water**, hair can be shampooed, set on rollers and dried by heat into a new shape. **When hair is saturated with water, the hydrogen and salt bonds are weakened, leaving the hair more pliable.** Then, by wrapping it around a roller under tension and drying it, the hair takes on a new shape because new hydrogen and salt bonds are formed between the protein chains. However, this set is only temporary because **exposure to water will break the new bonds. Even the humidity in the air can break the new bonds** and restore the original ones.

Using rollers or a blow dryer and curling iron to create a thermal design is referred to as a physical change since it is only the physical characteristics of the hair that change.

The sulfur-containing side bond, the disulfide bond, is the most important to your work. When these sulfur-type side chains join with other sulfur-type side chains, they form the disulfide bond. This bond is a chemical bond that forms between protein structures. A lot of your chemical services, particularly perming and relaxing, directly affect the disulfide bond by either breaking the disulfide bond or reforming it in a new shape. This process is a chemical change and creates lasting results.

The side bond known as **van der Waal's Forces** is based on the theory that atomic groups prefer an environment with other groups that have structures similar to theirs. This type of bonding is not important for your work as a hair designer other than to know that it exists and plays a role in bonding protein chains.

HAIR'S CHEMICAL STRUCTURE

1. Hair begins with individual atoms, the smallest unit of matter.
2. These atoms unite by sharing electrons to become molecules of amino acids.
3. One end of one amino acid bonds to the opposite end of another amino acid to form the peptide or end bond.
4. The amino acids create polypeptide protein chains.
5. The individual protein chains bond, side-to-side, to other chains by hydrogen bonds, salt bonds, disulfide bonds and van der Waal's Forces.
6. The bonding of protein chains to other protein chains makes human hair.

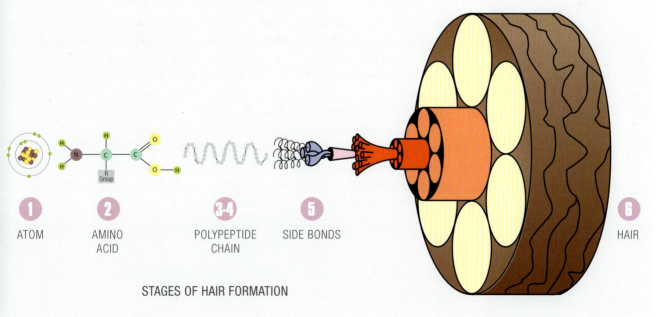

STAGES OF HAIR FORMATION

5.2 THE pH SCALE

pH (potential hydrogen) is a unit of measurement that indicates whether a substance is acidic, neutral or alkaline. Alkaline is sometimes called "base." Just as degrees measure temperature and inches measure distance, **pH numbers measure the amount of acid or alkali in a water-based solution.** As a salon professional, you need to understand pH and its effects on hair, skin and scalp. This means knowing which products have high or low pH and why. **Only solutions containing water and/or which dissolve in water can have an acidic or alkaline nature.** A solution is acidic or alkaline depending on the number of negative hydroxide ions or positive hydrogen ions it contains (an ion is an atom that has gained or lost electrons). If a solution has more positive hydrogen ions than negative hydroxide ions, it is *acidic*. If it has more *negative* hydroxide ions, it is *alkaline*. When a solution has an equal number of hydrogen and hydroxide ions, it is neutral.

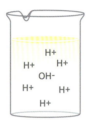 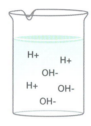 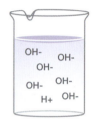

A solution is acidic if it has more positive hydrogen ions than negative hydroxide ions.

When a solution has an equal number of positive and negative ions, it is neutral.

A solution is alkaline if it has more negative hydroxide ions.

0 – 6.99 = Acid
7 = Neutral
7.01 – 14 = Alkaline

The pH measurement scale ranges from 0 to 14 with number 7 as neutral. Numbers less than seven indicate acid while numbers greater than seven indicate alkaline. The scale is **logarithmic**, which means *each step or number increases by multiples of 10*. pH 6 is 10 times more acidic than neutral 7; however, 6 is 10 times less acidic than 5, which falls in the range of the average pH of hair, skin and scalp. So, when you are using products that are pH 6 or "only one number" away from the average pH of hair, it is actually 10 times less acidic. That is a big difference. For example, have you ever peeled an orange and, as the juice from the orange came in contact with your skin, you felt a slight tingle? The pH of an orange is approximately 2, which is 3 steps away from the pH of your skin (4.5 to 5.5).

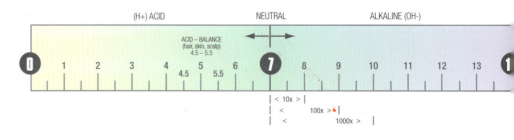

CHEMISTRY

116

Three methods of testing any product to determine the pH level include pH (Nitrazine) paper, pH pencil or a pH meter. The acid mantle that coats the skin and hair can also be measured with these.

At the top of the scale is 14, which is 10 million times more alkaline than 7. As you can see, a very slight variation in pH will greatly affect the acidity of any salon product.

pH balanced and acid balanced are two terms that are sometimes confused in the cosmetology industry. pH balanced means the pH is balanced at a certain number, but not necessarily at 4.5 to 5.5 (average pH range of hair, skin and scalp). **Acid balanced means just that, balanced within the acid range of 4.5 to 5.5.** Acid balanced is the term applied to most professional shampoos and conditioners. Your task as a salon professional is to use products that will help maintain the acid balance of the hair and skin at the 4.5 to 5.5 acid range level.

Understanding pH measurements and values will greatly assist your ability to keep the hair, skin and scalp in the best condition possible. Reading labels correctly, selecting the right products for clients and recommending products for home hair care will also be based on a good understanding of pH values.

ITEM	pH VALUE (approx.)	ACID, ALKALINE OR NEUTRAL
Lemon Juice	2.5	Strong Acid
Diet Cherry Coke	3.0	Weak Acid
Distilled Water	7.0	Neutral
Toothpaste	8.5	Weak Alkaline
Ammonia	12.5	Strong Alkaline

BRAIN BALANCING
Unscramble these words from the pH section for a "brain-balanced" feeling!

OAIICLGTHMR   EIAANLKL   CDNEAALB   DCAI   EUALRTN   OEDNGYRH

COSMETOLOGY FUNDAMENTALS

5.3 CHEMISTRY OF COSMETICS

The Food and Drug Act of 1938 defines cosmetics as "articles intended to be rubbed, poured, sprinkled, or otherwise applied to the human body or any part thereof for cleansing, beautifying, promoting attractiveness or altering the appearance." As a salon professional it is important to understand the physical and chemical characteristics of cosmetics in order to better serve your clients.

COSMETIC CLASSIFICATIONS

Six general classifications are assigned to categorize cosmetics used in the cosmetology industry. Knowledge of these cosmetic classifications will help you understand product labels and directed use. These classifications are based on how well the substance combines with another as well as the physical characteristics of each.

A mixture is two or more substances that are physically combined.

6 CLASSIFICATIONS

1 SOLUTIONS   2 SUSPENSIONS   3 EMULSIONS

4 OINTMENTS   5 SOAPS   6 POWDERS

1 SOLUTIONS

Solutions are mixtures of two or more kinds of molecules, evenly dispersed. For example, solution made by mixing a package of instant soup and a cup of hot water. The dry soup would be called the solute, which is any substance that dissolves into a liquid and forms a solution.

Water is considered a universal solvent because it is capable of dissolving more substances than any other solvent. Only oil and wax can not be dissolved in water.

The water would be called a **solvent,** which is any substance that is able to dissolve another substance. The soup would be called the solution. Solutions do not separate when left standing and are generally clear mixtures. Stirring is usually required when dissolving a solute. **Solutes** can be either solid, liquid or gas. Hydrogen peroxide would be an example of a gas mixed with a liquid to form a solution. There are three classes of solutions:

- Dilute solution contains a small quantity of the solute in comparison to the quantity of solvent.
- Concentrated solution contains a large quantity of the solute in comparison to the quantity of solvent.
- Saturated solution cannot take or dissolve more of the solute than it already holds at a given temperature.

2 SUSPENSIONS

Suspensions are also mixtures of two or more kinds of molecules. Unlike solutions, however, suspensions have a tendency to separate when left standing and therefore need to be shaken before using. An example of a suspension would be vinegar and oil as a salad dressing preparation.

Immiscible = liquids not able to be mixed

Miscible = liquids able to be mixed together without separating

If left standing, the mixture of vinegar and oil separates and needs shaking before being used. Many lotions used in the cosmetology industry are suspensions. Calamine lotion is another example.

③ EMULSIONS

Emulsions are formed when two or more nonmixable substances (like oil and water) are united with the help of a binder or gum-like substance. The gum-like substance might be a soap. General classifications of emulsions are oil-in-water (perm solutions) and water-in-oil (cold creams). Most emulsions used in the cosmetology industry are classified as oil-in-water.

④ OINTMENTS

Ointments are mixtures of organic substances and a medicinal agent, usually found in a semi-solid form. Water is generally not present in this mixture. Ointment-type preparations come in the form of sticks (like lipstick), pastes (like some eye shadows or blush) and mucilages (thick liquids, such as styling lotions).

⑤ SOAPS

Soaps are mixtures of fats and oils converted to fatty acids by heat and then purified. Soaps used in the cosmetology industry generally fall into the categories of deodorant soaps, beauty soaps, medicated soaps and liquid soaps.

⑥ POWDERS

Powders are equal mixtures of inorganic and organic substances that do not dissolve in water and that have been sifted and mixed until free of coarse gritty particles. Perfume and shades of color are usually added for purposes of enhancement.

SHAMPOOS

You are now ready to take a look at the chemistry of products and procedures for services in the salon. The natural place to start is with the service most often performed...shampooing. **You shampoo primarily to clean the hair and scalp and to remove all foreign matter, including dirt, sebum (natural scalp oil), cosmetics, hair spray and skin debris without adversely affecting either the scalp or hair.** Shampooing the hair is an important function as it is often the first impression the client has of the salon and of the designer. Shampooing, as part of a salon service, can be a highly therapeutic experience when done in a caring, organized and confident manner. Remember, **the shampoo should be a soothing, relaxing experience, as it sets the climate for all future services.**

Hair should be shampooed as often as necessary depending on how quickly the scalp and hair become soiled. Frequency varies from individual to individual. **Improper or irregular cleansing allows a breeding place for disease-causing bacteria** and can lead to scalp disorders and even hair loss. Generally, oily hair needs to be shampooed more often than normal or dry hair. Strong alkaline shampoos are not recommended as they may make the hair dry and brittle.

HOW SHAMPOO WORKS

Even though the hair fiber beyond the scalp is dead (i.e., biologically inactive), a mixture of secretions from the sebaceous glands and perspiration from the sweat glands helps maintain the hair and scalp at its natural pH of 4.5 to 5.5, allowing a shiny, alive appearance. These scalp secretions can be spread by simply running the fingers through the hair or by brushing or combing. Failure to remove these scalp secretions on a regular basis will allow a build-up of oily film. The oily film is an emulsion, a combination of oil, sweat, dead epidermal cells and dirt particles.

Most shampoo is water-based and contains an ingredient known as a **surfactant** or *cleansing agent*. **Surfactants, also called surface active agents, are used to remove oil from the hair.**

A surfactant is necessary because water alone cannot attack and dissolve oil. For example, if you just wet the remains of a greasy dinner plate of spaghetti, the water simply beads up. Once you add soap, the grease breaks up and is easily washed away. It is necessary to add detergents, soaps or other surface active agents (surfactants) to do the job.

The molecule of a surface active agent is a two-part molecule. **It has a water-loving part (hydrophilic) and an oil-loving part (lipophilic).** During a shampoo, the water-loving part is attracted to water, while the oil-loving part is attracted to oil on the hair. The resulting "push-pull" action causes the oil to "roll up" into droplets, which are then lifted into the water and washed away. By removing the oil from the hair shaft and scalp, the water can wet the hair and scalp and the debris can be washed away.

Some shampoos contain both a surfactant and conditioner. Together they not only cleanse the hair but help condition it as well. These conditioners can contain many ingredients, including hydrolyzed protein derivatives. These derivatives strengthen damaged areas of the hair by depositing protein fragments along the hair shaft.

THE ROLE OF WATER

Water plays an important part in the success of your shampoo. Water can be classified as either hard or soft, depending on the amount and kinds of minerals present. Hard water or well water contains certain salts of calcium, magnesium and other metals that prevent the shampoo from lathering. It can be softened by a chemical process. Soft water contains very small amounts of minerals and is preferred for shampooing as it lathers more freely.

Emulsion (ee-**MUL**-shun), n. a substance formed when two or more non-mixable substances, such as oil and water, are united with the aid of a binder or an emulsifier.

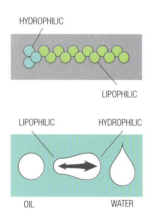

Water is usually the first ingredient listed on most shampoos, which indicates it is the primary ingredient. This is usually pure or deionized water. Remember—water is electrically charged, neutral on the pH scale and earns the title of "universal solvent."

WATER PURIFICATION

Sedimentation and filtration are two methods used in the purification of water. During sedimentation undesirable substances, such as clay, sand, etc., sink to the bottom and then during filtration, pass through a porous substance. Chlorine is added to kill bacteria and complete the purification process. Water boiled at a temperature of 212° (100° Celsius) will also destroy most microbic life.

Key points to remember about shampooing:

- The natural pH of hair, 4.5 to 5.5, is maintained by the mixture of secretions from the sebaceous glands and perspiration.
- Shampoos contain surfactants, that remove oil from the hair.
- Hard water contains certain minerals which prevent shampoo from lathering; soft water is preferred due to its low amount of minerals.
- Shampoos should be formulated to conform to the natural pH of the acid mantle of the hair and scalp.

TYPES OF SHAMPOOS

Many varieties of shampoos are available today to the professional designer. It is important that you familiarize yourself with all of them to learn which will bring the best results to your individual clients. Remember to always read and follow the recommended directions for successful results.

1 **ALL-PURPOSE SHAMPOOS** contain a low alkaline content and a low concentration of surface active agents. They are designed to cleanse the hair without correcting any special condition. They do not strip color and are very mild. Some even include anti-fungus and anti-dandruff agents.

2 **ACID-BALANCED (NON-STRIPPING) SHAMPOOS** are formulated to have the same pH as the hair and skin (4.5 to 5.5) and can be used on almost all types of hair. They are made especially to cleanse chemically treated hair without removing permanent hair coloring or toners. Always use a mild non-stripping shampoo on bleached hair and dry, damaged hair.

3 **"PLAIN" SHAMPOOS** are usually strong and contain a high alkaline or soap base. They can be used successfully on virgin hair in good condition, but are not recommended for chemically treated or damaged hair. When using this type of shampoo, always follow with an acid rinse to restore the acid balance of your client's hair and scalp.

4 **SOAPLESS SHAMPOOS** are able to lather without harsh alkaline ingredients. They are made by a process in which the oils from synthetic detergents have been treated with sulfuric acid, resulting in substances known as wetting agents. These soapless shampoos or surfactants are effective in both soft and hard water and rinse out easily.

Water (H_2O) makes up approximately 60% of the human body and covers 75% of the earth's surface.

5 **MEDICATED SHAMPOOS** may be available from your local beauty supply house, but often can be obtained only by prescription from your client's doctor. They contain ingredients designed to treat scalp and hair problems or disorders.

6 **CLARIFYING SHAMPOOS** often have a higher alkalinity in order to be able to remove residue, chlorine, minerals or product buildup. Clarifying shampoos are often used before chemical services.

7 **ANTI-DANDRUFF SHAMPOOS** are formulated for either a dry or oily scalp and contain an anti-fungus or germicide ingredient and conditioners to control dandruff conditions or other scalp conditions that could breed infections. When using an anti-dandruff shampoo, always follow the manufacturer's directions, massage the scalp vigorously and rinse thoroughly.

8 **LIQUID DRY SHAMPOOS** are used to cleanse the scalp and hair when the client is unable to receive a normal shampoo. The shampoo loosens the dirt and oil from the hair and scalp when applied with saturated cotton. Liquid dry shampoos are effective in cleaning wigs and hairpieces because ordinary shampoos deteriorate the wefting (base material to which the hair is sewn). The basic procedure is to apply the solution to the scalp and small strands of hair, rubbing briskly along each section. Follow the application by blotting with a towel. Any remaining solution will evaporate. Liquid dry shampoos are very drying to the hair and should be used only when necessary. They are highly flammable and should be used with caution. Always use in a well-ventilated room away from open flames or appliances. Never smoke cigarettes or allow clients to smoke when using liquid dry shampoos.

9 **POWDER DRY SHAMPOOS** are formulated for clients who are bedridden and cannot wet the hair. These shampoos contain orris root powder that absorbs soil and oil as the product is brushed through the scalp and hair. After applying the powder, brush it out of the hair with a long-bristled brush until all traces of powder are removed. Between strokes wipe the brush with a clean towel. Do not give a powder dry shampoo before a chemical service.

10 **CONDITIONING SHAMPOOS** contain small amounts of animal, vegetable or mineral additives that penetrate into the cortex or coat the cuticle layer of the hair. These additives can improve the tensile strength and porosity of hair and will usually be removed with the next shampoo. Protein substances found in penetrating shampoos/conditioners can last through several shampoos.

11 **COLOR SHAMPOOS** are temporary color molecules that adhere to the outer cuticle of the hair and deposit color. The effects of these shampoos, available in enhancing and vivid colors, last from shampoo to shampoo.

12 **SHAMPOOS FOR THINNING HAIR** are formulated as gentle shampoos, with a lighter molecular weight that does not cause damage or weigh hair down. These shampoos may also contain ingredients to provide a healthy environment for the maximum amount of hair growth.

This wide variety of shampoos has one desired result—a satisfied customer with healthy hair. It is essential for you, as a salon professional, to realize that not all shampoos that claim pH balance are necessarily acid balanced. An acid-balanced shampoo has the natural 4.5 to 5.5 pH of the hair and scalp. If the natural acidic conditions are maintained during a shampoo, the cuticle scales are kept in a more compact state and therefore a minimal amount of swelling of the cuticle fibers occurs. Hair is strongest at a pH of 4.5 to 5.5 because it is compact and least swollen. If the pH of a shampoo is too alkaline (or too acidic), the hair fiber can swell. This swelling weakens the hair, making it more susceptible to other forms of distress, such as dryness and cuticle damage. Strong, compact hair is more pleasing in appearance and easier to manage.

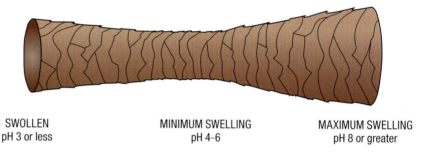

SWOLLEN
pH 3 or less

MINIMUM SWELLING
pH 4-6

MAXIMUM SWELLING
pH 8 or greater

RINSES AND CONDITIONERS

Hair's chemical composition is changed with perm and color services. Bonds are broken that can never be rejoined. Hair becomes chemically and mechanically damaged through daily care. The tools of your profession—thermal styling irons, blow dryers, teasing combs, brushes and even rollers—can cause a degree of damage. Other factors that can affect hair condition are the environment and products such as alkaline shampoos. Once the natural bonds in the hair are broken, nothing can be done to actually reconnect them and repair the hair.

As a designer, it is your responsibility to be aware of products that can strengthen hair, add body and protect it from further damage. Scientists have formulated products that can smooth rough hair cuticles, add protein molecules to the hair shaft and add humectants (moisturizers) to replace moisture to dry hair. It is important for you to investigate these products, to help your clients' hair to be as cosmetically pleasing as possible and to prepare their hair properly for chemical services. To achieve this, it is important for you to know why and when each product type is used and the results you can expect to achieve.

COSMETIC APPEARANCE is the luster or shine of the hair. If the layers of the outer cuticle stand away from the hair shaft, the hair will appear rough and dull.

POROSITY refers to the ability of the hair to absorb moisture, liquids or chemicals.

MANAGEABILITY is determined by how easily a comb can pass through wet or dry hair.

ELASTICITY is the ability of the hair to stretch and return to its natural shape without breaking. Healthy hair can be stretched about 50% when wet and up to 20% when dry. Tensile strength measures the amount of tension that can be applied before the hair breaks.

RINSES

Rinses affect mostly the surface of the hair. Rinses are usually applied to the hair and rinse off immediately. They sometimes leave a coating that surrounds each hair strand. Some rinses can actually be detrimental to the hair because they contain ingredients that "build up" on the hair's surface. This "build up" can make the hair feel limp, attract dirt and make it difficult to control. Rinses are applied to the hair to help close the cuticle and make hair feel soft and manageable.

There are several effective rinses on the market today. Many rinses (and conditioners) are formulated for specific types of hair by chemists who specialize in the study of hair. At one time, however, all rinses had to be prepared in the salon or by the consumer "at home." Rinses you should be familiar with include:

① **VINEGAR AND LEMON (ACID) RINSES** help keep the cuticle compact. The vinegar rinse is mixed by using two tablespoons of white vinegar with a pint of tepid water. Lemon rinse uses the strained juice of two lemons or 15 drops of concentrated lemon extract. Adjust with water to a pH of 4.5 to 5.5. Acid rinses usually have a very low pH (2 to 3) and are designed to dissolve soap scum and curds, untangle and separate the hair and add sheen. Soap scum, caused by the combination of the minerals in the water and the fatty acids of soap, is the residue remaining on the surface of the hair after shampooing. An acid rinse can also be used to counteract the alkalinity present after a chemical service.

② **CREME RINSES** soften and add luster, making tangled hair easier to comb. A creme rinse is creamy in appearance and adheres to the hair shaft, even after ordinary rinsing, thus leaving the hair with a soft feel and much easier to comb and handle. Creme rinses are only slightly acidic and do not have the same function as acid rinses. In selecting a creme rinse, be sure to select one with a proper pH level for your needs.

③ **MEDICATED RINSES** are designed with ingredients that control minor dandruff and scalp conditions. They can usually be applied with cotton or poured over the scalp followed by a one-minute scalp massage, but be sure to follow manufacturer's instructions. Their active ingredients, such as benazlkonium chloride, lauryl isoquinolinium bromide and polysorbate leave the hair lustrous and manageable.

CONDITIONERS

Conditioning is an important step in your client's hair needs. Sometimes a client's hair may be in great condition and only require a rinse to smooth the cuticle. But in many cases the hair has been dried out and damaged by strong alkaline shampoos, chemical damage or heat styling. Any amount of heat can damage the cuticle layer over time, leaving a rough, dry feeling. In these cases, a conditioning treatment may be needed.

Conditioners usually penetrate deep into the hair so they are formulated differently from rinses. In order to achieve maximum penetration, they are usually kept on the hair for a specific length of time. The length of time a conditioner should be left on the hair depends on its formulation and purpose.

Sometimes the addition of heat is recommended to open the cuticle, which allows for better penetration. Read the manufacturer's instructions before applying.

Remember, hair "damage" generally refers to bonds (disulfide, etc.) that have been broken through the application of chemical services or thermal styling. Conditioners don't actually repair broken bonds, but rather fortify the damaged areas of the hair and protect it against further damage from chemical services or heat. They may also alter the way hair behaves, giving it less stretch or reducing the relaxation of a set. Conditioners provide a temporary remedy for existing hair problems.

1 **INSTANT CONDITIONERS** coat the hair shaft and restore moisture and oils, but do not penetrate into the cortex or replace keratin in the shaft. Instant conditioners usually have a vegetable oil base, an acidic pH and are not recommended for fine and limp hair. They are generally left on the hair for 1 to 2 minutes, then rinsed off.

2 **NORMALIZING CONDITIONERS** also usually contain a vegetable protein and have an acidic pH, which causes the cuticle to close after alkaline chemical services. They are generally applied for approximately 2 minutes and rinsed off.

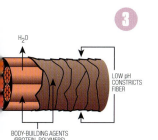

3 **BODY-BUILDING CONDITIONERS** are required when hair is fine and limp and contains too much moisture to maintain a good style. The formula, with protein, will penetrate into the damaged hair shaft and deposit proteins into the cortex. The proteins displace the excess moisture, providing more body to the hair. This modifies the delicate moisture/protein balance and makes the hair more manageable and able to hold a style for a longer period of time. Protein conditioners may be used before chemical services to help ensure their success. They are usually left on about 10 minutes. However, always follow manufacturer's instructions.

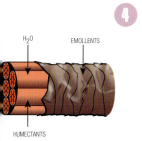

4 **MOISTURIZING CONDITIONERS** contain hydrolyzed animal proteins and are recommended for dry, brittle hair that has been mechanically or chemically damaged. The humectants (moisturizing ingredients) in a moisturizing conditioner will penetrate into each hair shaft to bind and hold moisture in the hair. These conditioners form a thin film on the cuticle, acting as a barrier to keep moisture from escaping. Moisturizing conditioners should not be used for several days after a perm or it will go limp. Follow manfacturer's directions for the length of time to leave on the hair after shampooing.

5 **CUSTOMIZED CONDITIONERS** are formulated to meet special needs. When a client's hair requires a combination of moisturizing and body-building properties, you may customize the treatment, mixing a moisturizing conditioner with a body-building protein product to improve the condition of your client's hair.

INGREDIENTS FOR CONDITIONERS

Most protein conditioners are derived from animal or vegetable materials, and a few come from minerals. A common animal protein found in conditioners is bovine serum, a refined and sterilized cattle tissue such as blood and bone marrow. The refined placentas of female cattle and sheep and collagen are also popular animal proteins found in hair conditioners.

The vegetable proteins found in conditioners are usually made from soybeans, balsam tree, olives, wheat germ and tong beans. These vegetable and animal proteins are refined through a very complex method (with various combinations of chemicals into the formulation of a conditioner). A conditioner need not contain protein. However, since hair is largely made up of protein, it becomes the logical choice and a major component in most conditioning products.

Additional ingredients found in conditioners include:
- **Amines/Quats** make hair easier to comb and control static.
- **Dimethicones** give softness to the feel of hair without weighing it down. They are a form of silicone.
- **Fatty alcohols** and acids give hair a smooth feel when dry and make it easier to comb. Fatty alcohols are creamy in texture and help retain moisture.

Conditioners should be used sparingly and only when necessary for clients with fine, thin hair. However, a heavier conditioner may be needed for thick or curly hair. In some cases, a leave-in product may be used to help control curl and waves. Some clients may be concerned that using a conditioner will make their hair "too soft" or "weigh it down." Just remember, the right conditioner for each client should provide the needed result, great looking, healthy and well-conditioned hair.

PERMS

ORIGINAL STRAIGHT HAIR

The three major chemical services, perm (also known as permanent waving), chemical relaxing and hair color, are covered in depth in each respective chapter of Unit 2. In this section of Chemistry, you are given an overview of the information that pertains to the chemical ingredients with which you will be working when performing these services.

Perms allow designers to chemically reform hair into a wavy or curly formation.
- First, the client's hair is wrapped around perm tools chosen to reflect the desired curl pattern.
- Then, a processing lotion (also called waving lotion) is applied to break disulfide bonds. This softens the protein structure and allows the protein chains to assume the shape of the perm tool.

SHIFTING AND BREAKING OF DISULFIDE BONDS

- Rinsing removes the processing lotion.
- A second chemical, the neutralizer (also called rebonding lotion), reforms the disulfide bonds into the new configuration. The resulting chemical change in the hair holds the hair in its new position.

Perms fall into two primary categories:
1. Alkaline waves (cold waves), which are processed *without* heat and have a pH of approximately 8.0 to 9.5.
2. Acid waves (heat waves), which are processed *with* heat and must be wrapped with tension. Acid waves have an approximate pH of 6.9 to 7.2.

The main chemical ingredient found in alkaline waves is *thioglycolic acid* or its derivatives and ammonium hydroxide. *Ammonium hydroxide* is added to the formula to shorten the processing time. It is also responsible for the swelling that occurs during this process, which makes it easier for the thioglycolic acid to penetrate the hair structure and break the disulfide bonds. Processing begins as soon as the chemical has been applied to the hair.

DISULFIDE BONDS REFORMED

The main chemical ingredient found in **acid waves** is *glyceryl monothioglycolate*. In acid waving, speed is sacrificed for a more controlled curl and less damage to the hair when procedures are carefully followed. Heat is sometimes used to assist in the penetration of the hair structure.

The main ingredient found in most neutralizers (or bonding lotions) is either hydrogen peroxide, sodium perborate, or sodium bromate. All three of these ingredients can cause additional damage to the hair if left on longer than specified by the manufacturer.

RELAXERS

Just as a perm adds curl and body to hair by changing its molecular structure, a chemical relaxer reduces curl in tightly curled or wavy hair by changing its molecular structure.
- The reforming (relaxing) product, which is usually formulated in a heavy cream base, is applied to the hair and holds the hair in a straight position while it is being processed. In addition a smoothing or pressing action is applied to the softened hair, causing the entire protein structure to relax to the straighter position.
- The neutralizing (bonding) step utilizes a neutralizing shampoo or lotion to reduce the swelling caused by alkaline formulas. This chemical change causes the hair to be held in the new straight configuration.

ALERT!

Sodium hydroxide and thioglycolate are not compatible. A sodium hydroxide relaxer should never be given on hair that has been relaxed with a thioglycolate relaxer or vice versa. The straigtened hair must grow out before additional chemical services can be performed.

There are two popular types of products used to chemically relax hair:
1. Sodium hydroxide type – formulated with 2% to 3% sodium hydroxide in a heavy cream base with an alkaline pH of anywhere from 11.5 to 14.
2. Ammonium thioglycolate type – formulated with 4% to 6% thioglycolic acid or its derivatives with 1% ammonium hydroxide and an 8.5 to 9.5 pH. A cream base is also usually added.

When chemically relaxing hair with sodium hydroxide, the disulfide bonds are broken at point "X" between the first sulphur atom and the adjacent carbon atom, resulting in one sulphur atom being lost. This process is called lanthionization and results in a lanthionine bond (contains only one sulphur atom). Once the disulfide bond has been broken in this manner, the hair cannot be reformed or permed because the ammonium thioglycolate chemical process requires that the disulfide bonds remain in tact. **It is important to remember that the chemical action of sodium hydroxide is irreversible.** Thioglycolate breaks the disulfide bond at point "Y" between two sulfur atoms.

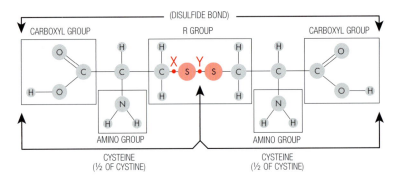

CURL REFORMATION

A soft curl perm (which will be referred to as curl reformation or curls) is a service used to loose the texture of curly to tightly curled hair. The hair is first smoothed into a relaxed shape by usin the back of a comb and fingers combined with the application of a thioglycolate-based product in a gel or cream form. Once the hair has achieved a straightened shape, the thioglycolate product is rinsed from the hair. A curl booster is applied and perm rods are used to achieve the curl formation. **Once the test curl displays the desired curl formation, the hair is rinsed and a neutralizing (bonding) lotion is applied to reform (fix) the curl into a lasting shape.**

The chemical change that occurs with this service is the same as in a perm service. **The application of the processing solution prior to wrapping the hair on perm tools serves to soft and rearrange the disulfide bonds. The chemical rearranger is rinsed before a complete relaxation (straightening) of the hair takes place, allowing the disulfide bonds to take on the shape of the selected perm rod.**

Extreme care must be taken during this service to ensure satisfactory results. **Extended processing time, combined with dual application of processing solution can damage the hair.** Follow manufacturer's directions closely.

HAIR COLOR

Manufacturers create an array of colors and lighteners that give the designer the ability to create subtle to dramatic hair color changes. Hair color products fall into the following general categories:

- Nonoxidative Color
- Oxidative Color
- Lighteners
- Developers
- Vegetable, Metallic and Compound Dyes

Oxidants (often called developers) are products that have the ability to release oxygen, which is needed for a chemical change. Oxidative colors are mixed with an oxidant (developer) such as hydrogen peroxide. Nonoxidative colors are not mixed with oxidants and are used straight from the bottle. In the oxidation process a substance loses an electron and oxygen is acquired. When a substance gains an electron and oxygen is released, the process is called reduction (redox). This process not only occurs in hair color services, but in perming/relaxing services as well. Overprocessed hair can also be the result of reduction or redox.

NONOXIDATIVE COLORS

1 **TEMPORARY COLORS** are nonreactive, direct dyes that only coat the surface of the hair shaft. There's nothing to lighten the hair and no chemical changes occur in the solution. These colors are called certified colors and are accepted by the government for use in foods, drugs and cosmetics. Temporary colors last only until they are shampooed out.

2 **SEMI-PERMANENT COLORS** last through several shampoos, then the color molecules generally shampoo out. Semi-permanent colors are dye molecules in a solution that are able to penetrate the cuticle layer of the hair versus coating the hair shaft as with temporary colors. Semi-permanent color molecules are smaller in size and weight than the molecules found in temporary color products, and they are slightly alkaline in pH. Semi-permanent colors use a direct dye process, which means the color is present without the need to chemically develop it. Direct dye colors need no mixing and the color you see in the bottle is the color that is deposited on the hair.

OXIDATIVE COLORS

1 **LONG LASTING SEMI-PERMANENT COLORS** (sometimes referred to as demi-permanent or oxidative without ammonia) use a low volume peroxide to develop the color molecules and aid in the color processing. Ammonia is a colorless gas with a strong odor, composed of hydrogen and nitrogen. Peroxide alone does not lift color from the hair. It needs an alkaline substance such as ammonia to lift color. Therefore, long lasting semi-permanent or demi-permanent colors are only able to add color to the hair. They cannot subtract, lift or lighten. Long lasting semi-permanent colors are available in liquid, cream and gel forms.

2 **PERMANENT HAIR COLORS** (sometimes referred to as oxidative with ammonia) use an oxidation system that starts out with colorless molecules. When these molecules are combined with peroxide, a chemical reaction (change) occurs, building colored molecules. The small molecules enter the hair with the aid of an alkaline substance such as ammonia and then, as they oxidize in the cuticle and the cortex, they link together to form a permanent colored molecule. When this happens, they are permanently anchored in the hair. It is the combination of the ammonia and hydrogen peroxide that is also responsible for the permanent color's ability to both lighten the hair's natural color and deposit artificial color.

ALERT!
Because allergies to aniline tints are unpredictable, manufacturer labels prescribe a patch test to be given 24 hours before any application.

Permanent hair colors are also referred to as aniline derivative tints. These colors penetrate the cuticle and the cortex, remaining in the hair until they are removed by chemical means or the hair grows out and is cut off. Their primary ingredient is usually paraphenylene diamine or a related chemical. It's usually possible to reproduce natural hair shades without losing shine or condition when using an aniline derivative color. Aniline derivative colors can safely be applied over hair that has been previously permed or colored.

LIGHTENERS

Lightening the hair is also referred to as bleaching or decolorizing. It is one of the oldest methods used in a hair color service. Before permanent tints were formulated to lift and deposit color in one application, bleaching was the first step to any permanent hair coloring service in which lighter hair was desired.

Lightening hair always involves oxidation of the natural melanin in the hair. Oxidation in the lightening process means that peroxide is mixed with an alkaline product such as ammonia. The release of oxygen from the peroxide chemically alters other molecules, changes the melanosome (pigment) structure of the hair and lightens the color of the hair. It does this by breaking down pigment granules into tiny fragments that are no longer able to absorb light to the same degree as they did before. The longer this lightening solution remains in contact with the hair, the more the melanin is changed. This process is called oxidation. The melanin doesn't immediately lose its color when oxidized. The hair goes through several color changes as the pigment disperses and each change lightens the hair to a new level.

Lighteners or bleaches are made up of a combination of ingredients including an alkaline substance such as ammonia. Some also contain conditioning and thickening agents for control in application. They need to be mixed with peroxide immediately before application because only then is the oxidation process at full strength. The solution quickly begins to weaken.

 ON-THE-SCALP LIGHTENERS are gentle enough to be applied directly on the scalp and are available in two forms.

Oil lighteners use a certain amount of ammonia to give high lift. Because of the added oil, this is a mild form of lightener. For this reason it can be used directly on the scalp with no ill effects. When mixed with peroxide, its pH is around 9.

Cream lighteners are the most popular form of lightener because added conditioners make them gentler and the creamy consistency keeps them in place on the hair and prevents running or dripping. They are also used directly on the scalp. Their pH is about the same as that of the oil lighteners.

Activators can be added to oil or cream lighteners to boost their strength. These activators increase the pH of a lightener toward the alkaline side, thus increasing the speed of the oxidation process. The pH is increased by chemicals called alkali salts and persulfates. Since activators can double the strength of hydrogen peroxide, no higher than 20 volume is recommended when mixing for an on-the-scalp application.

2 **OFF-THE-SCALP LIGHTENERS** (powder bleaches) contain alkaline salts and a strong oxidizing agent that, when mixed with peroxide, become a strong lightening product. These lighteners are much stronger than the oil or cream lighteners and lighten the hair faster. Because they have no added oils or cream, they can irritate the scalp causing burns and blisters. For this reason they are usually used for off-the-scalp lightening procedures, such as highlighting.

Conditioning agents provide some protection to the scalp and the hair, however. Some off-the-scalp bleach powders have protein conditioning agents that help prevent chemical damage to the hair during the lightening process. This type of powder bleach has a distinct advantage over ones that do not contain conditioning agents. During the bleaching process, the conditioner can protect the hair's internal protein structure and the surface of each hair shaft. The pH of powder lighteners when applied to the hair is about 10.3.

DEVELOPERS

Hydrogen peroxide (H_2O_2) is the most common developer or oxidizing agent used in hair coloring and in hair lightening. It is mixed in various proportions and various strengths. The strength most often used is a 20 volume solution. Volumes refer to the amount of oxygen gas that would be removed from a peroxide solution if **the molecule was broken into its components, water and oxygen.** Hydrogen peroxide is also called a developer **or oxidizing agent** because permanent colors require peroxide to develop their color molecules. Peroxide comes in different forms such as clear, cloudy, creamy and gels. Its pH is between 2.5 and 4.5.

In hair lightening, ammonia or other alkalis are used to activate or raise the peroxide's pH, therefore making it more alkaline. Once activated by the higher pH substance, the peroxide can act as an oxidizer and lift or subtract hair color.

A hydrometer is used to measure the strength (volume) of hydrogen peroxide. A hydrometer indicates the potency (strength) of hydrogen peroxide and allows you to dilute higher strength liquid peroxide to lower volumes. A hydrometer is also beneficial if there is a question about whether hydrogen peroxide that has been stored over a long period of time is still potent. Manufacturer recommendations will indicate **shelf life (usually 3 years) of hydrogen peroxide and instruct that it be stored in a cool, dry place.**

VEGETABLE, METALLIC AND COMPOUND DYES

A less professional category of hair color includes natural vegetable dyes, metallic salts and the combination of the two called a compound dye. **Henna** is an example of a vegetable dye and, in its purest form, produces reddish highlights in the hair. It is one of the oldest forms of hair coloring and is derived from the Egyptian privett plant. Natural colors other than the characteristic henna reds are produced by combining henna with metallic salts, such as lead, silver and copper. There are problems when using henna and henna compounds because repeated use coats and builds up causing damage to the hair.

The more these colors are used the more color change takes place. For this reason these dyes are called progressive colors. Hennaed hair sometimes cannot be permed because the reforming solution can't penetrate evenly through the buildup. In addition, the metals in a henna compound may react violently with other chemicals used in salon chemical services causing hair breakage or discoloration. There are certain formulas designed to remove henna buildup, but they are not very effective. The best solution is to let it grow completely out before any chemical service.

Pure metallic dyes seem relatively harmless but can also cause complications. They too are incompatible with other chemical services such as perms and oxidative hair coloring. These colors depending on the metals used, may fade into peculiar or unnatural shades. With exposure to the sun and chlorine, silver dyes may appear to have a green cast, lead dyes a purple cast, and copper may turn green. Metallic coatings have a tendency to look and feel dry.

Metallic colors can be purchased over the counter at local drug stores or supermarkets. Some clients might not know they are using metallic dyes. That makes communicaton before chemical services very important. If you suspect that your client has used metallic colors and doesn't know it, perform the test for metallic salts featured in *Color, Chapter 13*. Metallic dyes are toxic and both you and your client should wash your hands thoroughly after exposure. Special shampoos and cleansers are available to remove metallic dyes from the hair.

PRODUCT INFORMATION

The understanding of specific ingredients in the products you use and what effects they have will mark you as an above ordinary professional. Material Safety Data Sheets from the manufacturer are the best source of specific information about a product. Additional resources can include the Food and Drug Administration (FDA), which regulates cosmetics in the United States, and the United States Pharmacopeia (U.S.P.), which is a book that lists and standardizes drugs. Informatic can also be found in the International Cosmetic Ingredient Dictionary, which is published by the Cosmetic, Toiletries and Fragrance Association and is available at many public libraries.

COSMETIC INGREDIENTS

When you read a product label, the ingredients are listed in order of their concentration. The first ingredient on the list appears in the largest amount and so on. At present, the cosmetic industry selects from more than 5,000 different ingredients. Here are some common ingredients and their usual function:

05

MOISTURIZERS function as a moisture barrier or to attract moisture from the environment:

- CETYL ALCOHOL (fatty alcohol) – Keeps oil and water from separating; also a foam booster
- DIMETHICONE SILICONE – Skin conditioners and anti-foam ingredient
- ISOPROPYL LANOLATE, MYRISTATE, and PALMITATE
- LANOLIN AND LANOLIN ALCOHOLS and OIL – Used in skin and hair conditioners
- OCTYL DODECANOL – Skin conditioner
- OLEIC ACID (olive oil)
- PANTHENOL (vitamin B-complex derivative) – hair conditioner
- STEARIC ACID and STEARYL ALCOHOL

PRESERVATIVES and antioxidants (including vitamins) prevent product deterioration:

- TRISODIUM and TETRASODIUM EDETATE (EDTA)
- TOCOPHEROL (vitamin E)

ANTIMICROBIALS fight bacteria:

- BUTYL, PROPYL, ETHYL, AND METHYL PARABENS
- DMDM HYDANTOIN
- METHYLISOTHIAZOLINONE
- PHENOXYETHANOL (also rose ether fragrance component)
- QUATERNIUM-15

THICKENERS and waxes are used in stick products such as lipsticks:

- CANDELILLA, CARNAUBA, and MICROCRYSTALLINE WAXES
- CARBOMER and POLYETHYLENE THICKENERS

SOLVENTS are used to dilute:

- BUTYLENE GLYCOL and PROPYLENE GLYCOL
- CYCLOMETHICONE (volatile silicone)
- ETHANOL (alcohol)
- GLYCERIN

EMULSIFIERS break up and refine:

- GLYCERYL MONOSTEARATE (also pearlescent agent)
- LAURAMIDE DEA (also foam booster)
- POLYSORBATES

COLOR additives:

- SYNTHETIC **ORGANIC** COLORS derived from coal and petroleum sources (not permitted for use around the eye):
  - D&C Red No. 7 Calcium Lake (lakes are dyes that do not dissolve in water)
- **INORGANIC** PIGMENTS – approved for general use in cosmetics, including for the area of the eye:
  - Iron oxides
  - Mica (iridescent)

HAIR COLOR – phenol derivatives used in combination with other chemicals in permanent hair colors:

- AMINOPHENOLS

COSMETOLOGY FUNDAMENTALS

pH ADJUSTERS stabilize or adjust acids and bases:

- AMMONIUM HYDROXIDE in skin peels and hair waving and straightening
- CITRIC ACID – adjusts pH
- TRIETHANOLAMINE pH – adjuster used mostly in transparent soap

OTHERS

- MAGNESIUM ALUMINUM SILICATE – absorbent, anti-caking agent
- POLYMERS AND PLASTICIZERS – hair stiffening agents used in hairsprays
- SILICA (silicon dioxide) – absorbent, anti-caking, abrasive
- SODIUM LAURYL SULFATE – detergent
- STEARIC ACID – cleansing, emulsifier
- TALC (powdered magnesium silicate) – absorbent anti-caking
- ZINC STEARATE – used in powder to improve texture, lubricates

U. S. Food and Drug Administration, Center for Food Safety and Applied Nutrition, Office of Cosmetics Fact Sheet, February 3, 1995

SALON PRODUCTS AND THEIR pH RANGES

Today's salon professionals need to understand the pH of the chemicals they use and its effects on hair, skin and nails. Remember that there are three ways of testing pH in professional products: nitrazine paper, pH pencil and the pH meter.

Nitrazine paper, or pH paper, is one of the most familiar methods. To use this testing method, just dip the paper into the solution. A product with a 4.5 pH or below will not change the paper from its original yellow shade, while a higher pH will change the color to dark blue (4.6 to 7.4). Any product with a pH of more than 7.5 will turn the paper purple.

The pH pencil can be used in several ways. One way is to rub the pencil all over a small sheet of paper. Now you can dip the paper into the solution. It will turn yellow if the solution is acidic, or purple if the solution is alkaline.

The pH meter provides the most accurate method for measuring pH because it registers the exact pH of the product. It can also measure the pH of the acid mantle that coats the skin and hair.

Remember that products in the pH range of 4.5 to 5.5 will keep hair, skin and scalp closest to their natural, healthy state. When using alkaline products, it is important to restore the acid balance once the service is complete. Keep in mind that in order for a product to have a pH rating or be tested for pH, it must contain water and/or have the ability to dissolve in water. The chart below identifies general pH ranges for common professional hair, skin and nail products.

SHAMPOOS AND CONDITIONERS

Acid-Balanced Shampoo	4.5 -	5.5
Alkaline Shampoo	7.0 -	9.0
Acidifying Conditioner	2.2 -	5.5
Deep Penetrating Conditioner	3.5 -	5.5

PERMS AND RELAXERS

Acid Perm	6.9 -	7.2
Alkaline Perm	8.0 -	9.5
Sodium Hydroxide Relaxer	11.5 -	14.0
Ammonium Thioglycolate Relaxer	8.5 -	9.5
Neutralizer	2.5 -	7.0

COLORS AND LIGHTENERS

Oil Bleach	8.0 -	9.5
Powder Bleach	10.0 -	11.0
Tints	9.5 -	10.5
Hydrogen Peroxide	2.5 -	4.5

FINISHING PRODUCTS

Mousse	5.5 -	6.0
Gel	4.5 -	5.5
Hairspray	5.0 -	6.0

SKIN PRODUCTS

Cleanser	4.5 -	5.5
Toner	5.5 -	6.0
Moisturizer	5.5 -	6.0

NAIL PRODUCTS

Polish Remover	5.0 -	6.0
Cuticle Creme	5.5 -	6.0
Hand Lotion	4.5 -	5.5

ACTIVITY

Under the direction of your instructor, test various products you bring from home using nitrazine paper. Compare the results with those identified on the chart on the previous page.

HEALTH RISKS

Possible health effects of chemicals you work with depend on the following:

- The amount of the chemical in the product
- Its toxicity
- The length of time you are exposed
- How the chemical enters your body
- Your own individual sensitivity

Check each product's Material Safety Data Sheet (MSDS) for more information.

As a salon professional you will be using a variety of chemicals to improve the personal well-being of your clients. Your knowledge of the proper use of these chemicals will be necessary as you provide a safe and comfortable experience for client visits and for your personal health.

CONNECTING THEORY TO REAL-WORLD PRACTICE

CHEMISTRY	PERSONAL CONNECTION: IMPROVE YOURSELF	INDUSTRY CONNECTION: BECOME PROFESSIONAL	CLIENT CONNECTION: SERVE THE GUEST
MATTER	Make the connection between protein atoms and the structure of hair	Heighten respect for hair and the industry that cares for it	Explain how hair's structure affects its appearance and treatment
THE pH SCALE	Understand the nature of acidity and alkalinity and how to measure them	Demonstrate how the pH scale affects the delivery of salon services	Use products that align with pH of clients' hair, skin and nails
CHEMISTRY OF COSMETICS	Recognize the chemical properties of common cosmetic products	Advance professional stature through in-depth knowledge of the "tools of the trade"	Choose the right products for individual needs and excellent results

IN OTHER WORDS

As you work with clients in the salon, your understanding of chemistry will help you select the most appropriate products for enhancing their appearance, their health and their overall well-being.

LESSONS LEARNED

- The bonding of protein chains to other protein chains makes human hair.
- The pH scale indicates whether a substance is acidic, neutral or alkaline to assist professionals in keeping the hair, skin and scalp in the best condition possible.
- Knowledge of the six classifications of cosmetics helps professionals understand product labels and usage directions.

06

SALON BUSINESS

6.1 THE SALON INDUSTRY
WHAT YOU NEED TO KNOW
YOUR PROFESSIONAL GOALS

6.2 JOB SEARCH
RESUMÉS
JOB INTERVIEWS
EVALUATING THE SALON

6.3 PROFESSIONAL RELATIONSHIPS
NETWORKING
BUILDING A CLIENTELE
THE DESIGNER-CLIENT RELATIONSHIP
THE DESIGNER-STAFF RELATIONSHIP
PERFORMANCE REVIEW

6.4 SALON OWNERSHIP
SELF-APPRAISAL
TYPES OF SALON OWNERSHIP
REQUIREMENTS OF A SALON
GETTING THE RIGHT ADVICE
SPACE REQUIREMENTS AND FLOOR PLANS
BORROWING MONEY
RENTAL AGREEMENTS
TYPES OF INSURANCE
TAXES
EXPENSES AND INCOME
SALON PHILOSOPHY, POLICIES AND PROCEDURES
SALON OPERATION

6.5 SALON RETAILING
SELLING
PROFESSIONAL PRODUCTS
CLOSING THE SALE
BUYER TYPES
FOLLOW-UP
EFFECTIVE DISPLAYS

THE ABILITY TO SELECT THE RIGHT SALON AND TO BE FAMILIAR WITH SALON BUSINESS PRACTICES WILL LEAD TO FINANCIAL REWARDS AND PROFESSIONAL GROWTH

FOLLOWING THIS LESSON
YOU WILL BE ABLE TO:

Establish short- and long-range professional goals within the salon industry

Identify which job offer to accept by recognizing:

- The steps necessary to search for a job
- Questions to be asked during a job interview
- Personal qualities that will be evaluated during the interview
- Potential job benefits that an employer might offer

List the steps used to develop and maintain professional relationships, including building a clientele

Describe salon ownership types, structure, operations and requirements for the practice of good business

Define the techniques used to recommend retail product sales to clients

CONNECTING THEORY TO REAL-WORLD PRACTICE

UNDERSTANDING THE SALON INDUSTRY FROM A BUSINESS PERSPECTIVE WILL HELP YOU:

PERSONAL CONNECTION: IMPROVE YOURSELF	**INDUSTRY CONNECTION:** BECOME A PROFESSIONAL	**CLIENT CONNECTION:** SERVE THE GUEST
Set and achieve goals that will lead to personal, career and financial success	Expand the horizons of a salon job into a high-level career with multiple growth opportunities	Serve clients from a position of greater confidence, authority and insight that goes beyond technical ability

As a salon professional, you will perform many creative services for clients. But to have a successful salon career, it's important to see "the big picture" of how the salon industry works as a whole. Knowing how to get a job, keep a job and move up in your career are valuable insights that, combined with your artistic talents, will pave the way to a fulfilling professional life.

6.1 THE SALON INDUSTRY

The salon customer depends on and seeks out the advice of the expert designer. The designer is no longer a beauty "operator," but an artistic business professional, offering solutions and creativity on behalf of the client.

WHAT YOU NEED TO KNOW

It takes more than design talent to be successful in today's cosmetology world. You'll need to be knowledgeable in many areas of business, including:
- Communications
- Public Relations
- Sales Promotions

The areas in which you choose to develop your expertise will shape your career's future.

Your future will also be affected by today's constantly changing lifestyle. These changes have created an increasing demand for the services of the salon professional. Today's fast-paced lifestyle has resulted in an increased awareness of good grooming habits and the popularization of many new products. Several hair, skin, and nail care products have now become so important to our everyday life that they have actually become household names, such as mousse, gel, etc.

Another important reason for the popularization of specific products is "consumerism." That is, most people have become label readers. They regularly analyze the contents and quality of the products they purchase. They have also become more discriminating in their purchases. They have likes and dislikes and will not accept second best.

Because of these changes, there is an increasing demand for your advice. Manufacturers, distributors and industry organizations conduct and sponsor educational seminars, clinics and training programs designed to upgrade your technical and business skills and product knowledge on a regular basis. These educational events will give you a very important edge that will help you stay ahead in all aspects of the professional business.

At no other time in history has a career in the cosmetology field been more attractive or lucrative than today. The public continues to bestow well-earned respect, prestige and rewards on those who strive to be the best. Through the services you perform, you can take pride in your contributions to society and your unique artistic creations. You can be both a businessperson and an artist.

YOUR PROFESSIONAL GOALS

A goal states and defines what path your career will take. You may want to own a salon… become a platform artist…teach in a school…or anything else that appeals to you. Your goals will motivate you on a daily, monthly and yearly basis. Listed below are four easy-to-follow guides that will help you determine your goals.

Establish a long-range goal. It identifies where you want your career to be in 5 years.
- Write it down.
- Discuss the obstacles that you might encounter with someone who has accomplished a similar goal.
- Make a commitment to yourself to dedicate your actions toward the goal.

Determine your short-range goals. They identify what you would like to achieve in the next year.
- Decide on immediate activities you can undertake to achieve this short-range goal. Examples would include job interviews, part-time work in a salon, etc.

Create a plan to achieve your goals.
- Be specific as you create a set of objectives and tasks. Examples would include continuing education, saving 5 dollars per week, etc.
- Consider your budget and include ways to support the plan financially.
- Include alternate plans.

Review your goals periodically.
- Change them if they no longer reflect your chosen personal and professional life directions.
- This is where alternate plans come into play. You may need to save 10 dollars per week or attend more seminars than you originally planned.

6.2 JOB SEARCH

Searching for a job can be an exciting and rewarding experience. As your search progresses you'll be learning a lot about the inner workings of the industry and yourself. Remember, when searching for a job, do not compromise your goals.

Listed below are several methods you can use to find out about salons that are hiring personnel or interviewing for future positions:

1. Talk to designers who work in the salons you admire. They might know of positions about to open up.
2. Check the classified section of your local newspaper. Many salons advertise there. The salon name may not be listed under the "Beauty Salons" section. Instead you may discover an ad under "Hair Designer," "Professional Salon Stylist," "Makeup Artist," "Cosmetologist," or other special headings. The Sunday classified section generally has the widest range of employment opportunities.

06

3. Talk to distributor sales consultants (from companies that sell hair, skin and nail care products to schools and salons) who may visit your school. Salons often inform these distributor consultants of their personnel needs.

4. Almost all cosmetology schools have job placement services for their graduating students. Refer to your school's bulletin board for job postings and ask your instructors to give you some ideas about seeking employment.

5. You may want to check with your city or state unemployment office for listings in the cosmetology field. While there, you can place your name on file and they will contact you with openings in the field.

6. A very good idea is to canvass the area where you would like to work. Then make a list of those salons where you would like to be employed. Call or visit the salons that impressed you most and ask if they are hiring.

7. You can also mail out resumés, attaching a cover letter to each, requesting that the owner or manager contact you for an interview if an opening becomes available.

RESUMÉS

If you do decide to send a **resumé**, be sure to develop one that describes your attributes in a brief, concise manner, including:

- Personal data (name, address, phone, email)
- Educational background (schools attended)
- Additional training (seminars attended, etc.)

- Previous employment (if applicable)
- Special skills or areas of expertise
- Any special awards or recognition

Also include:

- References (professional/personal)
- Interests (hobbies, skills)
- Most important: WHY you want to work in this particular salon

NOTE: Be sure your resumé is neat, accurate and up-to-date. There are professional business service offices that offer resumé creation and writing at a very reasonable cost. You may want to use their services for printing your resumé on professional paper stock or for assisting you in the creation of your resumé. Always address your letter and resumé to the owner or manager of the salon. If you don't know the owner's and/or manager's name, call and find out. Some salons may allow you to submit your resumé electronically.

USING TECHNOLOGY TO YOUR ADVANTAGE
A major key to job-seeking success is the competitive edge gained by taking advantage of technology to help you create a professional online resumé and portfolio. Social networking sites like LinkedIn are used solely for professional networking and job-seeking. They provide a professional platform that allows you to highlight specific skills, additional training and other accomplishments that set you apart from your competition.

	Name
	Address
	City, State, Zip
	Email
	Phone
OBJECTIVE:	A beginning job in hair design leading to a position as a platform artist.
EDUCATION:	XYZ Academy
	Chicago, Illinois
	Diploma in Cosmetology, 2013
	Professional training in all areas of hair artistry as well as skin care, nail care and personal and professional communications. Specialized training in color and long hair design
	ABC High School
	Chicago, Illinois
	Diploma in General Education
EXPERIENCE:	Cashier - Touhy & Western Standard
2012-Present	Chicago, Illinois
	Duties include maintaining inventory as well as operating electronic cash registers
AWARD:	1st Place in Color and 1st Place in
RECEIVED:	Evening Makeup

Even though you may have to write much of the same data on the application form, a resumé can give the salon information about you that would not normally be asked on the application form. You have the option of including a photo of yourself with your resumé. If you are applying for a position within a large salon and you know that many people complete the interview process, it might be good marketing to include your photo. The person interviewing you would appreciate having a visual reminder of who you are. Legally you are not required to supply a photo.

A **cover letter** is a necessity as a companion piece to your resumé. The cover letter introduces you to the salon, offers a brief summary of why you would like to be employed at the salon and also provides a brief description of the qualities you feel you could bring to the salon. This letter should be well-written and concise, in a business letter format, and contain the date, your address, salon address, greeting, closing and your signature.

JOB INTERVIEWS

Your first **job interview** for a position as a designer or a specialist in a salon may seem too far away to consider if you're just beginning your cosmetology course or make you nervous because you are about to graduate. Or perhaps, after months of study and practical experience, you're excited about obtaining a new job.

While interviews can be "nerve-wracking" for everyone, just remember to stay calm and be yourself. It won't take long for your skills, talents and positive attitude to outweigh your concerns. Proper preparation takes away most of the nervousness.

PERSONAL APPEARANCE

Before going to your interview, remember that your personal appearance and grooming habits are very noticeable. If you are neat and fashionably dressed and if you have a contemporary hairstyle that flatters your face and physical features, if your skin looks healthy (makeup applied properly for females), you will begin the interview with a very good first impression. This initial impression will set the tone of your interview.

INAPPROPRIATE

APPROPRIATE

SALON BUSINESS

APPLICATION

Before the interview begins, you may be asked to fill out an application for employment. Aside from standard information such as your name, address and telephone number, you will list where and when you graduated from cosmetology school, the date you completed your State Board of Cosmetology Examination and any additional educational training you may have had. If you have attended special classes, seminars or additional career-related training activities, list this information also.

PUNCTUALITY

The first relationship you form with the prospective employer will be while applying for your job. The impression you make as a professional is your responsibility. You alone will have to promote yourself and your skills to the potential employer. An interviewer may intentionally schedule an appointment time that is early in the morning to determine your ability to be punctual. Be sure you arrive early for the appointment and that you have confirmed the exact location, parking availability and cost, if appropriate, and the approximate travel time you will need.

TECHNICAL AND COMMUNICATION SKILLS

The salon owner/manager will be interested in the skills and services you perform. Salons are always eager to have talented, capable staff members. The fact that you recently graduated from school can actually be an advantage since many salons will see you as having acquired no bad working habits.

Very often during an interview for a designer's position (or other related position), you will be asked to demonstrate your skills to determine your level of technical expertise. The interviewer may do several things:

1. Ask you to demonstrate your skill level by bringing a model to cut, color or perm
2. Contact your school to get an appraisal from instructors

During the course of your conversation with the management or while demonstrating your skills, your interviewer will also be evaluating your communication skills and your ability to develop interpersonal relationships. Be as calm and professional during the interview and demonstration as you would be with a client.

In the United States, illegal interview questions are those that discriminate on the basis of:

- Age
- Disability
- Color
- National origin
- Race
- Religion or creed
- Gender

PERSONAL QUALITIES

Another area the interviewer will be evaluating is your personal qualities. The salon management may evaluate you on such qualities as your:

- Sincerity and honesty
- Motivation and enthusiasm toward the industry
- Understanding of the salon's goals
- Realistic career objectives
- Obvious desire to work

- Ability to promote a new service or retail product
- Willingness to work as a member of the salon team
- Ability to organize and manage your time
- Educational and professional goals
- Ability to accept constructive criticism

EVALUATING THE SALON

Correctly evaluating your future workplace is very important, for it is there you will be spending most of your days developing your career. To evaluate a salon in terms of its advantages and disadvantages, ask the owner/manager questions about the prospective job and consider some of the following criteria:

1. What is your impression of the salon management? Does the owner/manager appear to be someone who communicates with and encourages the members of the staff? Does he or she seem to be easy to talk to about goals and desires?
2. What services are performed there? Are the salon's products professional? Is the work performed of a high quality?
3. What does the salon charge for the services performed? Are the prices in line with the quality of the work done? Is the salon competitive with other salons in the area?
4. How large is the salon staff? Are you comfortable working with a group of people this size?
5. Which product line does the salon use and recommend to clients for use at home? Is it the same product line used on clients in the salon at the backbar?
6. What type of clientele does the salon have? (Students, business people, etc.)
7. Is the salon "growth-oriented?" What are its goals?
8. What is the salon's policy on advanced education for members of the staff?
9. What benefits does the salon offer its employees? (Medical insurance, retirement, paid holidays, educational advancement)
10. Does the salon have well-developed advertising and promotional programs to help bring in new clients?
11. What are the policies and procedures of the salon?
12. Who schedules clients? How?
13. What are the working conditions? (Will you be comfortable?)
14. What are the job responsibilities? (Will the job be a challenge?)
15. What will you be paid? (What are the advancement possibilities and benefits?)

If any of these questions remain unanswered after your initial interview, be sure to find out the answers during your final interview.

HINT

The size of the salon is probably the least important factor in deciding whether to accept a position. The physical size of a business is not an indication of its potential for growth or your potential to be successful. A small salon can be more successful in many ways (including financially) than a larger salon that is not working to its full potential.

Do not be overly influenced by the physical appearance or the busy activity that goes on inside a salon. Take time to evaluate each salon to make certain it will be a stimulating place to work. Determine if it is a professionally operated business that allows you to grow and achieve your goals. Spend enough time in the salon to get a feeling for the atmosphere and teamwork there.

BE PREPARED

In the space provided below, write your answers to typical questions a salon interviewer might ask you:

How would your best friend describe your personal characteristics?
___

What amount of time does it take you to apply oxidative color to a 1" (2.5 cm) regrowth area?
___

What amount of time does it take you to wrap a conventional perm on hair that is 5" (12.5 cm) long?
___

What would your instructor say is your strongest technical skill area?
___

What would your instructor say is your strongest professional characteristic in dealing with people?
___

JOB BENEFITS

Job benefits are a key factor that will determine whether you accept one job over another. Remember, when viewing the potential of a job, consider not only your salary or commission on services or retail, but also the benefits provided. Often a job that pays less in salary is actually giving you more by providing you with costly benefits (extras) such as:

1. Paid holidays, bonuses
2. Number of sick days allowed each year (paid or not)
3. Insurance benefits (health, accident, life)

4. Retirement plan
5. Paid vacations
6. Opportunities for travel
7. Opportunity for advancement, new positions, responsibilities
8. Educational seminars and events (Does salon share cost?)
9. Ongoing salon educational programs and guest artist classes
10. A motivating and comfortable workplace
11. Length of lunch or dinner break and number of breaks during the day or evening

Tell your employer about any conflicts you may have with your work schedule during the interview. Before you accept employment with a salon, school or product manufacturer, etc. look at all the benefits offered. Determine which ones are important to you. Will you be happy without the benefits you want most?

YOUR NEW JOB

In a salon, there are several approaches used to instruct new employees. Two of the most common approaches are:

1. Many salons have a **general orientation program** to familiarize the new employee with the work habits and standards of the salon. Most salons have Employee Handbooks, detailing such information. General orientation might also include a few days of technical training to familiarize you with techniques that are particular to your new salon position.

2. Another approach has the new designer assigned as an **assistant** or **apprentice** to an experienced designer in the salon until he or she is totally familiar with salon procedures and practices. This method varies in length of time based on your skill level and expected expertise. Some salons prefer to offer a combination of assisting and assigning you new clients, which provides you an opportunity to build a clientele of your own.

NOTE: A combination of a general orientation program and assisting is also a common practice with new employees.

6.3 PROFESSIONAL RELATIONSHIPS

The salon industry is multifaceted, drawing on a multitude of job descriptions, positions and career directions. Building solid professional relationships with other professionals is your foundation for the future.

NETWORKING

Professional relationships are based on open, honest, well-developed communication with everyone you meet during your career. Whether these people are clients, staff members, salon owners, managers or others you meet at seminars, trade shows or other industry-related programs, each can be important to your growth.

As these relationships grow, they reflect the strengths, creativity, dedication and tremendous effort of progressive salon professionals throughout the world. It is a rewarding challenge for everyone beginning a career to form professional relationships with fellow industry members.

The most important relationships you form at the beginning of your career are those that develop within the salon. Like all relationships, those in the salon begin with the first impression you create.

BUILDING A CLIENTELE

There are many techniques you can use to build a clientele. Some of the most effective techniques include the following:

WORD-OF-MOUTH ADVERTISING
Word-of-mouth advertising is probably the most effective way of building your clientele. Clients who are pleased with your services will recommend your services to their friends. Your expertise, your care with people, and your willingness to teach, all help bring clients and their friends into the salon.

BUSINESS CARDS
If your salon has business cards printed with logo, name, address and phone number, ask the management if you can have cards printed with your name on them. Give these cards to current and potential clients. If the salon in which you are working does not provide cards, ask permission from the owner and consider supplying the cards yourself in an effort to build your business.

REFERRALS
Referrals are important because they increase your client base. If clients are telling their friends about you (referrals) and those friends are calling the salon and asking for you (requests), you're improving your reputation and income opportunities.

PREBOOKING

It sounds so simple, but one of the most effective ways to build your clientele is to ask clients to make a future appointment before they leave the salon. Taking the initiative to assist clients in maintaining regular appointments is one of the most effective tools for retaining a client base which builds success.

PROMOTIONAL LITERATURE

If the salon has printed promotional literature, such as flyers, newsletters or postcards, print your name on them, carry them with you and give them to people you meet. You'll be pleasantly surprised at the number of new clients you gain from this little extra effort.

GUEST APPEARANCES

If you enjoy speaking before an audience, you might try offering your services as a guest speaker or demonstrator. Civic groups, clubs, charities, high schools and college groups all enjoy hearing about the latest trends in fashion and style. They also like seeing the makeovers that you can present. Guest appearances can be an enjoyable experience and potentially develop a clientele that will ask for you by name. Be sure to check your area's regulating agency rules governing performing demonstrations outside the salon.

HINT

If you perform at a fashion show or a civic organization, pass out your cards to interested members of the audience. These cards will refer new clients to you.

CORRESPONDENCE

Send thank-you cards to every client after every appointment or call all new clients after their first visit to follow up. Send reminder notes one week before each appointment or call. With approval from the salon owner, send a birthday card to every client with a gift certificate for $5.00 off her next service or offer discounts on high-ticket services, such as colors or makeovers. Send "I miss you" cards to clients who have not visited you in two months or longer.

YOUR PERSONAL TOUCH

Spending a little extra time sharing a styling tip or suggesting a new style or product to you clients are all examples of your personal touch. If a client mentions a need for more time in the mornings, you might suggest an easier-to-care-for design. It is this personal touch that will keep your clients returning to you for future services.

THE DESIGNER-CLIENT RELATIONSHIP

A solid pattern of communication with clients must be established on their first visit to the salon. If your clients feel that you are anxious to please them, they will develop a loyalty toward you. But first they must be convinced of your credibility and your abilities as a salon professional.

ALERT!

You must continually be expanding your clientele. A certain percentage of your clients will leave the salon each year, so you need to be prepared to constantly keep your business growing.

06

To develop this credibility, you will need to establish a professional relationship with your clients. This designer-client relationship is critical to your success as a salon professional and to the salon that employs you.

To communicate effectively with a client, you must first understand the individual. A large part of this understanding will occur during your initial contact with the client. At the beginning of the service you will consult with your client and this conversation will "set the tone" for your relationship. During this conversation it is essential to determine the client's desires and needs and explain what might be best for overall appearance. You need to learn how clients feel about making changes to their appearance and what service objectives they have in mind. Other information you will need to learn from clients regarding specific services is covered in detail in upcoming chapters.

KEYS TO SUCCESSFUL CLIENT RELATIONSHIPS

- Determine the client's needs.
- Clearly explain to the client what the "finished look" will be before beginning any service.
- Suggest alternative styles, if the client only wants to make a minor change, rather than a dramatic one. Further changes may be suggested later.
- Teach the client how to maintain the hair design, makeup application, nail care or other service at home.
- Provide the client with information on the correct product regimen to use at home and proper product application.
- Show the client pictures of new styles and suggest any additional services that would enhance the client's appearance. (Do not suggest to the client that the outcome will look "just like" the photograph.)
- Introduce change periodically so the client's appearance is both attractive and current.
- Accommodate the client whenever possible. If it is possible to adjust your appointment schedule for a client, do so (without inconveniencing other clients).
- Share new information about cosmetology and fashion with your clientele. It will generate excitement and enthusiasm for your services and for the salon.
- Treat your clients with the same respect and concern you would like them to exhibit toward you.
- Manage downtime constructively by helping others, performing tasks around the salon and maintaining client base. Organize your work and prepare to have products and implements ready for each client. Serve clients promptly when they arrive. However, do not rush one client in order to serve the next. When making an appointment, be sure the time allotted for each person allows you to remain on schedule.
- Notify your clients in advance if you plan to be absent for an appointment or on vacation and "prebook" (reschedule) their appointments with fellow designers through the salon receptionist.

THE DESIGNER-STAFF RELATIONSHIP

All successful businesses depend upon a strong team approach, involving all members of the staff. This team concept revolves around several factors, some of which are listed below. See if you can think of some others.

COMMON GOALS

Each team member sets his or her own personal goals for a day, month and year. Salons, research institutions and manufacturers also set goals for themselves, such as:

- Financial goals
- Sales volume goals
- Educational goals

Teamwork flourishes when a blending of personal and business goals occurs.

SHARING KNOWLEDGE

As a member of the working staff, you are expected to share your knowledge and techniques with your fellow team members and other professionals. Sharing results in loyal, satisfied clients as well as in encouraging others to share with you. Should a special challenge or problem arise during your business day, you should consult with your fellow team members. As with the medical field, it is a sign of professionalism to consult with your colleagues about specialized or problem areas.

Because you are a team member, you should express your ideas, thoughts and feelings to create an open professional relationship with others. Dreams and aspirations, as well as frustrations and anger, may be expressed maturely with other members of the team. Problem situations will be quickly resolved through the application of good communication skills.

HELPING OTHERS

Although staff members have their own clientele to serve, sometimes you'll have extra time, so use it to help your co-workers. In return, they will help you when you need assistance. Perhaps the most important factor of teamwork cannot be taught. It is the all-important sense of togetherness and friendship that will hold your team together. The strong, positive, professional relationship that develops between you and other designers in the salon will not be built overnight. Instead you must establish a rapport with each person and continue to work toward good communication, understanding and teamwork every day. The people you work with can become your friends and your professional associates.

Remember these valuable concepts used by successful business people in any industry:
1. Plan ahead
2. Create a professional image
3. Define your goals
4. Develop good professional relationships

Education + Skill + Confidence = SUCCESS!

NOTE

Good teamwork involves referrals. A client booked into a salon for a design service might be referred to a specialist for skin care needs, or vice versa. In each case, the designers reinforce the salon's concern for the client by suggesting treatments and services. Working as a team, you can provide each client with special care.

PERFORMANCE REVIEW

At regular intervals throughout your employment, the salon management will discuss your job performance with you. Called performance reviews, they have several common characteristics:

- Performance reviews occur at predetermined intervals. It is important to do a self-appraisal prior to each performance review.
- You will be given suggestions to help you capitalize on your strong areas.
- You will receive constructive criticism about the areas where you could improve.

6.4 SALON OWNERSHIP

Perhaps your dream, maybe even one of your long-term goals, is to run your own salon. The successful salon owner, through ambition and hard work, can enjoy personal and financial security and the creative freedom to develop and build a lucrative business. Even if you have never thought of salon ownership or already know that you do not have a desire to own a salon, it will be beneficial for you to know the fundamental principles of various salon ownership models and operations. Understanding the inner workings of salons will create a foundation that will allow both you and the salon owner to meet goals together. This section of the chapter will explore how to begin the process of owning a salon.

SELF-APPRAISAL

A salon owner does not have to be all things to all people. The designer planning to open a salon should assess his or her own skills carefully to pinpoint any areas of weakness. Locating weaknesses allows the potential salon owner to hire employees for whom those same areas are strengths. Skills essential to a successful salon owner are:

1. The ability to recognize hair fashion trends and technical expertise (While the salon owner need not excel in every salon service performed, it is important to recognize great color skills or perm techniques and hire staff accordingly.)
2. The ability to communicate with the public, not only in ordinary situations, but also in unusual or difficult instances
3. The ability to accept suggestions and criticism from clients and staff
4. The ability to exert self-control
5. The ability to manage the financial operations of a salon or to work with a professional bookkeeper or accountant to create a budget that predicts income and expenses
6. The ability to establish and adjust salon pricing in accordance with local economic factors
7. The knowledge to create business through promotion
8. The ability to set realistic business goals
9. The ability to organize a business plan into an executive summary:
   - Goals
   - Market potential
   - Marketing strategy
   - Financial projection
   - Exit plan

COSMETOLOGY FUNDAMENTALS

These skills can be learned and developed through study and hard work. The experience you gain working as a designer in someone else's salon will provide you with invaluable opportunities to watch and learn. Poor or inexperienced management and/or poor bookkeeping systems have been the cause of failure for many salons. Many local colleges and universities, however, offer management and business training that can combine with your cosmetology education to help you become the owner of a successful salon.

FINANCIAL STATUS

Anyone thinking of opening a business must have money to invest. Few people have the thousands of dollars needed to equip and supply a salon. Therefore, you must prove you are a "good risk" before a bank or savings and loan will lend you money. Preparing a personal financial statement is the first step toward securing a loan.

PERSONAL FINANCIAL STATEMENT

A personal financial statement contains three basic elements:

- **A list of all the property you own, your assets.** Assets include physical property, such as a house, car, recreational vehicle, antiques, jewelry, gold or silver, collections of valued goods, like stamps or coins, or any item for which you could receive payment. The best assets are cash-valued items, such as certificates of deposit, IRAs, life insurance policies, savings bonds, stocks/bonds, cash in money market, and checking and savings accounts. Together these are your **total assets.**
- **A list of all the money you owe, your liabilities.** Any outstanding loan balances on your assets (on a house or car), bills from credit cards or charge accounts, or student loans are liabilities. Together these are your **total liabilities.**
- **Final figure, net worth, calculated by subtracting your liabilities from your assets.** Assets minus liabilities equal net worth. For example:
  - if you had . . . . $50,000 assets
  - minus . . . . $30,000 liabilities
  - you would have a . . $20,000 net worth

A bank might loan only 10% of personal net worth. With a net worth of $20,000, for example, you could borrow approximately $2,000. A 5-chair salon will cost on the average from $5,000 to $50,000, depending on location, improvements and equipment needed. It is possible to borrow money with a low personal net worth, but then you are categorized as a "high risk" and may have to pay interest rates 5 to 8 points higher than the usual rate.

As you can see, a future salon owner should begin accumulating cash or physical assets and paying off all liabilities from the day of graduation. Getting the help of a certified financial consultant is a step in the right direction. Some areas offer this service without charge.

Your personal finances must be in order before you can go into business. Once you have determined your net worth and your ability to borrow money, you must have a plan. Now is the time to determine the kind of salon you want and can afford.

TYPES OF SALON OWNERSHIP

There are four types of ownership:

1. **A sole proprietorship is a business owned by one person** who is in complete control of the business, receives all profits from the business and is responsible for all debts and losses.

2. **A partnership is a business owned by two or more persons.** All costs of opening, operating and maintaining the business are shared by the partners as agreed. Partnerships can be between persons with different management or salon skills. One may be an excellent designer while the other has management ability. This relationship builds on the strengths of each and avoids weaknesses. Caution: A partnership agreement should be legally written. The agreement should specify the rights and obligations of each partner. In the event that a partner decides to leave the partnership or sell his or her portion, there should be a written buy-out agreement. Verbal agreements lead to misunderstandings. A solidly based relationship between partners is essential for a partnership to work.

3. A **corporation** is a legal entity, separate from its shareholders, which is formed under legal guidelines. A corporation has a charter or articles of incorporation describing the purposes of the corporation and the structure of the company. **A corporation is actually owned by its shareholders.** The shareholders elect representatives known as the board of directors. The board of directors then appoints officers (such as the president, vice president and treasurer) to run the day-to-day business. Shareholders receive income based on the profits of the corporation. Corporations may be privately held by just a few stockholders or publicly held. If publicly held, stock of the corporation is owned by many people and is available for sale on one of the stock exchanges. As a general rule, stockholders are not liable for the corporation's debts or losses as long as the corporation is operated as a separate legal entity. Laws concerning liability or damage to persons or property as a result of a corporation's activities may be different according to where the corporation is formed and the place where it conducts its business. A lawyer and an accountant should be employed to ensure that the corporation is properly established and conducts its business in accordance with the local laws.

4. A **franchise** is more a form of operation than a form of ownership. **A franchise is simply an operating agreement in which a fee is paid to a parent corporation in exchange for fixtures, promotion, advertising, education and management techniques. The owner of a franchise agreement can be a sole proprietor, partnership or corporation.** Certain rules must be observed in the operation of a franchise. An initial purchase fee plus a monthly service charge is paid to the parent corporation. A franchise is an excellent way to share in the expertise of industry experts. However, simple policies about hours, products used, benefits for employees, salaries and even the color of the salon are decided by the parent corporation.

REQUIREMENTS OF A SALON

To begin the process of salon planning, you will need to research the following:

1. **Location**. The most important factor in opening a salon business is location. What are the available locations in your area? You need to assess parking conditions, high-traffic activity (walk-by, drive-in or bus service), and rental fees per square foot.

2. **Market Need**. How many salons and designers are there in the area? What are the salon services offered, prices charged, types of potential clientele (age, income and social groups)? A ten-year forecast of the economic future of the community can usually be obtained from the local Chamber of Commerce or Economic Development Agency.

3. **Cost of Necessary Improvements**. Improvements include dollars that must be spent to meet a salon's unique plumbing and lighting requirements, such as shampoo bowls and color areas, and to upgrade electrical wiring, heating, air conditioning and so forth. A landlord will sometimes share in this expense. Salon equipment is a separate expense not included in improvements.

GETTING THE RIGHT ADVICE

At this point any serious future salon owner will need the advice of some experts.

1. An **accountant** can tell you what a bank is likely to lend you, based on your net worth. An accountant is a financial advisor, not an expert on the salon industry. He or she is generally paid on a monthly or quarterly basis. The accountant's tasks would include:
   - Informing you about types of business ownership and their tax benefits and liabilities
   - Evaluating a rental agreement
   - Setting up a basic bookkeeping system, including periodic income statements to evaluate profit or loss
   - Recording and preparing tax payments to various government agencies
   - Representing you if you are audited by the Internal Revenue Service

2. An **insurance agent** will provide advice on insurance needed to safely open and operate a business. (See types of insurance in this chapter.) Insurance is a form of risk management. When you buy insurance, you are paying a fee to a company to assume your risk of loss. For example, car insurance is a set dollar amount of assumed risk on your car. The insurance company is betting you won't have an accident. You're betting your premium that you might have an accident. The rule of insurance is, "If you can easily afford to totally replace an item, don't insure it," unless you could in some way be held responsible for personal injury if the item malfunctioned or if property for which you were responsible caused an accident. There are requirements that certain insurance, such as Workers' Compensation, be carried to protect the consumer and the employee. As an owner, you must have this type of insurance. Select a reputable agent and company that offer the whole range of insurance policies needed by the salon. An agent is paid on a commission basis according to the policies of the company or companies represented.

3. A lawyer is an advisor on the legal obligations of business ownership, borrowing money, signing rental (lease) agreements and assuming tax responsibilities. You should consult a lawyer when documents are being signed or when establishing a type of ownership requiring a written agreement (a partnership or corporation). **You may also want to contact a lawyer prior to signing a purchase or rental agreement to determine the existence of any outstanding debt against the building or business.** Lawyers are normally paid on an hourly basis for all phone calls, in-person consultations or preparation of documents. Ask the rate before consulting with a lawyer.

COMPLIANCE

The salon owner's responsibilities also include being in compliance with all local, state/province and federal rules, regulations and laws. Examples include city zoning and building codes, city or county waste disposal rules, assigned state/province regulatory agency licensure regulations, the Internal Revenue Service, OSHA, and various acts such as Americans with Disabilities Act (ADA), which allows access and fair treatment in the business and educational environment to disabled persons. A lawyer is able to assist the salon owner to be in compliance with all regulations.

4. A distributor sales consultant representing a full-service, professional-only distribution (beauty supply) house is the link between the manufacturers of products and equipment and the salon. It can be beneficial to develop a strong relationship with one distributor. The full-service distributor will carry all products and equipment needed to open a salon. The distributor may have financing available, may help in salon design, may help find good salon locations, may aid in locating prospective employees and may provide in-salon education and large-scale educational seminars or workshops. The distributor sales consultant earns a commission on the dollar amount you purchase in supplies. However, he or she may be able to provide you with an efficient, cost-saving inventory control system that ensures a maximum return on every dollar invested in retail and professional-use products. If you don't make money, neither will the distributor sales consultant. The distributor-owner is a key professional relationship a salon owner must develop.

There are also discount and cash-and-carry beauty supply houses throughout the country that provide products or equipment with few or none of the above-mentioned services. In addition some manufacturers sell directly to salon owners. A salon owner must decide what is important to his or her salon operations when selecting a distributor.

SPACE REQUIREMENTS AND FLOOR PLANS

In general, it takes 120 to 150 square feet per designer to create an efficient working space. Square footage is obtained by multiplying the length of the location by its width. For example, a 15 by 30 foot space is a total of 450 square feet (15 x 30 = 450). A distributor sales consultant could help you design a sample salon layout based on 3 to 4 designers working in a 450 square foot space. **Some regulating agencies have specific minimum space requirements for each designer.** In this instance, the salon will be licensed to employ a maximum number of designers working at one time.

As the owner you could give more space per designer, but you would need to be aware that your investment costs would rise, which may cost the salon more than is profitable. The ideal salon arrangement has an efficient traffic pattern. The best design requires the fewest steps for the client and designer to travel.

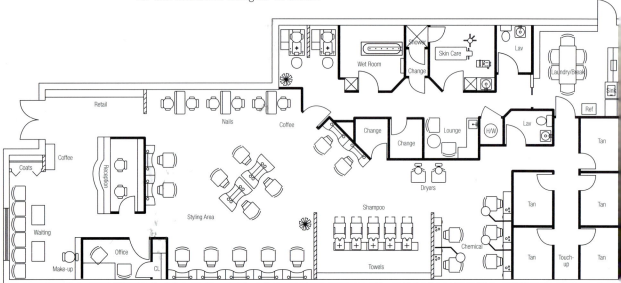

All salons require a reception area with seating and a desk for receiving guests, a dispensary, a restroom, and service areas such as shampoo and drying areas. In addition, many salons have a retail display and promotion area, a lounge, laundry and utility room.

Develop a floor plan for a proposed location before trying to determine any details on cost of equipment or interior decorating. If a location cannot be arranged with an efficient floor plan (with a minimum capital improvement cost), look at other locations. Salons can be installed with an investment from $1,000 up to $10,000 per designer. Weigh the cost of installation for the salon you want. Sometimes a location is priced right, with good traffic and the type of clientele desired, but the cost of installation is too high. Examine many alternatives. Then work out the decorating details. Remember, this is *your* salon. Make it one you'll enjoy working in and one that will pay off.

BORROWING MONEY

After you have found a location, determined a suitable and affordable floor plan, determine the cost of fixtures and estimated the capital improvements necessary, you must determine how much money you will need to borrow. It is important to note that you should not sign a rental agreement until you have received your loan approval. Your accountant should advise you of the operating capital needed to open the salon and to pay the expenses of your business for at least six months. Generally, you must be willing to invest some of your own money in the salon for an institution to grant a loan. It is important to make all your loan payments on time to avoid default (failure to repay), since you will be granted future loans based on your ability and willingness to do so.

RENTAL AGREEMENTS

Upon obtaining a loan, you can enter into a rental agreement (called a lease). Normally a lease should extend for 5 years with an option for 5 more years, in order to avoid unexpected rent increases. It is unprofitable to install a salon for less than 5 years, due to the time needed for a new business to grow and flourish. You should negotiate for all or part of the capital improvements to be paid by the owner of the building or lessor. Such a request is reasonable because these improvements will stay in the building when you move out. **As the renter or lessee, you promise to pay rent and use the property according to the agreement**. It is common for salons to need extra water pipes, larger water heaters, more electric outlets, washer and dryer facilities, installation of shampoo bowls and large window areas. These special features will probably have to be paid for by the lessee (you). However, arrange for the maintenance or repairs on normal building equipment, such as furnace and air conditioner, to be the lessor's (owner's) responsibility.

A large portion of the expense of the salon is the rent. There are two kinds of rent:
1. A **fixed rent** is a set dollar amount paid each month to the lessor. A fixed rent allows you to predict your monthly expenses carefully.
2. A **variable rent** includes a set dollar amount paid per month plus a percentage of the total monthly income. Variable rents are common in malls and large shopping centers. However, with the small percentage of profit earned by an average salon, a variable rent could be a serious mistake. Have your accountant predict the results of a variable rent system before signing a lease.

Have a lawyer evaluate a tentative lease and make suggestions for change. You can negotiate changes in any lease. Remember, don't sign a lease unless you, your lawyer and your accountant are satisfied that it is fair and reasonable.

TYPES OF INSURANCE

As stated previously, insurance is a form of risk management. It protects you from the financial difficulties that can follow unexpected loss of property, income and/or life. The following are types of insurance available to eliminate some of the risks of being in business.

- **Malpractice insurance is a policy that protects the salon owner from financial loss that can result from employee negligence while performing hair, nail and skin care services on salon clients.** Every salon professional should be insured by the salon owner. This insurance covers the cost of a lawsuit or settlement resulting from damage caused to a client during any service.
- **Property or premise insurance** is a policy that covers the actual salon equipment and physical location in case of natural disasters, fire, theft or burglary, or accidents occurring at the business. It covers replacement of lost items and carries a liability clause that will pay a claim if someone is injured on the premises.
- **Product liability insurance** is a recent addition to available insurance coverage. With the huge number of products found within the cosmetology industry, a need for protection has

developed. This coverage protects against financial loss arising because of injury or damage resulting from the use of a product.

- **Unemployment insurance** is required by federal law for all qualified employers. Employers pay into a central fund that offers compensation to laid off, displaced or otherwise eligible employees until suitable employment can be found and/or a designated amount of time has passed.

- **Workers' Compensation is a state-controlled insurance required by law.** This insurance is paid directly to the state on a quarterly basis to cover any expense resulting from an injury to an employee. If the employee is injured while working in the salon, all medical expenses are paid by the state, and the state provides the employee with a guaranteed income until the employee can return to work.

TAXES

Internal Revenue Service (IRS) rules require you to register a daily log of all your tips, which is income. Keep a copy for yourself and submit a copy to your employer. Did you know that as a salon owner, you are responsible for reporting your employees' tips?

The salon owner is responsible for withholding from an employee's income for payment of certain taxes and for paying these withholdings to the government. In the U.S., these include federal, state and local income taxes and social security tax. The salon owner also has a tax obligation to the employee. **For every dollar of social security tax paid by the employee, the salon owner must pay the same amount to the federal government. Social security is a planned savings/retirement fund for every worker in the United States.** Medicare is part of your social security tax and provides medical insurance coverage during retirement. In Canada, the salon owner is responsible for withholding Federal and Provincial tax, Employment Insurance (EI) and Canadian Pension Tax.

The salon owner must also provide an annual W-2 form for each employee. The W-2 form will indicate all taxes paid for the past year. It is important for all employees to verify that the salon owner is submitting taxes under the correct social security number so appropriate credit is given.

States have sales taxes on products and services. **The salon owner is responsible for collecting and paying these monies to the state on a monthly or quarterly basis.** A permit is required to collect taxes, and the payments are a permanent record of the salon's dollar volume. A salon owner must apply for a state sales tax permit before collecting tax on products or services sold.

Income tax is paid on the profits (earnings) of a business. The Internal Revenue Service establishes criteria for reporting profit and loss.

EXPENSES AND INCOME

In very basic terms, the financial success of a salon will be achieved when the salon's income is significantly greater than its operating expense. Income refers to all payments received from clients for services performed and home care products purchased.

Operating expense refers to all the costs incurred in running the salon each day. **If the salon's income is greater than the operating expense, the salon is operating at a profit. If the operating expense is greater than the income, the salon is operating at a loss.** The salon may operate at a loss, as clientele develops, during the first few weeks, months and even years it is open. Your accountant should help you take that fact into consideration when your initial financing is arranged.

If you make a profit, you pay a percentage of that profit to the federal, state and local governments. If you suffer a loss, you receive a tax credit (pay little or no tax). You can see that careful planning and control of expenses are essential.

Careful record keeping is required by law. It is wise to keep all records of your daily sales and service for 5 to 7 years. If you are audited by the IRS, these records are proof of your income. Failure to keep records is against the law in most areas.

Independent Contractor is an IRS term that can be applied to designers who rent or lease workstations from a building owner. Rental or leasing fees can vary, depending on urban or rural location. The building owner provides a location in which to work and pays the utilities. The designer (lessee) provides all professional supplies, a telephone line and products for retail sale to clients.

In this system, the designer—who is considered self-employed by the IRS—reports income and pays "self-employment tax" directly to the government each quarter. There are no benefits provided to the lessee/designer by the salon owner, other than a place to work.

The average cost of operating a business (by percentage of income) breaks down as follows:

COMPENSATION 50%
Salaries or commissions for yourself and your employees, including payroll taxes

RENT. 12%
Fixed or variable

SUPPLIES 5%
Professional products used (consumption/consumable), retail products sold and
miscellaneous equipment and tools

ADVERTISING. 3%
Promotion of the salon

UTILITIES. 2%
Water, electricity, gas, sanitation, phone

INSURANCE. 1.5%
All types

EMPLOYEE BENEFITS. 1.5%
Education, paid vacations, pension plans or profit-sharing, health insurance

MAINTENANCE 2%
Repairs, laundry, cleaning and replacement of equipment

COST OF DOING BUSINESS 2%
Accounting, legal, licenses, subscriptions, professional dues, etc.

SERVICES OF DEBT 5%
Capital improvements, equipment and original loan expense

DEPRECIATION. 3%
An account established to save for replacement of equipment;
creates tax credit

MISCELLANEOUS. 1%
All other expenses

TOTAL OPERATING EXPENSE: . . . . 88% OF INCOME

REMEMBER

Income minus Expenses equal Profit. The better you control your expenses, the faster you will pay off your debt and be able to see higher profits from the salon.

All the above expenses can be controlled. If your operating statement shows a particular expense that is too high, you can take steps to reduce costs. Expenses shown above may be higher or lower for your salon, depending on climate, size of community and region. Of course increasing your profits in ways that have minimal effect on increasing your expenses will yield higher net. Retail displays, for example, use existing space and require a one-time expense for the display unit. The only ongoing expenses are the costs of keeping the display well-stocked and, perhaps, retail commissions paid to your designers and salon coordinator or receptionist on their retail product sales. Staff compensation is the largest ongoing salon expense.

SALON PHILOSOPHY, POLICIES AND PROCEDURES

A salon should have a professional philosophy or standard of ethics. Creating a Policies and Procedures Handbook is the first step in developing these standards. It provides a set of rules for the owner and staff to work by and can be revised as needed. A salon handbook should thoroughly outline the salon owner's expectations of employees. Information contained in a salon handbook might include: job descriptions, educational and professional requirements, client relations policies and employee conduct guidelines, location of MSDS information, guidelines on dealing with client or staff disabilities, hours, prices, service standards, record-keeping policies, benefits, infection control standards, care of equipment, absence policy, complaint policy and causes for termination of employment.

A salon handbook should also inform the employee about what to expect from management. The employer is expected to provide a safe and pleasant working environment, reasonable working hours, equitable salary structure, products and supplies, and sanitation services.

The employer should also provide a format, such as weekly or biweekly salon meetings, in which employees can offer suggestions and opinions and expect unbiased consideration to be given to the topics and ideas they might bring up. These provisions could be covered in the handbook as well.

SALON OPERATION

Now that you have explored the steps to opening a salon, it's time to consider important aspects of salon operation: hiring, compensation, pricing, advertising, retailing and receptionist duties.

HIRING

Hire employees who meet your standards of honesty and professionalism. You might consider conducting 2 to 3 interviews to determine if a designer is the right candidate for employment in your salon.

The salon owner needs to apply for a Federal Employer Identification Number before hiring employees.

U.S. Federal Law states that you must determine if the employee is a legal citizen prior to final hiring by requesting proof of valid social security card, driver's license and/or birth certificate and completing what is called an I-9 form. A copy of the completed I-9 form, along with a photocopy of the supporting proof documents, should be placed in the employee's file.* After hiring, introduce the new employee to your entire staff and make him or her feel a part of your salon team.

*In Canada, a Social Insurance number is required as proof of ability to work.

COMPENSATION

There are three common ways an employee can be paid:

1. A **commission structure** is based on a percentage of the dollar income the individual designer creates by servicing clients. Perhaps the designer does 10 cuts at $10 per cut in an 8 hour day. The total (or gross) income is $100. A percentage up to 50% is normally paid. At 50% the designer receives $50 or $6.25 per hour worked. This pay structure is based on the number of clients and the amount of work done.

2. A **salary structure** is a compensation system that guarantees a set income on a weekly or monthly basis. This salary is similar to salaried positions in all professions. Salon owners like salaries because educational costs and employee benefits such as health insurance, pension plans, and paid vacations can be budgeted if the payroll is based on fixed salaries.

3. A **salary plus commission structure** guarantees a certain amount of money on a regular basis and allows additional payment based on the number of clients the designer brings into the salon. This system gives the designer a steady paycheck, while rewarding the designer for building his or her clientele.

PRICING

Service prices should be determined by conducting a market survey before opening the salon. Price the services at a reasonable rate to fit the income range of the clients you want to attract. Create a profile of the clientele you hope will visit your salon and target them with your advertising. Determining what other salons are charging can be helpful. But remember price is not the only reason clients select a particular salon. The community image of the salon, the quality of work performed, the personalities of the designers, the ambiance and the salon location are major incentives for a client to return to your salon.

ADVERTISING

Advertising tells the public about your salon—the services you perform, the quality of work you produce and any other reasons that clients should patronize your salon. **The best form of advertising is word of mouth.** Satisfied clients tell others about your salon, as do unsatisfied clients. Advertising in the printed media can be very effective. Direct mail advertising involves sending postcards or flyers to prospective clients encouraging them to try your salon. Daily or weekly newspaper ads can create an image in the consumers' minds through the repetition of your name and logo. Magazines or periodicals that reach the type of clientele you are trying to attract can also be effective.

Television and radio ads can be effective but costly. Billboards, bus stop seats and public relations efforts, including holding styling shows or fund-raising events for charity, can also promote your professional pursuits.

Involvement in community affairs, the chamber of commerce or service organizations can also promote your personal and professional image in the area. Be known as a worker. People will try your professional services if they like you and trust you as a person.

Plan a yearly advertising budget and stick to it. Alternate expensive forms of advertising with inexpensive methods. If one form of advertising works, repeat it. If something fails, drop it. Consider surveying your clients once a year for their opinions about your services, your community image and your advertising program.

INVENTORY AND PRODUCT CONTROL

Products are purchased by the salon owner and brought into the salon for use during client services and for retailing to the client. These products are referred to as inventory or stock in quantity. Inventory is generally identified by two categories, professional and retail. In order for the salon to operate at a profitable margin, it is important that a strong inventory system is in place that will allow close management of these valuable products. Proper inventory practices also indicate that emphasis must be placed on ensuring timely ordering of products. Not having a product available to perform a service or meet a purchasing need of a client is not good business practice.

Inventory control is a term applied to procedures used in the salon that will ensure that products are accounted for from the time they are brought into the salon until they are sold or used. In addition, inventory control guidelines are established to monitor the number of sales made of a specific product within an assigned time frame. Determinations on whether specific products should be continued as retail items are based on the number of "turnovers" or "turns," which means calculating the amount of time it takes to sell the product once it is on the shelf. It is not to an owner's business advantage to invest money in products that don't turn over in a timely fashion.

A salon owner should expect the designers to sell products for home care to their clients. Setting a sales goal is essential to providing retail income to both the salon owner and the designer. It is an industry-recommended goal that for each dollar in services a designer performs on a client, that client should be purchasing a dollar in home-care products. A client who visits a salon for a cut every 6 weeks, at the average cost of $15, could easily spend another $15 on the retail products he or she will need for use at home. That same client, through careful product recommendations, may eventually spend more on retail products than on salon services by purchasing additional hair care products, skin care products and/or cosmetics.

Many salons pay a commission ranging from 8% to 15% of the designer's total retail sales to the designer. Some salon owners pay lower commission for lower dollar volume sales. A sliding scale creates the incentive to sell more. The salon owner is responsible for keeping an inventory of products for designers to sell.

RECEPTIONIST DUTIES

Keeping client records easily accessible in a central location may be one of the receptionist's responsibilities.

In many cases the receptionist is the first person to greet the clients as they arrive. If the salon does not have a full-time receptionist, the salon owner usually appoints a designer to serve in this capacity as needed or the designers rotate throughout the day, meeting the needs of this area. In some cases, the receptionist also acts as the cashier, managing the operations of the cash register.

The receptionist position is very important and primary duties are to:
1. Promote good will and client satisfaction.
2. Schedule appointments in a fair and efficient way.
3. Manage incoming and outgoing calls regarding appointments.
4. Inform designers of client arrival in the salon.
5. Supervise the reception area to ensure organization and efficiency.
6. Promote retail products and additional services to clients.
7. Handle pressure and client complaints efficiently.
8. Ensure client services are all paid and documented.
9. Ensure messages are handled in order of priority and with efficiency.
10. Work with designers to ensure punctual schedules.

A poor receptionist can ruin a salon's operations. Clients often judge the salon by how phone calls are handled and how they are treated as they arrive in the salon the first few minutes. It is crucial that the receptionist be cheerful and able to handle most situations. A great receptionist can make everyone's day go more smoothly and less stressfully.

MAKING CHANGE

Cash operations are important to every business and the salon is no exception. The receptionist or assigned cashier needs to ensure accuracy and efficiency, providing the correct denomination of bills and coins for cash transactions and trouble-shooting during credit transactions. When giving change, always count back from the smaller denomination, usually coins, and move to the larger, usually bills.

> For example, if the client's bill for services and products totals $32.97 and the client offers $35, the client would hear counted back "98, 99, 33, 34 and 35." This would indicate that you have offered the client change of 3 cents (to total $33) and then 2 singles (to total $35).

The most efficient method of offering change is to always give the client the fewest bills necessary to complete the transaction. Therefore, it is necessary that an adequate inventory of various bill and coin denominations is on hand. A client might say it is okay to receive 25 pennies because you are out of other coins, but in reality it is not good business, takes more time and is not as efficient.

TELEPHONE TECHNIQUES

Your telephone answering technique creates the first impression a client will have of the salon. The telephone is used to make appointments, answer questions, receive messages, handle complaints and remind clients of future appointments. Because the telephone plays such an important role in the salon's business, it is imperative that anyone answering the phone is well-trained and answering procedures are carefully planned. Telephone answering tips include:

1. Answer the phone within two rings.
2. Greet the client by saying:
   - The salon name
   - Your name
   - "How may I help you?"
3. Listen carefully for:
   - Client's name
   - Service desired or other information (ask client to repeat if unclear)
4. Book appointment and repeat back to client:
   - Designer requested
   - Time and date of appointment
   - Exact service to be done
   - "Thank you for calling, (client's name)"

5. If you cannot help the client personally:
- Ask the client, "Would you please hold?"
- Wait for a response (yes or no)
- Then place the line on hold and go get help
- Return to client within 1 minute

6. If a message is being left, include:
- Date and time
- For whom the message is intended
- Name of caller
- Phone number of caller
- Exact message
- *Repeat back the entire message* to caller
- Deliver the message at an appropriate time

NOTE: Booking appointments can be done more effectively if the person answering the phone is aware of the designers' skills, their speed, prices and availability.

Here are some additional phone tips:
- Do not talk to others in the salon while on the phone.
- Avoid sounding harsh, shrill or irritated.
- Use good grammar.
- Speak clearly, calmly and with enthusiasm.
- Be courteous, speak at a moderate pace and avoid interrupting the caller.
- Handle complaints tactfully by asking the client to come into the salon, so everything possible can be done to please her/him. If a client refuses, offer to compensate the client (according to salon policy) or ask the client, "What would make you happy?" Take a complaint very seriously. Just one unhappy client can directly affect your salon's reputation, the designer's reputation and your future income.
- Always maintain self-control.
- When informing clients of pricing, be exact. A client expects to pay a quoted price unless informed that a preliminary stylist-client consultation is required.
- Don't promise that a chemical service can be performed without hair analysis if an analysis is salon policy. Performing a chemical service on chemically damaged hair can result in even greater hair damage and can possibly result in a malpractice lawsuit against the salon and/or designer.
- In a salon without a full-time receptionist, take turns answering the phone. Distribute new clients who don't request a particular designer among all designers with openings. Book others, and they will book you when they are answering the phone.

Remember, telephone techniques are tremendously important. Skillful handling turns a price inquiry phone call into a new client for your salon, soothes the ruffled feelings of a customer who might otherwise leave your clientele, and generally increases your salon's business.

SCHEDULING APPOINTMENTS

The process of scheduling appointments is of primary importance within the operation of the salon. Generally appointments are scheduled according to the type of service and the speed of the designer. Important information that is noted on the appointment book includes the following:

- Designer's name
- Scheduled service
- Appointment time
- Client's name
- Date
- Client's phone number

Frequently additional information is added to the appointment book by using codes that represent various types of clients. Codes used for identifying client types might include the following:

Walk-in clients might be represented by placing a "W" next to the client's name to indicate the client did not call ahead for an appointment.

Request clients could be indicated by placing an "R" next to the client's name to identify a specific designer has been requested to perform the service. In an effort to serve the needs of the client, the salon could notify this client if the requested designer is absent on the day of the scheduled appointment.

Transfer clients might be indicated by placing a "T" next to the client's name to indicate that this client is able to be transferred to another designer. This code is very helpful if a designer is running behind schedule or in the case of absence of the assigned designer.

6.5 SALON RETAILING

Retailing in the salon—selling products for client home care—will help make you a successful designer and will show your clients you are interested in their grooming needs. It is an ongoing process that requires effort and dedication, just as the services you learn to perform. Successful retailing in the salon requires you to look for new ways to interest your clients in the products you recommend.

SELLING

Selling is the international pastime of exchanging service for product, money for expertise. This system of exchange is as old as human existence. Even in stone-age society, humans bartered to acquire daily needs. Bartering, which gradually became selling, represented a simple exchange for the essentials of life.

Today, selling combines psychology and sociology in a sophisticated system. Selling has become an important form of expression in society. The systems of exchanging are the same but the approach has become more subtle, more directed. **Successful selling could best be defined as the art of professional recommendation.**

In your daily communication you may be practicing recommendation without even knowing it. When you try to convince someone of the merits of an idea or your ability to get the job done, you are really asking them to believe in you. In the professional beauty industry, you take this a step further and begin to use confidence and expertise to recommend a product or service. You are, in effect, persuading someone else to trust and believe in your professionalism.

The keys to retail selling in a salon are remarkably similar to convincing others to like and believe in you. As a professional "recommender," you will be selling two important things:

1. Your artistic abilities, services, credibility and professionalism
2. Retail products, grooming aids and implements

RECOMMENDING

When you begin working in a salon, you will be well-trained in sculpting and designing hair and will feel confident providing those and other related services to clients. Your clients will learn to trust and believe in you and your talents as a professional and most will be very willing to listen to your recommendations.

Clients who come to you will want to learn how to take care of their hair, skin and nails at home between visits. A logical extension of your salon service is recommending the kind of quality products for use at home that will complement your design services. Clients will appreciate your concern and will usually accept your recommendations of hair, skin and nail care retail products. Professional product recommendations will help you establish a clientele that will remain loyal to you and to the products you recommend. Retailing is part of a total professional concept, a complete approach to client service. Successful salons are those whose staff members are effectively recommending their services and a quality line of retail products.

Become an invaluable asset to any salon staff by:
- Listening to clients
- Recognizing their needs
- Offering sound advice
- Recommending the best products for home use
- Communicating professionally while performing services

KNOWLEDGE AND CONFIDENCE

To promote retail products effectively you must have confidence in yourself and the products you recommend. That confidence comes from thorough knowledge of each item and through first-hand experience with the product.

The more experienced you become while in school, the more successful you will be on the job. The next time someone comes in for a haircut, suggest something that will enhance the hair and benefit the client.

PROFESSIONAL PRODUCTS

It is your responsibility as a professional to familiarize yourself with the finest products for hair, skin and nails. Practice recommending products to your clients in school, and check with them periodically to be certain that the product is producing the expected results. Maintaining a binder that serves as a source of information about product ingredients, costs and promotions will assist you in remaining current with product information. Unless you are thoroughly familiar with a product, its uses and benefits, you will be unable to offer effective recommendations. It is necessary that you learn as much as possible about a line of products and try them yourself to become completely familiar with them. If you don't use and believe in products you're promoting, you'll have much more difficulty in being a success at getting others to try them.

Salons do have advantages over drugstores, department stores and supermarkets when retailing grooming aids. They have the opportunity to prove that a product works by demonstrating its use and effectiveness. Salons provide licensed professionals like you to give your recommendations about products that will most benefit the consumer. A salon will want to be certain that the products offered for retail are safe and that designers do not overstate any warranty criteria. An in-depth knowledge of professional products begins with an understanding of their features and benefits.

FEATURES AND BENEFITS

Features of a product are its characteristics, which might include the size of the container, the aroma, or a specific ingredient. Benefits of a product are things that the product will do to enhance the appearance or improve the condition of the client's hair, skin or nails.

When you begin working in a salon, study the features and benefits of all the retail products offered for sale. You'll soon discover this simple formula for success:

Features + Benefits = Incentive to Buy

If features are presented in an appealing manner, benefits explained thoroughly, and both customized according to individual need, the client will most likely buy the product. Following are examples of features and benefits:

FEATURES	BENEFITS
1. Size - bottle is small	**1.** Perfect for travelling
2. Ingredients - product contains protein	**2.** Reconditioning effect
3. Concentrated formula - small amount required	**3.** Economical purchase

One of the keys for successful recommendations is to customize the product's features and benefits to fit the needs of the client. In order to customize home care programs, first ask your clients questions to determine their needs, lifestyle, style desired and any hair and scalp problems they might have. Start with general questions like the following (your client's answers will give you additional direction):

- Who recommended you to the salon?
- When did you have your last (perm, haircut, manicure, etc.)?
- What do you want from a (perm, haircut, permanent color, etc.)?
- What didn't you like about that (perm, haircut, permanent color, etc.)?
- Which (shampoo, conditioner, moisturizer, nail polish, etc.) works best for you? Why?

INVOLVE THE CLIENT

Describe a product's features and benefits, and you will interest clients and gain their attention. The next step in successful recommendation is to let the client hold, smell or sample the product. The more the senses are used in examining a product, the more involved the client becomes with the product and the more personally he or she will identify with that item. It would be very difficult for a client to gain a feeling about the product if it were out of reach or behind glass. To effectively promote a product's benefits, you may wish to demonstrate the product for the client and make testers available to examine and try. With a skin care product, for example, you could give a "mini facial" and then have the client feel the effects on the skin's surface.

Personal referrals and recommendations of retail products provide your most effective advertising.

COSMETOLOGY FUNDAMENTALS

SUGGEST NEW PRODUCTS

As new products are introduced in the salon, think of the clients who would benefit from their use. When those clients come in for a visit, present the products' features and benefits. Then suggest that they try the items at home. You are once again reinforcing your concern for your clients and your professionalism in the salon.

Your clients will return again and again to buy those items that they believe are best suited for them and this is the start of your successful repeat business. Having been "sold" on a product once and having used it and liked the results, clients will more than likely continue to buy products on their own initiative, leaving you time to teach new clients about home grooming care.

CLOSING THE SALE

The next time you make a retail purchase of some sort, listen to the salesperson's presentation. Evaluate it in terms of the features and benefits of the product.

Just as important as presenting a product's features and benefits is the closing of the sale. If you are afraid to ask the client for a commitment after all your effort to present products, you have just wasted time!

You, as a salon professional, cannot earn a retail commission or bonus unless you promote and conclude your professional recommendation of the retail items. Nor can you expect the professional services that you perform on clients, such as haircoloring or perms, to last and look attractive unless clients care for their hair at home with the right products.

The conclusion of a retail sale is something that you build up to from the beginning of the recommendation process. Your positive attitude, your knowledge of the product, your explanation of the product benefits and how it is to be used, and your customized treatment program for the client, all reinforce the fact that you expect the client to purchase the product.

State the price. If the client has an objection to the price of a retail product, that person is actually saying to you, "Prove to me that it's worth the investment."

If the product's features and benefits have been clearly and personally related to the client's needs, price will be less important. If a client does raise a price objection, you haven't presented the features and benefits thoroughly enough to convince them to make the purchase. By returning to the important points that have been missed in your presentation (such as personal need), you will give the doubtful client more reasons to buy the item. With the proper in-salon education, the client will plan to spend a certain amount of money each month on the right home hair-care products.

BUYER TYPES

Understanding different types of potential consumers and what motivates them to buy will help you in closing the sale.

IDENTIFY BUYERS

- The **Ready Buyer** is open-minded and will take a chance on new products without hesitation. Be sure to keep this buyer aware of any new products the salon is offering.
- The **Logical Buyer** wants to know all the facts about a product, thinks carefully about buying without much regard for who else likes or uses the product. Explain to the logical buyer what a product will do, how it should be used, then supply him/her with available literature. Leave the client alone for a moment to make a decision.
- The **Emotional Buyer** bases purchases more on personal reasons than facts. Maybe the client's friend has a similar product. The emotional buyer is quite often an impulsive, spontaneous person who reacts to color of packaging or aroma of product. Describe how the product will improve cosmetic appearance, show results with proper use, and demonstrate the product's use for the customer. Make sure this buyer understands the benefits.
- The **Bargain Buyer** wants to save money at all costs and is not as interested in quality of product as price. Be sure to keep this buyer aware of any sale items or salon promotions offered. Don't push the client.
- The **Stubborn Buyer** puts up a struggle and has a strong desire to debate with you. Offer all the facts, describe results. Then, if the client still isn't convinced, send product literature home or offer a complimentary trial size if available.

These buyer types are only generalizations and can be found in several combinations. To effectively recommend products, you must believe in yourself and your professional ability to offer the proper treatments for your clients.

WHAT MOTIVATES BUYERS

Needs are fairly easy to identify if you observe and listen to your clients during each appointment.

Each buyer is unique. However, all clients share similar motivations for buying, including need, desire to look good, profit or gain and impulse.

Need is perhaps the easiest buyer motivation to recognize in the salon. For example, virtually everyone needs shampoo. Anti-dandruff shampoos, shampoos for color-treated hair, damaged hair, baby fine hair, dry or oily hair, all fill a need for your clientele.

Another need would be rinse to detangle the hair once it has been shampooed or a conditioner for damaged hair.

Creating need for a product means that you will be making clients aware of a product that will benefit them. By giving clients enough evidence that products are needed and will enhance their appearance, you convince the clients that they must have them.

Creating a need for a product in the mind of the client can be done through effective promotional displays in the salon, through client classes or individual conversations and analysis between the designer and the client. If, for example, a client comes to you for a haircut, and through hair analysis you find that the hair shows a deficiency, you should identify the need to the client and recommend a conditioning product.

If clients are willing to care for their hair at home, you can write out customized formulas for them and recommend the necessary conditioning products. Follow these steps for successful recommendation.

1. Observe and listen
2. Identify/create the need
3. Recommend products

Salon services will last longer when the hair is properly cared for at home with the right products purchased at your recommendation.

Desire to look their best causes people to make retail purchases. Clients are very consciou of their appearance. They will welcome advice from you on how they can keep their hair and skin looking their best. Salons have a built-in market for skin treatment items and hair care products, such as conditioners and thinning-hair enhancement products. Clients who have experienced hair loss or aging of the skin require very little convincing to try a quality, professionally recommended series of products.

The next major category of buyer motivation is **Profit or Gain**. People like to believe that they make intelligent purchases, no matter what the items. If clients believe that they will benefit from using a particular type of product, they will make those purchases.

If clients need convincing a product is right for them, recommend that they try a small size an item to see if it is effective for their needs. Once they have determined with the designer that the product is beneficial, the designer can recommend a larger, more economical size that item on the next visit.

Be careful not to prejudge the clients' ability to afford an item or their desire for a product. Even clients who have carefully budgeted their incomes will also appreciate information on more economical sizes of retail products and will feel complimented by your attention. If you have convinced your clients, they will plan for these retail purchases in advance.

Grooming aids lend themselves to **impulse buying**. Their retailers have created the need for these products through fashion magazines, television advertising and promotion. Salons have a built-in market of clients who want to be fashionable and attractive and who will respond to the need for new hair care and skin care products if the needs are effectively created through display and in-salon promotion. Statistics show that 45% to 65% of all purchases stem from impulse buying.

FOLLOW-UP

Some clients simply forget how to use the products that you have recommended. To avoid confusion and to reinforce your recommendation of the home hair care program, you might take a product brochure and write instructions on the back regarding the frequency of use. Many salons have printed their own forms with their salon logo, name, address and phone number for additional product recommendations. The designer or specialist merely fills in the client's name, the products recommended and any special instructions.

Benefits of written special instructions:
1. Reinforce the professionalism of your services and of the salon.
2. Clarify product use for clients so that they won't leave out an important step.
3. Remind clients to do the treatments, if they post the product recommendation form somewhere at home.
4. Help clients remember the products that have been suggested for their use.
5. Help the receptionist with retail recommendations before the client leaves the salon. Enable the designer to select merchandise from the retail shelves for the client to purchase at the conclusion of the salon visit.
6. Offer referral opportunities. Clients often take product recommendation forms home and show them to their families, friends and neighbors. This sharing could create new clientele for the salon.

Keep in mind that recommending a product one time doesn't guarantee that the client will continue using that item. The record cards that you maintain on each client will help you to see when the last purchases were made and to judge whether the client will be needing additional products on his or her next visit to the salon.

It would be an excellent idea for you to examine the condition of each client's hair, skin or nails several weeks after you have sold them products. If the client has experienced any reactions or if there seems to be no appreciable change in their condition, you will want to change the recommendation for the client. If there have been no problems and even minor improvement, encourage the client to continue with the original program.

It is advised that you not only check the hair, skin and nail condition when a client returns for service appointments but also pay particular attention to seasonal weather changes and how these affect the client.

A customized skin care program, for example, that suits a client perfectly during the warm summer months may not be adequate to protect the skin against the ravages of the cold winter. When necessary, revise your recommendations and explain why you are changing them.

EFFECTIVE DISPLAYS

Appreciating the value of salon displays will be most helpful to your future as a professional designer. When you begin working in a salon, you may be asked to help in the development and maintenance of salon displays. Promotional ideas do much more than brighten the area of the salon where your retail products are displayed. The following information will help you perform those duties in a professional and creative manner. Allocate adequate floor space for retail merchandise. Remember that the salon owner pays rent for every inch in the salon…even empty space! Don't let usable space stay empty; build a retail display to make that space pay. Display shelves for retail products, known as stock or stock inventory, should blend attractively with the salon decor but shouldn't disappear from sight because of their bland appearance. Use your imagination. Place displays in interesting areas of the salon.

Images courtesy of The Spa

RETAIL DISPLAY GUIDELINES

ORGANIZE STOCK
- Display the products by category.
- Put top-selling products and sizes at eye level on the display. This saves time and allows the client to shop on his or her own.
- Display product using island shelving (available on all sides) if possible. Utilize ends of island displays by placing shelving facing outward. This is called an "end cap" and is designed to catch the eye of the client as they enter the aisles.
- Rotate and rearrange the product to gain attention, prevent fading and ensure freshness of product.
- Place the latest shipment of same product in the back of the display when it arrives.
- Place displays in interesting areas, including high traffic areas, walls, windows, corners and workstations.

PRICE THE MERCHANDISE
- Price all retail products individually.
- Display price where a client can easily find it.

ENSURE QUALITY CONTROL
- Keep products on the edge of the shelves, facing the client. This creates easy access and high visibility of the product.
- Dust products daily and clean the shelves thoroughly at least once a week.
- Light the retail display area of the salon well.

CREATE PROMOTIONAL DISPLAYS
- Use product identification cards below each product on the shelves.
- Display literature on each retail item near the retail shelves so that clients have additional information to read and take home.

MAINTAIN INVENTORY CONTROL
- Use an inventory control form so you can monitor what products are selling well. This also helps account for product sales and makes reordering easier.
- Ensure that ordering of products is timely and controlled.
- Keep sufficient quantity of stock on the shelves at all times.

LEARN FROM THE DISPLAY EXPERTS
- The image of your retail area should attract a client's eye. View what other professional retailers are doing. Grocery stores, department stores and other specialty boutiques can give you great ideas on how their merchandising displays work for them.

As you reviewed earlier in this chapter, there has never been a time in history better than now to attain a career in the cosmetology field. A career as a salon professional will lead the way to many exciting opportunities and rewards. Your effort to select the job best suited for you, establish career goals, maintain professional relationships and recommend products to clients will help put you on the path to success.

CONNECTING THEORY TO REAL-WORLD PRACTICE

SALON BUSINESS	PERSONAL CONNECTION: IMPROVE YOURSELF	INDUSTRY CONNECTION: BECOME A PROFESSIONAL	CLIENT CONNECTION: SERVE THE GUEST
THE SALON INDUSTRY	Reach your goals in a dynamic, growing field	Contribute to the future of the industry	Provide the services clients want and need
JOB SEARCH	Reward yourself with the job that fits your individual needs	Expand your future career opportunities	Deliver your best to clients when you're in the right job environment
PROFESSIONAL RELATIONSHIPS	Connect with others for emotional balance and financial growth	Build a network for mutual support	Promote client confidence in a harmonious, team environment
SALON OWNERSHIP	See the salon from the owner's perspective	Understand the risks and rewards of owning a salon	Attract clients to a smoothly operating business
SALON RETAILING	Develop the ability to sell with ease	Improve your overall value to the salon	Recommend products that increase client satisfaction

IN OTHER WORDS

Selecting the right salon environment for you to work in and understanding the basics of how the salon business operates set a strong foundation for achieving your professional goals.

LESSONS LEARNED

- Establishing short- and long-range goals and following a plan to achieve those goals support the professional in reaching clear-cut levels of achievement.

- Evaluating the advantages and disadvantages of working at a particular salon is a prerequisite to accepting a job offer.

- The ability to develop meaningful relationships with the general public and professionals at all levels of the industry is a necessity for career success.

- Knowing the principles of salon ownership operations allows a professional to work productively with employers or to eventually own a salon.

- Recommending products to clients and teaching them how to use those products to achieve their desired image will help grow a loyal, appreciative client base.

07

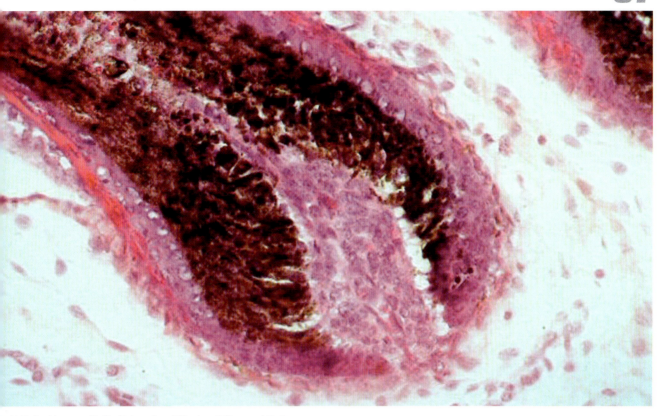

David B. Fankhauser, Ph.D.; University of Cincinnati Clermont College

TRICHOLOGY

7.1 HAIR THEORY
   HAIR BULB FORMATION
   HAIR GROWTH
   HAIR STRUCTURE AND BEHAVIOR
   NATURAL HAIR COLOR

7.2 HAIR CARE
   HAIR EVALUATION
   COMMON HAIR CONDITIONS
   COMMON SCALP CONDITIONS
   HAIR LOSS

7.3 DRAPING, SHAMPOOING AND SCALP MASSAGE
   DRAPING THEORY
   SHAMPOOING AND CONDITIONING THEORY
   SCALP MASSAGE THEORY
   DRAPING, SHAMPOOING AND SCALP MASSAGE ESSENTIALS
   INFECTION CONTROL AND SAFETY
   BASIC DRAPING, SHAMPOOING AND CONDITIONING
   BASIC SCALP MASSAGE

AWARENESS OF
HAIR'S GROWTH
AND STRUCTURE
AND OF COMMON
HAIR AND SCALP
CONDITIONS IS
THE FOUNDATION
FOR ATTENTIVE AND
SKILLFUL CLIENT
CARE SERVICES

FOLLOWING THIS LESSON
YOU WILL BE ABLE TO:

Define the theory of hair, including formation, growth, structure, behavior and color

Recognize how to care for the hair by doing an evaluation for common hair and scalp conditions, including hair loss

Explain and demonstrate proper draping, shampooing and scalp massage services

CONNECTING THEORY TO REAL-WORLD PRACTICE

ENGAGING YOURSELF IN THE STUDY OF HAIR WILL HELP YOU:

PERSONAL CONNECTION:	**INDUSTRY CONNECTION:**	**CLIENT CONNECTION:**
IMPROVE YOURSELF	BECOME A PROFESSIONAL	SERVE THE GUEST
Enhance your individual style by maintaining healthy hair and scalp	Demonstrate respect and commitment to the profession by attaining in-depth knowledge of hair	Educate clients about the condition of their hair and scalp to improve their appearance and general well-being

For your clients, nothing equals the security of being able to put themselves in the hands of a caring and competent salon professional. This sense of security unfolds during the opening, preparatory parts of the service, which include evaluating the condition of the client's hair and scalp and then draping, shampooing and conditioning, and massaging the scalp. Applying trichology, the study of hair, to these opening services is an important element in creating client peace of mind.

7.1 HAIR THEORY

The main purposes of hair are adornment and protection from heat, cold and injury. The technical name for the study of hair is trichology.

Living matter. What does it mean to say that something is alive? By definition, to say that matter has life means that it grows, it can reproduce, and it responds to stimulation. That is, it can act. It can react.

Is hair alive? Even though hair is primarily protein and protein is the basis for all living matter, **only the cells of the hair bulb are alive. The hair *fiber* or *strand* itself is not alive.**

HAIR BULB FORMATION

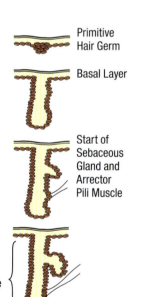

To understand more about hair, you need to know how the hair bulb is formed. In fetal life, **the hair follicle forms from a cluster of cells in the upper layer of skin**, technically referred to as the *basal layer* of the *epidermis*. This cluster of cells, called the *primitive hair germ,* needs nourishment to grow into a fully developed hair follicle. To get nourishment, it works its way down into the lower (dermal) layer of the skin. As it does, the cell cluster pulls the upper layer down with it, creating **a follicle or tube-like "pocket" called the root sheath, out of which the hair will grow.** At the base of the hair follicle is a large structure called the *papilla*.

The shape of this follicle will determine the shape (round, oval, elliptical, etc.) of the hair shaft as it grows from the follicle. Since the hair shaft actually grows out of the hair follicle, the diameter of the hair fiber will be the same as the diameter of the inside of the follicle.

In straight or wavy hair, hair follicles are more or less vertical to the surface of the scalp, with a slight "tilt." The angle of the hair follicle determines the natural flow or wave pattern of the hair. **The follicle in straight or wavy hair is typically round or oval.**

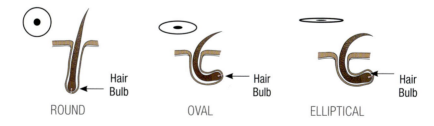

TWO PRIMARY PARTS OF HAIR
THE HAIR ROOT IS THE PORTION OF HAIR THAT IS INSIDE THE HAIR FOLLICLE UNDER THE SKIN'S SURFACE. THE HAIR FIBER, SOMETIMES REFERRED TO AS THE HAIR SHAFT OR STRAND, IS THE PORTION OF THE HAIR THAT EXTENDS ABOVE THE SKIN'S SURFACE.

In hair that is tightly curled, the hair follicles grow from the scalp at a much stronger angle. The follicle is almost parallel to the surface of the scalp. Furthermore, the hair bulb itself is nearly doubled back over the follicle in a growth shape resembling a golf club. **The hair follicle that produces a tightly curled hair has a flattened, elliptical shape.**

HAIR GROWTH

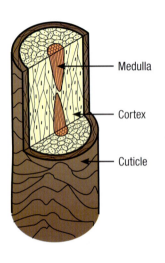

Hair pulled out from the roots will grow again unless the papilla (origin of hair) is destroyed.

As this primitive hair germ continues its growth downward into the dermis and joins a small number of dermal cells, these cells eventually become the dermal **papilla**. **The papilla is filled with capillaries (small blood vessels) that supply nourishment to the cells around it, called germinal matrix cells. The germinal matrix** is the area of the bulb where cell division (mitosis) takes place. These germinal matrix cells produce the cells that ultimately *keratinize (harden)* and form the three major layers of the hair:

1. **Cuticle** - the outer covering of the hair shaft made up of overlapping layers of transparent scales
2. **Cortex** - the second layer consisting of unique protein structures (gives hair most of its pigment and strength [elasticity])
3. **Medulla** - the central core of the hair shaft, also called the pith or marrow (often absent in fine or very fine hair)

Attached to the side of the root sheath are bulges. These bulges are the beginnings of the sebaceous glands. **The sebaceous, or oil, glands produce sebum (oil) and send it up through the hair follicles to the surface of the skin to prevent the hair and skin from becoming too dry. Sebum mixes with the body's perspiration to form the "acid mantle."** The acid mantle is important because it protects the cuticle, or outer covering, of the hair fiber and maintains the acid balance of hair and skin.

The arrector pili muscle comes from cells in the dermis that attach to the follicle just below the sebaceous gland. This is the muscle that causes the hair to stand on end when a **person is scared or cold.** It also aids in the secretion of sebum from the sebaceous glands. The other end of the arrector pili muscle attaches to the dermis (or lower layer) just beneath the basal layer of the epidermis.

CELLS FORM PARTS OF THE HAIR

As cells begin their journey upward through the hair follicle, they are separated into specific types. In other words, some cells will become cuticle scales, others will make up the cortex and others will have the particular formation of medulla cells.

The journey that began deep in the skin, then grew through the outer layers now becomes the visible hair fiber (shaft or strand). Another result of this process of traveling upward is keratinization. **Keratinization is a process whereby cells change their shape, dry out and form keratin protein.** Once keratinized, the cells that form the hair fiber or strand are no longer alive.

AMINO ACIDS = PROTEIN = HAIR

Hair is made up primarily of protein, which is made from the linking together of amino acids. The cortex of the hair is made of chains that take the shape of a helix or coil. These amino acid chains coil around each other and become protofibrils. Protofibrils then twist around each other to become microfibrils. Microfibrils follow the same process and become macrofibrils that also spiral together. This process, when complete, forms the cortex of the hair. The cortex is then covered with the cuticle scales, which also contain protein. **This twisting gives hair the ability to stretch like a spring without breaking.**

The prefix PROTO means first, the prefix MICRO means small and the prefix MACRO means large. Other examples would be prototype, microscope and macrobiotics.

STAGES OF HAIR GROWTH

Genes determine the growing stages of the hair. There are three stages of hair growth:

1. **The anagen or *active growing stage***, during which time each hair bulb has an attached root sheath. On the average 90 percent of a person's hair is in this stage which lasts from 2 to 6 years. Hair color is darker during the anagen stage.
2. **The catagen, a *brief transitional stage,*** when all cell division stops. This stage lasts only a few weeks.
3. **The telogen or *resting stage,*** when each hair bulb has no attached root sheath. At this time the hair falls out. On the average 10 to 15 percent of hair is in the resting stage, which generally lasts 3 to 4 months. Eventually, cell division is again stimulated, producing new hair, and the growth cycle starts again.

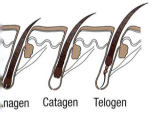

In humans, a mosaic pattern of hair growth occurs because each hair follicle has its own unique growing cycle. **Illness and lack of necessary vitamins and minerals can also affect hair and hair growth.** In fact, anything that alters the physiological state of the body can affect the hair follicle and hair growth.

In humans, the average rate of hair growth is ½" (1.25 cm) per month.

ANAGEN

CATAGEN

TELOGEN

Contrary to an old myth, hair does not grow after death of a human body. Hair never grows on palms, soles of feet, lips and eyelids.

Disease and medication can also affect hair growth by either stimulating the onset of the telogen phase or by causing the production of abnormal, brittle hairs. If a person has been ill or taking any medication, chemical services can damage hair that may be weak already.

Eyebrows and eyelashes are replaced every 4 to 5 months. Eyelashes are technically called cilia. Supercilia is the technical name for the hair of the eyebrows. Capilli is the technical name for the hair of the head.

HAIR STRUCTURE AND BEHAVIOR

There are three factors that affect the behavior of hair.
1. The first factor is *heredity*. The genes that people inherit from their parents will determine many things about the makeup of the hair, such as its color, shape and diameter.
2. The second factor is the *environment* or weather. If it's rainy or humid, hair will absorb moisture from the air. This extra moisture will alter some of the bonds that give hair its shape and, depending on the type of hair, it may become either limp or frizzy. On the other hand, wind may dry out the hair and sun may damage it. Both of these weather conditions, usually wet or dry, can cause a need for products that either take excess moisture out of the hair or put more moisture back in.
3. The third factor is the *products* or *appliances* used on the hair. For example, shampoos, conditioners, hair dryers, curling irons, perms, relaxers and hair color all affect the structural organization of the hair.

To better understand the differences in peoples' hair, you will need to take a closer look at hair's structural organization. The following series of slides taken of hair magnified hundreds of times show differences in the diameter of hair.

FINE　　　　　　　　　　MEDIUM　　　　　　　　　　COARSE

In the next series, observe the difference between Caucasian hair, Asian hair and Afro-centric hair. Notice that the structural organization of hair as shown by diameter and amount of pigment is very different among the three races. Keep in mind that diameter and amount of pigment may vary within each race as well.

CAUCASIAN　　　　　　　ASIAN　　　　　　　AFRO-CENTRIC

RATIO OF CUTICLE TO CORTEX

One result of genetic coding is the diameter of the hair shaft. In the picture on the left, notice the cuticle of a cross-sectional view of fine hair. Next, notice the picture of coarse hair.

As you've already seen, the cuticle is the protective part of the hair shaft and is made up of a harder protein than the cortex. If the hair is fine, treatments will affect it differently than if it's coarse. Examples include how well the hair holds a set and how the hair takes a perm or relaxer. It's an exaggeration to say that fine hair is "all cuticle," but that is often how it behaves. In cross section, up to 40% of fine hair can be cuticle, compared with 10% or 12% in coarse hair. The diameter of coarse hair is much larger than fine hair.

The cuticle is a hard, resistant layer of protein compared with the soft, elastic quality of the cortex. If a particular hair is 90% cortex and 10% cuticle, then that hair behaves like the cortex. That means it has more elasticity and ability to be molded and reshaped. But if the cuticle (which is harder or firmer and not easily stretched) makes up 40% of the hair fiber, then that hair will behave more like the cuticle and be more resistant to perms, relaxers or holding a set.

FINE HAIR　　　　　　　COARSE HAIR

NATURAL HAIR COLOR

One of the most fascinating aspects of hair is how it gets its color. Many people know that a pigment (coloring matter) called chlorophyll gives plants their green color. Most people don't know that a pigment called **melanin** gives skin and hair their color. In the hair, melanin is found mainly in the cortex, the hair strand's second layer. Here is how the natural coloring process works:

1. Melanin is produced by melanocytes, cells that exist among the dividing cells within the hair bulb.
2. Melanocytes rest near the hair bulb's nourishment center, the dermal papilla, and form bundles of a pigment protein complex called melanosomes.
3. Genes in the human body determine the amount and type of melanin produced by the melanocytes.

In simple terms, melanocytes produce melanosomes which contain the pigment melanin.

There are two types of melanin that create the large variety of hair colors, eumelanin and pheomelanin. **Eumelanin** is brown/black in color and **pheomelanin** is red/yellow in color. It is the amount, size and distribution of one or both of these melanins that influence the resulting hair color.

EUMELANIN
Brown/Black

PHEOMELANIN
Red/Yellow

If the amount of pheomelanin is very concentrated and near the cuticle layer, the hair color will appear more red. People with very dark, black hair may even have melanin in the cuticle layer, while lighter hair has melanin only in the cortex. **When there is a total lack of pigmentation in the hair and skin, the resulting condition is called albinism. A person with this condition is called an albino.**

Gray hair is caused by reduced color pigment, melanin, in the cortex layer of the hair. Gray hair is sometimes referred to as mottled hair, indicating white spots scattered about in the hair shafts. Gray hair grows from the papilla with the gray color, not as some might believe, turning gray after it has protruded above the skin. The natural aging process in humans is the cause of graying hair. However, some serious illnesses or emotional conditions may cause the hair to turn gray. A hereditary condition occurring at birth may cause some to gray prematurely. This is usually a defect in pigment formation.

07

MELANIN IN THE SKIN

Melanin in both the skin and hair serves as protection from the sun's damaging rays. For instance, if skin is exposed to sunlight, more melanin is created and sent to the surface to protect these sensitive cells, resulting in more color, or what is commonly called a "suntan." Although skin color is passed on through the genes, races that originated closer to the equator developed a higher content of melanin in their skin to better protect it against the sun. The same is true for hair. For example, white hair, which lacks melanin, is at the greatest risk for sun damage and can turn yellow from too much exposure. Therefore, you should recommend products with sunscreen and encourage your clients to wear hats when they anticipate spending extended periods of time in the sun.

7.2 HAIR CARE

Each person you'll work with is unique. The condition of each person's hair will differ, at least slightly, from any other you may have seen before. Sometimes those differences will be dramatic. Hair in poor condition will not hold a style or show off your design talent. Before you pick up shears or a comb, you will need to evaluate your client's hair.

HAIR EVALUATION

Hair is a fiber, and like all natural fibers, hair has different characteristics. Becoming familiar with your clients' hair prior to any service will allow you to support their individual hair needs.

1. **Determine your client's hair type and density**
   Knowing whether your client's hair type is fine, medium or coarse tells you what it can and cannot do on its own. You will usually determine your client's hair type by touch and visual examination. **The degree of coarseness or fineness in the hair fiber is referred to as texture.** The texture of coarse hair has the feel of wool, medium hair, the feel of cotton, and fine hair, the feel of silk. Other terms used to describe the feel of the hair include rough, wiry or soft. Once you know that, you're on your way to determining the particular cleansing and conditioning products that will best meet the hair's needs.

   Visual examination will give you a lot of clues. You can usually see whether the hair is dry or oily but, when you suspect it's been chemically altered, confirm this with your client. Ask the client, "Is your hair currently permed or tinted? Relaxed?" These are key questions to determine which cleansing and conditioning products will work best.

   A damaged or rough cuticle can cause hair to snag, look dull or be hard to manage. You can test for cuticle damage by running your thumb and finger along a strand of hair against the direction of growth. The more "drag" you feel, the more damage you can assume. Additional visual examination would include determining hair density. **The density of the hair is judged by the number of active hair follicles per square inch on the scalp.** For instance, a person with a thick head of hair will have many more active hair follicles than a person with thin hair. Density is usually referred to as light, medium or heavy (sometimes as thin, medium or thick). Density of the hair influences the amount of hair that should be parted and wrapped around a perm tool, roller or curling iron. Heavy density requires smaller subsections than light hair to allow for absorption of styling and processing lotions. In addition, placing too much hair on a perm tool or roller weakens the expected curl. Larger subsections can be used for light density hair.

2. Determine your client's hair condition
   Once you know the type of hair fiber with which you will be working, you need to know the condition of that fiber. The condition of the hair is usually determined by two key factors:

   a. **Hair porosity, the ability of the hair to absorb moisture, liquids or chemicals.** Raised cuticles influence the amount of liquid that can penetrate the hair. *Resistant porosity* describes hair that is able to absorb the least amount of moisture, usually due to the closeness of the cuticle layers. Resistant porosity is also called "poor porosity." *Average porosity* describes hair with the normal ability to absorb moisture. Such hair is in good condition, suitable for most services. *Extreme porosity* describes hair that is damaged from chemical services, such as overprocessing or the environment. Hair with extreme porosity is not in good condition and would require treatments prior to chemical services. Uneven porosity is a combination of two or more different porosities.

   b. **Hair elasticity, the ability of hair to stretch and return to its original shape without breaking.** Elasticity is also referred to as resiliency. Additional descriptive words to use when discussing elasticity with your client include pliability, buoyancy and springiness. Hair with normal elasticity is lively, able to spring back and usually has a shiny appearance. **Normal dry hair is capable of being stretched about $\frac{1}{5}$ (20%) of its length. Wet hair is able to be stretched 40% to 50% of its length.**

TEST FOR STRUCTURAL STRENGTH

While visual examination for elasticity is not absolutely accurate, it can tell you a great deal. Just by looking at the hair and handling it, you'll make judgments about what it needs. You can also perform this test for elasticity. (Note that this test is intended for straight or wavy hair.)

- Remove a strand of hair from the side of the head above the ears.
- Hold it between your thumb and forefinger and, with your thumbnail and index finger of the other hand, run the distance of hair rapidly as you would curl a ribbon with scissors. This will create a series of small curls.
- Gently pull the hair taut for 10 seconds and release. If the hair completely, or almost completely, returns to the curl pattern, it is in good condition. If it returns only 50% or less, it is structurally weak and needs conditioning.

GOOD　　　　WEAK

3. Consider the effects of your climate

   Once you have thoroughly evaluated the fiber, it's important to consider the climate in which you live. Is your climate primarily dry or humid? Because the amount of moisture in the air governs the amount of moisture in the hair, predominant humidity makes a big difference in the way hair looks and feels and, thus, a difference in the shampoo and conditioners you'll use. In humid regions, where hair becomes heavy with moisture, curl retention is a challenge, and protein conditioning may be needed to balance the moisture intake. In dry climates, hair tends to be flyaway, so moisturizing and surface conditioning become very important to reduce static and soften the hair fiber.

The more information you can gain from the client, the easier it will be to achieve good results. You will want to give your client's hair whatever it needs to look, feel and behave beautifully, beginning with the right hair analysis and followed by proper shampooing and conditioning.

COMMON HAIR CONDITIONS

Each hair strand has about 7 to 12 layers of cuticle scales. The cuticle layers protect the inside of the strand, which is called the cortex.

In healthy hair, the scales should lie flat along the cortex. The acid mantle lubricates the outermost layer of the cuticle and reduces friction. **Friction, as in combing and brushing, is one way in which the cuticle can be damaged.**

During your professional analysis of the hair fiber, a number of observations will alert you to possible problems you might encounter as you service the client's hair:

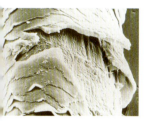

BROKEN HAIR

1. **Broken hair.** One of the most common causes of hair breakage is excessive stretching or traction. Hair subjected to excessive chemical processes, sun exposure and chlorine exposure may also exhibit breakage. The technical term for broken hair is **abraded hair**. One of the most common types of cuticle damage is called an **abraded cuticle. Abrasion can result from brushing or manipulating the hair while performing salon services, especially when it's still wet. Wet hair is more fragile than dry hair.** Rubber bands, tight hair clips and braids can actually break the cuticle. So can wrapping hair too tightly around a roller.

SPLIT ENDS

2. **Split ends.** The technical terms for split ends are fragilitis crinium (frah-JIL-I-tas KRI-nee-um), brittle hair or trichoptilosis (tri-kop-ti-LOH-sis). Split ends start as small cracks in the cuticle that deepen into the cortex. Eventually the hair is split entirely. Often there is no cuticle left in the region of a split and, if not cut off, the ends become frayed and unsightly. Split ends can be temporarily "sealed" by protein reconditioning. However, the process must be repeated frequently to keep the splits closed. In severe cases, it is advisable to cut off the split ends and reinforce the hair with a protein conditioner to prevent the freshly cut ends from splitting.

3. **Matting**. Excessive matting, called **pilica polonica** (**PIL**-i-ca **POL**-a-ni-ca), is characterized by a mass of hair strands tangled together in a mat that cannot be separated. The only remedy lies with a pair of shears. The cause of pilica polonica is usually excessive chemical hair lightening. In some cases, excessive friction can be the cause, as in repeated backcombing.

4. **Nodules**. Trichorrhexis nodosa (**TRIK**-o-rek-sis no-**DO**-sa), or knotted hair, **is characterized by the presence of lumps or swelling along the hair shaft**. These lumps are broken or partly broken places on the hair shaft. They can be caused by poorly performed chemical services, mechanical damage from curling irons or backcombing or by an inherited defect in the hair's keratin protein structure. Physical knotting of the hair (known as trichonodosis) results from friction of the scalp, as in vigorous towel drying or rubbing against a pillow.

5. **Canities** (ka-**NEESH**-eez). **Canities is the name given to grayness or whiteness of the hair.** Congenital canities occurs at or before birth primarily in albinos and occasionally in people with normal hair. Acquired canities refers to the loss of pigment in the hair as a person ages (graying of hair) or an onset may happen in early adult life. Causes of acquired canities may be extended illness, nervous strain or heredity.

6. **Ringed hair**. When alternating bands of gray and dark hair exist, the condition is referred to as ringed hair.

7. **Hypertrichosis** (hi-per-tri-**KOH**-sis) **describes an abnormal coverage of hair on areas of the body where normally only lanugo or babyfine hair appears. Hypertrichosis is also referred to as hirsuties (hur-sue-sheez) or superfluous hair.** Removal methods range from tweezing to electrolysis, depending on the amount of hair to be removed, location and client preference.

8. **Monilethrix** (mo-**NIL**-e-thriks). **Beads or nodes formed on the hair shaft is a condition referred to as monilethrix.** Breaks in the hair occur between the beads or nodes. Treatments may be given to improve the hair condition.

Mechanical damage results from the incorrect use of salon tools. Some brushes can pull the hair and stretch it until it breaks or they can wear down and loosen the cuticle cells. If a dryer is used too close to the hair or a hot curling iron is left on too long, the hair may become brittle and the cortex could possibly melt.

Usually, if the cortex is damaged, the cuticle has been damaged, too. However, sometimes the hair is damaged inside with only barely noticeable damage to the cuticle scales. Compare the picture of a normal cortex with the picture of the melted cortex. Other examples of heat styling damage include blistering and fracturing of the hair fiber due to improper heat-styling or use of low quality salon appliances.

NORMAL CORTEX

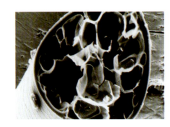
MELTED CORTEX

07

COMMON SCALP CONDITIONS

Listed below are the more common scalp disorders or diseases which you may come in contact with as a salon professional.

DISORDER OR DISEASE	MEDICAL TERM	DESCRIPTION	TREATMENT
Psoriasis *Disorder*	Psoriasis (soh-REYE-ah-sis)	Thick, crusty patches of red irritated scalp resulting from an autoimmune disease of the skin	Refer client to a physician
Dandruff *Disorder*	Pityriasis (pit-i-REYE-ah-sis)	Chronic scalp condition with excessive flaking, which accumulates on the scalp or falls to the shoulders, as well as itchiness, tightness and irritation of the scalp	Frequent shampooing with an anti-dandruff shampoo containing either pyrithione zinc, selenium disulfide or ketoconazole
Dry Dandruff *Disorder*	Pityriasis capitis simplex (kah-PEYE-tis SIM-pleks)	Dry flakes attached to the scalp or on the hair which can appear translucent	
Greasy or Waxy Dandruff *Disorder*	Pityriasis steatoides (ste-a-TOY-dez)	Oily flakes combine with sebum which stick to the scalp in clusters and can appear yellowish in color	

The leading cause of dandruff is a naturally occurring microscopic fungus called **Malassezia** (mal-uh-SEEZ-ee-uh). The fungus feeds on the scalp's natural oils and creates by-products that cause irritation on the scalp. The body reacts to the irritation by accelerating the amount and rate of flaking of dead skin cells.

EXTERNAL PARASITES

Be advised that the conditions listed on the chart below are contagious. Refer clients with these conditions to a physician before performing any salon services.

DISORDER OR DISEASE	MEDICAL TERM	DESCRIPTION	TREATMENT
Ringworm *Disease*	Tinea (TIN-ee-ah)	Red, circular patch of small blisters; caused by a vegetable parasite	Refer client to a physician
Ringworm of the Scalp *Disease*	Tinea capitis	Enlarged open hair follicles that are surrounded by clusters of red spots (papules); hair is likely to break in area infected; black spots may also be visible	Refer client to a physician
Honeycomb Ringworm *Disease*	Tinea favosa (fa-VO-sah) or **Favus** (FAY-vus)	Dry, yellow, encrusted areas on the scalp called scutula (SKUT-u-la); may have a peculiar odor; shiny pink or white scars may result	Refer client to a physician
Itch Mite *Disorder*	Scabies	Red and watery vesicles or pus-filled areas caused by an animal parasite (itch mite) burrowing under the skin	Refer client to a physician
Head Lice *Disorder*	Pediculosis capitis (pe-dik-u-LOH-sis)	Infestation of head lice on the scalp causing itching and eventual infection	Refer client to a physician

HAIR LOSS

As a salon professional, you are often the first person asked to to respond to questions about hair loss. So knowing how to adequately address client concerns will greatly affect your client's well-being.

NUMBER OF HAIRS ON HEAD

Red = 90,000   Brown = 110,000
Black = 108,000 Blond = 140,000
There is an average of 1,000 hairs to a square inch on the average head.

NORMAL HAIR LOSS

Hair actually covers most of your body before you are born. **Lanugo** is the term assigned to this baby fine, silky hair, which is shed shortly after birth. Lanugo is replaced with vellus, which covers most of the body including the head, and is often not visible to the naked eye. **Vellus** is short, fine, non-pigmented hair found more abundantly on women. Certain follicles are predetermined to produce long, thick pigmented hair, like normal scalp and eyebrow hair. This hair is referred to as terminal hair and replaces vellus hair around the time of puberty.

Everyone loses some hair every day. **Actually between 40 and 100 strands of hair is the average daily hair loss.** That's not as much as it sounds, considering that the average head has about 100,000 individual strands of hair.

ANDROGENETIC HAIR LOSS

Alopecia, or excessive hair loss, may be caused by a fungal or bacterial infection or inflammatory disease of the scalp. This abnormal condition occurs in both men and women If the scalp appears abnormal at all, do not attempt any services. Instead suggest that your client see a dermatologist. When there is no apparent scalp abnormality, hair loss may be caused by nutritional deficiency, drugs, emotional trauma and other physiological changes.

The most common form of alopecia is **androgenetic alopecia,** a combination of heredity, hormones and age that causes progressive shrinking, or miniaturization, of certain scalp follicles. This shrinking causes a shortening of the hair's growing cycle. Over time, as the active growth phase (anagen) becomes shorter, the resting phase (telogen) becomes longer. Eventually, there is no growth at all.

RECOGNIZING ANDROGENETIC ALOPECIA

In general, asking questions about family history will give a good indication of whether the hair loss is androgenetic or another type of alopecia. Ask your client if any relatives, including parents or more distant relatives, have hair loss, whether thinning has been gradual over several years or sudden or patchy. If the hair loss was sudden or patchy, advise your client to talk to a physician. If your client is a woman, ask her about crash diets, oral contraceptives and medications for certain cardiovascular conditions, vitamin deficiencies, and thyroid disorders to rule out hair loss created by these factors.

Because hair length and thickness are determined by how long the hair is allowed to grow before entering the next resting and shedding phase, the hair-loss process is thus a gradual conversion of terminal hair follicles to vellus-like follicles.

The net result is an increasing number of short, thin hairs that are barely visible above the scalp surface, and eventually no more hair is produced out of these follicles. In addition, more follicles are in the resting phase at the same time. Consequently, there is less scalp coverage.

PROGRESSIVE MINIATURIZATION OF THE HAIR FOLLICLE

Despite the dramatic reduction in follicle size with androgenetic alopecia, the follicle is not altered in structure nor does the number of follicles change.

In men, androgenetic alopecia is known as male-pattern baldness and frequently progresses to the familiar horseshoe-shaped fringe of hair. In women, it appears as a generalized thinning of the hair over the entire crown of the head. A significant difference between the genders is that most women exhibit scattered hair thinning. It is extremely rare for a woman to "go bald." **Alopecia prematura**, refers to baldness that occurs early in life, beginning as early as late adolescence.

Women with androgenetic alopecia usually first notice a gradual thinning of their hair, mostly on top of their heads as their scalp becomes more visible. Over time, the hair on the sides may also become thinner. Women retain their frontal hairline, which may be straight or "M"-shaped.

In the area where the scalp shows the most, look for a large number of miniaturized follicles that are producing shorter, thinner, fewer hairs than the long ones. Hold an index card near the scalp to help you see the miniaturized hairs. If you see a lot of miniaturized hairs, your client has androgenetic alopecia.

In addition to identifying miniaturized hairs by holding an index card close to the scalp, in the case of female clients, you may:

1. Part the hair in the middle of the scalp and look at the width of the part. A part that shows more scalp than normal indicates hair loss (a part on a normal head is very narrow).
2. Ask if the diameter of the ponytail has become smaller over the years (if applicable). A smaller diameter is one of the signs of androgenetic alopecia.
3. Ask your client if there are many hairs left on the brush after brushing once or if there are many hairs in the shower drain after shampooing. Check if your client has excessive shedding by simply running your hand through her hair. In general, anyone who has unusual, excessive shedding should see a doctor.

In the case of men, ask the client if the size of the bald spot has progressively increased over the years. In frontal balding, ask if the hairline has been progressively receding. With male clients, it is important to evaluate pattern separately from density because a man with a small pattern but a poor density may not respond to treatment as well as a man with a large area of hair loss and a fair density.

The degree of hair loss can be evaluated by rating pattern and density:

- Pattern refers to the shape and location of the area with hair loss.
- Density refers to how much hair is covering the scalp in the area of hair loss.

NOTE
Because women experience a single pattern of hair loss, only density needs to be evaluated.

DEGREES OF MALE-PATTERN BALDNESS

NORMAL

FRONT HAIRLINE

HAIRLINE/CROWN

Hair loss is identified according to various measurement systems. Each system identifies the pattern and density of the hair loss. Pattern refers to the shape and location of the hair loss, while density refers to how much hair covers the scalp in the area of the hair loss. These types of illustrations are often labeled so you can record and track your client's hair loss from one visit to another.

OTHER TYPES OF HAIR LOSS
POSTPARTUM ALOPECIA

Some women experience a "loss of hair" after having a baby. This temporary hair loss at the conclusion of pregnancy is called postpartum alopecia. The cause of this phenomenon is simple. During pregnancy, hair stays longer in the anagen cycle. Then, after childbirth, these hairs enter the telogen phase. Many women become concerned about this "sudden" loss of hair. But, actually, loss of hair is the result of the body's hormonal balance returning to its previous state. It isn't long until the amount of hair seems balanced again.

ALOPECIA AREATA

The National Alopecia Areata Foundation estimates that 6.5 million men, women and children suffer from alopecia areata.

Sudden loss of hair in round or irregular patches without display of an inflamed scalp is referred to as **alopecia areata.** This type of hair loss occurs in individuals who have no obvious skin disorder or serious disease. Alopecia areata is an autoimmune skin disease that is confined to a few areas and is often reversed in a few months, though recurrences may occur. A form of alopecia areata that presents itself as the total loss of hair on the scalp is alopecia areata totalis. The rarest form of alopecia areata is alopecia areata universalis, which presents itself as the loss of hair over the entire scalp and body.

TELOGEN EFFLUVIUM

Premature shedding of hair in the resting phase (telogen) can result from various causes such as childbirth, shock, drug intake, fever, etc. This premature shedding of hair during the resting phase is called **telogen effluvium.** Some women also experience sudden hair loss when they stop taking birth-control pills or if they follow a crash diet too low in protein. The hair loss is usually reversed once the condition is corrected.

TRACTION OR TRAUMATIC ALOPECIA

Hair loss due to repetitive traction on the hair by pulling or twisting is called **traction** or **traumatic alopecia.** Traction (excessive stretching or pulling) alopecia may be caused by wearing tight chignons or pony tails, tight rollers, tight corn rows or excessive tension during brushing and combing, especially when hair is wet. This hair loss is often caused by mechanical damage. However, it can also be caused by chemical damage, such as the excessive application of permanent wave solutions. This condition is usually reversed once the trauma has stopped.

HAIR LOSS TREATMENTS
TREATMENT OF ANDROGENETIC ALOPECIA

The Food and Drug Administration (FDA) has ruled that products claiming hair regrowth or hair loss prevention cannot be marketed without prior FDA review and approval.

Several products have been developed to treat androgenetic alopecia. If your client is working with a physician who has prescribed one of the treatments available to regrow hair and has requested assistance from you in applying product treatments, read and follow the manufacturer's directions.

Other hair loss treatments that your client might consider include:
1. FDA-approved products that regrow hair or prevent hair loss.
2. Products that provide an ideal environment for possible hair regrowth or loss prevention.

3. Surgical options are available mostly for men. Hair transplants, hair plugs and scalp reductions are performed by physicians or dermatologists. Several visits are necessary to achieve gradual results that allow periods of recuperation for the patient.
4. Wigs, toupees, hair additions or hair weaving are available as non-medical options. For additional information, refer to *Chapter 11, Wigs and Hair Additions*.
5. Cosmetic hair thickeners are products designed to volumize the hair. These products do not grow hair or put a halt to hair loss. They simply coat the hair, therefore giving it more body.

Hair loss today is often associated with cancer treatments. As a professional, it is important for you to know what resources are available to help your clients.

One of these resources, **Look Good... Feel Better (LGFB)** is a free, national, public-service program created from the concept that if a woman with cancer can be helped to look good, her improved self-esteem will help her approach her disease and treatment with greater confidence.

Look Good...Feel Better is offered through a national partnership of:
The Cosmetic, Toiletry, and Fragrance Association (CTFA) Foundation, a charitable organization established and supported by the trade association that represents the U.S. cosmetics industry. The CTFA Foundation provides makeup, materials and financial support (through the cosmetics industry).

The American Cancer Society (ACS), the nationwide, community-based, voluntary health organization dedicated to eliminating cancer as a major health problem. ACS administers the program nationwide and serves as the primary source of information to the public.

The National Cosmetology Association (NCA), a national organization of more than 45,000 hairstylists, wig experts, estheticians, makeup artists and nail technicians. NCA organizes and helps train the volunteer cosmetologists.

The three sponsoring partners work together to provide:
- Patient education, through group or individual sessions
- Free program materials, including videos and pamphlets
- Free makeup kits for patients in group workshops

For more information, go to: lookgoodfeelbetter.org or call 1.800.395.LOOK

7.3 DRAPING, SHAMPOOING AND SCALP MASSAGE

Draping, shampooing and scalp massage are quite often the first service contacts you have with a client in the salon. Making this contact a delightful, memorable service experience can have enormous impact on building client loyalty to you and the salon.

The safety, comfort and protection of the client's skin, hair and clothing are all part of the salon professional's responsibility and important considerations for overall client satisfaction.

Proper maintenance of the hair and scalp begins with a hygiene practice that many of you perform each and every day, shampooing. **The purpose of shampooing is to cleanse the scalp and hair by removing dirt, oils and product build-up. The hair must be shampooed as often as necessary with a shampoo specifically designed for the type and condition of hair.** If the hair is not cleansed properly, an accumulation of oil and dirt can lead to scalp disorders. If the client has any infectious diseases or disorders, refer him or her to a physician and do not proceed with the service.

Massage is a scientific method of manipulating the body by rubbing, pinching, tapping, kneading or stroking with the hands, fingers or an instrument. Massage dates back to antiquity and was used for health, beauty and medical reasons. Many believed that massage had beneficial qualities such as improving blood circulation, relieving headaches, reducing fat, diminishing fatigue, inducing sleep and preventing disease. Today, massage is not only a service in itself, but is included in other services such as shampooing, manicures and facials. This section of your chapter will focus on scalp massage offered alone or during a shampoo service. Your review of draping, shampooing and massage will begin with the important area of proper draping procedures.

DRAPING THEORY

Draping is performed prior to hair care services, such as shampooing and scalp massage, to protect the client's skin and clothing. Prior to draping, ask the client to remove any jewelry (necklace, earrings, hair pins and eyeglasses) and store it in a safe place. For your protection and the protection of others in the service area, ensure that jewelry and other valuables, such as purses, are stored in a safe place and are not blocking traffic areas, where they could cause an accidental fall or injury.

In ancient times, many people believed that their heads were protected by the gods or spirits and that shampooing might injure these spirits. Shampooing the hair became a ceremonial practice performed once a year in honor of a god's or goddess' birthday.

Many regulating agencies require that shampoo capes used to drape the client during salon services must be laundered in a solution capable of disinfecting the cape. Guidelines to protect the client also include making sure that the neck of the cape does not come in direct contact with the client's skin. Therefore, always use a neck strip and/or towel between the client's neck and the neckband of the cape.

GUIDELINES TO DETERMINE PROPER PROCEDURES FOR DRAPING

TOWEL
- In general, a towel and plastic or waterproof cape is used for shampooing, wet hair sculpting and designing, and chemical services.

PLASTIC CAPE
- The plastic cape protects the client and the client's clothing from becoming wet or damaged during the services mentioned above.

NECK STRIP
- A neck strip is usually used to replace a towel following a shampoo service if a hair sculpting service is going to be performed next. The neck strip is less bulky and will allow the hair to fall naturally. The neck strip is also used during dry hair sculpting to help prevent loose hairs from embedding into the client's clothing.

CAPE
- A cloth cape is usually used for designing and sculpting services on dry hair. The cloth cape is lighter weight and therefore more comfortable for the client and allows dry hair to slide to the floor more easily.

SHAMPOOING AND CONDITIONING THEORY

The shampoo service is performed prior to most hair services except certain hair color or chemical straightening services. Since most hair colors are applied to dry hair, the hair is not shampooed unless it is extremely oily or dirty. However, in some instances color products require that color be applied to towel-dried hair, following a shampoo service. Always read manufacturer's directions to be sure. For example, shampooing is not performed prior to chemical relaxing services since it could cause increased irritation, a burning sensation or actual burning once the chemical product is applied to the hair.

Understanding the pH (potential Hydrogen) level of shampoos and conditioners will help you make the right selection for each hair type and condition. **For instance, shampoos with a high pH level can make the hair dry and brittle, so for dry brittle hair, an acid-balanced shampoo would be recommended.** Shampoos and conditioners are reviewed more in depth in *Chapter 5, Chemistry*.

WATER

Water (H_2O) is classified as soft or hard. **Soft water is generally preferred for shampooing. Soft water is rain water or water that has been chemically treated. Hard water contains minerals and does not allow the shampoo to lather freely. However, it can be softened by a chemical water softening process.** Knowing which type of water you are working with in the salon will enable you to make the proper choice of shampoo. For more information on water, refer to "The Role of Water" on page 122 in *Chapter 5, Chemistry*.

You always need to remember to **monitor the temperature of the water before applying the water stream to your client's scalp** and during the rinsing portion of the service. This can be done by holding the shampoo hose and positioning a finger in the water stream. In addition, make sure the amount of water pressure is moderate and not so forceful that it is uncomfortable for your client. Excess water pressure is a primary cause of water-spill accidents.

Sometimes water may be present on the floor in the shampoo area. **Always wipe up any water-spill areas to prevent accidents that may occur if someone slips when crossing a wet traffic area in the school or salon.**

BRUSHING AND COMBING

Prior to the shampoo service, the hair should be brushed to remove tangles from the hair. Brushing also stimulates blood circulation to the scalp while removing dust, dirt and product build-up from the hair. Combing with a large-tooth comb or plastic brush with wide spacing is generally performed after a shampoo service to remove tangles from wet hair.

Usually brushes made from natural bristles are recommended, since they have many overlaying bristles that aid in cleaning the hair better than nylon bristles. **Keep in mind that brushing the hair prior to a chemical service or if any cuts or abrasions are evident is not recommended.** Since there are different ways to brush the hair, consider the following factors: Does the hair have extreme product build-up that makes it difficult to part the hair prior to brushing? Is the hair long or short? Is the hair naturally straight or curly? Under all circumstances, **you should begin brushing the hair from the ends first, then work toward the scalp.**

This will allow you to detangle the hair without adding additional stress or more tangles to the hair. Once the hair is free of tangles you can brush the hair thoroughly from the scalp to the ends.

REMOVING TANGLES FROM WET HAIR

After the shampoo, tangles should be removed in a specific, methodical manner:

- Always start at the lowest point of the tangled area, in this photo, the nape section. While lifting the weight of the tangled hair, release a section of hair with a large-tooth comb. Starting at the ends of the hair and progressing toward the scalp, comb downward through the hair. You may wish to hold the hair at the base to minimize discomfort while detangling. Keep in mind that chemically treated hair tends to tangle more easily than normal hair.
- Continue combing this section until all tangles are removed. To remove stubborn tangles, use short, gentle strokes.
- Part off another section immediately above the first section.
- Remove tangles in the same manner as before, starting at the ends. Comb through these two untangled sections and blend the hair together.
- Continue this procedure throughout the crown, sides and finally the top section.

In addition to knowing the importance of proper draping and shampooing, it will be key for you to understand the theory behind scalp massage and the relaxing and/or stimulating effects caused by this beneficial component of your client's shampoo experience.

SCALP MASSAGE THEORY

Scalp massage involves manipulations performed on the scalp to relax the muscles and stimulate blood circulation. Scalp treatments combine the benefit of massage with the use of products designed to improve the condition of the scalp. The relaxation experienced by the client during scalp massage is a "value-added" benefit that helps build client loyalty.

Although products such as essential oils, lotions or creams used in scalp treatments provide a specific benefit, these products may leave a residue on the hair. Plus the stimulation from the massage may cause scalp sensitivity for the client. For these reasons, you should avoid performing a scalp treatment immediately prior to a chemical service. Be guided by the condition of the client's hair and scalp, as well as manufacturer's directions.

When massaging the scalp, it is important to:

- Establish a soothing or stimulating "rhythm" when performing the manipulations.
- Maintain contact with the client throughout the manipulations to maintain a relaxing or stimulating experience.
- Carry out manipulations with firm, controlled movements to maximize the full benefit of massage and gain your client's confidence.
- Keep your nails at a moderate length to avoid scratching the scalp.

Just as products vary, so will the manipulations you choose to use during the scalp massage. Customizing your own sequence of manipulations is another method you may use in creating client satisfaction and loyalty. Listed here are the basic massage manipulations and the effects they cause. As you review this area, be aware that effleurage, petrissage and tapotement are the three primary scalp manipulations, with petrissage being the most important. Petrissage stimulates the sebaceous glands, which produce natural oil (sebum). This oil is often lacking in the case of dry hair and scalp.

THE FIVE BASIC MANIPULATIONS OF MASSAGE

MANIPULATION	MOVEMENT	EFFECT
EFFLEURAGE (ef-**LOO**-rahzh)	Light, gliding strokes or circular motions made with the palms of the hands or pads of the fingertips; often used to begin and/or end a treatment; also used on the face, neck and arms	Relaxing, soothing
PETRISSAGE (**PAY**-tre-sahzh)	Light or heavy kneading and rolling of the muscles; performed by kneading muscles between the thumb and fingers or by pressing the palm of the hand firmly over the muscles, then grasping and squeezing with the heel of the hand and fingers; generally performed from the front of the head to the back; also used on the face, arms, shoulders and upper back	Deep stimulation of muscles, nerves and skin glands; promotes the circulation of blood and lymph
TAPOTEMENT (tah-**POHT**-mant) or Percussion or Hacking	Light tapping or slapping movement applied with the fingers or partly flexed fingers; also used on the arms, back and shoulders	Stimulates nerves, promotes muscle contraction; increases blood circulation
FRICTION (**FRIK**-shun)	Circular movement with no gliding used on the scalp or with a facial when less pressure is desired; applied with the fingertips or palms	Stimulates nerves; increases blood circulation
VIBRATION (vi-**BRAY**-shun)	Shaking movement; your arms shake as you touch the client with your fingertips or palms	Highly stimulating

DRAPING, SHAMPOOING AND SCALP MASSAGE ESSENTIALS

There are many types of shampoos available and designed for specific hair types and conditions. Shampoos are designed for dry, oily, normal, color-treated and gray hair to name but a few. As a salon professional, making the proper selection will allow you to achieve the desired results. For shampoo ingredients, refer to *Chapter 5, Chemistry*.

Hair conditioners and rinses are used on shampooed hair to condition, soften and make the hair tangle-free for ease in combing. They are also used to restore the hair to its normal pH and remove soap residue. There are liquid rinses, thick creams and leave-in conditioners all of which yield different effects. The liquid rinses and thick creams are applied and left in the hair anywhere from a few seconds to 10 minutes. The leave-in conditioners are left in the hair until the next shampoo. **Frequent use of cream rinses and conditioners can result in product build-up that can leave the hair dull and lifeless.** Clarifying shampoos are designed to remove this product build-up.

DRAPING, SHAMPOOING AND SCALP MASSAGE PRODUCTS

PRODUCT	FUNCTION
SHAMPOOS	
ALL-PURPOSE	Cleanse the hair without correcting any special condition
ACID-BALANCED (NON-STRIPPING)	Cleanse all hair types, especially lightened, color-treated or dry, brittle hair
PLAIN	Cleanse normal hair but not recommended for chemically treated or damaged hair
SOAPLESS	Cleanse hair with either soft or hard water
MEDICATED	Prescribed by the client's doctor to treat scalp and hair problems and disorders; note: medicated shampoos may affect color-treated hair
CLARIFYING	Remove residue such as product build-up
ANTI-DANDRUFF	Control dandruff and scalp conditions
LIQUID DRY	Cleanse the scalp and hair for clients who are unable to receive a normal shampoo; effective in cleaning wigs and hairpieces
POWDER DRY	Cleanse the hair of clients whose health prohibits them from receiving a wet shampoo service

PRODUCT	FUNCTION
SHAMPOOS (CONT'D)	
CONDITIONING	Improve the tensile strength and porosity of the hair
COLOR	Enhance color-treated hair and tone non-color-treated hair temporarily; available in a variety of colors
THINNING HAIR	Cleanse the hair without weighing it down
RINSES	
VINEGAR AND LEMON (ACID)	Keep the cuticle compact, remove soap scum, return the hair to its pH balance and counteract the alkalinity present after a chemical service
CREAM	Soften, add shine and smoothness to the hair while making the hair tangle-free for ease in combing
ANTI-DANDRUFF	Control dandruff and scalp conditions
ACID-BALANCED	Close the cuticle after a color service to prevent the color from fading
ACID	Remove soap scum
COLOR	Add temporary color to the hair, which lasts from shampoo to shampoo; for more information on color rinses, refer to nonoxidative colors in *Chapter 13, Color*
CONDITIONERS	
INSTANT	Coat the hair shaft and restore moisture to the hair
NORMALIZING	Close the cuticle after alkaline chemical services
BODY BUILDING	Displace excess moisture, providing more body to the hair; made from protein
MOISTURIZING	Add moisture to dry, brittle hair
CUSTOMIZED	Moisturize and build body
SCALP TREATMENTS	
ESSENTIAL OILS	Provide invigorating, stimulating or soothing scents; allow fluid movement on the scalp
SCALP TONER	Adds a refreshing, stimulating feeling to the scalp; may have mild antiseptic properties and cleansing ability
MOISTURIZING AGENT	Replenishes or restores moisture to dry scalp; formulated as creams, oils or lotions

DRAPING, SHAMPOOING AND SCALP MASSAGE IMPLEMENTS AND SUPPLIES

IMPLEMENTS/SUPPLIES	FUNCTION
TOWELS	Protect the client's skin and clothing; also used to dry the hair
PLASTIC CLIENT CAPE	Protects the client and his/her clothing during wet and/or chemical hair services
CLOTH CLIENT CAPE	Protects the client and his/her clothing during dry hair sculpting or designing
NECK STRIP	Protects the client's skin
NATURAL-BRISTLE HAIR BRUSH	Increases blood circulation to the scalp, removes dirt, debris and product build-up from the hair prior to the shampoo service
ALL-PURPOSE COMB	Detangles and distributes the hair after the shampoo service
PLASTIC CAP	Covers hair to allow deeper penetration of conditioning treatment

DRAPING, SHAMPOOING AND SCALP MASSAGE EQUIPMENT

EQUIPMENT	FUNCTION
SHAMPOO CHAIR	Allows client to sit or lie down during the shampoo service
SHAMPOO BOWL	Holds and drains water and product during a shampoo service
SHAMPOO DISPENSARY	Displays shampoos and conditioners
TOWEL SHELVES OR CABINET	Store towels

INFECTION CONTROL AND SAFETY

Infection control and safety are essential while performing draping, shampooing and scalp massage services in order to protect the health and well-being of you and your client.

1. Do not brush the hair prior to a chemical service. If any cuts or abrasions are evident, a chemical service should not be recommended.
2. If shampoo gets into the client's eye, rinse immediately with tepid water. An eye wash cup (a cup that is held over the eye and is used to flush the eye with water) is recommended. If irritation persists, recommend that the client see a physician.
3. Disinfect shampoo bowl and implements as required by your regulating agency.
4. Discard contaminated and non-reusable materials (neck strip, cotton, etc.)
5. Wipe up any water-spill areas immediately.
6. Always test the temperature of the water prior to applying the water stream to your client's scalp. Continue to monitor the water temperature during rinsing by keeping one finger under the nozzle.
7. Ensure that the amount of water pressure is moderate to strong and not so forceful that it is uncomfortable for your client. Excess water pressure is a primary cause of water-spill accidents.
8. Decrease pressure during massage manipulations if client expresses sensitivity.
9. Keep the back of the cape on the outside of the chair during the shampoo service to prevent the water from running down the client's back and dampening the clothes.
10. Remember to detangle the hair thoroughly prior to and after the shampoo service.
11. Wash your hands with liquid soap prior to the shampoo service.
12. Avoid giving a scalp massage:
    - When scalp abrasions or a serious scalp disorder are/is present
    - Immediately prior to the application of a chemical service, such as perming, relaxing, lightening or coloring
    - When the client has a history of high blood pressure or a heart condition; ask client to consult with physician before proceeding, since scalp massage may increase the circulation of the blood.
13. Wear gloves if required during a shampoo or scalp massage service; check with your area's regulating agency for guidelines.

CAPE OUTSIDE CHAIR

WORKSHOP 01
BASIC DRAPING, SHAMPOOING AND CONDITIONING

Draping, shampooing and conditioning preparation and procedures vary based on the timing allowed for the service and each client's needs. For example, you may find it necessary to use a booster chair when shampooing a young child or, in some cases, is recommended that elderly or disabled clients lean forward into the shampoo bowl rather than lean back for medical or comfort purposes. Clients in a wheelchair may need to remain in the wheelchair rather than transfer to the shampoo chair.

There are several types of shampoo bowls and chairs available. Some bowls allow you to stand behind the client, which helps reduce back fatigue. Other units may have a hydraulic control that allows you to adjust the height of the chair or move it into a reclining position.

WET HAIR SERVICE DRAPING, SHAMPOOING AND CONDITIONING PREPARATION

The following is a list of draping and shampooing materials that are required for a wet hair service. Draping and shampooing for chemical services will be reviewed in *Chapter 12, Texture*. Assemble the following materials prior to draping, shampooing and conditioning your client:

- Towels
- Plastic cape
- Booster chair (if applicable)
- Shampoo, rinse or conditioning products

It is assumed in this procedure that you are moving directly from draping to shampooing. If there is a time lapse between draping and shampooing, it will be necessary for you to wash your hands again with liquid soap prior to shampooing.

WET HAIR SERVICE DRAPING, SHAMPOOING AND CONDITIONING PROCEDURE

- Wash and sanitize hands
- Ask client to remove jewelry and glasses and secure in a safe place
- Clip client's hair out of the way (if applicable)
- Turn client's collar inward (if applicable)
- Place towel lengthwise over client's shoulders, cross ends in front
- Position plastic cape over towel and secure; remove clip(s) from client's hair (if applicable)
- Examine the client's hair and scalp
- Position cape over shampoo chair
- Brush the hair
- Test the temperature and pressure of the water
- Wet the hair
- Apply shampoo
- Perform scalp massage manipulations
- Rinse thoroughly
- Repeat shampoo and rinse procedures if necessary
- Apply rinse or conditioner
- Rinse thoroughly
- Towel dry client's hair
- Detangle the hair

07

WET HAIR SERVICE DRAPING, SHAMPOOING AND CONDITIONING—STANDING IN BACK

Wash and sanitize your hands. Ask client to remove jewelry and glasses and secure in a safe place. **Clip client's hair out of the way (if applicable)** with a simple twist and clip placement. Turn client's collar inward if applicable, making sure that you are taking precaution not to damage client's clothing. **Place towel lengthwise over client's shoulders, and cross ends in front** to secure the towel.

02 Position plastic cape over towel and secure. Be careful not to catch neck hair in the fastener. Fold towel outward over the neckband of the cape for protection. Adjust for client comfort.

03 Test the temperature and pressure of the water to be sure it is warm and comfortable for your client.

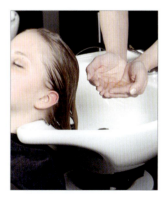

Wet your client's hair thoroughly. Ensure that the hair and scalp are saturated with water. Cup your hand over the front hairline, ears and nape to protect your client from becoming wet.

05-06 Apply shampoo into your palm first, then into the hair, and work into lather.

COSMETOLOGY FUNDAMENTALS 205

07-08 Perform scalp massage manipulations, starting at the front hairline. Use the cushions of your fingers, and circular or backward stroking (effleurage) manipulations. Maintain contact with the scalp and continue manipulations while you glide your hands gently toward the crown. Muscles affected during this time will be the frontalis (high on the forehead) and the aponeurosis (a-po-noo-RO-sis) (tendon connecting the frontalis and occipitalis). Repeat this and the following manipulations at least twice.

09 Glide back to the hairline and repeat the circular or backward stroking motion from the temporal area to the crown and then from in front of the ears to the crown. Maintain contact with the scalp while gliding.

10 Glide your hands behind the ear (auricular superior and posterior), and repeat effleurage manipulations up the back of the head (occipitalis). Use kneading (petrissage) movements at the nape area and work upward toward the crown, crossing over the occipitalis.

11 Massage the entire scalp area with attention to the hairline, crown and nape. Complete scalp massage manipulations. Remove excess shampoo.

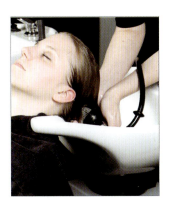

-13 Rinse thoroughly, protecting eyes, ears, etc., from spray and ampoo with your hand. When the spray is on, keep one finger curled er the edge of the nozzle so you can monitor any temperature changes he water. Also keep in mind that the pressure of the water from the zzle can range from a moderate to strong spray. Ensure that the spray strong enough to rinse all the shampoo from the hair. Rinse the entire alp area with additional attention at the nape. **Repeat the shampoo d rinse procedures if necessary**.

14 Apply rinse or conditioner. Work through the hair using gentle, stroking (effleurage) movements for 30 to 60 seconds. Follow manufacturer's directions for conditioning treatments that may need to be left on the hair for a longer period of time and may require a plastic cap and heat.

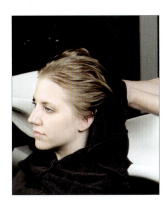

Rinse thoroughly, protecting nsitive areas from finishing rinse d/or water spray. Lift the hair d allow the water to run down e length of the strands. Squeeze cess water from the hair ends.

16 Towel-dry client's hair with a fresh towel. Wipe away any excess moisture from client's face.

17 Detangle the hair, beginning at the nape to avoid tangling the hair. Comb outward from the ends of the hair and work toward the scalp.

COSMETOLOGY FUNDAMENTALS

ALERT!

Never use firm massage manipulations when shampoo is to be followed by any kind of chemical service. In these instances, massage during shampoo should be very brief and very light. This light massage will help avoid the undesirable penetration of any chemicals into the skin, since deep massage can open pores into the dermis.

OPTIONAL NECK AND SHOULDER MASSAGE

Before detangling the hair after the shampoo procedure, you may wish to perform this additional massage treatment:

- Place fingers over muscles near shoulder joints.
- Begin a combination of effleurage and petrissage manipulations to bottom of neck.
- Move fingers up the outside of the neck, back down toward spine and back up and out to shoulder muscle joints.
- Repeat.

SHAMPOOING AND CONDITIONING – STANDING AT THE SIDE

Remember that shampooing and conditioning procedures basically remain the same, whether you are standing behind or at the side of your client. However, your body position will change and you may choose to include slightly varied scalp manipulations.

01 Wet your client's hair thoroughly. Protect your client's face, eyes and ears by positioning your hand along the hairline and cupping the ear. Monitor the water temperature with one finger positioned under the nozzle.

02 Perform scalp massage manipulations by using a circular motion with the cushions of your fingers from the front hairline to the crown. Perform petrissage manipulations with your thumbs.

3 Work from the center front
irline to the crown. Then return
 the front hairline, this time 1"
 5 cm) away from the center,
d repeat manipulations. Work
ward each side.

04 Lift and support the head. Work from side to side in the nape using a stroking movement.

05 Then use a scissoring movement throughout the entire head. Repeat a few times.

6-08 Rinse the hair thoroughly from the front hairline toward the crown and ends. Use one hand to lift and
pport the head. Cup your other hand over the nozzle and rinse to remove the shampoo at the nape. Use both
nds to gently squeeze remaining water from the hair.

COSMETOLOGY FUNDAMENTALS

LONG HAIR CONSIDERATIONS

Long hair requires special considerations during shampooing and conditioning. Lift longer lengths upward while rinsing to remove the hair from the shampoo suds that have accumulated in the bowl. Shampoo bowls designed for long hair have extended basins that allow the hair to fall naturally, which prevents the hair from becoming tangled.

WET HAIR SERVICE DRAPING, SHAMPOOING AND CONDITIONING COMPLETION

- Clean shampoo service area before continuing with client; disinfect comb and brush following the entire service.
- Ensure there is no water left standing in the shampoo service area.
- Discuss the products you used on your client and proceed to the next service.

WORKSHOP 02
BASIC SCALP MASSAGE

Basic scalp massage treatments involve scalp manipulations designed to relax your client's muscles and increase blood circulation. Treatments can vary according to the products and machines used. For instance, a dry scalp treatment may include a moisturizing scalp cream along with a scalp steamer or warm towels to help product penetration. Be sure to follow manufacturer's directions when using scalp treatment products.

BASIC SCALP MASSAGE PREPARATION
Assemble the following materials prior to providing a scalp massage service:
- Moisturizing agent, scalp toner or essential oils
- Towel
- Client Cap

BASIC SCALP MASSAGE PROCEDURE
- Wash and sanitize hands
- Drape client for a wet hair service
- Detangle hair
- Apply scalp product
- Perform effleurage scalp manipulations
- Perform petrissage scalp manipulations
- Perform effleurage scalp manipulations
- Perform tapotement
- Rotate the scalp
- Conclude scalp massage
- Shampoo client's hair
- Rinse hair
- Dry hair or move to next service

BASIC SCALP MASSAGE

01 Wash and sanitize your hands. Seat the client in a comfortable chair. Drape client for a wet hair service.

02 Detangle the hair. Apply **scalp product** according to the treatment being performed and according to manufacturer's directions.

03 Perform effleurage scalp manipulations. Stand behind your client and begin the stroking manipulations at the front hairline (frontalis), gliding at approximately 1" (2.5 cm) intervals to the nape area. Return to the front hairline and repeat until all areas are covered.

04 Perform petrissage scalp manipulations. Starting at the front hairline, massage with a kneading action in a circular motion. Keep your fingers and thumbs spread out and firmly pressed to the scalp as you massage. Release your hands from the scalp only as you move to another part of the scalp. Begin the movements at the front of the head and finish in the nape.

05-06 Perform effleurage scalp manipulations. Use lighter, circular manipulations as you move from the front hairline to the area above the ears at the crest (parietal) and then slowly returning to the top and repeating the manipulations. Cover the entire head. Then **perform tapotement**. Use the tips of your fingers and tap the scalp. Begin at the front hairline and work from side to side. Complete the tapotement technique at the nape. Customize your manipulations using a series of rotations with your thumbs, stroking movements with the palms of your hands or light strokes with the cushions of your fingers.

07-08 Use the palms of your hands and your fingers to **rotate the scalp** gently. Squeeze the head and release.

COSMETOLOGY FUNDAMENTALS 211

09-10 Conclude the scalp massage by using long, gentle effleurage strokes from the nape to the front hairline. Use a feather-like motion to remove hands from the scalp. Then use a light stroking motion from the front hairline to the nape. **Shampoo the client's hair** thoroughly, being careful to remove all scalp treatment product from the hair. **Rinse the hair** thoroughly and repeat shampoo and rinse if necessary. **Dry the hair or move on to the next service** scheduled for the client.

BASIC SCALP MASSAGE COMPLETION

- Offer to prebook your client's next visit. Discuss the next appropriate time to repeat this service based on the client's needs.
- Recommend appropriate retail products to your client.
- Clean your work area.

AROMATHERAPY FOR THE SCALP

The term aromatherapy is used to describe the combination of our sense of smell and the use of plant extracts and their healing abilities. "Aroma" refers to the natural fragrance of plants and "therapy" means "cure." The therapeutic effects of aromatherapy are incorporated into many salon services including scalp treatments.

Essential oils and scalp products containing vitamins and plant extracts address many health and wellness concerns. Therapeutic effects include invigorating the scalp, encouraging renewed hair growth, relieving flaking associated with dryness or dandruff, increasing blood flow circulation and calming and soothing the mind and body.

Aromatherapy expert, Dr. Blossom Kochhar from India, shared the following list of recommended essential oils she uses in her custom recipes for the scalp. Note that essential oils should not be used directly on the skin, but blended with a base oil such as sweet almond oil or grapeseed oil. When blending oils, follow the recommended usage chart shown below.

RECOMMENDED USAGE

Essential Oil
- 20 - 60 drops
- 7 - 25 drops
- 3 - 5 drops

Base Oil
- 3.5 fl oz (100ml)
- 1 fl oz (25ml)
- 1 tsp (5ml)

Pre-mixed scalp therapy oils, whether purchased from a manufacturer or mixed by you, can be applied directly to the scalp prior to manipulations. Essential oils can also be mixed with shampoo, which can then be applied to the scalp prior to the manipulations of a scalp treatment or incorporated into a shampoo service.

NORMAL HAIR AND SCALP
- Rosemary
- Chamomile

OILY HAIR AND SCALP
- Patchouli
- Cedarwood
- Clary Sage

DRY HAIR AND SCALP
- Ylang Ylang
- Sandalwood
- Lavender

OILY DANDRUFF
- Lemon
- Rosemary
- Cedarwood
- Thyme

ALOPECIA (HAIR LOSS)
- Sandalwood
- Bay
- Lavender
- Clary Sage
- Rosemary

Your understanding of the structure, growth and condition of the hair, along with your application of basic draping, shampooing and scalp massage techniques will serve as the foundation of your client's first contact with your skill level. Strive to display your best ability as you proudly offer your expertise. Remember how powerful your "touch" can be to the client. As you move through the service, ask how your client is doing. Be sensitive to your client's needs, making adjustments and recommendations for hair condition, water temperature and massage manipulations. You will soon be hearing these important words from your client, "I can't wait until my next visit!" or "My hair looks great when I leave, but I really come for the massage during the shampoo service!"

CONNECTING THEORY TO REAL-WORLD PRACTICE

TRICHOLOGY	PERSONAL CONNECTION: IMPROVE YOURSELF	INDUSTRY CONNECTION: BECOME A PROFESSIONAL	CLIENT CONNECTION: SERVE THE GUEST
HAIR THEORY	Expand your personal knowledge of your own hair and the medium you work in	Contribute to the development of salon procedures that require technical understanding	Help clients better understand and appreciate the growth, structure and behavior of their own hair
HAIR CARE	Gain confidence in recognizing and managing a broad range of hair and scalp conditions	Share a high level of expertise related to diseases and conditions of the hair and scalp	Identify hair and scalp problems and recommend effective treatments and courses of action
DRAPING, SHAMPOOING AND SCALP MASSAGE	Develop ease and competence in frequently used procedures	Demonstrate the attention to detail and client comfort that marks a true professional	Instill client trust, comfort and sense of security

IN OTHER WORDS

Clients will know they are in excellent hands when you demonstrate your knowledge of the hair and scalp in your preparatory client services.

LESSONS LEARNED

- The hair strand consists of three layers: the medulla, the cortex and the cuticle

- Two types of the pigment melanin give hair its variety of hair colors.

- Evaluating the texture, density, porosity and elasticity of clients' hair and determining if there are noteworthy hair or scalp conditions are done before beginning the client service.

- Proper draping is important to protect clients' skin and clothing.

- The shampooing and conditioning procedure is designed to ensure client comfort as well as to cleanse and prepare the hair for additional services.

- Scalp massage can both relax muscles to soothe the client and stimulate blood circulation to improve the condition of the hair and scalp.

08

DESIGN DECISIONS

- **8.1 DESIGN COMPOSITION**
  - SEE AND THINK AS A DESIGNER
  - DESIGN ELEMENTS
  - DESIGN PRINCIPLES
  - BALANCE
  - CREATE AND ADAPT AS A DESIGNER

- **8.2 DESIGN ADAPTABILITY**
  - PROPORTION
  - HAIR
  - CLOTHING
  - LIFESTYLE

- **8.3 CLIENT COMMUNICATION**
  - THE FOUR SERVICE ESSENTIALS
  - CONTRIBUTORS TO EFFECTIVE COMMUNICATION

CLIENT SATISFACTION
DEPENDS ON HAVING
A SYSTEM FOR MAKING
DESIGN DECISIONS THAT
LEAD TO THE CREATION
OF PERSONALIZED
HAIR DESIGNS

FOLLOWING THIS LESSON
YOU WILL BE ABLE TO:

Identify the design elements and design principles used to compose designs

Describe how hair designs can be adapted to complement different body and face shapes

Explain how each of the four Service Essentials supports effective client communication and decision-making

CONNECTING THEORY
TO REAL-WORLD PRACTICE
HAVING A DEFINED APPROACH FOR MAKING DESIGN DECISIONS WILL HELP YOU:

PERSONAL CONNECTION:	**INDUSTRY CONNECTION:**	**CLIENT CONNECTION:**
IMPROVE YOURSELF	BECOME A PROFESSIONAL	SERVE THE GUEST
Bring a true designer's point of view to everything you do	Elevate your career by using professional design standards in every client service	Guide clients through a process that results in the best design decisions for their unique needs

Some decisions are quick and easy, like what to eat for breakfast, and others are more difficult and require time and effort, like which career to pursue. When making decisions about the hair designs you will create for your clients, it's also true that some will come more easily than others. Having a system to rely on will give you the confidence to make decisions that will result in a great hair design for your client. Pivot Point's *A Designer's Approach* to hair design—seeing, thinking, creating and adapting as a designer—provides a foundation for decision-making that will help you excel at creating personalized designs that will lead to building a large and loyal clientele.

8.1 DESIGN COMPOSITION

Design is the arrangement of shapes, lines and ornamental effects to create an artistic whole. Design is all around you and impacts your life every day and in many ways. The way your furniture is designed will affect not only whether it is pleasing to look at, but also whether it is functional. The same holds true for fashion and architecture. This is why the profession you are learning is called "hair design"—because you will be arranging your clients' hair in ways that will be both functional and aesthetically pleasing.

Hair design is an art form, like sculpting, painting, architecture and fashion design, you have a lot in common with the designers and artists in these fields. To produce creative compositions, all of these professions require a medium to work with—your medium is hair—as well as specialized tools, training and skills. You will also need an understanding of design elements and design principles along with a healthy dose of inspiration.

Inspiration can come from many sources. It can come from nature, art, architecture, music, dance, movies, fashion, anything that you see, hear, taste, smell and touch, and your own imagination. You can be inspired by a line, a shape, a texture or a color, by a detail or by an overall impression.

As a hair designer, the more open you are to inspiration around you, the more creative you will be. Once inspired, your ability to see and think as a designer improves, enabling you to create personalized hair designs based on universal design elements and design principles.

THE FORM OF THE DANCE INSPIRES THE FORM OF THE ARCHITECTURE

Don Klumpp - Getty Images; Nederlanden Building in Prague, Czechoslovakia

COLOR PATTERNS IN NATURE INSPIRE HAIR COLOR DESIGNS

SEE AND THINK AS A DESIGNER

A big part of your satisfaction as a hair designer will come from creating functional and aesthetic hair designs for your clients. Training yourself to see and think as a designer will help you form a mental picture of the design you want to create, which includes the big picture as well as the specific details that are related to the design.

Seeing as a designer means observing the objects in the world around you and making connections among the different things you see. Thinking as a designer means analyzing what you see, visualizing a new design that you want to create, and organizing a plan that will enable you to actually create the design you have in mind. Without the ability to see and think as a designer, your brain will have less "food for thought" as you try to make design decisions for your clients and you'll find yourself producing the same designs over and over again.

Seeing and thinking as a designer begins with learning how to separate the parts from the whole, analyze those parts individually, and then put them back together again. Using qualitative and quantitative analysis as part of the three levels of observation will help you develop your seeing and thinking skills.

Jennifer Eckstein

QUALITATIVE AND QUANTITATIVE ANALYSIS

In qualitative analysis, you observe, name and list the parts of an object. You also list the properties of those parts. Using qualitative analysis, the dress you see here consists of a square neckline and a tight-fitting bodice leading into a full skirt.

In quantitative analysis, you begin to determine the amount of each part relative to size, proportion and dimension. **Proportion** is defined as any portion or part in relation to the whole. When you apply quantitative analysis to the same dress, you now see that $1/3$ of the dress is a tight-fitting bodice, while $2/3$ of the dress is a full skirt.

COSMETOLOGY FUNDAMENTALS

THREE LEVELS OF OBSERVATION

Many of the things in the world around you, including hair, can take on a variety of appearances, including different shapes, textures, colors and lengths. With so much diversity in front of you, it's important to have a system for analyzing what you see and talking about it. Selective seeing through the three levels of observation provides this system.

The **three levels of observation** are:

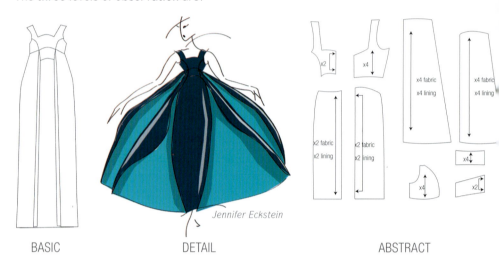

BASIC   DETAIL   ABSTRACT

These levels give designers a system for studying, categorizing and communicating the reality around them in a common language. Using these levels together with qualitative and quantitative analysis supports clear thinking and lays the foundation for design creativity.

BASIC
At the basic level, you are simply looking at an object and observing its silhouette or its three-dimensional form. When viewing a dress at the basic level, you would see only the outer shape or overall form of the dress, irrespective of any details. In this example, the overall shape of the dress is triangular.

DETAIL
Upon closer look at the detail level, you are observing the textures and/or color characteristics, along with any ornamental effects (qualitative analysis). Looking at the same dress at the detail level, you will register the type of material(s) the dress is made from such as silk, along with the specific color(s) such as teal and aqua blue. Upon closer analysis, you will even notice the specific pleated detail below the waistline.

ABSTRACT
Finally, at the abstract level, you use the information from the basic and detail levels to view the object in a more conceptual and less literal, concrete way (quantitative analysis). At the abstract level, you see "a step beyond" the object's face value of how it initially appears to you. Upon closer analysis of the dress, for example, you visualize the pattern that would allow you to recreate the overall shape and its component parts that make up the dress along with the proportional relationship of one part to another.

Anna Fehr

DESIGN ELEMENTS

The three **design elements** of form, texture and color are the major components of an art form, or a part of the artistic whole. Every object in the world, whether it is natural or man-made, consists of the three design elements. The design elements interplay and affect one another within a composition, so observing and analyzing the design elements individually and together help you understand and create complete designs.

In hair design, form is the design element that serves as the foundation for every design composition. Once the form is determined, texture and color are added to enhance the form. Viewing a design from all angles enables you to see each of the design elements from different perspectives, and how each view relates to the whole.

FORM

Form is the three-dimensional representation of shape. Form consists of length, width and depth. Shape is a two-dimensional representation of form consisting of length and width. In hair design, the terms form and shape are often used interchangeably when describing the outer boundary, outline, or silhouette of a design. There are three major categories of form and shapes, which are rectilinear, triangular and curvilinear. Rectilinear forms and shapes consist of horizontal and vertical lines. Triangular forms and shapes consist primarily of diagonal lines, while curvilinear forms and shapes consist of curved lines.

THREE DIMENSIONAL (3D)

Rectilinear

Triangular

Curvilinear

TWO DIMENSIONAL (2D)

Square

Triangle

Trapezoid

Circle

Half-Circle

Crescent

TWO DIMENSIONAL (2D)

Rectangle

Diamond

Kite

Oval

Oblong

DESIGN DECISIONS

The properties of form are point, line and shape. The illustrations on this page show how these three properties relate to one another to define a form.

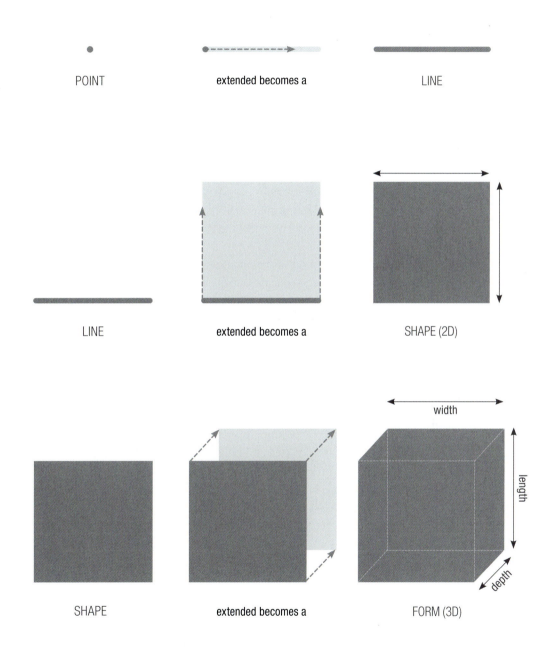

LINE

Analysis of form begins with an understanding of its most basic component, the point. A **point** is a mark, which, when set into motion, becomes a line. A **line** is a series of connected points. The path or direction of a given line can be straight, curved or any combination. Different types of lines can trigger different emotional responses, depending on their characteristics. The characteristics of a line can range from thin and delicate to thick and bold. Lines can express strength, delicacy, boldness, femininity or masculinity. Lines direct your eyes from one point to another. Used properly, lines can produce continuity and unity within a design.

The three basic straight lines are:
- Horizontal
- Vertical
- Diagonal

Horizontal lines are parallel to the horizon or floor and give the impression of stability, weight and calmness. Vertical lines are perpendicular to the horizon or floor and imply strength, weightlessness and equilibrium. Diagonal lines are energetic and imply motion.

Curved lines can be represented by any of the three basic straight lines. Curved lines also include concave and convex lines. Concave lines curve inward like the inside of a sphere, while convex lines curve outward, like the outside of a sphere. The path of a curved line can be slow and passive or fast and energetic. Curved lines imply softness and can lead your eye fluidly and rhythmically throughout a composition.

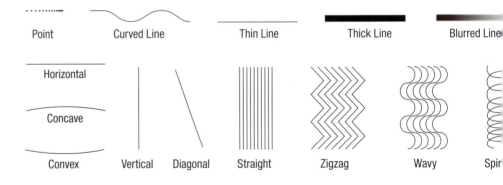

DESIGN DECISIONS

SHAPE

As a two-dimensional representation of form consisting of length and width but not depth, a **shape** is generally seen as a flat space, or plane, enclosed by a line that has turned to meet itself. A shape consists of angles and, when extended into space, a shape becomes a form.

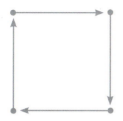 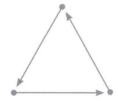 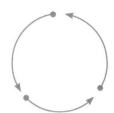

CELESTIAL AXIS

In your day-to-day work with clients in the salon, it will be important for you to identify and interpret the lines of their current and desired hair designs. The **celestial axis** is a symbol that will support you in identifying straight and curved lines, angles and directions. When observing lines in a hair design, include the outer boundary of the form (form line), the direction of the overall form and the lines within the form.

COSMETOLOGY FUNDAMENTALS 225

OBSERVING FORMS: NATURE, MAN-MADE AND HAIR
Nature creates an unlimited number of forms based on three basic characteristics: rectilinear, triangular and curvilinear. Human beings have interpreted these forms and through their imagination developed new forms. Studying forms and shapes in the natural and man-made worlds will enable you to create inspirational, new three-dimensional forms in hair. The world of fashion provides many examples that hair designers can draw on for inspiration, as do jewelry, the arts and architecture, to name just a few.

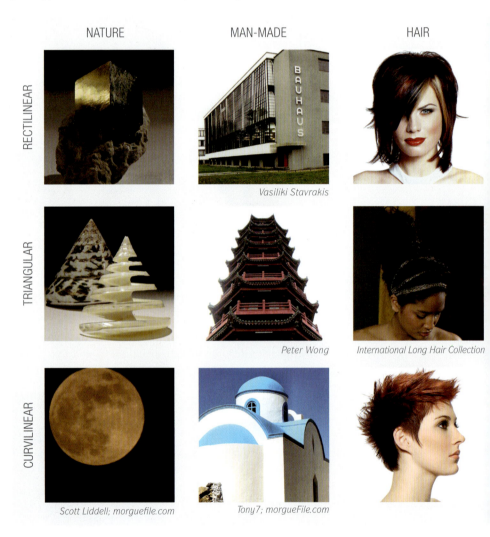

Vasiliki Stavrakis

Peter Wong   *International Long Hair Collection*

Scott Liddell; morguefile.com   *Tony7; morgueFile.com*

DESIGN DECISIONS

In hair design, forms are created through sculpting techniques, as well as hair design techniques and long hair design techniques.

SCULPTURE DESIGN

HAIR DESIGN

LONG HAIR DESIGN

TEXTURE

Texture is the visual appearance or feel of a surface, and it's the design element that creates interest within a design. Surface textures are divided into two main categories:
- Unactivated (smooth)
- Activated (rough)

OBSERVING TEXTURES: NATURE, MAN-MADE AND HAIR

Nature provides a myriad of textures, from soft, smooth surfaces to rough, edgy patterns. Fabrics are rich in textural qualities from smooth silks to soft cashmeres to coarse, scratchy woolens. Observing and feeling textures in the world around you will strengthen your observational skills and sense of touch. This in turn will provide you with inspiration from which to draw upon when creating textures in hair.

NATURE   MAN-MADE   HAIR

SMOOTH (unactivated)

ROUGH (activated)

T. Liedes; morguefile.com

Anna Fehr

228   DESIGN DECISIONS

In hair design, textures can also take on individual qualities of a line such as straight, zigzag and curved.

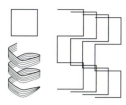 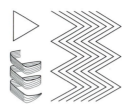 

Texture can be created through perming techniques and reduced through chemical relaxing techniques. Hair design, long hair design and sculpting techniques can add texture variables.

PERM DESIGN

RELAXER DESIGN

LONG HAIR DESIGN

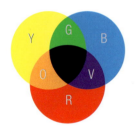

Y = Yellow   G = Green
R = Red   O = Orange
B = Blue   V = Violet

COLOR

Color is the visual perception of the reflection of light. The design element of color can add depth, dimension and the illusion of texture to a form. All colors are created by a combination of three primary colors:

- Yellow
- Red
- Blue

The primary colors are referred to as "pure" colors because they cannot be created by mixing any other colors.

When combining two primary colors together in varying proportions secondary colors are created, which are:

- Green
- Orange
- Violet

Every color can be categorized into one of three categories: warm, cool or neutral. Colors that contain yellow, red or orange are referred to as warm colors, while colors that contain blue, green or violet are referred to as cool colors. Colors that are neither predominately warm nor cool are referred to as neutral colors. Neutral colors, sometimes known as "earth tones," can include various shades of brown, beige, and gray.

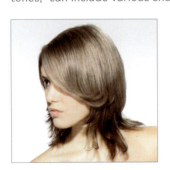  

DESIGN DECISIONS

OBSERVING COLORS: NATURE, MAN-MADE AND HAIR

Color and color patterns in nature are limitless, and can provide inspirational ideas for hair designs. Colors also communicate emotions, which you can use to personalize the hair designs you create. Warm colors like reds, oranges and golds give hair designs a passionate, energetic or exciting feel. Cool colors in a hair design, like blues, violets and greens can add a strong, edgy or confident quality. Using predominately neutral colors can give your clients a flexible canvas that is adaptable to many hair design choices. When creating hair color designs, you can reproduce the colors you see in nature in literal or symbolic ways to capture the essence of what you see.

Scott Liddell; morgueFile.com

In hair design, color can be added to hair through the use of hair color products or hairpieces. Color can lead your eye through a design or it can draw the eye to one particular point of interest. Color can also break up the surface appearance of the hair to create the illusion of texture.

HAIR COLOR PIECES

HAIR COLOR DESIGN

DESIGN PRINCIPLES

Design principles are the artistic arrangement patterns for the design elements of form, texture and color to follow. The four design principles are: repetition, alternation, progression and contrast. Understanding these four principles enables you to analyze a composition so you can recreate and adapt designs according to individual preferences. The following pages offer some examples of the design principles as they apply to form, texture and color.

REPETITION

With the design principle **repetition**, all units are identical except for position. Think of a classic pearl necklace. Repetition can be created throughout a composition or within a specific area. In hair design, repetition creates a feeling of uniformity.

REPETITION OF FORM

REPETITION OF TEXTURE

REPETITION OF COLOR

ALTERNATION

Alternation is a sequential repetition in which two or more units occur in a repeating pattern. Think of the colors on a checkerboard. In hair design, alternation can break up the surface of an object, creating interest.

ALTERNATION OF FORM

ALTERNATION OF TEXTURE

ALTERNATION OF COLOR

PROGRESSION

With **progression**, all units are similar yet gradually change proportionately in an ascending (increasing) or descending (decreasing) scale. Think of the notes in a musical scale. In hair design, progression can lead the eye rhythmically within a design or draw attention to a point of interest.

PROGRESSION OF FORM

PROGRESSION OF TEXTURE

PROGRESSION OF COLOR

CONTRAST

Contrast is a desirable relationship of opposites. Think of the look of a black tuxedo with a starched white shirt. Contrast creates variety and stimulates interest within a design.

CONTRAST OF FORM

CONTRAST OF TEXTURE

CONTRAST OF COLOR

BALANCE

Balance is an important part of any design composition. **Balance** is the state of equilibrium existing between contrasting, opposite or interacting elements. When a design is in balance, the arrangement of elements and the proportions within the design are harmonious and pleasing. Research has shown that lack of balance causes the eye to wander aimlessly through a design; the viewer will feel a sense of discomfort and eventually lose interest in the design altogether.

There are two types of balance:

SYMMETRICAL   ASYMMETRICAL

Symmetrical balance, or harmonious arrangement, is created when weight is positioned equally on both sides of a center axis, creating a mirror image. The focus remains on the silhouette of the design.

Asymmetrical balance, or off-center arrangement, is created when weight is positioned unequally from a center axis. Visual balance can still be achieved even though the actual mass of the hair is off center. Asymmetry creates a sense of movement and drama and should be personalized to the client. Extreme asymmetry would generally result in a design losing its balance.

CREATE AND ADAPT AS A DESIGNER

As a hair designer, your ultimate goal is to help clients look and feel their best with the design compositions you're able to create. Seeing and thinking as a designer give you a frame of reference for approaching all your design compositions. Creating as a designer means dedicating yourself to practice all aspects of hair design to build your expertise and to perform them with focus and precision. Adapting is the highest level of design proficiency. Adapting as a designer means that you are able to compose innovative and artistic hair designs by drawing upon your knowledge, skill and vision.

Pivot Point's levels of observation, design elements and design principles provide the foundation for creating professional hair designs. Mastering the process of seeing, thinking, creating and adapting as a designer will set you apart from the average stylist in the salon.

CREATE AND ADAPT AS A DESIGNER: FORM

CREATE AND ADAPT AS A DESIGNER: TEXTURE

CREATE AND ADAPT AS A DESIGNER: COLOR

8.2 DESIGN ADAPTABILITY

Fashion and style are important to culture as a whole and to people as individuals. People's fascination with the latest trends is driven by their desire to look and feel their best. As a salon professional, you have the ability to help clients accomplish this by offering sound design decisions, adapting what you know about design composition to each client's particular needs. Providing your clients with their best look requires careful analysis and communication to determine the design decisions that will help them achieve a hair design that flatters their unique physical features and also meets the needs of the way they live their lives every day. Adaptability involves modifying a chosen design to complement your client as much as possible and requires an understanding of the client's proportions, hair, clothing preferences and lifestyle.

08

PROPORTION

How is it possible that a hair design can look great on one client but absolutely terrible on another? The answer lies in the concept of proportion. The Greek philosopher Plato described beauty as existing in the proportion of things. Today's expert thinking confirms that proportion plays a major role in people's perception of beauty.

As a hair designer, you don't have the power to change another person's body type or face shape, but you do have the power to enhance your client's attractiveness by creating a more proportionate harmony between the hair design and the client's face, and between the client's head and body. As you read on, keep in mind that the suggestions for creating ideal proportions are just that: suggestions, and by no means are they hard rules. For you as a designer, it is most important that you are aware of the effects your design decisions can have on how a client's body proportions are perceived.

As artists throughout history sketched, painted and sculpted the human body, they discovered some golden rules about the ideal proportions between the body and the head, including the hair. Today those proportions have become a standard that is taught in art classes all over the world. When you incorporate these standards into your work as a hair designer, you will increase your ability to make the best design decisions for your clients.

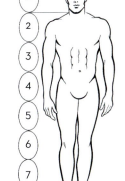

THE STANDARD PROPORTION BETWEEN HEAD AND BODY

According to the standard proportion most artists use, the head of a woman should be $1/7$ of her overall body height, while the head of a man should be $1/8$ of his overall body height. When creating hair designs for your clients, it is important to keep these proportions in mind because designs that are too large or too small for the client's stature will negatively affect the ideal proportions between the head and the body.

COSMETOLOGY FUNDAMENTALS

BODY SHAPES

The variety of human **body shapes** falls into three main categories, identified by height and bone structure. They are: tall and lanky, average, and short and sturdy. Analyze your client's body shape at the beginning of the service by having him or her stand in front of the mirror so you can both see the overall body height and proportions.

TALL AND LANKY BODY SHAPE

Clients with a **tall and lanky body** shape have an overall elongated and narrow bone structure. Neither their hips nor their shoulders are dominant. They generally have long legs, arms and necks. Women in this category are approximately 5'10" (1.7 m) or taller and men are approximately 6'1" (1.8 m) or taller. Due to their height, the heads of clients with a tall and lanky body shape appear small in proportion to their bodies and, therefore, these clients benefit from hair designs with added volume and/or length to make the head appear larger and in better proportion to the rest of the body. In the illustrations below note the different illusions that are created by short, small hair designs versus longer, fuller hair designs.

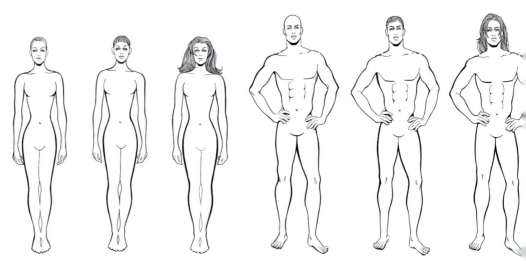

AVERAGE BODY SHAPE

Clients with an **average body shape** are people with normal height, dominant shoulders and average hips. Their bodies usually have a more balanced proportion. Women in this category are generally between 5'5" (1.6 m) and 5'9" (1.7 m) while men are usually between 5'7" (1.7 m) and 6'1" (1.8 m).

These clients can wear almost any hair length, from short to long, and any type of hair design, from close to the head to full. The decisions you make, however, will affect the clients' proportions. For example, a design that is short with volume on top will make an average body shape look taller, and a design that is shoulder length or longer with volume at the bottom will make people with this body shape look shorter.

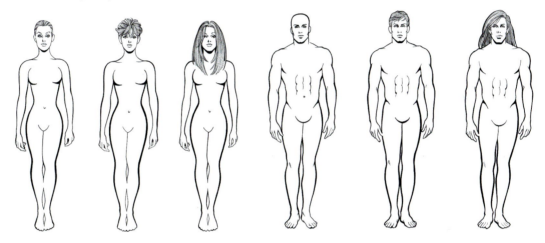

SHORT AND STURDY BODY SHAPE

Clients with a **short and sturdy body shape** are shorter and have a heavy or robust bone structure. They often have wide shoulders and hips and short arms, legs and necks. Women in this category are generally 5'4" (1.6 m) or shorter while men are 5'7" (1.7 m) or shorter. They benefit from hair designs with height and volume on the top to balance out their proportions. Hair designs that touch the shoulders or have a lot of overall volume tend to bring unwanted emphasis to the shortness and sturdiness of the client's stature.

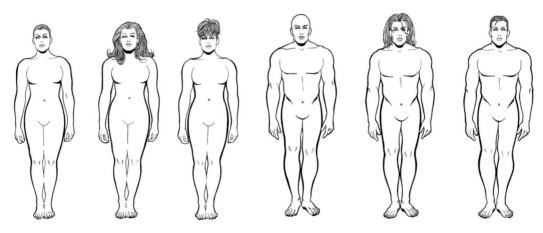

ENTIRE BODY SHAPE
When considering the entire body shape, identify the widest area of the body. As you visualize the client's overall body silhouette, imagine the amount of volume needed for the hair design to bring this widest area into proportion with the rest of the body. If the design is too small for a large figure, the proportion will be unbalanced and the body will look even larger. A short, small-boned body will easily become overpowered by a large hair design and, therefore, will appear even smaller.

LARGE FIGURE – MORE HAIR

Better balance

SMALL FIGURE – LESS HAIR

Better balance

BODY FEATURES

Besides the overall height and body proportion, there are also individual **body features** that, if dominant, need to be considered separately. The two main body features needing particular consideration are the neck and the shoulders.

NECK

Although the length of the neck often corresponds to a client's overall body shape, the neck should also be considered on its own when making design decisions.

Clients with short necks should generally not have a hair design with volume at the neck area as this accentuates the shortness of the neck. Long, wispy lengths are a good option since they visually elongate. Any outlining around the neckline should be narrow and elongated.

SHORT NECK
Keep hair close or off the face

Long necks can be enhanced by surrounding the neck with mass and fullness of the hair. Longer, fuller hair at the perimeter is a good design choice for clients with a long neck. If the client likes shorter hair, choose a design that still shows hair along the neck from the front view. Leave the nape area longer and fuller. Sculpt a horizontal design line at the bottom to imply weight or fullness.

LONG NECK
Frame with hair

SHOULDERS

As much as the neck reflects the overall body shape, so in most cases do the shoulders. A tall and lanky client will often have narrow shoulders, while a short and sturdy client will have wide shoulders. Although this is generally true, be sure to analyze each client's individual shoulder shape and make your design decisions accordingly.

Wide shoulders can benefit from a hair design with a narrowing design line in the back. The design lines could be any lines that imply a narrow or a steep "V" shape. These lines give the illusion of narrowing the shoulders and stretching the body.

WIDE SHOULDERS
Add elongation

Conversely, hair designs for narrow shoulders can feature design lines that imply horizontal lines or an "A" shape. Flat and wide, oval lines also work well. All of these lines need to be sculpted at low angles in order to add fullness and weight.

NARROW SHOULDERS
Add width

FACE

Facial structure often reflects body structure. Many tall and lanky clients have elongated faces while short clients often have wide faces. Any face can be beautiful if it is framed by the right hair design. To determine the most appropriate design, it is important to analyze the face using criteria such as bone structure and hairline, and by identifying the widest and most dominant areas.

Use these questions as a guide to help you easily and clearly determine which facial shape is present:
- Is the face long and narrow or short and wide?
- Is the shape of the face angular or rounded?
- Which area of the face is most dominant?

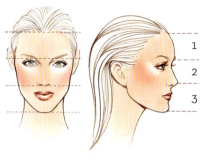

THREE-SECTIONING

Three-sectioning is an effective way to measure the proportions of the face. It is done by measuring the three sections of the face: section one is the front hairline to the middle of the eyebrows; section two is the middle of the eyebrows to the tip of the nose; section three is the tip of the nose to the tip of the chin. These sections are considered harmoniously proportioned if they are of equal length. If there is more than ½" (1.25 cm) difference between any of these sections, they are not considered harmonious. Hair designs and makeup can be used to create the illusion of balance. Having the client observe in the mirror while you are three-sectioning is a good way to lay the foundation so the client will understand the reasons behind the design decisions you will be recommending.

To measure the face using the three-sectioning technique:
- Comb and pin all the hair off of the face
- Place client in front of a mirror
- Remove the client's glasses and jewelry
- Measure the three sections with a tape measure or sculpting comb

COMMON FACIAL SHAPES

Illustrated here are the seven most common **facial shapes**. Being familiar with the different characteristics of each will help you adapt hair designs so that they flatter your client's face to its best advantage, whatever shape it may be. The majority of illustrations in this and upcoming portions of the chapter show women's faces because, in general, women's hair presents many more design options than men's hair. Be aware, however, that the same principles of hair design in relation to an individual's facial shape also apply to men.

OVAL   ROUND   SQUARE   OBLONG (Rectangle)   PEAR (Trapezoid)   DIAMOND   HEART (Triangle)

OVAL FACIAL SHAPE

The **oval face** is rounded, long and narrow rather than wide and short. It has no dominant areas. Oval faces look harmonious because the three sections of the face are in approximately equal proportions to one another. Oval faces look good with almost any hair design, length or texture. Sometimes the oval facial shape lacks a particular point of interest and can look plain. A stronger statement with the hair design may be used to create interest.

OVAL
Many choices

Standards of beauty change, but generally, oval is considered the ideal face shape. The following guidelines will give you ideas to help balance other face shapes to create the illusion of a more harmoniously balanced oval shape.

ROUND FACIAL SHAPE

The **round face** looks circular and tends to look short and wide rather than long and narrow. Round faces often have a low, round hairline and a short chin with a rounded jawline. These faces can look good with a geometric or linear hair design. An asymmetrical hair design can also offset the roundness of the face. Added height can be flattering and long, wispy side areas can make the cheeks look narrower. Avoid volume at the sides since this would add width. A few wisps of hair can be more attractive on a round face than a heavier fringe. Curls can emphasize the roundness of the face, so many designers will avoid them. If the client has naturally curly hair, create an angular shape. Placing volume either below the jawline or above the temple area can balance the width of the face.

ROUND
Avoid width

DESIGN DECISIONS

SQUARE FACIAL SHAPE

The **square face** is short and wide. It looks angular with straight lines. The front hairline and jawline are almost horizontal with cheekbones that protrude very little on the sides. The jawline is usually dominant on the square face. Square-shaped faces look good with hair designs that elongate the face—with height on top and narrowness on the sides. Very short hair with height on top can be flattering on a square face if the look suits the client's style. Curly texture and wisps of hair around the face can add softness to the angular lines of the face. People with square faces generally shouldn't wear horizontal fringes or designs that have width at the jawline.

SQUARE
Avoid straight lines

OBLONG FACIAL SHAPE

The **oblong (rectangle) face** is long, narrow and angular. The jawline is wide and almost horizontal. The hairline on the oblong face is only slightly curved. The sides sometimes look vertical since the cheekbones barely protrude. In many cases one area of the face is longer, such as at the forehead, the chin or the middle section. Oblong faces benefit from softness and width and often look good with longer, curlier hair. Chin-length hair with volume on the sides can also be flattering. A fringe can shorten the look of the oblong face. Avoid adding any more height to the oblong face. Also avoid flat, long, straight hair, which can also make the face look even longer.

OBLONG
Add softness

PEAR FACIAL SHAPE

The **pear-shaped (trapezoid) face** is most often elongated, with a narrower forehead and a wide jaw. The pear-shaped face can wear graduated forms very well since these designs can push the volume up and above the jawline into the narrower areas. If the hair is short, volume at the upper crest area works well. If the client wears the hair long, it should reach past the jawline. Long, wispy side areas can be used to slenderize the cheeks and jaw. In general clients with a pear facial shape should avoid extremely short hair and designs with a solid form (bob) that ends at the jawline.

PEAR
Add volume above jawline

DIAMOND FACIAL SHAPE

The **diamond-shaped face** appears elongated and angular. The widest area is at the cheekbones, while the forehead and chin are narrower. The diamond facial shape resembles the oval face, but tends to looks more angular. Diamond-shaped faces look softer with narrow sides and fullness at the chin. Solid form (bob) hair sculptures work well for this facial shape. Short hair also looks good on this shape with longer, wispier nape lengths to visually soften the pointed chin. Long, pointed side areas are not helpful since they emphasize the sharpness of the chin. Height on top, volume at the sides (width at the cheekbones), or a short, cropped nape will accentuate the appearance of a diamond-shaped face.

DIAMOND
Reduce width at sides

HEART FACIAL SHAPE

The **heart-shaped (triangle) face** is long and angular. The chin area is sometimes elongated and pointed, while the forehead is wider. Volume at the jawline and little or no volume on top is often recommended for this face shape. Curls can help to soften the features. If the hair is shorter, the nape still needs to be full, as short, cropped napes can make this face appear too harsh. Too much volume at the top of the hair design can make the face look more triangular. Diagonal-forward lines and long pointed side areas should be avoided.

HEART
Add volume at jawline

When communicating with clients about their facial shape, it is important that you use terminology that expresses your knowledge without labeling the client. For example, rather than saying to a client that she has a pear-shaped face, refer instead to fullness at the jaw and the narrow forehead area. Information presented this way is much more useful to the client. The shape descriptions are intended as a reference tool to aid in your understanding, not as a way to label clients as you consult with them. The art of client communication includes finding the right words to encourage and support the client while making professional recommendations. Remember, as people embrace their individuality, your efforts need to be focused on celebrating your clients' individual beauty, thus emphasizing their most attractive features.

FACE SHAPES

	DO	DON'T
	Oval Enhance features Balance body proportions	Add too much height
	Round Add height to crown Add width below jawline or above temple Create angular shapes	Add a full fringe Add width on sides Add equal fullness around entire face
	Square Sweep short hair up over ears Add soft movement to conceal square corners Begin side fullness at temples	Add solid lines at jawline Add height without width Style hair straight and flat
	**Oblong** Keep short hair equally full on top and above the ears Add width at sides Use a side parting and diagonal fringe	Add height without width Style hair straight and flat
	Pear Add width at forehead (in short or medium styles) Let long hair cover the jawline to conceal its width	Accentuate pear shape with narrowness at temples and width at jawline
	Diamond Use a side part and diagonal fringe Add width at forehead and jawline	Add width at cheekbones
	Heart Add width at jawline Leave fullness at nape that can be seen from front	Add width at forehead or cheekbones

DESIGN DECISIONS

PROFILE

A **profile** is an outline of an object from the side, especially the side view of the face and head. Since your clients are viewed from various angles, it is important that their hair design complements their profile as well as the front view. The most notable features of the profile are the forehead, the nose and the chin. You may wish to give your clients a hand-held mirror to help them view their profile as you make style recommendations. **There are three different types of profiles: straight, convex and concave.**

STRAIGHT PROFILE

A **straight profile** has a very slight outward curvature from the front hairline to the tip of the nose and from the tip of the nose to the chin. Straight profiles are considered to be the ideal and can be left totally exposed by a hair design.

CONVEX PROFILE

A **convex profile** has a strong or exaggerated outward curvature resulting from either a protruding nose or a sloping forehead or chin. For the convex profile, it is advisable to create the illusion of a straight profile. Adding volume to the fringe area and the forehead will help to visually shorten the length of the nose. To balance a sloping chin, keep the shape of the hair tighter in the nape so the chin doesn't appear too small in comparison to the hair volume. With a solid form hair sculpture, create a diagonal-forward perimeter line that points directly to the chin to make it appear larger. A receding chin on a male client can be camouflaged by a full beard and mustache.

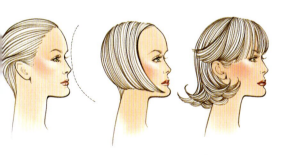

CONCAVE PROFILE

A **concave profile** has an inward curve, which is most often the result of a dominant, protruding forehead and chin or a small nose. To compensate for the dominant chin, build fullness in the nape and avoid short nape lengths and diagonal-forward lines, since this would cause the chin to stand out even more. To cover a large forehead, sculpt fringes and design them with minimal volume. Moving the hair off and away from the face will compensate for a smaller nose if the forehead and/or chin are not also protruding.

COSMETOLOGY FUNDAMENTALS

FACIAL FEATURES

Other features that may need special consideration when determining proper proportions include a receding hairline, protruding ears and eyeglasses.

RECEDING HAIRLINE

When a client has a receding hairline, avoid a side part directly in the center of the recession area. Try to design the hair without any direct part and let it fall slightly forward to cover the receding area.

PROTRUDING EARS

Although not technically part of the face, protruding ears have a significant effect on a client's facial appearance. Large or protruding ears should be covered with longer hair or designs should have more volume and fullness at the sides if the hair is short.

EYEGLASSES

A client who wears eyeglasses may pose two different types of challenges. The first challenge involves giving advice on the type of frame shape to select. The second challenge is adapting the client's hair design to the glasses already being worn. In general, the client's facial shape is the main factor that should guide the type of eyeglass frames that would best flatter the client and the same principles of proportion apply as in hair design. Selection of the eyeglass frames should also take into account the client's overall body shape, personality, lifestyle and clothing preferences.

When you keep the shape, size and color of the glasses in mind, you'll be better able to recommend an eyeglass design that works with your client's total image.

GUIDELINES FOR SELECTING EYEGLASSES

- Select large glasses for a larger face and small glasses for a smaller face.
- Determine if your client considers eyeglasses to be a fashion accessory or a necessity. A client who views glasses as a fashion accessory may be happy with a pair that draws attention through shape or color. A client who is not happy about wearing glasses and sees it as a necessity will probably be more satisfied with a delicate frame in gold or silver or possibly unframed lenses.
- The shape of the frame can also be used to enhance or compensate for the shape of the face. A square-shaped pair of glasses can give a round face more interest while a round pair of glasses can soften a square face. A wide frame can add width to a narrow face.
- Select an eyeglass frame color that corresponds to the tone of the client's coloring. Generally, a cool-toned frame such as silver, blue or teal will be better suited to clients with cool coloring and frames with warm colors such as gold or crimson will flatter clients with warm coloring.

HAIR

A salon professional could never make a design decision without analyzing his or her primary working material—the hair. It is important to determine several factors first about the hair before deciding on a particular design. These factors include: color, texture, density, length, condition and growth pattern.

HAIR COLOR AND NATURAL COLORING

When consulting with clients who want a change in their hair color and/or makeup, analyzing their natural coloring is an important first step in order to make the right design decision. The right hair color can emphasize the natural skin tone or eye color and make the client look fresher and more radiant. The wrong hair color can have the opposite effect.

To determine which colors are most flattering for your clients, you first need to analyze the pigmentation of your client's hair, skin, eyes and lips. Use the following chart to determine whether your client's color scheme tends to be warm, cool or neutral and whether the intensity of those colors is mild or strong. Keep in mind that warm colors contain yellow, orange and/or red, and cool colors contain blue, green and/or violet. Neutral colors contain all three primary colors, yellow, red and blue.

Use this chart to develop your ability to identify clients' natural coloring. Place an X in the square that most closely identifies your client's natural color scheme and count the number of X's in each column. The totals will help you make the best hair color decisions as well as makeup choices for your clients. Note that neutral colors tend to be balanced. Clients who have a neutral color scheme can look good in either warm or cool colors.

MILD STRONG

Warm   Cool   Warm   Cool

PIGMENTATION FACTORS

	WARM			COOL	
	MILD	STRONG	NEUTRAL	MILD	STRONG
HAIR					
Natural Hair Color					
Childhood Hair Color					
SKIN					
Scalp					
Skin Behind Ear					
Skin on Face					
Cheek Color					
Freckles on Arms and Shoulders					
Shadows Around Eyes					
EYES					
Eye Color					
Circle Around Eyes					
Whites of Eyes					
LIPS					
Natural Lip Color					
TOTAL:					

The following images show the influence that colors have on the overall look of a client and whether they are chosen correctly or incorrectly. The first image shows the client without any makeup. Analyze the skin color, eye color and lips. Then look at the other two images and note the positive and negative effects that colors have on the total image. As you can see, the hair color as well as the makeup color should parallel the client's natural coloring and intensity in order to emphasize the natural beauty.

HAIR TEXTURE

As mentioned earlier, **hair texture** refers to the surface appearance or feel of the hair as well as the diameter of the hair strand itself. Texture can be described as either unactivated, having a smooth and unbroken surface, or activated, having a rough surface. It can also be described as fine, medium or coarse.

UNACTIVATED

ACTIVATED

With unactivated designs you will find no hair ends exposed on the surface. The hair is often straight and is sculpted in a blunt line. With activated designs you will see a rough surface and lots of movement. Activation is created either through curls or when the hair ends are exposed on the surface, such as with hair that is layered. The surface appearance of the hair can be altered with a variety of salon services, such as sculpting the hair blunt or in layers, perming and relaxing, as well as with different finishing techniques or products as shown in the examples on the left.

The texture of the hair strand itself, the hair's diameter, will have an impact on the type of design that will work best for your client. Hair with fine texture is usually easy to design but the hair design may collapse quickly. By contrast, coarse hair is more difficult to design at first but, when done properly, the design lasts for a longer period of time. Note that curly, coarse hair tends to create a wider silhouette.

HAIR DENSITY

Density describes the number of hair follicles per square inch on the scalp and is usually referred to as light, medium or heavy (or thin, medium or thick). Hair density will determine the feasibility of certain hair designs. For example, clients with light density generally won't have enough fullness for longer designs that go past the shoulders. Clients with heavy density hair generally won't look as good with curly perms or feel comfortable with upswept hair because of the additional weight. The amount of volume you are able to achieve in a hair design often depends on the density of the hair.

Another factor to consider with hair density is the use of styling products. Styling products offering manageability, lasting power and conditioning effects can all supplement varying degrees of hair density. The styling product label usually indicates appropriate usage and hold factor for various hair types. You may need to consider this hold factor when attempting to match the right product with the desired volume. For instance, thick hair may require a heavier styling product for better control. Thin density hair, on the other hand, may require a lighter styling product that won't weigh down the hair while providing volume and mobility.

HAIR LENGTH

A client's existing hair length might not be long enough to carry out a chosen design immediately. It might be necessary to let some areas of the hair grow. If this is the case, it's helpful to inform clients about this delay to avoid disappointments.

HAIR CONDITION

The condition of the hair, especially in relation to the client's history of chemical services, is an important consideration. The hair's present condition determines which additional chemical services can be performed without jeopardizing the integrity of the hair. It is important that the salon professional and client work together to achieve and maintain healthy hair. It is your responsibility to recommend appropriate chemical services and proper home care maintenance with the appropriate products.

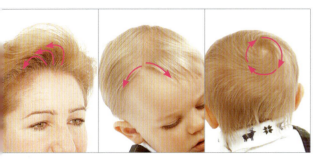

GROWTH PATTERN

Every client has certain growth patterns in the hair. The natural growth pattern determines the angle and direction at which the hair grows out of the scalp. This angle and direction are usually very strong and can seldom be altered. Before sculpting, analyze the client's hair growth pattern and directions. Your analysis will affect your choice of length and design line decisions. A client with strong patterns may end up with hair that "stands up" if the hair is sculpted too short.

CLOTHING

The strongest looks are the ones presented fully from head to toe, so clothing style is another important aspect to consider when designing the hair. Remember – the way your clients are dressed for a salon visit might not be the way they usually dress. Some clients don't dress up to visit the salon. Other clients might be dressed more formally than usual due to plans they have after the service. It's best to ask clients a few questions about their clothing style to get the full picture. Internationally, designers and the fashion industry identify six general clothing styles: natural, romantic, dramatic, gamine, classic and casual.

NATURAL

Clients in the **natural** category like to wear colors and materials that are found in nature. Their clothes, for example, will often be made from fabrics like cotton and wool and their jewelry will be made from materials such as stones and wood. Clients who favor a natural clothing style generally prefer that their hair design be low-maintenance and not require them to use a lot of styling products. They like their hair to look and feel healthy. Natural hair coloring products are popular among these clients, and the rest of their salon product choices also reflect their concern about personal health, the environment and animal testing.

ROMANTIC

Clients in the **romantic** category love silk, flower prints, lace, beads and pastel shades of color. They often shop at vintage stores to purchase accessories, such as shawls and small, detailed jewelry. They often dress tone-on-tone. Soft and feminine hair designs are good for these clients. They like curls, whether natural or permed, and soft hair colors, such as highlights of golden blond, light brown and strawberry blond.

DRAMATIC

Clients in the **dramatic** category gravitate to things that are out of the ordinary. They often want to draw attention and make heads turn. When it comes to their personal style, these clients seek out change and embrace new and exciting ideas. They may wear loud and colorful clothing and accessories and they are not afraid to experiment with hair designs and hair colors that reflect their bold style. Dramatic clients will give you the opportunity to stretch your creativity.

GAMINE

Clients in the **gamine** category are playful and very feminine. They are very fashion-oriented and enjoy wearing the latest looks. They wear small jewelry, often geometric in shape. They have an eye for interesting detail. Their hair is usually short. Side parts are common.

CLASSIC

Clients in the **classic** category are coordinated in their wardrobe. Every piece of clothing is well-chosen and usually exemplifies a design look, often in classic colors, such as navy, black, white, cream, beige, brown and gray. Female clients in this category like their hair to be well-designed, in good condition and an appropriate color, preferring natural blonds, reds and browns sometimes with thin highlights. Sophisticated short hair is popular, along with classic solid form bobs. If the hair is long, it is often worn in a ponytail or in a bun. Hair is usually the same color throughout and may be colored to brighten up the natural color, to tone down blond shades or to cover gray. Male clients in this category usually keep their hair short and well-groomed.

CASUAL

Clients in the **casual** category like their clothing and everything in their environment to be comfortable and low-maintenance. Their wardrobe often includes flat, comfortable shoes and sneakers. They like to wear blue jeans, T-shirts and sweatshirts. Even for elegant events they will find a way to be practical and comfortable. Their hair has to be easy for them to style and maintain on their own. Often the hair is longer and worn in a loose ponytail.

LIFESTYLE

When making a design decision, it is important to take into account your client's lifestyle since it will help determine a hair design's practicality. Some of the **lifestyle factors** that need to be considered are: job/career, hobbies (such as sports), family, time availability, hair care skills and finances.

JOB/CAREER

Consider the functional demands of the client's job and the type of image the job requires. Since many clients spend most of their time at work, those requirements cannot be neglected.

HOBBIES

A lot of things clients like to do for fun, fitness or relaxation will challenge their hair in different ways. Be sure to ask your clients whether their spare time activities pose any restrictions or create needs for their hair that should be considered.

FAMILY

Some clients find their partner's and family's preferences important. Asking your clients directly about this factor will help clear up any doubts and avoid later disappointment. Whether or not your clients have young children may also influence the type of design they can wear. For some parents, a low-maintenance design would probably be appreciated.

TIME

The amount of time a client is willing and able to spend on hair care can give you an immediate indication of how elaborate the hair design can be. Clients who would prefer spending as little time as possible for daily hair care and styling are better suited with a design that is simple, low-maintenance and requires relatively few products and tools.

SKILLS

Even though clients may be willing to invest all the time and money necessary for a certain look, some clients may not have the necessary skills required to achieve it at home. That makes it your responsibility to provide as much support for the client as you can through explaining the proper tools or products for the client to use for home maintenance. Demonstrate for your clients the correct methods and techniques they can use to achieve the best possible results.

FINANCES

Finally, the costs involved with the client's selected design need to be made clear. The costs for the initial design change as well as its ongoing maintenance, both recurring salon costs and at-home care, need to be discussed. If the client is aware of the whole picture ahead of time, there will be no unpleasant surprises and you will have a satisfied, loyal client.

8.3 CLIENT COMMUNICATION

Creating a good client relationship is just as important and as much of an art as creating a unique new hair design. Knowing how to develop clear, open and respectful communication between you and your clients is the key to developing the kind of client relationships that w make every client visit pleasurable and productive.

Although there are many benefits to effective client communication, three of them are particularly important to you as a hair designer. Effective communication allows you to:
- Uncover your clients' true wants, needs and expectations regarding the salon service.
- Gain your clients' trust and confidence so they will participate productively in the desig decision process and be more open and accepting of your design recommendations.
- Establish and maintain long-term relationships that keep clients returning to you and open the door for new client referrals.

THE FOUR SERVICE ESSENTIALS

The four **Service Essentials,** also known as the Four C's, will help you create an exceptional salon experience for your client and an environment that supports effective communication They provide a road map for every client service to help you address specific communicatio goals along the way. The Four C's are **Connect, Consult, Create and Complete.** Use the following chart as you practice the Four C's needed for a successful salon service. More information about the Four C's can be found in the *Salon Success* coursebook.

THE FOUR C'S

	HOW	WHY	WHAT YOU NEED
CONNECT 	Welcome guest with a smile, eye contact and handshake; introduce yourself to first-time guest	Build rapport and put guest at ease; demonstrate your interest in guest; for first-time guests, confirm their name, how they prefer to be addressed and get first clues on personality tendencies	Professional appearance and hygiene for positive first impression; friendly smile; upright posture; firm handshake; communication skills

08

THE FOUR C'S

	HOW	WHY	WHAT YOU NEED
CONSULT 	Ask questions about previous salon experiences, current hair design needs, lifestyle, clothing style, personal likes and dislikes; analyze body height and structure, face shape, condition and natural color of hair, personality tendencies	Get a complete understanding of guest's needs to determine design and service options	Hair design selector; color chart; comb; hand mirror; full body mirror; communication skills, client record card
	Summarize the design decisions; explain the services, the cost of upkeep and home care for the chosen design; gain guest feedback and approval	Ensure you and your guest have a common understanding about the design change and services to be provided and are in agreement about the plan to move forward; avoid misunderstandings and/or disappointment for guest or designer	
CREATE 	Ensure guest's comfort during service; explain steps and actions that are taking place; demonstrate use of products; commit to delivering the highest quality possible	Satisfy guest's needs; meet or exceed guest's expectations; create artistically crafted and flattering hair designs	Essential tools, products and equipment; service skills; communication skills
COMPLETE 	Gain feedback; ask questions; give home hair care tips; recommend and explain retail products; schedule next appointment; guide guest to front desk; say "thank you" and "goodbye"	Ensure guest is satisfied and understands how to maintain the design at home; reinforce positive relationship with guest; encourage new client referrals	Professional appearance; friendly smile; upright posture; firm handshake; appointment book; business cards; communication skills

CONTRIBUTORS TO EFFECTIVE COMMUNICATION

Effective communication is really about creating a two-way street in which both parties are equal participants in the communication process. Speaking, listening and body language all play important roles in communicating effectively. A skilled communicator pays attention to body language, speaks clearly and professionally, uses active listening skills and asks questions to demonstrate interest in the client. These communication basics are reviewed in more detail in the *Salon Success* coursebook.

In addition to these communication skills, there are other factors that contribute to your ability to communicate with clients during their salon visit. The main factors that influence effective communication are:

- Personality—Your own personality tendencies, the personality tendencies of your clients, and how they interrelate
- Schedule—The impact that time pressures and scheduling constraints can have on communication
- Environment—How elements within the immediate environment can help or hinder effective communication
- Professional Appearance—The effect that your appearance and hygiene can have on client perceptions

Being aware of these contributing factors and managing them in ways that enhance communication and minimize barriers to communication will help your clients feel accepted, put them at ease and build mutual respect and rapport. Controlling these factors to avoid communication problems will help make the "people" side of your job as enjoyable and fulfilling as the creative side of hair design.

PERSONALITY

In your own personal experience, you've probably noticed that you get along better with some people than with others. It's not that there's anything wrong with those other people, it's just that your personalities don't seem to be compatible. When you don't understand what drives someone's personality, it's difficult to communicate. This is why understanding personality differences is critical to your success in the salon.

Personality is defined as the outward reflection of inner thoughts, feelings, values and attitudes. Personality is an individual's distinctive pattern of thinking, feeling and acting. Salon professionals who have insight into their own personality and can identify their clients' personalities and adapt the way they communicate will be better able to establish rapport, make good design decisions and maintain client relationships over time.

Although an individual's personality remains fairly constant and predictable over time, it is not fixed in stone. A generally outgoing person can sometimes be quite withdrawn, just as a generally reserved person can sometimes be quite sociable. As a salon professional, the more you are willing to observe the actions and language of your clients, the more you will understand their personality tendencies, which will lead to much more productive communication between you.

There are four major behavior patterns that explain personality. This section will provide an overview of them, along with the behaviors usually associated with each and how to modify your own behavior to improve communication. The *Salon Success* coursebook contains an expanded discussion of personality.

The four personality behavior patterns are:
- Getting energized by being either introverted or extraverted
- Managing information by being either sensing or intuitive
- Making decisions by being either thinking or feeling
- Organizing work by being either structured or flexible

INTROVERTED/EXTRAVERTED

People who tend to be **introverted** get energized internally from thoughts and ideas, whereas people who tend to be **extraverted** get energized externally from other people and the environment. That's why introverted people don't mind spending time alone—they actually enjoy it—while extraverted people prefer being around other people.

INTROVERTED/EXTRAVERTED BEHAVIOR PATTERN

	YOU MAY OBSERVE THAT THE CLIENT	YOU CAN IMPROVE COMMUNICATION BY
INTROVERTED	• Sits still • Prefers to listen • Thinks before speaking	• Speaking and acting calmly • Giving client time to think before responding • Not interrupting
EXTRAVERTED	• Moves around; approaches others • Talks easily; interrupts • Thinks out loud	• Being lively • Encouraging client to talk • Engaging in conversation with client

COSMETOLOGY FUNDAMENTALS

SENSING/INTUITIVE

People who tend to be **sensing** manage information by focusing on concrete facts and practical details whereas people who tend to be **intuitive** manage information by focusing on abstract ideas and original solutions. The sensing personality relies on the five senses for information and the intuitive personality gives more weight to gut feelings and intuition.

SENSING/INTUITIVE BEHAVIOR PATTERN

	YOU MAY OBSERVE THAT THE CLIENT	YOU CAN IMPROVE COMMUNICATION BY
SENSING	• Speaks simply and directly • Talks about the present • Focuses on details and practicality	• Being direct, efficient and realistic • Providing costs, details and specific directions • Using a common-sense, no-nonsense approach
INTUITIVE	• Asks for options • Talks about the future • Focuses on the big picture and image	• Offering options that fit client's lifestyle • Demonstrating creativity and cutting edge approaches • Using visual images

THINKING/FEELING

People who tend to be **thinking** make decisions based on what is logical, objective and impersonal whereas people who tend to be feeling make decisions in a more subjective, personal way. The thinking approach uses the head more than the heart and relies strongly on reason. The **feeling** approach uses the heart more than the head and relies strongly on values.

THINKING/FEELING BEHAVIOR PATTERN

	YOU MAY OBSERVE THAT THE CLIENT	YOU CAN IMPROVE COMMUNICATION BY
THINKING	• Appears detached, hides emotions • Asks for pros and cons • Expresses disagreement and dissatisfaction readily • Decides easily, based on logic	• Speaking concisely • Providing facts, statistics and logic • Avoiding emotional displays
FEELING	• Talks about feelings and relationships • Gives long explanations • Agrees readily, avoids disagreeing • Decides slowly, based on social standards	• Speaking warmly with embellishments • Providing endorsements of respected people • Giving client time to make decisions

STRUCTURED/FLEXIBLE

People who tend to be **structured** organize work by planning routines and schedules whereas people who tend to be **flexible** organize work by adapting the way work is done and adjusting schedules based on changing circumstances. In this behavior pattern, the labels of structured and flexible very clearly represent the way these personalities operate.

STRUCTURED/FLEXIBLE BEHAVIOR PATTERN

	YOU MAY OBSERVE THAT THE CLIENT	YOU CAN IMPROVE COMMUNICATION BY
STRUCTURED	• Is on time and values punctuality • Appreciates organization and order • Focuses on end results and what is essential	• Being predictable, organized and on time • Notifying client about changes in advance • Focusing on essential information
FLEXIBLE	• Arrives late; is not concerned with schedule changes • Appears indecisive and disorganized • Asks for information beyond what is essential	• Accommodating client's flexible schedule • Encouraging client's questions • Guiding client through decision process

SCHEDULE

Time pressures and scheduling constraints can affect the quality of your communication with clients. You probably can think of situations from your own personal experience when feeling rushed prevented you from performing at your best or caused your communication with another person to be abrupt or incomplete. That's why it's important that your scheduling system leaves enough time to communicate calmly and thoroughly during each phase of the client visit.

There are several variables that determine how client visits are scheduled and how much time is allotted for each of the four Service Essentials. These variables include whether the client is new or returning, the level of experience of the hair designer, the type of service being delivered, and the number of services being scheduled during the day. Here are some **schedule** guidelines to keep in mind:

- During the Connect Service Essential, a lot can be accomplished in a short amount of time. Because it sets the tone for the entire client visit, it is important to devote your complete attention to the client. For a first-time client, allow ample time to connect with your client as it will set the tone for your ongoing relationship. Even when a previous appointment runs late, don't allow yourself to be distracted or omit the Connect phase.

- Allow sufficient time for the Consult Service Essential. Although you will probably need more time for new clients, be sure you also consult with returning clients and don't assume that you know what they are expecting from this day's service. Some salons see a detailed Consult as a service by itself, which means that the client may be booked for an extra 30 to 60 minutes to discuss his or her specific needs with the hair designer. Depending on salon policy, there may be an extra charge for this Consult service and the client may be scheduled for the hair service immediately following or at a scheduled time in the future.
- Some salons, when scheduling new clients, allow an additional 15 minutes to give the designer more time to conduct the Connect and Consult Service Essentials to ensure the communication necessary to establish a good relationship.
- The amount of time scheduled for the Create Service Essential depends on the type of service the client has asked for. If the client wants to change or add a service, check with the front desk to ensure you have the time available. Take the time to let the client know your decision about whether to do additional or changed services is based on what is in the client's best interest.
- The Complete Service Essential need not take a lot of time but don't neglect it since it can reinforce the positive relationship developed throughout the service. If rushed, however, the Complete phase can cause more damage than good. Recommend product for the client to take home, but be careful not to push. If you are late for your next appointment, do only as much as you can do calmly and respectfully, but always let the client know that you appreciated his or her visit and continued patronage.

ENVIRONMENT

You are probably well aware that the **environment** affects your ability to communicate well. Excessive noise and activity, poor lighting, interpersonal conflict and disorganization are all barriers to effective communication. During the Consult Service Essential in particular it's important that the environment be conducive to conversation. Make sure you can hear what your client is saying and that your client can hear you without either of you having to raise your voice. Minimize distractions. If you notice your client's attention is wandering, don't continue talking; wait until eye contact is restored or gently tap your client on the arm or shoulder to regain his or her attention.

Having the proper materials with you will also help you communicate effectively. Anything that adds a visual dimension will make it easier for clients to understand what you are saying. A full body mirror helps when discussing the proportions between body and hair design. Color swatches help your client get an accurate picture of your color design recommendations. Photo images in a design book, or in a photo library on a handheld device make it easier for you and your clients to discuss and agree on different sculpture, texture and color design options.

The environment can also help keep your client relaxed and comfortable, which in turn increases client satisfaction and makes communication easier. Music, beverages and reading material in the waiting area are examples of aspects in the environment that aid client relaxation. Availability of fresh towels for drying the client's skin and a brush to wipe hair off the client's neck and clothing will help you keep your client comfortable during the service. Taking charge of your environment to provide the best possible salon experience demonstrates your commitment to your clients and to your profession.

PROFESSIONAL APPEARANCE

Clients often see their salon professional as an image-maker. They observe and evaluate their designer's look very carefully. Your **professional appearance** is immediately connected to the expectation the client has of your job performance. In other words, a salon professional exhibiting a poor image will be expected to have poor skills as well. A designer exhibiting a professional image will generate more interest and excitement from the client. Equally important, your professional appearance will inspire trust and confidence from clients, which will open the lines of communication for successful results.

Personal hygiene is an aspect of professional appearance that is sometimes uncomfortable to discuss, but cannot be ignored. Poor hygiene, which includes such things as ungroomed fingernails, bad breath (halitosis), unkempt clothing and perspiration marks and odor, can be an immediate "turn off" to your clients and can shut down communication in a hurry. It will be up to you to monitor yourself closely in this area, since others may be reluctant to point out hygiene problems to you.

The loyalty of your clients is only as strong as the last hair design you create for them. And the success of every hair design depends on making the best design decisions you can. This chapter has presented the three essential cornerstones for making design decisions: design composition, design adaptability and client communication. Mastering these skills won't happen overnight, but practicing them from the beginning of your career will put you on the fast track to career success.

CONNECTING THEORY TO REAL-WORLD PRACTICE

DESIGN DECISIONS	PERSONAL CONNECTION: IMPROVE YOURSELF	INDUSTRY CONNECTION: BECOME A PROFESSIONAL	CLIENT CONNECTION: SERVE THE GUEST
DESIGN COMPOSITION	Understand the world around you using design elements and principles	Reproduce any hair design you see and create any hair design you can imagine	Explain to clients how and why a hair design can achieve a particular effect
DESIGN ADAPTABILITY	Analyze how an overall image can be enhanced through proportion and balance	Exemplify a true customer-centered attitude through your commitment to adapting to each client's needs	Help clients look and feel their best by maximizing strengths, minimizing flaws and enhancing their personal style
CLIENT COMMUNICATION	Improve your ability to communicate with all types of people	Build your professional credibility by demonstrating excellent communication skills	Provide an exceptional salon experience with a communication strategy that supports openness and respect

IN OTHER WORDS

Knowing the concepts behind design composition and adaptability and how to communicate effectively with clients will help you make the most appropriate design decisions for meeting the unique image needs of each client.

LESSONS LEARNED

- The three levels of observation are: basic, detail and abstract.

- The three design elements of form, texture and color are also the major components of an art form.

- The four design principles of repetition, alternation, progression and contrast are the patterns used to arrange design elements within a composition.

- Proportion plays a major part in how people perceive beauty and compose designs.

- Hair designs should be adapted to each client's body and facial shape and features, hair, clothing and lifestyle.

- Connect, Consult, Create and Complete are the four Service Essentials that provide an exceptional salon experience and support effective client-designer communication.

- Personality, schedule, environment and professional appearance are key factors that contribute to effective client-designer communication.

09

SCULPTURE

9.1 SCULPTING THEORY
  HAIR SCULPTURE ANALYSIS
  FOUR BASIC FORMS
  COMBINATION FORMS

9.2 SCULPTING TOOLS
  SHEARS
  TAPER SHEARS
  RAZORS
  CLIPPERS
  COMBS

9.3 SCULPTING SKILLS
  PIVOT POINT'S SEVEN SCULPTING PROCEDURES
  TEXTURIZING TECHNIQUES
  SHORT HAIR TECHNIQUES
  SCULPTING CONSIDERATIONS
  SCULPTING ESSENTIALS
  INFECTION CONTROL AND SAFETY
  SCULPTING SERVICE ESSENTIALS
  SCULPTING PROCEDURE OVERVIEW

SCULPTURE IS THE FOUNDATION OF ALL HAIR DESIGNS, CREATING SUBTLE TO DRAMATIC CHANGES IN PEOPLE'S APPEARANCE

FOLLOWING THIS LESSON
YOU WILL BE ABLE TO:

Identify the two ways to analyze the structure of a hair sculpture

Describe the four basic sculpted forms and combination forms

Describe the five main sculpting tools and how each is used to sculpt hair

Explain the skills needed to create hair sculptures, including Pivot Point's Seven Sculpting Procedures, texturizing techniques, short hair techniques and sculpting considerations

CONNECTING THEORY TO REAL-WORLD PRACTICE
SCULPTING HAIR INTO THE FOUR BASIC FORMS AND COMBINATION FORMS WILL HELP YOU:

PERSONAL CONNECTION:	**INDUSTRY CONNECTION:**	**CLIENT CONNECTION:**
IMPROVE YOURSELF	BECOME A PROFESSIONAL	SERVE THE GUEST
Use the theory of form and structure to produce a variety of results in the medium of hair	Master the art and science of hair sculpting to build respect from both clients and colleagues	Provide the essential foundation for hair designs, which can be adapted to changing trends

A child's first haircut, just like his or her first steps and first day of school, is often considered a milestone. Many parents, i fact, will keep a lock of hair from that first haircut as a memento. As people grow up, the way their hair is cut, or sculptec becomes more important to them. The hair sculpture is the foundation upon which an entire hair design is built, reflectin a person's image and sense of style. This is why your skill in the art and science of hair sculpture will play a major role building a successful salon career.

268
SCULPTURE

09

9.1 SCULPTING THEORY

Throughout history, the length and shape of hair have fascinated and inspired people. In some cultures, the length of a man's hair was associated with his strength and virility, as described in the story of Samson who lost his strength when Delilah cut off his hair. Many ancient Egyptians shaved their heads, possibly for religious or sanitary reasons. In the ancient Greek culture, both men and women wore their hair long.

Today, the length and shape of hair still fascinate and inspire. People know that their hair sculpture makes a significant personal statement. This is why the study of hair sculpture is at the heart of the salon profession. At Pivot Point, **hair sculpting is defined as the artistic carving or removing of hair lengths to create various forms and shapes.** Just as a sculptor molds and carves clay into a work of art, so too does a hair designer shape a head of hair. Only the tools and the medium are different.

Hair sculptures often get labeled with names that attempt to reflect their forms or shapes. You may be familiar with some names, such as the "bob," the "wedge" or the "shag." In the Pivot Point system, hair sculptures are identified according to their structure, also called the length arrangement. This language is clear, consistent and "scientific." It leaves no doubt as to how to sculpt the client's hair, or how to analyze an existing hair sculpture.

UNIFORMLY LAYERED FORM

The length arrangement of hair produces the form of a hair sculpture. For example, when the length arrangement of hair is all one length, its form will be uniformly layered. Although this type of terminology may seem strange to you at the moment, you will soon realize how this way of thinking about sculpture will make you a better hair designer. In other words, as a Pivot Point designer you will understand each hair sculpture from the inside out. You will know why the sculpting techniques work instead of just how they work.

Hair sculpting can stand alone as a core salon service or serve as the foundation for other services, such as a perm or color. Because the *sculpture* is the foundation of all the other hair services, it is crucial that the fundamentals of hair sculpting become second nature to you. Without a good sculpture, the overall design you and your client have in mind will be difficult to achieve and maintain.

COSMETOLOGY FUNDAMENTALS   269

To understand how to sculpt hair, you need to understand the relationship between the hair's length arrangement and the form that arrangement produces. This chapter, *Sculpture*, takes you through a step-by-step process that will prepare you to create all the sculpted forms you can imagine.

HAIR SCULPTURE ANALYSIS

Hair can assume an infinite variety of forms. This includes differences in shape, texture and structure. Hair sculpture analysis begins by using a consistent system of communication, which is based on "selective seeing" through the three levels of observation: basic, detail and abstract.

Analyzing a hair sculpture using the levels of observation helps train your eye to gather information that will allow you to recreate what you see and inspire design adaptation.

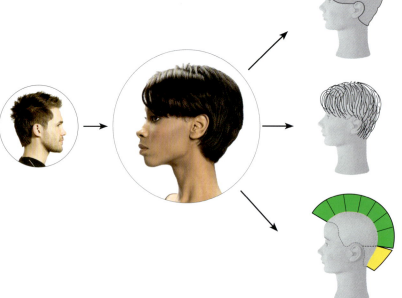

BASIC
Identify the basic form or shape by simply observing the outer boundary or silhouette, known as the **form line**.

DETAIL
Identify the detail in the texture or surface appearance.

ABSTRACT
In the abstract level, the hair is viewed as if is standing straight out from the head in order to identify the structure and how it was created.

SHAPE
Form analysis begins with the basic identification of the form or shape of the sculpture. Only the silhouette of the design is analyzed, while blocking out any extraneous information, such as the texture or color.

TEXTURE
The next step is to look at the detail of the surface appearance to determine the type of texture you see. There are two categories of surface appearance: unactivated texture with smooth, unbroken lines and activated texture with broken lines and exposed ends.

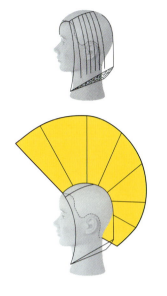

Some sculptures feature a combination of activated and unactivated textures. For example, a sculpture may have stacked ends in the exterior that display activated texture, while smooth, unactivated texture is maintained in the interior.

STRUCTURE

Structure is defined as the arrangement of lengths across the curves of the head. The various length arrangements create the shape of a sculpted form. A **structure graphic** is a diagram that provides an abstract view of the length arrangement to scale and proportion. The structure graphic serves as a blueprint for the final sculpture similar to the details of an architect's blueprint for a building.

In hair sculpture, there are two basic ways to analyze the structure:
- Natural fall
- Normal projection

CIAL ZONES
Apex   E - Chin
Hairline   F - Neck
Eye   G - Shoulder
Ear Lobe

NATURAL FALL

Natural fall describes the hair as the lengths lay or fall naturally over the curves of the head. Viewing a hair sculpture in natural fall allows you to observe and analyze the texture of the hair, the direction and character of the form line and the overall shape.

Natural fall describes the length or level to which the hair falls on the anatomy, such as the ear lobe, chin or neck.

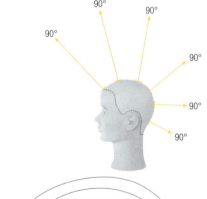

NORMAL PROJECTION

Another way to analyze the structure or length arrangement of a hair sculpture is in **normal projection**. With normal projection, the hair is viewed abstractly as if it were projected at a 90° angle from the various curves of the head.

Understanding the abstract structure of the form gives you the ability to duplicate any given design as well as develop your own creativity.

COSMETOLOGY FUNDAMENTALS

FOUR BASIC FORMS

The Pivot Point approach features four basic forms that, when used alone or in a combination, make up all hair designs. Each form has a unique shape, structure and texture and each can be sculpted at a variety of lengths.

The four basic forms are:
- Solid form
- Graduated form
- Increase-layered form
- Uniformly layered form

Each form is described in this section along with its color-coded structure graphic.

The shape of a hair sculpture is largely determined by where the weight is positioned. **Weight** is created by the concentration of length within a given area. Understanding how to work with weight allows you to reposition the amount of expansion within a design, changing its shape to better suit the client.

The **crest area**, which is the widest area around the head, divides the **interior**, the area above the crest, from the **exterior**, the area below the crest.

SOLID FORM

The **solid form** consists of lengths that progress from shorter in the exterior to longer in the interior. In natural fall all lengths fall to one level, resulting in an unbroken, unactivated surface texture. Near the top, the shape echoes the curves of the head; at the bottom, the shape reflects the build-up of weight at the perimeter. A solid form is sometimes referred to as a one-length cut, bob, Dutch boy, blunt cut or 0° angle cut.

COLOR-CODED: Blue
SHAPE: Rectangle
TEXTURE: Unactivated
STRUCTURE: Shorter exterior progressing to longer interior
WEIGHT: Maximum weight develops at the form line since all lengths fall to the same level

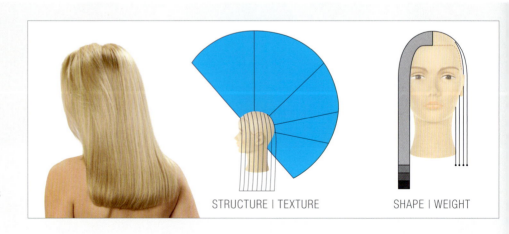

STRUCTURE | TEXTURE

SHAPE | WEIGHT

SCULPTURE

GRADUATED FORM

The **graduated form** consists of shorter exterior lengths that gradually progress toward longer interior lengths. In natural fall the ends appear to stack up along an angle. The result is a combination of unactivated texture in the interior and activated texture in the exterior. The line that divides the two textures is known as a ridge line. The weight in a graduated form occurs above the perimeter form line, creating the visual impression of a triangular shape. A graduated form is sometimes referred to as a wedge or 45° angle cut.

COLOR-CODED: Yellow
SHAPE: Triangle
TEXTURE: Unactivated/Activated
STRUCTURE: Shorter exterior gradually progressing to longer interior
WEIGHT: Found above the perimeter form line, where the unactivated and activated textures meet

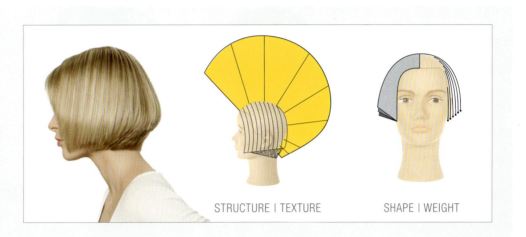

STRUCTURE | TEXTURE   SHAPE | WEIGHT

INCREASE-LAYERED FORM

The **increase-layered form** consists of shorter interior lengths that progress toward longer exterior lengths. In natural fall this progression creates a totally activated surface texture with no visible weight. Because the lengths of hair are dispersed across the curves of the head, the increase-layered form generally has an elongated or oval shape. An increase-layered form is sometimes referred to as a shag or 180° angle cut.

COLOR-CODED: Red
SHAPE: Oval
TEXTURE: Activated
STRUCTURE: Shorter interior progressing to longer exterior
WEIGHT: No concentration of weight since lengths disperse across the curves of the head

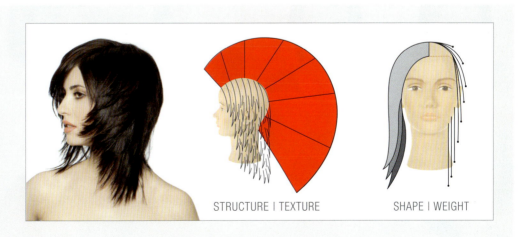

STRUCTURE | TEXTURE   SHAPE | WEIGHT

COSMETOLOGY FUNDAMENTALS

UNIFORMLY LAYERED FORM

The **uniformly layered form** has consistent lengths throughout the design. In natural fall this repetition of lengths produces a totally activated texture with no noticeable weight. Lengths disperse over the curve of the head, creating a rounded shape that follows the curves of the head. A uniformly layered form is sometimes referred to as a layered cut or 90° angle cut.

COLOR-CODED: Green

SHAPE: Circular

TEXTURE: Activated

STRUCTURE: Same length throughout

WEIGHT: No concentration of weight since lengths disperse across the curves of the head

STRUCTURE | TEXTURE SHAPE | WEIGHT

MEN

The four basic forms and their individual characteristics apply to both the female and male client. Although not considered a fifth form, **gradation**, also color-coded yellow, is a very short version of the graduated form. With gradation, shorter exterior lengths gradually progress to longer interior lengths and are generally combined with other forms. Fades and bald fades are examples of gradation.

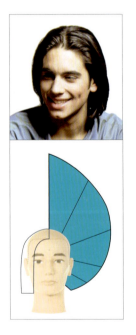    

274 SCULPTURE

COMBINATION FORMS

A large percentage of the designs that you will create for your clients will consist of **combination forms**, which include two or more of the four basic forms within a sculpture. The properties of the four basic forms can be combined in an infinite number of ways to create designs that are perfectly suited for each individual client.

The proportional relationship of each form within a combination produces the shape, texture and position of weight in the final design.

INCREASE/SOLID
When an increase-layered interior is combined with a solid exterior, the illusion of an activated surface appearance is achieved while maintaining maximum perimeter weight.

INCREASE/UNIFORM/GRADATED
Gradated exterior lengths create a close-fitting contour that blends with the uniformly layered lengths, while the increase-layered fringe elongates the form and creates height and fullness.

UNIFORM/GRADUATED

In this uniform graduated combination, shorter exterior lengths progressively blend to uniformly layered interior lengths creating a totally activated surface texture.

UNIFORM/INCREASE

Uniform interior lengths are combined with increase-layered exterior lengths for a highly activated surface and elongation toward the perimeter.

GRADUATION/UNIFORM/GRADATION

Gradation creates a close-fitting exterior and blends to uniformly layered lengths creating a rounded interior. Graduated interior lengths create weight to achieve a focal point toward the face.

SQUARE (RECTILINEAR) FORM
In this combination form, all four basic forms are combined in one sculpture. A weight area is created where the increase-layered form meets the graduated form, resulting in a square form.

9.2 SCULPTING TOOLS

Sculpting tools are the hand-held tools used for sculpting hair. Because different tools have different effects on the hair, the tools you use impact the final sculpture result, allowing subtle variations in texture, particularly at the form line. Through the design decision process, you will determine not only the form to be sculpted, but also the most appropriate tools and techniques to use. Being familiar with the various sculpting tools, will enable you to make the proper tool selections for the particular results.

The five tools used most often for sculpting hair are:
- Shears
- Razors
- Combs
- Taper shears
- Clippers

The tool together with the proper technique produces the desired result. Sculpting tools require disinfection after each use.

SHEARS
Shears, also called straight shears, produce a clean, blunt edge. By varying the position of the shears as you sculpt, you can create subtle variations in the hair strand.

TAPER SHEARS
Taper shears consist of one straight blade and one serrated blade. They produce a distinct and regular alternation of shorter and longer lengths. Taper shears with more, closely spaced teeth will remove a greater amount of hair, and taper shears with fewer, widely spaced teeth will remove less hair.

RAZOR

A **razor** produces tapering or an angled effect on the end of each strand, which results in more mobility and a softer, somewhat diffused form line. This tapering may occur on the top or bottom of the strand, depending on the sculpting technique you use. The razor may be used to sculpt the entire form or to texturize within the form.

CLIPPERS

Clippers are an electric tool that can achieve a variety of effects, depending on the blade attachment, or guard, used. Clippers can be used, for example, to create clean, precise lines or a soft, broom-like effect.

COMB

A **comb** is used to distribute and control the hair before and during sculpting. The amount of space between the teeth of the comb is very important in determining which comb best suits your purpose. The wider the spaces are between the teeth of the comb, the less tension is placed on the hair before or during sculpting. This results in softer finished lines. Closely spaced teeth will ribbon the hair more, allowing you to sculpt very precise lines.

SHEARS

Shears come in many different styles and lengths and are made from a variety of materials, ranging from porcelain to cobalt steel. Blade lengths range from as short as 4" (10 cm) to as long as 7½" (18.75 cm). As a rule, short shears are used for more precision or detailed sculpting, while longer shears are used for overcomb techniques and for sculpting larger sections of hair. As with every tool, shears are an investment. Select a quality pair and care for them as you would any fine instrument. It is important that your shears be kept very sharp. To avoid dulling your blades prematurely, never sculpt or cut anything with your shears other than hair. Be sure to disinfect your shears before and after every service.

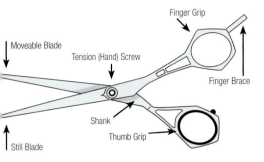

PARTS OF THE SHEARS

A pair of shears consists of a still or stationary blade, which is controlled by the finger grip, and the moveable, or action blade, which is controlled by the thumb grip. The two blades are joined by the tension or hand screw. The thumb and finger grips may be even with each other or they may be offset. Some shears have a finger brace on which the small finger rests for comfort and balance. The finger rest may or may not be removable.

HOW TO HOLD THE SHEARS AND COMB

Being comfortable with your tools is the first step to overcoming any concerns you may have about hair sculpting, so it is important to learn how to hold them properly.

INSERT RING FINGER
Insert your ring or third finger into the finger grip to control the still blade.

INSERT THUMB
Insert the tip of your thumb into the thumb grip to control the moveable blade. Note that placing more of your thumb into the thumb grip lessens the amount of control you have. Place your index and middle fingers on top of the shears for greater control. Rest your finger on the finger brace if your shears have one.

REMOVE THUMB AND PALM SHEARS
When combing the hair or making a parting during a hair sculpture, it is necessary to hold the comb and shears in the same hand. To make this possible without jeopardizing your client's safety, "palm" your shears by releasing your thumb from the thumb grip and closing your palm over the shears.

An alternative method for palming the shears is to rest the blade of the shears on the outside of the palm.

HOLD COMB
Hold the comb between your thumb and index finger of the same hand. Once the hair is distributed (combed), transfer the comb to the opposite hand for sculpting.

When sculpting against the skin or to refine a perimeter, the palm may be positioned toward the head with the still blade against the skin.

SCULPTING POSITIONS

The sculpting position you choose will depend on the area of the head on which you are working, the desired results and how comfortable the position is for you. In most cases, you will work with finger, shears and shoulder positions that are parallel. Some common sculpting positions include: palm down, palm up (or out), palm to palm, and on top of the fingers.

PALM DOWN
Position the palm of your sculpting hand downward.

PALM UP
Position the palm of your sculpting hand upward.

PALM TO PALM
Position the palm of your sculpting hand so that it faces the palm of your other hand.

ON TOP OF THE FINGERS
In most cases you will sculpt under, or inside, your fingers as shown in the previous two photos. When lifting the lengths on top of the head, however, you will need to sculpt the hair along the top of your fingers.

TAPER SHEARS

Taper shears, also known as thinning shears, are used for creating shorter lengths within the form or on the ends of the hair to reduce bulk and create mobility. One blade of the taper shears is straight and the other is notched (serrated). The purpose of the notch is to hold the hair. As the blade closes, only the hair held in the notches will be sculpted. The remaining hair will be pushed between the teeth and remain at the original length. The distance between the notches (teeth) of the taper shear blade will determine the amount of hair that will be sculpted and/or the degree of taper. Taper shears can be used on both damp or dry hair. Taper shears also require disinfection. Follow manufacturer's directions and disinfection guidelines.

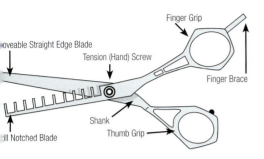

PARTS OF THE TAPER SHEARS

Taper shears have the same parts as shears except, as mentioned before, instead of having two straight edge blades, taper shears have one straight edge blade and one notched blade. The notched blade has teeth that are spaced at different intervals. Taper shears are held the same way as shears.

TAPER 8

Taper 8 shears have teeth that are spaced ⅛" (.3 cm) apart. Taper 8 shears are the best choice when a lightly tapered effect is desired, since it removes a minimal amount of hair within a parting.

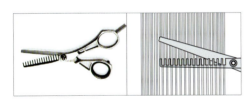

TAPER 16

Taper 16 shears have teeth that are spaced ¹⁄₁₆" (.15 cm) apart. Taper 16 shears are used to remove a medium amount of hair within a parting.

TAPER 32

Taper 32 shears have teeth that are spaced ¹⁄₃₂" (.08 cm) apart. Taper 32 shears are best for maximum hair removal and highly textured effects.

CHANNELING SHEARS

Channeling shears have wider notches that produce dramatic chunky effects. Channeling shears are primarily used for special effects such as extreme length variations and heavy fringes or notched perimeter lengths.

RAZORS

There is a variety of razors available to the professional hair designer that suits different styles of sculpting and levels of comfort. Some razors are foldable and some are not. Some include a guard that is used over the blade for protection or for texturizing techniques. Some razors have blades made from high-quality surgical steel, while others may have a soft, flexible steel blade.

When sculpting with a razor, it is essential that the hair be damp throughout. If the hair is too dry, sculpting will be more difficult and possibly uncomfortable for the client.

PARTS OF A RAZOR

The razor consists of a blade and usually a guard, which is used to protect you from coming in direct contact with the edge of the blade. The shank is used to hold the razor, while the handle, which is sometimes foldable, is used to rest your fingers. The tang is used to rest the little finger.

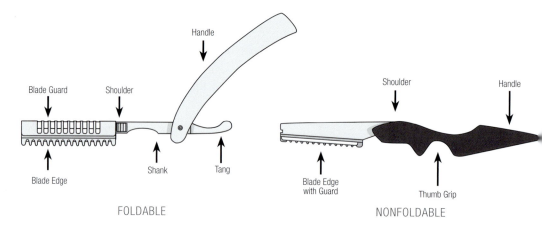

FOLDABLE NONFOLDABLE

HOW TO HOLD THE RAZOR

There are several ways in which you can hold the razor. The descriptions that follow explain how to hold a foldable razor and a nonfoldable razor.

With a foldable razor, the handle is generally positioned straight out while you are sculpting. Position your thumb at the bottom of the shank and position the rest of your fingers on top of the shank.

When sculpting in tight areas, such as around the perimeter hairline, you may wish to rest your little finger on the tang.

When working with a nonfoldable razor, position your thumb in the thumb groove and position your remaining fingers on top of the razor. This hand position works well when using texturizing techniques along a section of hair.

As an alternative, you can position your index finger on top of the razor while holding the razor with your thumb and remaining fingers. This hand position allows greater flexibility.

IMPORTANT SAFETY TIPS FOR USING A RAZOR

- Check with your area's regulating agency to determine whether you may remove nape or sideburn hair with the blade of a razor.
- Use the razor on damp-to-wet hair for the comfort of the client and ease in sculpting.
- Use a guard when applicable.
- Disinfect your razor before and after every service using general disinfection guidelines.
- Read manufacturer's directions before changing the blade of your razor.
- Replace the blade of your razor when it becomes dull.
- Use extreme caution when sculpting around moles, scars and skin lesions.
- Discard used razor blades in a puncture-proof or sharps container.

REMOVING AND INSERTING THE RAZOR BLADE
REMOVING
- Carefully remove the guard by first tightly grasping the razor handle and shank with the sculpting edge pointing upward, and then carefully slide the guard toward the end of the shank.
- Push the blade out using the guard. Place the flat side of the guard against the shank, with the razor blade positioned between the teeth of the guard.

INSERTING
- Hold the razor handle and shank with the blade slot directed upward.
- Grasp the razor blade with the sculpting edge pointing upward.
- Align the blade with the blade slot and insert the blade into the blade slot until it is secure.
- Position the outer edge of the blade between two teeth of the razor guard. Notice the teeth are locked into position in the blade slot. Maintain constant pressure and firmly push the blade into the full slot position.

COSMETOLOGY FUNDAMENTALS 283

RAZOR DISPENSER

Some razors come with a razor blade dispenser, which makes replacing razor blades safer and easier. Simply use the dispenser to slide on the new blade once the old one has been removed. Discard the old blade in a puncture-proof container.

CLIPPERS

Clippers are generally chosen to quickly sculpt larger sections of hair. Some clippers come with attachments called guards, which range from $1/8$" (.3 cm) to 1" (2.5 cm). These guards enable you to consistently sculpt the hair at the same length as the size of the guard (i.e., a $1/8$" [.3 cm] guard will sculpt the hair $1/8$" [.3 cm] from the scalp). When extremely short lengths are desired, no guard is used. Another way to determine and vary the distance from the scalp while sculpting is the clipper-over-comb technique. With this technique the clippers are positioned on top of the comb while sculpting. Clippers are available with different blade sizes. Small clippers, known as trimmers or edgers, are used to outline and refine the hairline, beard, mustache and sideburn areas.

PARTS OF THE CLIPPERS

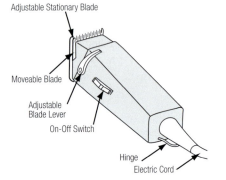

The stationary blade of clippers, also called the heel, is similar in function to the stationary blade of the shears. The moveable blade moves in a side-to-side motion as it sculpts the hair. The adustable blade lever is used to adjust the stationary blade. Some clippers have an electrical cord while others are cordless. A stiff-bristle clipper brush is used to clean the tool after each use. Blades should be removed for cleaning. Do not clean the clippers while they are turned on. The detachable blade and heel should be kept disinfected. Clipper oil provides lubrication for the moving parts of the tool to keep them good working condition, but should be used sparingly. Read manufacturer's directions for cleaning guidelines.

HOW TO HOLD THE CLIPPERS

The clippers can be held in a number of different ways, depending on the area of the head, the line or angle sculpted and your level of comfort.

One way to hold the clippers is to position your palm over them and positio your thumb on the side.

ALERT!
Never use clipper blades that have broken teeth, and always align a new set of blades.

SCULPTURE

Another way to hold the clippers is to position your thumb on top of them and position your remaining fingers underneath.

COMBS

Various comb sizes and shapes are used to control the hair. In particular, the main differences in combs are the sizes of the teeth, the spaces between the teeth and the desired results.

SHAMPOO COMB
The shampoo comb is designed to detangle wet hair in preparation for a hair sculpture.

MASTER SKETCHER
The Master Sketcher is used for controlling or distributing larger amounts of hair, as well as for the clipper-over-comb and shear-over-comb techniques.

SCULPTING COMB
The sculpting comb has both fine and wide teeth for distribution when working with medium-sized sections of hair.

TAPER COMB
The taper/contour or barber comb allows you to sculpt as close to the scalp as possible. It can also be positioned against the skin.

9.3 SCULPTING SKILLS

This section on sculpting skills explains the sequence of seven steps used every time you sculpt, followed by the texturizing techniques, short hair techniques and other sculpting considerations that increase your ability to sculpt professionally and meet the needs of a wide range of clientele.

A PROFESSIONAL AND PERSONALIZED SCULPTURE IS THE RESULT WHEN YOU:
- Follow Pivot Point's Seven Sculpting Procedures
- Perform the appropriate texturizing techniques
- Use short hair techniques when appropriate
- Address the considerations that apply to each individual client

PIVOT POINT'S SEVEN SCULPTING PROCEDURES

The Seven Sculpting Procedures are Pivot Point's unique system for producing predictable sculpture results. Developing your technical skills and following Pivot Point's systematic sculpting procedures will allow you to achieve accuracy and consistency in all of your work. Pivot Point's Seven Sculpting Procedures are: section, position head, part, distribute, project, position fingers/shears, and sculpt design line.

SEVEN BASIC SCULPTING PROCEDURES

1. SECTION
2. POSITION HEAD
3. PART
4. DISTRIBUTE
5. PROJECT
6. POSITION FINGERS/SHEARS
7. SCULPT DESIGN LINE

SECTION

Many successful hair sculptures begins with sectioning. **Sectioning** involves dividing the hair into workable areas for control. One common sectioning pattern divides the hair into four sections by parting from the center front hairline to the nape and from ear to ear. The numbers of sections and the types of sectioning patterns you choose depend on the type of hair sculpture you will be creating.

Sectioning and subsectioning are also determined by changes in design lines, projection angle or distribution, and are sometimes affected by the hair's natural growth patterns. If forms are combined, you may choose to section according to the proportion of one form to the other.

The most common terms used to identify the reference points of the head are: crest area (parietal), interior, exterior, front, back, top, sides, nape, crown, occipital, apex, fringe and perimeter.

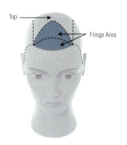
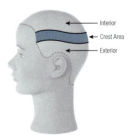
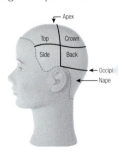

The front and back of the head are divided by a line that runs from ear to ear. The **side** is the area in front and on top of the ear. The **apex** refers to the top or highest point of the head. In the back of the head, right below the crest area, the protruding bone is referred to as the **occipital**. The area below the occipital is the **nape**. The area in front of the apex and which may extend to the outer corner of each eye is referred to as the **fringe** area. The area all around the hairline is referred to as the **perimeter**.

POSITION HEAD

The **head position**, upright, forward or tilted, directly influences the fall of the hair, which affects the texture and the direction of the sculpted line. You will usually want the head position to remain constant while sculpting a given area. The most common head positions are upright, forward or tilted to either side.

UPRIGHT
Sculpting the hair with the head in an upright position achieves the most natural, pure result.

FORWARD
When the head is in a forward position, the neck is stretched. Sculpting with the head in this position produces hair lengths that are shorter in the nape, and longer surface lengths. This results in a slight underbevel effect with ends that turn under when the head is returned to its normal upright position. The forward head position is often used when refining form lines.

TILTED
The head may be tilted to one side or the other to refine form lines.

PART

Partings are lines that subdivide sections of hair in order to separate, distribute and control the hair while sculpting. The size of the parting is determined by the density of the hair. The parting pattern used is generally parallel to the design line, which is the guideline used while sculpting. For maximum ease, efficiency and precision when making partings, the hair is combed in the direction that the parting will be made. The most common parting lines are horizontal, vertical, diagonal back, diagonal forward, concave and convex. **Concave lines curve inward, like the inside of a sphere, while convex lines curve outward, like the outside of a sphere.**

The **celestial axis** is a symbol used to identify straight and curved lines, directions and projection angles.

COSMETOLOGY FUNDAMENTALS

| HORIZONTAL LINES | DIAGONAL BACK | DIAGONAL FORWARD | VERTICAL LINES | CONCAVE | CONVEX |

④ DISTRIBUTE

Distribution is the direction the hair is combed in relation to its base parting. The four types of distribution are: natural, perpendicular, shifted and directional.

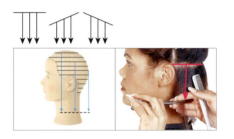

NATURAL DISTRIBUTION

Natural distribution is the direction the hair assumes as it falls naturally from the head due to gravity. Gravitational pull and natural growth patterns will affect this direction to some degree, especially over the crest area. Natural distribution is used from horizontal, diagonal-left and diagonal-right partings, primarily to create solid forms.

PERPENDICULAR DISTRIBUTION

With **perpendicular distribution,** the hair is combed at a 90°, or right, angle from its base parting. This type of distribution can be used from any line—horizontal, diagonal or vertical—and is primarily used to sculpt graduated and layered forms.

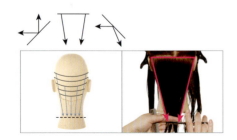

SHIFTED DISTRIBUTION

With **shifted distribution** the hair is combed out of natural distribution in any direction except perpendicular to its base parting. Shifted distribution, also known as overdirection, can be used when sculpting most forms except solid form. It is generally used for exaggerated length increases and blending within the form.

STRAIGHT UP

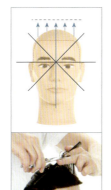

DIRECTIONAL DISTRIBUTION

When the hair is distributed straight up (vertically) or straight out (horizontally) from the curve of the head, it is called **directional distribution**. To maintain consistency, the lines of the celestial axis are used to visualize the distribution. Directional distribution results in length increases due to the curve of the head and is often used when sculpting along a plane. In hair sculpture, a plane is an imaginary two-dimensional flat surface that is sculpted in space along horizontal, vertical or diagonal lines.

STRAIGHT OUT

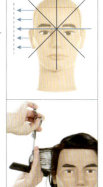

Directional distribution is also used to sculpt a square or rectilinear form using the **planar sculpting** technique. Planar sculpting is a technique in which the hair is sculpted along horizontal and vertical planes. At the top, the hair is directed straight up from the curves of the head and sculpted horizontally or parallel to the floor. Along the sides and in the back, the hair is distributed straight out from the curves of the head and sculpted vertically or perpendicular to the floor.

When using the planar sculpting technique, a weight area or corner is automatically achieved where the two planes meet, thus being referred to as a square form or rectilinear form.

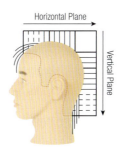

PROJECT

Projection, also known as elevation, is the angle at which the hair is held in relation to the curve of the head prior to and while sculpting. The most common projection angles used in hair sculpting are 0°, 45° and 90°. Angles between 0° and 30° are considered to be low projection, between 30° and 60° is medium projection and between 60° and 90° is high projection. Projecting below 90° produces (builds) weight. Projection angles 90° and above begin to layer the hair and diminish weight.

A quadrant of the celestial axis is used to determine projection angles from the straight and curved surfaces of the head. Once 0° has been established, 45° and 90° angles can be determined in any direction.

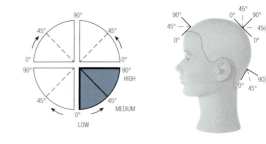

PROJECTION FOR SOLID FORM

Natural fall is the natural position hair assumes due to gravitational pull. In some areas of the head, natural fall may also be 0°. This will be relative to the shape of the individual head. When the hair is in natural fall, it is neither lifted from the scalp nor moved toward the scalp, particularly in the nape area. Minimal tension is applied to the hair.

With 0° projection the hair is held flat to the surface of the head while sculpting. This may occur naturally (natural fall) or the hair may be placed in this position with distribution. A solid form with a slight underbevel is the result of sculpting with 0° projection throughout the area, and with the head tilted slightly forward.

PROJECTION FOR GRADUATED FORM

Projection angles between 0° and 90° will result in a graduated form. The standard projection angle used to sculpt graduated forms is 45°. Since graduation is sculpted from the perimeter upward, the first section that is projected will determine the line of inclination. The **line of inclination** is the angle at which the graduation progresses in length. The higher the projection angle, the greater the amount of graduated texture and the higher the resulting line of inclination.

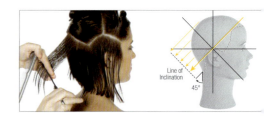

PROJECTION FOR INCREASE-LAYERED FORM

When sculpting increase-layered forms, the projection angle of the stationary design line establishes the location where all other lengths are converged. The farther the hair travels to the design line, the longer the result. You will generally use a projection angle of either 0°, 45° or 90°. Directing all the lengths to the stationary design line opposite the area of desired length increase is known as the conversion layering technique. The **conversion layering** technique is the primary sculpting technique used to sculpt increase-layered forms.

PROJECTION FOR UNIFORMLY LAYERED FORM

The projection angle used to sculpt uniformly layered forms is 90° from the curve of the head. This is also called normal projection. Maintaining a consistent 90° angle from the various curves of the head is important for uniformly layered forms since inconsistency will result in uneven lengths.

6 POSITION FINGERS/SHEARS

Finger/shear position refers to the position of the fingers and the shears relative to the base parting. The two basic types of finger/shear position are parallel and nonparallel.

PARALLEL FINGER/SHEAR POSITION

With a **parallel finger/shear position,** the fingers are positioned at an equal distance away from the parting while sculpting. Sculpting in this manner will result in the purest reflection of the chosen line. Since the shears will follow the fingers, this is also known as parallel sculpting.

NONPARALLEL FINGER/SHEAR POSITION

With a **nonparallel finger/shear position,** the fingers are positioned unequally away from the parting while sculpting. This position is used to create exaggerated length increases, to blend between contrasting lengths and to control weight development.

COSMETOLOGY FUNDAMENTALS 291

7. SCULPT DESIGN LINE

A **design line** is the artistic pattern or length guide used while sculpting and can be stationary or mobile. Any straight or curved line of the celestial axis can be used to create or analyze a design line. In some instances, the design line may also be the perimeter form line. An example would be a solid form structure.

STATIONARY DESIGN LINE

A **stationary design line** is a constant, stable guide to which all lengths are directed. This design line is used when a progression of lengths in the opposite direction is desired. A stationary design line is used to sculpt solid and increase-layered forms and to achieve a weight area (concentration of lengths) in graduated forms.

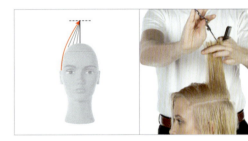

MOBILE DESIGN LINE

A **mobile design line** is a moveable guide that consists of a small amount of previously sculpted hair, which is used as a length guide to sculpt subsequent partings. A mobile design line, sometimes called a traveling guide, is used to sculpt graduated and layered forms and square combination forms.

CROSS-CHECKING

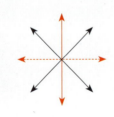

Cross-checking is the final stage in sculpting, in which the balance and accuracy of the sculpture is checked by using the line opposite the original parting pattern; for example, when sculpting vertically, you cross-check horizontally. Cross-checking may be performed periodically throughout the service. If unwanted lengths are found, they should be sculpted with the original parting pattern used to sculpt the form.

09

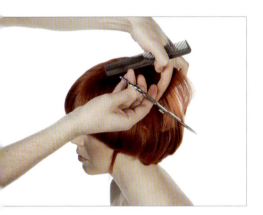

TEXTURIZING TECHNIQUES

Texturizing, sometimes referred to as tapering or thinning, involves sculpting shorter lengths within the form or at the perimeter to reduce bulk and create support, closeness, fullness, mobility and visual texture in the hair sculpture without shortening the overall length appearance of the hair. Texturizing can be done with a variety of tools to create various results. Although texturizing techniques are generally performed after the hair sculpture, texturizing techniques can also be used to create the sculpted form.

Always consider the hair's natural texture in order to determine where on the hair strand to perform the technique. For instance, **fine hair can be texturized closer to the scalp than coarse hair, since fine hair needs the extra support of the shorter lengths underneath in order to achieve a fuller-looking effect.** When coarse hair is texturized too close to the scalp, the shorter lengths will not blend with the surface hair, creating an uneven, spiked effect.

As a general rule, coarse hair should be texturized at least 1½" (3.75 cm) away from the scalp. Medium hair should be texturized 1" (2.5 cm) away from the scalp, and fine hair can be texturized as close as ½" (1.25 cm) from the scalp. A very light stroke must be used when texturizing to avoid a chunky effect.

Curly hair requires some special considerations. Although it is generally recommended to texturize hair while it is damp, curly hair should be texturized while it is dry to allow for more control and the shrinkage factor.

As a professional designer, you will need to determine which types of texturizing techniques will be used and the amount of texturizing needed for each client according to hair type and desired results. When in doubt, remember that it's always better to remove less hair than too much. **Avoid thinning around the hairline.** Such thinning creates short, uneven hairs that are difficult to control.

TEXTURIZING AREAS OF THE STRAND

Texturizing techniques can be performed at any of the three areas of the hair strand: base, midstrand and ends.

Base texturizing, which is performed from the scalp up to 1" (2.5 cm) away from the scalp, creates expansion and fullness. This technique removes weight at the base area, allowing the hair to lift away from the head. The shorter lengths support the longer lengths to encourage natural texture and movement.

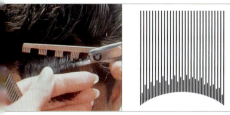

COSMETOLOGY FUNDAMENTALS

293

Midstrand texturizing, which is performed between the end of the base area up to 1" (2.5 cm) before the ends, reduces bulk and weight. The shorter lengths support the longer lengths to create fullness or a contoured effect.

End texturizing, which is performed on the ends of the hair, reduces bulk and weight to allow for mobility. End texturizing also softens the ends and helps to blend weight lines.

TEXTURIZING CATEGORIES

There are three main categories of texturizing: form line tapering, contour tapering and expansion tapering.

FORM LINE

CONTOUR

EXPANSION

FORM LINE TAPERING

Form line tapering refers to texturizing the ends of the hair along the form line to reduce bulk by releasing the ends to allow mobility. It also softens and helps blend weight lines. This technique is also known as end tapering. The types of form line tapering discussed in this section are: bevel-up, bevel-under, notching, pointing, end tapering with taper shears, razor etching, slithering technique and slide cutting.

BEVEL-UP TECHNIQUE

The **bevel-up** technique produces a slight upward turn of the ends, or "flip," by texturizing with the blade on top of the section of hair. The length of the stroke and the amount of pressure that you apply is determined by the amount of flip you wish to achieve.

BEVEL-UNDER TECHNIQUE
To encourage a **bevel-under,** or turned-under effect, the blade is positioned behind the section of hair and moved in curved strokes. As with the bevel-up technique, the amount of pressure you use and the length of your strokes will vary the amount of end taper achieved.

NOTCHING TECHNIQUE
The **notching** technique creates irregular lengths, usually for a chunkier texture along the hair ends. It can be used to sculpt the form line or the design line as well as for texturizing. This technique is ideal for curly or wavy hair. Weight is removed, encouraging mobility and adding textural interest to the design.

POINTING
For the **pointing** technique, the tips of straight shears are moved from the fingers toward the ends to create irregular lengths. The amount of end taper depends on the position of your fingers and the number of strokes.

The pointing technique can also be used at the base or midstrand on shorter hair lengths to release weight or create subtle textural interest.

END TAPERING WITH TAPER SHEARS
For a more distinct, regular alternation of shorter and longer lengths, tapering is performed with taper shears. Taper shears with more, closely spaced teeth will remove a greater amount of hair, while fewer, widely spaced teeth will remove less hair.

RAZOR ETCHING

Razor etching, which is used to reduce weight or remove length, is a technique in which the ends of the hair are carved into with a razor using a back-and-forth motion. The blade may be positioned at the side or at the top of a section. The length of the stroke will determine the amount of end taper that occurs within the section.

SLITHERING

Slithering, which is also referred to as effilating, is a technique in which the shears are opened and closed rhythmically while moving upward from the ends. **Slithering removes bulk and creates mobility.**

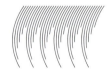

SLIDE CUTTING

Slide cutting is a technique in which slightly closed shears slide along the strand to produce a rapid length increase. Frequently used to maintain maximum length and weight in forms, slide cutting is also used for blending and framing areas around the hairline.

CONTOUR TAPERING

This texturizing technique is performed at the midstrand and ends to reduce bulk and allow the hair to lie closer to the head

RAZOR ROTATION

The **razor rotation** technique is performed by rotating the razor and the comb in a light, circular motion to reduce bulk and blend the form. **The hair should be damp when performing razor rotation in order to avoid client discomfort.**

EXPANSION TAPERING

This technique is usually performed near the base or midstrand to create expansion and volume. It removes weight throughout the strand, allowing the hair to lift away from the head. The shorter lengths support the longer lengths.

STRAND TAPERING WITH TAPER SHEARS
Strand tapering with taper shears creates expansion and volume within the form.

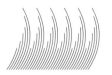

SLICING
The slicing technique is performed by gliding the open shears along the surface of the hair to achieve mobility. The amount of texture activation is controlled by how wide the shears are opened while sculpting. Slicing on the surface is used to create mobility and expansion.

SHORT HAIR TECHNIQUES

When sculpting shorter forms there are additional sculpting techniques you can use. These include overcomb and outlining techniques that achieve close-fitting contours with well-defined perimeter hairlines. These techniques can be applied to both male and female clients to achieve various designs, from classic to progressive. In addition, considering how male clients wear their facial hair, whether it be a beard, goatee or mustache, will allow you to adapt your overcomb and outlining techniques to personalize designs for them.

OVERCOMB TECHNIQUES

Overcomb techniques are used to sculpt short exterior lengths, generally gradation, which progress to longer lengths toward the crown. **Overcomb techniques** use a comb as a guide to hold lengths while the hair protruding over the comb is sculpted with shears, taper shears or clippers. There are generally two ways to hold a comb while performing overcomb techniques. The most common way is to place the index finger on the teeth and the thumb on the spine. Another way is to hold the comb between the thumb and fingers on both sides of the spine.

SHEAR-OVER-COMB TECHNIQUE

With the **shear-over-comb** technique a comb is used to control the hair while the shears are opened and closed repeatedly to sculpt the protruding lengths. Whether using straight shears or taper shears, the shears are positioned parallel to the comb and both the shears and the comb move upward in unison. This technique is performed as many times as necessary to complete the form.

CLIPPER-OVER-COMB TECHNIQUE

With the **clipper-over-comb** technique a comb is used as a guide to hold the lengths while the hair protruding over the comb is sculpted with the clippers. The clippers are positioned on top of the comb, which can be positioned horizontally, diagonally or vertically. The clipper-over-comb technique allows you to remove hair lengths very close to the scalp or to create square forms, such as the flat top.

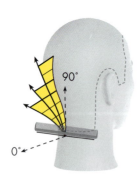

COMB CONTROL

Various comb sizes can be used to control the hair while sculpting. A large comb such as the Master Sketcher is used to quickly remove lengths. A sculpting comb is then used to sculpt shorter lengths, while a taper comb is used to define design lines and to refine the perimeter. The angle at which the comb is held and the distance between the comb and the scalp determine the amount of hair to be sculpted. The higher the angle of the comb, the greater the amount of transparency, or visibility, of the scalp that will be achieved. Overcomb techniques produce three types of gradation: low, medium and high.

LOW GRADATION

Low gradation creates the least amount of transparency and is generally located above the perimeter hair line, to just below the occipital. Note that the line of inclination, which is controlled by the angle of the comb, quickly moves away from the head, thereby creating a low line of inclination.

MEDIUM GRADATION

Medium gradation creates a medium degree of transparency and generally extends into the occipital area. The line of inclination moves closer to the head as the amount of gradation increases. Note that with medium gradation, the angle of the comb is positioned closer to the scalp than with low gradation.

HIGH GRADATION

High gradation creates maximum transparency and extends above the occipital and into the interior. The line of inclination is close to the head in high gradation. Note that the closer the comb is angled to the head and the closer the distance between the comb and the scalp, the higher the line of inclination and the greater the degree of transparency.

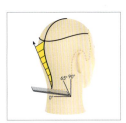

OUTLINING TECHNIQUES

Outlining the hair is a sculpting technique used to define the perimeter hairline. It is usually performed on short sculptures to accommodate the client's unique hairline, particularly at the nape. Be sure to analyze and follow the natural growth pattern when outlining the nape hairline.

Outlining can be performed with shears, a razor, clippers or trimmers. The tips of the shears may be used to outline the entire hairline, including the sideburns, ears and nape. Generally the tips of the shears are used first to create the outline. Then clippers, trimmers or a razor is used to sculpt the hair beyond the outlined area. Some regulatory agencies prohibit the use of a razor on the skin for certain licensed practitioners.

ALERT!
Use extreme caution when sculpting on the skin with the razor. Cosmetologists may not be allowed to perform this service. Be guided by your regulatory agency.

Clippers or trimmers can also be used for outlining. The clipper or trimmer blades are placed against the skin and the hair is sculpted section by section.

OUTLINING SPECIAL DESIGNS

Outlining special designs with the clippers or trimmers is an art form. Once you've planned your design, the hair is carved carefully. Stencils may be used to perform this creative art.

 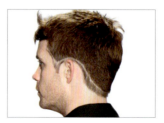

09

FACIAL HAIR

Designing facial hair—beards, goatees and mustaches—is a special service you can offer your male clientele. Facial hair can be worn as a fashion statement or to enhance or conceal facial features. You will usually use overcomb and/ or outlining techniques to trim eyebrows, beards, goatees, mustaches and sideburns. Maintaining the shape of a beard, goatee or mustache can be done with trimmers.

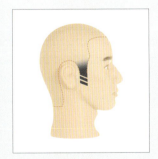
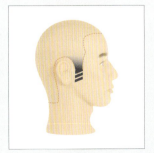

COSMETOLOGY FUNDAMENTALS

SCULPTING CONSIDERATIONS

There are important considerations that serve to check your work and enhance the final results. For example, considering the client's natural growth patterns to determine which hair sculpture will work best as well as personalizing that sculpted form are important steps that lead to client satisfaction. The sculpting considerations described in this section are: growth patterns, fringe and nape variations, curly hair considerations, and children as clients.

GROWTH PATTERNS

You will need to adapt your sculpting techniques to accommodate natural growth patterns. These growth patterns are determined by the angle and direction at which the hair grows out of the scalp. Strong patterns may cause the hair to "stand up" if sculpted too short. Natural parts may influence the overall design proportions and symmetry.

When sculpting shorter lengths, particularly those that require the use of the shear-over-comb technique, it is often advisable to work against the growth patterns while refining. This technique is most often performed on dry hair so that growth patterns are more obvious.

A **widow's peak** is a prominent hair growth pattern that forms from a point at the front hairline and curves to one side. Leave the fringe area longer to avoid a spiking effect with the hair sticking straight up.

A **cowlick,** characterized by a strong growth pattern that moves to the right or left, is usually found in straight or wavy hair at the front hairline or crown. Sculpt the hair following the same direction it naturally grows and falls. Allow additional length in this area to avoid spiking.

A **whorl** is a strong circular directional growth on either side of the nape or crown. Allow additional length so the hair will remain flat or sculpt the hair very close to the scalp to avoid spiking.

FRINGE AND NAPE VARIATIONS

The fringe is the hair that partially or completely covers the forehead in a hair design. The nape is the hair that covers the area at the back of the neck. It is important to adapt the fringe to the shape and features of your client's face and to the hair sculpture, as well as to consider the length and width of your client's neck when determining the right nape design. Here are a few examples:

A solid fringe can frame the eyes.

A longer fringe can be swept to the side to expose the forehead.

A layered fringe area adds texture, fullness and height.

Nape variations can be customized according to the hair's growth patterns and the dimensions of the client's neck and shoulders.

CURLY HAIR CONSIDERATIONS

When sculpting curly hair, there are some particular techniques that will help you create the desired result. Prior to sculpting curly hair, consider how the hair will be worn.

If the hair will be worn straight, you may wish to shampoo, air form (blow dry) and/or thermal press the hair straight before sculpting. By straightening the hair first, you will see how long the hair actually is and be able to sculpt the hair accordingly.

If the hair will be worn naturally curly, you may first wish to shampoo and towel-dry the hair. Drying the hair thoroughly will allow you to observe the natural curl formation. After observing the hair in its natural state, spray the hair with water to lightly moisten it. Sculpting the hair while damp rather than wet reduces the amount of stretching. Sculpting hair partly wet and partly dry will result in an uneven effect.

You may also use a comb instead of your fingers to control curly hair while sculpting. The comb allows for minimal tension so that you can view how the hair will fall naturally.

SCULPTING DRY VERSUS WET HAIR

Generally designers sculpt their client's hair after the shampoo while the hair is still damp. The advantages to dry sculpting include being able to see how the hair falls naturally and observing the shape of the sculpture as it is being created. Ultimately, it is a matter of preference and situation that determine whether to sculpt wet, dry, or both. Tool choice is another consideration: choose clippers for dry hair, a razor on damp hair, and shears on dry or wet hair.

CHILDREN AS CLIENTS

Although many children pose no challenge when performing a hair sculpture, some children do need to be treated more carefully to help alleviate their fears and concerns. You can offer reassurance to a timid child, or calm down a boisterous one, by taking a few simple steps prior to and during a professional hair service.

- In the reception area, kneel down and make eye contact with the child or sit down next to the child.
- Introduce yourself and, if the child is very young, explain what is about to take place. Use fun language when explaining the process. For example, talk about the "ride" in the chair when you pump it up and that you have a cape that he or she can wear, just like the superheroes wear.
- If the parent and child allow you, take a young child by the hand as you lead him or her to your workstation.
- While performing the service, maintain continual eye and voice contact. Keep the child informed of everything you are doing. Use firm, but not rough or jerky, contact with the head and hair to instill confidence.
- Keep in mind that many young children do not know the difference between left and right. You might try putting different color hair clips on their shoelaces and refer to them when you need the child to move his or her head in a certain direction.
- To keep a child from squirming, offer a reward, such as a balloon, if he or she cooperates. You can also remind the child that squirming may cause you to cut yourself. Do not, however, tell a child that you might cut him or her.
- If an older child or teenager comes into the salon without a parent and requests a sculpting service, consider calling the parent first to gain permission. Ask your salon manager for the salon's policy regarding unaccompanied minors.

SCULPTING ESSENTIALS

The following charts summarize what you've already learned about tools and will help you become familiar with the sculpting products, tools, supplies and equipment you will use in the salon. Hair sculpting products are available from a variety of manufacturers. Hair sculpting equipment includes the furnishings and provisions necessary for a professional sculpting service. Keep in mind that Material Safety Data Sheets (MSDS) for all products used in the salon are required to be available within the salon for your review.

SCULPTING PRODUCTS

PRODUCTS	FUNCTION
SCULPTING LOTION	Controls hair while sculpting
GEL	Creates wet-look finishes
MOUSSE	Defines texture; creates light hold to firm hold on wet or dry hair
POMADE	Adds gloss and sheen to dry hair; creates texture separation; also referred to as polisher, glosser, lusterizer and brilliantine

SCULPTING TOOLS/SUPPLIES

TOOLS/SUPPLIES	FUNCTION
SHEARS	Provide a clean, blunt edge or line
TAPER SHEARS	Create a distinct and regular alternation of shorter and longer lengths for mobility
RAZOR	Creates a tapered effect on the edge of each strand, which produces a softer, somewhat diffused line
CLIPPERS	Create clean, precise lines or a soft, broom-like effect; various blade attachments (guards) allow the hair to be sculpted at various distances from the scalp
TRIMMERS	Used to outline the hairline, beard and sideburns
SHAMPOO COMB	Detangles wet hair in preparation for hair sculpture
MASTER SKETCHER COMB	Controls and distributes larger amounts of hair; also used for overcomb techniques
SCULPTING COMB	Parts and distributes the hair; primary comb for sculpting and overcomb techniques
TAPER/BARBER COMB	Helps to sculpt short lengths and refine the perimeter when used against the skin
TOWEL	Protects client from getting wet during shampoo service
PLASTIC CAPE	Protects client's clothing during the shampoo and hair sculpting service
CLOTH CAPE	Protects client's clothing during a dry hair sculpting service
NECK STRIP	Protects client's skin from contact with the cape; replaces towel during the hair sculpting service
SPRAY BOTTLE	Holds water; used to keep the hair damp while sculpting

SCULPTING EQUIPMENT

EQUIPMENT	FUNCTION
HAIR SCULPTING STATION	Provides a place for tools to be displayed and organized
HYDRAULIC CHAIR	Provides proper back support for client during the hair sculpting service; adjustable
WET DISINFECTANT CONTAINER	Holds solution for disinfecting tools
SHAMPOO BOWL	Supports client's neck and holds water and shampoo products during a shampoo service

ALERT!
Always follow manufacturers' directions for the proper use, disinfection and maintenance of sculpting essentials.

INFECTION CONTROL AND SAFETY

The following is a list of safety precautions you must follow prior to and during a hair sculpting service.
1. Practice infection control guidelines.
2. Wash and sanitize hands.
3. Protect the client and his or her clothing with proper draping procedures. Refer to the "Draping" portion of *Chapter 7, Trichology*.
4. Check the scalp for any diseases or disorders. If any are evident, refer the client to a physician and do not proceed with the service.
5. Disinfect and sanitize all tools after each use.
6. Discard disposable razor blades after each individual use and place in a puncture-proof container.
7. Sweep and dispose sculpted hair prior to performing an air-forming service.

SCULPTING SERVICE ESSENTIALS

As with all hair services, communicating with your client prior to the service will help you avoid misunderstandings and ensure predictable results. Use photos and magazines while talking with your client to clarify your design intentions.

CONNECT
- Meet and greet the client with a firm handshake and a pleasant tone of voice.
- Communicate to build rapport and develop a connection with the client.

CONSULT
- Ask questions to discover client needs. Questions such as, "Did you have a specific reason for selecting this particular look?" and "What haven't you liked about your previous look?" will help bring out what the client really wants and areas of concern the client might have.
- Ask questions about his or her lifestyle, such as "How much time do you have to spend on your hair?" Remember, if the client is leading a hectic lifestyle, you probably won't want to suggest a design that requires a high degree of maintenance.

- Ask specific questions such as, "Would you like layers in your hair?" or "Would you like your ears or your neck exposed?" to uncover client expectations about his or her hair design. Refer to *Chapter 8, Design Decisions,* for further guidelines.
- Analyze your client's face and body shape, physical features, hair and scalp. Refer to *Chapter 8, Design Decisions,* for further guidelines.
- Assess the facts and thoroughly think through your recommendations.
- Explain your recommended solutions and the price for today's service(s) as well as for future services.
- Gain feedback from your client and obtain consent before proceeding with the service.

CREATE
- Ensure your client is protected by draping with a towel and plastic cape during the shampoo process. Replace the towel with a neck strip for the actual sculpting procedures.
- Ensure client comfort during the service.
- Stay focused on delivering the sculpture service to the best of your ability.
- Teach the client how to perform at-home hair care maintenance.

COMPLETE
- Request specific feedback from your client. Ask questions and look for verbal and nonverbal cues to determine your client's level of satisfaction.
- Escort client to the retail area and show at least two products you used. Recommend products to maintain the appearance and condition of your client's hair.
- Invite your client to make a purchase.
- Suggest a future appointment time for your client's next visit.
- Offer sincere appreciation to your client for visiting the school or salon.
- Complete client record card for future visits; include recommended products.

SCULPTING PROCEDURE OVERVIEW

Once you understand the theory behind sculpture, you are ready to use your knowledge and apply it to hair. You can achieve a variety of results by combining techniques and forms within a single design. Fortunately, your mannequins won't complain, so practice, practice, practice. The *Sculpture, A Designer's Approach* coursebook will show you step-by-step procedures for individual sculpture services in greater detail.

SCULPTURE PREPARATION

- Clean sculpting station with disinfectant
- Arrange sculpting essentials, including shears, razor with guards and disposable blades, sculpting combs, sectioning clips and spray bottle
- Wash your hands with liquid soap
- Ask the client to remove jewelry and store in a secure place
- Drape client for a wet service
- Perform analysis of hair and scalp
- Shampoo and condition client's hair
- Replace client's towel with neck strip

SCULPTURE PROCEDURE

- Perform the Seven Sculpting Procedures to achieve desired results
    1. Section the hair into workable areas for the purpose of control
    2. Position head as either upright, tilted or forward
    3. Part to separate, distribute and control the hair (horizontal, vertical or diagonal)
    4. Distribute the hair (natural, perpendicular, shifted and/or directional)
    5. Project the hair appropriately for the desired structure (natural fall, 0°, 45°, or 90°)
    6. Position fingers/shears (parallel or nonparallel)
    7. Sculpt the appropriate design line (stationary or mobile)
- Texturize the sculpted form as appropriate (base, midstrand or ends)
- Cross-check for accuracy
- Perform finishing design procedures

SCULPTURE COMPLETION

- Reinforce guest's satisfaction with the overall salon experience
- Make professional product recommendations
- Prebook guest's next appointment
- End guest's visit with a warm and personal goodbye
- Discard non-reusable materials, disinfect tools and arrange workstation in proper order
- Wash your hands with liquid soap
- Complete client record card
- Provide follow-up after the salon visit

The theory and procedures you learned in this chapter will form the basis for advanced work in the ever-growing field of hair sculpting. Your future awaits as you practice mastering them.

CONNECTING THEORY TO REAL-WORLD PRACTICE

SCULPTURE	PERSONAL CONNECTION: IMPROVE YOURSELF	INDUSTRY CONNECTION: BECOME A PROFESSIONAL	CLIENT CONNECTION: SERVE THE GUEST
SCULPTING THEORY	Recognize the characteristics of the four basic sculpted forms	Possess strong fundamentals that are the foundation for creating successful hair sculptures	Consult with clients regarding the effects of different sculpted forms
SCULPTING TOOLS	Relate each part of a tool with its functionality	Use a variety of sculpting tools safely, skillfully and artistically	Select the proper tool for producing the intended sculpting effect
SCULPTING SKILLS	Understand how different sculpted forms are achieved using specific skills and techniques	Excel at delivering consistent, high-quality hair sculptures	Exceed clients' expectations with sculptures that support and complement their desired look

IN OTHER WORDS

Using the four basic forms, individually and in combination, along with the appropriate sculpting tools and skills, allows you to create versatile, subtle-to-dramatic sculpture designs for your clients.

LESSONS LEARNED

- The two ways to analyze the structure of a hair sculpture are natural fall and normal projection.

- The four basic forms are: solid form, graduated form, increase-layered form and uniformly layered form.

- Combination forms include two or more of the four basic forms.

- The five main sculpting tools are: shears, taper shears, razors, clippers and combs.

- Pivot Point's Seven Sculpting Procedures are: section, position head, part, distribute, project, position fingers/shears, and sculpt design line.

- Texturizing techniques, short hair techniques and sculpting considerations are skills used in conjunction with the Seven Sculpting Procedures that allow adaptation to a wide variety of clientele and the creation of special sculpture effects.

10

HAIR DESIGN

10.1 HAIR DESIGN THEORY
HAIR DESIGN ANALYSIS
TOOLS FOR HAIR DESIGNING
SETTING
BASE CONTROL
FINISHING
HAIR DESIGN ESSENTIALS
INFECTION CONTROL AND SAFETY
HAIR DESIGN SERVICE ESSENTIALS

10.2 WET DESIGN TECHNIQUES
FINGERWAVES
PINCURLS
SKIP WAVES
ROLLERS
WET DESIGN PROCEDURE OVERVIEW

10.3 THERMAL DESIGN TECHNIQUES
AIR FORMING
HAIR PRESSING
THERMAL IRONS
THERMAL DESIGN PROCEDURE OVERVIEW

10.4 LONG HAIR DESIGN THEORY
LONG HAIR DESIGN ANALYSIS
CLIENT CONSIDERATIONS
LONG HAIR DESIGNING
LONG HAIR DESIGN ESSENTIALS
INFECTION CONTROL AND SAFETY
LONG HAIR DESIGN SERVICE ESSENTIALS

10.5 LONG HAIR DESIGN TECHNIQUES
TWISTS
KNOTS
OVERLAPS
BRAIDS
LOOPS
ROLLS
LONG HAIR DESIGN PROCEDURE OVERVIEW

THE SUCCESS OF
ANY HAIR SERVICE
LIES IN THE DESIGN
OF ITS FINISHED FORM,
TEXTURE, DIRECTION
AND MOVEMENT

FOLLOWING THIS LESSON
YOU WILL BE ABLE TO:

Identify the theoretical foundations for a successful hair design service

Explain the primary techniques for wet design

Explain the primary techniques for thermal design

Identify the theoretical knowledge required for a successful long hair design service

Explain the primary techniques for long hair design

CONNECTING THEORY TO REAL-WORLD PRACTICE

LEARNING THE DIFFERENT WAYS TO DESIGN HAIR WILL HELP YOU:

PERSONAL CONNECTION:	**INDUSTRY CONNECTION:**	**CLIENT CONNECTION:**
IMPROVE YOURSELF	BECOME A PROFESSIONAL	SERVE THE GUEST
Wear hair designs that are flattering and reflect your personality	Attract and retain clientele by delivering consistently excellent hair designs	Fulfill client needs by offering a wide array of hair design options

Through the art of hair design, you will be able to completely change your clients' appearance to reflect their persona style. As you experiment with different tools, techniques and products, you'll learn to create an endless number c flattering design options. Hair design temporarily transforms a head of hair into creative and personal expressions that w make your client look and feel amazing.

10.1 HAIR DESIGN THEORY

Hair design is the art of dressing and arranging hair to create temporary changes in the form and texture of the finished hair design. Altering texture or adding volume can change the entire feeling of a design. Mastery of the components of movement and direction, along with balance and proportion, will serve you well in any design service that you perform.

Getty Images

Just as a sculptor chisels stone and a fashion designer sews cloth, hair designers use the medium of hair to express their artistic vision. Only the boundaries of your imagination can limit your creative expression.

As you become stronger and more proficient in your hair design skills, you can offer more interesting and varied options to your clients. This chapter will guide you through the three major areas of hair designing:
- Wet design
- Thermal design
- Long hair design

All three are interrelated and important for you to understand.

Wet designing includes molding, fingerwaving and setting the hair with rollers and pincurls to create classic to progressive hair designs.

Thermal designing, which uses blow dryers, brushes and thermal irons, has become the most popular styling method today. It requires minimal time and clients are able to closely duplicate results at home.

Long hair designs are most often requested for formal occasions, The long hair design techniques that you use will vary according to the client, her hair and the reason she has come to the salon.

The temporary nature of the form, texture and direction changes produced through hair design not only provides you with many creative opportunities, it also provides clients with a high degree of flexibility. Your hair design abilities give clients the freedom and confidence to change their look as often as they like. Educating your clients on the best techniques and products for styling their hair at home gives them even more options for day-to-day wear and allows your work to always look its best.

In the salon, hair design is a core service and can be performed as a stand-alone service or as the final phase of a sculpture, texture or color service. Being able to offer a variety of design options and performing them consistently and professionally builds client loyalty and satisfaction. While fashions and hair trends may change, understanding the theory of hair designing will be essential to achieving success as a salon professional.

HAIR DESIGN ANALYSIS

In hair design there are primary considerations for you as a hair designer. These primary considerations include the design's:

- Form and shape
- Texture
- Direction

When creating hair designs, you will need to consider the whole design as well as its separate parts. Analyzing a hair design using the basic, detail and abstract levels of observation provides you with a basis to re-create what you see and the ability to envision your own unique designs.

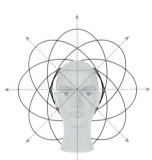  

BASIC – FORM AND SHAPE
Consider the three-dimensional form from all directions, determining where *volume* (mass or fullness) and *indentation* (hollowness) are positioned. Consider the overall shape, such as circular or triangular.

COSMETOLOGY FUNDAMENTALS 315

 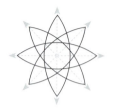 

DETAIL – TEXTURE
Determine whether the surface texture is unactivated (smooth) or activated (rough). Also determine the types of textures you see, such as straight, wavy, curly, tightly curled or combination.

ABSTRACT – DIRECTION
Consider the overall direction in which the hair is moving, as well as the directions within the form.

FORM AND SHAPE

In hair design, form is the result of volume and indentation. The form of a design can expand in any direction. Analyzing the position of volume and indentation from all angles allows you to view the outer shape of the design.

When analyzing form, people naturally try to find equilibrium within the design. Developing a sense of balance in any art form requires strong observational skills as well as intuition. Balance, whether symmetrical or asymmetrical, plays an integral part in the dynamics of a design and must be analyzed from all angles.

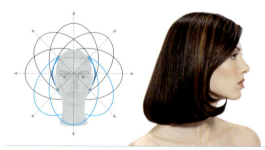

With the sculpted form as the foundation, hair designing allows you to subtly or drastically alter the shape of the form. A common design for the solid form is accentuating the perimeter weight area.

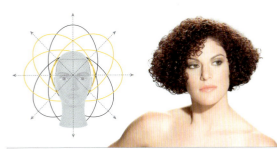

Graduated forms can be altered with the addition of texture to the sides and/or interior.

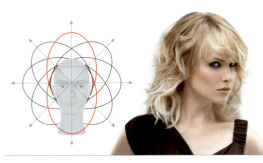

Texture added throughout the increase-layered form can further accentuate the activated texture.

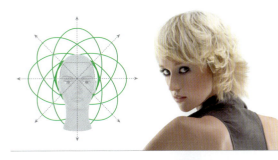

Uniformly layered forms can be altered throughout or within a given area depending upon the desired position of volume.

Reducing the amount of texture creates smooth, sleek finishes.

In long hair designs, the final composition may bear little or no resemblance to the shape or form of the underlying hair sculpture.

TEXTURE

Texture as a design element helps you determine the influence it has on the total design. For instance, some texture changes expand the form or change the direction of the hair. Identifying the texture also helps to determine the finishing technique or type of tool needed to create the desired texture pattern.

Your client's natural texture, whether it is straight, wavy, curly or tightly curled, can be temporarily changed through wet setting or thermal designing. The shape or pattern of the new texture is influenced by the shape of the tool you use and the position of the tool. Textures include waves, curls, spiral curls, crimped textures or any combination.

WAVES

CURLS

SPIRAL

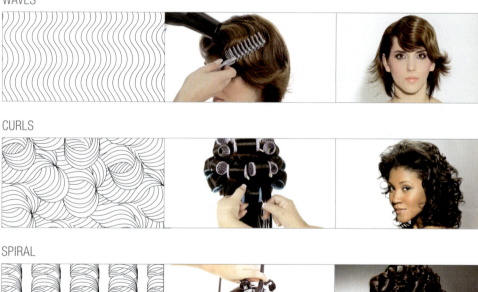

10

Texture patterns created in a hair design service can range from slow, undulating wave patterns to fast, highly activated curls, depending mainly on the diameter of the tools used. Large-diameter tools produce slow waves and smaller diameters produce faster curls.

A LONG, SLOW WAVE   A MEDIUM-SPEED CURL   A FAST-SPEED CURL PATTERN

Thermal design tools such as curling irons and crimping irons add texture to the hair, while flat irons are used to straighten the hair.

DIRECTION

The overall direction of a design can be analyzed according to where the hair moves in relation to the face. Directions are often described as hair moving forward, or toward the face, backward, or away from the face, to one side, or any combination of these. The direction in which the hair is worn can make a major change in a client's appearance.

COSMETOLOGY FUNDAMENTALS

Besides the overall design direction, directional changes within the design can also be analyzed. These directional changes are lines that can be straight, curved or angled. They lead the eye through the design, giving the impression of motion. Curl patterns on longer hair will unfold, forming clockwise and counterclockwise directions.

TOOLS FOR HAIR DESIGNING

Tools play an important role in the creation of a hair design. These tools include blow dryers and their attachments, brushes, combs, rollers and clips. Electrical tools should be handled with care to ensure the safety of you and your clients.

BLOW DRYERS
Blow dryers and their attachments are used to air form wet hair while using brushes, combs and your fingers to create temporary direction and texture changes. Concentrators focus the air flow to a small area while diffusers spread a gentle air flow over larger areas and are used for creating scrunched textures.

AIR FORMING BRUSHES
Brushes such as vent and 9-row air forming brushes allow the greatest air flow to the hair so that the lengths can be dried quickly while directing them into the lines of the design.

ROUND BRUSHES
Round brushes are tools used to create volume and curved end texture. They are available in different diameters, with different types and spacing of bristles. Some have metal interiors that retain heat to strengthen the curl pattern.

> #### COLOR
> Remember that the combination of the three design elements—form, texture and color—creates a final design. As you create changes in texture and form, consider how color patterns influence the final design.

CUSHION BRUSHES

Cushion brushes have a soft, padded base and, generally, nylon bristles. They are used on dry hair to relax a set, backbrush or smooth the surface of the hair. The density and length of the bristles on a brush will influence the surface appearance.

ROLLERS

Cylinder (straight) rollers are available in a range of lengths and diameters and are used within straight shapes. Cone-shaped rollers are used in curvature shapes. The cone-shaped roller has a progression of speeds because of its wide and narrow ends. Both types of rollers are applied to wet or damp hair, which must be dried with these tools in place. Wet sets using rollers have a more structured finish.

Self-adhering rollers can be applied to dry or semi-dry hair to reinforce the curl or to wet hair for a more structured finish. Hot rollers are used on dry hair to quickly add volume and texture. Follow disinfection guidelines provided by your regulatory agency.

CURLING IRONS

Curling irons use heat to create temporary curvilinear texture patterns. They can have individual electric cords or can acquire heat from an electric base or stove. Professional curling irons, also referred to as marcel irons, come in a variety of diameters.

PRESSING COMBS

Pressing combs are used to apply heat and tension to temporarily straighten tightly curled hair.

FLAT IRONS

Flat irons consist of two flat plates. Hair is positioned between the heated plates to temporarily straighten and silk the hair.

COSMETOLOGY FUNDAMENTALS

UNDULATING IRONS
Undulating irons consist of two undulating or curved irons and are used to create an "S" pattern or wave formation.

CRIMPING IRONS
Crimping irons consist of angular or serrated plates that, when heated, are used to create crimped texture.

COMBS
The main features of a comb are its size and the spacing between its teeth. Some combs have a pointed end, called the tail, which is used to part or lift the hair. When a comb has widely spaced teeth, the resulting texture patterns in the hair reflect the shape and interval of the teeth.

MOLDING COMB
The molding comb is used for distributing and molding the hair, especially in fingerwaving. Half of the comb has larger-spaced teeth that are used to initially distribute the hair, and the other half has finer spaced teeth that are used to further refine the lines of distribution.

MASTER SKETCHER
The Master Sketcher is a type of comb used for backcombing and smoothing the surface of the hair.

FINE-TOOTH TAIL COMB
The fine-tooth tail comb, also known as a drawing comb, is used for distribution, molding, parting and scaling. When a comb has fine-spaced teeth, the hair can be distributed smoothly since the teeth firmly grasp the hair.

10

WIDE-TOOTH TAIL COMB
The wide-tooth tail comb is used for backcombing and finishing techniques. When a comb has wide-spaced teeth, the texture patterns reflect the shape and interval of the teeth.

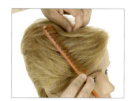

LIQUID TOOLS
Styling products, or liquid tools, are used before, during and after designing to add shine and a range of support to the hair. Product usage is very important to the success of your design and becoming knowledgeable in this area will help you use and recommend the best products. Products such as mousse offer additional styling control and strengthen the set and finish. They can be applied to wet or dry hair. Styling gels have a thicker viscosity and offer increased strength. Gels are applied to wet hair. A polisher or glossifier is added to dry hair for shine and detailing textures.

SETTING

Whether you are setting hair with rollers or pincurls, air forming or iron curling, the procedural steps you will use for the various types of wet and thermal designing are very similar. The physical actions and tools will vary, but the principles behind controlling the hair remain the same. Visualizing the finished design helps you identify the procedural steps required to create the design.

WET-SETTING PROCEDURES

DISTRIBUTE   **MOLD**   **SCALE**   **PART**   **APPLY**

THERMAL SETTING PROCEDURES

DISTRIBUTE/MOLD   **SCALE/PART/APPLY**

COSMETOLOGY FUNDAMENTALS

DISTRIBUTE AND MOLD

Distribution is the direction the hair is combed or dispersed over the curve of the head. **To mold, or shape, the hair refers to designing wet hair in straight or curved lines after the hair has been distributed to create a pattern.**

Some finished designs are the result of distributing and molding wet hair after a styling product has been applied. The hair can be dried and combed out or left molded to create a "wet look."

Molding can also serve as a design blueprint prior to setting. In this example the molded pattern has been scaled or carved out according to the predetermined size and proportion required for the roller set.

Distribution and molding can occur simultaneously, such as when air forming a design.

In some instances, hair may be wrapped around the head, known as hair wrapping. The smooth curvature finish reflects the large curves of the head.

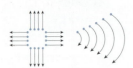 

PARALLEL DISTRIBUTION   RADIAL DISTRIBUTION

Distribution begins from a point of origin. A **point of origin** is the place where motion begins, or the beginning of a design. In hair design, there are two types of distribution: parallel and radial. With **parallel distribution**, the hair is distributed from multiple points of origin. With **radial distribution**, the hair is distributed from one point of origin.

PARALLEL DISTRIBUTION

Parallel distribution refers to straight or curved lines that originate from many points of origin and travel at an equal distance from one another. Curved parallel lines result from distributing the hair in a curved motion while molding.

RADIAL DISTRIBUTION

Radial distribution refers to straight or curved lines that originate from a single point of origin and radiate outward in any direction, like the spokes of a wheel. Curved radial lines are distributed straight and then curved while molding.

SCALE

To *scale* or section means to carve out shapes in the proper predetermined size and proportion to establish the lines of the design. Pre-sectioning, or the scaling of shapes, is done to ensure that tools fit properly and to serve as a blueprint for the entire design. Sections will very often take on the form of a geometric shape, which is scaled according to the desired proportion. The scaling of a shape also takes into consideration the size of the client's head, as well as individual growth patterns, such as cowlicks and a widow's peak.

In hair design, geometric shapes are the components that make up a composition. Understanding the characteristics of each shape helps you to create the desired directions and movements within a design.

Some of the straight and curved geometric shapes that are used in hair design are: rectangles, triangles, kites, circles, ovals and oblongs. Some shapes dictate that specific distribution patterns, such as parallel or radial, be used. It is important to remember that an entire design will always be composed of some combination of shapes.

STRAIGHT SHAPES

Straight shapes or sections include rectangles, triangles and trapezoids. Straight shapes are generally combined with curvature shapes to create an infinite number of hair design compositions.

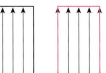

RECTANGLE

Rectangular shapes consist of parallel distribution. Once the shape is molded, a tail comb is used to scale the shape according to the size desired.

TRIANGLE

Triangular shapes consist of radial or parallel distribution. In some instances, a tail comb is first used to distribute the hair from a single point of origin. Parallel distribution is then used to distribute the hair within the triangle. Finally, a tail comb is used to scale out the shape according to the size desired.

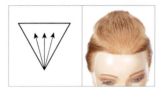 

DIAMOND AND KITE

Shapes can be combined to encompass a larger area. For instance, back-to-back triangles can create diamond or kite shapes.

TRAPEZOID

A trapezoid is a straight shape that includes two parallel and two nonparallel sides. Trapezoid shapes consist of parallel distribution and can also be combined with other shapes.

CURVATURE SHAPES

Curvature (curved) shapes or sections include circles, ovals and oblongs. They imply motion and are generally used to create curvature directions or waves. Any of these curvature shapes can be distributed to move in either a clockwise or counterclockwise direction.

CIRCLE

A *circle* is a geometric, closed-curve shape bounded by a circumference and having equal radii from a center point of origin. Generally in hair design only a portion of the circle, such as the half-circle, is used. A half-circle is used to move the hair in equal proportions from a center poin of origin. Straight radial lines are used from a single point of origin to establish the position of the ha circle. Then, curved radial lines are molded to create the half-circle shape in a clockwise or counterclockwise direction. Finally the shape is scaled according to the size desired. A tool may be used as a guide to scale the shape.

EXPANDED CIRCLE

An expanded circle, which is an extension of the half-circle, is used to encompass a larger area than a half-circle. The same distribution and molding rules apply as with the half circle, except that a larger area is scaled according to the size desired.

OVAL

Just like the half-circle, only a portion of the oval is used in hair design. An oval is a geometric curved shape bounded by a circumference, having unequal radii from a point of origin. The unequal radial lines produce fast to slow speeds that result in unequal movements from the point of origin. The hair is distributed in straight lines from an off-center point of origin. The shape is then molded in a clockwise or counterclockwise direction and scaled according to the size desired.

EXPANDED OVAL

The expanded oval, which is an extension of the half-oval, is used to encompass a larger area than a half-oval. The same distribution and molding rules apply as with the half-oval, except that a larger area is scaled according to the size desired.

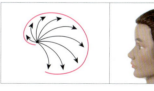

OBLONGS

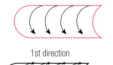

An **oblong** is an elongated curvature shape with parallel "C" lines, consisting of a convex (closed) end and a concave (open) end. Oblongs contain many points of origin and parallel curved distribution, which can move in a clockwise or counterclockwise direction. Generally two or more oblong shapes are used in hair design to create an alternating wave (S-shaped) pattern.

Oblongs consist of a first and second direction. The first direction, or top half of the shape, moves toward the convex end. The second direction, or bottom half of the shape, moves toward the concave end. The oblong shape is scaled according to the size desired.

PART

After molding and scaling the design, the hair is parted and subdivided for control. Partings are lines that subdivide shapes or sections to help distribute and control the hair. These subsections are often called bases and generally are the areas of hair on which you will apply the various tools and techniques. Bases are created from parallel and radial parting patterns.

PARALLEL

RADIAL

Parallel horizontal partings are used within a rectangle shape to create rectangle-shaped bases. Horizontal partings can also be used within a triangle shape to create trapezoid-shaped bases.

HORIZONTAL

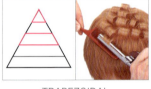
TRAPEZOIDAL

A radial parting pattern is used within curvature shapes, such as the circle, to create triangle- and trapezoid-shaped bases, and within an oval to create triangle-shaped bases.

RADIAL

Parallel diagonal partings are used to create rhomboid-shaped bases within an oblong. A rhomboid is a straight shape with two sets of parallel lines and no right angles.

PARALLEL

APPLY TOOLS

Once straight- or curved-shaped sections have been parted, the hair is set by applying a tool, such as a roller, round brush or curling iron. This will produce the desired amount of volume, indentation and degree of texture and movement.

Defined curls and waves are achieved in hair design by applying rollers, thermal irons and/or round brushes, and pincurl techniques. The size of the curl will be determined by the diameter of the tool or the diameter of a pincurl. Tools with smaller diameters create tighter or faster curls, while larger-diameter tools produce slow waves.

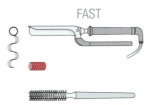
FAST

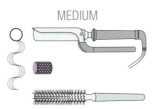
MEDIUM

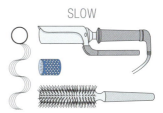
SLOW

There are three components of every curl:
- Base
- Stem (Arc)
- Circle

The base is the area between straight or curved partings within a shape or, in other words, the section of hair on which the roller, thermal iron or round brush is placed. The **stem**, or **arc**, is the hair between the scalp and the first turn of the hair around the roller, thermal iron or round brush. The stem determines the amount of movement of the section of hair. Longer stems create more movement and shorter stems create more base strength (support) and less movement. The **circle** of a curl is the hair that is positioned around the roller, thermal iron or round brush. It determines the size of the curl. The diameter of the tool you choose will determine the size of the circle.

BASE CONTROL

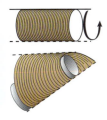

Base control refers to the size of the base in relation to the diameter of the tool, and the position of the tool in relation to the base. The base control used within a hair design affects the amount of volume (lift, fullness, mass) or closeness (flatness) achieved. Base control is used within straight and curvature shapes to create three-dimensional forms.

STRAIGHT VOLUME AND INDENTATION BASE CONTROL

Straight volume base control creates lift and straight indentation base control creates areas of hollowness or depression. Regardless of the technique or tool being used, straight volume and straight indentation base controls are performed within straight shapes, such as the rectangle and triangle. The base shapes within straight shapes include the rectangle, triangle and trapezoid. With straight volume, the base and strand are lifted and the ends turn under. With straight indentation, the base and strand are flat and the ends turn upward. Straight indentation is usually combined with straight volume to create a contrast in direction.

STRAIGHT VOLUME

STRAIGHT VOLUME AND STRAIGHT INDENTATION

BASE SIZE

Base size includes both the width and the length of the base. With rectangular bases, the base width is measured according to the diameter of the tool and the length of the base is measured according to the length of the tool.

The most commonly used base sizes are 1 diameter (1x), 1½ diameters (1½ x) and 2 diameters (2x). In the case of pincurls, the size of the base is related to the diameter of the circle.

1X   1½X   2X   1X

STRAIGHT VOLUME TOOL POSITION

The position of the tool in relation to the base will affect the lift or volume achieved as well as the amount of base strength. The base controls that are used in hair designing are the same regardless of the technique or tool being used (rollers, pincurls, round brush, thermal irons):

TOOL POSITION	BASE SIZE	PROJECTION ANGLE	DESCRIPTION	EFFECT
On Base (Full Base)	1x	45° above the center of the base	Tool sits completely within the base	Maximum volume, maximum base strength
Half-off base (Half-Base)	1x Optional: 1½x, 2x	90° from the center of the base	Tool sits half-off and half-on the bottom parting	Less volume, less base strength
Off Base	1x Optional: 1½x, 2x	45° below the center of the base	Tool sits completely off the bottom parting	Least volume, least base strength
Underdirected	1½x Optional: 2x	90° from the center of the base	Tool sits in the lower portion of the base, but not on or below the parting	Reduced volume and base strength
Overdirected (Volume Base)	1½x Optional: 2x	45° above the center of the base	Tool sits in the upper portion of the base, but not on or above the parting	Exaggerated direction and volume, reduced base strength

STRAIGHT INDENTATION TOOL POSITION

With indentation the position of the tool and the size of the base influence the amount of hollow space or flatness achieved. Tool position also influences the strength of the base and mobility of the curl.

TOOL POSITION	BASE SIZE	PROJECTION ANGLE	DESCRIPTION	EFFECT
On Base	1x	60° below center	Tool sits completely on its base, rolled in an upward direction	Maximum base strength and volume
Half-Off Base	1x Optional: 1½x, 2x	30° below center	Tool sits half-off and half-on its base, rolled in an upward direction	Medium base strength, allowing more curl mobility
Off Base	1x Optional: 1½x, 2x	0° below center	Tool sits completely off its base, rolled in an upward direction	Minimum base strength, maximum curl mobility
Underdirected	1½x Optional: 2x	45° below center	Tool sits within the base close to the bottom of the parting, rolled in an upward direction	Medium base strength, strong curl flare

CURVATURE VOLUME AND INDENTATION BASE CONTROL

Curvature volume is set within curvature shapes, such as the oblong, circle or oval. The base and strand are lifted and the ends turn under. With curvature indentation the base and strand are flat and the ends turn upward. Curvature indentation is usually combined with curvature volume and curvature indentation techniques are used to create three-dimensional forms. The base shapes used for curvature volume and indentation include the rhomboid, trapezoid and triangle; these are described on the following page. The most common base sizes used for curvature volume and curvature indentation are 1x, 1½ x and 2x the diameter of the tool chosen.

CURVATURE VOLUME

CURVATURE VOLUME AND CURVATURE INDENTATION

COSMETOLOGY FUNDAMENTALS

RHOMBOID

For rhomboid-shaped bases, which are used within an oblong, base width is measured by the large end of the cone-shaped roller, while base length is measured by the length of the tool.

TRAPEZOID

For trapezoid-shaped bases, used in the outer portion of an expanded circle, base width is measured by the large end of the cone-shaped roller, while base length is measured by the length of the tool.

TRIANGLE

For triangle-shaped bases, such as within a half-circle or half oval, base width is measured with the large end of a cone-shaped roller at the outer circumference of the shape. Base length is measured one diameter of the small end of the cone-shaped roller, plus the length of the tool away from the point of origin.

CURVATURE VOLUME TOOL POSITION

Curvature volume tool positions include on base, underdirected, half-off base and off base. There are no overdirected tool positions for curvature volume.

1X ON BASE
45° ABOVE CENTER

1½X UNDERDIRECTED
90° FROM CENTER

1X HALF-OFF BASE
90° FROM CENTER

1X OFF BASE
45° BELOW CENTER

TOOL POSITION	BASE SIZE OPTIONS
On Base	1x
Underdirected	1½ x , 2x
Half-Off Base	1x, 1½ x, 2x
Off Base	1x, 1½ x, 2x

Although the position of the tool changes when setting curvature indentation, the base controls are the same.

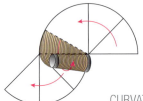 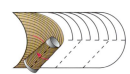

CURVATURE INDENTATION

HAIR DESIGN

CURVATURE PINCURLS

Curved partings are used for setting pincurls within curvature shapes. The base controls used for curvature pincurls are the same as the ones used for rollers. The size of the base and position of the circle in relation to the base affect the amount of volume achieved.

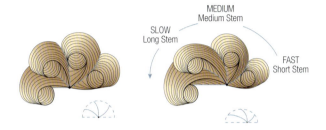

CURVATURE VOLUME AND INDENTATION AIR FORMING

When air forming volume or indentation, it is the position, direction and continual motion of the brush that control the amount of volume or indentation achieved. Keep in mind that the same base controls used for rollers can also be used with a round brush.

In summary, base size and tool position determine the amount of volume or indentation in a hair design. The tools you work with will be determined by the desired results, your client's hair and your personal preferences.

FINISHING

This finishing phase of hair design is often referred to as the "comb-out." At this point in the service, you will address any areas of the design that require blending. You'll also create support, add volume and refine the form while adding any personal touches.

The steps used to finish a design are:

- Relax
- Dry mold
- Backcomb or backbrush
- Define the form
- Detail

RELAX

Once the set is dry, the hair is relaxed with 1 or 2 cushion brushes. Relaxing is done by brushing all the way to the scalp to integrate the bases and soften the curl texture. You will want to work within as well as against the set lines to ensure thorough relaxing.

DRY MOLD

Dry molding reinforces the established lines of the design. To do this you will use a cushion brush to retrace the lines of the set, following each movement with the other hand on top of the hair to control lengths with the heat of your palm.

BACKBRUSH/BACKCOMB

Backbrushing and **backcombing** are optional techniques used to increase height and control form in a hair design by creating a cushion or mesh at the base. Keep in mind that backbrushing and backcombing are most effective when the hair has been texturized since the shorter lengths get directed down to the base, creating support for the longer lengths. In addition to following the movements of the set, you will want to use the base control of the set as a guide to determine how much volume or closeness you need to create in a specific area of a design. Backcombing is also called French lacing, teasing, ratting, matting and ruffing.

Backbrushing is done on the surface of the hair to achieve a light, airy effect. A small section of hair is held taut with one hand, while the other hand gently slides the brush from the ends toward the base. Finally, the brush is turned outward to carefully remove the hair from the brush. The bristles of the brush are then used to pick up the next section and the backbrushing technique is repeated until the desired effect is achieved.

When backcombing underneath the surface of the hair, the fine teeth of the comb are used to direct the lengths to the base to create a firm cushion. One hand is used to hold the hair taut, while the other hand is used to direct the lengths with the comb underneath the surface of the hair toward the base. The cushion created at the base expands the form and connects the shapes for a more structured and controlled finish.

A large-tooth comb can be used on the surface of the hair to lightly blend the bases and to create detailed texture finish with an airy effect.

DEFINE THE FORM

Defining the form includes smoothing the surface of the hair, redefining the lines of the design, and controlling the amount of desired volume. This can be the final step of the hair design process.

DETAIL

Detailing is adding finishing touches, such as piecing or pleating the hair for additional texture and personalizing the form. At this point you can really emphasize your client's personal style. Detailing requires a light touch and a certain amount of restraint on your part. Too much "detail" can overwhelm the integrity of the design, resulting in a fussy or overworked design.

COMB-OUT VARIATION

Depending on the finished design you are trying to achieve for a particular client, you may not need to use all of the finishing procedures. For example, backbrushing may be omitted for a more casual feeling, and relaxing, dry molding and/or backcombing may not be required for some air-formed designs.

HAIR DESIGN ESSENTIALS

To achieve the design effects desired, you should become familiar with the tools, supplies, products and equipment used during hair design services. The following charts identify these design essentials and define their basic functions. Styling products are also called liquid tools and are essential to achieving lasting designs.

HAIR DESIGN TOOLS/SUPPLIES

TOOLS/SUPPLIES	FUNCTION
COMBS	
MOLDING COMB	Distributes and molds the hair; half of the comb is used for distribution, half is used to refine the lines
FINE-TOOTH TAIL COMB	Distributes, molds, parts and scales the hair; also known as a designer comb, drawing comb and tail comb
LARGE-TOOTH TAIL COMB	Backcombs; used also for finishing techniques
MASTER SKETCHER COMB	Detangles and backcombs hair
RAKE COMB	Detangles; separates curls and defines texture
LIFTER	Details; lifts; backcombs
BRUSHES	
VENT BRUSH	Achieves lift or volume when air forming smoother textures or creating directional emphasis
7- OR 9-ROW AIR FORMING BRUSH	Smoothes wavy or curly textures; allows greater air flow to the hair for quicker drying while adding directional emphasis when air forming
ROUND BRUSH	Imparts varying degrees of curved or curled texture and volume; available in different diameters, type and spacing of bristles; some have metal interiors that retain heat to strengthen the curl pattern
CUSHION BRUSH	Relaxes sets; backbrushes; dry molds; defines the form

TOOLS/SUPPLIES	FUNCTION
ROLLERS, PINS AND CLIPS	
CYLINDRICAL ROLLER	Creates uniform curl formation/diameter across width of base; used in straight-shape roller setting
CONICAL OR CONE-SHAPED ROLLER	Creates progression of curl diameter from narrow end of base toward wide end; used in curvature-shape roller setting
PICK	Secures rollers in place while hair dries
SINGLE-PRONG CLIP	Secures pincurls
DOUBLE-PRONG CLIP	Secures molded shapes/sectioning; secures rollers if picks are not used
BOBBY PIN	Secures hair in place for finished design, especially in long hair designs
HAIRPIN	Secures hair in place for finished design, especially in long hair designs
LONG HAIRPIN	Defines textural detail and movement
WAVE OR STYLING CLAMP	Holds fingerwaves in place
THERMAL DESIGNING	
BLOW DRYER	Air forms wet hair while using brushes, combs and your fingers to create temporary direction and textural changes
DIFFUSER	Spreads a gentle airflow to a large area of hair; attachment for a blow dryer
CONCENTRATOR	Focuses the air flow to a small area of hair; attachment for a blow dryer
HOT BRUSH/COMB	Dries hair while creating waves or curls
PRESSING COMB	Straightens tightly curled hair
CURLING IRON	Adds curled or waved texture to the hair by utilizing a heated barrel powered by an electric cord, base or stove
FLAT IRON	Straightens and silks the hair
CRIMPING IRON	Creates crimped or angular type texture
UNDULATING IRON	Creates undulating wave pattern

HAIR DESIGN PRODUCTS

PRODUCTS	FUNCTION
GEL	Creates maximum control and support of the hair especially for wet setting; varying strengths available
MOUSSE	Supports volume and movement; used to define texture and directional patterns; foam consistency; may or may not contain conditioners

PRODUCTS	FUNCTION
STYLING LOTION	Supports volume and movement; liquid consistency
SPRAY GEL	Supports volume and movement; used for wet-look finishes; firmer hold than lotion; liquid consistency
NON-AEROSOL HAIRSPRAY	Holds finished design in place; liquid dispensed through pump
AEROSOL HAIRSPRAY	Holds finished design in place; available in a variety of strengths; liquid dispensed through compressed gas and spray
POMADE/POLISHER	Adds high intensity gloss and sheen; adds texture separation and definition; adds weight to the hair
PRESSING OIL/CREAM	Prepares and protects hair during pressing service; helps prevent scorching and breakage; conditions and adds shine; helps hair stay pressed longer; use less pressing oil to avoid smoke or burning

AIR DESIGN EQUIPMENT

EQUIPMENT	FUNCTION
HAIR DESIGN STATION	Provides a place for tools to be displayed and organized
HYDRAULIC CHAIR	Provides proper back support for client during the service; adjustable
WET DISINFECTANT CONTAINER	Holds solution for disinfecting tools
SHAMPOO BOWL	Supports client's neck and holds water and shampoo products during a shampoo service
MIRROR	Displays hair design to client and hair designer for communication and balancing design

INFECTION CONTROL AND SAFETY

Below is a list of safety precautions you should follow prior to and during a hair design service. Additional infection control and safety precautions specifically for long hair design services are listed later in this chapter.

1. Practice infection control guidelines.
2. Wash and sanitize hands with liquid soap.
3. Protect the client and his or her clothing with proper draping procedures. Refer to the "Draping Procedures" later in this section.
4. Analyze the scalp for any diseases or disorders. If any are evident, refer the client to a physician and do not proceed with the service.

5. Ensure that the client does not have sensitivities to any styling products that will be used during the service, such as mousse or gel. Avoid using excessive amounts of styling products on the scalp, which might cause irritation.

6. Detangle the hair from the ends to the base prior to shampooing the hair.

7. Check occasionally on clients that are placed under a hair dryer to ensure the client is comfortable and not being adversely affected by the heat.

8. Avoid using excess tension on the hair and scalp when backcombing or backbrushing, which may be uncomfortable for your client and unduly stress the hair.

9. Check the air-intake area on the blow dryer to ensure it is free from debris before beginning the air forming procedure.

10. Perform thermal iron procedures only on dry hair.

11. Test the temperature of thermal irons or pressing combs before applying them to the client's hair.

12. Exercise caution when using thermal irons on chemically treated hair. Since this hair is more sensitive, improper usage of thermal irons can cause damage; therefore, use lower temperatures and shorter contact time on hair that has been chemically altered or shows signs of mechanical damage or recommend a wet set.

13. Protect the client's scalp from thermal irons by positioning a hard rubber or nonflammab comb underneath the iron. Avoid having the teeth of the pressing comb or hot comb com in contact with the client's scalp to guard against burning and/or heat irritation. Exercise increased caution when working with thermal design tools near the hairline and especially near the ears to avoid burning the client's skin.

14. If a burn occurs on you or your client, flush with cold water and let the skin completely cool. Blot dry and apply a first aid cream to the burn. If blisters appear, see a physician immediately. Blistering is a sign of a severe burn that can scar if left untreated.

15. Avoid pressing hair too often. Frequently pressed hair may suffer progressive hair breakage.

16. Remember to disconnect or turn off all appliances and tuck all cords out of reach when leaving your station unattended.

17. Disinfect all tools after each use. If you notice brown or black residue on tools, clean metal portions with fine steel wool around the diameter of the barrel. Always use disinfected combs, rollers, clips and brushes for each client.

ALERT!

Always follow manufacturers' directions for any products used during a hair design service.

DRAPING PROCEDURES FOR A HAIR DESIGN SERVICE

Generally a plastic cape is used during the shampooing, conditioning and wet designing phases of a service to protect the client's skin and clothing. A styling cape of lighter weight, cloth or fabric, may be selected during the dry designing phases of the service. Refer to *Chapter 7, Trichology*, for details on the proper draping procedures.

HAIR DESIGN SERVICE ESSENTIALS

All hair services require that you communicate with your client prior to the service to ensure predictable results that meet your expectations and your client's. Use photos and magazines to facilitate the dialogue between you and your client. Concentrate on changes that can be made in the form, texture and direction of the design. If possible, show your client hair design options that were created on the same or a similar hair sculpture as the one he or she has.

It's also a good idea to teach your client some basic techniques for maintaining the hair design after leaving the salon. Knowing some options he or she can do at home will increase the longevity and enjoyment of the hair design.

CONNECT
- Meet and greet the client with a smile, a firm handshake and pleasant voice.
- Communicate with the client to help build rapport and develop a relationship.

CONSULT
- Ask questions to discover your client's needs. You might ask questions such as: "What brings you in for a new hair design today?" Answers might be, "I have an important business dinner to attend this evening," or "My cousin is getting married and I'm a bridesmaid," or "I can't do my own hair anymore so I would like to schedule weekly appointments for a shampoo and set."
- Ask if the client has any particular ideas about the hair design. Get as much information as you need to find out what your client really wants.
- Ask questions to determine the amount of volume and type of texture the client desires. These are two areas in which miscommunication between client and hair designer can easily occur. Make sure you understand your client's specific desires.
- Analyze your client's face and body shape, physical features, hair and scalp. Refer to Chapter 8, Design Decisions, for further guidelines.
- Assess the facts and thoroughly think through your recommendations.
- Explain your styling recommendations and clarify the price for today's service(s) as well as for any future appointments.
- Gain feedback and approval concerning your recommendations from the client.
- Seek clarification if your client is hesitant with your recommendations.

CREATE
- Ensure your client's protection by using the proper draping procedures.
- Ensure client comfort during the service.
- Stay focused on delivering the hair design service to the best of your ability.
- Teach your client how to perform at-home maintenance of the new hair design.

COMPLETE
- Reinforce guest's satisfaction with his or her overall experience.
- Make professional product recommendations.
- Prebook guest's next appointment.
- End guest's visit with warm and personal goodbyes.
- Discard non-reusable materials, disinfect tools and arrange work station in proper order
- Wash your hands with liquid soap.
- Complete the client record card.
- Provide follow-up after the salon visit.

10.2 WET DESIGN TECHNIQUES

Wet design refers to the area of hair designing in which the hair is manipulated into the desired shapes and movements while wet and then allowed to dry. Wet designing includes molded designs such as fingerwave designs, roller sets and pincurl sets. Once the wet hair is "set," it is allowed to dry completely. Then it is finished using any combination of combs, brushes and/or fingers and additional liquid tools, if desired. Roller sets generally result in the firmest set and are longer lasting compared to the other wet design techniques. Your review of wet design in this chapter will include fingerwaves, pincurls, skip waves and rollers

FINGERWAVES

Fingerwaving, the art of shaping and defining the hair in graceful waves, was once popular for everyday wear. They are now most often used in conjunction with other design technique

Learning to fingerwave, you're developing:
- Dexterity
- Coordination
- Strength

You're also exercising your visual imagination as you design wave patterns to follow the curves of the head and reflect the trends seen throughout history. A complete understandin of the correct fingerwaving procedure is necessary to accurately create a fluid movement o balanced design.

In some instances, two combs are used to create tight waves on tightly curled textures.

A fingerwave is created by molding two complete alternating oblong shapes—using your fingers and a comb—that are joined and connected by a ridge. In the photograph, the open end of the oblong is identified by a dashed line and the closed end by a solid line. Notice how the shaping creates a series of parallel curved lines. Also, notice the **hollow** (recess) and the ridge (high ledge) areas of each wave movement. Pinching or pushing the ridge will create overdirection of the wave and is not recommended. Fingerwaves with low ridges are known as shadow waves.

Fingerwave patterns can be designed diagonally, vertically or horizontally. Some patterns include a part, while others move directly off the face. The size of the wave pattern can also vary.

PINCURLS

Pincurls are one of many ways you are able to temporarily change the direction and texture of the hair. Generally pincurls are used on straight, permed or naturally curly hair that has been properly texturized. Pincurls are not recommended for tightly curled hair. Used primarily to create temporary effects or specialized closeness, pincurls allow a wide range of movement. Forming pincurls relies on your dexterity and smooth handling of the hair to create clean, smoothly wound curls without the use of a tool such as a roller, and to control the consistency of the curl shape. If the pincurls are not smooth, the resulting curl or wave will not be smooth.

COMPONENTS OF A PINCURL

A section of hair that forms a pincurl is commonly described in three parts:
- Base
- Stem (arc)
- Circle

The pincurl base is the area of the strand at the scalp between partings within a shape.

The stem (arc) is the beginning portion of the strand that demonstrates the direction of the curl (between base and first turn). The stem determines the amount of movement a pincurl will have.

The pincurl circle is the remaining end of the strand that forms the curl. The size of the circle determines the width and strength of the wave. A closed circle will produce a much smaller and stronger wave for a fluffy effect. An open circle will produce a wider wave pattern with uniform curls.

BASE SHAPES FOR PINCURLS

Various shaped bases are used when working with pincurls. The primary reason for this variation of base shapes is to avoid splits in the finished hair design. Generally, straight-shaped bases are used within straight shapes and curved-shaped bases are used within curved shapes. Pincurl base shapes that are used most often are triangle, square/rectangle and crescent.

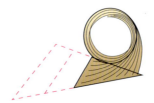 

TRIANGLE
Used within straight shapes and along the hairline; alternating triangles help to avoid splits.

SQUARE/RECTANGLE
Usually used within an overall square shape.

CRESCENT
Also known as arc, curved, half-moon or C-shaped base; used within curvature shapes such as circles, ovals and oblongs. Curvature or carved pincurls are curls that are carved or sliced from a curved shaping.

Keeping bases consistent within a shape will allow you to work with equal amounts of hair in each pincurl and, therefore, have more consistent results in your finished curls and waves.

BASE CONTROL FOR PINCURLS

The sizes of pincurl bases are usually related to the diameter of the circle, which, in turn, determines the resulting wave or curl. Pincurl base control refers to the size of the base in relation to the size of the circle or curl and the position of the curl relative to the base. The size of the base and the base control used will affect the length of the stem of each pincurl. The length of the stem will determine the movement of the curl. The base controls that are most often used are on base, half-off base, off base, underdirected and overdirected.

ON-BASE PINCURL
A correct on-base pincurl control requires that the entire circle of the curl be positioned on the base. This base control is used to produce lift or strong curl effect, or when used in a series, to create a strong wave line. On-base pincurls are also referred to as no-stem pincurls.

HALF-OFF-BASE PINCURL
In a correct half-off-base pincurl control, half of the circle is positioned below the base. This base control is used when an equal degree of predetermined direction and volume is required. Half-off-base pincurls are also referred to as half-stem pincurls.

OFF-BASE PINCURL
With off-base pincurl control, the stem and circle are positioned below the base. This base control is used when design closeness and mobility are required, usually in the nape area or along the hairline. Off-base pincurls are also referred to as full-stem pincurls.

UNDERDIRECTED
With underdirected base control the circle sits on the lower portion of the base. This base control is used to create reduced volume.

OVERDIRECTED
With overdirected base control, the circle sits in the upper portion of the base. This base control is used to create exaggerated direction. An overdirected base control is not used with curvature pincurls.

STRAIGHT PINCURLS
Straight volume pincurls are large, stand-up pincurls that achieve a similar effect to hair wound around a roller, but result in weaker (less) volume. Straight volume pincurls are used within straight shapes to create fullness and height. Straight volume pincurls are also referred to as stand-up, cascade pincurls and barrel curls. In some instances, you will need to create a blend or transition from areas of volume to areas of closeness. Transitional or semi-stand-up pincurls will achieve this blend. These pincurls are not quite stand-up curls and not quite flat curls.

To create a straight volume pincurl, distribute the hair smoothly and reinforce the arc with the tail comb. Smooth the ends in the direction of the circle formation, also known as ribboning the hair. Place the ends inside the circle and secure with a clip.

Reinforce Arc   Smooth (ribbon)   Form Circle   Secure

CURVATURE PINCURLS

Consulting with your client and visualizing the finished design will help you determine where lift (volume) and where a closer effect are desired. **The three common types of curvature pincurls are: flat, volume and indentation.** Flat, volume and indentation pincurls are set here within an alternating oblong pattern to create closeness, fullness and dimension. Flat pincurls are also known as carved or sculpture curls.

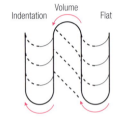

FLAT PINCURLS

With flat pincurls the base, arc and circle are flat. **Flat pincurls are used for closeness.** Since the hair does not travel any distance from the base before the arc begins, the result is a no-stem curl. To create a flat pincurl, a clockwise oblong or shaping is molded at the front hairline. Flat pincurls begin at the concave end of the shape. A tail comb is used to part the hair from the center of the shape in the second direction, toward the concave end. The hair is then smoothed to create a ribbon-like effect. The base remains flat while the stem is curved and the circle is formed. The flat pincurl is secured in the second direction. This technique is repeated until the remaining shape is completed.

VOLUME PINCURLS

With volume pincurls the base and arc are lifted away from the head and the circle turns under. **Volume pincurls are used to create fullness and height.** They can be positioned anywhere on the head.

To create a volume pincurl, a counterclockwise oblong is molded first. Volume pincurls begin at the convex end of the shape. A tail comb is used to part the hair toward the first direction or convex end. The comb is used to create lift at the base and to reinforce the stem. The circle is then formed. The volume pincurl is secured inside the circle in the first direction or convex end of the shape. This technique is repeated until the remaining shape is completed.

INDENTATION PINCURLS

With indentation pincurls the base is flat and the arc and circle are lifted. **Indentation pincurls are used to create hollow space and flare.** Generally, indentation pincurls follow volume pincurls in a hair design.

To create an indentation pincurl, a clockwise oblong is molded first. Indentation pincurls begin at the concave end of the shape. A tail comb is used to part the hair from the center of the shape in the second direction. The index finger is used to keep the base flat while curving the stem with the comb. The circle is then formed up and away from the base. The indentation pincurl is secured through the circle in the second direction. This technique is repeated until the entire shape is completed.

PINCURLS: HALF-CIRCLE AND HALF-OVAL

When setting curvature volume pincurls within a half-circle, all pincurls are positioned at an equal distance away from the point of origin. When setting curvature volume pincurls within a half-oval, the pincurls are positioned at an unequal distance away from the point of origin to achieve fast, medium and slow speeds.

SKIP WAVES

Skip waves are composed of two alternating oblongs connected by a ridge, in which one oblong is molded and one is set. The first oblong is molded (skipped), and the next oblong is set with pincurls, rollers or a round brush. The oblong that is set supports the molded shape and gives more dimension to the design. The pattern can be repeated in order to create a series of skip waves. Flat, volume or indentation pincurls can be used to create a variety of undulating patterns. Skip waving achieves wide, deep-flowing waves that are generally positioned on the side of the head, either vertically or horizontally.

A strong wave pattern that combines fingerwaves and flat pincurls is one specific example of a skip wave. The first oblong remains molded and the next oblong is set in flat pincurls. One oblong followed by a row of pincurls is called a ridge curl. An alternation consisting of at least two oblongs and two rows of pincurls creates a skip wave and produces a strong wave pattern.

COSMETOLOGY FUNDAMENTALS

ROLLERS

Rollers are used to set the hair and can achieve many of the same effects that are achieved with pincurls. So why would you choose rollers over pincurls? For starters, one roller, depending on its length, sets the same amount of hair as two to four pincurls. This means that your setting time can be greatly reduced. Second, setting with rollers allows you to set the hair with tension, which will result in a firmer, longer-lasting set. Earlier in this chapter, you learned about the components of a curl as well as the various base controls that are used when setting the hair. Now you'll look at some additional points that you will need to know in order to create easy-to-finish roller hair designs.

  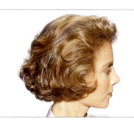

ROLLER DIAMETER

The diameters of rollers are chosen according to the desired curl pattern. Smaller rollers usually produce curlier effects, but the exact results will vary according to the length of your client's hair.

ROLLERS IN STRAIGHT SHAPES

Cylindrical rollers are usually used within straight shapes such as rectangles and triangles. Depending on the width of the rectangle shape, rollers of the same length are used to encompass the shape. On the other hand, short and long rollers may be used within a bricklay pattern to accommodate a larger rectangle shape. For triangle shapes, a progression of tool lengths is used to accommodate the narrow to wide shape. Depending on the desired result, the roller diameter(s) you choose can create repetition, alternation or even a progression of curl.

A **rectangle** set with rollers will achieve straight directional movement and is generally used as a "fill-in" or "blending" shape with curvature shapes set on either side. Generally, rectangle shapes are set from multiple points of origin and with any of the straight volume base controls depending upon the desired effect. Straight indentation base controls used within a rectangle shape are generally positioned near the perimeter hairline for a "flip" effect.

HAIR DESIGN

Triangle shapes are used to achieve straight movement in any direction and can be positioned at the top and sides of the head. In this example, triangles radiate outward from one point of origin positioned at the crown. A progression of tool lengths is used to accommodate the narrow-to-wide shape. The crown is set with on-base controls that diminish to half-off base. The result is a movement of texture that radiates outward from the crown and gradually diminishes toward the perimeter.

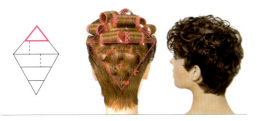

Back-to-back triangles are often used to create diamond or kite shapes. This achieves maximum texture at the widest area of the shape that gradually tapers toward the narrow points of the shape.

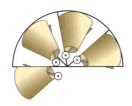

ROLLERS IN CURVATURE SHAPES

The most efficient way to set rollers within a curvature shape, such as the circle, oval or oblong, is to use cone-shaped, also known as tapered, rollers. Because of the way cone-shaped rollers fit into a curvature shape, they allow you to create stronger curvature movements that are not achievable with straight rollers.

A **half-circle** set with rollers will achieve curvature volume that directs hair with equal radial lines. Half-circles are commonly positioned at the fringe area or at the sides to direct an equal amount of hair off the face and on the face. Equal length rollers are positioned 1x away from a single point of origin. In this example, a progression of base controls from on-base to off-base achieves maximum to diminishing volume toward the hairline. Adapt the size and proportion of a circular shape to the client's head size and the design desired.

Expanded circles are larger circles that extend the curvature direction from the circle or half-circle while maintaining equal radial lines. Expanded half-circles are most often positioned at the sides to create curved direction that extends to the back. An inner-and-outer technique is used to set expanded circles. The inner half-circle is set as a normal half-circle. The outer circle is set by aligning the base partings to follow the same point of origin as the inner circle. Rollers in the outer circle are positioned within their bases, versus 1x away from the point of origin.

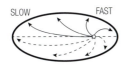

A **half-oval** set with rollers will achieve curvature volume that directs hair with unequal radial lines. When positioned at the front or sides, half-ovals can be used to direct a greater amount of hair off the face than on the face or the reverse, a smaller amount of hair off the face and a greater amount on the face.

Unequal length rollers are positioned 1x away from a single point of origin. In this example, a progression of base controls from on-base to off-base achieves maximum to diminishing volume.

Expanded ovals are an extension of a half-oval. Expanded ovals are positioned at the front or sides of the head to create curvature movement that travels toward the back. An indirect technique is used to set the expanded oval. Each individual roller is set from its own point of origin that is established at the front bottom corner of each roller. Rollers are positioned 1x away from their point of origin.

Generally, two or more oblongs are set in alternating directions to create a strong wave pattern. Oblongs may be positioned anywhere on the head and in any direction. Rollers are positioned diagonally and set from multiple points of origin.

In this example, alternating volume oblongs are set at the top of the head to create a strong wave pattern that moves from the front hairline to the crown.

In this example, alternating volume oblongs are followed with indentation oblongs from a side part to achieve a strong wave pattern with a flip effect.

Partial roller sets are often combined with molding techniques to create customized designs.

WET DESIGN PROCEDURE OVERVIEW

This section contains guidelines for performing fingerwaves and skipwaves with flat pincurls, followed by a Procedure Overview, which reviews the Preparation, Procedure and Completion phases, for wet design setting and finishing. By understanding the following design guidelines and procedure overview, you will be able to create a multitude of hair designs to please even the most particular clients. The *Hair Design, A Designer's Approach* Coursebook will show you step-by-step procedures for individual wet hair design services in greater detail.

FINGERWAVES AND FLAT PINCURL GUIDELINES

- Mold the first direction toward the closed end of an oblong shape and mold the second direction by positioning your index finger in the center of the shape and molding the hair toward the open end.

- Create the ridge by positioning the teeth of the comb along your index finger and sliding the comb approximately 1" (2.5 cm) toward the concave end of the oblong. Then, flatten the comb, switch fingers to position the ridge between your index and middle fingers; turn the comb and distribute the hair in the opposite direction to complete the ridge.

- Pivot carefully to avoid overdirecting the hair at the crown area; continue fingerwaving around the curve of the head to the other side.

- Begin the ridge of the next oblong at the concave end; work from the front hairline around the head to the other side.

- Complete the fingerwaves; strive for equally spaced waves.

- Begin to set flat pincurls beginning at the concave end of the last oblong, taking care not to disturb the ridge.

- Complete the flat pincurls and use finishing procedures to style as desired.

SKIP WAVES WITH FLAT PINCURLS GUIDELINES

- Mold two oblongs with a connecting ridge. The first shape travels in a counterclockwise direction and the second oblong travels clockwise.

- Set flat pincurls in the second oblong. Begin setting at the open or concave end. Do not disturb the shapes or the ridge as you position the pincurls.

- Complete the row of pincurls. Mold two more oblongs. Leave the first oblong undisturbed and set the second in flat pincurls. Dry the hair completely before combing this pattern out.

WET DESIGN: SETTING AND FINISHING PROCEDURE OVERVIEW
SETTING AND FINISHING PREPARATION
- Clean work station with disinfectant
- Arrange hair design essentials that include tools/supplies such as various length rollers, picks, clips, tail comb, large-tooth comb, cushion brush, setting lotion and finishing products
- Wash your hands with liquid soap
- Ask the client to remove jewelry and store in a secure place
- Drape client for a wet service
- Perform analysis of hair and scalp
- Shampoo and condition the hair using products appropriate for the client's hair type
- Towel dry and detangle the hair

SETTING AND FINISHING PROCEDURE

- Perform the appropriate setting procedures to achieve desired results
  - **Distribute** the hair into the desired direction in relation to the client's face
  - **Mold** the hair into straight and/or curved lines, using parallel and/or radial distribution
  - **Scale** (section) the hair into straight and/or curvature shapes to establish the lines of the design
  - **Part** the hair to create shapes or subsections or to control the hair, as needed
  - **Apply** the appropriate tools and wet design techniques, using appropriate base control
- Perform the appropriate finishing procedures to achieve desired results
  - **Relax** the hair with a brush to blend the partings and smooth the texture
  - **Dry mold** the hair with a cushion brush and your hands to reinforce the lines of the design
  - **Backbrush and/or backcomb** to create volume and indentation, expand the design's shape and/or connect shapes within the design
  - **Define the form** to achieve the desired look
  - **Detail** the hair, if needed, to add particular finishing touches and/or to personalize the design

SETTING AND FINISHING COMPLETION

- Reinforce guest's satisfaction with the overall salon experience
- Make professional product recommendations
- Prebook guest's next appointment
- End guest's visit with a warm and personal goodbye
- Discard non-reusable materials, disinfect tools and arrange work station in proper order
- Wash your hands with liquid soap
- Complete client record card
- Provide follow-up after the salon visit

10.3 THERMAL DESIGN TECHNIQUES

Thermal designing is the technique of drying and/or designing hair by using a hand-held dryer while simultaneously using your fingers, a variety of brushes, pressing comb and/or a thermal curling iron. "Thermal" means relating to or caused by heat. It is important to remember that heat is a form of energy that needs to be handled with great care, especially when used on hair.

Blow dryers and thermal irons are the thermal tools available to the hair designer. Using these tools in conjunction with a variety of designer brushes and combs, you can achieve any number of creative and practical design solutions.

Hair is composed predominantly of proteins connected by both physical and chemical bonds and by the hair's physical hydrogen bonds that can easily be broken down by either water or heat. When the hydrogen bonds of the hair are weakened by the heat of the thermal service, the protein chains are able to shift accepting a new position. When the heat is removed and the hair cools, the bonds are reformed in the new configuration.

After applying the thermal tool, the hair needs to cool completely prior to brushing or combing. If the hair is stretched while it is still warm, with the bonds still in a weakened state, the new texture pattern will not hold. Exposure to water, as in rain, humidity and shampooing, will also cause the hair to return to its original shape. Since heat and water can so readily reverse any changes in the hair achieved by reforming the physical bonds only, thermal designs are considered to be temporary.

There are also many styling products available that are formulated to prepare the hair for and protect it from the heat of thermal tools. Using these products sparingly will help ensure good results while maintaining the condition and integrity of the hair.

AIR FORMING

The term **air forming**, also called blow drying, refers to the process of simultaneously drying and designing the hair to create a new form. Blow dryers and their attachments are used to air form wet hair while using brushes, combs and your fingers to create temporary direction and texture changes.

Blow dryers are available in different sizes and shapes and also vary in the amount of wattage, generally from 1,000 watts to 1,800 watts. A blow dryer consists of a slotted nozzle, a heating element, a small motor or fan, temperature and air flow controls and, of course, a handle.

Blow dryer attachments that fit on the nozzle of the unit include concentrators and diffusers. Concentrators focus the air flow to a small area, which allows you to control the air flow and heat more specifically.

REMEMBER

Chemically treated hair is more fragile and additional care is required. Use thermal-protectant products and avoid high temperatures from the blow dryer and iron.

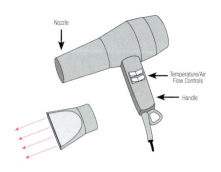

Diffusers spread a gentle air flow over a larger area and are generally used for freeform drying techniques such as scrunching. Temperature controls on the blow dryer provide a cool to hot setting, allowing for client comfort and design control.

TO PROPERLY HOLD THE BLOW DRYER
Loop the electric cord over the wrist when holding the blow dryer. This will allow the cord to travel in the same direction as the blow dryer and will also prevent the cord from hitting the client or trailing on the floor.

AIR FORMING GUIDELINES

- Always use a heat-protective styling lotion or other styling product before any air-forming process to reduce friction and form a clear, protective barrier against mechanical damage or the drying effects of heat. Excessive air forming can cause hair to lose elasticity or create split ends and has an overall drying effect.
- To save time and energy, remove approximately 90% of the water from the hair before thermal designing by towel blotting to eliminate excess water and then blow drying. Because hair that is too wet does not transfer heat effectively and because water keeps the hydrogen bonds in a softened state, designing with heat at this overly wet stage is more difficult.
- Dry the hair on the high setting, move to the medium setting for designing and set the design with cool air. A progressive decrease in temperature helps smooth the transition from wet, slippery hair, to hair that is more fixed and formable. Set your designs with cool air to reduce the warmth that curls retain. Retained heat makes the curls pliable and therefore more likely to "fall" back to their natural bond formation.
- Air form in the direction of the cuticle scales, not against them. Keep the dryer's airflow pointing down the hair strand from the scalp to the ends. Drying in the direction of the cuticle will protect the scalp and improve the hair's sheen when dry.
- Always keep the dryer 3" to 5" (7.5 cm to 12.5 cm) from the hair and constantly move it back and forth to reduce the potential of hair and scalp damage from heat.
- Use caution with damaged and lightened (bleached) hair. The greater the degree of chemical damage, the more susceptible the hair is to breakage, friction and heat damage. Therefore, remove all the water you can from the hair with a towel. Complete drying on the medium setting, air form the hair on low, and set the design with cool air. Since this type of hair is easily broken, choose your brushes carefully to avoid excessive tension.

AIR FORMING WITH ROUND BRUSH

Air forming with a blow dryer in one hand and a round brush in the other hand allows you to dry the hair quickly as you change the form, direction and texture of the hair. The diameter of the round brush you choose will influence the resulting texture pattern. Smaller brushes are used for curlier designs or short hair. Larger brushes are used for smoother results or for longer hair. Some brushes have metal cores, which retain heat and allow you to create stronger curl patterns. Determine the size and firmness of the curl by selecting a brush with the diameter that matches the size of the desired texture pattern.

When air forming for volume and indentation, it is the position, direction and continual motion of the brush that control the amount of volume or indentation achieved. For volume, the brush is positioned underneath the hair. For indentation, the brush is positioned on top of the hair. Refer to the "Base Control" section of this chapter for additional information.

VOLUME   INDENTATION

FINGER STYLING

Finger styling is a technique in which the fingers are used to manipulate and design the hair as it is dried with the blow dryer. The hair is lifted or held flat while drying to create the desired finish. The fingers are used to separate and define the texture. **Scrunching, a form of finger styling, involves gently squeezing the hair lengths as the hair is dried using a diffuser to introduce a texture patter that the hair responds to naturally.** Scrunching creates the best response on wavy or curly hair and does not work as well on straighter textures. Generally, a diffuser is attached to the blow dryer to soften the air flow while the hair is scrunched with the fingers to create the texture pattern.

HAIR PRESSING

Hair pressing, or **silking**, is a technique for temporarily straightening curly and tightly curled hair. Once the hair is shampooed and conditioned, it is air formed dry with tension to begin to reduce the natural curl pattern. A pressing oil or cream is applied to the hair, and then a hot pressing comb or silking (straightening) iron is used on small sections of hair to further straighten the curl. Because the pressing service can require heating the hair for a longer period of time than other thermal services, analyzing the type, texture and condition of the hair is particularly important. Frequent conditioning of the hair will help protect against breakage, dry scalp, split ends and dull appearance. Avoid pressing chemically damaged hair and pressing the hair too often, which can cause breakage. Hair pressing results last until the next shampoo. Exposure to high humidity can cause curl patterns to revert back to the natural texture.

Hair pressing is considered less damaging to the structure of the hair in comparison to a chemical relaxer service, thus leaving the hair with more strength and body. Clients also have more color options available to them when selecting a temporary pressing service versus a chemical change.

Analyzing the diameter of the hair is also important to a successful hair pressing service. Fine hair is especially delicate and must be treated gently. Less heat and pressure should be applied to fine hair than to other types of hair to avoid breakage. Medium hair is the least difficult to press and requires no particular precautions. Coarse and/or tightly curled hair can be quite resistant to hair pressing. Even though this type of hair can tolerate more heat and pressure than fine or medium hair, you need to guard against carelessness that can lead to hair damage. Remember that burned hair cannot be reconditioned.

The pressing comb is used to apply heat and tension to temporarily straighten tightly curled hair. The pressing comb is used on totally dry hair in preparation for the silking (straightening) iron application, which usually follows. There are two types of pressing combs, regular and electric. Regular pressing combs have a wooden handle since wood does not absorb heat. Regular pressing combs are heated in what is called a "stove" or "stove heater." Electric pressing combs have either an "on and off" switch or a thermostat with a control switch that allows the hair designer to select either high or low heat settings. Pressing combs are made of stainless steel or brass.

It is of the utmost importance that you protect the hair from excessive heat. Most thermal design tools are manufactured so that the temperature is maintained at a level that is safe for the hair. When working with stove-heated pressing combs or thermal irons, you'll need to check the temperature by testing the pressing comb or thermal iron on a piece of white paper towel. If the paper towel changes to yellow or brown, or scorches after about five seconds, you will need to let the comb or iron cool a bit prior to using it on the hair.

PRESS AND CURL SERVICE
A "press and curl service" involves curling or waving the hair with a thermal iron after it has been pressed. This service provides additional texture options for clients who have naturally curly or tightly curled hair.

Smooth effects with a pressing comb are accomplished by the pressing action of the heated spine of the comb against the hair. The number of times you repeat the pressing action on the same subsection depends on the amount of curl you wish to remove. Some hair designers prefer to use narrow partings and press once or twice on one side only. Others prefer to take larger sections and press once or twice on both sides of the subsection. A **soft press** means pressing the hair once with less pressure and heat. A **hard** or **double press** means pressing the hair twice with more pressure and heat. You'll need to adjust the pressure and temperature of the iron according to your client's hair condition and texture.

THERMAL IRONS

There are several different types of thermal irons and a variety of ways they may be used to create complete designs and to impart texture patterns on dry hair. Curling irons are a widely used type of thermal iron and they come in a variety of sizes. Other types of thermal irons include straightening or flat irons, crimping irons and undulating irons.

Thermal curling is the process of temporarily adding curl texture to the hair through the use of curling irons or other types of thermal irons. The earliest thermal irons were curling irons, first introduced by Marcel Grateau in 1875. These irons are now often called "marcel curling irons." These irons are some of the most frequently used styling tools available toda Thermal waving or curling is achieved by applying heat to dry hair from either an electric or stove-heated curling iron to create curls or waves for a finished hair design.

CURLING IRONS

The curling iron has four parts:
- Rod handle
- Shell handle
- Barrel, or rod (the round heating cylinder)
- Groove, or shell (the clamp that holds the hair against the barrel)

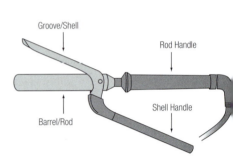

Electric curling irons have a swivel at the base of the handle that permits the electric cord to turn, without twisting, as the iron is being manipulated. For best performance, curling iron barrels and grooves are made of stainless steel to retain heat. Various barrel sizes and shapes are available.

The electric curling iron contains a heating element controlled by a thermostat that maintains a constant temperature during use. A good iron should be able to be left on for an entire day and still maintain the correct temperature. Lower temperatures are recommended for fine, chemically altered, lightened and damaged hair.

TO PROPERLY HOLD THE CURLING IRON
The best method for holding a curling iron will be determined by comfort and control. Some hair designers prefer to use only the little finger to open the iron, and the other fingers to close the iron. Others find it easier to use the little finger and ring finger to open the iron.

Practice these two methods of holding the iron to determine which is most comfortable for you, while allowing you to maintain the greatest control as you turn the iron to create a cur As the iron is turned in downward circular movements, a swivel at the base of the handle w permit the iron to turn without twisting the cord. As you continue to turn the iron, you will need to shift your thumb to aid in the turning motion.

PRACTICE MANIPULATIONS WITH THE CURLING IRON
Because curling irons can be difficult to use and can burn the hair strand if used incorrectly practice is recommended. Practice with a cold iron on your mannequin in the beginning unt you are comfortable with the manipulations.

Practice rolling the iron toward you (standing in back of your model, this will be a downward rotation) while opening and closing the clamp at regular intervals.

Practice rolling the iron away from you (standing in back of your model, this will be an upward rotation) while opening and closing the clamp at regular intervals.

Practice rolling the hair first in one direction and then in another. End each curling rotation by releasing the hair, which is done by opening and closing the clamp in a quick "clicking" movement.

CURLING IRON TECHNIQUES

Following are examples of different curling iron techniques and various texture patterns that can be achieved by varying the position of the curling iron along the hair strand. Curling irons are usually cylindrical in shape and create the texture pattern that reflects their diameter. Refer to the "Base Control" section in this chapter for volume and indentation base control information.

BASE-TO-ENDS TECHNIQUE

With the base-to-ends technique, the curling iron is first positioned slightly away from the base.

Next, the curling iron is turned one-half revolution toward the scalp.

The curling iron is then turned away from the scalp one-half revolution in the same direction, to make one complete revolution. This technique is repeated until the entire hair strand is gradually fed into the curling iron.

A heat-resistant (nonflammable) comb is positioned between the curling iron and the scalp to protect the client's scalp from accidental burning.

The base-to-ends technique creates volume and support at the base and a consistent curl pattern throughout the strand. For a volume base control, position the barrel of the curling iron underneath the hair strand. For an indentation base control, position the barrel of the curling iron on top of the hair strand. Depending on the length of hair, there are several ways to direct the hair within the curling iron.

Always feed the ends of the hair all the way through the curling iron to avoid crimped "fishhook" ends.

With short hair, the ends of the hair are directed into the center, also known as the Figure 4 technique.

With medium lengths of hair, the ends of the hair are directed to one side, also known as the Figure 6 technique.

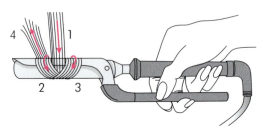

When working with longer lengths of hair, the ends of the hair are directed to both sides, also known as the Figure 8 technique.

ENDS-TO-BASE TECHNIQUE

With the ends-to-base technique, the curling iron is positioned at the ends of the hair and then rotated upward, toward the base. For a volume effect, the barrel of the curling iron is positioned underneath the hair strand. For an indentation effect, the barrel of the curling iron is positioned on top of the hair strand. The ends-to-base technique is appropriate on shorter hair lengths. On longer hair, the curl pattern achieved using this technique is generally stronger at the ends and weaker toward the base.

ENDS TECHNIQUE

With the ends technique, the curling iron is positioned to add curl texture at the ends only. This technique can be used to create a curved-under or flipped-up (indentation) effect.

MARCEL TECHNIQUE

The curling iron can be used to create marcel waves, or alternating oblongs, along the hair strand. The hair strand is placed into the curling iron with the barrel of the curling iron positioned on top of the strand and the shell of the iron beneath the strand. A comb is used to help direct the hair in alternating directions to form the wave.

SPIRAL TECHNIQUE

Elongated spiral curls can be created with a curling iron using a spiral technique. The curling iron is positioned vertically or diagonally at the base. The curling iron is then turned while gradually feeding the hair strand into the curling iron until the entire strand is fed through and the ends are within the iron. Another way to perform the spiral technique is to position the curling iron on the ends of the hair then turn the curling iron upward in a vertical or diagonal position toward the base

Detangling and combing the hair smoothly prior to applying the thermal iron ensures a consistent texture pattern throughout the hair strand.

SPECIAL-EFFECTS THERMAL IRONS

Special-effects thermal irons that allow you to create textures other than traditional curvilinear and curled textures are available. Following are some examples:

STRAIGHTENING OR FLAT IRONS
Straightening or flat irons consist of two flat plates. The hair is placed between the two plates near the base and then brought down to the ends in one smooth, flowing movement. This technique is referred to as straightening or silking the hair.

CRIMPING IRONS
Unlike straightening irons that consist of two flat plates, crimping irons consist of two plates that have an angular or serrated pattern. The hair is positioned between the two crimped plates, which are then closed upon the hair. The resulting texture is angular, which is often referred to as crimped hair.

UNDULATING IRONS
Undulating irons consist of two undulating or curved plates that create an "S" pattern. The hair is positioned between the two plates, which are then closed upon the hair. The result is an undulating wave pattern.

THERMAL IRON CONSIDERATIONS

Cleaning thermal irons (or pressing combs) can be accomplished by running fine-grade steel wool along the barrel of the iron while it is still slightly warm to remove any styling residue. Clean the iron in the direction that the hair flows across the barrel. That is, move the wool pad around the circumference of the barrel, not vertically (base to tip). This precaution ensures that hair will not flow against the grain and be damaged. This steel wool method should not be used on barrels with Teflon or other coatings. Steel wool can chip and wear off the coating, leading to abrasion during use. Use only a gentle cleaning method on coated irons.

Close a hot iron lightly on a damp towel before curling extremely damaged or bleached hair. This step is not necessary for most hair types, but with damaged hair, you want to cool the iron and assess the heat before it is applied. Some tinted hair, white hair and very fine hair will also benefit by testing the iron and proceeding with a lower iron temperature. This testing can prevent scorching or dryness.

Choose an iron with even heat distribution. Use appliances that heat up uniformly across the barrel with no cool spots. Uniform heat will avoid uneven curls. Remember that a metal curling iron holder retains heat. If you use a metal holder be sure to test the temperature of the iron before using it on your client's hair. Never test an iron's heat by touching it with your fingers or placing it near your nose to smell if it is hot. You can sufficiently judge the amount of heat an iron is giving off by bringing your hand very near the barrel, without touching it.

THERMAL DESIGN PROCEDURE OVERVIEW

This section contains guidelines for performing press and curl techniques followed by a Procedure Overview, which reviews the Preparation, Procedure and Completion phases, for an air forming and curling iron service. Reviewing the following design guidelines and procedure overview will help you prepare to perform these hair design skills to meet the needs of a variety of clients. The *Hair Design* coursebook will show you step-by-step procedures for individual thermal design services in greater deta

PRESS AND CURL GUIDELINES

- Section hair for air forming and air form to reduce natural curl pattern
- Section hair for thermal pressing, apply pressing oil/cream and test the temperature of pressing comb
- Insert teeth of pressing comb underneath parting
- Turn comb and press hair with spine as you work from base to ends
- Feed hair slowly through comb as you work down toward the ends
- Complete the back using horizontal partings; press the front using diagonal partings; press hairline
- Heat thermal iron(s); test the temperature of the iron(s)
- Curl hair as desired
- Finish the hair design

AIR FORMING AND CURLING IRON PROCEDURE OVERVIEW
AIR FORMING AND CURLING IRON PROCEDURE PREPARATION
See "Wet Design: Setting and Finishing Preparation" within the "Wet Design Procedure Overview" section of this chapter

AIR FORMING AND CURLING IRON PROCEDURE
- Perform the appropriate air forming and curling iron procedures to achieve desired results
  - **Distribute**, **mold** and **scale** the hair simultaneously to establish the directional pattern of the design prior to air forming and during air forming; control the form and the lines of the design as the molded directions are air formed
  - **Part** the hair and **apply** the proper base control using a round brush in a repetitive, constant motion to control the amount of volume, indentation and direction within the design while blending between bases and shapes
  - Part and apply the appropriate curling iron base controls; safely test the iron prior to applying it to the hair; position the comb underneath the curling iron to protect the scalp; use only a hard rubber or nonflammable comb, if applicable
- Perform the appropriate finishing procedures to achieve desired results
  - **Relax**, **dry mold** and **backbrush and/or backcomb**, if needed, to create volume, expand the design's shape and/or connect shapes within the design
  - **Define the form** by selecting the appropriate tool to affect the surface texture appearance of the design
  - **Detail** the hair by adding any finishing touches, such as pleating, to create separated texture definition and complete the design

AIR FORMING AND CURLING IRON PROCEDURE COMPLETION
See "Wet Design: Setting and Finishing Completion" within the "Wet Design Procedure Overview" section of this chapter.

10.4 LONG HAIR DESIGN THEORY

Hair designers approach the subject of long hair designing with attention to the elements of:
- Form
- Texture
- Color

Their compositions are three-dimensional and incorporate universal design principles such as:
- Repetition
- Alternation
- Progression
- Contrast

Every hair designer would benefit from understanding the mechanics of long hair design as a way to expand his or her clientele. Those who are passionate about long hair designing see it as a creative art form that requires their full attention and time, and, therefore, specialize exclusively in long hair design for special occasions, such as weddings.

LONG HAIR DESIGN ANALYSIS

Understanding how to look at a photograph using the basic, detail and abstract levels of observation not only allows you to reproduce what you see, it also allows you a means of communicating clearly with your client. Once you are able to reproduce what you see, you have set the foundation for creating a repertoire of ideas to choose from, and eventually you begin to adapt unique designs of your own.

BASIC—FORM AND SHAPE
At the basic level, the outer shape or outline of the three-dimensional form is identified by the position of volume.

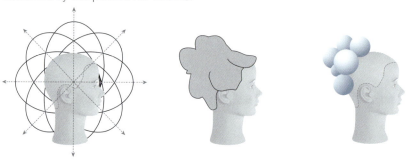

DETAIL—TEXTURE
The detail level allows you to determine the type(s) of textures you see such as smooth (unactivated) or rough (activated), which in turn allows you to determine the techniques that were used to create the texture.

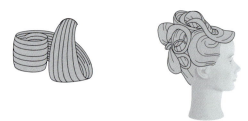

ABSTRACT—DIRECTION
With the abstract level, the overall direction and the directions within the form are identified.

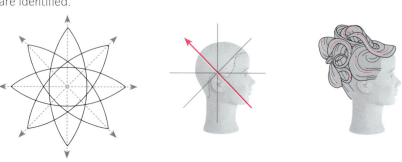

FORM OR SHAPE

In long hair designing, it is not the length arrangement but the placement of mass, or volume, within the design that creates the overall shape or three-dimensional form. Volume may be positioned in a specific area or throughout the design.

EQUAL HEIGHT AND WIDTH
When volume is positioned equally throughout a long hair design, attention is not focused on any particular area.

International Long Hair Collection

MORE HEIGHT THAN LENGTH
Volume positioned in a specific area, such as the crown or nape, automatically draws the eye to that area. Some designs may include more height than length, which will draw attention diagonally to the crown or vertically straight up or to the top. The position of volume within a long hair design becomes the **focal point**.

 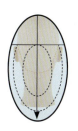 

MORE LENGTH THAN HEIGHT
Designs that include more length than height focus attention at the nape or below the shoulders.

MORE WIDTH THAN HEIGHT OR LENGTH
Shapes that consist of more width than height or length will draw the eye horizontally across the design.

The overall shape of a design can be broken down further by analyzing the shape(s) and form within the design. Keep in mind that the size and position of individual shapes influence the feeling of the design, allowing you unlimited creative options.

In some instances, fillers (loose fibers), can be used to expand a design or to create specific forms or shapes.

TEXTURE AND COLOR

In long hair design, texture is identified as unactivated (smooth) and activated (patterned). Both the technique and amount of existing or designed curl influence the resulting texture. For example, loops are considered smooth, while tightly formed twists are considered activated. In long hair designs, it is not uncommon to see a combination of textures. The design element color plays an integral role in hair designing. Color can lead your eye through the movements of a design or it can create a focal point within a design.

DIRECTION

The direction of a form is established by the flow of the shapes within a design. The celestial axis, which consists of all the straight and curved lines, can be used to analyze the overall direction of the form.

The direction of the hair implies motion and plays an important part in the dynamics of a design. Directions within the form can be identified as clockwise, counterclockwise, vertical, horizontal and/or diagonal and can lead your eye rhythmically throughout the design.

PROPORTION AND BALANCE

The proportional relationship between size, shape, texture and color should be considered when planning a well-balanced design, which can be symmetrical or asymmetrical. The size and position of individual shapes influence the overall feel and impression of the design, allowing you unlimited creative options.

CLIENT CONSIDERATIONS

Long hair designing is a service that is often performed for special occasions, so you will want to give extra emphasis and attention to exceeding the client's expectations by creating a beautiful and flattering design. Communicating the relationship between the considerations discussed in this section and the final long hair design to your client will not only help her understand and accept your design recommendations, it will also help build your professional reputation along with client trust and loyalty.

Here are some specific considerations to keep in mind as you communicate and work with your client to ensure that successful design decisions will be made.

CLIENT CONSIDERATIONS	DESIGN DECISIONS
FACIAL FEATURES	• Determine whether detailing around the face should be a component of the design. Soft facial features may become overpowered with too much detailing. A long hair design that is pulled away from the face may be more flattering to softer facial features, while bolder facial features can carry off more detail around the face.
BODY STRUCTURE	• Identify your client's particular body shape and factor it into your design approach. Consider that clients who are short and sturdy benefit from a design with height and volume, while just the opposite is true for tall and lanky clients. Refer to *Chapter 8, Design Decisions*, for additional information.
HAIR LENGTH, DENSITY AND TEXTURE	• Analyze the condition of the hair to determine any limitations for the long hair design. Clients with short hair who want an upswept design will present more limitations than those with longer lengths. For short-haired clients, hairpieces are an option. Refer to *Chapter 11, Wigs and Hair Additions*, for additional information.
OCCASION	• Consider the nature of the occasion. Is she attending a wedding, or is she the bride-to-be? Is she attending a black-tie affair or a prom? Answers to these questions will guide you in your decision-making process.

CLIENT CONSIDERATIONS	DESIGN DECISIONS
WARDROBE	• Consider what the client will be wearing. A gown that is strapless will offer you different design options than one with a high or closed neckline. The fabric of the gown also plays a critical role. Smooth, sleek gowns may be complemented with smooth, controlled hair designs, whereas intricate, beaded textured gowns may lend themselves to more intricate, yet simple, hair designs.
IMPRESSION	• You'll want to find out what kind of impression your client wants to make. Does she want to look elegant, soft and romantic, or perhaps is she striving for a more fashion-forward look?

In long hair design, there is always more than just one choice—the options are endless. Listening to your client and gaining insight into her personality, fashion sense and perceptions of the "perfect" long hair design will help you blend your professional knowledge with your client's expectations to create a long hair design she'll be thrilled with.

LONG HAIR DESIGNING

Once the desired shape, direction and position of volume are identified, you will follow a step-by-step procedure to ensure control of the form as it is being created. The long hair design procedures are:

• Distribute   • Section   • Part   • Apply   • Detail

DISTRIBUTE

In long hair designing, **distribution** defines the overall direction of the design. Distribution is performed throughout the long hair service. At first, overall distribution, including distributing the hair away from the face, toward the crown, toward the nape, or downward from a part, is performed to prepare the hair for the position of ponytail(s) or volume.

In the absence of a ponytail, distribution is generally performed in the direction the hair will be worn, including upward toward the crown, away from the face, or from a part.

SECTION

In long hair designing, **sectioning** is used for the purpose of control. The number of sections you choose to use within a design will depend on the desired results.

Common sectioning patterns include subdividing the front from the back, the nape, occipital, crown, fringe and/or perimeter. The hair is then distributed into those areas to position ponytails, resulting in a concentration of volume in those specific areas. In many instances, the ponytails are further sectioned before the chosen technique is applied.

Increasing the number of ponytails or sections within a design allows you to vary the position of volume and, therefore, influence the shape.

If no ponytails are used, you may need to section as the design is being created to control the hair and the position of volume.

PART

Partings are used to subdivide the hair and larger sections for control. Any straight or curved line from the celestial axis can be used to part the hair. In most cases, partings are performed in the direction the hair will be distributed.

Distribution from individual partings or shapes is performed along any straight or curved line from the celestial axis in preparation for the chosen technique. Distributing the hair neatly from the parting is of utmost importance in long hair designing to achieve smooth, clean lines.

APPLY

Once the hair has been distributed, sectioned and/or parted as appropriate to achieve the final design, you will **apply** long hair techniques, such as twists, knots, overlap, braids, loops and rolls. Each of these techniques is described later in this chapter. The techniques chosen will determine whether the finished texture will be unactivated (smooth) or activated (patterned). Where you position the technique will determine the position of volume.

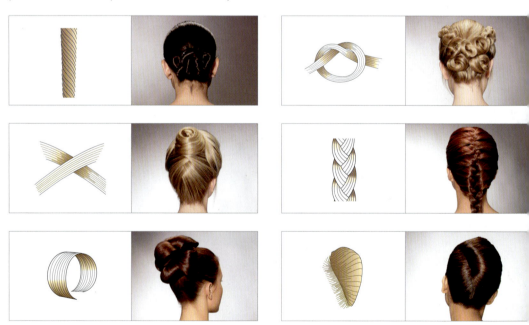

BACKCOMBING/BACKBRUSHING

As with wet and thermal hair design techniques, you will also apply backcombing and backbrushing techniques in long hair designing to control the overall shape of the design and individual shapes within the design. In most instances, backcombing and backbrushing techniques are performed with loop and roll designs to increase the amount of volume or expansion. The surface of the hair is smoothed in the direction the hair will be worn without removing the support achieved through backcombing or backbrushing.

SECURING THE DESIGN

A hallmark of beautiful long hair designing is being able to create designs without exposing the hairpins and bobby pins that were used to secure the design. Strategically positioning hairpins or bobby pins underneath the surface of the hair or within shapes are examples of ways to secure the hair.

DETAIL

Detailing is the finishing touches that can be performed during, or as a final phase of the design to personalize the form. Detailing includes using long hairpins to control the formation of shapes, textural detail and movements within a design. Once the hair is properly secured underneath the surface, the long hairpins are removed.

Detailing also includes ornamentation that can be used both aesthetically and functionally to conceal hairpins and bobby pins, or in place of them.

COSMETOLOGY FUNDAMENTALS

LONG HAIR DESIGN ESSENTIALS

To perform professional long hair services, you need a selection of products, tools, supplies and equipment—from hairpins to hair nets, from hairpieces to hair accessories.

Long hair design tools also include the tools that you will use to properly prepare the hair prior to creating the long hair design, such as rollers and thermal irons. Properly preparing the hair sets the foundation from which to build upon. Once the hair is properly prepared, you will use a variety of combs, brushes, hairpins, and finishing tools such as hairspray to create your designs.

Because many of the essentials used for wet and thermal design are also used for long hair design, refer to the "Hair Design Essentials" section earlier in this chapter for information about additional products, tools, supplies and equipment.

LONG HAIR PRODUCTS

PRODUCTS	FUNCTION
NON-AEROSOL HAIRSPRAY	Holds finished design in place; liquid dispensed through pump
AEROSOL HAIRSPRAY	Holds finished design in place; available in a variety of strengths; liquid dispensed through compressed gas and spray
POMADE	Adds shine and texture definition; smoothes the hair; adds weight to the hair; provides hair control; silicon-based product
SHINE SPRAY	Adds shine and provides hair control
OIL SHEEN	Adds shine and provides hair control

LONG HAIR TOOLS/SUPPLIES

TOOLS/SUPPLIES	FUNCTION
BOBBY PIN	Secures hair in place for finished design, especially in long hair designs
HAIRPIN	Secures hair in place for finished design, especially in long hair designs
LONG HAIRPIN	Defines textural detail and movement; controls the formation of shapes while creating the design; u-shaped hairpins without ridges
ELASTIC BAND	Holds ponytails in position
FINE-TOOTH TAIL COMB	Sections, parts and distributes the hair
LARGE-TOOTH TAIL COMB	Backcombs; used for finishing techniques
MASTER SKETCHER COMB	Detangles and backcombs hair

TOOLS/SUPPLIES	FUNCTION
CUSHION BRUSH	Relaxes sets; backbrushes; dry molds, defines the form
HAIR NET	Controls and secures a hair design or portion thereof; delicate, open-meshed fabric, usually knotted or woven and attached to a fine elastic band
FILLER	Expands a design or creates specific forms using loose hair fiber
HAIRPIECE	Covers specific areas of the head for definite purposes; used to add length, color or shape to a design; made of human hair or artificial hair
HAIR FORM	Expands a design by using a fiber-filled shape
HAIR ACCESSORY	Provides ornamentation and/or a method to secure the hair; ranging from plastic combs to jewel-encrusted clips

HAIR DESIGN EQUIPMENT

See listing earlier in this chapter.

INFECTION CONTROL AND SAFETY

The following is a list of safety precautions to follow prior to and during a long hair service.

1. Practice infection control guidelines.
2. Wash and sanitize hands.
3. Ask client to remove jewelry (earrings, necklace) to avoid catching the comb on the jewelry and injuring the client and/or damaging the jewelry.
4. Check the scalp for any diseases or disorders. If any are evident, refer the client to a physician and do not proceed with the service.
5. Protect the client and his or her clothing with proper draping procedures. Refer to the "Draping" portion of *Chapter 7, Trichology.*
6. Avoid securing ponytail and/or hair too tightly, causing discomfort to the client and possibly hair breakage.
7. Protect the client's scalp by gently securing hair with bobby pins and hairpins that have a protective plastic coating on the ends.
8. Avoid spraying finishing products into the client's eyes, onto hair accessories and/or clothing.
9. Disinfect and sanitize all tools after each use.

ALERT!

Always follow manufacturers' directions for the proper use, disinfection and maintenance of long hair essentials.

LONG HAIR DESIGN SERVICE ESSENTIALS

As with all hair services, communicating with your client prior to the service will help you avoid misunderstandings and ensure predictable results. When discussing the hair design service with a client, use photos and magazines to clarify your design intentions. Make sure that you reach clear agreements concerning the service to be performed.

CONNECT
- Meet and greet the client with a smile, firm handshake and a pleasant tone of voice.
- Communicate to build rapport and develop a connection with the client.

CONSULT
- Ask questions to discover client needs, such as: "What is the event or special occasion you are attending?" "What role will you have in the event?" The answers to these questions will help y make the most appropriate design choices for your client.
- Ask your client to describe what she will be wearing. A strapless gown will allow you different design options than a gown with a high or closed neckline. The amount—or lack of—detail on a gown will help you determine the amount of detail in the hair design.
- Ask your client if she has any accessories that she would like to include in her long hair design such as a veil or ornate hair clips.
- Ask questions such as, "What type of impression would you like to convey?" Is it "romantic," "classic" or maybe an "avant-garde" or "fashion-forward" look?
- Ask questions to better understand your client's personality. For example, a woman who doesn't wish to call too much attention to herself may not benefit from a bold, edgy or fashion-forward design.
- Analyze your client's face and body shape, physical features, hair and scalp. Consider where t volume should be positioned and how your client would look from all angles, including the pro view. Refer to "Design Adaptability" in *Chapter 8, Design Decisions*, for further guidelines.
- Assess the facts and thoroughly think through your recommendations.
- Explain your recommended solutions and the price for the services you are recommending.
- Get feedback from your client and obtain consent before proceeding with the service.

CREATE
- Ensure your client is protected by draping with a towel and plastic cape during the shampoo process. Once the hair is properly dried, replace the cape with a cloth cape for the actual long hair service.
- Ensure client comfort during the service.
- Stay focused on delivering the long hair design service to the best of your ability.
- Teach the client how to use a light holding spray if necessary as the day and the event progre

COMPLETE
- Request specific feedback from your client. Ask questions and look for verbal and nonverbal cues to determine your client's level of satisfaction.
- Escort client to the retail area and show at least two products you used.
- Invite your client to make a purchase.

- Suggest a future appointment for your client's next special occasion.
- Offer sincere appreciation to your client for visiting the school or salon.
- Complete client record card for future visits; include recommended products.

10.5 LONG HAIR DESIGN TECHNIQUES

Long hair designing is a temporary service, so be creative and have fun practicing. The more you practice, the more efficient you will become and the more fun you will have.

The long hair design techniques mentioned earlier—twists, knots, overlaps, braids, loops and rolls—will now be explored more closely. Designs created from ponytails are known as off-the-scalp designs; designs created directly from the scalp are known as on-the-scalp designs.

 ## TWISTS

Twists consist of one, two or three strands of hair intertwined and/or rotated to form a rope-like appearance. The size of the strand and the tension applied determine the appearance of the twist, which can range from large to small and from loose to tight.

Single-strand twists consist of one strand of hair that is rotated in a clockwise or counterclockwise direction.

Multiple single tightly twisted strands can create a highly textured intricate pattern.

  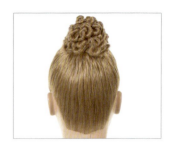

Two strands lightly twisted can create a loop-like effect.

Three strands intertwined and twisted can create a tight, rope-like appearance.

KNOTS

Knots consist of an interlacing or tying together of a strand or strands of hair. Knots can vary from large to small and may be positioned along the base, midstrand, ends or any combination.

Single-strand knots, such as those used on a day-to-day basis, are created by forming a circle with one strand and bringing the ends through the center.

2-strand knots are created by tying two strands of hair together.

OVERLAPS

Overlaps consist of two strands crossed to opposite sides, in a downward or upward direction, to create a crisscrossed effect. The size and number of strands within a design can dramatically influence the amount of crisscross pattern in the finished result.

Two strands alternately crossed over one another in a downward direction can create a draped-like effect.

Two strands alternately crossed over one another in an upward direction can create a tight crisscrossed effect.

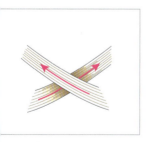  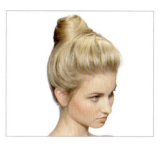 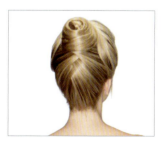

BRAIDS

A **braid** consists of the crossing or weaving of three or more strands of hair. Twine, plait, pleat, weave, intertwine and interlock are just some of the terms associated with the age-old art of braiding. Whether piled high on the head, pinned close in the nape or free-falling past the shoulder, braids offer an artistic, individualistic design opportunity.

Braids can be classified according to the number of strands used in the technique, which can range from 3 to 5, 7, 9 and more. The 3-strand braid is the foundation of all the braids. Once the 3-strand braid has been established, adjacent strands are woven toward the center. Any of these braids can be performed off-the-scalp from a ponytail or on the scalp.

   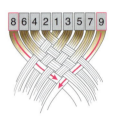

The two most common braiding methods are 3-strand overbraid, also known as the French or invisible braid, and the 3-strand underbraid, also known as the visible braid. The difference between the two techniques is whether a strand of hair is crossed over or under a center strand.

The **3-strand overbraid** has an inverted appearance, which is why it is referred to as an invisible braid. This technique can be used to create one 3-strand braid that conforms to the curve of the head or for multiple braids that can either be worn straight or elaborately formed into shapes.

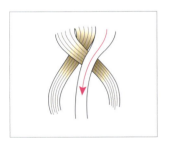   

Unlike the 3-strand overbraid, where the outside strands are crossed over the center strand, for the **3-strand underbraid**, the outside strands are crossed under the center strand. Crossing the strands under the center strand creates a projected or visible braid pattern.

When performed on the scalp, the 3-strand underbraid is also known as cornrowing. Cornrowing can be a combination of on-the-scalp braiding that then extends off the scalp. Three-strand underbraids may be positioned in any number of ways.

Multiple-strand braids create a wider pattern of intricate woven texture.

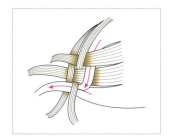  

LOOPS

Loops are the folding, bending or encircling of hair strands, which are then secured in a curvature shape. Loop compositions are timeless and offer the designer maximum freeform creativity. Varying the size, dimension and position of each loop allows the designer to create and achieve a multitude of design possibilities.

Loops can vary in shape. For instance, circular loops take on a more rounded appearance, while elongated loops can look more cylindrical or triangular. Loops can be open or closed on one end or both. As the number of loops in the design increases, the pattern becomes more intricate.

A single loop consists of folding and pinning a section of hair to create one loop.

Double loops consist of two loops created with one section of hair.

ROLLS

Rolls consist of hair that is wrapped or wound within itself. In addition to fashion trends and personal preference, the size and shape of the roll is predetermined by the length of the client's hair. Rolls can be cylindrical or conical in shape and positioned along any line of the celestial axis. In many instances, roll designs are combined with other techniques such as loops.

LONG HAIR DESIGN PROCEDURE OVERVIEW

Once you understand the theory behind long hair designing, you are ready to use your knowledge and apply it to the medium of hair. You can achieve a variety of results by combining techniques within a single design. The *Hair Design* coursebook will show you step-by-step procedures for individual long hair design services in greater detail.

LONG HAIR DESIGN PREPARATION

- Clean long hair design station with disinfectant
- Arrange long hair design essentials, including hairpins, bobby pins, elastic bands, combs, brushes, accessories, hairspray and shine spray
- Wash your hands with liquid soap
- Ask the client to remove jewelry and store it in a secure place
- Drape client for a wet service
- Perform analysis of hair and scalp
- Shampoo, condition and dry client's hair
- Replace client's draping with cloth cape and neck strip once the hair is dried

LONG HAIR DESIGN PROCEDURE

- Perform the long hair design procedures to achieve desired results
  - **Distribute** the hair to reflect the overall direction of the design (away from the face, toward the crown, toward the nape, downward from a part)
  - **Section** the hair into workable areas for the purpose of control (one or multiple ponytails, ponytail with perimeter lengths left free, individual partings with no ponytails)
  - **Part** the hair in the appropriate parting pattern (any straight or curved line from the celestial axis)
  - **Apply** the appropriate long hair techniques to achieve the desired results (twists, knots, overlaps, braids, loops or rolls)
  - **Detail** the hair (ensure hairpins and bobby pins are properly concealed, include ornamentation when applicable, control flyaways, use shine spray, hairspray)
- Check the form for balance (symmetrical or asymmetrical)

LONG HAIR DESIGN COMPLETION

- Reinforce guest's satisfaction with the overall salon experience
- Make professional product recommendations
- Prebook guest's next appointment
- End guest's visit with a warm and personal goodbye
- Discard non-reusable materials, disinfect tools and arrange workstation in proper order
- Complete client record card
- Provide follow-up after the salon visit

The theory and techniques you learned in this chapter will form the basis for advanced work in the ever-growing field of hair design. Your future awaits as you practice to gain mastery.

CONNECTING THEORY TO REAL-WORLD PRACTICE

HAIR DESIGN	PERSONAL CONNECTION: IMPROVE YOURSELF	INDUSTRY CONNECTION: BECOME A PROFESSIONAL	CLIENT CONNECTION: SERVE THE GUEST
HAIR DESIGN THEORY	Know how form, texture, direction and movement combine for an overall hair design	Develop a reputation for professional hair design by relying on a strong theoretical foundation	Use proven approaches to analyze, set and finish hair designs for your clientele
WET DESIGN TECHNIQUES	Work with wet hair to produce a variety of new design looks	Expand your salon talents with artistic and creative wet designs	Provide customized hair designs that add body and wave
THERMAL DESIGN TECHNIQUES	Achieve softer-looking hair designs with thermal techniques	Offer contemporary and creative thermal designs	Satisfy a wide range of clients who want a quick, efficient hair design
LONG HAIR DESIGN THEORY	Explore a discipline that provides unlimited creative possibilities	Display innovation, passion and leadership in a specialized salon skill	Consider personal traits and the specific occasion to create appropriate long hair designs
LONG HAIR DESIGN TECHNIQUES	Take advantage of the many options for creating designs with long hair	Raise your industry standing by creating high-profile long hair designs	Apply a variety of artistic techniques to achieve classic and progressive long hair designs

IN OTHER WORDS

Hair design is at the heart of your profession because it is the service most closely related to your clients' satisfaction with their finished looks.

LESSONS LEARNED

- Hair design consists of working with form, texture, direction and movement to achieve the final design look.

- Wet design is achieved by manipulating the hair into set positions while wet and then maintaining it in these positions while drying.

- Thermal design uses heat energy to form the hair into new texture patterns.

- Long hair design combines long hair techniques and creativity to transform the hair into distinctive, dramatic or formal designs.

- Hair design, achieved by thermal design, wet design and long hair design, is considered temporary because the results can be undone by brushing, combing and shampooing.

11

WIGS AND HAIR ADDITIONS

11.1 WIGS AND HAIRPIECES
HISTORY
COMPOSITION, COLORS AND CONSTRUCTION
WIG AND HAIRPIECE ESSENTIALS
INFECTION CONTROL AND SAFETY
WIG AND HAIR ADDITION SERVICE ESSENTIALS
WIG SERVICES
HAIRPIECES

11.2 HAIR ADDITIONS
HAIR ADDITION METHODS

THE ABILITY TO OFFER A FULL RANGE OF WIGS AND HAIR ADDITIONS WILL HELP CLIENTS WITH SPECIAL HAIR NEEDS LOOK AND FEEL THEIR BEST

FOLLOWING THIS LESSON
YOU WILL BE ABLE TO:

Explain why clients wear wigs and hairpieces

Explain the composition, colors and construction of wigs and hairpieces

List the professional wig services performed in the salon

Describe five methods of attaching hair additions

CONNECTING THEORY TO REAL-WORLD PRACTICE

DEVELOPING SKILL AND SENSITIVITY IN WORKING WITH WIGS, HAIRPIECES AND HAIR ADDITIONS WILL HELP YOU:

PERSONAL CONNECTION:	**INDUSTRY CONNECTION:**	**CLIENT CONNECTION:**
IMPROVE YOURSELF	BECOME A PROFESSIONAL	SERVE THE GUEST
Appreciate the value these products bring to people with serious needs and to design originality	Exemplify versatility in hair artistry and client care	Address a wide array of client care needs, from bold looks to solutions for concealing hair loss

A hair designer, who uses wigs, hairpieces and hair additions, will have the power to help people with hair loss regain the self-confidence, as well as to satisfy people who want an exciting or daring change.

11.1 WIGS AND HAIRPIECES

Maybe you have always wanted to work with community theater or help cancer patients who have experienced hair loss following medical treatments. The first section of this chapter deals with wigs and hairpieces. **Wigs** are designed to cover the entire head and **hairpieces** are designed to cover only specific areas of the head.

HISTORY

Wigs have been worn, by women and men, for both aesthetic and practical reasons for as long as history has been recorded. It is believed that ancient Egyptians began to wear wigs to protect their heads from the heat of the sun. Originally worn by the upper classes, wigs were eventually worn by all levels of Egyptian society, other than priests and laborers.

Other ancient cultures, such as those of the Romans and the Greeks, also wore wigs to varying degrees, depending on the fashions and customs of the moment. In Imperial Rome, the 'orbis' hairstyle required that a woman brush her hair forward and create a mass of tight curls at the front. Usually built up on a wire frame (a very early hairpiece), these curls were quite often not the wearer's own hair.

Several centuries later, during the Elizabethan era, the aristocracy sported curled wigs generously studded with precious gems.

Historically, wigs and hairpieces have risen and fallen in popularity according to trends, fashions and even politics. During various periods, those that created and tended to the making of wigs for the aristocracy have been both reviled and revered. In ancient times, slaves were often responsible for the care and styling of their master's wigs and hairpieces. While they may have possessed talents and skills, they were still treated as slaves. Later, particularly in the French courts, hairdressers had a more elevated status. Their creations were instrumental in establishing fashion trends and indicating a lady's or gentleman's social status.

The extraordinary height and complexity of wig designs were, in many ways, indications of the extremes that led to the French Revolution. Yet the prevailing trends, regardless of the extravagant expense and effort, were still followed by those who wished to maintain their status as fashion-conscious members of the aristocracy.

During the 1950s and 1960s, wigs and hairpieces rose tremendously in popularity. The development of synthetic fibers, known as modacrylics, made mass production and lower prices a possibility. Wigs and hairpieces were worn as fashion accessories, especially for evening, with no social stigma.

The majority of clients that schedule salon visits for wig services do so because they are experiencing hereditary hair loss or hair loss due to illness. For other clients, wigs can offer a quick color or length change.

Wigs have also been worn by actors and actresses, to great effect, throughout the ages. Theatrical wigmaking, especially of period designs, for theater and opera stages, is an art form in itself. Many of these actresses and celebrities have come to know the benefits of wearing wigs in their personal lives as well. The advances in technology and design have made it so much easier for them, and your clients, to take advantage of the wide range of wigs available.

11

The beautiful actress Raquel Welch is so appreciative of the benefits of wigs that she has endorsed a line of them. The examples shown here were personally chosen by Ms. Welch for inclusion in her signature collection. Note the natural effects of the color designs and the softness and fluidity of the haircuts. Whether your clients just want to change their look, like Ms. Welch, or need to wear a wig for prescriptive purposes, wigs that look this real make it easier than ever before to offer this service with confidence.

COMPOSITION, COLORS AND CONSTRUCTION

Before performing wig services for your clients, it is important to have a good understanding of the composition, colors and construction of wigs.

WIG COMPOSITION

Wigs and hairpieces can be made of human hair, animal hair, synthetic fibers or a blend of these. Asian, Indian or European hair is generally used to make human-hair wigs, European being the most costly. Generally, hair from India is wavy while hair from Asia is straight. The hair is specially treated to protect against possible damage from styling services. Since the appearance and texture of human-hair wigs and hairpieces are the most natural, they are preferred by those wanting a wig to look like their own hair. Since the supply of human hair for the manufacturing of wigs is limited, these wigs are the most expensive.

Modacrylic (synthetic) wig fibers are formulated from petroleum products and are produced as very long threads (monofilaments), which are then rolled onto spools. These fibers make it very cost effective and efficient to produce wigs. Shades are almost unlimited, so human hair colors can be closely duplicated. While modacrylic fibers may not always resemble human hair, modern technology has produced very realistic results.

If you're not certain whether a hairpiece is made of human hair or modacrylic fiber, pull out several strands and hold them over a match flame. **A human hair strand will burn slowly and produce an odor. A synthetic fiber will either "ball up" on the end (melt) and extinguish itself or burn very rapidly and produce no odor.**

Animal hair wigs and hairpieces, most often made of yak, angora, horse or sheep hair, have even less resemblance to human hair than modacrylic fibers. Animal hair is most often used to produce fantasy hairpieces, theatrical wigs or wigs meant to be worn by display mannequins.

WIG COLORS

All the colors used for wigs and hairpieces are standardized according to the 70 colors on the **J and L ring**, the standard hair color ring used by wig and hairpiece manufacturers. The ring contains numbered samples from black to palest blond. This ring allows wig manufacturers to select from a variety of colors and to create special effects such as highlighted hair.

11

WIG CONSTRUCTION

Wig construction falls into two general categories: cap wigs and capless wigs. **Cap wigs** consist of an elasticized mesh-fiber base to which the hair fiber is attached. Cap wigs are available in several sizes and are produced most often as handmade wigs.

In recent years, capless wigs have become the more prevalent and popular form of wigs. **Capless wigs** consist of rows of hair wefts sewn to strips of elastic. Because of their construction, many capless wigs weigh only a few ounces and are, therefore, very light, cool and comfortable.

Hair and/or synthetic fibers may be attached to the wig cap or base in one of three methods. They may be hand-tied, machine made, or semi-hand tied. A hand-tied (hand-knotted) wig or hairpiece is produced by actually hand tying strands of hair into a fine meshwork or foundation. Patterns are used to simulate natural growth patterns that closely resemble human hair growth and create a natural look. The hair is attached at close intervals and generally duplicates the density of a fairly thick head of human hair. Since this process is labor intensive and time consuming, these wigs tend to be the most expensive.

Wigs known as "machine made" consist of hair fiber sewn into long strips called wefts, which are then sewn to the cap of the wig in a circular or crisscross pattern. Machine-made wigs can be very difficult to design since the direction of the hair is determined by the position in which the weft is sewn to the cap.

Combinations of hand-tied and machine-made wigs and hairpieces are called semi-hand tied. The best toupees, a wig or patch of false hair worn to replace a bald area, are semi-hand tied to create sturdy, natural-looking, reasonably priced hair replacements.

When helping your client select a wig, the wig's construction is significant in determining the best value in the client's price range. Capless wigs or caps that allow the scalp to "breathe" prevent excessive perspiration that may cause odors. These wigs need to be cleaned less frequently. Another factor of importance is that many wigs have flesh-colored sections designed to look like human skin. These sections give a realistic look when the hair is parted or moves. Most clients, of course, desire as natural a look as possible.

COSMETOLOGY FUNDAMENTALS

WIG AND HAIRPIECE ESSENTIALS

To perform a professional service for a client with a wig, you need a selection of products, implements and equipment. Refer to Material Safety Data Sheets (MSDS) for all products used in the salon.

WIG AND HAIRPIECE PRODUCTS

PRODUCT	FUNCTION
NONFLAMMABLE LIQUID SHAMPOO	Cleans human-hair wigs and hairpieces
CONDITIONER	Keeps the wig in good condition
MILD SHAMPOO	Cleans synthetic wigs and hairpieces
SYNTHETIC WIG SHAMPOO	Cleans synthetic wigs and hairpieces
SYNTHETIC WIG CONDITIONER	Keeps synthetic wigs and hairpieces in optimum condition
HOLDING SPRAY	Holds finished wig designs in place

WIG AND HAIRPIECE IMPLEMENTS/SUPPLIES

IMPLEMENTS/SUPPLIES	FUNCTION
COMB	Detangles and styles wigs and hairpieces
BRUSH	Styles wigs and hairpieces
SHEARS	Sculpt and customize wigs and hairpieces
THINNING SHEARS	Taper and blend; remove bulk and excess fiber
RAZOR	Tapers and blends; removes bulk and excess fiber
ROLLERS	Allow temporary curl placement for human-hair wigs
PINCURL CLIPS	Allow temporary curl placement for human-hair wigs
WIG CAP	Holds client's hair in place and helps wig to stay in place
BOBBY PINS	Secure client's hair under wig; sometimes used to hold wig in place
HAIRPINS	Secure hair, especially for chignons and other 'updo' effects
NEEDLE AND THREAD	Create darts and tucks in wigs; secure wefts in track-and-sew technique; used to sew wefts for fantasy hairpieces
WIG PINS	Hold wigs and hairpieces in place on canvas block during designing, cleaning and maintenance services
STYROFOAM HEADS	Store and display wigs
CHIN STRAP	Holds wig in place on client's head during services
J AND L (JL) COLOR RING	Allows client and salon professional to choose wig or hairpiece color

IMPLEMENTS/SUPPLIES	FUNCTION
MEASURING TAPE	Measures client's head to determine correct wig size
PLASTIC BAG	Covers and protects canvas blocks
PORCELAIN OR GLASS BOWL	Holds cleaning solution and wigs or hairpieces during cleaning and sizing service
CLOTH CAPE	Protects client during designing and fitting services

WIG AND HAIRPIECE EQUIPMENT

EQUIPMENT	FUNCTION
CANVAS BLOCKS (VARIOUS SIZES)	Hold wig while services are being performed
WIG DRYER	Dries wigs that have been wet set (on canvas blocks)
HYDRAULIC CHAIR	Allows client to sit at proper height for salon professional to perform services

INFECTION CONTROL AND SAFETY

The majority of wig services are performed while the wig is on a wig block, so safety concerns are somewhat minimized. However, it is essential to keep your client's safety in mind at all times.

- Disinfect all tools and implements properly.
- Explain to your client points of maintenance and hygiene specific to each service.
- Ensure that a wig or hairpiece has sufficient air flow if it will be worn for long periods of time.
- Work with products, such as liquid dry shampoos, in a well-ventilated area.
- Observe carefully, when performing a hair addition service, the direction in which the client's hair naturally grows. Avoid going against the natural growth pattern, since doing so could cause discomfort to the client and damage to the hair.
- Teach your clients how to maintain and care for any hair addition service. Although your artistry may make the additions look like their own hair, they cannot treat the additions in the exact same way.

WIG AND HAIR ADDITION SERVICE ESSENTIALS

There are several things to keep in mind when communicating with a client for a wig, toupee or hair addition service. Regardless of the reason(s) that the client desires the service, discretion is of great importance. Whether hair loss is hereditary or caused by illness or medication, many clients will be very self-conscious about their need to seek your services. First and foremost, make sure the client feels comfortable and safe in the environment of the salon. Second, the client needs to trust you as the salon professional.

Since you will often be dealing with the adverse conditions that cause hair loss, you need to be especially sympathetic and emotionally supportive.

Carefully observe and record details about hair length, texture and colors during your conversation with the client. Discuss with your client certain design options that may make it easier to attain realistic-looking results. In the case of illness or hereditary hair loss, most clients are not looking forward to the prospect of wearing a wig. It is your job to help them realize how very helpful and positive the experience can and should be. Much of the client's comfort level with the service and the wig itself will be determined during your conversation with the client, so make the most of this opportunity. Serve your client with dignity, respect and a positive, supportive attitude.

WIG SERVICES

Hand-tied wigs may be custom made or purchased "ready to wear." When selecting and/or designing a wig for a client, remember that your client's comfort is as important as the way the wig looks. Therefore, it is important that you can offer special wig services that will help ensure your client's satisfaction. These services may include wig measurement and fitting, instructions on how to put on a wig, as well as blocking, cleaning, sculpting, coloring and styling wigs.

WIG MEASUREMENT AND FITTING

In order that your client's wig fits comfortably, it is important that you understand how to properly measure and fit the wig to your client's particular head size and shape. Although wig manufacturers may require additional, specific measurements for their products, following these basic measurement guidelines will allow you to properly fit the majority of wigs for your clients.

WIG MEASUREMENT AND FITTING GUIDELINES

- Brush the client's hair as smoothly as possible. If the hair is long, pin it flat.
- Measure the circumference of the head, beginning at the hairline in the middle of the forehead and circling the entire head, running the tape just above the ears, around the back and returning to the starting point. Be sure the client's ears are not caught under the tape measure. The average hairline circumference is 22 inches.

- Measure the distance of the hairline from the center of the forehead over the crown to the nape hairline. For the most comfortable fit possible, bend the client's head back to find the spot at the base of the skull where the wig will rest.

- Measure the distance from ear to ear over the crown of the head.

- Measure the distance from temple to temple (just above the ear) over the occipital bone. Some manufacturers may request that you measure the distance from ear to ear, along the nape hairline, and also the width of the nape area.

PUTTING ON A WIG

Along with selecting and/or creating the perfect wig for your client, it is important to teach your client the easiest way to put on a wig. This will help the client feel more comfortable wearing the wig and eliminate frustrations.

PUTTING ON A WIG GUIDELINES

- Brush your client's hair back from the face and up from the back hairline. Pin to secure. Long hair can be swept up or secured in large, flat pincurls.
- Cover the client's hair with a fine net or wig cap made specifically for the purpose of controlling the client's hair and making the wig stay more securely in place.

- Place the front hairline of the wig over and slightly lower than the client's front hairline. Hold the front of the wig in place and position the wig over the rest of the head to the nape. You may also ask the client to hold the front of the wig in place as you position the wig over the sides, back and nape. Adjust the wig as needed for security and comfort.

- Adjust and form the wig perimeter to better fit the client's head shape and hairline. Many wigs contain wire at the sideburn area for this very purpose.

COSMETOLOGY FUNDAMENTALS

WIG BLOCKING

When performing wig services, such as designing or cleaning, it is important that the size and shape of the wig are not compromised. Proper sizing procedures, called **blocking**, will help maintain the wig's original size. Canvas-covered head forms, called **wig blocks**, are manufactured for use during these services. The blocks are available in six sizes: 20, 20.5, 21, 21.5, 22 and 22.5 inches (50, 51.25, 52.5, 53.75, 55 and 56.25 cm). One of these sizes should closely match the circumference measurement of the client's head. If the wig needs to be stretched, it is placed on a block larger than the client's head; if shrunk, on a smaller block. The block is placed on a swivel clamp for control.

WIG BLOCKING GUIDELINES

- Select the correct size canvas block. You may need slightly larger or smaller blocks than the wig for stretching or shrinking.
- Cover the block with clear plastic and then secure the plastic tightly with wig pins to protect the canvas during the service.

- Place the wig on the block and secure it with wig pins at the following places:
  - Center front
  - Both temples
  - Center of the nape
  - Corners of the nape

CUSTOMIZING OR FITTING A WIG

Custom-ordered wigs can be quite expensive and, therefore, cost prohibitive for many clients. Fortunately, the majority of clients will be able to use a ready-to-wear wig, one that will not require any alterations from a salon professional. However, if alterations are necessary, you will want to be able to offer this service to your clients.

Many wigs have elastic bands through the nape or crown that allow for easy adjustments. Almost all have adjustable elastic bands at the bottom back or at either side of the nape. Some are secured with small hooks and many are adjusted with small strips of Velcro®. Many salon professionals will use a small safety pin for added security. The elastic may be sewn in place with top stitching that allows the stitches to be removed, since occasional readjustments may be needed. Also the elastic band itself may need to be replaced occasionally.

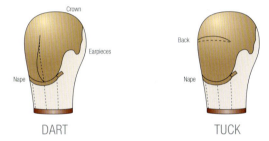

Darts are alterations made vertically to remove width in the nape area (from ear to ear). Tucks are alterations made horizontally to shorten a wig from the front to the nape. Both darts and tucks are made by turning a wig inside out and sewing a fold, like a seam, inside the cap. Horizontal alterations are usually made with the tuck near the crown to avoid excess bulk close to the perimeter.

These simple adjustment techniques will help ensure your clients' satisfaction with their wig purchases, as well as their confidence in your abilities as a salon professional.

STRETCHING OR SHRINKING CAP WIGS

In some instances you will be able to adjust the size of a wig without making tucks or darts, by either stretching or shrinking the wig. You might need to stretch a wig if it is just a little too tight or if it has somehow shrunk a bit.

STRETCHING CAP WIG GUIDELINES

- Turn the wig inside out and thoroughly moisten the cap of the wig by spraying with hot water.
- Turn the wig right side out and carefully stretch it over a wig block one size larger than the circumference of the wig itself.
- Secure the wig to the block along the hairline using wig pins.
- Design the hair if desired and allow the wig to dry.

SHRINKING CAP WIG GUIDELINES

- Select a block one size smaller than the wig's circumference.
- Turn the wig inside out and moisten the cap with hot water.
- Turn the wig right side out and place it on the smaller block.
- Dry the wig under a warm dryer only if the wig is human hair; heat can distort curl patterns of synthetic fibers.
- Adjust the wig, if it is still too big, by sewing darts and tucks into the over-stretched areas.

CLEANING AND CONDITIONING

Many wig and hairpiece manufacturers will give you guidelines as to the proper care of their product. Some manufacturers also have specific products available that you can offer your clients. Regardless of the specific brand of products, the following information will serve you well as you work with your clients' wigs and hairpieces.

Human-hair wigs and synthetic wigs will require slightly different methods of cleaning and conditioning. **Human-hair wigs or hairpieces should be cleaned every two to four weeks, depending on how frequently the piece is worn.** Conditioning should follow each cleaning, since some wig-cleansing products, like liquid dry-cleaning shampoos, can be very drying.

Because modacrylic fibers aren't as porous, synthetic wigs do not require cleaning as frequently as their human-hair counterparts. Cleansing a synthetic wig once every 6 to 12 weeks should be sufficient in most cases. Synthetic wigs do not require conditioning as human-hair wigs do. However, many manufacturers recommend synthetic conditioning sprays that will keep the fibers in optimum condition.

HUMAN-HAIR WIGS: CLEANING AND CONDITIONING GUIDELINES

Since hand-tied wigs generally have a delicate construction and are more expensive, extra care should be taken in their cleaning.

- Clean the perimeter of the wig and the inside foundation with a toothbrush or cotton ball, using liquid cleaner. The remainder of the cleaning is done with the wig on the block.

- Prepare the canvas block by covering it with a plastic bag and securing the bag with wig pins.
- Block the wig and secure it to the form with wig pins. Mark the block with additional wig pins along the hairline to assist you in proper blocking after you've cleaned the wig. Brush or comb the wig to remove tangles and to loosen dirt and styling product residue.
- Place three-to-five ounces of nonflammable liquid dry shampoo or cleanser in a large porcelain or glass bowl.
- Remove the wig from the block and turn it inside out. Soak the wig for three-to-five minutes while very gently rubbing the hairline to remove debris and stains. Swirl the hair gently in the product for about one minute and remove the wig from the liquid.
- Blot the inside of the cap of the wig thoroughly to remove excess moisture. Turn the wig right side out and blot the hair gently.
- Stretch the wig gently over the block. Use the hairline markings you made on the plastic to guide your placement of the wig. Secure with wig pins.

- With the wig on the block, use a wide-tooth comb to distribute conditioner through the hair. Be sure to follow manufacturer's directions.

ANOTHER OPTION
- Hand-tied wigs may also be soaked right on the wig block, after gently cleaning the hairline with cleaner and a small brush.

SYNTHETIC-HAIR WIGS: CLEANING GUIDELINES

- Cover the canvas block with plastic and secure with wig pins.
- Block the wig and secure it to the form with wig pins. Mark the block along the hairline to assist you in proper blocking after you've cleaned the wig. Brush the hair to remove tangles and loosen dirt and wig spray residue. Remove the wig from the block.
- Shampoo the wig by turning it inside out and soaking it in a mild shampoo solution. Work the debris from the hairline and inside with a toothbrush.

- Turn the wig right side out and swish hair in the solution. Allow the wig to soak for 5 to 10 minutes and then rinse thoroughly with lukewarm water.
- If necessary, repeat cleansing and soak longer.
- Rinse and blot the excess moisture with a towel.
- Place on the block to dry, following the blocking guidelines you indicated on the plastic-covered canvas head form.

COLORING SERVICES

Although most wig manufacturers can custom color their wigs and hairpieces in almost any shade you can imagine, it is an extra benefit to your clients if you can offer this service to them in cases where a desired color doesn't exist for their particular choice. Color should not be applied to synthetic wigs and hairpieces, since the non-porous fiber will not allow the hair shaft to be coated or penetrated.

Human-hair wigs and hairpieces can be effectively colored with temporary rinses that last from shampoo to shampoo, semi-permanent colors, fillers or low-level (darker) oxidative colors. The hair used to create human hairpieces and wigs has already been chemically treated and has most likely been decolorized and bleached. Therefore, it is advisable to avoid oxidative colors that lighten the hair and lighteners since it may be hard to predict the results. Refer to the *Color* chapter for more information on these types of colors. Before coloring a wig or hairpiece, be sure to perform a strand test. Also keep color off the wig cap as much as possible, since color may eventually dissolve the fabric.

HUMAN-HAIR WIGS: COLORING GUIDELINES

- Clean the wig following the "Cleaning and Conditioning Guidelines."
- Apply the appropriate color on the wig hair according to product directions, distributing evenly through the hair with a wide-tooth comb. Allow the color to process and remain on the hair according to manufacturer's instructions.
- Remove the color and condition hair according to the manufacturer's directions.
- Apply desired styling products and set the hair with rollers, or distribute hair in the desired direction and allow the wig to dry.

SCULPTING

The majority of wigs are available "pre-cut." The hair or fiber is attached to the cap so that the resulting length arrangement creates a finished hair sculpture. Keep in mind, though, that human-hair wigs are more likely to require a full shaping than their synthetic counterparts.

Most wigs are produced with about twice as much hair as on a typical human head. Therefore, it is often necessary to taper or thin a wig in order to decrease bulk and create a more natural-looking appearance. You may use a razor or thinning shears to thin a human-hair wig. It is not recommended to use a razor on synthetic wigs, since they tend to frizz easily. Be sure to sculpt synthetic fiber when it is dry to avoid additional frizzing.

The majority of thinning should be done near the base to remove bulk, especially near the front hairline and behind the ears. Be especially careful to avoid cutting into the cap or the wefting. On a hand-tied wig, be sure that the knotting remains secure and that you have not cut any of the knots.

You may need to do some customizing on a pre-cut wig so that it perfectly suits your client's features. The fringe and front hairline areas are very common areas that require customizing. Thinning or tapering may also be performed closer to the hair ends as needed.

If a full sculpture is required, it is best to establish the length and basic lines while the client is wearing the wig so you can relate to your client's facial features. Moving the wig to a block after the basic lines have been established will simplify the remaining blending and shaping efforts by allowing you more movement and control. Remember, make sure the wig is properly positioned and secured to the block.

TIP

Backcombing the hair very close to the front hairline of the wig can help you soften the hairline and create a more natural-looking result.

ALERT!
Don't put synthetic wigs and hairpieces under a dryer, since excessive heat can melt the fiber.

SETTING AND FINISHING

Human-hair wigs can be either wet set or set when dry. Setting a human-hair wig is very much like setting the hair growing on a human head, except that particular attention should be paid to creating closer shapes at the nape and making sure the hairline is covered. Note that pincurls can be used where closeness is required and that wig pins can be used on the block instead of picks to hold rollers or pincurls in place.

Synthetic wigs are pre-designed with predetermined curl patterns. This curl pattern is not intended to be altered by the client or the salon professional. The predetermined curl patterns in synthetic wigs require only minimal designing after cleaning.

Wigs provide a wide range of solutions and fashion statements for you and your clients. Understanding how to provide customized services for your clients allows you another method of retaining a satisfied, loyal clientele.

HAIRPIECES

Hairpieces are worn for coverage in specific areas or simply to create particular effects. They consist of a man-made base with attached hair fiber. Hairpieces are most often worn with your client's own hair to create a fashion statement or a special-occasion look. Synthetic hairpiece manufacturers usually produce their own color samples based on the modacrylic fiber they use. A full range of colors and special effects is available.

- A wiglet consists of hair fiber usually 6 inches (15.2 cm) or less in length attached to a round-shaped, flat base. A wiglet is a hairpiece usually worn to create fullness or height at the top or crown area of the head. Wiglets are designed to be blended into the wearer's own hair. Most wiglets have clips attached in order to secure them to the client's own hair.
- A cascade consists of long hair fiber attached to an oblong-shaped dome base. A cascade is a hair piece worn to create bulk or special effects.

11

- A fall is a hairpiece with a base that covers the crown, occipital and nape areas. Falls are available in various lengths, usually between 12 and 24 inches (30.5 cm and 61 cm) and create the look of a full, thick head of hair. Variations of the fall include demi-falls, demi-wigs and three-quarter wigs. The front of your client's hair is incorporated into the design of these pieces.
- A switch is a long weft of one to three swatches of hair, mounted on a loop base, worn primarily as a braid or ponytail. Switches may be worn hanging or incorporated into an updo and are used particularly for evening designs.
- A chignon is a fairly long, bulky segment of looped hair, usually sewn to a wire base or tied into a strong cord. Chignons are usually pre-formed into a specific shape and are most often worn at the crown of the head or at the nape.

- A curl segment consists of individual pieces of curly hair that vary in bulk depending on the desired effect. Colors can be natural or dramatic fantasy colors since curl segments are most often worn to create specific fashion statements.
- A braid is a switch that has three swatches of hair braided together, often with a thin wire running through it. The wire helps hold the braid in the shape that you have designed.
- A toupee is a hairpiece worn by men to cover bald or thinning hair spots, particularly on top of the head. Some men, however, may require a full wig. Toupees are usually attached with an adhesive.

Many manufacturers offer a variety of hairpieces that do not fall into the more traditional categories. These include small clip-on pieces, ponytail wraps, artificial ponytails, and many other designs worn for fun and fashion.

An integration hairpiece has many openings in the base that allow the client's hair to be pulled through for blending purposes. Primarily used to add length and volume to a hair design, the integration hairpiece is lightweight and adaptable.

Many fashion hairpieces are designed so that attachment is as simple as possible. A variety of clips, combs or interlocking combs is used to allow for quick and easy changes.

Other hairpieces can include elaborate hair ornaments like those used in the HairWorld Championships or International Hairstyling Competitions. These hairpieces are often custom-made by the contestants and incorporated into the overall design according to the rules of the competition.

TOUPEES

Toupees are hairpieces designed specifically to cover balding areas, especially for men. Many men will wish to be as discreet as possible about attaining this particular service from you, so again you should exercise discretion and propriety while communicating with the client.

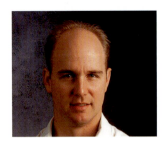

Headstart™ Hair for Men

GUIDELINES FOR MEASURING TOUPEES

Most toupee manufacturers require that the salon professional submit an impression of the client's head. This impression is used to customize the toupee to the specific size and shape of the client's head and his particular needs. When creating a plastic head form, accuracy is obviously very important.

- Place a length of clear plastic wrap over your client's head, from ear to ear. Twist the ends until the plastic molds tightly to the head.

- Create an outline of the intended shape of the toupee by placing tape over the plastic parallel to and slightly beyond the area of hair loss.

- Create a cap for the toupee by criss-crossing strips of plastic tape within the outlined area. Position each strip, one at a time, and mold to the head. Create a complete cap with tape. Once the impression is complete, use a felt tip pen to indicate the exact size and shape of the toupee.

- Have the client raise his brows to wrinkle his forehead. Approximately ½" (1.25 cm) above the top wrinkle indicates a generally ideal position for the center hairline. An alternative is to measure four finger widths above the brow line. Generally, this will give you an appropriate and acceptable front hairline position. An extremely low hairline position is one of the "giveaways" of a poorly fitted toupee.

- Extend the line to cover the bald area. It is advisable to extend the pattern ½" (1.25 cm) over the hairline. If the client's hairline continues to recede, he will still be able to wear the toupee.
- Identify the crown/cowlick area by clearly marking this area on your form.

- Carefully draw a part, if it is desired, and indicate the hair growth direction to be positioned on either side.

- Remove taped form carefully and trim excess. Tape underside if necessary.
- Clip hair samples from behind the ear and nape to guide the manufacturer in blending the right color for the client.

NOTE

Some manufacturers require a plaster form of the client's head. This form is sent to the manufacturer who creates a latex cap and attaches hair to the cap. A latex cap creates the best fit but may not allow perspiration to escape.

Clients who wear toupees are in need of your continued expertise, even after the toupee has been created. Careful sculpting and blending with the client's own hair are absolute necessities to ensure that the finished design looks as natural as possible. Advise your client to maintain the natural hair with regular haircut appointments. If the natural hair becomes too long, it will not blend with the perimeter lengths of the toupee. It is also necessary to advise the client that his natural hair may alter in color, possibly through graying. Color change may create a situation in which the toupee and the client's hair no longer match or blend. At that time it may become necessary for your client to invest in a new toupee.

Headstart™ Hair for Men

11.2 HAIR ADDITIONS

Unlike wigs and hairpieces, hair additions consist of loose hair fiber intended for attachment to the base of the client's own hair. Hair additions offer a whole new spectrum of designing options for you and your clients. You can add length, density, texture and/or color all over or in just the right places to accent your design. Match the color and texture of your client's hair for the most natural-looking results, or create stunning new effects by introducing contrasting elements in the hair additions. Materials for extensions most commonly include human hair, animal hair such as camel, yak or horse, and synthetic fibers such as Kanekalon, nylon, and polyester. One of the highest grades of human hair is referred to as Remy hair which is hair with the cuticle intact and facing the same direction.

Products, implements and equipment needed to perform a hair addition service include extension fibers, a hackle, which is a metal plate with rows of pointed needles used to blend or straighten hair, and drawing boards, which are flat mats used to hold hair extension fibers during a hair addition service.

HAIR ADDITION METHODS

On these pages, you will find highlights of several of the most popular and commonly used methods of creating hair additions. Keep an eye on industry publications to learn about new methods that are being developed on an ongoing basis.

OFF-THE-SCALP BRAIDING, LOOSE HAIR/FIBER

Off-the-scalp braiding uses a standard three-strand braiding technique to attach loose fiber or hair. It is achieved by incorporating the hair or fiber, along with the natural hair, as it is braided. The additional hair can be added to one side or both sides of the braid.

The size of the base is determined by the desired thickness of the braid. Divide the base into three sections. Then select the length and density of the hair to be added. Position the addition as shown, joining it with the outside strands. An underbraid technique is used in this example. Grasp the center strand with the thumb and index fingers of your right hand. Then turn your right hand in order to cross the outside right strand (with the additional hair) under. This now becomes the center strand. Next, turn your left hand to cross the left strand (with additional hair) under. This now becomes the center strand. Continue this alternating pattern to the ends.

COSMETOLOGY FUNDAMENTALS

As you work, you may equalize the density of the strands by borrowing a small amount of hair from the added strands and joining this hair with the strand that did not get additional hair.

This model's hair additions combine on-the-scalp and off-the-scalp braiding with loose fiber. Note the consistency of the base sizes and the tension used to create these additions. Notice that the ends are not braided, since they will be incorporated into the finished, sculpted design.

Pamela Ferrell, Cornrows & Co.

ON-THE-SCALP BRAIDING, LOOSE HAIR/FIBER

With this technique, known as interlocking, a three-strand, on-the-scalp braid is used as a base to which fiber or hair is added. You can add loose fiber to every left and right strand for maximum density or you can space the additions along the braid to create a progression of density.

Begin by parting off a strip of hair to be braided. This strip is called a track. At the top of the track, part off a small square and section it into three strands. Begin a three-strand underbraid, crossing the right strand under the center and then the left strand under the center.

Join a strand of hair or fiber to the right strand, with the end of the fiber at the ends of the outside strand. Then cross these combined strands to the center.

Use your thumb and index finger to pick up hair from the track, and add it to the center strand.

Then add a new strand of fiber to the left strand and cross the combined strands to the center to lock the new strands at the base. Continue using the same technique, picking up hair at the scalp, as you work through the track. You may alter the pattern by adding more or less fiber. You can also alter the number of crosses between the added fiber, depending on the desired results. Remember: the amount of fiber you add along the braided track will determine the density in any given area.

 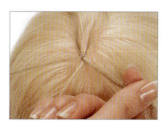  

This model is wearing a beautiful example of on-the-scalp braids with loose fibers. Note that the hair additions create a fashionable texture statement as length is added.

Pamela Ferrell, Cornrows & Co.

TRACK AND SEW

With this method, a three-strand on-the-scalp braid is used as a support structure to which a hair weft, a strip of human or artificial hair, is then sewn.

TRACKING

The tracks used in this technique are similar to the tracks described in on-the-scalp braiding. The difference is that these tracks will be used to support hair wefts as opposed to having loose fiber added to them. Tracks can follow the curves of the head or relate to the desired form line. They may be positioned horizontally, vertically or diagonally as well as along convex or concave curved lines. Clean, precise tracks depend on clean, precise parting lines. Once you have parted the track, secure the remaining hair on either side out of the way.

Plan your track so that the ends of the braids can be camouflaged by the sewn-on wefts. Generally, position the tracks 1 inch (2.5 cm) behind the hairline so they are not visible.

On finer or straighter hair, crimped fiber may be added to the braided track for additional stability.

SEWING METHODS

Straight and/or curved needles with blunted ends are used to sew wefts to the braided tracks. These blunted ends help avoid discomfort or injury to you or your client. Generally, a cotton/polyester blend thread is used to sew the wefts to the tracks.

LOCK STITCH

Thread the needle, making sure the thread is long enough to be doubled across the length of the weft/track. Sew through the weft first and then bring the needle through the track. Pull the thread through, forming a small loop. Bring the needle through the loop and wrap the thread around the needle. Pull the loop tight to form a "lock stitch" that will keep the end of the weft more secure.

OVERCAST STITCH

An "overcast" stitch is used to secure the weft to the track. For this stitch, the needle and thread are passed under the track and the weft and then brought back over. Move slightly to one side to complete the next stitch. This is the simplest and quickest stitch used to secure the weft to the track. A lock stitch is used at either end of the track for added security.

LOCK STITCH THROUGHOUT

You may also use a lock stitch across the length of the entire weft/track. Spacing the stitches equally will help to distribute the weight of the weft more evenly.

DOUBLE-LOCK STITCH

A double-lock stitch can be used to secure a weft at either end or across the length of the weft/track. This stitch is similar to the lock stitch except that the thread is wound around the needle as shown to create a "double lock."

For this model, the track-and-sew technique is used to attach synthetic hair that matches her color and curl texture. Three curved tracks are braided and an overcast stitch is used to secure the wefts to the tracks.

Pamela Ferrell, Cornrows & Co.™

Make sure that the partings are clean and neat. Keep the hair outside of the track isolated with clips to ensure accuracy. Note that the loose ends of the braids have been crossed over and sewn as the weft is being sewn on.

BONDING – WEFTS

Bonding is the attachment of additional hair fiber to a client's own hair with a special adhesive. The adhesive is applied along partings of the client's hair and to the sewn edge of the weft being added. Since some clients may have an allergic reaction to ingredients in the adhesive it is necessary to perform a patch test prior to the application of bonded hair additions. It is also necessary to advise your clients of the duration and longevity of this type of hair-addition service, which may vary according to factors such as frequency of shampooing, oiliness of the scalp and products used. Note that oil will break down the adhesive.

After creating the part, measure the length of the weft and cut it accordingly. Remember that both the client's hair and the weft need to be completely dry prior to performing the service.

Apply the liquid adhesive to the hair along the parting. Make sure the adhesive is applied consistently to ensure proper bonding.

Apply the adhesive along the sewn edge of the weft, then place the weft along the part and apply gentle pressure. Make sure that contact is made along the entire length of the weft.

For this model, bonded additions are performed on the sides and layered to create a dynamic shape.

BONDING - STRAND BY STRAND (FUSION METHOD)

This technique utilizes a bonding agent that is activated by a heating element to affix loose hair fiber to small sections of the client's own hair. Since the hair is attached in such small increments, the results can be very natural-looking and undetectable.

Small rectangular sections are taken within rows and isolated with a plastic disc. The additions are placed behind the sections of hair. The heating element, in this case tongs, is applied until the bonding agent has softened. Then the fingers are used to roll the bonded area until the natural and added hair have bonded. It is essential that natural growth patterns are carefully observed and noted prior to the service. Going against these patterns can result in discomfort to your client and possible damage to the hair and scalp.

The placement of color within the pattern of additions is also important to consider so that the additions blend with the client's natural or artificial colors attractively. This model gets it all: additional length, texture and color. Strand-by-strand bonded additions are terrific for achieving high-fashion looks but are also used for prescriptive purposes to improve self-esteem.

Great Lengths

Once you add the wig and hair additions services described in this chapter to your repertoire, you will be able to provide all of their unique benefits to your clientele.

CONNECTING THEORY TO REAL-WORLD PRACTICE

WIGS AND HAIR ADDITIONS	PERSONAL CONNECTION: IMPROVE YOURSELF	INDUSTRY CONNECTION: BECOME A PROFESSIONAL	CLIENT CONNECTION: SERVE THE GUEST
WIGS AND HAIRPIECES	Be aware of options and opportunities for unique self-expression and for dealing with hair loss	Demonstrate ability and desire to be proficient in a full spectrum of salon and client care services	Provide solutions for clients who need or want to improve their appearance without altering their natural hair
HAIR ADDITIONS	Stay current with methods for augmenting one's own hair	Increase both your technical and artistic range of skills	Offer a range of natural and dramatic options that enhance clients' own hair

IN OTHER WORDS

With special knowledge and skills, you will be able to provide clients with the wigs, hairpieces and hair additions that can help them overcome hair loss or achieve dramatic new looks.

LESSONS LEARNED

- Wigs and hairpieces have been worn throughout history for both practical and aesthetic reasons.

- The fiber composition of a wig or hairpiece—human hair, animal hair, synthetic fibers or blends—affects the design services that can be performed and the products that can be used.

- A positive, supportive and respectful attitude helps build trust and rapport in clients who need wig services due to hair loss.

- The primary goals of most wig services are to achieve a look that resembles the client's own hair and to maintain the wig in good condition.

- Hairpieces are available in a variety of configurations, including: wiglets, cascades, falls, switches, chignons, curl segments, braids and toupees.

- Hair additions are loose fibers that are attached to the base of the client's own hair and are used to achieve added length, density, texture and color.

TEXTURE

12.1 PERMING THEORY
HISTORY OF PERMING
PHYSICAL PHASE OF PERMING
CHEMICAL PHASE OF PERMING
PERM ESSENTIALS
INFECTION CONTROL AND SAFETY
PERM SERVICE ESSENTIALS
PERM PROCEDURE OVERVIEW
PERM PROBLEMS AND SOLUTIONS

12.2 RELAXING THEORY
HISTORY OF RELAXING
BASIC RELAXING THEORY
ADVANCED RELAXING THEORY
RELAXER ESSENTIALS
INFECTION CONTROL AND SAFETY
RELAXER SERVICE ESSENTIALS
PRODUCT OVERVIEW
RELAXER PROCEDURES OVERVIEW
RELAXER PROBLEMS AND SOLUTIONS

TEXTURE SERVICES THAT GIVE CLIENTS A VARIETY OF LONG-LASTING STRAIGHT, WAVY AND CURLY LOOKS ARE IN DEMAND IN THE SALON

FOLLOWING THIS LESSON
YOU WILL BE ABLE TO:

Explain the theory, techniques and procedures for perming

Explain the theory, techniques and procedures for relaxing

CONNECTING THEORY TO REAL-WORLD PRACTICE

UNDERSTANDING THE THEORY, TECHNIQUES AND PROCEDURES OF CHEMICAL TEXTURE TRANSFORMATION WILL HELP YOU:

| **PERSONAL CONNECTION:** | **INDUSTRY CONNECTION:** | **CLIENT CONNECTION:** |
IMPROVE YOURSELF	BECOME A PROFESSIONAL	SERVE THE GUEST
See the wide range of hair texture options and the methods for how each of them can be achieved	Expand your professional skills to create popular and original texture designs	Transform your clients' hair texture to give them the volume, design options and long-lasting results they want

Perming and relaxing services represent the process of using physical and chemical actions to permanently change the texture of hair, giving your clients the straight-to-curly and curly-to-straight looks they desire. Perming adds texture to the hair and relaxing reduces texture in the hair.

TEXTURE

12

12.1 PERMING THEORY

Perming is a service to be offered in conjunction with other salon services. Since the sculpted form is the foundation of every design composition, your clients will often need you to sculpt their hair so that the texture added by the perm service will achieve the desired look. When your client wants a look that requires added texture, consider how all the design elements of form, texture and color will work together. Using the design concepts discussed in *Chapter 8, Design Decisions,* along with the perming concepts you will learn in this chapter will allow you to create professional texture design compositions for your clients based on tried and proven techniques.

Clients request perms to add volume, texture and movement to their hair.

HISTORY OF PERMING

ELECTRIC PERMANENT WAVING MACHINE

SPIRAL

The desire for curly or wavy hair dates back to ancient cultures. The ancient Egyptians wrapped hair around wooden sticks, applied mud from hot springs and then baked it in the sun. When the mud was dry, it was removed. Sometimes the results lasted a few weeks, possibly because of sulfur derivatives in the mud.

The ability to create long-lasting curls and waves, which today is called perming or permanent waving, became a reality in the 20th century. **In 1905, Charles Nessler made the first real breakthrough with his heat permanent waving machine.** The machine heated the rollers, around which the hair was tightly wrapped in a spiral fashion. **This spiral method involved wrapping the hair from scalp to ends,** which was only suitable for clients with long hair. These first permanents consisted of a solution of strong alkalis similar to the sodium hydroxide used today for hair relaxing. Once applied, the solution was heated to about 212°F (100°C) with the aid of electrical heaters.

COSMETOLOGY FUNDAMENTALS 413

CROQUIGNOLE

After World War I, this spiral method was no longer adequate because women began cutting their hair much shorter. Consequently, in 1926, **the croquignole method of wrapping hair from the ends to the scalp** became practical and popular. Croquignole is a French word and refers to the movement of the fingers against the thumb while wrapping. **This croquignole method, also known today as the overlap method, led the way to the use of clamps that were preheated on a separate electric unit and then placed over the hair. This preheated clamp process was called the preheat or machineless method.** Again strong alkali chemicals were used with the heat to produce a lasting curl.

In 1931 at the Midwest Beauty Show in Chicago, Ralph I. Evans and Everett G. McDonough introduced another method of perming. Instead of electricity, this heatless technique used bi-sulphides that worked fairly well. The process produced a chemical reaction that reformed the hair from straight to curly or wavy. Sometimes the client would have the wave wrapped in the salon, go home and then return in the morning for her finished design, which led to the name the "overnight wave."

All three methods used various combinations of strong alkalis, heat, tightly wrapped hair and long processing times to produce a permanent curl. These early methods caused scalp burns and severe hair damage.

COLD WAVES: THIOGLYCOLIC ACID AND ALKALINE

Because of the many drawbacks and unwanted side effects of the early perms, there was an increasing need for a safer and more practical perm process. By 1938 Arnold F. Willatt had invented the first cold wave. It was called "cold" because no machines were used and chemicals created no heat reactions. **With this machineless method, the hair was still wrapped on perm tools while a waving lotion (thioglycolic acid or a derivative) processed the hair without heat.** Once the hair was processed, the waving lotion was rinsed out. Then a chemical with an acid pH, called a neutralizer, was applied to reform the hair to the shape of the perm tool. These first cold waves took six to eight hours to complete at room temperature.

Today's highly improved cold waves are called alkaline waves and generally take only 15 to 30 minutes to process. **Alkaline waves are currently formulated with thioglycolic acid (or its derivatives) and ammonia,** which create a compound called ammonium thioglycolate. Ammonia is a strong alkaline and, when added to thioglycolic acid, creates a waving lotion with a pH between 8.0 and 9.5 that penetrates the hair much faster, even without heat, than thioglycolic acid alone. Neutralizers bring down the pH of the hair and rebond the curl pattern to make it permanent.

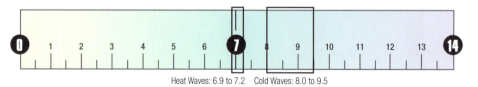

Heat Waves: 6.9 to 7.2   Cold Waves: 8.0 to 9.5

HEAT WAVES: ACID/ENDOTHERMIC AND EXOTHERMIC

Acid waves appeared on the market in the early 1970s. **Acid waves contained a thioglycolic derivative called glycerol monothioglycolate** and did not contain ammonia. They were also called "buffered waves" because they were gentler on the hair and penetrated the hair strand more slowly than cold waves. To speed up the processing time, **heat was added by placing a plastic cap on the client's head and placing her under a preheated dryer. This method of processing is called endothermic because heat is absorbed from the surroundings.** Heat causes the pH to rise gradually, leaving the hair in much healthier condition. **Today's acid perms are in the pH range of 6.9 to 7.2.**

Appearing on the market next were exothermic perms. These perms are able to generate their own heat, without an external heat source, because an additive is mixed with the perm solution to create heat through a chemical reaction. Exothermic perms are self-timing, self-heating, and range from acid to alkaline, depending upon the manufacturer.

NEW TECHNOLOGY

Perm products on today's market include neutral, low pH alkaline and low/no thio perms, which may or may not require heat.

Today's perms involve two major phases. The first phase is the physical action of wrapping the hair around specifically selected perm tools in particular patterns and directions. The second step is the chemical phase, which involves applying the perm solution, rinsing it from the hair, applying the neutralizer and rinsing it from the hair. Both phases of the perm process are of equal importance.

> As a salon professional, it is your responsibility to stay current with the latest technology and products and always follow the manufacturer's directions.

PHYSICAL PHASE OF PERMING

In the physical phase of perming, the desired size and shape of the new wave or curl pattern are achieved by wrapping the hair around perm tools with corresponding sizes and shapes. The hair needs to be wrapped smoothly and evenly around each tool, using appropriate tension without stretching it, to ensure the hair takes on the desired shape. Because wrapping the hair is key to achieving the final result and requires a significant amount of time, your skill in performing the physical phase is an important part of a successful perm service.

PHYSICAL PHASE

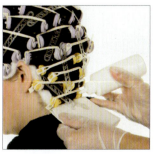
CHEMICAL PHASE

FINAL PHASE

To perform the physical phase of a perm service, you will need to be familiar with:
- Distribute and section
- Wrap
  - Perm tools (rods)
  - End paper techniques
  - Base control
  - Perm patterns

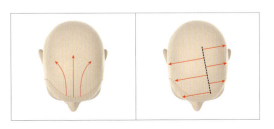

DISTRIBUTE AND SECTION

Proper distribution and sectioning are important to successful perming. You will begin by distributing the hair in the direction you want it to move. The hair can be distributed away from the face, toward the face, downward from a side part, or in alternating clockwise and counterclockwise directions with the face as a reference.

After distributing, you will then section the hair according to the length of the perm tool and the wrapping pattern you've chosen. You will usual divide the hair into two types of sections: large sections that help you control the hair and smaller subsections, called bases, from which you will wrap the hair onto the tools.

WRAP

There are two basic wrapping techniques for rotating strands of hair around a perm tool: overlap, also called croquignole, and spiral.

OVERLAP (CROQUIGNOLE)

To perform the **overlap** (croquignole) technique, the hair is rotated or revolved around a tool from the ends of the hair strand up to the base. The hair overlaps itself with each revolution. To create a complete curl pattern, the strand should overlap around the perm tool at least 2½ times. The overlap technique produces curls and undulating waves and is also used to achieve base lift and strong end curl. It is best suited for short- to medium-length hair.

SPIRAL

The **spiral** wrapping technique positions revolutions of hair next to one another to create an elongated texture pattern, which is consistent along the length of the strand and reflects the shape and diameter of the tools used. This technique is most often used on medium to long hair.

There are two ways to perform the spiral technique: ends-to-base and base-to-ends. With the ends-to-base spiral method, you begin by placing the perm tool at the end of the hair strand, then rotate under twice, move the tool to a vertical position, wrap the hair around the tool in a corkscrew fashion until you reach the base and finish by securing the tool. With the base-to-ends method, you begin at the base, wrap the hair around the tool, which is held vertically, until you reach the end of the hair strand and secure the tool. Both methods produce a hanging curl with reduced volume at the base.

PERM TOOLS

Perm tools come in various lengths, diameters and shapes. Each diameter is color coded so you can more easily select the correct tools during the perm service. Colors vary with individual perm tool manufacturers.

The most common perm tool used is a rod that is cylindrical in shape and generally straight or concave. Straight perm rods produce curls or waves that are uniform throughout the hair strands. The hair on the ends travels approximately the same distance as the hair in the center, producing the consistent curl pattern.

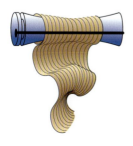

Concave perm rods are narrower in diameter in the center of the rod and wider in diameter at the ends of the rod. With concave rods, therefore, the hair on both ends travels farther to make one complete turn around the rod than the hair in the center of the rod. This difference produces a smaller, tighter curl in hair wrapped around the center of the rod and a wider, more spiraling pattern in hair wrapped around the ends of the rod.

Perm tools with different diameters produce different degrees of curl activation, which range from slow to medium to fast.

Large-diameter tools produce large curls, wave formations or body waves with a slow undulation. Large patterns like these work well when perming only certain areas of the head, also known as a zonal or partial perm, because they blend easily with the unpermed areas.

Medium-diameter tools produce texture with a faster rate or speed of activation than large diameter tools. These results are often described as curly or wavy.

Small-diameter tools produce small, firm curls and create a fast texture with an energetic feeling. When using small perm tools, keep in mind that the fast curl produced will greatly reduce the appearance of the hair's length.

Soft rods are flexible tubes that allow hair strands to be wrapped around the length of the tool to produce a natural-looking curl.

LENGTH REDUCTION

This chart shows wefts of the same length permed on different diameter perm tools. Notice that as permed texture is added to a design by using smaller and smaller tools, the hanging hair length becomes progressively shorter. Although the hair itself does not actually become shorter, the addition of permed texture creates the illusion of shorter lengths. Also keep in mind that the number of revolutions the hair makes around the tool varies the texture pattern. For instance, a large perm tool used on shorter hair will achieve a loose wave. The same perm tool used on longer hair will produce a distinct undulation. Analyzing the relationship between the hair length and the tool diameter will help you accurately anticipate the amount of length reduction that will take place.

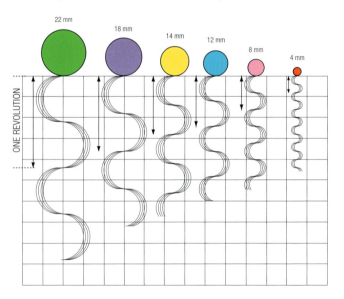

TEXTURE

END PAPER TECHNIQUES

End papers are used to control the hair ends and keep the hair smoothly wrapped around the perm tool to ensure a smooth, uniform curl formation. End papers are available in several sizes and are chosen according to the hair length and the amount of hair being wrapped. These porous papers cover the ends of the hair to control uneven lengths, minimize breakage and eliminate crimps or "fishhooks" on the ends of the hair. There are four basic techniques for applying end papers to the hair: bookend, double-paper, single-paper and cushion.

The **bookend technique** uses one end paper folded in half horizontally. This technique is generally used to control sections of hair when a shorter tool length is selected or to wrap sections of very short hair.
- Position end paper and fold it over the ends, or pre-fold an end paper and place it over the strand.
- Slide the end paper partially past the ends of the strand without converging (bunching) the hair. Keep the ends of the hair flat and completely covered by the end paper.
- Optional: Fold the end paper vertically, creating an elongated bookend technique, for longer hair or very narrow sections of hair.
- Position the perm tool and wrap.

The **double-paper (double-flat) technique** incorporates two end papers, one on the top of the strand and one on the bottom. It is the most common end paper technique, also called double-flat, because it allows you maximum control of tapered ends and avoids bunching the ends. Longer end papers are available for this technique and are helpful for controlling large sections of hair and for protecting color-treated and fragile hair.
- Position the first end paper under the strand, partially past the ends of the hair.
- Position the second end paper on top of the strand, slightly past the first end paper.
- Position the perm tool and wrap.

The **single-paper technique** is a more advanced version of the double-paper technique. It requires more practice because only one paper is used to control the ends of the hair. It is most often used with healthy, competent hair.
- Position the end paper on top of the strand and slide it down partially past the ends.
- Position the perm tool and wrap.

COSMETOLOGY FUNDAMENTALS

The **cushion technique** incorporates several end papers. It begins with a double-paper technique and then additional end papers are positioned on top of the strand as you wrap the perm tool. This technique layers end papers to provide cushioning and support to fragile hair and controls shorter lengths within the hair section. It is recommended for chemically treated or highly porous hair to allow even absorption of the processing solutions and is used primarily in alkaline perming to keep the hair smooth and provide for expansion when the hair swells.

- Position the first two end papers as in the double-paper technique.
- Wrap the perm tool to within ¼" (.6 cm) of the end of the first two papers.
- Place another paper on the top of the strand overlapping the first paper.
- Wrap the hair toward the base. Continue the cushion technique up the strand as needed.

ALERT!

When using multiple end papers, be sure to rinse and blot thoroughly since the extra papers hold more moisture than a single end paper. Water left in the end papers after rinsing the perm solution will dilute the neutralizer and weaken the curl formation.

BASE CONTROL

Base control refers to the combination of two related aspects of perming: (**1**) the size of the base in relation to the diameter of the tool, (**2**) the position of the tool in relation to the base. A base is the area between two partings for an individual perm tool. A base is also known as a panel, blocking or subsection.

STABILIZERS

Stabilizers or picks are plastic support tools designed to maintain the positioning of perm tools. Positioned under the bands of perm tools, stabilizers are generally placed in the same direction as the wrapping direction.

BASE SIZE

The length and shape of a base change according to the section that is being wrapped. Bases can be rectangular, triangular or rhomboidal in shape and positioned vertically, horizontally or diagonally.

Base size is defined by the base's length and width. The length of a base is usually determined by the length of the perm tool being used. It is important that the base is not longer than the length of the tool. If it is, excess hair at both ends of the tool will be dragged toward the center, creating an uneven curl pattern that is wider at both ends than it is in the center.

The width of the base is determined by the diameter of the perm tool being used. A one-diameter (1x) base size is equal to the tool's diameter. Larger base sizes, such as 1½ and 2 times the diameter of the perm tool, are also used. When you use larger base sizes, more hair will be wrapped around the tool, reducing the amount of base lift and producing a looser curl, which may be the desired result. Be careful, however, since too much hair on the perm tool will prevent the solutions from penetrating properly, causing an uneven curl result. Too much hair on the perm tool can also cause the tool bands to cut into or crease the hair. This creasing produces a crimp or a ridge causing a stress point on the hair, which may eventually cause the hair to break.

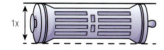

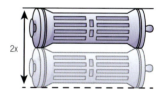

A one-diameter (**1x**) base size is most frequently used in perm design.

To achieve a one-and-a-half diameter (**1½x**) base size, measure one full diameter plus one half.

A base that is measured with two full diameters of the chosen tool is called a two-diameter (**2x**) base.

TOOL POSITION

Tool position refers to the placement of the wrapped perm tool in relation to its base. It is determined by the size of the base and the angle at which the hair is projected while wrapping. Tool position affects the degree of lift from the base, which is important because base lift creates volume and many clients ask for a perm because they want more volume in their hair. Tool position also affects the degree of blending between bases. There are four basic tool positions: On base, half-off base, underdirected and off base. They are described here in order of the amount of base lift achieved (from most base lift to least).

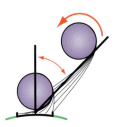

ON BASE
To achieve an **on-base tool position**, you will use a 1x base, project the hair at a 45° angle above the center of the base and wrap the tool so it is positioned between the two base partings. **On base is the tool position that creates the most volume.** On-base control is not recommended for alkaline perms, since expansion is limited at the base and tension may cause breakage.

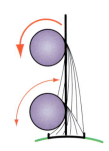

HALF-OFF BASE
The most commonly used base control is half-off base. Generally, a 1x base size is used. To achieve half-off base control, project the hair at a 90° angle from the center of the base. **With half-off base control, the perm tool will be positioned half on its base and half off its base, directly on the lower parting.** The benefits of half-off base control include medium base lift and maximum blending between bases.

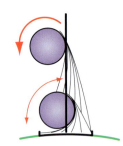

UNDERDIRECTED
With an **underdirected tool position**, the base size is at least 1½x and the hair is projected a a 90° angle from the center of the base. This angle positions the tool in the lower half of the base to achieve moderate base lift. Underdirected tool position is used in perimeter areas where less volume is desired.

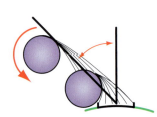

OFF BASE
With an **off-base tool position**, there will be no curl at the scalp. The hair is held at 45° below the center of the base while wrapping so that the tool is positioned completely off its base. **An off-base tool placement is used only where you want a minimal degree of volume or base lift** and a curl pattern concentrated on the midstrand and ends. Off base is effectively used near the perimeter and within a design for blending permed and unpermed areas. Any base size can be used for the off-base tool position.

PERM PATTERNS

"Perm pattern" is the term used to refer to the way perm tools are arranged around the client's head while wrapping. Perm patterns, also known as wrapping patterns, help you organize and control how you perform the perm service and they also affect the final look of the new curl pattern. Of the many possible perm patterns, the most commonly used are: rectangle, contour, one-two bricklay, spiral bricklay and alternating oblong.

The **rectangle pattern**, or 9-block, consists primarily of rectangular sections subdivided into rectangular bases. The basic direction is downward. The rectangle pattern is generally considered the most basic perm pattern and can be performed on any sculpted form.

The **contour pattern** is a versatile pattern because it adapts to the contours or curves of the head. This pattern includes a central rectangle and slight diagonal and horizontal partings at the sides.

The **one-two bricklay pattern** positions tools in a staggered configuration. This pattern gets its name because it resembles the way a bricklayer deliberately arranges the bricks in a building, alternating their position row by row. This wrapping pattern generally uses rectangle-shaped bases, which can be positioned in any direction. It is wrapped with an overlap technique and positioned horizontally or diagonally, depending upon the curves of the head. The one-two bricklay pattern is used to create consistent curl and to help avoid splits between the bases.

The **spiral bricklay pattern** features horizontal rows that are subdivided in a staggered bricklay pattern. Tools are positioned vertically within the rectangular bases. The spiral wrapping technique is used in conjunction with the bricklay perm pattern to achieve an elongated curl pattern on medium to longer lengths of hair.

The **alternating oblong pattern** positions perm tools using diagonal partings within oblongs, which are elongated shapes that create strong wave patterns. Alternating oblongs can be positioned horizontally, vertically or diagonally within a design.

> **ALERT!**
> Always read and follow manufacturer's directions before you begin wrapping. A special shampoo or a pre-wrap solution designed to be applied before you wrap the hair may be included in the perm you have selected. Some manufacturers may recommend applying the perm solution to individual sections prior to wrapping.

ADVANCED PERM TECHNIQUES AND PATTERNS

There are also many advanced techniques and patterns you can use to achieve a variety of customized texture results.

- Strand variations differ from the basic wrapping techniques in that they allow you to place texture on certain parts of the hair strand rather than along the entire strand.
- Base variations provide alternatives to the standard base control techniques, allowing you to create different texture looks.
- Advanced perm patterns, also called custom wrapping patterns, position new texture in specific areas or zones of the head and can be used with other advanced techniques to create truly unique looks.

STRAND VARIATIONS

Base perming refers to adding texture only at the base of the hair strand—the part of the hair strand closest to the scalp. It is ideal for clients who need lift and support but not end curl. It is also used when the previous perm retains enough curl but lacks support at the base. In either case, it is essential to determine the amount of the strand that will be permed.

With base perming wrapping begins at a desired point along the strand, and ends are left free, and controlled as you wrap down to the base. You may wish to coat the ends with a conditioner or protective cream before processing the perm.

Away from the base perming, sometimes referred to as end perming, refers to adding texture anywhere along the strand *except* at the base to create contrasting textures that can result in progressive designs or a natural-looking finish. You will determine the proportions of texture to be added at the ends and/or the midstrand according to the final result you and your client want to achieve. A popular example of away from base perming is end perming, sometimes known as perimeter perming, which adds texture at the ends of the strands only.

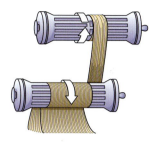

A combination of base perming and away from the base perming is sometimes referred to as a piggyback perm. In this technique, two (or more) perm rods are positioned along the length of the hair strand. The first perm rod is wrapped like a base perm and the second rod is wrapped in the opposite direction from the ends to the midstrand and positioned on top of the first rod. The perm rods are wrapped in alternate directions to create a continued wave pattern. Both rods can be the same diameter to create a consistent texture or the rods can be customized to create more than one texture along the strand. For clients with very long hair, using the piggyback technique can help to ensure complete saturation of the perm chemicals.

BASE VARIATIONS

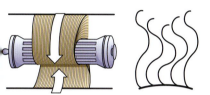

Compression bases are larger than 2x and the perm tool is positioned within the base. They are used to wrap a larger amount of hair on a perm tool in order to create more texture at the ends and less at the base. Since the size of the base is much larger than normal, less texture and support will be created at the base.

Woven bases, or zigzag bases, are usually used for blending between directional or texture changes. This technique can be used between bases or between larger sections. Often, woven partings are used to blend into areas that are left natural.

ADVANCED PERM PATTERNS

Zonal patterns, also called partial perms, involve adding texture in certain areas, or zones, of the head rather than throughout the entire hair design. This type of pattern can add volume and directional movement to otherwise straight hair in selected areas. It also works well for clients with short hair. Zonal patterns are generally used in areas such as the fringe, crown and nape.

Freeform patterns are those that do not use the standard perm patterns and techniques. They are often constructed by intermingling a variety of perm tool diameters and alternating wrapping directions for a soft, freeform texture result.

ERGONOMIC TIPS FOR PHYSICAL PHASE OF PERMING
- When wrapping the hair, stand directly behind the section to be wrapped, not to one side or the other.
- Be sure the perm tools, end papers and spray bottle are within easy reach of your free hand. You will find it difficult to perform a smooth, even wrap if you need to shift to reach for supplies.
- Do not bend over, stoop or raise your shoulders uncomfortably while wrapping. Raise or lower the styling chair and tilt the client's head to the proper angle. These adjustments help you keep your back erect, distribute weight evenly on your legs and eliminate shoulder cramps.

CHEMICAL PHASE OF PERMING

Once the hair has been wrapped on perm tools, the chemical phase begins. The chemical process transforms the hair into lasting perm texture. Two chemicals are used during the chemical phase: the perm solution, which is a reducing agent, and the neutralizer, which is an oxidizing agent. Perm solution is also known as waving lotion or reforming lotion. Be sure to follow manufacturer's directions to ensure the best possible results when using perm solutions and neutralizers.

The procedures that you follow during the chemical phase may vary with perm products developed for individual hair types, such as fine, normal or color-treated hair. The basic steps of the chemical phase include:

PROCESSING
- Applying perm solution
- Timing and testing
- Rinsing
- Blotting

NEUTRALIZING
- Applying neutralizer
- Rinsing
- Removing perm tools

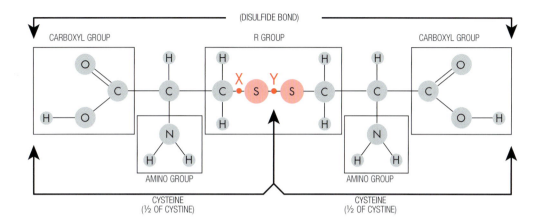

PROCESSING

To permanently change the hair from a straight to a curly state, strong disulfide bonds found in the cortex are softened and broken. The disulfide bond is a chemical bond formed between two sulfur (S) atoms found in the amino acid called cystine. The perm solution breaks the disulfide or S-S bonds. This softening process allows the disulfide bonds to shift to a new configuration.

In alkaline (cold) waves, the perm solution chemically breaks, or reduces, the strong disulfide bonds while the hair is wrapped on the perm tools. With acid (heat) waves, heat, tension, and the perm solution break the disulfide bonds. With both types of perm solutions, the processing action softens the protein structure and allows the disulfide bonds to shift, assuming the shape of the tool.

An accurately performed perm pattern and smoothly wrapped hair will allow for proper saturation of the perm solution. Once the hair is wrapped, a barrier cream is applied around the client's hairline and cotton is positioned on top of that. Cotton should be replaced when it becomes saturated. Leaving the cotton on the client's skin could cause chemical burns.

APPLYING PERM SOLUTION

After the hair has been wrapped, the processing solution should be applied carefully, one perm tool at a time, to ensure complete and even saturation. Make sure to saturate the hair on every perm tool. Missing tools will produce an inconsistent curl formation.

If the manufacturer's directions state that heat is required for processing, a plastic bag should be attached around the hairline and the client should be placed under a hooded dryer. Heat is sometimes required for acid perms but generally not for alkaline perms. Resistant hair may require heat and a longer processing time.

TIMING AND TESTING

Getting the desired texture result depends on leaving the perm solution on the hair for the correct amount of time. Some perms are designed by the manufacturer to be self-timing. When using a self-timing perm, be sure to set a timer for the amount of time recommended by the manufacturer.

For perms that are not self-timing, you will need to test the hair to determine when processing is complete. A test curl allows you to see how well the bonds are softening and shifting to their new shape. To perform a test curl, you will unwind 1½ to 2 turns of the rod, allowing the hair to unfold naturally. Do not push the hair toward the head in an attempt to force a desired curl formation to appear. If processing is complete, you should see a definite "S" shape or pattern that tends to subdivide into groupings and the wave dimension should match the diameter of the perm tool. This is known as a positive test curl.

RINSING

After processing is complete, as evidenced by a positive test curl, you will rinse the hair thoroughly with water. Rinsing stops the processing action and removes all of the perm solution from the hair before neutralizing. Some perms require you to rinse for a full five minutes. Long or thick hair may require more rinsing time. Take care not to disturb the position of the perm tools while rinsing, because the hair is in a swollen and softened state. Use gentle water pressure to avoid disturbing the hair on the perm tools.

BLOTTING

After the perm solution is thoroughly rinsed from the hair, you will blot the top and bottom of each perm tool with a terry cloth towel to remove excess water. This is important because excess water left in the strands before neutralizing dilutes the neutralizer chemical and results in incomplete rebonding. Insufficient blotting, therefore, can lead to weak curls that relax sooner than they should.

NEUTRALIZING

Neutralizing is the final chemical step in the perm process. It reforms the disulfide bonds while lowering the pH of the hair. **The main ingredient found in most neutralizers is hydrogen peroxide, sodium perborate or sodium bromate. The pH can range from 2.5 to 7, depending on the type of neutralizer.** Neutralizing is also known as rebonding or oxidation.

APPLY NEUTRALIZER

Be sure to thoroughly saturate the hair on each perm tool with the neutralizing solution. Follow manufacturer's directions and be careful not to leave the neutralizer on the hair any longer than recommended, as this might dry out the hair or, in severe cases, cause breakage.

The neutralizer reduces the swelling caused by the alkalinity of the perm solution and rebonds and restores the disulfide bonds. This change rehardens, or fixes, the disulfide bonds into the new shifted position, which is determined by the size of the perm tool, making the texture change "permanent."

It is interesting to know that oxygen from the air (air oxidation) can achieve the same results as the neutralizer. Air oxidation is impractical, however, because the hair must dry naturally on the perm tools, without heat, for 24 to 48 hours, depending on the length and texture of the hair.

RINSING

After the hair is neutralized, it needs to be rinsed with water again to remove all chemicals. Handle the hair carefully while rinsing because it is still swollen and can be easily damaged. There are two methods for rinsing the neutralizer. With the first method, and for a stronger curl result, leave the perm tools in position and thoroughly rinse the neutralizer. With the second method, remove the perm tools, work the neutralizer through to the ends and rinse. The chemical phase is now complete and the hair will retain the shape of the tool, resulting in a new texture configuration.

CATEGORIES OF PERM SOLUTIONS

ALERT!
Always follow manufacturers' directions to achieve the best results from their perm products.

Manufacturers have created a wide variety of perm solutions so that you can select the most appropriate one according to the pre-perm analysis of your client's hair and the strength of the curl desired. There are two general categories of perms used in the salon, alkaline (cold) perms and acid (heat) perms. As their names in parentheses imply, **alkaline perms are processed without heat and acid perms are generally processed with heat.**

ALKALINE PERMS

Alkaline perms have a pH of approximately 8.0 to 9.5. The alkalinity softens and swells the hair fibers, making it easier for the chemicals to penetrate the hair structure. These perms are excellent for resistant hair or when strong curl patterns are desired. **Because of the high alkalinity, it is necessary to use caution and skill to prevent damage to the hair structure or chemical burns to the skin.** Alkaline perms are not recommended for highly porous hair. Another kind of perm in this category is the low pH alkaline perm, created for textures and types of hair that do not respond well to other kinds of perm solutions. With a pH of 8, it is less alkaline than the typical cold perm.

Alkaline perms should be wrapped without tension (minimal stretching or straining of the hair) because alkaline reforming lotion causes the hair to swell. This swelling creates the necessary tension on the hair. Wrapping the hair with too much tension prior to applying an alkaline perm solution could result in an uneven penetration of the lotion and lead to breakage. Instead, hair should be held just taut enough to control the hair, creating a smooth, even wrap from ends to scalp. Keep in mind that, because the hair swells, it is easier to rinse and blot the hair when using an alkaline solution.

With alkaline perming, the hair starts to process as soon as the solution is applied. Because of its higher pH, it processes faster than an acid perm, increasing the risk for hair damage, which is why it is so important to watch the process carefully. Remember that alkaline perms are applied without heat.

ACID PERMS

Acid perms are in the pH range of 6.9 to 7.2. Acid perms in the market today are now capable of processing without heat. They start out with a higher pH and heat is an option for a firmer curl. Unlike alkaline perms, acid perms cause only minimal swelling, therefore, it is essential that the hair be wrapped with firm, even tension. Without uniform tension throughout the strand, the perm will not process correctly, which may produce an uneven curl pattern.

Heat and wrapping with even tension boost the penetration of the glycerol monothioglycolate into the hair strands where it breaks the disulfide bonds. The heat needed for acid perms is often just the client's body heat that is trapped by placing a plastic bag over the perm wrap. Additional heat is achieved by placing the client under a hooded dryer.

Acid perms are slower acting than alkaline perms and are recommended for damaged, highly porous and previously permed hair. Since the lower pH of an acid perm requires longer processing time, there is less chance of damage from overprocessing; however, you still want to monitor the process carefully.

It is essential to completely rinse the perm solution from the hair before neutralizing. Since acid perms cause little swelling, it takes more time (at least 5 minutes) and attention to remove the perm solution from the hair than with an alkaline perm. Insufficient rinsing before neutralizing can trap odor in the hair.

ADVANTAGES OF ALKALINE AND ACID PERMS

ALKALINE PERMS	ACID PERMS
• Strong curl pattern	• Soft, natural curl pattern
• Faster processing time	• Gentler to the hair
• Better for resistant hair	• More control due to slower processing time
• No need for heat	• Better for fragile or tinted hair

LOW/NO THIO

The low/no thio perm, introduced in 1992, has a different reducing agent known as cysteamine hydrochloride (hi-dro-CLOR-id). There are many benefits to using this type of perm, such as deeper penetration of the solution for longer-lasting and more consistent curls, less dilation of the cuticle layer, and the ability to reform up to 60% more bonds during neutralization. The low/no thio option makes perming available to people who may have an allergic reaction to thioglycolic acid, which is found in both alkaline and acid perms.

HAIR ANALYSIS

For best results, it is important to perform a hair analysis before any perm service. An analysis of the porosity, elasticity, texture and density of the client's hair will help you:
- Choose the right base size and tool size for optimum curl development
- Select the proper perm solution for effective results
- Manage processing time safely and efficiently

More information on hair analysis is located in *Chapter 7, Trichology*.

POROSITY

Porosity refers to the ability of the hair to absorb moisture, liquids or chemicals.
The more porous the hair, the more able it is to absorb the perm solution. For perming porous hair, therefore, a mild acid perm would be desired. Hair that lacks porosity is called "resistant." Resistant hair requires a stronger alkaline solution in order to pre-soften the cuticle and allow the perm chemicals to be absorbed. Highly or excessively porous hair is usually in some stage of chemical or physical damage from highly alkaline shampoos, hair color treatments or thermal styling. Highly porous hair needs to be reconditioned before any perm service with a pre-wrapping product to equalize its porosity. In addition, you will need to select a gentler, slower-acting type of perm that gives you greater control during processing.

ELASTICITY

Elasticity is the hair's ability to be stretched and return to its original shape. If hair has poor elasticity, it will not return to its original state after it is gently stretched. Hair that lacks elasticity can react adversely to perm solution, so it is not advisable or safe to perm hair that is weak or shows any signs of breakage.

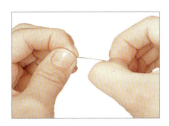 

> Tenacity is a term meaning the ease or difficulty with which a product can penetrate the cuticle layer of the hair.

FINE, MEDIUM AND COARSE TEXTURE

The texture of hair is often categorized as either fine, medium or coarse. It is essential for you to consider texture in this way so you can select both the proper perm formula and size of perm tool for your clients' hair. Although not always true, you will usually find that fine an coarse hair are more challenging to perm than hair with medium texture. Manufacturers wil often label their perm products according to the results you can expect to achieve for fine, medium or coarse hair.

DENSITY

Density refers to the number of hair follicles per square inch. Remember that **hair density does not always correspond to hair texture.** Hair with a fine texture can be very dense (thick) or not very dense (thin). Likewise, hair with a coarse texture is not necessarily dense, but can be thick or thin. Analyzing the density of the hair helps determine the amount of ha that will be wrapped on each perm tool. Because the amount of hair placed on a perm tool directly affects the absorption of perm solution and neutralizer, adjusting for the density of each client's hair is important for proper sectioning and wrapping and, ultimately, for achieving a successful perm. Denser hair will require smaller base sizes to ensure that there is not too much hair wrapped around the perm tools.

Manufacturers label their perm products according to hair texture, porosity and desired curl:

- **Texture:** Fine, medium, coarse
- **Porosity:** Normal, resistant, previously permed, tinted, bleached
- **Desired Curl:** Firm; true to tool size; soft, body waves

Analyzing your client's hair and choosing the desired curl formation will help you to select the appropriate perm products for your client and make appropriate decisions on how to section, wrap and process the hair to achieve the best results.

PERM ESSENTIALS

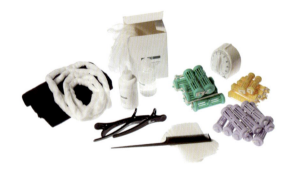

To deliver a professional perm service, you need an organized selection of products, tools, supplies and equipment. Manufacturers produce a wide range of perm products designed for all types of hair. Refer to Material Safety Data Sheets (MSDS) for all chemical products used in the salon. Perm service equipment includes furnishings and provisions necessary to provide a professional service.

PERMING PRODUCTS

PRODUCTS	FUNCTION
PERM SOLUTION	Reduces disulfide bonds so hair can assume new shape of perm tool
NEUTRALIZER	Fixes, locks in, restores bonds to make new shape of hair permanent
BARRIER CREAM	Protects client's skin when applied to hairline before using chemicals
PROTECTIVE CREAM	Protects parts of hair strand not being processed during a retouch service

PERMING TOOLS/SUPPLIES

TOOLS/SUPPLIES	FUNCTION
APPLICATOR BOTTLE	Controls and applies perm solution or neutralizer
PERM TOOLS (RODS)	Determine the size and shape of new curl configuration
PLASTIC SHAMPOO CAPE	Protects client from chemicals and water
CLOTH TOWELS	Absorb and remove water, perm solution and neutralizer through blotting
PERM BIB/NEUTRALIZING CAPE	Catches excess chemicals as they run off the scalp; protects client
COTTON STRIPS	Protect client's face from chemicals when applied around hairline
PLASTIC SECTIONING CLIPS	Hold hair in place in controlled sections before and during wrapping procedure
STYLING COMB	Controls, distributes and parts hair to be wrapped within a section
TAIL COMB	Parts off sections of hair and individual bases when wrapping
END PAPERS	Control the hair ends when wrapping; equalize porosity and absorbency during processing, rinsing and neutralizing
SPRAY BOTTLE	Holds water used to keep hair damp for more control of hair while wrapping
PROTECTIVE GLOVES	Shield designer's hands from chemicals during processing

PERMING EQUIPMENT

EQUIPMENT	FUNCTION
HEAT EQUIPMENT: PLASTIC CAP, INFRARED LAMPS, HOODED DRYER	Provide heat for acid perms during processing as required by the manufacturer's directions
TIMER	Alerts designer to check for test curls, processing and neutralizing times as recommended by the manufacturer
SHAMPOO BOWL	Holds client's head and hair for shampooing prior to service and for rinsing perm solution and neutralizer from hair
STYLING CHAIR	Provides comfortable seat for client; adjustable for best working height

INFECTION CONTROL AND SAFETY

It is always important to use safety precautions to protect yourself and your clients during a salon service. Safety precautions help you to maintain the integrity of your clients' hair. The following list describes safety precautions to be followed prior to and during a perm service. After the list you will find a more detailed explanation of several of these steps.

1. Practice infection control guidelines. Wash your hands with liquid soap.
2. Protect yourself. Wear gloves when applying chemical solutions.
3. Protect your client's clothing with proper draping. See "Draping for Chemical Services" in the next section.
4. Check the scalp for abrasions or diseases. Do not proceed with perm services if abrasions or diseases are present. See "Scalp Analysis" later in this section.
5. Conduct a test curl to help determine how your client's hair will react to a perm. See "Preliminary Test Curls" later in this section.
6. Avoid perming damaged hair that shows breakage. If the hair is dry, brittle or over-porous, recondition it first. Cut off damaged hair ends and select a mild perm formula.
7. Never perm hair that has been treated with a sodium hydroxide or a no-lye relaxer. The results could be severe breakage and/or irreversible damage.
8. Analyze your client's hair to determine the correct perm formula to be used. Identify if the hair has been tinted, bleached, highlighted or previously permed.
9. Perform a test for metallic salts if there is a possibility that such a product is on the hair. See "Testing for Metallic Salts" later in this section.
10. Determine if your client has experienced an allergic reaction to any other previous perm service prior to beginning the current perm service.
11. Protect your client's skin by applying cotton around the hairline. Replace the cotton when it becomes saturated. Note that solution-saturated cotton could cause chemical burns if left on the skin.

12. Throw away any opened, unused perm solution or neutralizer. These products can change in strength and effectiveness if they are not used soon after being opened.
13. Follow manufacturer's directions. Do not dilute or add anything to the solution or the neutralizer unless indicated by the manufacturer's directions.
14. Keep all products out of the eyes and away from the skin as much as possible. If the products come into contact with these areas, rinse immediately and thoroughly with cool water.
15. If a plastic bag is used during processing, do not allow it to rest on the skin. It should be attached over the cotton strip that is positioned around the hairline.

DRAPING FOR CHEMICAL SERVICES

Proper draping procedures for chemical services protect the client's clothing as well as help prevent skin irritations or burns caused by the chemicals you apply. Draping for chemical services is not the same as draping for a shampoo.

1. Ask the client to remove neck jewelry, earrings and eyeglasses (if applicable) and place them in a purse or pocket for safekeeping.
2. Turn client's collar under.
3. Place a towel around the client's neck and fasten a plastic shampoo cape over the towel. Be sure the cape covers the back of the chair. Check with the client to be sure that the cape is not too tight, yet fits snugly enough to prevent water or solution from dripping onto clothing.
4. Fold the edge of the towel down over the cape and drape a second towel over the shampoo cape. Fasten it securely with a clamp.
5. Check before applying chemical solutions and performing rinsing procedures that the cape has not fallen inside the back of the chair.

SCALP ANALYSIS

Since perming involves the use of chemicals, it is important to examine and analyze the condition of your client's scalp before the service in order to ensure client safety. When the scalp is healthy, you may proceed with the service, provided the hair is structurally competent. Look for any abnormalities on the scalp, such as cuts, scratches, sores or abrasions. If you find any of these irregularities, postpone the perm service until the scalp is healthy again. **Never apply chemicals over any abnormal scalp condition.** To do so could cause chemical burns and scalp problems.

PRELIMINARY TEST CURLS

Preliminary **test curls** help determine how your client's hair will react to a perm. Take the time to test hair that is bleached, overporous, damaged or has been colored with henna.

1. Shampoo the hair once and gently towel-dry. Use light manipulations.
2. Wrap one perm tool in a concealed area that represents the overall condition of the hair, following perm directions.
3. Apply protective cream to the surrounding area and cover with plastic.
4. Wrap a coil of cotton around the perm tool to protect the surrounding hair from the chemicals.
5. Apply perm solution to the wrapped hair; keep the chemicals away from the unwrapped hair.
6. Set a timer and process according to manufacturer's directions.
7. Check the test curl at least every five minutes.

To check a test curl, unfasten and carefully unwind the curl 1½ to 2 turns of the rod. Do not let the hair loosen or unwind completely from the tool. Hold the thumbs together on the back of the tool and turn it back toward the head. Do not push the perm tool toward the head. If an "S" shape or pattern is not evident, rewrap the tool and continue processing. Observe the hair carefully and look for overly softened hair. When the undulation is ready, the hair will automatically form a strong, well-defined "S" shape or pattern. When you achieve a positive test curl, proceed with the rinsing and neutralizing steps. Examine the finished curl. If desired results are achieved, proceed with perm service. Note that this is the same procedure used for testing curls during the actual perm processing time.

TEST FOR METALLIC SALTS

Color products that contain metallic salts (see *Chapter 13, Color*) form a residue on the hair that interferes with the chemical action of a perm. The results can be uneven curls, distinct discoloration, hair damage or breakage. If you suspect metallic salts are present, perform a "1:20 test" prior to performing a perm service. This test is done by mixing 1 ounce (30 ml) of 20 volume (6%) peroxide and 20 drops of 28% ammonia in a glass bowl. Remove at least 2 strands of hair and immerse in this mixture for 30 minutes. At the end of 30 minutes, look for any of these possible results:

- If the hair strands lighten slightly, there are no metallic salts present. You may proceed with the perm.
- If the hair strands lighten quickly, the hair contains lead. Do not perm.
- If there is no reaction after 30 minutes, the hair contains silver. Do not perm.
- If the solution begins to boil within a few minutes, giving off an unpleasant odor, and if the hair degrades and pulls apart easily, the hair contains copper. Do not perm.

ALERT!

Do not perm until the metallic product has been cut out of the hair. Before giving any future perms, repeat the test for metallic salts.

PERM SERVICE ESSENTIALS

As with all professional services, communicating with your client prior to the actual service will ensure predictable results and will help you avoid misunderstandings. As you review the four basic steps of the perm service essentials, remember the impact of active listening, critical thinking and analysis on the overall success of the service.

CONNECT
- Meet and greet the client with a firm handshake and pleasant tone of voice.
- Communicate to build rapport and develop a connection with the client.

CONSULT

- Help your client fill out a consultation form.
- Analyze your client's wants and needs by asking questions: Determine what type of design the client expects. Identify how much texture is needed. Use photos or a styling guide for clear communication.
- Consider your client's lifestyle. Does your client have a busy lifestyle or enough available time to spend styling the hair? Can the client handle a high-maintenance design or is a low-maintenance design required?
- Ask about your client's perming history: Have there been problems with perming in the past? Are there particular details your client can share about the behavior and reactions of the hair?
- Analyze your client's face and body shape, physical features, lifestyle, climate effects, hair and scalp type, condition, prior product usage and results from previous services. Assess the facts and thoroughly think through your recommendations.
- Document on the record card everything that is important to the successful outcome of this service, as well as future services.
- Have your client sign a Release Form, which is required by some malpractice insurance companies. This standard Release Form states that the school or salon is not responsible for damages that may occur.
- Always use extreme care when working with chemicals.
- Explain your recommended solutions as well as the price for the service(s). Think about future services as well as today's service.
- Focus on the physical and emotional needs of your client by building rapport and clarifying communication. Reinforce what you began in the Connect phase if your client is hesitant with your recommendations.
- Gain feedback from your client and obtain consent before proceeding with service.

CREATE
- Ensure your client is protected by draping with a plastic cape and towel.
- Ensure client comfort during the service. Pay particular attention to preventing the perm chemicals from dripping onto your client's face and neck and irritating the scalp.
- Deliver all steps of the perm service to the best of your ability.
- Teach the client how to perform home hair care to keep the new waves or curls looking healthy and vibrant and to maintain the overall look of the new texture design.

COMPLETE

- Request specific feedback from your client. Ask questions and look for verbal and nonverbal cues to determine your client's level of satisfaction.
- Recommend products to maintain the healthy condition of your client's hair.
- Suggest a future appointment time for your client's next visit.
- Offer sincere appreciation to your client for visiting the school or salon.
- Accompany your client to the reception/payment area or to the door. Send the client off with a warm farewell.
- Complete the record card with accurate information for future services and file it in a secure area with other record cards.

PERM PROCEDURE OVERVIEW

The steps for performing a perm service are fairly consistent, no matter which perm pattern and wrapping techniques you are using. These steps, which are listed here, apply to all the basic and advanced perm patterns you learned about earlier in this chapter. The *Texture, A Designer's Approach* coursebook will show you the step-by-step procedures for individual perm patterns in greater detail.

PERM PREPARATION

- Clean workstation with disinfectant
- Arrange perm design essentials including perm tools, stabilizers, end papers, sectioning clips, tail comb, plastic cap, gloves, cotton, perm solution and neutralizer
- Wash your hands with liquid soap
- Ask the client to remove jewelry and store in a secure place
- Drape the client for a chemical service
- Perform analysis of hair and scalp
- Shampoo hair lightly without scalp manipulations
- Perform preliminary test curl

12

PERM PROCEDURE

- **Distribute** the hair in the direction the hair will be worn
- **Section** the hair according to the desired wrapping pattern
- **Wrap** using a 1x half-off base control or other base control depending on desired result
  - Secure perm tools with stabilizers or picks
  - Place barrier cream and cotton along hairline
- **Process** according to manufacturer's directions
  - Apply processing solution

- Take test curls, if needed
- Rinse processing solution and towel blot each perm tool
- **Neutralize** according to manufacturer's directions
  - Apply neutralizer
  - Rinse
  - Remove perm tools
- Finish perm design

PERM COMPLETION

- Reinforce guest's satisfaction with the overall salon experience.
- Make professional product recommendations.
- Prebook guest's next appointment.
- End guest's visit with a warm and personal goodbye.
- Discard non-reusable materials, disinfect tools and arrange workstation in proper order.
- Wash your hands with liquid soap.
- Complete client record card.
- Provide follow-up after the salon visit.

PERM PROBLEMS AND SOLUTIONS

The following section alerts you to some problems that may occur with perms, along with their possible causes and solutions.

WEAK OR LIMP CURL

Cause: Underprocessing; perm solution not left on the hair long enough
Solution: Follow manufacturer's self-timing recommendations; use a timer for accuracy; take accurate test curls

Cause: Using perm tools that are too large for desired curl
Solution: Make sure hair completes at least 2½ revolutions around the perm tool, or reduce tool diameter

Cause: Hair is wrapped too loosely around perm tools
Solution: Wrap with smooth, even tension; acid perms generally require more tension than alkaline perms; always read and follow manufacturer's directions

Cause: Incorrect choice of perm product
Solution: Analyze your client's hair and match your findings to the perm performance description listed by the manufacturer

COSMETOLOGY FUNDAMENTALS

439

UNEVEN CURL

Cause: Inconsistent application of perm solution and/or neutralizer
Solution: Apply chemicals in a systematic method to avoid missing any perm tools

Cause: Incomplete rinsing or blotting
Solution: Be consistent; rinse and blot all tools thoroughly

Cause: Too much hair wrapped on perm tools or hair is not evenly distributed on tool
Solution: Base sizes equal to the diameter of the tool will give you the most consistent curl pattern; avoid bunching hair and wrap it as smoothly as possible around tools

FRIZZINESS

Cause: Overprocessing; perm solution left on the hair too long; may look curly when wet but frizzy when dry
Solution: Take frequent test curls; use timer to accurately track time

Cause: Hair is stretched or manipulated too much after perm when thermal designing
Solution: Use finishing products designed to define curl patterns; dry with warm heat using little tension on the hair

BREAKAGE OR DRYNESS

Cause: Hair is wrapped on perm tools with too much tension
Solution: Avoid excessive stretching; moderate tension is advisable

Cause: Hair is too fragile for perming
Solution: Perform thorough pre-perm analysis of hair to determine if perming is advisable; perform preliminary test curl if in doubt

Cause: Perm tool band places pressure on hair during processing
Solution: Lift band off hair by placing picks under it

SKIN IRRITATION

Cause: Cotton or neck towel is allowed to remain on skin after it was saturated with perm solution
Solution: Replace with fresh cotton or towel as needed; do not allow solution-soaked cotton to remain on skin, especially under plastic cap

UNPLEASANT ODOR AFTER PERMING

Cause: Insufficient rinsing of perm solution before neutralizing
Solution: Rinse hair for a full 5 minutes or longer; check for proper rinsing by smelling hair, as you should not smell perm solution; rinse more carefully when using acid or low/no thio perms since they take longer to remove from hair

HAIR LIGHTENS AFTER A PERM SERVICE

Cause: Many neutralizers contain hydrogen peroxide, which will lighten the hair slightly; lightening effect is more apparent on porous hair
Solution: Apply a temporary color to deposit missing tones; book hair color appointment, if needed, one or more weeks after perm; follow manufacturer's directions for same day perm and color services

PERM DID NOT LAST AS LONG AS EXPECTED
Cause: Hair not in proper condition before perm service
Solution: Recondition weak hair before perming

Cause: Incomplete neutralization; insufficient blotting after rinsing perm solution, which dilutes the neutralizer
Solution: Remove excess water by blotting the entire head first and then each perm tool before applying neutralizer

12.2 RELAXING THEORY

Relaxing refers to the loosening or reducing of the hair's existing texture as when straightening curly or tightly curled hair. Clients choose relaxer services to go from tightly curled, curly or wavy hair to less curly or wavy textures. The maximum degree of relaxation results in straight hair; which means a small amount of texture is left in the hair. It is not recommended that more than 85% of the texture is removed, as it can damage most types of hair.

Relaxing, like perming, is a specialized service that is often performed in conjunction with other salon services, like hair sculpture, and can help you increase your income and build a loyal clientele. Although relaxer products continue to improve, making them easier to use, there is more to a successful relaxer service than knowing how to apply the products correctly.

HISTORY OF RELAXING

Relaxing hair with chemicals appeared early in the 20th century as a means of controlling extremely curly hair. The first chemical relaxers were made of potash (wood ashes), lye, white potatoes and lard. Mixed together, these ingredients produced a harsh mixture strong enough to chemically straighten tightly curled hair. In its pure form, lye is a caustic chemical with a pH of 14. It has the ability to eat away or erode the cuticle layer of the hair, making it very limp and straight, as well as easier to manage.

Because the relaxing mixture contained domestic household ingredients, it was an unstable formula that produced unpredictable results. The mixture was usually so strong that it caused hair loss and severe scalp burns. Yet, in spite of these risks, people were willing to accept the consequences in order to achieve the desired results.

In the early 1900s a temporary method of hair relaxing, called hair pressing, was conceived by Sarah Breedlove (1867-1919), who was better known as Madam C. J. Walker. With this method, petroleum jelly was applied to the hair after it had been washed and dried. A metal comb, which had been heated over a small gas burner, was then pressed against and pulled through the hair using tension, temporarily straightening it.

By the late 1950s, several commercially produced chemical relaxers were available. Even though they remained highly caustic with the potential to cause damage to the hair and scalp, the new formulas were more consistent, making the results more predictable.

BASIC RELAXING THEORY

This section on basic relaxing theory will introduce you to the most widely used relaxer services and to the products, skills and knowledge needed to perform them.

BASIC RELAXER SERVICES

There are four basic relaxer services: curl diffusion, virgin relaxer, retouch relaxer and zonal relaxer. These four services comprise the relaxer services you will perform most frequently in the salon.

A **curl diffusion** service, also known as a chemical blow-out, is a technique used to loosen or relax tightly curled hair patterns by approximately 50% of their natural shape.

A **virgin relaxer** service is a technique used on natural, untreated or "virgin" hair to straighten the hair up to 85%.

A **retouch relaxer** service is performed on the new growth only to match the previously relaxed hair.

A **zonal relaxer** service is performed only in selected areas of the head. A zonal relaxer is usually performed when the client's nape area and sides are closely tapered or when the perimeter hairline is frizzy.

TYPES OF RELAXER PRODUCTS

Although there are many relaxer products used in the professional salon, they fall into two major categories that correspond to the two main relaxer chemicals: sodium hydroxide and ammonium thioglycolate. Sodium hydroxide is the stronger of the two chemicals and, therefore, has more relaxing power than ammonium thioglycolate. Because they are stronger, sodium hydroxide products are also more caustic and harsher to clients' hair, scalp and skin. Generally, sodium hydroxide relaxers are used on curly, tightly curled and resistant hair, while thio relaxers are used on wavy, curly or nonresistant hair. Understanding each type of relaxer product will enable you to choose the most appropriate product for each individual client.

SODIUM HYDROXIDE

Sodium hydroxide (sodium) relaxers are strong alkaline products that have a pH of 11.5 to 14, and are designed to straighten tightly curled hair. Sodium hydroxide relaxers are also known as sodium relaxers or lye relaxers. Prior to the 1960s, sodium relaxers were called base relaxers. These relaxers required that a base cream be applied prior to the relaxer service to protect the scalp. Following the 1960s, no-base sodium hydroxide relaxers were developed. They have a high oil content and conditioning agents that help protect the hair and scalp from irritation, which can eliminate the need to apply additional base cream to the client's scalp, hence the name "no-base." No-base sodium relaxers are generally the choice of salon professionals because they are gentler to the hair and scalp than base relaxers. Keep in mind, however, that no-base sodium products still contain a caustic chemical, so skill and thorough product knowledge are required, and base cream may still be needed for clients with sensitive scalps. As with all chemical products, be sure to follow manufacturer's directions for safe and accurate results.

ALERT!

Do not apply sodium hydroxide relaxer to extremely porous hair that has been colored with permanent hair color or lightened hair (decolorized, bleached). Also, do not apply sodium hydroxide to hair that has been permed with ammonium thioglycolate or to hair that is going to be permed with ammonium thioglycolate. Multiple services performed over the hair reduce the number of bonds in the hair, which can cause severe breakage.

No-lye relaxers contain a derivative of sodium hydroxide. They contain calcium, potassium, guanidine, lithium hydroxide, or bisulfate as the active ingredient. The name, no-lye, derives from the fact that sodium hydroxide is not the active ingredient. No-lye chemical relaxers are usually recommended for less resistant hair and require frequent follow-up conditioning treatments.

Ammonium Thioglycolate Relaxers: 8.5 to 9.5   Sodium Hydroxide Relaxers: 11.5 to 14.0

AMMONIUM THIOGLYCOLATE

The **ammonium thioglycolate** (thio) relaxer, with a pH of 8.5 to 9.5, is a chemical reducing agent that causes the hair to soften and swell. Hydrogen and disulfide bonds in the hair are affected during thio processing. With the thioglycolate relaxer, the disulfide bonds break between the two sulfur atoms in the cystine amino acids. The neutralizing process then causes the split cystine amino acids to rejoin.

Relaxer strengths for ammonium thioglycolate are usually categorized as mild (delicate), regular (normal), and super (resistant).
- Mild is used on healthy, color-treated hair, fine-textured or porous hair.
- Regular is used on curly to medium-textured hair.
- Super is used on tightly curled, coarse-textured or resistant hair.

Sodium, no-lye and thio relaxer formulas consist of three principle ingredients: an active alkaline agent (sodium, potassium, lithium or guanidine hydroxide), oil (surfactants or surface-acting agents that protect the hair and scalp) and water. These components control the relaxer's effectiveness and efficiency. It is important to remember that the formulation of the chemical relaxer requires quick application, processing and removal to prevent damage. Correctly applied, relaxers provide maximum relaxing action as well as optimum conditioning effects with minimal or no scalp irritation or hair loss. As a result, the hair feels soft and looks shiny and healthy.

HAIR ANALYSIS

Before beginning any chemical service, including a relaxer service, you will perform a hair analysis to properly assess the condition of your client's hair. The porosity, elasticity, texture, density, type of curl pattern and overall condition of the hair will help you determine the appropriate type of service, type and strength of relaxer product, and processing time.

RELAXING AND COLORING
Hair color services requiring hydrogen peroxide should not be performed on the same day as the relaxer service. Generally the client should wait a minimum of 10 days. Relaxer services should never be combined with color services that require lightener (bleach).

Conducting several preliminary tests before a chemical service will help you gain the most accurate assessment possible of your client's hair to ensure successful results. As you perform these tests, carefully analyze the condition of the hair and scalp. If you see signs of breakage in the hair or abrasions on the scalp, postpone the service until the condition improves. Refer to *Chapter 7, Trichology*, and to the "Infection Control and Safety" section in this chapter for additional information on how to assess the hair for a chemical relaxer service.

POROSITY

Porosity refers to the ability of the hair to absorb moisture, liquids or chemicals. Porosity is also one of the determining factors in selecting the appropriate chemical relaxer strength and processing time. The more porous the hair, the faster the hair will accept the product. With porous hair, choose a product labeled as mild. When the hair is more resistant, you will need to select a product labeled as super strength. The porosity test is also known as the finger test and is described in *Chapter 7, Trichology*.

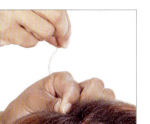

ELASTICITY

Elasticity describes the hair's ability to stretch and return without breaking, much like the action of a rubber band. Elasticity can range from very good to very poor. If the hair flexes back and forth as it is gently pulled, it shows good elasticity. Hair with good elasticity can usually tolerate stronger chemicals, while hair with weaker elasticity requires milder chemicals. If the hair has very poor elasticity, chemicals should not be used. In the case of extreme breakage, you may need to cut off the damaged hair. If the damage is not extreme, you can chemically relax the hair and then offer a course of treatment following the relaxer service. **The elasticity test is also known as the pull test,** which is explained in *Chapter 7, Trichology*.

FINE, MEDIUM AND COARSE TEXTURE

One of the aspects of texture relates to the actual size or diameter of an individual hair strand. When analyzing the hair for a chemical relaxing service, texture can be categorized as fine, medium and coarse. It is common for one head of hair to have several different textures, such as very fine hair in the nape area and coarse hair in the crown. When conducting strand tests, therefore, it is important to test each type of hair texture found on the client's head with its proper strength of relaxer, even if this means testing in several different areas of the head.

DENSITY

Density refers to the number of hair follicles per square inch and can be classified as either light, medium and/or heavy (sometimes thin, medium, thick). Knowing the hair's density helps you determine the proper size partings to use during the relaxer application, for example, thick hair will require smaller and, therefore, more partings than thin hair. Partings can range from ¼" (.6 cm) to ½" (1.25 cm).

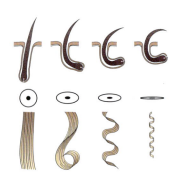

IDENTIFYING EXISTING TEXTURE (CURL) PATTERNS

Natural texture patterns, also called curl patterns, can be identified by their visual characteristics. The four major texture patterns as determined by the shape of the hair follicle are:

- **Straight**–Round Follicle
- **Wavy**–Oval Follicle
- **Curly**–Elliptical Follicle
- **Tightly Curled**–Elliptical Follicle

Tightly curled hair is also referred to as flat-cell hair because its follicle has a flat, elliptical shape. Although certain ethnicities are often associated with particular textures, all of the texture patterns can be found in people of every ethnicity and race. It is also common for one person's head of hair to have several different texture patterns, such as both straight and wavy.

Three curl patterns that primarily relate to relaxing services are:

WAVY   CURLY   TIGHTLY CURLED

STAGES OF RELAXING TIGHTLY CURLED HAIR

It is not advisable to relax tightly curled hair to the 100% relaxation level because this can overprocess the hair, leaving it limp and susceptible to breakage. Even without removing 100% of the hair's texture, relaxing tightly curled hair can give clients a wide range of hair design options.

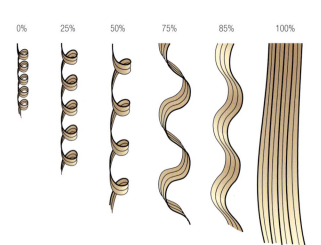

Tightly Curled Texture Pattern
- 0%–Not Relaxed

Relaxing
- 25%–Minimum Relaxing
- 50%–Curl Diffusion
- 75%–S-Curl Pattern

Optimum Relaxing
- 85%

Overprocessed
- 100%

12

THE PHASES OF A RELAXER SERVICE

As in perming, relaxing the hair involves both chemical and physical steps.

In relaxing, the chemical and physical phases are not as clear-cut as in perming, because the relaxer chemical is applied early in the procedure, then the physical steps of smoothing the hair and testing are performed, followed by the rinsing of the relaxer chemical and applying and rinsing the neutralizer. However, just like perming, the chemical and physical phases are equally important in producing successful relaxing results.

CHEMICAL PHASE
- Sectioning the hair
- Applying the relaxer product

PHYSICAL PHASE
- Smoothing or combing
- Timing and testing
- Rinsing, blotting and neutralizing

CHEMICAL PHASE

The main chemical step of the relaxer service is the application of the chemical relaxer product to the hair. Before applying the product, sectioning the hair allows you to control the hair and organize your approach to be sure all the hair is appropriately saturated with the relaxer chemical.

SECTIONING THE HAIR

Once you and your client have agreed on the relaxer service you're going to perform, the first step is to section the client's hair for organization and control of the chemical application process. Generally, you will create four or five large sections when relaxing the entire head. When doing a zonal relaxer, you will probably need fewer sections.

Along with sectioning, and **before applying the chemical relaxer product on the client's hair and scalp, it is important to protect the skin around the hairline and ears with a base cream (basing).** Sometimes it is applied to the entire scalp if the client has a history of scalp sensitivity, or when a sodium hydroxide-based product is used. Petroleum is the main ingredient in base creams. Body heat liquefies the base, providing a light, oily film that helps protect the scalp from irritation during chemical processing.

APPLYING THE RELAXER PRODUCT

Applying the proper strength relaxer product based on the client's hair type is critical to the success of the relaxer service. The primary method for applying the relaxer chemical is with a brush. The relaxer product is applied to one or both sides of the strand depending on the requirements of the service being performed. You may also sometimes see relaxer being applied with the comb or fingers, but these methods are generally not recommended. It is critical to apply relaxer evenly without missing any areas. If the relaxer is not evenly applied or if areas are missed, there will be an uneven pattern of straight or curly hair or ridges that could be hard to control.

CURL DIFFUSION

For a curl diffusion service, the product is generally applied to shorter lengths of hair. A tail comb is used to section and control the hair, while a brush is used to apply the product to the surface of the hair.

VIRGIN RELAXER

With a virgin relaxer service, the chemical relaxer is first applied to the most resistant area (usually the crown or lower). The product is first applied ¼" (.6 cm) to ½" (1.25 cm) away from the scalp area and up to the porous ends. Next, the product is applied to the scalp area, if necessary. Chemical relaxers have a tendency to spread toward the scalp due to body heat, so further application may not be needed.

RETOUCH RELAXER

A retouch relaxer service uses the same procedures as a virgin application, except that the product is applied only to the new growth area at the scalp. Overlapping the product onto the previously relaxed hair may result in breakage. To protect previously treated hair from the chemical product, a protective cream should be applied.

ZONAL RELAXER

For a zonal relaxer service, the product is applied to selected areas of the head using the curl diffusion application technique or the virgin relaxer application technique, depending on the desired result.

PHYSICAL PHASE

The success or failure of a chemical relaxer service is strongly influenced by the physical phase of the service. The physical phase begins by smoothing or combing the chemical relaxer product to facilitate the relaxation of the curl pattern. After timing and testing to determine that the desired level of relaxation has been achieved, the relaxer is rinsed completely from the hair and excess water is blotted to ensure the neutralizer can work properly.

SMOOTHING OR COMBING

The action of spreading the chemical relaxer through the hair with the spine or back of a comb as it processes is called smoothing. **Smoothing** redistributes the relaxer on the hair strand and helps relax and reform the bonds to a new straighter position.

In a curl diffusion service, you will comb instead of smoothing the relaxer through the hair because you want to reduce the curl pattern only by about 50%. Combing with the teeth of the comb, rather than smoothing with the back of the comb, ensures that the hair is not overly relaxed beyond the 50% level.

TIMING AND TESTING

Knowing how long to smooth the relaxer product through the hair is critical to achieving the desired texture result and, therefore, to a successful relaxer service. Rinsing the relaxer out too soon without sufficient smoothing or leaving the relaxer on the hair too long while continuing to smooth are both recipes for a dissatisfied client. The two primary ways to know when you can stop smoothing and rinse the relaxer from the hair are:

1. Timing according to manufacturer's directions and/or standard salon guidelines
2. Performing relaxation tests

TIMING GUIDE

When the chemical relaxer is applied to the hair, it softens and swells the hair, allowing penetration through the cuticle into the cortical layer where the sulfur and hydrogen bonds are altered. These bonds contribute to the hair's elasticity, strength and resilience, while helping retain its curly state. How quickly or slowly the chemical relaxer penetrates depends on the hair's texture and porosity. Coarse-texture hair generally has less cuticle and more cortex than fine hair, which slows product absorption. Slower absorption increases processing time, especially if the hair is nonporous (highly resistant).

By contrast, fine-texture hair has more cuticle and less cortex. Initially, the relaxer product may take longer to penetrate to the cortex, yet the product can quickly damage the inner layer of hair. This type of hair requires a sound knowledge of its structure and the effects of chemicals on it.

FOR THIO RELAXERS (INCLUDES APPLICATION AND SMOOTHING)

STRENGTH	CONDITION OF THE HAIR	TIMING
MILD	Fine Texture Hair	Up to 15 minutes
REGULAR	Curly to Medium Texture Hair	Up to 20 minutes
SUPER	Tightly Curled to Coarse Texture Hair	Up to 25 minutes

FOR SODIUM HYDROXIDE RELAXERS (INCLUDES APPLICATION AND SMOOTHING)

STRENGTH	CONDITION OF THE HAIR	TIMING
MILD	Color Treated to Fine Texture Hair	10 to 15 minutes
REGULAR	Curly to Medium Texture Hair	Up to 20 minutes
SUPER	Curly to Coarse Texture Hair	Up to 20 minutes

RELAXATION TEST

Depending on the type of relaxer service that is being performed, there are two ways to perform a relaxation test.

For curl diffusion services, testing is based on the designer's visual perception to know when the desired degree of curl has been achieved. During the combing phase, the designer watches for the hair's ability to "spring" back. If the curl is too tight, additional combing will need to be performed.

For all other relaxer services, the **relaxation test**, also known as the comb test, allows you to determine if additional smoothing is required. The relaxation test is performed with the spine or back of the comb. The first step is to smooth excess product from the scalp area. The second step is to press the back of the comb against the scalp area to determine the degree of relaxation. If a minimal amount of indentation occurs and the curl pattern reverts or "beads," additional smoothing may be required depending upon the desired results. If a strong amount of indentation occurs, the hair has reached optimum relaxation. You are now ready to thoroughly rinse and blot the hair.

RINSING AND BLOTTING

Because of the high alkalinity of relaxers, the hair must be rinsed for a long period of time to stop the chemical action and completely rid the hair of any chemical residues. It is important to check closely in the nape area and behind the ears, which are areas that are more difficult to rinse. Any chemicals left in the hair will remain active and could cause serious skin and/or hair damage.

Blotting the hair to remove excess water after rinsing is also very important. Excess moisture left on the hair can adversely affect the ability of the neutralizer to work properly. The blotting process also gives you the opportunity to check carefully throughout the entire scalp area to detect any chemicals that have not been rinsed.

NEUTRALIZING

When you are certain the hair is free of chemicals and excess moisture, proceed with the neutralizing shampoo procedure. **It is important to use an acid-balanced neutralizing shampoo or stabilizer to reharden (lock) the hair into its new, straighter shape.** The neutralizer causes oxidation, which restores the broken disulfide bonds. Always be guided by the manufacturer's directions about how many times you must shampoo the hair and how long the neutralizing product is to be left on the hair.

CREATING THE NEW RELAXED TEXTURE PATTERN

The following steps provide an overview of how you will create new, relaxed texture patterns for your clients. They reflect how the theory reviewed in this section—types of relaxer products, hair analysis, types of relaxer services, and phases of a relaxer service—is integrated when performing relaxer services in the salon.

1. Identify the existing texture pattern: wavy, curly, tightly curled
2. Determine the desired texture pattern: straight, wavy, curly
3. Analyze hair competency: porosity, elasticity, density
4. Select the appropriate relaxer service: curl diffusion, virgin, retouch, zonal (or partial)
5. Choose the relaxer product and formula: thio or sodium; mild, regular, super
6. Perform the relaxer service

ADVANCED RELAXING THEORY

Advanced relaxer services build upon the fundamental concepts used in basic relaxer services while taking advantage of unique techniques or products to deliver more customized options for relaxing clients' hair. Thermal reconditioning and curl reformation are two specialized services that are offered in many salons to further meet the needs of clients.

Reading and following product directions is even more important with advanced services since procedures vary from manufacturer to manufacturer. It is also important to perform a thorough hair analysis with preliminary tests before applying chemicals to determine the hair's porosity, elasticity, density and texture. The information learned from the hair analys will help ensure successful results.

THERMAL RECONDITIONING

Thermal reconditioning is an advanced relaxer service that results in straight hair by using heat to restructure the bonds in the hair. A thermal reconditioning service is designed to straighten wavy to curly hair up to 100%. If the client does not want his or her hair straightened to this degree, thermal reconditioning is not the appropriate service. It is also not recommended for clients with tightly curled hair. In some instances, thermal reconditioning is performed on coarse, straight hair to make it more manageable. Thermal reconditioning is also known as Japanese straightening, ionic retexturizing, thermal restructuring or thermal rebonding.

Thermal reconditioning presents a higher level of difficulty than other relaxer services. Because the process incorporates both chemicals and heat, pay special attention to performing thermal reconditioning precisely and accurately.

The technique that sets thermal reconditioning apart from other relaxer services is the use of a flat iron with ceramic plates. The ceramic plates allow higher temperatures to be maintained without scorching the hair, as metal plates might.

Prior to beginning a thermal reconditioning service, you will shampoo and section the hair. Sectioning for thermal reconditioning is minimal and will generally include a horizontal parting pattern. The main steps performed for thermal reconditioning are:
- Relax the hair with an ammonium thioglycolate-based product
- Straighten the hair using a flat iron
- Neutralize the hair with a designated product

RELAX
To prepare for the application of the relaxer product, a base cream is applied to the client's hairline and tops of the ears after the hair has been sectioned. Since a thio-based product is used, it is not necessary to apply the base cream to the entire scalp. A porosity control product, usually in the form of a spray, is then applied to the hair.

TEXTURE

For a virgin thermal reconditioning application technique, the hair is relaxed using the same techniques as with that of the virgin thio relaxing procedure. The product is first applied ½" (1.25 cm) away from the scalp area and up to the porous ends. Next, the product is applied to the scalp area and ends, if necessary. Chemical relaxers have a tendency to spread toward the scalp due to body heat, so further application may not be needed.

For a thermal reconditioning retouch service, the amount of new growth needs to be significant, generally 3 to 4 inches (7.5 to 10 cm) or 8 months of new growth. The chemical relaxer product is applied only to the new growth being especially careful to avoid overlapping the product onto the previously relaxed hair.

Both the virgin and retouch thermal reconditioning services are smoothed by combing the chemical product through the lengths that are being straightened.

Once the desired degree of straightening has been achieved, the relaxer product is thoroughly rinsed from the hair. Unlike traditional relaxing services, the hair is not neutralized after rinsing the relaxer chemical. For both the virgin and retouch thermal reconditioning services, the hair is dried until approximately 80% of the moisture is removed in preparation for the flat iron procedure, but always follow specific manufacturer's directions.

STRAIGHTEN

Both the virgin and retouch thermal reconditioning services achieve complete straightening by flat-ironing the hair from base to ends using very fine partings. Usually ⅛" (.3 cm) partings are recommended so that the flat iron can be placed close to the scalp without converging lengths, which may create kinks or bends in the hair. It is essential that the plates of the flat iron are ceramic and not metal. The combination of ironing the hair using small sections with a special thermal iron that reaches temperatures of 356° Fahrenheit (180° Celsius) produces the straightened effect.

NEUTRALIZE

Thermal reconditioning services require neutralizer to be applied to dry hair that has been meticulously flat-ironed. Neutralizing dry hair after flat-ironing ensures the straightest results. Neutralizer is applied to ½" (1.25 cm) partings and each parting is combed smooth again. Sections are combed together slightly to blend. Remember to always follow manufacturer's directions for timing and rinsing.

IMPORTANT GUIDELINES FOR THERMAL RECONDITIONING

- Following a thermal reconditioning service, the hair should not be shampooed for 48 to 72 hours. Keeping the hair dry for this period of time will ensure optimum results for the client. Once the 48-to-72 hour period has passed, the hair should be shampooed as often as necessary.
- It is critical that no accessories such as barrettes, pins or bands are used on the hair for 48 to 72 hours after the thermal reconditioning service. Recommend that clients not tuck their hair behind their ears or wear ponytails as these may also adversely affect the newly straightened hair.

CURL REFORMATION

Curl reformation is a chemical service designed to change tightly curled hair to curly or wavy hair. Curl reformation is also known as soft curls, reformation curls or double-process perm. The hair is first relaxed to reduce the curl pattern and then permed to create a new curl pattern.

The curl reformation process involves three main steps:
- Reduce the existing curl pattern
- Reform to produce a new curl pattern around perm tools
- Rebond to fix (neutralize) the chemical bonds and lock in the new curl pattern

REDUCE

The first step is to reduce the hair's natural curl by applying a chemical product known as a curl rearranger. The curl rearranger is applied ½" (1.25 cm) away from the scalp and out to the porous ends. Next, the product is applied to the scalp area if necessary and the hair is smoothed from the scalp to the ends.

Ammonium thioglycolate is the main ingredient found in curl rearrangers. Thio is an alkaline chemical available in cream, lotion or gel. It is called a curl rearranger because it shifts and rearranges the polypeptide chains and disulfide bonds of the hair, the same as in perming. It is available in mild for fine hair, regular for average hair, and super for resistant hair. Since the descriptions of strengths may vary among manufacturers, be sure to read the manufacturer's directions carefully. For additional information on ammonium thioglycolate relaxers, refer to the "Types of Relaxer Products" section earlier in this chapter.

The curl rearranger is applied to the hair using the same application procedures as in chemical relaxing. It is important not to over-relax the hair because it must maintain enough bonds to create a successful curl pattern in the next step. The curl rearranger is rinsed, but not shampooed, from the hair before proceeding to the reforming step.

With a virgin application, the curl rearranger is applied ¼" (.6 cm) to ½" (1.25 cm) away from the scalp and up to ½" (1.25 cm) away from the ends. The product is applied to the ends last, since this is the most porous area of the strand. A curl reformation retouch uses the same procedures as the virgin application, except that the curl rearranger is applied to the new growth only. It is important that the curl rearranger product not overlap with the previously treated hair, since overlap could cause breakage. Refer to the client's record card for documented information about previous chemical services.

REFORM

In the reforming step, a curl booster, or perm solution, is applied to the hair. A mild creamy form of ammonium thioglycolate is the main ingredient found in the booster. Then the hair is wrapped with the desired perm tools to begin forming the new curl pattern. Any perm pattern, such as the rectangle or bricklay, may be used to wrap the hair. Once the hair is completely wrapped, additional booster is applied to the hair to ensure thorough saturation. When the processing is complete, the hair is rinsed and towel-blotted with the perm tools remaining in the hair.

An alternative method for reforming is to first wrap the hair in the desired pattern and then apply the booster to each tool ensuring thorough saturation.

When performing a curl reformation service, the perm tool diameter chosen is generally at least two times larger than the diameter of the natural curl pattern. Since this service results in some natural texture remaining in the hair, thinner partings are used while wrapping.

REBOND

The third and final step, rebonding, involves neutralization. The neutralizer locks in the new curl pattern that was created in the reforming step. The neutralizer is applied to the perm tools and remains on the hair for the full processing time. Neutralizing with the perm tools in the hair will result in a firmer curl pattern. For a looser curl pattern, apply neutralizer to the perm tools, then remove the tools and apply additional neutralizer to the hair for the remaining processing time.

RELAXER ESSENTIALS

To achieve a successful relaxer service, you need an organized selection of products, tools, supplies and equipment. Relaxer products are produced by many different manufacturers, are disposable and must be frequently replaced. Refer to Material Safety Data Sheets (MSDS) for information on all salon products. Relaxer tools are the hand-held tools you use, and relaxer equipment includes all items necessary to provide a professional service.

RELAXER PRODUCTS

PRODUCTS	FUNCTION
SHAMPOO	Cleanses/removes dirt and oils from scalp and hair
BASE CREAM	Protects scalp, hairline and ears from chemicals; petroleum-based product
PROTECTIVE CREAM	Protects parts of hair strand not being processed during a retouch service
CHEMICAL RELAXER PRODUCT	Relaxes hair texture
NEUTRALIZER OR NEUTRALIZING SHAMPOO	Rehardens, fixes and restores bonds to make new shape of hair permanent; contains oxidizing agent
PROTEIN/MOISTURIZING CONDITIONER/SEALER	Restores protein and/or moisture balance lost during processing
STYLING LOTION	Provides extra control and lasting quality of design
HAIRSPRAY OR STYLING PRODUCTS	Provides extra flexibility and holding qualities of design

ADDITIONAL PRODUCTS FOR CURL REFORMATION

PRODUCTS	FUNCTION
CURL REARRANGER	Reduces peptide bonds so hair can relax; thio-based product
CURL BOOSTER	Helps hair assume new shape of perm tool; milder form of thio
CURL ACTIVATOR	Helps new curl configurations retain their shape and provides moisture; applied frequently after every shampoo
INSTANT MOISTURIZER	Helps replace natural moisture and oils lost during chemical processes

RELAXER TOOLS/SUPPLIES

TOOLS/SUPPLIES	FUNCTION
PROTECTIVE SHAMPOO CAPE	Protects client from chemicals; large, loose protective covering fastened at the neck area
CLOTH TOWELS	Absorb and remove water, relaxer product and neutralizer when blotting; also curl rearranger product and booster during curl reformation
NEUTRALIZING BIB/ NEUTRALIZING CAPE	Catches excess chemicals as they run off the scalp; protects client
PROTECTIVE GLOVES	Shield designer's hands from chemicals during processing
SPATULA	Removes relaxer and/or other products from containers for application, keeping supply of original product uncontaminated
SECTIONING CLIPS	Hold hair in place in controlled sections for easier application of relaxer products
APPLICATOR BRUSH	Applies relaxer, perm solution (during curl reformation), and neutralizer to hair with less product waste, greater control and efficiency
TAIL COMB (NON-METAL)	Parts out sections of hair; used for smoothing during processing
SHAMPOO COMB	Distributes neutralizer through the hair, eliminating tangles and minimizing damage to swollen hair using smooth, wide teeth of the comb
BOWL	Holds relaxer for application

ADDITIONAL TOOLS/SUPPLIES FOR THERMAL RECONDITIONING

TOOLS/SUPPLIES	FUNCTION
BLOW DRYER	Dries the hair
FLAT IRON	Straightens the hair

ADDITIONAL TOOLS/SUPPLIES FOR CURL REFORMATION

TOOLS/SUPPLIES	FUNCTION
PERM TOOLS (RODS)	Determine the shape and size of the new curl; selected by shape, diameter and length
COTTON STRIPS	Protect hairline, neck and area above ears from chemicals
END PAPERS	Control the hair ends when wrapping; equalize porosity and absorbency during processing, rinsing and neutralizing
STABILIZERS (PICKS)	Hold perm tools in position when placed under the perm tool band
PLASTIC BAG	Covers the hair during processing and sometimes during reconditioning treatments

RELAXER EQUIPMENT

EQUIPMENT	FUNCTION
HEAT EQUIPMENT: PLASTIC INFRARED LAMPS, HOODED DRYER	Provide and capture heat when conditioning following relaxer service; help restore hair's structural integrity
TIMER	Alerts designer to check for maximum amount of time allowed for relaxer to be on hair and scalp; also for monitoring neutralizing times as recommended by the manufacturer
SHAMPOO BOWL	Allows client's hair to be rinsed and shampooed; needed for rinsing relaxer chemicals and neutralizer from hair
STYLING CHAIR	Adjusts for designer's working needs and comfortable seating for client

INFECTION CONTROL AND SAFETY

It is important to practice infection control and safety procedures in order to prevent the spread of any harmful bacteria. Always use combs, brushes and relaxer tools that have been disinfected for every client, every time.

1. Advise client not to shampoo within 48 hours before the sodium hydroxide relaxer service. The natural oils can help protect the scalp when performing this relaxer service. Shampoo the client's hair lightly prior to the other relaxer services: thio relaxer, thermal reconditioning and/or curl reformation.

2. Protect your client's clothing with proper draping. See "Draping for Chemical Services" later in this section.

3. Perform a strand test to determine the hair's competency. If the hair is dry, brittle or overporous, recondition it first and/or cut off damaged ends to avoid overprocessing. See "Preliminary Strand Testing" later in this section.

4. Examine the scalp for any irregular conditions, such as scratches, abrasions, irritations or cuts. If you discover any of these, do not proceed. Postpone and reschedule the relaxer service when the scalp is healthy again.

5. Perform a test for metallic salts if there is a possibility that such a product is on the hair. See "Testing for Metallic Salts" later in this section.

6. Avoid brushing or pulling the hair before giving any chemical service to prevent scalp irritation.

7. Never use sodium hydroxide to relax hair that has been treated with a thio product or vice versa. The results could be severe breakage and/or irreversible damage.

8. Cut off all hair that has been previously treated with sodium hydroxide if curl reformation is desired.

9. Take special care with lightened (bleached) hair. Most lightened hair is unable to receive relaxer services.

10. Apply base cream around the hairline and ears to prevent skin irritation when performing all relaxer services.

11. Wear protective gloves during chemical services to shield your hands from the harsh effects of chemicals.

12. If a client experiences burning during a sodium hydroxide relaxer service, rinse the hair with warm water, apply neutralizing shampoo and proceed with remaining service.

13. Perform several test strands to avoid overprocessing.

14. Monitor timing guidelines closely.

15. Avoid chemical burns and irritation to the skin, eyes, ears and nose by keeping all products away from them. If chemicals accidentally get on the skin, flush the area with cool water. If product gets into the eyes, flush them thoroughly with lukewarm water and consult a physician immediately.

16. Secure cotton strips around the hairline before applying neutralizer to keep it off the skin. When the cotton becomes wet, replace it immediately. For added protection (optional), place a neutralizing bib around the hairline with the elastic bands on top of the cotton to prevent skin irritation or chemical burns when rinsing.

ALERT!

Avoid leaving a client unattended while the hair is processing.

DRAPING FOR CHEMICAL SERVICES

Proper draping procedures for chemical services are very important. Draping protects the client's clothing and helps prevent skin irritations or burns caused by the relaxer chemicals. When draping your client for a chemical service, you will place a towel under the cape and a towel on top of the cape. Refer to the "Perming Theory" section of this chapter for details on this draping procedure.

PRELIMINARY STRAND TESTING
FOR THIO AND SODIUM RELAXER SERVICES

Strand testing evaluates the overall condition of the hair to determine if it can withstand the chemical service. To perform a strand test:

- Part off a small section of hair in the most resistant area of the head.
- Apply the chemical relaxer to the test strand.
- Follow the manufacturer's timing guide and check the test area frequently.
- Smooth the hair to straighten it.
- Rinse, then use a neutralizing shampoo and towel-dry the test area thoroughly.
- Test in another area using a stronger relaxer strength if the test strands did not relax enough.

FOR A CURL REFORMATION SERVICE

Preliminary strand testing is a good predictor of how your client's hair will react to the curl rearranger, booster and neutralizer. Always take the time to test tinted, bleached, over-porous or damaged hair.

- Shampoo and towel-dry the hair.
- Apply base cream on the scalp and hairline.
- Follow the manufacturer's directions and test the most delicate areas of the hair.
- Wrap a coil of cotton around the strand to isolate it from the rest of the hair.
- Apply curl rearranger to the hair, then smooth, rinse and blot it. Apply the booster and wrap the strand on a perm tool. Set a timer and process according to the manufacturer's directions.
- Pay close attention to the process and check the hair frequently.
- Unfasten and carefully unwind the hair about 1½ to 2 turns of the rod to check the test curl. Do not permit the hair to loosen or unwind from the perm tool completely. Hold the hair firmly by placing a thumb at each end of the tool. Turn it gently toward the scalp so that the hair falls easily into the wave pattern. Do not push the perm tool toward the head. Continue checking until a firm curl pattern forms, equal to the tool's diameter.
- Process, rinse and neutralize the test strand.
- Evaluate and document the results.

Shampoo only once before a curl reformation service to avoid sensitizing the scalp. Use light finger pressure and moderate water pressure with a mild temperature.

TEST FOR METALLIC SALTS

Color products that restore or progressively darken the hair (sometimes called hair restorers) contain metallic salts. These form a residue on the hair that interferes with the chemical action. Performing a chemical service on hair with metallic salts can result in uneven texture, distinct discoloration, hair damage or breakage. To avoid such negative results, perform a test for metallic salts, also called a 1:20 test, before performing a relaxer service. Review the "Perming Theory" portion of this chapter for details on testing for metallic salts.

RELAXER SERVICE ESSENTIALS

Before applying any chemicals to the hair, have a thorough conversation with the client. Success comes from listening carefully and recording all the important information on the record card. One of the most important considerations for a successful service is being sure you understand the new texture pattern that your client desires. Asking clients questions to determine how much of the existing texture they would like reduced and gathering a complete history of their past chemical services, including any problems they may have had, will enable you to make the proper decisions for a successful relaxer service.

CONNECT
- Meet and greet the client with a firm handshake and pleasant tone of voice.
- Communicate to build rapport and develop a connection with the client.

CONSULT
- Help your client fill out a consultation form.
- Ask questions to discover the client's wants and needs. How much curl or texture does your client want reduced? Use photos or a styling guide for clear communication.
- Check into your client's relaxer history. Have there been problems with relaxers used in the past? Are there particular details that your client would like to share about her hair, such as breakage, thinning, etc.?
- Analyze your client's face and body shape, physical features, lifestyle, climate effects, hair and scalp type, condition, prior product usage and results from previous services. Assess the facts and thoroughly think through your recommendations.
- Document on the record card everything that is important to the successful outcome of this service, as well as future services.
- Ask the client to sign the Release Form before the service begins. A standard Release Form, required by some malpractice insurance companies, states that the school or salon is not responsible for damages that may occur.

COSMETOLOGY FUNDAMENTALS

461

- Explain your recommended solutions as well as the price for the service(s). Think about future services as well as today's service.
- Focus on the physical and emotional needs of your client, building rapport and clarifying communication, reinforcing what you began in the Connect phase if your client is hesitant with your recommendations.
- Gain feedback from your client and obtain consent before proceeding with the service.

CREATE
- Ensure your client is protected by draping the client with a plastic cape and towel.
- Ensure client comfort during the service.
- Deliver all steps of the relaxer service to the best of your ability.
- Teach the client how to perform home hair care to keep the hair healthy and maintain the overall look of the new texture design.

COMPLETE
- Request specific feedback from your client. Ask questions and look for verbal and nonverbal cues to determine your client's level of satisfaction.
- Recommend products to maintain the healthy condition of your client's hair.
- Suggest a future appointment time for your client's next visit.
- Offer sincere appreciation to your client for visiting the school or salon.
- Accompany your client to the reception/payment area or to the door. Send the client off with a warm farewell.
- Complete the record card with accurate information for future services and file it in a secure area with other record cards.

PRODUCT OVERVIEW

The following chart summarizes the different types of chemical relaxer products along with the advantages and disadvantages of each. This chart can be used as a guide when choosing the proper relaxer for any type of hair. Remember to also consider the strength of the relaxer.

TYPE AND DESCRIPTION (listed by main ingredient)	ADVANTAGE	DISADVANTAGE
Sodium Hydroxide Category: Lye, Base, No Base pH: 11.5 - 14	Faster processing time; better for resistant hair and/or coarse hair	Irritates the scalp; may cause severe damage; strict time constraints; base application required and/or recommended
Calcium or Potassium Hydroxide Category: No Lye	Better for less-resistant hair; less irritating to scalp	May be more drying; slower processing time; requires frequent conditioning treatments

TYPE AND DESCRIPTION (listed by main ingredient)	ADVANTAGE	DISADVANTAGE
Guanidine Hydroxide Category: No Lye, Mix (contains calcium hydroxide and guanidine carbonate)	Better for less-resistant hair; less irritating to scalp	Processes slowly; not recommended for tightly curled hair
Lithium Hydroxide Category: No Lye, No Mix	Better for less-resistant hair; less irritating to scalp	Process slowly: not recommended for tightly curled hair
Ammonium Bisulfate Category: No Lye, No Mix	Better for less-resistant hair	Requires the addition of heat; not recommended for tightly curled hair
Ammonium Thioglycolate pH: 8.5 - 9.5	Better for less-resistant hair; more control due to processing time; better for fragile, fine or tinted hair	Not recommended for tightly curled hair

RELAXER PROCEDURES OVERVIEW

The following overview describes the basic steps for performing the curl diffusion service as well as virgin and retouch services using both sodium hydroxide and ammonium thioglycolate products. The preparation steps will only be shown once since they are the same for all of the relaxer services. Then, the procedural steps for each of the basic relaxer services will be given. The completion steps, which are the same for all of the relaxer services, will conclude the overview. The *Texture, A Designer's Approach* coursebook will show you step-by-step procedures for basic relaxer services and advanced relaxer services, such as curl diffusion and thermal reconditioning in greater detail.

PREPARATION

Before beginning any relaxer procedure, there are a series of steps you will perform to prepare yourself, your work area and your client, ensuring a safe and successful service.

RELAXER PREPARATION
- Clean workstation with disinfectant
- Assemble relaxer essentials that include sectioning clips, a non-metal tail comb, gloves, base cream, relaxer, bowl and applicator brush
- Wash your hands with liquid soap
- Ask client to remove jewelry and store in a secure place
- Drape client for a chemical service
- Perform analysis of hair and scalp
- Perform preliminary strand test and elasticity test

ALERT!

Never apply a thio relaxer over hair that has been relaxed with a sodium hydroxide relaxer or vice versa, since these two chemicals are not compatible. Severe damage and breakage can occur.

COSMETOLOGY FUNDAMENTALS

CURL DIFFUSION PROCEDURE OVERVIEW

With this technique the chemical relaxer is applied and gently combed through the lengths for even distribution and coverage. As the hair is combed in its growth direction, you will need to carefully watch for the desired texture pattern. When the hair attains the desired texture pattern, the product will need to be rinsed out before you apply a neutralizing shampoo. You will then need to comb the hair in the final design direction and allow it to air dry.

CURL DIFFUSION PROCEDURE

- **Section** hair for control if necessary
- Apply base cream around entire hairline and tops of ears
- **Part** hair horizontally and lift using tail comb beginning at back right section
- **Apply** relaxer starting at back right section below the part and work toward nape without applying directly to scalp; avoid applying to hairline; work from the back to the sides, to the top section and then from the front hairline to the nape hairline
- **Comb** (or **smooth**) through hair using a wide-tooth comb starting at right nape section and working upward; avoid touching the scalp; work from the back to the sides then to the top
- Perform visual strand **test**
- Rinse thoroughly and **neutralize** according to manufacturer's directions
- Finish texture design

NOTE
Prior to thio application, the hair should be shampooed and base cream should be applied only to the hairline and ears. For sodium hydroxide application, however, the hair should not be shampooed prior to the service, and base should be applied to the entire hairline, scalp and ears.

SODIUM HYDROXIDE RELAXER PROCEDURE OVERVIEW

Sodium hydroxide relaxers can be used on any type of hair but are especially designed for tightly curled hair. A sodium hydroxide relaxer is a progressive product, which means that once you apply the product, the hair cannot return to its original state, nor can you perform a curl reformation service afterward. A sodium hydroxide relaxer, therefore, is used to permanently relax or straighten the hair.

For a virgin application of a sodium hydroxide relaxer, the product is applied to the most resistant area and ¼" (.6 cm) to ½" (1.25 cm) away from the scalp up to the porous ends. To ensure a thorough application, partings should be approximately ¼" (.6 cm) and product should be applied to both sides of the strand. The heat from the scalp will allow the product to spread toward the scalp. However, if you need to apply product closer to the scalp, do so only after you have applied it to the midstrand throughout the head first. Never apply product directly on the scalp. The relaxer product is applied to the perimeter hairline last since the hairline is sensitive to breakage and is usually finer in texture.

The above application procedure is a guideline. Other application techniques are also acceptable. For example:
- You may begin the application at the ridge of the first curl.
- To equalize processing time on long hair, you may begin application farther away from the scalp to avoid overprocessing the hair.

Your instructor may have additional guidelines that are equally acceptable for you to follow.

VIRGIN SODIUM HYDROXIDE RELAXER PROCEDURE

- Assemble virgin sodium hydroxide relaxer essentials
- DO NOT pre-shampoo the client's hair
- **Section** hair into 5 sections
  - Apply base cream around entire hairline, tops of ears and to scalp of each section using checkerboard technique and ¼" (.6 cm) to ½" (1.25 cm) partings; apply base using horizontal and vertical partings
  - **Apply** relaxer starting at top of back right section using ¼" (.6 cm) horizontal partings applying ½" (1.25 cm) from base through midstrand, avoiding ends; apply relaxer to top and bottom of parting; work toward bottom of section; bring lengths down; work from the back to the sides to the top; avoid touching scalp
  - Apply relaxer starting at top of back right section to top and bottom of base and porous ends using ¼" (.6 cm) horizontal partings; follow the same parting and working pattern used previously to apply to the midstrand; do not apply directly to scalp
  - Apply relaxer to entire hairline starting at front hairline working toward nape on both sides
- **Smooth** top and bottom of each ¼" (.6 cm) parting starting at top of back right section from base to ends using back of comb; bring lengths down; work from the back to the sides to the top
- Perform comb relaxation **test** using spine or tail of comb
- Rinse thoroughly and **neutralize** according to manufacturer's directions
- Finish texture design

RETOUCH SODIUM HYDROXIDE RELAXER PROCEDURE

- DO NOT pre-shampoo the hair
- **Section** hair into 5 sections
  - Apply base cream around entire hairline, tops of ears and to scalp of each section using checkerboard technique; apply base using horizontal and vertical partings
  - Apply protective cream to previously relaxed hair starting at top of back right section; apply to top and then bottom of ½" (1.25 cm) horizontal partings from line of demarcation to ends; work from the back to the sides to the top of the head
  - **Apply** relaxer starting at top of back right section; apply to top and bottom of new growth area only; avoid touching scalp, and use ¼" (.6 cm) horizontal partings; work from the back to the sides to the top; avoid applying to hairline; bring lengths down
  - Apply relaxer to entire hairline starting at front hairline working toward nape hairline on both sides

- **Smooth** top and bottom of ¼" (.6 cm) partings in new growth area; start in top of back right section using back of comb; bring lengths down; work from the back to the sides to the top of the head
- Perform curl relaxation **test** using spine or tail of comb
- Rinse thoroughly and **neutralize** according to manufacturer's directions
- Finish texture design

AMMONIUM THIOGLYCOLATE RELAXER PROCEDURE OVERVIEW

When you are working with a thio relaxer, the first-time application is applied to the most resistant area and ¼" (.6 cm) to ½" (1.25 cm) away from the scalp out to the porous ends. Additional product may then be applied at the base (scalp area) if necessary. **Product is applied to the base last, since the hair near the scalp will process more quickly due to body heat.** A non-alkaline shampoo is recommended after the chemical relaxer has been rinsed from the hair. The natural oils that are removed during the chemical relaxing process are replaced with a conditioning treatment.

The above application procedure is a guideline. Other application techniques are also acceptable. For example:
- You may begin the application at the ridge of the first curl, which may be farther from the scalp.
- To equalize processing time on long hair, you may begin application farther away from the scalp to avoid overprocessing the hair.

Your instructor may have additional guidelines that are equally acceptable for you to follow.

VIRGIN THIO RELAXER PROCEDURE
- Pre-shampoo the hair lightly
- **Section** hair into 5 sections
  - Apply base cream around entire hairline and tops of ears
- **Apply** relaxer starting at top of back right section using ¼" (.6 cm) horizontal partings and applying ½" (1.25 cm) from base through midstrand, avoiding ends
  - Apply relaxer to top and bottom of each parting; work toward bottom of section; bring lengths down
- Work from the back to the sides to the front using diagonal-back partings at the sides and horizontal partings at the top
  - Apply relaxer to the base and porous ends in each section using same parting pattern and technique; avoid touching scalp
- **Smooth** top and bottom of each ¼" (.6 cm) parting starting at top of back right section from base to ends using back of comb; bring lengths down; work from back to sides to top
- Perform a comb relaxation **test** using spine or tail of comb
- Rinse thoroughly and **neutralize** according to manufacturer's directions
- Finish texture design

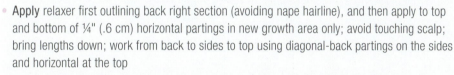

RETOUCH THIO RELAXER PROCEDURE
- Pre-shampoo the hair lightly
- **Section** hair into 5 sections
  - Apply base cream around entire hairline and tops of ears
  - Apply protective cream to previously relaxed hair starting at top of back right section; use ½" (1.25 cm) horizontal partings applying to top and then bottom of each parting from line of demarcation to ends; apply protective cream to remaining sections using same technique
- **Apply** relaxer first outlining back right section (avoiding nape hairline), and then apply to top and bottom of ¼" (.6 cm) horizontal partings in new growth area only; avoid touching scalp; bring lengths down; work from back to sides to top using diagonal-back partings on the sides and horizontal at the top
- **Smooth** top and bottom of ¼" (.6 cm) partings in new growth area, starting at top of back right section using back of comb; bring lengths down; work from back to sides to top
- Perform comb relaxation **test** using spine or tail of comb
- Rinse thoroughly and **neutralize** according to manufacturer's directions
- Finish texture design

RELAXER COMPLETION
After you have finished your client's relaxer design, the service is not yet complete. There are additional steps that reflect your professionalism and your interest in the total satisfaction of each and every client. These completion steps will be the same for all of the relaxer services.
- Reinforce guest's satisfaction with his or her overall experience.
- Make professional product recommendations.
- Prebook guest's next appointment.
- End guest's visit with warm and personal goodbyes.
- Discard non-reusable materials, disinfect tools and arrange workstation in proper order.
- Wash your hands with liquid soap.
- Complete client record card.
- Provide follow-up after the salon visit.

RELAXER PROBLEMS AND SOLUTIONS

The following section alerts you to some problems that may occur with relaxers, along with their possible causes and solutions.

EXTREME BREAKAGE SHORTLY AFTER RELAXING
Cause: Improper neutralizing allows active ingredients to remain in the hair strand
Solution: Allow the neutralizing product to remain in the hair no longer than specified in manufacturer's directions and ensure neutralizer is thoroughly rinsed

BREAKAGE WITHIN THE NAPE AFTER RELAXING

Cause: Overprocessing; Relaxer product left in the neck of the shampoo bowl comes in contact with client's nape when client leans back into bowl after rinsing product from hair

Solution: Rinse the relaxer from the neck of the bowl before leaning the client back into the bowl after rinsing product from the hair

IRRITATION OR SENSITIVITY AROUND THE HAIRLINE

Cause: Client cleansed his or her face and extended cleansing into the hairline before the relaxer service

Solution: Instruct clients to avoid cleansing into the hairline prior to the service

CONNECTING THEORY TO REAL-WORLD PRACTICE

TEXTURE	PERSONAL CONNECTION: IMPROVE YOURSELF	INDUSTRY CONNECTION: BECOME A PROFESSIONAL	CLIENT CONNECTION: SERVE THE GUEST
PERMING THEORY	Enhance appearance with added volume, body and curlier hair textures	Excel at producing professional straight-to-curly texture designs	Create specific curl patterns that produce natural or dramatic results
RELAXING THEORY	Achieve different looks with straighter, more manageable textures	Address a wide range of client needs by delivering expert chemical relaxer services	Give clients relaxed texture and more design options without damaging their hair

IN OTHER WORDS

Your specialized skill in providing chemical texture services will allow you to transform your clients' appearance, giving them the straight-to-curly and curly-to-straight looks they want, while building your clientele and professional reputation.

LESSONS LEARNED

- Chemical texture services offered in the salon include: perming, to transform hair from straight to curly; and relaxing, to transform hair from curly to straight.

- Perm results depend mainly on the distribution and sectioning, wrapping technique, base control, tool size and perm pattern used.

- Relaxer results depend mainly on the chemical relaxer product and smoothing technique used.

- Thermal reconditioning is designed to straighten hair up to 100% using a chemical service followed by flat-ironing the hair.

- A curl reformation service creates a new, looser curl pattern by first relaxing and then perming the hair.

13

COLOR

13.1 COLOR THEORY
WHAT IS COLOR?
THE LAW OF COLOR
CHARACTERISTICS OF COLOR

13.2 IDENTIFYING EXISTING HAIR COLOR
MELANIN
GRAY HAIR
IDENTIFYING NATURAL LEVEL AND TONE
IDENTIFYING ARTIFICIAL LEVEL AND TONE
ADDITIONAL CONSIDERATIONS

13.3 CHANGING EXISTING HAIR COLOR
COLOR CHEMISTRY
DESIGNING COLOR
HAIR COLOR ESSENTIALS
INFECTION CONTROL AND SAFETY
COLOR SERVICE ESSENTIALS
PRODUCT OVERVIEW
COLOR PROCEDURES OVERVIEW
HAIR COLOR PROBLEMS AND SOLUTIONS

COLOR DESIGN IS ONE
OF THE MOST VERSATILE
AND POPULAR SERVICES
OFFERED IN THE SALON

FOLLOWING THIS LESSON
YOU WILL BE ABLE TO:

Define color and the law of color

Explain the characteristics of color

Describe how to identify a client's existing hair color

Explain the techniques used to change existing hair color

CONNECTING THEORY TO REAL-WORLD PRACTICE

APPLYING COLOR THEORY AND THE PROFESSIONAL TECHNIQUES OF HAIR COLOR DESIGN WILL HELP YOU:

PERSONAL CONNECTION:	**INDUSTRY CONNECTION:**	**CLIENT CONNECTION:**
IMPROVE YOURSELF	BECOME A PROFESSIONAL	SERVE THE GUEST
Experiment with color combinations and techniques to create flattering color effects	Be recognized as an artistic, as well as highly skilled, hair designer	Enhance clients' appearance by changing their hair color using principles of color theory and design

People use their natural eye for color every day in coordinating their wardrobes and decorating their homes. As a salon professional, you will use your trained and experienced eye to create hair color designs that will enhance your clients' appearance.

13.1 COLOR THEORY

Color can define the lines and shape of a hair design, soften facial features, warm skin tones and accentuate a person's lifestyle and personality. Dispersed throughout a design, color can unify contrasting elements. It may be a background element, visually leading the viewer's eye to a focal area, or it may be the element that actually creates the focal point. In other words, color can play a supporting role—enhancing the overall effect of the sculpted form, or it can be the lead player—really standing out, with the rest of the design supporting it.

Hair coloring techniques have been used since ancient times. Cleopatra was said to have used henna to add reddish tones. Roman women used mixtures of wood ash, unslaked lime and sodium bicarbonate to lighten their hair. Eventually people realized that sitting in the sun could lighten hair. It wasn't until the mid-1800s that a German professor, August Wilhelm von Hofmann, and one of his students, William Henry Perk, accidentally discovered how to create permanent dyes. Their discovery led to the synthetic hair colorants that are used today, which change color in one of two ways:

1. Temporarily: by adding color pigment that shampoos out (immediately or over time)
2. Permanently: either by adding or removing color pigment

REASONS FOR CHANGING HAIR COLOR

TO CREATE A FASHION STATEMENT

TO ENHANCE EXISTING OR NATURAL HAIR COLOR

TO COVER OR BLEND GRAY

TO MIMIC OR CORRECT THE SUN'S LIGHTENING EFFECTS

WHAT IS COLOR?

Color is the visual perception of the reflection of light. Without light, there would be no color. In other words, color is a phenomenon of light. Isaac Newton discovered this fact in 1676 when he passed white light through a prism and found that the light broke out into continuous bands of color, ranging from red to orange to yellow, then green to blue to indigo and finally violet.

Each of these colors is a group of electromagnetic waves, also called wavelengths, traveling through space. Although many forms of electromagnetic waves, such as radio waves and infrared waves, are not visible to the eye, the waves that can be seen create color. These waves are known as "visible light."

Wavelengths cannot be seen unless they are reflected off of an object. The brain then interprets these waves of light as color. For example, when white light shines on a red bottle, the bottle absorbs most of the light waves except the red ones. These reflected red light waves are interpreted by the eye as the color red.

THE LAW OF COLOR

As a hair colorist, you will recommend hair color options for your clients. To do this, you need to be familiar with the law of color. **The law of color states that only three colors—yellow, red and blue, called primary colors—are "pure" colors,** meaning that they cannot be created by mixing together any other colors. The three primary colors create all the other colors.

When two of the three primary colors are mixed in varying proportions, they produce the three secondary colors: orange, green and violet. Orange contains varying proportions of red and yellow, green contains varying proportions of blue and yellow, and violet contains varying proportions of red and blue.

Mixing a primary color with its neighboring secondary color in varying proportions makes tertiary colors. There are six tertiary colors: yellow-orange, red-orange, red-violet, blue-violet, blue-green, and yellow-green.

PRIMARY COLORS

Yellow

Red

Blue

SECONDARY COLORS

Orange

Green

Violet

TERTIARY COLORS

Yellow-Orange

Red-Orange

Yellow-Green

Blue-Green

Red-Violet

Blue-Violet

COLOR WHEEL

A **color wheel** is a 12-hue color circle that is created from the three primary colors, yellow, red and blue. The color wheel can be used as a tool in which the 12 colors—three primary, three secondary and six tertiary—are positioned in a circle, allowing any mixed color to be described in relation to the primary colors. **The name of a color, also referred to as tone or hue, is identified by its position on the color wheel. The tone of a hair color can be described as warm, cool or neutral.**

The color wheel is a tool that you will continue to use in the salon to help you mix hair colors and neutralize unwanted tones.

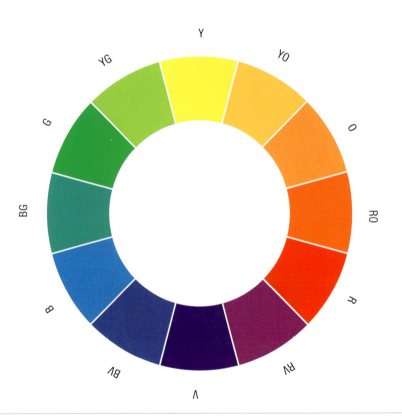

Depending on the concentration of pigment within a color, the outcome of mixing two colors can vary. For example, one manufacturer's "red" can lean toward a cool red, versus a warm red from a different manufacturer; plus, it can be lighter or darker. When mixing a "yellow" with a "red" to achieve "orange," begin with yellow and add red until the desired shade of orange is achieved.

COLOR WHEEL

Creating a color wheel out of white yak hair and nonoxidative colors will help you understand the law of color.

WARM AND COOL COLORS

Colors can be classified as either warm colors (warm tones) or cool colors (cool tones). **Warm color tones** generally fall into the yellow, orange and red half of the color wheel, while **cool color tones** generally fall into the green, blue and violet half of the color wheel. Yellow-green and red-violet can at various times be considered either warm or cool, depending on whether they contain more pigment, or coloring substance, from the cool side of the color wheel or the warm side.

You can get an expanded view of warm and cool tones from a color sphere, which is a three-dimensional version of the color wheel.

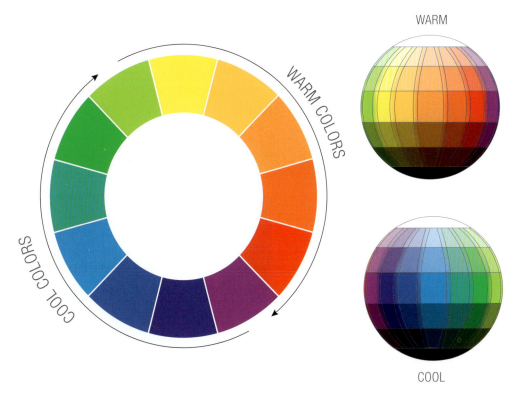

Based on this concept of warm and cool color tones, any colored object or substance can be categorized as either warm or cool. People may be referred to as warm or cool, based on their hair and skin tones. For example, **if someone is classified as warm, this means his or her hair and skin coloring fall into the yellow, red and orange category,** or has predominantly yellow, red or orange undertones.

When designing color for a "warm" client, you would usually keep the new hair color in the warm range. Likewise, for clients with cool coloring, it is usually more flattering to keep their hair color in the cool range.

COMPLEMENTARY COLORS

Colors found opposite one another on the color wheel are referred to as complementary colors. When two complementary colors are combined, the result contains all three primary colors. When complementary colors are mixed together in varying proportions, they neutralize or cancel one another out, eventually producing a neutral color, such as certain shades of gray, black or brown, depending on the proportions used. Colors that do not exhibit warm or cool tones are considered neutral colors.

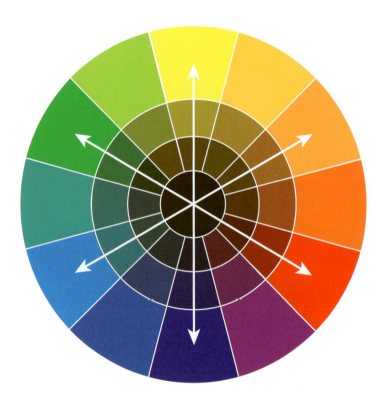

Understanding how complementary colors interact with one another is important because, in hair coloring, complementary colors are often used to correct or neutralize unwanted tones. For instance, a client's hair may have lightened to a brassy, orange tone. A correction is possible by using the color wheel to determine that blue is the complementary color to orange and, therefore, applying a blue-based color to the brassy tone will neutralize or correct it to achieve the desired final shade.

Varying proportions of the three primary colors create a range of brown and/or neutral colors. Light golden brown colors contain more yellow, while medium reddish-brown colors contain more red.

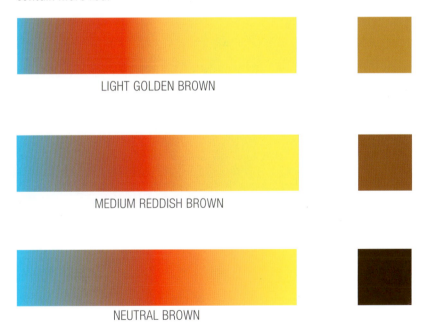

LIGHT GOLDEN BROWN

MEDIUM REDDISH BROWN

NEUTRAL BROWN

CHARACTERISTICS OF COLOR

In the language of color theory, color has three main characteristics: hue, value and intensity. Understanding what these characteristics are and how they translate from color theory into actual salon practice will give you a strong foundation for creating professional hair color designs for your clients.

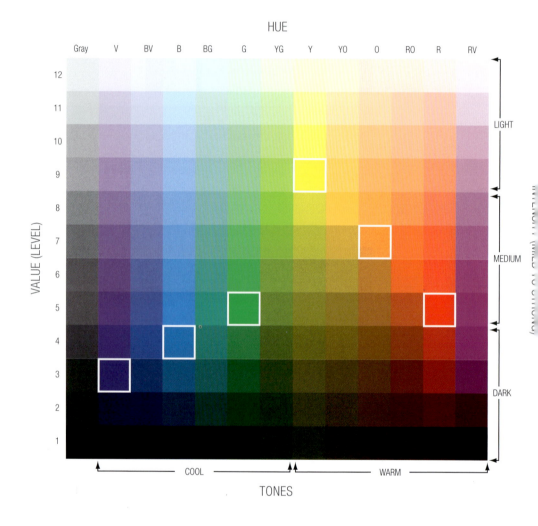

HUE

Hues are named and abbreviated for easy reference based on their position on the color wheel. The primary and secondary colors are all abbreviated by their first initial –Y for yellow, R for red, B for blue, G for green, O for orange and V for violet. The names of the six tertiary colors are combinations of the primary and secondary colors that combine to form them. The hue "red-orange," for example, which is positioned between the hues red and orange on the color wheel, is abbreviated as RO. Likewise, BV stands for blue-violet, which lies between blue and violet on the color wheel. These abbreviations are often used by manufacturers to identify the specific hues of hair coloring products.

VALUE/LEVEL

The second characteristic of color is value, also referred to within the salon industry as level. **Value, or level, is the degree of lightness or darkness of a color, relative to itself and to other colors.** For instance, when yellow is described as a light color, red as medium and blue as dark, what is really being described is the value of a color.

FIELDS OF COLOR

DARK   MEDIUM DARK   MEDIUM   MEDIUM LIGHT   LIGHT

There are two ways that hair color designers talk about the value of hair colors: fields and levels. All the hair colors in the world can be broadly categorized into three major fields:

- Dark (black)
- Medium (brown)
- Light (blond)

The fields can be further subdivided into medium dark and medium light. Broadly speaking, natural redheads would generally fall into the medium field.

The level system is a numbering system that identifies the lightness or darkness of hair colors in smaller specific increments. This system divides both natural and artificial hair color into 12 categories, called levels, which are numbered from 1 to 12: the higher the number, the lighter the hair color. The darkest hair colors are level 1, while the lightest hair colors are level 12. Some manufacturers and other industry professionals use a 1 to 10 level system rather than 1 to 12, but it operates in the same way.

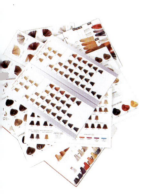

Because hair color design has a lot in common with art and painting, observing how painters use value to create different visual effects will help you incorporate the concept of value to create a variety of hair color effects for your clients. Begin by looking at a picture or a painting that has been photographed in black and white. You'll notice that each color appears as a shade of gray. What you are seeing is the relative lightness or darkness of each color—its value—not the colors themselves.

Painters use pigments of different values to create three-dimensional illusions. Note how the lighter colors seem to come forward while the darker colors seem to recede.

Hair colorists use the concept of value to classify hair color as light, medium or dark when measured against a gray scale. When designing hair color, it is helpful to think first in shades of gray. Consider if lights and/or darks should be positioned to create added depth, dimension or textural interest. Then visualize your design in color.

INTENSITY

Intensity refers to the vividness, brightness or saturation of a color within its own level. The intensity of a color can range from mild to strong. Words often used to describe the intensity of a color include deep, vibrant and rich to describe strong intensity and subtle, muted and soft to describe mild intensity. The most intense version of a color is also sometimes called "pure," as in "pure red" or "pure green," because it represents the most intense, most saturated, "truest" version of that color.

You can use the characteristics of a color chart to identify the intensity of colors and how intensity relates to value. Note how the primary colors, in their purest intensity, vary in level, with yellow being the lightest, blue the darkest, and red considered medium. Note how the most intense version of each color occurs at different levels from one another, but corresponds to the general value of that color. For example, the most intense blue occurs at level 4, the most intense red occurs at level 5, and the most intense yellow occurs at level 9. Since **blue is the darkest of the three primary colors,** its most intense form also has the darkest value of the three. Yellow is the lightest and the most intense yellow has the lightest value of the three. The most intense red is in the middle.

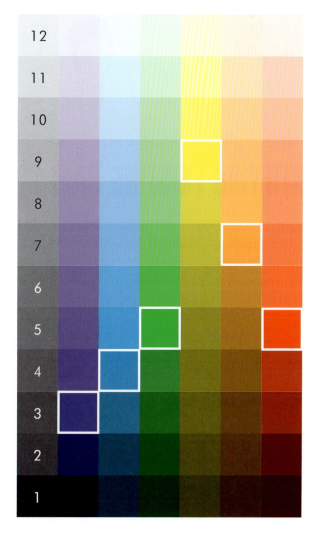

COSMETOLOGY FUNDAMENTALS

COLOR THEORY SUMMARY

Hair colors in the same field can vary in intensity, ranging from mild to strong.

- Color is the visual perception of the reflection of light; without light, there is no color.
- All colors are derived from red, yellow and blue, the primary colors.
- Colors found opposite one another on the color wheel are complementary and are used in hair coloring to neutralize unwanted tones.
- The hue or tone of a color is identified and named by its position on the color wheel.
- Every color can be described as being either a warm, cool or neutral tone.
- Level, or value, is the degree of lightness or darkness of a color ranging from 1 to 10 or 1 to 12.
- Intensity refers to the brightness or vividness of a color.

LIGHT	MEDIUM	DARK

13.2 IDENTIFYING EXISTING HAIR COLOR

Identifying your client's natural or existing color is one of the first steps in a hair color service. Unlike painting a white wall, you will apply color over natural or previously colored hair. Chemists create artificial pigments to imitate natural hair colors. When these colors are applied to virgin hair, or hair that has not been colored before, it is the combination of the natural melanin and the artificial pigment that creates the final color result. When working on previously color-treated hair, the final color is the result of the existing or contributing pigment and the artificial color applied. **Contributing pigment** is either the client's naturally present melanin or a combination of this melanin and any previously applied artificial color that is remaining on the hair.

 +  =

CONTRIBUTING PIGMENT + ARTIFICIAL PIGMENT = FINAL COLOR RESULT

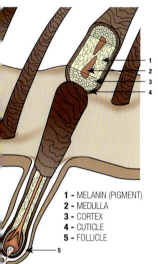

1 - MELANIN (PIGMENT)
2 - MEDULLA
3 - CORTEX
4 - CUTICLE
5 - FOLLICLE

MELANIN

Pigment that gives hair its natural color is known as melanin and is determined through genetic coding. This section reviews the information presented in *Chapter 7, Trichology*, to make sure you have a clear picture of how melanin gives hair its color.

The three layers of the hair are the cuticle, the cortex and the medulla. Down in the hair bulb are pigment-producing cells called melanocytes. These melanocytes produce small egg-shaped structures called melanosomes, which are protein packets that surround pigmented granules called melanin. The melanin eventually becomes incorporated into the keratin protein of the cortex as the hair grows.

The melanin created by the body is first developed at the bottom of each hair follicle. From here, the melanin becomes seated in the cortex of the hair shaft. As the hair grows from the follicle, it develops its color according to inherited characteristics.

There are two types of melanin found in the cortex of the hair, **eumelanin (brown/black pigment) and pheomelanin (red/yellow pigment)**. It is the amount, size, type and distribution of melanin that determine whether hair will be black, brown, red or blond. A dense concentration of eumelanin will produce very dark hair. A small population of eumelanin will produce light (blond) hair. A predominant amount of pheomelanin will create red hair.

BLACK RED BROWN BLOND

COSMETOLOGY FUNDAMENTALS

GRAY HAIR

When the melanocyte cells slow down in their production of melanin, as is common in the aging process, each hair strand gradually loses its color and the result is white hair. There are many things that affect melanosome production but heredity is the primary factor. Since each hair is individual, it is not unusual to find a mixture of nonpigmented (white) and pigmented hair on the same head, making the hair appear gray. As more and more melanocyte cells become inactive, there will be more white hair.

Different patterns of graying can occur with each individual. Some people gray around the front hairline and sideburn area first, while others may begin to gray at the top or crown area. Different percentages of gray can also occur from the front to the back. Gray hair is found in every field, from light gray to medium gray to dark gray.

PERCENTAGES OF GRAY HAIR

Prior to a color application it is important to determine the percentage of gray your client has, since you may need to use different color formulas to accommodate the different percentages of gray hair. Generally, gray hair can be categorized as 25%, 50% or 75% gray. With 25% gray hair, there is more pigmented hair and less nonpigmented hair. With 50% gray, there is an even mixture of pigmented and nonpigmented hair. If the client exhibits a very high percentage of gray (75%-80%), the hair will appear lighter overall. When creating a color formula for a client with this type of hair, you may need to adjust your color formula by applying a color that is one level darker than the desired level. **If the client has approximately 25%-30% gray hair, apply a color one level lighter than the desired shade.**

It is sometimes said that gray hair is more resistant to color applications than pigmented hair. This is not necessarily true. As the color molecules wash out or fade from sunlight, the hair looks lighter faster because there is no natural pigment or background color. Gray hair may be more coarse and less elastic, which can make it more resistant to chemical color services. **If you find that you are working with resistant hair, you may need to pre-soften or pre-lighten the hair first by mixing and applying a lighter shade to make it porous enough to receive the final color application.**

IDENTIFYING NATURAL LEVEL AND TONE

Before performing a color service, it is important to analyze your client's natural hair color in order to determine which products, formulas and techniques will give your client the best results. First, determine the general field (dark, medium dark, medium, medium light and light). Then, using manufacturer's color swatches, identify the specific level, from 1 to 10 (or 12). Finally, determine whether the tone is warm or cool. Keeping the color wheel theory in mind ask yourself: What is the predominant undertone you see? On which side of the color wheel would that fall? Level 9 blond hair, for example, can further be described as a level 9 warm (golden) blond or a level 9 cool (ash) blond.

As you learned earlier in this chapter, **the level of a hair color can be identified on a scale from 1 to 10 or 1 to 12, with 1 being the darkest and 10 or 12 being the lightest.** Levels are often given descriptive names such as "lightest blond." Keep in mind that the names and levels may vary with each manufacturer.

DARK	MEDIUM	LIGHT
1 BLACK	5 LIGHT BROWN	9 LIGHT BLOND
2 DARK BROWN	6 DARK BLOND	10 VERY LIGHT BLOND
3 MEDIUM DARK BROWN	7 MEDIUM BLOND	11 LIGHTEST BLOND
4 MEDIUM BROWN	8 MEDIUM LIGHT BLOND	12 PALEST BLOND

As you look around, you will see a multitude of hair colors from the deepest blue black to the whitest white and all the various shades of browns, reds and blonds in between. It is interesting to note that the majority of the world's population falls within the dark hair color category.

IDENTIFYING ARTIFICIAL LEVEL AND TONE

When clients come to you for a color change, sometimes they will already have had a prior color service. In these cases, you will not only need to identify the client's natural, or genetic, hair color; you will also need to identify the artificial color that has been added to his or her hair. Identifying the level and tone of artificial hair colors is also a necessary skill for choosing and formulating the color that you will be adding to the client's hair during the color service.

Manufacturers identify and name their artificial hair colors in several ways. For example:
- By level and tone, such as level 5RV (red-violet)
- By field and tone, such as medium red-violet
- By tone or name, such as red-violet or mahogany

COSMETOLOGY FUNDAMENTALS

In artificial hair coloring, the predominant tone, known as **base color**, identifies the warmth, coolness or neutrality of a color.

Artificial warm colors that contain base colors such as yellow or red-orange, may be described as golden blond or auburn. Artificial cool colors containing green or violet base colors might be described as ash or platinum. Be sure you know the base color of the formula you are planning to use before beginning any color service.

BASE COLOR	RESULT
Yellow or Gold	Golden blond tones
Red	Vibrant red tones
Blue	Minimize orange brassiness
Violet	Neutralize unwanted yellow tones

Understanding base colors will not only allow you to identify artificial hair colors, but it will also help you choose the correct level and tone to achieve the desired warm, cool or neutral results. Keeping the color wheel in mind, as well as the client's contributing pigment, will help you choose the right base color to achieve a specific hair color result.

TONES/BASE COLORS

The chart on the right will help you become familiar with some of the most common base colors and names for artificial hair colors. The first column shows base colors and their abbreviations. The second column shows artificial hair color names and their corresponding base colors. These hair colors come in a variety of levels and intensities and can be used alone or mixed together to create a wide array of tones. Keep in mind that artificial hair color names and level numbers may vary slightly with each manufacturer.

BASE COLORS

- Yellow (Y)
- Red (R)
- Blue (B)
- Gold (G)
- Violet (V)
- Ash (A)
- Neutral (N)
- Green (G)
- Red-Orange (RO)
- Red-Violet (RV)
- Blue-Violet (BV)

ARTIFICIAL HAIR COLORS

- Platinum (Violet)
- Golden Blond (Yellow or Gold)
- Ash Blond (Blue-Violet)
- Chestnut Brown (Green)
- Golden Brown (Gold)
- Copper Gold (Orange)
- Auburn (Red-Orange)
- Burgundy (Red-Violet)
- Mahogany (Red-Violet)
- Plum Brown (Red-Violet)
- Black Velvet (Violet)
- Blue Black (Blue)

When identifying artificial hair color, you'll also need to recognize its intensity. When referring to a red-orange hair color, for example, you might describe it as a mild red-orange compared to a strong red-orange. The intensity of an artificial hair coloring can be lessened, or neutralized, by adding a complementary color or it can be increased, or strengthened, by adding a concentrated color such as yellow, red, blue, green or violet. For example, the intensity of a red-orange color may become stronger by adding red-orange concentrate to the formula or become weaker by adding the complementary blue-green color.

ADDITIONAL CONSIDERATIONS

Along with the hair's level, tone and intensity, it is important to consider the texture (diameter) and porosity of your client's hair. These considerations will influence color absorption and processing time.

TEXTURE

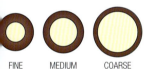

FINE   MEDIUM   COARSE

As you may recall from *Chapter 7, Trichology,* the degree of coarseness or fineness in the hair fiber is referred to as texture. Coarse hair may be resistant to lightening or it may appear to process slightly lighter than the intended level. On the other hand, fine hair, which has pigment grouped more tightly together and is generally less resistant, may appear to process darker when color is deposited. When lightening or removing pigment from fine hair, a mild lightener is usually recommended. Generally, medium-textured hair has an average response to color products.

POROSITY

Porosity refers to the ability of the hair to absorb moisture, liquids or chemicals. **Porosity is a main factor when selecting products, formulating hair colors and determining the appropriate application technique and amount of processing time.** The number of cuticle layers and how tightly they overlap determine the degree of porosity. When the cuticle layer is raised, it is easier for the product to penetrate through the cuticle into the cortex. This information is important in hair coloring because, depending on its porosity, the hair may or may not absorb enough color.

Some common factors that affect the porosity of the hair include sun exposure, alkaline shampoos and chemical products such as hair colors, lighteners, perms and relaxers. Even the heat from hair dryers and curling irons affects the porosity of the hair. The more the hair is exposed to these factors, the greater the porosity.

With **resistant porosity**, the cuticle layers are smooth, tightly packed and compact. Color absorption in this case may take longer or you may have to apply additional pigment to ensure color absorption.

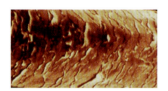

With **average porosity**, the cuticle is slightly raised, thereby accepting color products easily.

The condition in which the cuticle is lifted or missing is referred to as **extreme porosity**. With this type of porosity, the hair may take the color too intensely or not hold the color and fade quickly between salon visits. The cuticle is lifted and/or missing due to physical or chemical stress.

In many instances, you will note that a client has more than one type of porosity, which is called uneven porosity. Clients who have had previous chemical services often have hair with uneven porosity. The hair may exhibit extreme porosity on the midstrand or ends and average porosity on the new growth. **Often clients with long hair may exhibit uneven or variations in porosity because the hair on the ends has been more exposed to environmental elements.** These elements coupled with repeated shampooing and thermal designing can leave the ends with extreme porosity. Uneven porosity happens not only along the hair strand but throughout the head as well. An example of this would be a client with highlighted hair. The hair that has been lightened may be one type of porosity, while the hair that is natural may be another type. **In cases of uneven or extreme porosity, a filler may be required to equalize porosity throughout the hair strand prior to the color service to ensure even color absorption.** You will learn more about fillers later in the chapter.

To determine porosity, select a small section of hair. Hold the ends and slide your thumb and forefinger along the hair strand toward the scalp. The more rough the hair feels and the easier the hair backcombs, the greater the porosity.

13.3 CHANGING EXISTING HAIR COLOR

Hair color can be changed in one of two ways: either temporarily by adding pigment or permanently by adding and/or removing pigment. Deciding which method you will use will help you select the right products for the service.

When changing the color of the hair, remember that the final hair color will result from the combination of the natural melanin and any pre-existing artificial color (contributing pigment) and the new hair color (artificial pigment) applied to the hair. Before determining how much color to add or subtract, it is important to determine the level of the hair color, which corresponds to the amount, size, type and distribution of pigment contained in the hair—the darker the hair, the greater the concentration of pigment; the lighter the hair, the lower the concentration of pigment.

COLOR DESIGN SERVICES

Use the following steps to create a new hair color, and remember,
CONTRIBUTING PIGMENT + ARTIFICIAL PIGMENT = FINAL COLOR RESULT

CONTRIBUTING PIGMENT
Determine the client's existing level and tone. Identify the actual hair color, which may be natural, gray, previously color-treated, brassy or lightened by the sun. Use your swatches or swatches provided by the manufacturer. Also determine the porosity of the client's hair.

ARTIFICIAL PIGMENT
Determine the client's desired level and tone. Use your swatches or swatches provided by the manufacturer. Consider the porosity. Determine whether you need to go lighter, darker or remain in the same level and just change the tone (warmth or coolness) or intensity.

FINAL COLOR RESULT
Choose the color formula. The formula may include color(s), developer and/or lighteners. Identify the tones and levels you will use and their positions within the design. Keep in mind that darker colors recede and add depth, while lighter colors come forward and add brightness to the design.

COLOR CHEMISTRY

Manufacturers create an array of colors and lighteners that give the salon colorist the ability to create subtle to dramatic color changes. Before you can begin to use these colors effectively, you need to understand how each one works, including the physical and chemical effects they have on the client's hair. Being familiar with the color chemistry of artificial hair colors will help you avoid unwanted reactions so you achieve the color results you and your client want while keeping the client's hair in healthy condition.

The general categories of hair color products are:
NONOXIDATIVE COLORS (not mixed with developer)
- Temporary
- Semi-permanent

OXIDATIVE COLORS (MIXED WITH DEVELOPER)
- Long lasting semi-permanent (demi-permanent)
- Permanent
- Toners
- Fillers

LIGHTENERS
- On-the-scalp
- Off-the-scalp

DEVELOPERS

OTHER COLOR PRODUCTS
- Vegetable
- Metallic
- Compound Dyes

NONOXIDATIVE COLORS

Nonoxidative colors add pigment but do not lighten the existing hair color. Nonoxidative color products are used to darken the color, impart shine and add new tones as well as to neutralize unwanted tones. Nonoxidative colors are not mixed with an oxidant or developer (oxidizing agent) and are used directly out of the bottle. These types of colors create only a physical change to the hair, with no chemical change, by depositing colors that shampoo out. Although nonoxidative colors do not create a chemical change, they can penetrate the cortex, stain the hair and may become difficult if not impossible to remove. The major classifications of nonoxidative colors are temporary and semi-permanent.

TEMPORARY COLORS

Temporary colors, as the name implies, are used to create temporary color changes that last from shampoo to shampoo. They are non-reactive, direct dyes, which means no chemicals are needed to develop them. They contain large color molecules that coat only the surface of the cuticle, thereby creating a physical (and not a chemical) change to the hair. There's nothing in the product that will lighten the hair and no chemical changes occur in the solution or in the hair. They can neutralize unwanted tones, add tone to faded hair or add pigment to the hair without chemically altering the structure of the hair. These colors are called certified colors and are accepted by the Food and Drug Administration (FDA) for use in foods, drugs and cosmetics.

Temporary colors do not require that a predisposition or patch test (test for allergic reaction) be performed to determine if the client is sensitive or allergic to the product, since temporary colors do not contain aniline derivative substances.

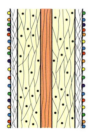

LARGE COLOR MOLECULES COAT THE CUTICLE

COLOR APPLICATION

FINAL COLOR RESULT

A polymer is a chemical compound or mixture of compounds that consists of many molecules in a long chain-like structure. It is found in many products including nonoxidative and oxidative hair colors. It can add shine or conditioning qualities to the hair or it can be used as a thickening agent in a hair coloring product. When applied to the hair, it acts as a coating.

Temporary colors, also known as color rinses, are made in a variety of different forms, including: weekly rinses, color mousses, color gels, color crayons, mascaras, color pomades, spray-on colors, color shampoos and rinses. Unlike other color products, once you apply temporary hair colors to the hair, you do not rinse the color. Temporary colors are simply applied to clean, towel-blotted hair, which is then finished as desired with the color remaining on the hair until the next shampoo.

Weekly rinses are generally applied at the shampoo bowl and are used to add tone to faded hair, neutralize unwanted tones or to temporarily add color to the hair without creating a chemical change.

Color mousses and gels come in a variety of colors and are used to brighten the existing color, tone gray hair and create dramatic effects. Since mousses are also designed to add volume to the hair, they aid in the designing process.

Color crayons and mascaras come in a variety of colors and are used for a number of effects ranging from blending in the new growth to creating fun, colorful designs.

Pomades also come in a variety of colors and, aside from adding shine to the hair, can add tone or create special color effects on the hair.

Spray-on colors come in an aerosol can, which may become flammable. Spray-on colors come in a multitude of colors and are a quick and easy way to add color to the hair for special effects.

Color-enhancing shampoos and conditioners are used to maintain the existing color after a color service or to add tones to the hair. They are also used to eliminate unwanted tones.

SEMI-PERMANENT COLORS
Semi-permanent colors deposit color and cannot lighten the hair. Since semi-permanent colors do not use chemicals to alter the hair, depending on the color chosen and porosity of the hair these colors will fade with each shampoo, leaving no line of demarcation. A line of demarcation is represented by an obvious difference between two colors along a hair strand, which can result from new growth or from overlapping product onto previously color-treated hair. Because semi-permanent colors leave no line of demarcation as they fade, retouches are not required. Semi-permanent colors use a direct-dye process, which requires no mixing—the color you see in the bottle is the color that is deposited on the hair. Semi-permanent colors contain small and large color molecules. The small color molecules are able to penetrate the cuticle layer of the hair and enter the cortex, instead of just coating the hair strand as with temporary colors.

A wide array of semi-permanent colors, referred to as glosses or color enhancers, are used to create subtle to dramatic color changes. They can add tone or deepen the existing color, refresh a faded hair color or neutralize unwanted tones. They can cover small percentages of gray hair and are used for blending higher percentages of gray. Semi-permanent colors can have a longer lasting effect when heat is applied to porous hair. **Although these types of hair colors are not mixed with a developer, a predisposition test for allergic reactions is required if the product contains an aniline derivative ingredient.** This type of test is explained and outlined later in the chapter.

Depending on the ingredients in the product and the porosity of the hair, repeated applications of semi-permanent colors may alter the structure of the hair, especially when applied to hair that has been previously treated with chemicals, such as permed or relaxed hair.

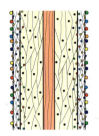

SMALL COLOR MOLECULES COAT THE CUTICLE, PENETRATE CORTEX

COLOR APPLICATION

FINAL COLOR RESULT

White
Light Field
Medium Light Field
Medium Field
Medium Dark Field
Dark Field
Dark/50% Gray

NONOXIDATIVE
Applying different manufacturers' nonoxidative products on different fields of hair color swatches allows you to analyze the results before working on clients. Remember, these products cannot lighten the existing hair color. The resulting color is a combination of the color applied and the existing hair color.

> Oxidative colors are not designed to lift or lighten artificial pigment. Color removers and dye solvents are designed to lift artificial pigment.

OXIDATIVE COLORS

Oxidative colors deposit color, or lift (lighten) and deposit color in a single-process technique. Oxidative colors are mixed with an oxidant (developer) to create a chemical change that has a longer-lasting effect than that of semi-permanent colors. There are two major classifications of oxidative colors: oxidative colors without ammonia, and oxidative colors with ammonia. Fillers act as a companion product to oxidative colors.

Oxidative colors without ammonia are also known as long-lasting semi-permanent (demi-permanent) which are designed to add tone or darken the existing hair color.

TONE

DARKEN AND TONE

Oxidative colors with ammonia are also known as permanent hair colors and are designed to add tone or darken the existing level to achieve a darker result. Oxidative colors with ammonia can also lighten and add tone to natural hair pigments to achieve a lighter result in a single process.

LIGHTEN AND TONE

Available in a wide range of levels and tones, manufacturers label their products with the level system and with descriptive words similar to the fields of color. Consider the fields of color a general classification and levels a more specific description of the lightness or darkness of the product. Keep in mind that darker oxidative colors contain more pigment, while lighter colors contain less pigment but have greater lifting ability.

DARK		MEDIUM DARK		MEDIUM		MEDIUM LIGHT		LIGHT	
1	2	3	4	5	6	7	8	9	10

COSMETOLOGY FUNDAMENTALS

LONG-LASTING SEMI-PERMANENT (DEMI-PERMANENT) COLORS

Long-lasting semi-permanent colors use a low volume of hydrogen peroxide to develop the color molecules and aid in color processing. Long-lasting semi-permanent colors are designed to deposit color, add tone to the hair, but not lift (lighten) the existing hair color. Long-lasting semi-permanent products contain small color molecules that penetrate the cortex, some of which join or link together. **Long-lasting semi-permanent products generally last 4 to 6 weeks depending on the porosity of the client's hair,** giving this process a longer-lasting effect than the results achieved with nonoxidative color products.

Long-lasting semi-permanent products contain very little or no ammonia, which is the reason these products do not achieve lift or lighten the hair. Color products require an alkaline substance such as ammonia to create lift.

Long-lasting semi-permanent colors are available in liquid, cream and gel forms. Since most long-lasting semi-permanent colors contain aniline derivatives, a predisposition test is required. **Long-lasting semi-permanent color products are also referred to as deposit only demi-permanent, or oxidative without ammonia colors.**

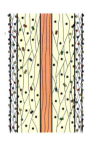
SMALL COLOR MOLECULES ENTER THE CORTEX; SOME COUPLE TOGETHER

COLOR APPLICATION

FINAL COLOR RESULT

PERMANENT COLORS

Permanent hair colors are mixed with hydrogen peroxide and are capable of both lightening natural pigment and depositing artificial pigment in a single process. Permanent hair colors can also add tone or darken the existing hair color. They are sometimes called oxidative tints with ammonia or aniline derivative tints. Paraphenylenediamine (para-**PHE**-ni-line-i-**DIA**-min) and paratoluenediamine (para-tol-**U**-ene-i-**DIA**-min) are two types of dye intermediates, either one of which can be found in permanent tints.

Nonoxidative colors and oxidative color formulas with low volume developers are a good choice for clients who relax their hair.

Permanent hair colors contain small colorless molecules (paradyes) that become colored when mixed with hydrogen peroxide. Once they are applied to the hair, the oxidative color swells the hair strand. The small colored molecules enter the hair with the aid of an alkaline substance (alkalizing ingredient) such as ammonia. Then, as they oxidize in the cuticle and the cortex, they link or couple together to form permanent colored molecules. When this happens, they are permanently anchored in the hair.

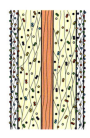

SMALL COLOR MOLECULES ENTER THE CORTEX; SOME COUPLE TOGETHER

COLOR APPLICATION

FINAL COLOR RESULT

It is the combination of the ammonia in permanent hair colors and hydrogen peroxide that allow for the lift and lightening of the hair's natural color. The stronger the hydrogen peroxide, the greater the lift achieved. Permanent hair colors, as the name implies, are permanent. In some instances, products such as a color remover or dye solvent can be used to remove unwanted artificial pigment. Once you have removed the unwanted pigment, you may recolor the hair as desired.

Permanent hair colors have become one of the most popular color products used in the salon, since they offer the colorist a wide range of color possibilities. The colorist can choose from many levels and tones to create an infinite number of hair colors. They are mixed with various strengths of developer, depending on the desired amount of lift and/or deposit. Generally, most permanent hair colors are mixed with 20 volume (6%) hydrogen peroxide. High-lift tints are designed to achieve lighter colors and are generally mixed with a double amount of 30 volume (9%) or 40 volume (12%) hydrogen peroxide. When mixing permanent hair colors, be sure to follow the manufacturer's directions since changing either the amount or the volume of the peroxide can affect the lift and deposit achieved.

As a general rule, 10 volume (3%) peroxide is used for deposit and minimal lift, 20 volume (6%) lifts two levels, 30 volume (9%) lifts three levels. The resulting color will be a combination of the pigment remaining (contributing pigment) and the artificial color that is deposited.

If you are not able to achieve the desired amount of lift using a single-process color, prelightening may be required.

Permanent hair colors come in three forms: liquids, creams and gels. Liquid hair colors are thinner than creams and gels and are generally applied with a bottle. They may contain fewer conditioning agents and greater ammonia content. These types of colors have good penetration ability. Cream hair colors are generally mixed with a cream developer and are applied with a bowl and brush technique.

ALERT!

Since permanent colors contain aniline derivatives, a predisposition test (patch test) is required.

COSMETOLOGY FUNDAMENTALS

They have conditioners and thickening agents. The consistency of gel colors is somewhere between that of a liquid and a cream. Gel colors are more penetrating than cream colors but have fewer conditioning agents. Gel colors have the same or more penetrating ability than liquids.

OXIDATIVE COLORS

Applying different manufacturers' oxidative products on different fields of hair color swatches allows you to analyze the results before working on clients. Remember, these products can add tone or darken the hair, or they can lighten and add tone to the hair in a single process. The resulting color is a combination of the color applied and the existing hair color.

TONERS

Toners are light pastel colors used to add warmness or coolness to prelightened hair. Toners are used to deposit color and neutralize unwanted pigment remaining after prelightening, such as brassy golds or yellows. Permanent toners are mixed with low volumes of developer. Nonoxidative toners are not mixed with developer and can be used where there is a mixture of natural and prelightened hair, such as after a highlight service.

The degree of prelightening will help determine the level of toner to be applied. All toners should be selected in relation to the law of color. As you know, complementary colors—colors across from one another on the color wheel—will neutralize one another. For instance, a violet-based toner will produce a light neutral blond on prelightened pale yellow hair. Remember to perform a strand test in order to predict results accurately. Since toners contain aniline derivatives, a predisposition test is also required.

COLOR APPLICATION

FINAL COLOR RESULT

FILLERS

Fillers provide an even base color by filling in porous, damaged or abused areas with materials such as protein or polymers. They equalize the porosity of the hair and deposit base color in one application. Although fillers are not considered oxidative colors, they are designed to be used prior to or in conjunction with oxidative colors.

Fillers come in a variety of colors and are generally chosen to replace the missing primary color. There are two types of fillers: conditioning and color. **Conditioning fillers** are used to recondition damaged hair prior to a color service. The color is then applied right over the filler and they both process simultaneously. **Color fillers** are used on damaged hair and when there is a question as to whether or not the color will hold, such as with porous hair.

Fillers have many advantages and will:
- Give more uniform color in a tint back (returning hair to its natural color)
- Deposit color on faded hair and ends
- Help hair hold color
- Prevent off-color results
- Prevent a dull color appearance

Extremely damaged hair may absorb more color than normal, but it also has a hard time holding on to these color molecules.

BEFORE

FILLER APPLICATION

COLOR APPLICATION

FINAL COLOR RESULT

Fillers can be applied directly to the hair before an oxidative color or they can be mixed with the color formula.

CONCENTRATES, INTENSIFIERS AND DRABBERS
Concentrates, intensifiers and drabbers are names given to products designed to increase the vibrancy of a color formula or to neutralize unwanted tones from the contributing pigment. They are concentrated colors (pigments) that can be mixed into the color formula or they can be applied directly to prelightened hair to create a desired result. These products come in a variety of colors such as yellow, red, blue, orange, violet, green, silver and ash. Concentrates can be used to brighten or neutralize tones while intensifiers are used to brighten and drabbers to neutralize tones.

LIGHTENERS

Lighteners, also known as bleach, are used to decolorize, remove or diffuse pigment. They can be used to create the final color result or create a new pigment on which to build the final hair coloring. Lighteners utilize ingredients such as ammonia and peroxide to facilitate the oxidation process. When this mixture is added to the hair it penetrates the cortex, causing the melanin to break into smaller pieces before removing or diffusing the color. The longer this lightening solution remains in contact with the hair, the more the melanin changes. Lighteners are generally applied to dry hair and are classified as either on-the-scalp lighteners or off-the-scalp lighteners.

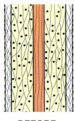
BEFORE

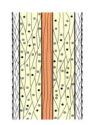
LIGHTENER APPLICATION DIFFUSES MELANIN

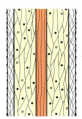
AFTER

DEGREES OF DECOLORIZATION

As natural hair is lightened, the eumelanin and pheomelanin pigments are decolorized and the hair goes through degrees of decolorization, or stages of lightening. Dark hair goes through approximately 10 stages or degrees of decolorization. The main degrees to look for are: red-orange, orange, yellow-orange (gold), yellow, pale yellow and palest yellow. Keep in mind that the **hair should never be lightened to white because this could cause extreme damage.** If the hair is overlightened, a toner may make the hair appear ashy, gray or cool, since most of the warm tones will be missing.

Black | Dark Red-Brown | Red-Brown | Red | Red-Orange | Orange | Yellow-Orange (Gold) | Yellow | Pale Yellow | Palest Yellow

There are no established times for how long it takes to lighten hair to any given degree. Time for decolorizing always varies with the individual client due to the amount, size, type and distribution of natural pigment as well as the texture and porosity of the hair. Different manufacturers' products may also have an effect on timing. The best way to find out the correct time, as well as to determine if the hair is in proper condition for lightening, is to perform a preliminary strand test and follow manufacturer's directions.

DOUBLE-PROCESS

If the desired color result is different from what can be achieved with decolorizing alone, color can be applied to recolorize the hair to the shade desired which is called a **double-process technique**. Before starting the decolorizing (lightening) and recolorizing (adding pigment back into the hair after decolorizing) process, you need to know the desired color result. This allows you to determine the proper degree of decolorization and the degree of new pigment you will need to add in order to produce the result you and your client want. Two common reasons for recolorizing are either to add more intensity or to neutralize the remaining contributing pigment. In either case, refer to the law of color and remember it is the combination of the color you apply and the contributing pigment that creates the final color result.

BEFORE

LIGHTENER APPLICATION
DECOLORIZES

TONER APPLICATION
RECOLORIZES

FINAL COLOR RESULT

The double-process technique involves two steps:
1. The hair is decolorized, or prelightened, to the desired degree, which is referred to as the contributing pigment. Decolorizing your client's hair is necessary when you want to lighten the natural pigment dramatically (more than 3-4 levels) to achieve dramatic finishes. You can lighten selected strands, areas within the design or the entire design.
2. The hair is recolorized by applying hair color to create the final color result. The hair color can be an oxidative color, a nonoxidative color or a toner.

The type of lightener you choose for your client depends on whether you will be applying product on the scalp, as in a full design, or off the scalp, as in highlighting.

ON-THE-SCALP LIGHTENERS
On-the-scalp lighteners are mild enough to be applied directly on the scalp and are available in two forms: oil and cream. Both of these lighteners have a pH around 9 and can be mixed with an activator (accelerator, booster) to increase the speed of the oxidation process. The main difference between oil and cream lighteners is their consistency. Besides having a thicker consistency, which prevents the product from dripping, cream lighteners also contain conditioners.

OFF-THE-SCALP LIGHTENERS
Off-the-scalp lighteners come in powder form and, when mixed with hydrogen peroxide, become a strong lightening product. As a general rule, off-the-scalp lighteners are stronger and work faster than on-the-scalp lighteners. Because they have no added oils or creams, they can irritate the scalp, causing burns and blisters. They are generally used for off-the-scalp procedures, such as freeform painting. Some powder lighteners contain buffering agents and conditioners, which allow them to be used on and off the scalp. To ensure client safety, always read the manufacturer's directions.

Some powder lighteners have color pigment already included in their mixture. These lighteners may be used to add desired tones or neutralize certain tones. These lighteners may be used to create the final color or to lighten the hair before recolorizing.

DECOLORIZING

Applying lightener to several swatches of dark hair and watching the hair decolorize will give you a better understanding of the stages or degrees of lightening. Removing the lightener at each degree will help you understand the amount of time it takes dark hair to decolorize to each degree, while allowing you to analyze the contributing pigment at each degree. The type of lightener you use, the strength of developer, and the length of time it remains on the hair will influence your results. Note that the lighter fields of hair color go through fewer degrees of decolorization and will, therefore, take less time to reach the lighter shades.

RECOLORIZING

Taking the decolorization process one step further by recolorizing the hair will enable you to see the role the contributing pigment plays on the final color result. Remember, it is a combination of the contributing pigment plus the artificial color applied that creates the final color result. Recolorizing the hair with toners to achieve warm, cool and neutral results will help you train your eye to the nuances of color. When using nonoxidative colors, vibrant results can be achieved. On these swatches, the original level is at the top followed by the decolorized degree without a toner. The remaining swatches were decolorized to the same degree, then recolorized to achieve various tonal results.

DEVELOPERS

Developers, with a pH of 2.5 to 4.5, are oxidizing agents used with demi-permanent and permanent colors, lighteners and toners. A developer may be referred to as a catalyst or conductor and needs to be mixed with ammonia or other alkaline compounds to become ac Developers come in a variety of strengths (volumes or percentages) and consistencies (liqui creams). Generally, lower strengths of developers are used for depositing, while higher stren are used to achieve greater lift. Follow the manufacturer's directions when selecting the stre and the amount of developer to use with an oxidative color. **Hydrogen peroxide (H_2O_2) is th** most commonly used developer (oxidizing agent) in hair coloring products.

13

> **ALERT!**
> Increasing the strength of hydrogen peroxide in a formula beyond the manufacturer's recommendations may cause damage to the hair and chemical burns to the skin and scalp.

In the United States developers are measured by volume, such as 10, 20, 30 and 40 volume, while in Europe they are measured by percentage, such as 3%, 6%, 9% and 12%. The strength of hydrogen peroxide or other developer you choose for your color formula will depend upon the amount of lift or deposit you desire, as well as what the color manufacturer recommends. The lower the volume, the less lift that will be achieved; the higher the volume, the more lift that will be achieved. It is important to immediately begin applying a color product that has been mixed with developer since the oxidation process begins immediately upon mixing them.

Demi-permanent colors are designed to deposit color, therefore, a low volume of developer (under 10 volume 3%) would be used to achieve minimal lift. On the other hand, a high-lift permanent tint may require 40 volume (12%) to achieve a greater amount of lift. Generally, 20 volume (6%) is used with the majority of hair coloring products. Always follow the manufacturer's directions for the proportional ratio when mixing color with developer, which may vary from manufacturer to manufacturer. Perform a strand test to avoid any problems.

Mixing hydrogen peroxide in a metal bowl may cause it to become weak. The metal ions in a metal bowl will have an adverse reaction with the hydrogen peroxide. **Therefore, always mix the formula in a glass or plastic bowl.**

Manufacturer recommendations will indicate the shelf life (usually 3 years) of hydrogen peroxide and instruct that it be stored in a cool, dry place.

If lower volumes of developer are not available, you can dilute 20 volume (6%) hydrogen peroxide with zero volume (0%) hydrogen peroxide using the following guidelines:

- 15 vol (4.5%). . . . . . . .3 parts 20 vol H_2O_2 + 1 part 0 vol (0%)
- 10 vol (3%) . . . . 1 part 20 vol H_2O_2 + 1 part 0 vol (0%)
- 5 vol (1.5%). . . . . . . .1 part 20 vol H_2O_2 + 3 parts 0 vol (0%)

For example: If 1 part = ¼ oz then 3 parts = ¾ oz

Cream developer may be diluted with zero volume cream developer while liquid developer may be diluted with distilled water.

Developer Strengths

40 vol = 12%
30 vol = 9%
20 vol = 6%
10 vol = 3%

Applying different volumes of developers with lightener on the same color hair for the same amount of time will allow you to analyze the resulting effects of the various strengths of developers. Lower volumes decolorize more slowly and higher volumes decolorize more quickly.

COSMETOLOGY FUNDAMENTALS

VEGETABLE, METALLIC AND COMPOUND DYES

Vegetable, metallic and compound dyes are the least common types of hair coloring products used in the salon today. Although there are some areas of the world that use vegetable dyes in the salon, metallic and compound dyes are discouraged since they are unreliable and, sometimes, unsafe.

VEGETABLE DYES

Vegetable dyes utilize natural products to color the hair. **The most common vegetable dye is known as henna, which, in its purest form, produces reddish highlights in the hair.** One of the oldest forms of hair coloring, henna is derived from the Egyptian privet plant. To create colors other than red, henna can be mixed with other substances, such as metals.

After a few applications, henna can penetrate the cortex of the hair and build up. When this happens, the color is permanent since the molecules are anchored in the cortex. **Hair that has been colored with henna sometimes cannot be permed since the resulting build-up doesn't allow the neutralizing solution to penetrate evenly.** Since there is not a reliable product available to completely remove henna from the hair, it is usually best to wait until the hair has grown out to perform a chemical service.

Chamomile is another vegetable product used to color the hair. It is found in shampoos and after-shampoo rinses and is relatively harmless to the hair. Chamomile produces a yellow stain on the hair, which resembles golden highlights.

METALLIC DYES

Metallic dyes are known as progressive dyes because the hair turns darker with each application. These are not considered a professional product, since their use is not recommended. The reason metallic dyes are not recommended is that the metals in the product do not mix successfully with other chemicals used in salon services, such as perm solutions. The result of mixing these products can cause discoloration and breakage. To avoid any problems with chemical services, it is advisable to cut hair that has been colored with metallic dye.

Depending on the metals used, these dyes may fade into peculiar or unnatural shades. With exposure to the sun and chlorine, silver dyes may appear to have a green cast, lead dyes a purple cast and copper dyes a red cast.

COMPOUND DYES

Compound dyes are a combination of metallic and vegetable dyes. Metallic salts are added to vegetable dyes to create a wider range of colors and a longer-lasting color than achieved with vegetable dyes alone. Compound dyes tend to be unpredictable and they are incompatible with other chemical services in the salon. Refer to "Infection Control and Safety" within this chapter for a description of how to test for metallic salts.

DESIGNING COLOR

Now you are ready to learn about designing color. Keep in mind that the color design is a part of the total composition, which also includes the other design elements of form and texture. Designing color includes the identification of the existing and desired color, along with the patterns, shapes and techniques that will be used to create the color design. A thorough conversation with the client is of utmost importance to ensure that you will produce what the client has in mind. When creating color designs, understanding how to break down a color design composition using the levels of observation will allow you to not only better communicate with your client, but it will also help you develop a keen eye for color.

BASIC

At the basic level you are looking at a color design and identifying if what you see is a light, medium or dark hair color. It may be the same color throughout or consist of a combination of colors. Visualizing the design in black and white can be helpful when determining its lightness or darkness.

DETAIL

Looking a bit closer will help you identify the family of hair color and the warmth or coolness of the hair. Is it a light, warm brown or a medium, cool brown? Is it a warm red, or a cool red?

ABSTRACT

Finally, at the abstract level, you imagine the placement of color to create the effects you see. A color graphic is a representation of the color scheme that identifies the placement of colors, patterns and shapes that were used to create the color design.

SCULPTED FORM

The sculpted form may serve as an inspiration for color placement. The smooth, interior surfaces of the solid and graduated forms offer a canvas for achieving maximum light reflection with a repetition of color. When more than one color is added to the surface, textural qualities are achieved. The activated surfaces of the increase-layered and uniformly layered forms can be further enhanced when multiple colors are used within the design.

EXISTING/DESIRED LEVEL

Identifying the existing and desired levels and where to position lights and/or darks can be an easy way to think about color placement before thinking about the design in color.

Questions you can ask include:
- Should I go lighter or darker, or stay in the same level and just add tone?
- Should I create textural interest by breaking up the light reflection with an alternation of colors?
- Should I create a dramatic effect by using contrasting colors?

ZONAL PATTERNS

Zonal patterns are patterns that subdivide the head into multiple areas to create a color design with a combination of colors. The fringe, top, crown, nape and perimeter are all examples of areas or zones that can be isolated and colored. Depending on the desired effect, keep in mind that some zones may be left natural. Color can create a focal point and interest within a color design ranging from subtle to dramatic.

COLOR WITHIN SHAPES

Aside from subdividing the head into zones, shapes are used to create color designs or patterns. The size and position of the shapes are determined by your design decision. Shapes used to create color designs include the rectangle, triangle and circle. These shapes may contain one or multiple colors depending upon the desired effect.

COLOR APPLICATION TECHNIQUES

Color application techniques are described according to the placement of color along the strand: base, midstrand, ends or any combination.

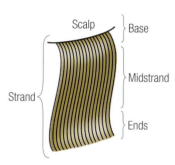

BASE TO ENDS (DARKER RESULT)

A base-to-ends application is used when you want to add tone to or darken the existing color along the entire strand. A base-to-ends application is also known as a virgin darker technique. The same procedure is used for both nonoxidative and oxidative colors.

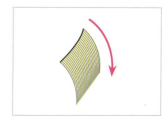

MIDSTRAND TO ENDS THEN BASE (LIGHTER RESULT)

The midstrand-to-ends-then-base technique is used to lighten the existing color by applying the new color or lightener to the midstrand, generally ½" (1.25 cm) away from the scalp, then up to but not including any porous ends. The product is applied to the base and porous ends later, since they will lighten faster. The base area lightens faster for two reasons: First, the new growth is not fully keratinized and is more receptive to chemical processes. Second, the heat from the scalp will accelerate processing time. When the hair is halfway to the desired degree of lightness, newly mixed product is then applied at the base. If your client's hair has porous ends, they will probably be lighter and won't need as much processing time as the midstrand. **The midstrand-to-ends-then-base application is also known as a virgin lighter technique.**

BASE (RETOUCH)

A base application is used for a retouch color service. During a retouch color service, color or lightener is applied to the new growth only to match the existing color, unless manufacturer's directions state otherwise. To maintain a consistent color and to prevent breakage, avoid overlapping product onto the previously colored hair, which may also result in a line of demarcation.

DIMENSIONAL COLORING TECHNIQUES

Not all color designs require a complete all-over color change. In many instances you may wish to break up the light reflection to create depth, dimension and the illusion of texture. In these instances, you can choose more than one color to add to the design. **Dimensional coloring** involves the positioning of highlights and/or lowlights on the surface of the hair or to selected strands throughout the design to create special effects.

The main idea in dimensional coloring involves the theory that darker colors recede and add depth, while lighter colors come forward and add brightness to the design. Note that the same hair color can appear lighter (highlight) or darker (lowlight), depending upon its surrounding color.

After determining the pattern or shape you will use to position the dimensional color, you will need to select the appropriate techniques to achieve the desired results. Widely used dimensional color techniques include weaving and slicing, in which isolated strands are lightened or darkened. Making isolated strands lighter is known as **highlighting** and making isolated strands darker is known as **lowlighting**. Freeform painting, generally performed on the surface of the hair, end lights, performed on the ends of the hair, and the cap method are additional dimensional coloring techniques that can be used for highlighting and lowlighting the hair.

WEAVING AND SLICING

Weaving and slicing techniques are generally used to add depth and dimension to the existing hair color. Lightener and/or color are used to create a highlighted or lowlighted effect. The number and size of weaves and/or slices within a design and the color chosen will determine the degree of lightness or darkness achieved.

With the **weaving technique**, a tail comb is used to weave out selected strands in an alternating pattern. These strands are then positioned over a piece of foil or thermal strip and the lightener or color is then applied. The woven strands are generally enclosed in foil or thermal strips to isolate them from the remaining hair.

The size of the weave refers to the amount of hair selected, while the density pattern refers to the amount of weaves within a particular area. The depth of the weave also influences the amount of hair selected. To ensure that highlights will be visible on curly hair, a medium or thick (chunky) weaving technique is used.

MEDIUM WEAVE

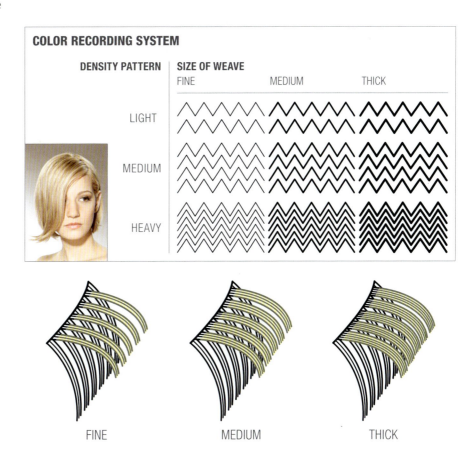

With the **slicing technique**, the tail comb is used to part off a straight line through the hair. These strands are then positioned over a piece of foil or thermal strip and the lightener or color is then applied. The foil or thermal strip is then folded to isolate the selected strands from the remaining hair.

FINE SLICE

COLOR RECORDING SYSTEM

DENSITY PATTERN	SIZE OF SLICE		
	FINE	MEDIUM	THICK
LIGHT	—— —— ——	—— —— ——	━━ ━━ ━━
MEDIUM	—— —— —— ——	—— —— —— ——	━━ ━━ ━━ ━━
HEAVY	—— —— —— —— —— ——	—— —— —— —— —— ——	━━ ━━ ━━ ━━ ━━ ━━

The size of a slice refers to the amount of hair selected, while the density pattern refers to the number of slices within a particular area. As a general rule, the finer the slice, the more blended the appearance. The thicker the slice, the bolder the color appearance.

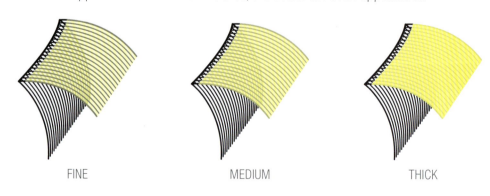

FINE   MEDIUM   THICK

When you select foils for either procedure, you will want to make sure they are wider and longer than the section you are weaving or slicing. If the sections become too wide, the hair product may seep out of the foil and cause "bleeding" or "spotting" on the untreated hair. If this happens, you can apply a darker color to the spotted hair to return it to the appropriate color.

FREEFORM PAINTING

Freeform painting is a technique in which a tool is used to strategically position color or lightener on the hair. Depending on the colors chosen, this can create a highlighted or lowlighted effect to either imitate the sun's natural lightening abilities or to create textural qualities, without a visible line of demarcation as the hair grows out.

When using the freeform painting technique, it is usually applied with a brush and painted on the surface of the hair vertically and in an alternating pattern. For this reason, freeform painting is also referred to as surface painting.

A color tool such as a stryper comb can be used instead of a brush to add color to the hair. Freeform painting can be used as a lowlighting technique to reduce the amount of gray and is an ideal option for clients who may not want an all-over color change.

When performed underneath the surface of the hair, freeform painting techniques can create an impression of inner lights, depending on how the hair moves.

END LIGHTS

Dimensional coloring can also be achieved by lightening only the ends of the hair, known as **end lights**. Lightener is applied to the ends only in a freeform, yet controlled, pattern.

COSMETOLOGY FUNDAMENTALS

Another way to create end lights is to add lightener to a sheet of foil. Then simply buff the foil across the surface in a back-and-forth motion to apply the product to the ends. This technique is also called shoe shining.

CAP METHOD

Another way to create highlights and/or lowlights is with the **cap method**. A crochet hook is used to pull hair strands through a perforated cap. The amount and the density of the strands pulled through the cap will determine whether a light or heavy amount of highlights or lowlights will be achieved.

After the hair strands are pulled through the holes in the perforated cap, lightener or color is then applied to the selected strands. If lightener is used, some manufacturers may recommend that a plastic bag or cap be positioned over the color-treated hair to facilitate processing and keep the product moist since the perforated cap reduces available body heat. Once the desired result has been achieved, the product is removed. If a permanent toner is used, shampoo and towel-dry the hair with the cap in place. Then apply toner to the prelightened strands. Process and rinse. Remove the cap and shampoo. If a semi-permanent toner is used, you can remove the cap, shampoo, towel-dry the hair and then apply toner to the entire head. Remove according to manufacturers' directions.

Highlighting or lowlighting with the cap method is generally performed on shorter hair, no longer than 6" (15 cm). Since the lightener will not come into contact with the scalp, this method is ideal when you want to avoid product touching the client's scalp. A powder or off-the-scalp lightener may be used as well as on-the-scalp lightener or color to achieve the desired results.

RETOUCH FOR DIMENSIONAL COLORING TECHNIQUES

Dimensional coloring will usually require a retouch application anywhere from 3 to 8 weeks after the original service, depending on the desired effect. If the untreated area at the base does not take away from the overall design, a retouch service could be done as long as 10 to 12 weeks after the original service.

Retouches may consist of introducing new highlights into the same area or applying lightener to the base area of previously lightened strands. If you select previously lightened strands, you will apply lightener only to the base area (new growth) and remove the ends from the foil before folding. With shorter hair, you will fold the foil upward just enough to cover the previously treated hair. Then you will fold the foil again to cover the product. This folding method will prevent the previously treated hair from coming into contact with the product.

HAIR COLOR ESSENTIALS

To perform professional color procedures, you need a selection of products, tools, supplies and equipment. Color products are produced by many different manufacturers, are disposable and must be frequently replaced. Employers are required to make Material Safety Data Sheets (MSDS) for all products available for your reference and use in the salon. Color tools are the hand-held tools you use. They must be disinfected or discarded after every use. Color equipment includes the furnishings and provisions necessary to provide a professional color service.

COLOR PRODUCTS

PRODUCTS	FUNCTION
NONOXIDATIVE	
TEMPORARY	Adds tonal value or highlights to specific areas; color washes out when hair is shampooed
SEMI-PERMANENT	Adds tonal value and imparts shine, but does not lighten the natural melanin; gradually fades, lasting up to 4 to 6 shampoos; can have a longer-lasting effect on porous hair or when heat is applied; can have a permanent effect on chemically relaxed and lightened hair
OXIDATIVE	
LONG-LASTING SEMI-PERMANENT/ DEMI-PERMANENT	Adds tone or darkens the existing color but does not lighten the natural melanin or previously colored hair; retouches may be required every 4 to 6 weeks
PERMANENT	Tones, darkens or lightens natural melanin in a single process; cannot lighten previously colored hair; remains on the hair until it is cut off or removed by chemical means such as with a lightener or color remover; retouches may be required every 4 to 6 weeks
LIGHTENERS	
ON-THE-SCALP LIGHTENER	Lightens (decolorizes) melanin or artificial pigment; used to achieve colors not attainable with a single process; gentle enough to be used on the scalp
OFF-THE-SCALP LIGHTENER	Lightens (decolorizes) melanin; used for off-the-scalp techniques such as highlighting, surface painting and the cap method or to achieve colors not attainable with a single process
ADDITIONAL COLOR PRODUCTS	
HYDROGEN PEROXIDE	Aids in the formation of color dye molecules; used as an oxidizing agent in hair coloring; available in different strengths
FILLER	Evens out the porosity of the hair or creates an even base color for the final color service; used before a color service; can be added to the color formula to help the hair hold color and prevent off-color results

13

PRODUCTS ADDITIONAL COLOR PRODUCTS	FUNCTION
CONCENTRATE/ INTENSIFIER/DRABBER	Intensifies or neutralizes colors; mixed into the color formula; used alone on prelightened hair to create a vibrant color statement
BARRIER CREAM	Protects the client's skin from irritation and stains; used around the hairline, sometimes called protective cream
TALCUM POWDER	Allows gloves to be put on and taken off with ease; used inside gloves
COLOR STAIN REMOVER	Removes color stains from skin

OLOR TOOLS/SUPPLIES

TOOLS/SUPPLIES	FUNCTION
GLASS OR PLASTIC BOWL	Holds the color formula; some have an edge that can be used to rest the color brush and a rubber base that prevents the bowl from slipping; some also have a measurement guide that is used for accuracy in mixing; generally, a bowl-and-brush application is used when working with products that have a thick consistency
COLOR BRUSH	Consists of nylon bristles on one end that are used to apply the color; the other end is pointed and can be used to part the hair; brushes come in a variety of shapes and sizes and are chosen according to the area you are working in and the effects desired
PLASTIC APPLICATOR BOTTLE	Holds color formula; consists of a pointed end that is used to part the hair and apply (distribute) the color; marked with numbers that are used as a measuring guide; generally, a bottle application is used when working with products that have a thinner consistency
MEASURING DEVICE	Indicates the units of measurement in ounces (oz), milliliters (ml) or cubic centimeters (cc); used to measure the formula
FOIL/THERMAL STRIPS	Isolate woven or sliced strands of hair from the untreated hair during a color service; also prevent colors from intermixing

COSMETOLOGY FUNDAMENTALS

TOOLS/SUPPLIES	FUNCTION
TAIL COMB	Used for combing and parting the hair; fine teeth on one end are used for combing the hair and pointed end is used for parting the hair
WIDE-TOOTH COMB	Combs in color for special effects and detangles the hair
STRYPER COMB	Holds color; used to distribute color on the hair
CLIP	Controls the hair while coloring
PROTECTIVE CAPE	Protects the client and his or her clothing
NECK STRIP	Protects the skin from coming into direct contact with the cape
TOWELS	Used as part of the draping procedure to protect the client's clothing; used for the shampoo service
COTTON ROLL	Protects the client's eyes from product drips when positioned around hairline; used at the base in between partings to avoid product seepage during lightener applications; used to perform patch tests
PROTECTIVE APRON/ SMOCK FOR COLORIST	Protects colorist's clothing from stains
PROTECTIVE GLOVES	Protect the hands during chemical services; in some areas, wearing gloves during any service, especially chemical services, is mandatory—check with your area's regulatory agency
CHEMICAL RECORD CARD	Documents client's personal and color information

COLOR EQUIPMENT

EQUIPMENT	FUNCTION
ROLLABLE COLOR/ PRODUCT TABLE	Provides a place for laying out some color tools, supplies and products
HYDRAULIC CHAIR	Provides proper back support to the client during the color service; has a lever that can be used to adjust the height of the chair to ensure the proper level and comfort for the hair colorist

EQUIPMENT	FUNCTION
TIMER	Allows colorist to keep track of processing time
WET DISINFECTANT CONTAINER	Holds disinfectant for disinfecting tools such as combs
HOODED DRYER/ HEATED LAMPS/ ACCELERATOR MACHINES	Used to speed up the action of the coloring process
SHAMPOO BOWL/AREA	Used to rinse and shampoo client's hair; holds shampoo and conditioning products

INFECTION CONTROL AND SAFETY

The following is a list of safety precautions that you should always adhere to prior to and during a color service to protect the client and yourself.

1. Practice infection control guidelines including disinfection procedures. Protect yourself by wearing a cape and gloves and by washing your hands before and after each client visit.

2. Perform a patch test 24 to 48 hours prior to the application of an aniline derivative tint. See "Predisposition (Skin Patch) Test" later in this section.

3. Perform the color service only if the patch test is negative and there are no metallic or compound dyes present.

4. Protect the client's clothing with proper draping. See "Draping for a Color Service" later in this section.

5. Check the scalp for abrasions. Do not proceed with the service if there are any cuts or irritations.

6. Perform a preliminary strand test and subsequent strand tests as needed. See "Strand Tests" later in this section.

7. Do not brush the hair prior to the color service; doing so will irritate the scalp.

8. If pre-shampooing is necessary, use light manipulations and tepid (lukewarm) water.

9. Use sanitized applicator bottles, brushes and combs. Only use plastic or glass bowls to mix the color formula.

10. Once you've mixed the formula, use it immediately. Discard any leftover product once the service is completed.

11. Do not permit the product to come into contact with the eyes. If it does, rinse the eyes immediately with tepid water and refer the client to a physician.

12. Monitor the color process to assess color development and to prevent any stress to the skin, scalp or hair. If the client experiences discomfort, remove the product immediately.

13. During a retouch color service, avoid overlapping the product, especially with lightener; doing so may cause breakage.
14. Avoid leaving the client unattended during a hair color service.
15. Never color hair that has been colored with a product that contains metallic salts. To test for metallic salts, immerse a small strand of the client's hair in a solution of 1 oz. 20 volume (6%) peroxide and 20 drops of 28% ammonia (mix in a glass container). Check the results after 30 minutes. The most common reactions that indicate metallic salts are present are discoloration, a "gummy" feeling and/or a foul smell. Future chemical services cannot be performed unless the previously chemically treated hair is cut off.
16. Rinse the hair with lukewarm or cool water, never hot.
17. Do not use aniline derivative tints to color eyelashes or eyebrows; if product enters the eyes it may cause blindness.
18. Complete client record card, noting any allergies or adverse reactions the client may have experienced.

ALERT!
Always follow manufacturers' directions and read Material Safety Data Sheets (MSDS).

PREDISPOSITION (SKIN PATCH) TEST

According to the U.S. Federal Food, Drug and Cosmetic Act, **all color products containing an aniline derivative ingredient require a predisposition (skin patch) test 24 to 48 hours prior to the hair color service.** This test will help determine if the client is sensitive or allergic to certain chemicals in the hair color product.

Once the predisposition test has been performed, it is important to analyze the results. If the results are negative (no reaction), it means that the color formula may safely be used. Positive results include redness, swelling, blisters, itching, burning of the skin and/or respiratory distress. If the predisposition test results are positive, do not proceed with the service and have the client seek medical assistance.

PREDISPOSITION (PATCH OR SKIN PATCH) TEST GUIDELINES

INSIDE ELBOW   **BACK OF EAR**

CLEANSE AREA
- Wash and sanitize hands.
- Cleanse test area (inside of the elbow or behind the ear).

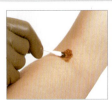

APPLY INTENDED FORMULA
- Apply intended color formula with cotton swab.
- Leave undisturbed for 24 hours.

CHECK FOR RESULTS
- Analyze results; determine if reaction is negative (no signs) or positive (signs of redness, swelling, blisters, itching or burning of the skin and/or respiratory distress).
- If reaction is negative, proceed with the service. If reaction is positive, do not proceed with the service.
- Record results on client record card.
- Clean work area.

DRAPING FOR A COLOR SERVICE

Keep in mind that draping for a chemical service is different from draping for a shampoo or hair sculpture service.

Proper draping is required in order to protect the client's skin and clothing during hair color services. Prior to draping the client, ask the client to remove neck jewelry, earrings and eyeglasses and store them in a safe place. To perform a proper draping procedure for a hair color service, you will need two towels and a plastic cape.

DRAPING GUIDELINES FOR A COLOR SERVICE

- Wash and sanitize hands.
- Have client remove jewelry.
- Clip client's hair out of the way.
- Turn the client's collar under.
- Cross towel over client's shoulders.
- Position cape over towel and fasten.
- Drape a second towel over cape.
- Detangle the hair and section according to the applicable service; avoid brushing the scalp.
- Apply barrier cream to entire hairline to prevent irritation and staining.
- Clean work area.

COSMETOLOGY FUNDAMENTALS 517

STRAND TESTS

A strand test is the process of isolating a section of hair for analysis. **A preliminary strand test is usually performed 24 to 48 hours before the actual hair color service to determine proper color formulation.** Another strand test, referred to as a color development strand test, is taken during the actual processing of a color application to monitor processing timing and to assess any stress on the hair or scalp.

A preliminary strand test can be performed immediately following a negative predisposition test. The important factors you'll discover by performing a strand test and analyzing the results prior to the service include:

- Correct formula and processing time to be used
- Reaction of the hair and what particular procedures may be needed to ensure proper color absorption (conditioning, filling, etc.)
- Possible presence of coating on the hair from previous applications that could be damaging or undesirable when new color is applied (metallic, henna, styling aid build-up, etc.)

The intended color formula is mixed and applied to a section of hair, somewhere that is visible for the client to see. You may do as many preliminary strand tests as necessary to achieve the desired result. For example, if the hair has not reached the desired degree (levels) of lightness, additional processing time and rechecking of the strand test would be required.

PRELIMINARY STRAND TEST GUIDELINES

- Wash and sanitize hands.
- Analyze the skin patch test results; if negative, proceed with preliminary strand test.
- Drape client for chemical service.
- Wear protective gloves and colorist apron.
- Isolate a small section of hair at the crown or another area of your choice (preferably an area where the results are visible to the client).
- Apply the intended color formula.
- Set the timer.
- Rinse out the color product from the test strand at the end of the processing time, then shampoo, rinse and dry the test strand.
- Analyze the results and make any necessary color formula adjustments. Perform another strand test if appropriate. Document your results.
- Clean color service area.

COLOR DEVELOPMENT STRAND TEST (DURING SERVICE) GUIDELINES

Strand testing during the processing time of the color service allows you to monitor color development and check for stress to the hair and scalp. You should perform strand tests in several areas, such as the most resistant area and the area of the initial application. Strand testing during processing is most often performed when you are working with oxidative colors and lighteners but can also be performed for nonoxidative colors. To perform a color development strand test, you will need a water bottle and white towel.

- Select a small section of hair.
- Position the selected strand on a towel.
- Spray water along the entire strand.
- Gently rub across the strand to remove the product thoroughly.
- Check results against a white towel.
- If results are desirable, rinse, shampoo and condition the hair.
- If results are not desirable, continue processing until proper results are achieved.

COLOR SERVICE ESSENTIALS

As with all hair services, communicating with your client prior to the actual service will ensure predictable results and will help you avoid any misunderstandings that may arise. Hair color swatches, magazines and pictures can be used as a guide while consulting with the client to reinforce the communication.

To avoid any false color analysis, be sure the area is well-lit, preferably in a room with a window. Proper lighting in the hair color area of the salon is essential for accurate analysis, color selection, application and final evaluation. Keep in mind that incandescent lighting generally makes the hair appear warmer, while fluorescent lighting makes the hair appear cooler. To create a more natural light reflection, use fluorescent lighting that is balanced for daylight.

Practice reflective listening skills by listening closely and then repeating what your client has said to you to avoid any misunderstandings.

CONNECT
- Meet and greet the client with a firm handshake and a pleasant voice.
- Communicate to build rapport and develop a relationship with the client.

CONSULT
- Ask questions to discover the client's needs and information about past color services. Open-ended questions such as, "What made you interested in a color service today?" can help you gain valuable insight into your client's wants and needs.

- Ask about clothing and lifestyle. Refer to *Chapter 8, Design Decisions,* for additional guidelines.
- Ask your client about maintaining the new color and make him or her aware of the financial commitment.
- Analyze client's face, body shape, physical features, eye and skin tones. Refer to *Chapter 8, Design Decisions,* for guidelines.
- Analyze the porosity and condition of the hair. Remember, you always want to maintain the best possible condition of the hair.
- Assess the facts and thoroughly think through your recommendations. Use photos, magazines and/or hair color swatches to better understand your client's desires. Don't be afraid to let your client know if you are unable to perform a service. Remember, not all requests are possible, even on healthy hair.
- Explain your recommended solutions and the price for today's service(s) and for future services as well.
- Ask additional questions related to the client's desired outcome if the client is hesitant about your recommendation.
- Gain feedback and approval from your client.

CREATE

- Ensure client protection by draping the client with towels and a chemical cape.
- Ensure client comfort during service.
- Stay focused on delivering the color service to the best of your ability.
- Teach the client how to perform at-home color care maintenance.

COMPLETE

- Reinforce guest's satisfaction with his or her overall experience.
- Make professional product recommendations to maintain the appearance and condition of your client's hair color, such as color shampoos and conditioners.
- Prebook guest's next appointment.
- End guest's visit with warm and personal goodbyes.
- Discard non-reusable materials, disinfect tools and arrange workstation in proper order.
- Wash your hands with liquid soap.
- Complete client record card with accurate information for future services and file it in a secure area with other record cards.
- Provide follow-up after the salon visit.

CLIENT RECORD CARD/RELEASE FORM

The key to successful client relationships that include ongoing hair color services and consistent chemical results is to keep accurate records. The client record card contains information such as the client's name, address and telephone number. The client record card also contains the color formulation and information about the condition of the client's hair and scalp. The client record card is used throughout the salon visit, from the communication period up until the client has left the salon.

A client release statement helps the school or salon owner avoid retribution as a result of any damages or accidents and may be required as part of some malpractice insurance policies. However, it is not a legal document and may not absolve the hair colorist from responsibility for any damage that may occur to the client's hair as a result of the chemical service.

PROMOTING AND RETAILING HAIR COLOR SERVICES

Credibility is the key to effective client communications. To build credibility with clients, you should become a personal advertisement for hair color services. In other words, having a good color design yourself will go a long way in selling that service. You must also be aware of basic color theory, use the best hair color products on the market and be able to communicate the value of hair color using current, professional terminology. Examples of professional terminology include:

- Lighten (versus bleach)
- Color (versus dye)
- Highlighting or weaving (versus frosting or streaking)

Rule number one in merchandising is to display your products and services. Because it may be impractical to display all your professional hair color products, you can certainly display your hair color services in other ways by:

- Decorating the salon with hair color pictures.
- Putting up signs at your workstation that promote hair color techniques in a positive and appealing way.

PRODUCT OVERVIEW

This portion of the chapter presents an overview of the hair color products you will use most often in the salon. Becoming familiar with these products will help prepare you for the many hair color service possibilities you'll encounter in the salon.

HAIR COLOR PRODUCTS

CATEGORY	LASTING POWER	FUNCTION	APPLICATION METHOD
NONOXIDATIVE (not mixed with developer)			
Temporary	From shampoo to shampoo	Deposits color	Base to ends at shampoo bowl; combed on
Semi-Permanent	4 to 6 shampoos; fades with each shampoo	Deposits color; adds shine; cannot lighten hair	Base to ends (heat may be required)
OXIDATIVE (mixed with developer)			
Demi-Permanent	Fades in 6 to 8 weeks New growth 6 to 8 weeks	Deposits color, but usually does not lighten hair	Base to ends (darker result) Base only
Permanent (also known as single-process tints)	Permanent New growth 3 to 6 weeks	Lightens and deposits color	Base to ends (darker result) Midstrand to porous ends, then base to ends (lighter result) Base only
LIGHTENERS (mixed with developer)			
On-the-Scalp	Permanent New Growth 3 to 6 weeks	Lightens existing hair color (safe enough to be used on scalp)	Midstrand to porous ends, then base and ends (lighter result) Base only
Off-the-Scalp	Permanent New growth 12 to 16 weeks	Lightens existing hair color (used off the scalp for special effects, i.e., highlighting, painting, etc.)	Slightly away from the scalp to the ends (lighter result) Base only

13

COLOR PROCEDURES OVERVIEW

By understanding the following color guidelines and procedures, you will be able to create an endless array of hair color designs for your clients. This section contains guidelines for applying a nonoxidative temporary rinse and semi-permanent color, followed by procedural overviews, which review the preparation, procedure and completion phases, for oxidative darker result, oxidative lighter result and double-process blond. The basic steps for a color procedure include, Section, Part, Apply, Test, Remove and Condition. Note, "Remove" may or may not include rinsing and shampooing the hair. Follow manufacturer's directions when removing hair color products. The *Color, A Designer's Approach* coursebook will show you step-by-step procedures for individual color services in greater detail.

NONOXIDATIVE TEMPORARY COLOR GUIDELINES

Temporary colors are usually applied to clean, towel-blotted hair and remain on the hair until the next shampoo. These colors are generally applied at the shampoo bowl with an applicator bottle because of their liquid consistency. Read the manufacturer's directions for application procedures. Listed below are general guidelines to follow for a temporary color rinse application.

- Wash and sanitize hands; gather and assemble color essentials; wear protective gloves and apron; drape the client for a color service.
- Shampoo and towel-blot the hair thoroughly.
- Apply color with an applicator bottle from scalp to ends for all-over coverage, or comb the color on for a blended effect.
- Blot excess color to prevent dripping; do not rinse the hair.
- Finish the hair design as desired.
- Record the results on the client record card; organize materials
- Clean workspace.

NONOXIDATIVE SEMI-PERMANENT COLOR GUIDELINES

For application and processing procedures, read manufacturer's directions, which may vary. Semi-permanent colors are usually applied to shampooed, towel-dried hair.

Retouches are scheduled whenever the color needs refreshing. An average is every 4 to 6 weeks but this is influenced by how frequently your client shampoos his or her hair, as well as how porous the hair is. When semi-permanent color needs refreshing, it is applied from base to ends, just like the original color application.

SEMI-PERMANENT COLOR GUIDELINES

- Part the hair into four sections
- Apply barrier cream
- Pour color into bottle
- Outline first back section
- Take 1" (2.5 cm) horizontal partings
- Apply color from base to midstrand, omitting porous ends
- Complete first section working from the top to the bottom
- Complete back section
- Outline front sections, then apply color to these sections from diagonal-back partings
- Apply color to remaining midstrand and ends
- Work color through for even saturation
- Apply cotton around hairline
- Place plastic cap over hair
- Position client under pre-heated dryer if applicable
- Set timer
- Perform strand test if desired
- Rinse, shampoo and remove any color stains
- Condition and finish hair design as desired
- Clean work area

OXIDATIVE COLOR: DARKER RESULT PROCEDURE OVERVIEW

When applying an oxidative color for a darker result, color is applied from base to ends. If the ends are porous, you may apply a filler to them first or delay application of color to the porous ends until later. This application technique is also called a virgin darker when it is performed for the first time. Retouches are applied to the base area only.

OXIDATIVE COLOR: DARKER RESULT PREPARATION

As with any professional service, it is important to have your area, products, tools, supplies and equipment in proper order. Before performing an oxidative hair color service, be sure to satisfy the following points:

- Perform predisposition test 24 to 48 hours before service (be guided by manufacturer's directions); if negative, proceed with hair color service
- Disinfect color area; arrange tools and supplies, including color bowl and brush, gloves, large-tooth comb, tail comb, sectioning clips, long-lasting oxidative hair colors, developer and barrier cream
- Wash and sanitize hands; drape the client for a color service; perform hair and scalp analysis; wear protective gloves and color apron; perform preliminary strand test
- Review previous client record card, if applicable

OXIDATIVE COLOR: DARKER RESULT PROCEDURE

- Apply barrier cream around hairline including top of ears
- **Section** the hair into four sections
- Measure and mix color formula
- Outline first back section
- **Part** the hair using ¼" (.6 cm) thick horizontal partings across back sections
- **Apply** color from base to ends; work from nape upward to top of section
    - Complete the section following the same procedures then outline hairline and bring hair down

OXIDATIVE COLOR: DARKER RESULT PROCEDURE (CONT'D)
- Repeat same color application on other back section
- **Apply** color to remaining front sections using diagonal-back partings; work from the top down; subdivide for control
  - Reapply around hairline, ensuring coverage, and bring hair down
  - Cross-check to ensure accurate product application
  - Remove any color stains on skin
- **Process** color according to manufacturer's instructions
- Perform a strand **test** to check color development
- Rinse and shampoo to **remove** color from hair and skin and **condition**
- Finish color design

OXIDATIVE COLOR: DARKER RESULT COMPLETION
- Reinforce guest's satisfaction with the overall experience.
- Make professional product recommendations.
- Prebook guest's next appointment.
- End guest's visit with warm and personal goodbyes.
- Discard non-reusable materials, disinfect tools and arrange workstation in proper order
- Wash your hands with liquid soap.
- Complete client record card.
- Provide follow-up after the salon visit.

OXIDATIVE COLOR: DARKER RESULT RETOUCH GUIDELINES

Depending on how fast your client's hair grows, retouches are generally performed every 6 to 8 weeks. Apply color to the new growth only. Do not overlap onto the previously colored hair. If the previously colored hair has faded, apply a semi-permanent or demi-permanent color in a matching shade.

OXIDATIVE COLOR: LIGHTER RESULT PROCEDURE OVERVIEW

When lightening your client's hair for the first time (virgin technique), the color is applied first from the midstrand out to the porous ends. The color is applied to the base area last, since the lightening action there is accelerated due to incomplete keratinization of the new growth as well as additional body heat at the base area. Very porous ends may also process faster and, therefore, require less processing time. The retouch application is at the base area only.

OXIDATIVE COLOR: LIGHTER RESULT PREPARATION

- Perform predisposition test 24 to 48 hours before service (be guided by manufacturer's directions); if negative, proceed with hair color service
- Disinfect color service area; arrange tools and supplies, including color bowl and brush, gloves, large-tooth comb, tail comb, sectioning clips, oxidative hair color(s), developer and barrier cream
- Wash and sanitize hands; drape the client for a color service; perform hair and scalp analysis; wear protective gloves and color apron; perform preliminary strand test; review previous client record card, if applicable

OXIDATIVE COLOR: LIGHTER RESULT PROCEDURE

- **Section** the hair into four sections; apply barrier cream around the hairline
- Measure and mix the formula
- Begin the application in the most resistant area, **part** using ¼" (.6 cm) thick partings and **apply** the color product ½" (1.25 cm) away from the scalp on both sides of the strand, out to the porous ends; if the ends are not porous, apply the color to the ends
  - Repeat same color application on remaining sections, working from the top of the section to the bottom
  - Cross-check to ensure even coverage and set the timer
- **Process** according to manufacturer's instructions
- Perform a color development strand **test**
- Apply newly mixed color product to the base and ends when the hair has reached 50% of the desired level, using the same parting pattern
- Set the timer and perform a color development strand test
- **Remove** color, rinsing thoroughly when the hair has reached the desired level; remove color stains around hairline; shampoo and **condition** hair
- Finish color design

OXIDATIVE COLOR: LIGHTER RESULT COMPLETION

See Oxidative Color: Darker Result Completion

OXIDATIVE COLOR: LIGHTER RESULT RETOUCH

New growth is more visible on lightened hair and generally requires more frequent retouches. Depending on the contrast between the lightened and the natural hair, some clients will need to schedule retouches every 3 to 6 weeks. Color is applied to the base area, avoiding the previously colored hair. If the remaining hair has faded, apply an oxidative product without ammonia in a matching tone to refresh the color.

DOUBLE-PROCESS PROCEDURE OVERVIEW

A double-process technique is a two-step process that involves lightening (decolorizing) the hair first and then recoloring the hair to the desired tone. **The lightener is first applied ½" (1.25 cm) away from the scalp out to the porous ends.** Once the color has reached approximately 50% of the desired lightness, a fresh mixture is applied to the base. If the ends are very porous, you will want to delay application of the lightener until after the base application, since the ends may develop more quickly. Generally ⅛" (.3 cm) horizontal partings are used throughout to ensure even penetration of product.

REMINDER
With a double-process technique, the lightener product is not applied immediately to the new growth because the body heat and incomplete keratinization near the scalp will cause the hair to lighten more quickly there, resulting in an uneven color formulation.

  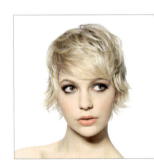

DOUBLE-PROCESS PREPARATION

As with any professional service, it is important to have your area, products, tools, supplies and equipment in proper order. Before performing a double-process hair color service, be sure to satisfy the following points:

- Perform predisposition (skin patch) test 24 to 48 hours prior to service if applicable for the toner application
- Disinfect color area
- Arrange appropriate color essentials, including on-the-scalp lightener, developer, toner, catalyst, color bowl, brush, color applicator bottle, cotton strips, gloves, large-tooth comb, tail comb, sectioning clips and barrier cream
- Wash and sanitize hands; drape the client for a color service; perform hair and scalp analysis; wear protective gloves and color apron; perform preliminary strand test
- Review previous client record card, if applicable

DOUBLE-PROCESS PROCEDURE

- **Section** the hair into four sections
  - Apply barrier cream around entire hairline
  - Begin at the back crown or most resistant area
- Decolorize the hair
  - **Part** hair using ⅛" (.3 cm) thick horizontal partings
  - **Apply** lightener ½" (1.25 cm) away from scalp through ends on both sides of the strand; if ends are porous, delay application of lightener until after base application
  - Place cotton at base between each parting to prevent seepage
  - Apply lightener generously, subdividing partings while working from the top of the section to the bottom; complete section
  - Repeat same procedure in next back section
  - Part along slight diagonal-back partings on front side to keep lightener away from client's face and repeat same application procedures as in back
  - Work from the top to the bottom of each front section using the same application procedures; bring each parting down
  - **Process** while monitoring for desired degree of decolorization
  - Perform a strand **test** for desired degree of decolorization, removing the lightener with a damp towel to see results clearly
  - Apply lightener to base when hair has decolorized halfway to desired degree of lightness by removing cotton and using same parting pattern used previously
  - Apply product around front hairline
  - Cross-check using a parting pattern opposite the initial application to ensure even coverage

DOUBLE-PROCESS PROCEDURE (CONT'D)

- Keep the lightener moist during development time by reapplying newly mixed product if necessary
- Process until an even degree of lightness is achieved from base to ends
- **Remove** lightener from hair and scalp rinsing thoroughly, then shampoo and towel-dry hair; check to ensure there are no scalp abrasions
- Recolorize the hair
  - Mix toner formula
  - **Section** hair for toner application with same pattern used previously
  - Outline each section then **part** the hair and **apply** toner from base to ends working from top to bottom of each section
  - Outline hairline for even coverage
  - **Process** according to manufacturer's directions
- Rinse and shampoo to **remove** toner and **condition** hair
- Finish color design

OPTIONAL

- An alternative application method for the double-process technique includes beginning at the nape and working upward, while applying the lightener to one side of the strand only.

DOUBLE-PROCESS COMPLETION
See Oxidative Color: Darker Result Completion

DOUBLE-PROCESS RETOUCH
Retouch applications are performed every 3 to 6 weeks depending on the rate of new growth and degree of contrast. **Lightener is applied to the new growth only.** Use ⅛" (.3 cm) partings to ensure consistent application. **Do not overlap the lightener onto the previously treated hair, since this may cause overprocessing and breakage.** Finally, a color may be applied over the hair to tone or blend the color.

13

To ensure even color, it is very important to decolorize the new growth to the same degree as the previously lightened hair. Once the lightener is shampooed from the hair, towel-dry the hair and apply the toner to the new growth. If the midstrands and ends need refreshing, distribute diluted color formula or a matching, nonoxidative hair color through the ends for the last few minutes of processing.

HAIR COLOR PROBLEMS AND SOLUTIONS

The following are a few problems that may occur as part of a hair color service along with some possible solutions.

THE COLOR FADED QUICKLY

Cause: The correct percentage of developer was not chosen.
Solution: Use a lower percentage of developer that will give you less lift. Remember, higher volumes give you more lift.

Cause: Repeated chemical overlapping caused uneven porosity.
Solution: Choose a deposit-only color when necessary to refresh the midstrand and ends.

Cause: Improper at-home maintenance.
Solution: Recommend a shampoo and conditioner for color-treated hair at the end of each color service.

THE COLOR RESULT IS TOO LIGHT

Cause: The color formula chosen was too light.
Solution: Choose a color with a heavier concentration of pigment.

Cause: Improper analysis of the existing level.
Solution: Use swatches to determine the existing color.

Cause: The strength of developer was too high.
Solution: Use a lower percentage when more deposit is desired.

Note: If the color result was too light immediately upon completion of the color service, you may wish to apply a nonoxidative or an oxidative color without ammonia throughout or add a few lowlights to create depth.

COSMETOLOGY FUNDAMENTALS

THE COLOR RESULT IS TOO DARK

Cause: The color formula chosen was too dark.
Solution: Choose a lighter color. Use swatches to determine the existing and desired field. Also take into consideration the porosity of the hair.

Cause: The developer volume chosen was too low.
Solution: Adjust the developer strength according to the lift and deposit desired.

Cause: Improper analysis of the type of porosity was made.
Solution: Check the porosity of the hair prior to color application. Remember, with extrem porosity, the color may at first take quite intensely and then gradually fade with each shampoo. If this is the case, wait about a week (after repeated shampoos have been performed) before re-evaluating.

Note: If the hair is too dark immediately upon completion of the color service, you may wish to use the following as a guideline to correct the situation: Additional shampooing may remove some of the unwanted pigment. If the color is still too dark, adding a few highlights to add brightness and lightness to the design may be enough. However, in extreme cases, lightener or a color remover may need to be used.

INSUFFICIENT GRAY COVERAGE

Cause: The proper formula was not chosen.
Solution: Be sure to include all three primary colors in your formula or choose a natural series that was designed for gray coverage.

Cause: The color selected was too light.
Solution: Choose a color with a heavier concentration of pigment. Remember that very light hair colors may not contain enough warm pigment.

Cause: The proper analysis for percentage of gray was not made.
Solution: Although an accurate analysis may be difficult, use the following as a guide: Determine whether the hair looks more or less than 50% gray. Then, approxima from that point. For very high percentages of gray, use a lower level than the desired level and add warmth to the formula for a natural effect. If the gray is hardly noticeable, do not adjust the color formula.

Cause: Color was not applied evenly.
Solution: Be sure to apply the color evenly from a consistent parting pattern. Always double-check the hairline.

Note: If the problem of insufficient gray coverage arises immediately upon the completion of the color service, reformulate using all three primary colors and apply the color throughout.

THE ENDS ARE TOO DARK

Cause: Color was applied to the ends too soon or when not necessary.
Solution: Delay the application until the last 5 to 15 minutes of the processing time, depending on the porosity of the hair. When a retouch is completed, apply color to the ends only if they are faded; then reformulate with an oxidative color without ammonia.

Note: If the ends became too dark immediately upon the completion of the color service, try to remove some of the unwanted pigment by re-shampooing the hair. In an extreme case you may need to use a lightener or color remover.

THE ENDS ARE TOO LIGHT

Cause: Color was applied too late to the ends. Not enough development time was allowed.
Solution: Apply the formula sooner or adjust the color formula with a very low volume of developer.

Cause: Improper at-home maintenance.
Solution: Recommend that a shampoo and conditioner for color-treated hair be used between salon visits.

Note: If the ends are too light immediately upon the completion of the color service, reformulate using a very low volume of developer and apply the color to the ends.

TINT BACK

Coloring the hair back to its natural color is called a "tint back" service. Tint back is a service that utilizes all your hair coloring skills and knowledge. The use of a color filler is generally recommended to provide an even base from which to work and to replace a missing primary color. The degree of porosity, the number of levels you are coloring back to, and the color you wish to achieve will determine whether you will apply the filler directly to the hair prior to the color application or whether you will mix it into the color formula. Follow manufacturer's directions and perform a strand test to ensure predictable results. Refer back to "Fillers" in this chapter for additional information.

TINT BACK GUIDELINES

- Perform a strand test.
- Subdivide the hair into four sections. Apply filler to desired areas.
- Process according to the manufacturer's directions.
- Re-section the hair and apply the color formula from the line of demarcation out to the porous ends.
- Process and strand test for color development. Then apply to the porous ends. Process accordingly. Note that a diluted color formula may be applied to the remaining hair to blend into the line of demarcation.
- Rinse with lukewarm or tepid water, followed by a shampoo.
- Apply conditioner to the hair, rinse and style as desired.
- Record formula results on the chemical record card. Complete the service by recommending at-home maintenance products.
- Disinfect tools, discard non-reusable supplies and clean work area.

HAIR COLOR REMOVAL TECHNIQUES

Occasionally it may become necessary to remove artificial pigment from the hair. Some reasons for removing artificial pigment may include:

- Repeated overlapped applications of hair color have left the hair too dark, dull or have caused an uneven band of color along the hair strand
- The client wants to return to his or her natural color, which is a lighter shade
- A fashion color was used, but the client now desires a more natural color
- Incorrect formulas were used, resulting in unwanted shades

Although there are products available to remove artificial pigment, caution must be exercised since the process can be difficult and damaging to the hair. In cases of extreme color-build up, it may not be possible to remove artificial pigment from the hair.

Products known as color removers and dye solvents are designed to remove artificial pigment. These products are sometimes mixed with hydrogen peroxide for a stronger effect and with distilled water for a milder effect. Always read manufacturer's directions. As with most color services, performing a strand test before attempting a color removal service is always advisable to avoid damaging the hair and to verify whether the service can be performed.

13

ALERT!

Avoid leaving the client unattended while performing a permanent color removal.

PERMANENT COLOR REMOVAL GUIDELINES

- Follow manufacturer's directions regarding shampooing the hair prior to the color removal application.
- Section the hair into four basic sections.
- Mix the product in a glass or plastic bowl.
- Begin the application in the darkest area and apply the product throughout the four sections.
- Complete the application and cover the hair with a plastic cap if applicable.
- Strand test frequently.
- Once the color is removed, rinse the product immediately.
- Gently and thoroughly shampoo the product from the hair.
- Towel-dry and analyze the hair. It may be necessary to re-apply the color remover product in some areas.
- Once the product has been shampooed out, condition and dry the hair if applicable.
- It is important to note that once the artificial color has been removed, the final hair color has not yet been achieved. Generally, the resulting color serves as a foundation for the final hair color. If no signs of scalp irritations are present, perform a strand test. If a filler is needed, choose one according to the missing primary color (refer to the color wheel). Then choose the appropriate color. Keep in mind that the hair has gone through several chemical services, leaving the hair porous, therefore, a low volume developer mixed with the desired color formula is advisable.

HENNA REMOVAL GUIDELINES

Hair coated with the vegetable dye henna is generally not compatible with other hair coloring or chemical services. To remove henna, follow these procedures:

- Apply 70% alcohol to the hair strand, avoiding direct contact with the scalp. Allow alcohol to remain on the hair for 5 to 7 minutes.
- Apply mineral oil directly over the alcohol, completely saturating each strand from scalp to ends.
- Cover the hair with a plastic cap and place the client under a preheated, hooded dryer for 30 minutes.
- Without rinsing, apply concentrated shampoo for oily hair and massage into the lengths. Allow shampoo to remain on the hair for 3 minutes.
- Massage the hair again, then rinse thoroughly with hot, but comfortable, water.
- Shampoo again. Several shampoos may be necessary.

COSMETOLOGY FUNDAMENTALS

CONNECTING THEORY TO REAL-WORLD PRACTICE

COLOR	PERSONAL CONNECTION: IMPROVE YOURSELF	INDUSTRY CONNECTION: BECOME PROFESSIONAL	CLIENT CONNECTION: SERVE THE GUEST
COLOR THEORY	Bring advanced color knowledge to all types of visual expression	Visualize innovative and client-centered color designs	Recommend subtle-to-dramatic hair color variations to meet individual client needs
IDENTIFYING EXISTING HAIR COLOR	Distinguish the multiple characteristics of natural and artificial hair color	Begin every color service correctly to ensure predictable results	Analyze clients' hair appropriately to ensure final color is achieved
CHANGING EXISTING HAIR COLOR	Match different color effects with the products and techniques used to produce them	Grow a loyal clientele by delivering high-quality color design services	Add depth, dimension, brightness, intensity and variety to your clients' hair color

IN OTHER WORDS

Knowing how to change your clients' hair color allows you to create an array of hair design effects for a wide variety of client needs.

LESSONS LEARNED

- Color is the visual perception of the reflection of light, and its main characteristics are hue, value and intensity.

- The color wheel is a tool used to describe any mixed color in relation to the primary colors. Colors opposite one another on the color wheel are complementary colors and are used in hair coloring to neutralize unwanted tones.

- Natural and artificial hair colors are identified by their level, which specifies the lightness or darkness of the color from blond to black, and their tone, which specifies whether the color is warm, cool or neutral.

- The client's final hair color is the result of its contributing pigment and the formula of artificial pigments, developers and/or lighteners applied to the hair.

- Nonoxidative colors produce temporary or semi-permanent results and oxidative colors produce long-lasting or permanent results. Lighteners are used to decolorize pigment and to achieve lighter color results.

- Color designs are achieved using zonal patterns, shapes and color application techniques.

- Dimensional color effects can be achieved through weaving and slicing techniques, as well as from freeform painting techniques and the cap method.

14

THE STUDY OF NAILS

14.1　NAIL THEORY
　　NAIL STRUCTURE
　　NAIL GROWTH
　　NAIL DISEASES, DISORDERS AND CONDITIONS

14.2　NATURAL NAIL CARE
　　NAIL SHAPES
　　NAIL ESSENTIALS
　　INFECTION CONTROL AND SAFETY
　　NATURAL NAIL CARE SERVICE ESSENTIALS
　　BASIC MANICURE
　　MALE MANICURE
　　PEDICURE ESSENTIALS
　　BASIC PEDICURE
　　SPECIAL NAIL SERVICES

14.3　ARTIFICIAL NAIL CARE
　　ARTIFICIAL NAIL ESSENTIALS
　　INFECTION CONTROL AND SAFETY
　　NAIL TIPS
　　TIPS WITH ACRYLIC OVERLAY
　　SCULPTURED NAILS
　　ADDITIONAL ARTIFICIAL NAIL SERVICES

NAIL THEORY AND NAIL
CARE PROCEDURES FOR
BOTH NATURAL AND
ARTIFICIAL NAILS
ARE KEY INGREDIENTS
FOR MEETING CLIENTS'
TOTAL IMAGE NEEDS

FOLLOWING THIS LESSON
YOU WILL BE ABLE TO:

Describe the structure, growth, diseases, disorders and
conditions of the nail

Explain and demonstrate the services for natural nail care

Explain and demonstrate the services for artificial nail care

CONNECTING THEORY
TO REAL-WORLD PRACTICE

KNOWING NAIL THEORY AND THE PROCEDURES FOR PERFORMING MANICURES AND PEDICURES WILL HELP YOU:

PERSONAL CONNECTION: IMPROVE YOURSELF	**INDUSTRY CONNECTION:** BECOME A PROFESSIONAL	**CLIENT CONNECTION:** SERVE THE GUEST
Keep the nails of the hands and feet healthy and beautiful	Deliver high-quality nail services within a full-service salon environment	Enhance clients' appearance, image and self-confidence with natural and artificial nails

Next to the face, the human hand is a person's most expressive feature. Hands nurture, caress, instruct and communicate.
Caring for clients' hands, as well as their feet, gives them confidence and composure. Knowing how to make this happen
for your clients will give you great satisfaction and an additional outlet for your professional skill.

REMEMBER
MANICURE = MANI (hand) + CURE (care)
PEDICURE = PEDI (foot) + CURE (care)

14

14.1 NAIL THEORY

Like the hair, the nail is an appendage of the skin. The technical name for the nail is onyx (ON-iks). The study of the structure and growth of the nails is called onychology (on-ih-KOL-o-gee).

NAIL STRUCTURE

The best way to learn nail structure is to examine a detailed diagram of the nail.
1. The **free edge** is the part of the nail that extends beyond the end of the finger or toe and protects the tips of the fingers or toes.
2. The **nail body** (nail plate) is the visible nail area from the nail root to free edge. Made of layers. No nerves or blood vessels can be found here.
3. The **nail wall** is the folds of skin on either side of the nail groove.
4. The **lunula** is the half-moon shape at the base of the nail, which appears white due to a reflection of light at the point where the nail matrix and nail bed meet.
5. The **eponychium** (ep-o-**nik**-ee-um) is the cuticle that overlaps the lunula at the base of the nail.
6. The **cuticle** is the loose and pliable overlapping skin around the nail.
7. The **nail matrix** is the active tissue that generates cells, which harden as they move outward from the root to the nail.
8. The **nail root** is attached to the matrix at the base of the nail, under the skin and inside the mantle.
9. The **mantle** is the pocket-like structure that holds the root and matrix.
10. The **nail bed** is the area of the nail on which the nail body rests. Nerves and blood vessels found here supply nourishment. Ligaments attach the nail bed to the bone.
11. The **nail grooves** are the tracks on either side of the nail that the nail moves on as it grows.
12. The **perionychium** (per-i-o-**nik**-ee-um) is the skin that touches, overlaps and surrounds the nail.
13. The **hyponychium** (heye-poh-**nik**-ee-um) is the skin under the free edge.

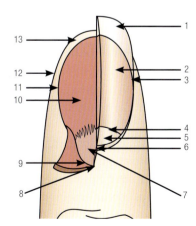

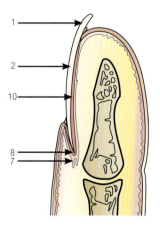

SIDE VIEW,
CROSS SECTION OF FINGER

NAIL GROWTH

Like the hair, the nail is made of keratin (hardened) protein. Although nail protein is much harder than the protein of hair, its growth is similar to the growth of hair.

Nail growth originates from active tissue known as the matrix, located in the mantle. The matrix contains lymph, blood vessels and nerves that create cells, which are pushed outward from the nail root. These cells keratinize (harden) as they continue toward the nail body (plate) and become fully hardened by the time they reach the eponychium. These hardened cells form the visible nail body (plate) that curves on the sides and travels in tracks found on the side of the nail called nail grooves. The nail plate can be thin, normal or thick, depending on the rate of production of cells in the matrix. **Under normal circumstances, growth of a new nail plate takes about 4-6 months.** The nail bed on which the nail body (plate) rests contains many nerves, as well as blood vessels for continuous nourishment.

Nails grow at an average rate of ⅛" (.3 cm) per month in adults. Nails grow more rapidly in younger people because general cell reproduction is occurring at a faster rate. Thus, as one ages, the growth of nails slows down.

Nail growth is faster in summer than in winter, and can be affected by nutrition, health or disease. The thumb nail grows slowest, while the nail on the middle finger grows fastest. Toenails are harder and thicker than fingernails but grow more slowly.

Injuries to the nail can result in shape distortions or nail discoloration. Most nail injuries are minor and resulting distortions and/or discoloration are temporary. Permanent distortions can occur when:

- A nail is lost due to trauma and, without the protection of the nail plate, the nail bed or matrix is injured.
- A nail is lost through disease or infection. The regrown nail, in these circumstances, is often distorted in shape.

NAIL DISEASES, DISORDERS AND CONDITIONS

Any disease, disorder or condition of the nail is called an onychosis (on-i-KO-sis).

- If a disease is present, no nail service can be performed; the client must be referred to a physician.
- If a disorder is present, nail services may be done with care; the client may want to consult a physician for help and information.
- If a condition is present, nail services can be performed, and the condition should improve with correct techniques, products or improved nutrition.

A STUDY OF ONYCHOSIS CONSIDERS 4 FACTORS

1. IDENTIFICATION
Identification of the disease, disorder or condition

2. CAUSE
Etiology (e-te-OL-o-je) or cause of the disease, disorder or condition
- Systemic (meaning throughout the system) causes are internal. They are related to illness, nutrition or heredity.
- Environmental causes include nail services or products (chemicals) that have adversely altered the skin or nail.
- Disease-related cause is often invasion of the skin or nail tissues by an agent like bacteria or fungi. These agents are contagious and spread by contact.

3. DIAGNOSIS
Diagnosis, the identification of an onychosis by the symptoms, and prognosis, the outlook for recovery

4. TREATMENT
In-salon treatments:
- Products used and recommended for home care
- Techniques used and taught to the client

HAND AND NAIL EXAMINATION

To discover problems associated with the hands, nails or growth of nails, begin with a hand and nail examination. As a salon professional, you observe the hands and nails to determine the type of services that should be performed to improve their condition and appearance. **There are six signs of infection in the nail and hands: pain, swelling, redness, local fever, throbbing and pus.** A healthy nail is smooth, curved, and without hollows or wavy ridges. It is flexible, translucent and pinkish in color.

Before performing an examination, wash and sanitize your hands and your client's hands. Then, hold the client's hands and turn front and back while observing:
- Temperature of skin (coldness may indicate poor circulation; heat may indicate infection)
- Skin texture/feel (may indicate need for moisture or possible diseases or disorders)
- Inflammations/redness on hand or nails (may indicate need for moisture/possible diseases or disorders)
- Color/condition of nail bed (may identify visible injuries, disease and/or indications of poor circulation)
- Condition and length of free edge (may identify nail biter or "picker" or indicate dry, brittle nails)
- Tenderness or stiff joints (special massage techniques may be required)
- Shape and thickness of nail plate (may indicate a disease or disorder and how to properly file)

On determining that a special condition exists, explain it to the client and suggest products and care techniques to help overcome the condition. **Certain nail irregularities (often disease-related), however, must be referred to a physician for diagnosis or treatment and no nail service performed until the condition is alleviated.** When in doubt, refer your client to a physician.

NAIL DISEASES

Clients with nail diseases must be referred to their physician for treatment before nail services can be provided. A few of the irregularities shown below may have a disease-related or systemic cause. Identification of nail diseases is important to protect the health of the client and yourself.

ONYCHOMYCOSIS/TINEA UNGUIUM/UNGUIS

Onychomycosis (o-ni-ko-mi-**KO**-sis) or **tinea unguium** (**TIN**-ee-ah **UN**-gwee-um) or **unguis** (**UN**-gwees) is ringworm of the nail.

Cause: Fungus, disease-related, can result from a nail injury invaded by fungus
Prognosis: Nail becomes thick and discolors from black to brown or beige to white; can develop white scaly patches with yellow streaks under nail plate; deformed nail may fall off; must be diagnosed and treated by a physician.
Treatment: No service may be performed.

TINEA MANUS

Tinea (**TIN**-e-ah) **manus** is ringworm of the hand.

Cause: Fungus, disease-related
Prognosis: Appears as rings containing tiny blisters, dark pink to reddish in color; can have dry flakes; can be confused with eczema or contact dermatitis; can spread to nails, scalp, feet or body. Must be diagnosed and treated by a physician.
Treatment: No service may be performed. Refer client to a physician.

TINEA PEDIS

Tinea pedis (**TIN**-e-ah **PED**-is) is "athlete's foot" or ringworm of the feet.

Cause: Fungus, disease-related; thrives in dark, moist places
Prognosis: Itching and peeling of the skin on feet; blisters containing colorless fluid form in group or singly on sores and between toes, leaving sore or itchy skin on one or both feet; must be diagnosed and treated by a physician.
Treatment: No service may be performed. Refer client to a physician.

PARONYCHIA

Paronychia (par-o-**NIK**-e-a), or felon, is inflammation of skin around the nail.

Cause: Bacterial infection, disease-related condition of the tissue surrounding the nail that can occur if a hangnail gets infected; prolonged exposure of hands to water can create conditions favorable for paronychia to develop
Prognosis: Red, swollen, sore, warm to touch, can lose the nail; must be diagnosed and treated by physician; healing takes 4 weeks; nail may grow out deformed but can recover shape.
Treatment: No service may be performed. Refer client to a physician.

ONYCHOPTOSIS
Onychoptosis (o-ni-kop-TO-sis) **refers to shedding or falling off of nails.**
Cause: Disease and injury related
Prognosis: If the disease causing the problem is cured, the nail will regrow; may occur on only one or two nails; nail bed will be sensitive and should be protected while nail regrows.
Treatment: No service may be performed on affected nails. Refer client to a physician.

ONYCHIA
Onychia (o-NIK-e-a) **is inflammation of the nail matrix.**
Cause: Bacterial infection, disease-related
Prognosis: Inflammation of the nail matrix; pus formation; red, swollen and tender; nail may stop growing, and plate may detach; nail may not grow back; if it does, it will probably be deformed; must be diagnosed and treated by a physician.
Treatment: No service may be performed. Refer client to a physician.

ONYCHATROPHIA
Onychatrophia (o-ni-ka-TRO-fe-a) **is atrophy of the nail or wasting away of nail.**
Cause: Injury or systemic disease
Prognosis: Nail shrinks in size and may separate from nail bed; if illness-related, may not improve if matrix is damaged; the nail may improve in 3 to 6 months.
Treatment: No service may be performed on affected nails. Refer client to a physician.

ONYCHOLYSIS
Onycholysis (o-ni-KOL-i-sis) **refers to a loosening or separation of the nail.**
Cause: Internal disorder, infection or drug treatment; systemic, disease-related
Prognosis: Loosening of the nail plate starting at the free edge and progressing to the lunula; nail doesn't come off; stays attached at root area; must be diagnosed and treated by a physician.
Treatment: Do not touch. No service may be performed on affected nails. Refer client to a physician.

NAIL DISORDERS
Unless infection is present, clients with nail disorders may receive modified nail services.

BLUE NAILS
Blue nails appear bluish in color.
Cause: Systemic problems of the heart, poor circulation or injury
Prognosis: "Blue" color in skin under nails; can be solved if cause is eliminated; common in older people.
Treatment: Make client aware of problem and possible causes; suggest seeing a physician; manicure with caution, using light pressure

EGGSHELL NAILS
Eggshell nails are very thin, soft nails.
Cause: Hereditary or nervous condition
Prognosis: Thin nails, almost see-through, transparent.
Treatment: Regular application of top coat, nail strengtheners or artificial nails as well as good dietary practices.

CORRUGATIONS

Corrugations (kor-u-**GA**-shuns) are horizontal wavy ridges across the nail.

Cause:	Injury, systemic conditions; uneven growth
Prognosis:	Easily recognizable; if injury-related, it may grow out and disappear; systemic conditions may cause permanent ridges.
Treatment:	Lightly buff to level the nail surface; apply a base coat or ridge filler to protect and even surface. Avoid overbuffing, since it is easy to thin the nail plate.

KOILONYCHIA

Koilonychia (koi-loh-**NIK**-ee-uh) or spoon nails are nails with a concave shape.

Cause:	Systemic or long-term illness or nerve disturbance
Prognosis:	Unusual nail shapes; unlikely to disappear.
Treatment:	File carefully; apply no pressure to nail plate; use polish to harden and protect nails.

FURROWS

Furrows are indented vertical lines down the nail plate.

Cause:	Injury to matrix that causes cells to reproduce unevenly; can be nutrition, injury or illness related; pushing too hard with pusher during nail service or exposure to harsh chemicals.
Prognosis:	Easily recognizable; may grow out; may be permanent.
Treatment:	Lightly buff; apply base coat or ridge filler to protect and even out surface; perform nail service as usual.

ONYCHOGRYPOSIS

Onychogryposis (o-ni-ko-**GRI**-po-sis) also called "claw nails" represent an increased curvature of the nail.

Cause:	Systemic
Prognosis:	Increased thickness and curving of the nail that may occur with age or injury to nail; most often occurring in the big toe; physicians may remove if severely deformed or difficult to keep clean.
Treatment:	Look for signs of infection; clean well under free edge; file with emery board and keep nails short; only a podiatrist should trim.

ONYCHOCRYPTOSIS

Onychocryptosis (o-ni-ko-**KRIP**-to-sis) are ingrown nails.

Cause:	Environmental or poor nail trimming practices; can become infected
Prognosis:	If the nail grows into the edge of the nail groove cutting the skin or becomes deeply embedded and/or infected, refer client to a physician who will remove the skin or portion of nail causing the problem. It may also occur on toes if shoes are too tight, or if the toenails are filed too deeply on sides.
Treatment:	Thoroughly soften skin, trim nail straight across to prevent pressure on the nail groove. If infection is evident, do not perform service. Refer to a physician.

MELANONYCHIA

Melanonychia (mel-uh-nuh-**NIK**-ee-uh) is a brown or black darkening of the nail.

Cause:	Increased production of melanin by melanocytes in the nail matrix due to trauma, systemic disease or medications.
Prognosis:	The incidence of melanonychia varies according to skin pigmentation with percentage being higher in persons with darker skin color.
Treatment:	Make client aware of problem and possible causes; suggest seeing a physician.

14

ONYCHAUXIS
Onychauxis (o-ni-KOK-sis) or hypertrophy is a thickening of the nail plate or an abnormal outgrowth of the nail.
Cause: Injury to nail or systemic
Prognosis: Easily recognizable; likely to disappear.
Treatment: Can be lightly buffed to even out the nail plate.

ONYCHOPHYMA (on-ih-ko-FEE-ma) is the swelling of the nail and is often associated with onychauxis.

NAIL CONDITIONS
Nail conditions are generally minor irregularities that allow the client to receive either full or modified nail services.

AGNAILS
Agnails (hangnails) are split cuticles; loose skin partially separated from the cuticle.
Cause: Cuticle is overly dry and splits; environmentally caused
Prognosis: Skin breaks at corners of nails; can be trimmed with cuticle nippers and may heal in 2 to 3 days; can be reoccurring.
Treatment: Trim only separated hangnail skin completely; moisturize and avoid massaging the area. Instruct the client to use cuticle oil daily. Hangnails may become infected if not properly treated.

BRUISED NAILS
Bruised nails (also called splinter hemorrhages) show dark purplish discoloration under the nail.
Cause: Trauma to nail; environmental; blood trapped under nails or small capillaries hemorrhage
Prognosis: Discoloration under nail; normal nail growth will continue; bruised area will grow out with nail.
Treatment: No pressure on nail plate.

LEUCONYCHIA
Leuconychia (loo-ko-NIK-e-a) are white spots appearing in the nail.
Cause: Injury to the nail, heredity, signs of systemic disorders or nutritional deficiency
Prognosis: A small separation from the nail bed; grows out with the nail.
Treatment: Make client aware of possible cause; perform nail service as usual.

PTERYGIUM
Pterygium (te-RIJ-e-ge-uhm) refers to the living skin that becomes attached to the nail plate either at the eponychium (dorsal pterygium) or the hyponychium (inverse pterygium).
Cause: Severe injury to the eponychium or hyponychium
Prognosis: Excess living skin that can remain attached to the nail plate and disrupt normal nail growth.
Treatment: No service on affected nails. If severe, refer the client to a physician.

BEAU'S LINES
Beau's Lines are indentations that run across the nail.
Cause: Growth at the area under the cuticle is interrupted by major injury or severe illness that has traumatized the body for an extended period of time such as uncontrolled diabetes or pneumonia.
Prognosis: Nail returns to normal after the trauma.
Treatment: Make client aware of possible cause; perform nail service as usual.

ONYCHOPHAGY

Onychophagy (o-ni-**KOF**-a-je) refers to bitten nails.

Cause: Nervous habit, stress related

Prognosis: Easily recognizable; if biting stops, the nails will regrow; may be sensitive to touch; nail plate will appear flat and may be deformed until an entire nail has regrown from the matrix; can completely recover.

Treatment: Perform nail service weekly; apply polish to nails.

ONYCHORRHEXIS

Onychorrhexis (o-ni-ko-**REK**-sis) are split or brittle nails.

Cause: Injury, improper filing or harsh chemical contact

Prognosis: Easily recognizable; file with emery board carefully; may be a permanent condition

Treatment: Soften nails well before trimming; hot oil manicure; advise client to perform moisturizing treatments daily at home. Wear rubber gloves when hands are in water or chemicals.

Bacterial infections are very contagious and are indicated in early stages by a yellow-green spot that eventually becomes black. At that stage the nail softens and smells bad. Refer clients with a bacterial infection to a physician.

PIGMENTATION PROBLEMS

Discoloration of the nail can indicate serious problems in the nail bed or nail plate. In general, all changes of color should be referred to a physician unless they can be removed by a cleansing agent like soap. Vitamin deficiencies, bacterial infections, fungal infestations, protein deficiencies, kidney or liver disorders or reactions to medications can all cause discoloration. They should not be ignored. **The condition of the hands and nails will often indicate the overall health of the body.**

14.2 NATURAL NAIL CARE

Nail care, like hair design, is a science, a service and an art. Nail care can be an "extra" service you provide to your client or it can be a creative specialty. Nail specialists are called nail technicians.

The purpose of a nail service is to improve the appearance of the hands and, in particular, the nails. A good nail service completes the picture begun by fantastic hair and skin and carefully selected clothing.

NAIL SHAPES

Although nails grow in assorted shapes and sizes from convex to concave, wide to narrow, round to angular, **there are five basic nail shapes: pointed, oval, round, square and squoval.** Generally, the more square the nail shape, the stronger it is. It will be your job to enhance the natural shape of your client's nails, the shape of their fingers and the overall appearance of their hands.

POINTED   OVAL   ROUND   SQUOVAL   SQUARE

NAIL ESSENTIALS

To perform a professional nail service, you need a selection of products, implements and equipment. Nail service products are produced by many different manufacturers, are disposable and must be frequently replaced. Material Safety Data Sheets (MSDS) for all products used in the salon must be available. Nail service implements are the hand-held tools you use. They must be disinfected or discarded after every use. Nail service equipment includes the furnishings and provisions necessary to provide a professional nail service.

NAIL SERVICE PRODUCTS

PRODUCT	DESCRIPTION	FUNCTION
DISINFECTANT	Chemical product	Destroys or kills bacteria and some viruses
ANTISEPTIC	Liquid or foam-based products	Reduces microbes on the skin
STYPTIC PRODUCT	Liquid or spray	Stops bleeding when applied
POLISH REMOVER	Acetone or non-acetone	Dissolves polish
COTTON BALLS OR PLEDGLETS	Absorbent; pledglets are cotton pads	Used to apply polish removers, powder feet, remove lotions from nail plate
CUTICLE REMOVER CREAM	Low percent hydrogen peroxide, sodium or potassium hydroxide	Loosens dead skin

PRODUCT	DESCRIPTION	FUNCTION
NAIL BLEACH	Lightener or high percent hydrogen peroxide	Removes stains and whitens nails
SOAKING SOLUTION	Liquid soap used with finger bowl	Softens skin, loosens dirt, aids in pushing back cuticle
CUTICLE CREAM OR OIL	Moisturizer	Softens cuticle skin, moisturizes brittle nails
HAND LOTION	Lubricant	Softens skin and aids when providing massage manipulations
BASE COAT	Colorless polish	Evens out nail plate, holds nail color to nail, prevents pigments from penetrating nail plate
LIQUID POLISH	Colored polish, enamel	Creates a colored effect
TOP COAT OR SEALER	Colorless hard polish	Protects colored polish from chipping, fading and peeling
SPEED DRY (NAIL DRYER)	Drying agent; spray or polish applied over top coat	Aids in fast drying of polish; protects from stickiness or matte finish to polish
NAIL CONDITIONER	Moisturizing ingredients	Applied to nails to avoid dryness
NAIL MEND FIBER	Mending material; fiberglass, silk, linen and nylon; also called fabric wrap	Repairs splits or cracks on the nail
NAIL STRENGTHENER (NAIL HARDENERS)	Usually a clear polish applied prior to the base coat; may contain strengthening fibers	Prevents nails from splitting and peeling
LIQUID NAIL WRAP	Polish consisting of tiny strengthening fibers; more fiber than a nail hardener	Hardens and protects the nail

NAIL SERVICE IMPLEMENTS/SUPPLIES

IMPLEMENTS/SUPPLIES	FUNCTION
EMERY BOARD	Shortens and shapes natural nails and smoothes rough edges by using sandpaper-like fine and coarse sides
CUTICLE PUSHER	Pushes back cuticle on the nail (rounded end) and pushes back cuticle in the corners of the nail (pointed end); can be metal or wood
ORANGEWOOD STICK	Loosens debris and is used to apply creams and clean under free edge

IMPLEMENTS/SUPPLIES	FUNCTION
CUTICLE NIPPER	Trims hangnails; check with your regulatory agency regarding usage
NAIL AND CUTICLE SCISSORS	Cuts nails or trims mending fiber
NAIL BRUSH	Cleans nails and removes debris before polishing
TWEEZER	Manages detail work such as nail art
BLOCK BUFFER/ 3-WAY BUFFER	Smoothes surface of the nail; some states do not permit use
COSMETIC SPATULA	Removes cream from jars in an effort to meet infection control guidelines
FINGER BOWL	Allows comfortable soaking of nails
TOWELS	Dries hands and nails

NAIL SERVICE EQUIPMENT

EQUIPMENT	FUNCTION
NAIL SERVICE TABLE	Provides a place for all tools to be laid out; is the proper height for comfort; may have an attached light
NAIL SERVICE STOOL	Allows easy access to all tools and the client because seat is adjustable
CLIENT'S CHAIR	Provides proper back support and comfort to client during nail service
NAIL SERVICE CUSHION	Forms a cushion to rest client's arm during service while drying hands (towels may be used in the absence of a cushion)
WET DISINFECTANT CONTAINER	Holds disinfectant for disinfecting implements under infection control guidelines
ELECTRIC HEATER	Heats cream for specialized nail services
GLASS CONTAINER	Holds absorbent cotton, cotton swabs and other accessories
LAMP	Lights the area for close detail work (most often purchased as part of the table or may be purchased separately and attached to table); generally uses a 40-watt bulb

INFECTION CONTROL AND SAFETY

Infection control and safety while performing nail services is essential in order to protect the health and well-being of you and your client. It begins with your conscientious efforts to keep your nail table clean and organized and continues throughout the service. Additional steps are:

- Wash your hands and have your clients wash their hands with liquid soap.
- Follow manufacturer's directions on all products being used.
- Avoid filing too deeply into the corners of the nails to prevent ingrown nails.
- Wash implements with soap and water then disinfect after every service; store in a dry, covered container and handle sharp-pointed implements carefully.
- Wear protective gloves during nail services, if required.
- Clean and disinfect nail service tabletop after every service.
- Check that all bottle tops and container lids are tightly sealed and labeled.
- Empty soaking solution from finger bowl. Disinfect and replace with fresh solution for every client.
- Clean the surface of the foot bath ensuring that all debris is removed from behind the drain screen; disinfect following manufacturer's directions.
- Arrange all products and implements in proper order.
- Handle all products carefully and avoid spillage. Use spatulas to remove creams from containers.
- Practice blood spill procedures if a blood spill occurs.
- Discard non-reusable materials such as emery boards in a closed (container) waste receptacle.

BLOOD SPILL PROCEDURE
If a blood spill should occur, use the following steps:

1. Stop the service; wash your hands; cover your hands with protective gloves when dealing with an injured party.
2. Apply antiseptic and/or liquid or spray styptic product to the injured party. If you are injured, stop the service and clean the injured area; apply antiseptic and/or liquid or spray styptic product.*
3. Dress or cover the injury with appropriate dressing.
4. Cover injured area with finger guard or glove as appropriate.
5. Clean and disinfect implements and workstation with a broad spectrum disinfectant.
6. Double-bag all blood-soiled (contaminated) articles and label the bag as hazardous waste or as directed by your area's regulating agency; remove your gloves and clean your hands with a liquid soap.
7. Return to client and continue the service.

*Do not allow containers, brushes, nozzles or styptic container to touch the skin or come in contact with the wound.

14

NATURAL NAIL CARE SERVICE ESSENTIALS

As with all professional services, communicating with your client prior to the actual service will ensure predictable results and will help you avoid any misunderstandings that may arise. As you review the four basic steps of the natural nail care service essentials, remember the importance of active listening, critical thinking and analysis on the overall success of the service.

CONNECT
- Meet and greet the client with a firm handshake and a pleasant voice.
- Communicate to build rapport and develop a relationship with the client.

CONSULT
- Ask questions to discover client needs.
- Analyze client's nails and hands.
- Assess the facts and thoroughly think through your recommendations.
- Explain your recommended solutions, the products that will be used and the price of the service.
- Think not only of today's service, but future services also.
- Gain feedback and approval from your client.

CREATE
- Ensure client comfort during service.
- Stay focused on delivering the service to the best of your ability.
- Teach the client how to perform home nail-care maintenance.
- Have a range of colors available and emphasize the importance of a base coat and a top coat.

COMPLETE
- Request satisfaction feedback from your client.
- Escort client to retail area and show him/her at least two products you used.
- Recommend products to maintain appearance and condition of your client's nails.
- Inform client that you keep these products in stock for purchase at all times.
- Invite your client to make a purchase.
- Ask your client for referrals for future services.
- Suggest a future appointment time for your client's next visit.
- Offer appreciation to your client for visiting the school or salon.
- Record recommended products on client record card for future visits.

WORKSHOP 01
BASIC MANICURE

Manicuring is the cosmetic care of the hands and fingernails. The Latin word "manus" means hand and "cura" means care.

As with any professional service, it is important to have your area, products, implements and equipment in proper order prior to your client's arrival.

BASIC MANICURE PREPARATION
- Clean nail table with disinfectant
- Place fresh soaking solution to the left of the client on the nail service table, near technician
- Clean, disinfect and place nail service implements on the nail table
- Review and arrange products conveniently, in order of usual use

BASIC MANICURE PROCEDURE
- Wash and sanitize hands*
- Perform visual examination of hands and nails
- Remove polish
- Analyze skin and nails thoroughly consult with client
- File and shape nails
- Apply cuticle remover
- Place hand in finger bowl
- Repeat filing, shaping and cuticle care on opposite hand
- Pat first hand dry
- Push back cuticles
- Scrub hand and nails
- Clean under free edge
- Pat hand dry
- Repeat cuticle care and cleaning on opposite hand apply massage lotion or cream
- Perform massage techniques
- Remove all traces of massage lotion or cream from nails
- Apply base coat
- Apply two coats of polish
- Apply polish at free edge
- Remove excess polish from skin
- Apply top coat and quick-dry product

OPTIONAL
File and shape nails, place hand in finger bowl, then apply cuticle remover
*Wear protective gloves if required by your regulating agency.

MANICURE

01 **Wash and sanitize your own** and your client's hands and nails and apply a topical antiseptic. Perform visual examination of the hands and nails. Continue if there are no noticeable diseases or disorders.

02 **Remove polish** from base to tip on the nails of both hands to prepare for the examination. Use polish remover and cotton, and wipe from the base of the nail to the tip to avoid leaving polish residue on the skin.

03 **Analyze skin and nails thoroughly.** Consult with your **client** about shape and length of nails desired.

NAIL PREP
04 **File and shape the nails** with an emery board.
- Begin with the little finger on one hand and shape from the outer edge of the nail toward the center to avoid splitting.
- Use 2 or 3 short strokes on each side of the nail and one longer stroke per side to blend. Round the top of the nail gently.

CUTICLE CARE
05 **Apply cuticle remover** cream to one hand.

06 **Place the hand in the finger bowl** to allow cuticles to soften. Repeat filing, shaping and cuticle care on the opposite hand.

07 **Pat the client's first hand dry** with a towel, and place the other hand in soaking solution. Gently **push back the cuticle** on each finger on the first hand with a cotton-wrapped orangewood stick or cuticle pusher.

If you trim the cuticle, try to use a cutting method that utilizes removing the cuticle as one segment.

COSMETOLOGY FUNDAMENTALS 553

Hangnails may be trimmed to the surface of the skin. Note that cutting or trimming cuticles is illegal in some areas. Check with your area's regulating agency.

REMINDER
- Ensure the comfort of your client throughout the service
- Work neatly
- Maintain professional communication

08 Scrub hand and nails with a nail brush in a downward direction and then dry hand.

09 Clean under the free edge of each nail with a cotton-wrapped orangewood stick. Pat hand dry. Repeat cuticle care and cleaning on the opposite hand.

MASSAGE

The massage portion of the manicure is key to the relaxation and pampering of the client. The following are some basic techniques. Be guided by your instructor for additional manipulations.

10 Apply massage lotion or cream from elbow to forearm and down to the fingertips to prepare for the massage. **Perform massage techniques** on both hands using long rhythmic effleurage strokes. Rotate in a circular motion to loosen the wrist.

11 Massage fingers using a circular motion called joint movement.

12 Knead palm with petrissage, moving thumbs in a circular motion from wrist to fingers.

13 Remove all traces of massage lotion or cream from nails before applying polish. Use a cotton-wrapped orangewood stick soaked in polish remover underneath and on the surface of the nail.

OLISH
Apply base coat, beginning
th the little finger of one hand
d working toward the thumb.
peat on opposite hand.

15 Apply two coats of polish, using light, sweeping strokes from nail base to free edge. Polish middle of nails first, then the sides. Repeat the second coat when all ten nails are polished.

16-17 Apply polish at the free edge to help prevent chipping. Remove excess polish from skin with orangewood stick, wrapped in cotton and saturated with polish remover. Apply top coat and a quick-drying product, which may be a spray, pump or polish.

BASIC MANICURE COMPLETION

Perform after every nail service:
- Offer a prebook visit to your client.
- Recommend retail products to your client.
- Discard non-reusable materials, replace used towels with fresh towels and arrange all products and implements in proper order.
- Disinfect your nail service implements and the top of the nail service table.
- Wash your hands with liquid soap.

Avoid causing air bubbles by rolling the nail polish bottle between your palms to mix. Shaking a polish bottle will cause the application to appear uneven.

WORKSHOP 02
MALE MANICURE

The procedure for a male manicure is basically the same as the basic manicure just described. There are a few variations to keep in mind.

01 File men's nails short usually into either a round or square shape.

02 Apply a clear base coat and top coat only, if polish is desired.

03 Use a 3-way buffer to create a natural shine or proceed to step 4 for an oil buff. Use horizontal movements, working from the base of the nail to the free edge. Buff with the black side, then buff with the white side, and finally the gray side. Lift the buffer from the nail to break contact between strokes, which will avoid overheating the nail.

04 Apply oil to the nail before buffing with the gray side to create an oil buff. Buffing should be limited to every 2 to 3 weeks t avoid overthinning the natural nai

PEDICURE ESSENTIALS

The following items are necessary to complete a pedicure service along with the items used for the basic manicure service.

PEDICURE SERVICE PRODUCTS

PRODUCT	FUNCTION
FOOT SOAK	Cleans and softens the foot
FOOT SPRAY	Removes germs from skin; acts as an antiseptic
SLOUGHING LOTION	Removes dead skin cells
FOOT LOTION	Moisturizes and stimulates the feet
FOOT POWDER	Dries and deodorizes

PEDICURE SERVICE IMPLEMENTS/SUPPLIES

IMPLEMENTS/SUPPLIES	FUNCTION
FOOT FILE	Softens and removes calluses; paddle with a gritty surface
FOOT BRUSH	Cleans nails and removes debris; stiff brush
TOENAIL CLIPPER	Shortens toenails
TOE SEPARATORS	Separate toes during polish technique; made of foam, rubber or cotton
SLIPPERS	Protect feet while polish dries

PEDICURE SERVICE EQUIPMENT

EQUIPMENT	FUNCTION
PEDICURE TABLE	Holds and stores all equipment, products and implements
PEDICURE FOOT REST	Props up the client's feet for the service
PEDICURE CHAIR	Provides comfortable chair for clients
FOOT BATH OR TUB	Serves as basin to soak feet

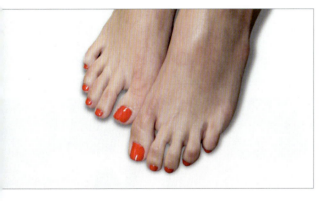

WORKSHOP 03
BASIC PEDICURE

Pedicuring is the cosmetic care of the feet and toenails.
The Latin word "ped" means foot and "cura" means care.

BASIC PEDICURE PREPARATION

Preparation for a basic pedicure is similar to that for a manicure along with the guidelines listed below:
- Clean and disinfect implements
- Set up equipment and lay out tools on sanitized table
- Review and arrange products conveniently, in order of use
- Gather products and solutions needed from the dispensary
- Prepare the foot bath with enough sanitizing solution to cover both feet
- Wash your hands with liquid soap

BASIC PEDICURE PROCEDURE

- Wash and sanitize hands*
- Sanitize client's feet
- Perform a visual examination
- Soak and dry feet
- Remove nail polish
- Examine feet
- Trim and file nails
- Apply cuticle remover cream
- Push back cuticles
- Apply sloughing lotion and massage to remove dead skin cells
- Repeat trimming, filing and cuticle care on opposite foot
- Soak and scrub both feet with brush to remove debris
- Dry thoroughly
- Massage with lotion
- Remove excess lotion from nail surface
- Apply powder and position toe separators
- Apply base coat
- Apply two coats of polish
- Apply top coat, followed by quick-drying product
- Allow drying time
- Remove toe separators when dry

*Wear protective gloves if required by your regulating agency.

PEDICURE

 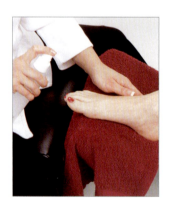  

01 Wash and sanitize hands by washing and applying antiseptic. Waterless or foam antiseptics are easy to use.

02 Sanitize your client's feet by spraying each foot with an antiseptic. Perform a visual examination. If there is no sign of disease or disorder, place client's feet in the foot bath and allow to soak according to manufacturer's directions, usually 5 to 10 minutes.

03 Remove client's feet from the foot bath, dry them and place on the foot rest. Remove nail polish, if any.

04 Examine the feet for any abnormalities. Use disposable spatulas to separate toes. If there are no problems, continue service

THE STUDY OF NAILS

05 **Trim and file nails.** If nails are too long, use a toenail clipper. Position the clipper horizontally.

06 **File straight across**, softening the corners to avoid ingrown toenails. Avoid clipping or filing too deeply into the corners.

07 **Apply cuticle remover cream** to each toe. **Push back cuticles** with a cotton-wrapped orangewood stick.

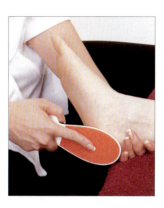

08 **Apply sloughing lotion** to entire foot and **massage to remove dead skin cells**. If needed, use a foot file or paddle. Repeat trimming, filing and cuticle care on the opposite foot. Scrub both feet with brush to remove any debris and clean under toenails. Remove each foot from bath and dry thoroughly.

MASSAGE

Foot massage is very similar to hand massage, but your movements can be firmer and larger. A benefit of foot massage is the prevention of foot and leg problems. In order to maintain relaxation, do not drop the foot or break contact during massage manipulation.

09 **Massage with lotion.** Use effleurage strokes to apply lotion to foot and calf.

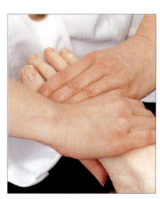

10 Then, use circular kneading movements, beginning at the knee and going down to the ankle and back up to knee avoiding the shinbone and area above the knee. Apply pressure to the muscular tissue on either side of the shinbone. Repeat three times.

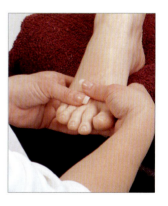

11 **Massage top of each foot** and toe.

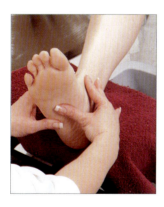

12 **Knead (petrissage) the sole**, using circular movements.

COSMETOLOGY FUNDAMENTALS

559

13 Remove excess lotion from the nail surface with a cotton-wrapped orangewood stick soaked in polish remover.

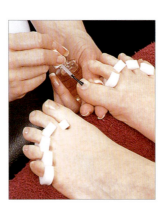

POLISH
14 Apply powder with cotton to the feet, then **position toe separators**. If desired, slippers may be put on prior to the toe separators. **Apply base coat** to the nails of both feet. Start at the little toe and work to the big toe.

15 Apply two coats of polish.

16 Apply top coat, followed by a quick-drying product. Allow drying time up to one hour. Remove the toe separators when polish is dry.

BASIC PEDICURE COMPLETION

- Offer a prebook visit to your client.
- Recommend retail products for your client.
- Discard non-reusable materials, replace used towels with fresh towels and arrange all products and implements in proper order.
- Disinfect your pedicure service implements and equipment.
- Wash your hands with liquid soap.

SPECIAL NAIL SERVICES

Additional services may sometimes be required to accommodate your client's special needs. Five of these special services will be described here.

FRENCH MANICURE

A **French manicure** is similar to the plain manicure with two exceptions:
- White polish is applied on the free edge.
- Pink or peach polish is applied to the entire nail.

NAIL REPAIR (MENDING WITH SILK)

Along with the products used for the basic manicure procedure, you will also need the following items for repairing nails: adhesive accelerator, silk, dehydrant and an adhesive. Split or broken (cracked) nails can be repaired to a smooth surface appearance using the steps on the following page.

NAIL REPAIR GUIDELINES

1. Smooth the surface of the nail gently over the broken or split area with the black side of a 3-way buffer to remove surface oil.
2. Apply dehydrant to the nail.
3. Cut a small piece of (silk) fiber, sized slightly larger, to cover split or break.
4. Apply adhesive to split or broken area of the nail. Do not touch skin or cuticle with adhesive.
5. Place silk, using tweezer, over split or broken portion of nail. Cut away any uneven edges.
6. Smooth repaired area with orangewood stick.
7. Apply second layer of adhesive to seal. Avoid touching the skin. You may apply adhesive accelerator to speed drying time.
8. Allow to dry thoroughly.
9. Buff smooth with 3-way buffer.
10. Soak and scrub nail repair area.
11. Continue with nail service.

HOT OIL OR CREAM MANICURE

These nail services involve the use of an electric heating device. Instead of placing a client's hand in a warm water soaking solution, the hand is placed in warmed oil or cream. All other procedures for this nail service are the same as in a basic nail service. This procedure is helpful for very dry, aging or abused hands and on ridged or brittle nails.

ELECTRIC NAIL SERVICES

Special electrically powered tools can perform the same procedures as a basic nail service. Emery discs file the length of the nails, vibrating devices aid in pushing cuticles, spinning nail brushes remove debris, and coarse sandpaper discs act like an abrasive on calluses. Nail buffing discs can not be used in certain areas. Take precautions to avoid heat friction and overthinning of nail plates when using any electric equipment on natural nails. Nail drills should be used only on artificial nail applications. Check with your area's regulating agency.

NAIL ART

Nail art is an additional service that some salons offer their clients. With this service, your creativity can be expressed in many different ways. Nail art can range from simple patterns to detailed landscape scenes. Flat nail art is created by using nail paints and striping tape. Three-dimensional nail art is created with rhinestones, feathers, painted acrylic beads, etc. Airbrush nail art is applied with an airbrush gun and airbrush paints. Nail jewelry is also a popular option.

14.3 ARTIFICIAL NAIL CARE

Artificial nails are used to improve the appearance of one's nails and help to conceal broken nails. There are several types of artificial nail products currently available for use in the salon. Each has special procedures individualized by the manufacturer of the product. Since each brand of artificial nails can vary greatly in application procedure, your review in this text will be centered around the basic product ingredients and procedures.

Artificial nails can be applied over a plastic tip or created directly on the nail. Prior to an artificial nail service, a basic manicure should be performed up to but not including the base coat.

There are three general product systems by which artificial nails can be created, which are:
1. **Acrylic Nails** (powder and liquid)
2. **Nail Wraps** (fiberglass, silk, linen and nylon)
3. **Gel Nails** (light-cured)

In the past, a discoloration found between the nail plate and an artificial nail was referred to as a mold, but was actually a bacterial infection caused by pseudomonas aeruginosa, a bacteria occurring naturally on the skin. In favorable conditions, such as a lack of oxygen, the bacteria grow unrestrained and cause an infection which leads to discoloration of the nail.

ARTIFICIAL NAIL ESSENTIALS

Just like natural nail manicure and pedicure services, artificial nail services require a selection of products and implements. The following items are necessary to complete an artificial nail service along with the items used for the basic manicure service. Each is described by name and function.

ARTIFICIAL NAIL SERVICE PRODUCTS

PRODUCT	FUNCTION
MONOMER	Mixes with the powder to form an acrylic nail; liquid in form
POLYMER	Mixes with the monomer to form an acrylic nail; powder in form
PRIMER	Ensures adhesion of acrylic product to nail
NAIL TIPS	Adhere to nail; they have a hollowed area on one end called the nail well, which is attached to the natural nail; plastic extension

PRODUCT	FUNCTION
NAIL FORM	Forms an acrylic extension to the natural nail; plastic, paper or metal templates
ADHESIVE	Bonds a plastic tip to a natural nail; specially formulated for the nail industry; tacky (sticky) substance
DEHYDRANT (ANTISEPTIC)	Reduces the amount of moisture in the nail when brushed over the nail plate; allows better adhesion of nail enhancements and reduces growth of bacteria
BRUSH CLEANER	Removes any residual nail enhancement product from the bristles of a brush

RTIFICIAL NAIL SERVICE IMPLEMENTS/SUPPLIES

IMPLEMENTS/SUPPLIES	FUNCTION
DAPPEN DISH	Holds monomer and polymer separately
ACRYLIC BRUSH	Builds the acrylic nail; may be flat, oval or rounded in shape and is made from natural hair, such as sable
NAIL FILE	Shortens, files and shapes artificial nails; coarse grit
BLOCK BUFFER	Smoothes nails; rectangular abrasive block
EYEDROPPER	Removes acrylic liquid from container to dappen dish

INFECTION CONTROL AND SAFETY

1. Wear protective goggles when using adhesive and filing acrylic nails.
2. Keep all lids on product containers tight to prevent vapor leakage.
3. Insure that ventilation is adequate and provides an intake of outside air and a return of salon air.
4. Avoid allowing primer (hydrant) to come in contact with skin since it may cause burning.
5. Dispose of all monomer and polymer together in a sealed plastic bag. Do not pour monomer or any nail liquid, including polish remover, down a drain.
6. Clean up any product spills immediately and dispose of them in a covered container.
7. Avoid unnecessary pressure at base of nail when filing. Nail root or matrix damage could result.
8. Follow manufacturer's directions exactly. Do not mix and match chemicals from different manufacturers.
9. Avoid overheating nail during buffing.
10. Do not allow food or drink in the general area of acrylic nails.
11. Do not allow smoking in the salon, as vapors from nail products, such as adhesives, are flammable.
12. Keep all products organized and labeled, and maintain MSDS guidelines for all products.

WORKSHOP 04
NAIL TIPS

The length of your client's natural nail can be extended through the use of plastic nail tips.

These come in sizes often numbered from 1-10 with number 1 the largest and 10 the smallest. Selecting the right size for each of your client's nails is a critical factor in the success of these extensions. Nail tips are reasonably strong and can be cut, filed and polished. Avoid damaging plastic nail tips by using non-acetone polish remover.

NAIL TIPS PREPARATION

In addition to following the same preparation procedures as outlined in the "Basic Manicure" section of this chapter, be sure to assemble the following products and implements:
- Nail tips
- Adhesive glue
- Dehydrant
- 3-way buffer

NAIL TIPS PROCEDURE

- Wash and sanitize hands*
- Perform visual analysis
- Remove nail polish
- Perform thorough hand and nail examination and consultation
- Select correct size of nail tips
- File and shape natural free edge
- Buff nail surface gently
- Apply dehydrant to nail surface
- Apply first drop of adhesive to well of plastic tip
- Roll tip onto natural nail slowly
- Hold nail for 15 to 30 seconds
- Apply second drop of adhesive on top of seam
- Spray with adhesive accelerator
- Trim free edge of nail tip
- Measure length of all nails
- File free edge
- File and buff top of seam
- Buff to shine or polish
- Blend and smooth imperfections

*Wear protective gloves if required by your regulating agency.

ALERT!

METHYL METHACRYLATE MONOMER

In the early 1970s, the Food and Drug Administration (FDA) received a number of complaints of personal injury associated with the use of acrylic monomers containing methyl methacrylate. On the basis of its investigations of the injuries and discussions with medical experts in the field of dermatology, the FDA concluded that liquid methyl methacrylate is a poisonous substance that should not be used in acrylic monomers. However, methyl methacrylate is safe to use in acrylic polymers.

NAIL TIPS

Wash and sanitize your hands and your client's hands. Perform **visual analysis** for signs of disease or disorder. If none are present, **remove nail polish**. Next, continue to **perform a thorough hand and nail examination and consultation.**

SIZING
01-03 Select **correct size of nail tips** to fit client's nail bed. Match the width of each nail. If they are too wide or too small, they may loosen. They must fit sidewall to sidewall. They should cover no more than ⅓ to ½ of the nail bed and extend ⅓ to ½ the length of the free edge. Bevel the well of the nail tip with a file to reduce the amount of filing after initial adhesion.

NAIL PREP
04 File and shape natural free edge and buff the nail surface gently to remove oil and prepare the natural nail.

05 Apply **dehydrant to the nail surface** to help reduce moisture and oil, prevent bacterial growth and maximize adhesion.

ADHERING NAIL TIPS
06 Apply first drop of adhesive to the **well of the plastic tip.** This helps to avoid air bubbles under the tip and excess adhesive, which sometimes occurs if you apply the adhesive to the natural nail. **Roll tip onto the free edge of the natural nail slow**ly so you can see the adhesive moving up the natural nail.

07-08 Hold the nail for 15 to 30 seconds. Do not force nail on. If it has to be forced, it probably does not fit correctly.

COSMETOLOGY FUNDAMENTALS

09 Apply a second drop of adhesive on top of the seam along the tip and natural nail. Apply the drop at the center and spread side to side.

10 Spray with an adhesive accelerator to help set the adhesive quickly.

TRIMMING
11 Trim the free edge of the nail tip with toenail clippers to the desired length. Always cut from the sides to the center.

12 You can also use a one-cut tool designed for this purpose. Do not use scissors, since it will cause lifting on one side of the tip and undue stress to the nail tip.

13 Measure the length of all nails and strive for symmetry.

FILING/BUFFING
14 File the free edge to the shape desired.

15 File and buff the top of the seam to create a smooth finish. Keep the file flat on the nail tip to avoid filing into the natural nail. Be careful not to overheat the nail with constant buffing. Periodically, check the seams with your fingers for smoothness and temperature. Continue with each nail.

16-17 Buff to a shine or polish. Blend and smooth imperfections between the tip and natural nail with a buffer block. Use a 3-way buffer to add shine. Buff with the black side, then white and finally the gray side. Note: Nail tips can be overlayed with acrylic for strength, as seen in the next procedure.

14

NAIL TIPS COMPLETION

- Offer a prebook visit to your client
- Recommend retail products for your client
- Discard non-reusable materials, replace used towels with fresh towels and arrange all products and implements in proper order
- Disinfect your nail tips service implements and equipment
- Wash your hands with liquid soap

WORKSHOP 05
TIPS WITH ACRYLIC OVERLAY

To create a more durable extension and a longer lasting service, acrylic material can be applied over the nail tip. The **overlay** is created with a combination of acrylic powder called a **polymer** and a liquid called a **monomer**. A sable brush is dipped first into the liquid and then into the powder to combine the two ingredients and create "beads or balls" of acrylic on the end or side of the brush. These beads are then deposited onto the nail and nail tip to create the overlay. The parts of the sable brush you should know are identified in the illustration to the left.

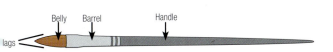

TIPS WITH ACRYLIC OVERLAY PREPARATION

In addition to following the same preparation procedures as outlined in the "Basic Manicure" section of this chapter, be sure to assemble the following products and implements:

- Sable brush
- Liquid in dappen dish
- Nail adhesive
- Regular nail implements and products
- Acrylic liquid and acrylic powder in dappen dishes
- Nail tips
- Dehydrant and primer

TIPS WITH ACRYLIC OVERLAY PROCEDURE

- Wash and sanitize hands*
- Perform visual analysis
- Remove nail polish
- Perform thorough hand and nail examination and consultation
- Prepare natural nail-buff, dehydrate, prime
- Apply tips
- Buff nails and tips
- Form bead on side or tip of acrylic brush
- Apply acrylic at free edge (zone 1)
- Pat and press with belly of brush to blend
- Blend acrylic toward middle of nail plate (zone 2)
- Place second acrylic bead in middle of nail plate (zone 2)
- Pat and press toward free edge
- Place third acrylic bead at cuticle area (zone 3)
- Pat and press toward middle of nail plate (zone 2)
- File and shape nail
- Buff to smooth finish

*Wear protective gloves if required by your regulating agency.

COSMETOLOGY FUNDAMENTALS

TIPS WITH ACRYLIC OVERLAY

01 Wash and sanitize your hands and your client's hands. Perform visual analysis for signs of disease or disorder. If none are present, remove nail polish. Next, continue to perform a thorough hand and nail examination and consultation. Prepare natural nails by buffing, applying dehydrant and primer. Apply tips as shown under nail tips procedure. Buff nails and tips.

ACRYLIC OVERLAY
02 Form a bead on the side or tip of your acrylic brush by dipping flags into liquid and laying or dragging the brush through the acrylic powder.

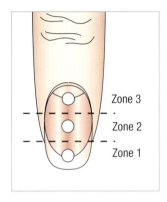

03 Think of the nail as subdivided into 3 zones to help build the overlay.

04-06 Apply acrylic at free edge (zone 1). This bead should be medium in size. Pat and press with the belly of the brush to blend from side to side. Blend acrylic toward the middle of the nail plate (zone 2) by stroking gently.

07 Place a second acrylic bead in the middle of the nail plate (zone 2) and spread from side to side. This bead should be medium in size. Pat and press toward the free edge, blending the acrylic with zone 1. The consistency you create is very important. The bead should melt a little but not touch the sides of the nail wall.

08 Place a third acrylic bead at the cuticle area (zone 3) and spread it from side to side. This should be the smallest and most moist of all beads. Pat and press toward the middle of the nail plate (zone 2) blending over this zone. Take care that the acrylic in zone 3 is kept thin and off the skin.

Keep all acrylic and products off the skin and cuticle. Contact could cause the acrylic to lift and/or produce an allergic reaction.

To determine when the acrylic is dry enough to file, tap it with the barrel of your brush, which should produce a clicking sound.

14

11 Buff to a smooth finish with a 3-way buffer.

ILING/BUFFING
9-10 File and shape the nail when the acrylic is dry. Hold the skin out of e way when you are filing. For the best leverage hold ⅓ of the file and se the remaining ⅔ of the file length.

AIL TIPS WITH ACRYLIC OVERLAY COMPLETION

- Offer a prebook visit to your client.
- Recommend retail products for your client.
- Discard non-reusable materials, replace used towels with fresh towels and arrange all products and implements in proper order.
- Disinfect your acrylic overlay service implements and equipment.
- Wash your hands with liquid soap.

WORKSHOP 06
SCULPTURED NAILS

Sculptured nails produced with a nail form rather than a tip can be used as an alternative to tips and overlays.

culptured nails are created by combining two ingredients, which are the polymer and the monomer. A powder acrylic is ixed with a liquid containing both a plasticizer, which keeps the mixture flexible while drying, and a catalyst, which creates chemical reaction that causes the acrylic and plasticizer to dry. Since you control the mixing, success is based on creating a onsistent combination of ingredients on each nail.

his mixture is applied to a nail form that extends the length of the nail plate and may extend beyond the free edge of the atural nail. After drying, the form is removed and the new nail is shaped, filed and polished. As the natural nail grows out, "fill-in service" (referred to as re-balancing) is needed every two weeks. Also, only non-acetone polish removers should be sed with sculptured nails. The problem reported most often by clients who wear sculptured nails is the formation of bacteria nder the artificial nail. Applying a dehydrating product to the nail and making sure the nail is completely dry before erforming a sculptured nail service will help avoid trapping moisture and the occurrence of a bacterial infection. In addition, nce most acrylic primers contain ingredients to help prevent the growth of bacteria, avoid touching the nail with your hands fter the primer has been applied.

SCULPTURED NAILS PREPARATION

In addition to following the same procedures as outlined in the "Basic Manicure" section of this chapter, be sure to assemble the following products and implements:

- Acrylic liquid and acrylic powder in dappen dishes
- Liquid in dappen dish
- Dehydrant and primer (if required)
- Sable brush
- Regular nail implements and products
- Nail forms (plastic, paper or metal)

SCULPTURED NAILS PROCEDURE

- Wash and sanitize hands*
- Perform visual analysis
- Remove nail polish
- Perform thorough hand and nail examination and consultation
- File free edge
- Buff surface of nail lightly
- Remove filing residue

- Apply dehydrant
- Apply nail form
- Apply primer if directed
- Measure out required amount of acrylic powder
- Form bead on side of brush
- Apply acrylic bead to form to create free edge (zone 1)
- Rotate brush

- Pat and press toward edges of nail form
- Define shape and length of free edge
- Create second acrylic bead
- Place second bead in middle section (zone 2)
- Pat, press and stroke acrylic into place

- Place smallest bead just below cuticle (zone 3)
- Pat, press and stroke acrylic down to base of nail
- Apply fourth bead (optional)
- Remove form
- File
- Remove nail dust and filings
- Buff with a buffer block and 3-way buffer

*Wear protective gloves if required by your regulating agency.

SCULPTURED NAILS

01 Wash and sanitize your hands and your client's hands. **Perform visual analysis** for signs of disease or disorder. If none are present, **remove nail polish.** Next, continue to **perform a thorough hand and nail examination and consultation.**

02 File the free edge and buff the surface of the nail lightly using a 3-way buffer to prepare the natural nail. **Remove filing residue** with cotton.

03 Apply dehydrant to the natural nail.

570 THE STUDY OF NAILS

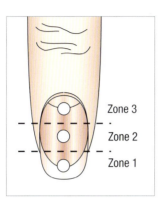

NAIL FORM

04 Apply the nail form by sliding the nail form under the client's nail, and allowing the adhesive tabs to attach to the sides of the client's finger. Do not force the form under the nail as it may cut the hyponychium. Make sure the form fits snugly under the edge, is positioned in a c-curve and is even with the client's nail.

Apply primer if directed by the sculpting brand you are using. Since most primers are acids, avoid any contact with the skin to prevent a burn or an allergic reaction. As you proceed with the application, use the art as a guide when determining the three zones.

05 Measure out the required amount of acrylic powder into the dappen dishes. Form a bead on the side of the brush by dipping the flags of the sable brush into the liquid, thoroughly moistening and laying or dragging the wet brush through the white acrylic powder. Avoid dipping the barrel of the brush as it will cause bristles to loosen. This should be the largest bead. More liquid in the brush allows you to draw more powder, producing a larger bead.

06 Apply acrylic bead to the form to create a free edge by placing the bead where the free edge meets the nail form (zone 1). Rotate the brush slightly as you deposit the acrylic bead. It will be formed into a half circle, often referred to as the smile line.

07-09 Pat and press toward the edges of the nail form with the belly of the brush spreading outward toward the edges of the nail form. Define the shape and length of the free edge. Some nail forms have a grid pattern on them, which will help you create symmetry.

COSMETOLOGY FUNDAMENTALS

571

10-11 Create a second acrylic bead, medium in size, by dipping your brush first into liquid then into the pink acrylic powder. Place the second bead in the middle section (zone 2). Pat, press and stroke the acrylic into place, gently overlapping zone 1.

12 Place the smallest bead just below the cuticle (zone 3), just below the cuticle area. Pat, press and stroke the acrylic down to the base of the nail. Move out to the sides and past the point where the free edge meets the nail form, overlapping the acrylic material previously applied. Apply a fourth bead for additional strength across the stress area where the free edge meets the nail bed, if needed.

FILING/BUFFING
13 Remove the nail form when acrylic is dry. File to create a smooth finish. Remove the nail dust and filings. Periodically break contact to reduce heat, check for smoothness and feel the temperature of the nail. Continue with each nail.

14-15 Buff with a buffer block and a 3-way buffer to create shine and a natural-looking blend between the tip and the natural nail. Buff with the black side, then white and finally the gray side. Wash hands to remove nail dust. Sculptured nails can be left natural or polished.

SCULPTURED NAILS COMPLETION
- Offer a prebook visit to your client.
- Recommend retail products for your client.
- Discard non-reusable materials, replace used towels with fresh towels and arrange all products and implements in proper order.
- Disinfect your sculptured nail service implements and equipment.
- Wash your hands with liquid soap.

FILL-INS AND RE-BALANCING ACRYLIC NAILS

Whenever you coat the entire surface of the nail with acrylic, the base of the nail (at the cuticle) will require fill-in services. These should be booked approximately every 2 weeks, when the nail has grown $1/16$" (.156 cm). This is very important because otherwise as the natural nail grows, the artificial nail will lift, which can lead to trapped moisture and growth of bacteria.

FILL-INS AND RE-BALANCING GUIDELINES

Preparation for the fill-in service is basically the same as the sculptured nails preparation other than the use of the nail form.

1. Wash and sanitize your hands and your client's hands. Perform visual analysis for signs of disease or disorder. If none are present, remove all polish, using a non-acetone polish remover and cotton. Next, continue to perform a thorough hand and nail examination.
2. File the cuticle area to remove any loosened acrylic material. Blend the line of demarcation by smoothing out the "edge" of acrylic material with your file in the new growth area. Be careful not to file the natural nail.
3. Re-balance the shape of the entire nail to keep it looking natural. Zone 1 should be thin, zone 2 should be thicker for strength and zone 3 should be thin. (See illustration to the right). File and buff to re-balance nail and blend remaining acrylic to new growth area.
4. Buff with the fine side of a block buffer to gently buff any exposed surface of the natural nail.
5. Cleanse nails with liquid soap and water; do not soak.
6. Push cuticles back.
7. Apply dehydrant to exposed natural nail only.
8. Apply primer to exposed natural nail only.
9. Apply acrylic bead to new growth area.
10. Pat, press and stroke in place.
11. Apply acrylic bead to stress point where the free edge meets the nail bed to complete.
12. File entire nail smooth with a file or 3-way buffer. Wash hands to remove nail dust.
13. Apply base coat and polish as desired.

If you see signs of a bacterial infection, you may remove the artificial nail, but wear gloves and use proper disinfection procedures. Send the client to a physician for treatment. Do not perform further nail services until the bacterial infection has cleared up.

REMOVING NAIL TIPS, TIPS WITH OVERLAYS AND SCULPTURED NAILS

To remove nail tips, tips with overlays and sculptured nails, soak nails in the product solvent recommended by the manufacturer. When adhesive is thoroughly softened, gently lift artificial nail product from natural nail using an orangewood stick. Cleanse entire nail using polish remover followed by cleansing solution.

ADDITIONAL ARTIFICIAL NAIL SERVICES

Additional artificial nail services include nail wraps and light-cured gel nails.

NAIL WRAPS

Nail wraps are woven materials that are applied to the natural nails or nails with tips to add strength. The material is held in place and an overlay is created by applying several layers of a thick adhesive called resin. The resin is chemically hardened by the application of an accelerator. A product that is sometimes referred to as "liquid nail wrap" acts as a nail strengthener. It is basically a polish that contains fibers and is generally applied in the same way as polish. Different types of fabric are used for wraps today, including:

- Fiberglass
- Silk
- Linen
- Nylon

Fiberglass is a synthetic fiber that is loosely woven and is almost invisible once applied. Fiberglass is a very strong and sturdy fabric to use. Silk is a natural fiber that is tightly woven. Silk is often recommended for shorter nails with ridges because when applied, it creates a very smooth overlay. Linen is a thicker fabric that remains visible on the nail after application. Clients typically wear a polish to hide the fact that they have a linen wrap overlay.

LIGHT-CURED OR GEL NAILS

This product is simply an acrylic gel that is applied to the nail plate, after which the hand is placed under a special light (ultraviolet or halogen) that creates a chemical reaction that causes the product to harden. This process is called "curing" the nail. This product is used to reinforce weak nails or can be used over tips to add sheen and strength. Manufacturers have created different gels to act as bonding agents for tips, nail builders or thickeners and nail glosses for shine. It is a fast and economical service for the client and an excellent way to help a client develop beautiful strong nails. Always follow manufacturer's directions carefully.

CONNECTING THEORY TO REAL-WORLD PRACTICE

THE STUDY OF NAILS	PERSONAL CONNECTION: IMPROVE YOURSELF	INDUSTRY CONNECTION: BECOME PROFESSIONAL	CLIENT CONNECTION: SERVE THE GUEST
NAIL THEORY	Understand the relationship between healthy nails and general health	Use scientific knowledge to develop high level skills in nail services	Protect client health and safety when delivering nail services
NATURAL NAIL CARE	Maintain personal nail hygiene that reflects your personal image	Build salon clientele by delivering consistently excellent nail services	Help clients improve the health and beauty of their natural nails
ARTIFICIAL NAIL CARE	Enhance your appearance with specialized nail products	Expand your professional range through specialized nail services	Offer clients additional options for special nail looks

IN OTHER WORDS

Providing specialized nail services enhances your clients' total image and helps you build a loyal clientele.

LESSONS LEARNED

- Understanding the structure and growth of nails and the diseases, disorders and conditions of the nail is essential in order to provide nail services that protect clients' health and safety.
- Well-groomed and cared-for natural nails improve clients' overall appearance.
- Artificial nail services enhance your clients' appearance and in turn assist you in retaining more loyal clients.

15

THE STUDY OF SKIN

15.1 SKIN THEORY
FUNCTIONS OF THE SKIN
COMPOSITION OF THE SKIN
TYPES OF SKIN
SKIN DISEASES AND DISORDERS

15.2 SKIN CARE
MASSAGE
FACIAL MASKS
SKIN CARE ESSENTIALS
INFECTION CONTROL AND SAFETY
SKIN CARE SERVICE ESSENTIALS
BASIC FACIAL

15.3 HAIR REMOVAL
HAIR REMOVAL ESSENTIALS
INFECTION CONTROL AND SAFETY
HAIR REMOVAL SERVICE ESSENTIALS
TEMPORARY HAIR REMOVAL
BASIC WAXING
PERMANENT HAIR REMOVAL

15.4 MAKEUP
FACIAL SHAPES
COLOR THEORY
MAKEUP ESSENTIALS
INFECTION CONTROL AND SAFETY
MAKEUP SERVICE ESSENTIALS
MAKEUP TECHNIQUES AND PRODUCTS
BASIC MAKEUP APPLICATION

HEALTHY, GLOWING, ATTRACTIVE SKIN CAN BE ACHIEVED THROUGH PROFESSIONAL SKIN CARE, HAIR REMOVAL AND MAKEUP APPLICATION

FOLLOWING THIS LESSON
YOU WILL BE ABLE TO:

Define the function, composition and types of skin

Identify disorders and diseases of the skin

Explain and demonstrate the steps and massage techniques used during a basic facial

Identify the difference between temporary and permanent hair removal and explain the techniques used for each

Explain the basic steps used during a makeup application

CONNECTING THEORY TO REAL-WORLD PRACTICE

APPROACHING PROFESSIONAL DEVELOPMENT AS A PRACTICAL SCIENCE WILL HELP YOU:

PERSONAL CONNECTION:	**INDUSTRY CONNECTION:**	**CLIENT CONNECTION:**
IMPROVE YOURSELF	BECOME A PROFESSIONAL	SERVE THE GUEST
Appreciate the beauty, complexity and importance of the body's largest organ	Broaden your expertise to include high quality skin care services	Give clients the self-assurance that comes with beautiful, healthy skin

There are many products with "derm" (skin) on the label and these reflect people's growing interest in health beautiful skin.

15.1 SKIN THEORY

The skin is the largest—and perhaps most magnificent—organ of the body. It is simultaneously sensitive and supremely durable and requires special attention and care to maintain its health, elasticity, color and vibrancy.

The study of the skin, its structure, functions, diseases and treatment is called **dermatology**. A dermatologist is a medical skin specialist. As a salon professional, it is important for you to have a basic understanding of skin and the skin care services offered in the salon. In the skin care industry, esthetics is known as the process of cleansing, toning, moisturizing, protecting, and enhancing the skin.

The skin, as the largest organ of the body, covers the entire body and protects it from invasion from outside particles. Except for the brain, the skin is the most complex organ of the body. Your skin is continuously working in its own efficient manner as an intermediary between your body and your environment, performing many functions. The skin and its layers make up the integumentary (in-**TEG**-u-men-tary) system of the body.

FUNCTIONS OF THE SKIN

The skin has six basic functions:

SENSATION
Feelings generated by the nerve endings just under the outer layer of the skin make you aware of heat, cold, touch, pain and pressure. The reaction to a sensation is called a reflex.

SECRETION
The skin secretes sebum, a complex mixture of fatty substances that keeps it soft, supple and pliable. The sebum on the skin, known as acid mantle, serves as a protective barrier to prevent bacteria from invading the skin.

ABSORPTION
The skin permits certain substances like water and oxygen to pass through its tissues.

REGULATION
The skin helps maintain the body's temperature.

PROTECTION
The skin shields your body from the direct impact of heat, cold, bacteria and other aspects of the environment that could be detrimental to your health.

EXCRETION
The skin eliminates sweat, salt and wastes from the body, therefore helping remove toxins from the internal systems.

COMPOSITION OF THE SKIN

The skin has three main layers:

1. **Epidermis, which is the outermost layer of the skin,** also referred to as cuticle or scarf skin
2. **Dermis, which is the underlying, or inner, layer of the skin,** also called derma, corium, cutis or true skin
3. **Subcutaneous** (also called subcutis or subdermis), **which is located below the dermis layer and composed primarily of fatty (adipose) tissue**

EPIDERMIS

The epidermis makes up the outer layers of the skin. It's almost like a bag that covers you and protects you from the environment. **The epidermis is composed of five layers of cells with differing characteristics and contains no blood vessels.**

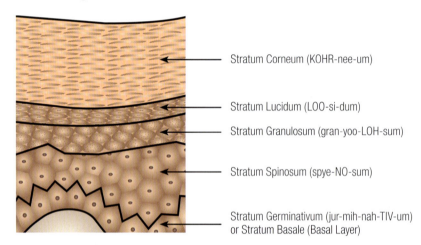

Stratum Corneum (KOHR-nee-um)
Stratum Lucidum (LOO-si-dum)
Stratum Granulosum (gran-yoo-LOH-sum)
Stratum Spinosum (spye-NO-sum)
Stratum Germinativum (jur-mih-nah-TIV-um) or Stratum Basale (Basal Layer)

STRATUM GERMINATIVUM

At the lowest level of the epidermis you will find the **stratum germinativum.** It begins with the stratum basale, or basal cell layer, which is a single layer thick. **It is here where skin cell growth occurs through mitosis or cell division.** Basal cells are constantly dividing and producing new cells that are pushed toward the surface of the skin to replace cells that have been shed. Keratinization, the chemical conversion of living cells into dead protein cells, begins when the newly produced cells are pushed toward the surface. As the newly produced cells move toward the surface and farther away from the stratum germinativum, they flatten out, lose most of their water, die and, as keratinized cells, are finally shed. This process takes from 25 to 30 days, depending mostly on the area of the body, age and/or health of the individual. **Melanocytes are also found in the stratum germinativum.** These cells produce the melanosomes or pigment granules containing melanin that give color to the skin. There are two types of melanin. Eumelanin is brown/black in color and pheomelanin is red/yellow in color. **The amount and type of melanin present will determine the skin's color.** Brown skin contains a large amount of melanin while skin with little melanin will appear pale or pinkish. Melanin protects the skin, particularly in layers closest to the surface, by screening out harmful ultraviolet rays.

STRATUM SPINOSUM

The **stratum spinosum** is the next layer up and is sometimes considered to be part of the stratum germinativum. It includes cells that have absorbed melanin to distribute pigmentation to other cells. The cells then become irregularly shaped and appear as spines between the cells.

STRATUM GRANULOSUM

The next layer is the **stratum granulosum**. In this layer the cells become more regularly shaped and look like many tiny granules. This layer of the epidermis gets its name from these granules. These granules (almost dead cells) are on their way to the surface of the skin to replace cells that are shed from the stratum corneum.

STRATUM LUCIDUM

On the palms of the hands and the soles of the feet only, where there are no hair follicles, there is another skin layer that is called the stratum lucidum. The cells in this layer are even more flattened and transparent (clear). They are called squamous (**SQUAW**-mus) cells due to their flat, scale-like appearance, thus making the skin thickest on palms of hands and soles of feet.

STRATUM CORNEUM

The uppermost layer, the **stratum corneum** (sometimes called the horny layer) is the toughest layer of the epidermis and is composed of keratin protein cells that are continually shed and continually replaced by new cells from below. Unlike the hard keratin found in nails and hair, the keratin produced by the skin remains soft throughout the keratinization and shedding process. The stratum corneum acts as a protective layer for the layers below it. It protects the skin's moisture balance by acting as a barrier to moisture loss. It, in turn, is protected by an acid mantle, a mixture of oil, secreted by sebaceous oil glands, and water secreted by sweat glands. The pH of the acid mantle averages 4.5 to 5.5.

The entire epidermis protects the dermis and the subcutaneous layers below it. Since the skin cells are constantly being sloughed off at the stratum corneum, the replacement of the cells is a continuous process.

DERMIS

The **dermis** layer is made up of connective tissues. Connective tissues are composed of a semifluid substance containing collagen protein and elastin fibers, both of which lend support to the epidermis and give the skin its elastic quality. Collagen protein fibers are strong and flexible while the elastin fibers are soft and pliable. It is in this layer that the collagen and elastin fibers deteriorate, causing the skin to sag and wrinkle during the aging process. Also found in the dermis are the sweat glands called **sudoriferous** (soo-dohr-IF-er-us) **glands**, oil glands called **sebaceous** (sih-BAY-shus) **glands**, sensory nerve endings and receptors, blood vessels, arrector pili muscles and a major portion of each hair follicle. Remember that hair is an appendage of the skin, as are the nails and sweat and oil glands.

The dermis is also called the 'true skin' or corium (**KOH**-reeum).

SUDORIFEROUS GLANDS

The sudoriferous (sweat) glands are controlled by the nervous system of the body. Each gland consists of a coiled base and tube-like duct opening on the surface of the skin to form a sweat pore. **The sweat glands have three major functions:**

1. **Control and regulation of body temperatures.** When the body becomes overheated, large quantities of sweat are secreted onto the skin's surface. This allows for rapid evaporation, which cools the skin and maintains the body temperature at 98.6°F (37°C).
2. **Excretion of waste products.** Waste materials, such as salt and other chemicals, are easily eliminated as sweat is produced.
3. **Helping to maintain the acidic pH factor of the skin.** A mixture of sweat and oil (called the acid mantle) keeps the surface of the skin slightly acidic, which helps prevent bacteria from entering the body.

Sweat and oil glands are called duct glands.

Sweat, the amount of which varies with your body temperature and activity, is a weak salt solution. Besides water and salt, sweat contains other substances including lactic acid and uric acid, both of which help create the acidic pH of sweat.

The sudoriferous glands, also called eccrine glands, are widely distributed over the body surface. They are found in the greatest concentration on the palms of the hands, soles of the feet, scalp and forehead, underarms, anterior trunk and genital region.

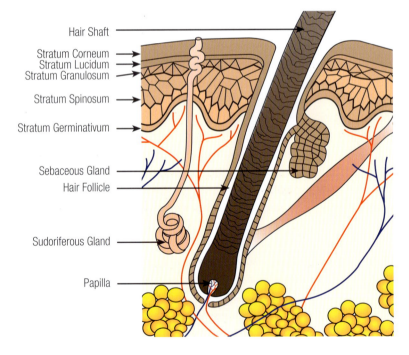

SEBACEOUS GLANDS

Sebaceous, or oil, glands are partially controlled by the nervous system and are sac-like glands that are attached to hair follicles. These glands are 2-3 times larger around facial hair follicles than they are around scalp follicles. When sebaceous glands produce an overabundance of sebum, the result is "oily skin." No oil glands are found on palms of hands or soles of feet.

Sebum is a complex secretion containing a high percentage of fatty, oily substances. The sebum mixes with the secretion of the sweat glands and spreads over the surface of the skin. It is this layer of oil and moisture that is called the acid mantle. The acid mantle keeps the skin smooth, prevents dirt and grime from entering the outer layer of the epidermis, and also prevents the skin from drying or chapping.

When we measure the pH of the skin, we are actually measuring the pH of the acid mantle.

The acid mantle is naturally acidic, ranging from a pH of 4.5 to 5.5 for most people. This is mainly due to lactic acid and sodium salt. The mantle protects against bacterial invasion by providing a hostile (acidic) environment for bacterial growth. Most of the problems encountered with skin are caused by the sebaceous gland, whether by underactivity or overactivity or blockage of the duct. The sebaceous glands are attached to the upper third of the hair follicles and the oil, or sebum, is secreted onto the surface of the skin by way of the papillary (**PAP**-e-lair-y) canal.

SUBCUTANEOUS

Below the dermis of the skin is a fatty layer called the subcutaneous tissue. **The subcutaneous tissue is a protective cushion for the skin.** It acts as a shock absorber to protect the bones and to help support the delicate structures such as blood vessels and nerve endings. This layer gives contour and shape to the body and acts as an emergency reservoir of food and water.

It is composed of adipose (fatty) and loose, connective tissue. The collagen and elastin fibers that run in all directions are continuous with those in the dermis. Depending upon genetics,

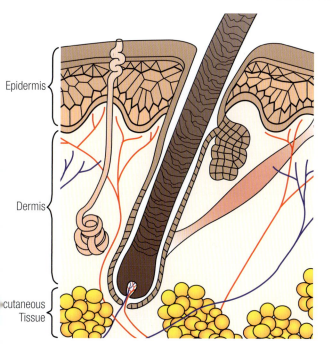

nutrition, exercise and general health of the body, varying amounts of fat cells are found in the subcutaneous tissues. This fatty tissue provides insulation, acts as padding and stores energy for the body. Subcutaneous fat storage is partly under the control of sex hormones, which account for some of the differences in body contours between males and females.

The subcutaneous layer contains large blood vessels that transport nourishment to the skin and nerves. Also in this layer are the glandular parts of some of the sudoriferous glands and some sense organs for touch, pressure and temperature. Nerves of the skin are found in the subcutaneous layer and in the lower epidermis layer. Nerve bundles found in the subcutaneous tissue branch into the stratum granulosum layer and respond to pain. Cold, heat and touch affect other nerves, located in lower levels of the epidermis.

SKIN PIGMENTATION

As previously mentioned, melanin-producing cells called melanocytes are located in the basal layer of the epidermis. These cells, loaded with melanin, move toward the surface at a faster rate than other cells. **Melanin is distributed throughout all epidermal cells and forms an effective barrier from the penetration of ultraviolet rays to the deeper layers of the skin.**

Melanin tans the skin to protect it from the burning rays of the sun. Light and dark skin do not differ in number of melanocytes they contain. They differ, rather, in the amount and type of melanin produced. Dark skin contains more melanin, which serves as a more effective barrier to the damaging rays of the sun than is seen in light skin. Skin with little melanin present is light, pale or may appear slightly pink. The "pink" tone visible in pale skin is the reflection of red blood through the epidermis. Carotene, a yellow pigment located primarily in the top layer, can give skin a sallow or yellowish cast. No matter what color, all skin needs protection from the ultraviolet rays of the sun.

Ultraviolet rays of the sun speed up the production of melanin, making your skin darker. The stimulation of the production of melanin and the tanning of the skin that results protect the dermis layer of the skin by absorbing these ultraviolet rays. Overexposure to the sun can cause damage to the skin, such as burning, peeling, wrinkling and even skin cancer.

Many products have been developed to further help the skin from absorbing ultraviolet rays. One such product is sunscreen, which comes in various SPF (Sun Protection Factor) strengths. This rating system allows you to determine how long you can stay out in the sun without burning. For example, an SPF 15 indicates that you can be out in the sun 15 times longer than you could without any protection at all.

The American Academy of Dermatology recommends the following tips to reduce the sun's harmful effects:
- Try to keep out of the sun between 10:00 am and 4:00 pm.
- Apply a sunscreen with Sun Protection Factor (SPF) of at least 30, and re-apply every two hours.
- Wear protective, tightly woven clothing.
- Stay in the shade whenever possible.
- Avoid surfaces, such as water, that can reflect up to 85% of the sun's damaging rays.
- Protect children by keeping them out of the sun and, beginning at six months of age, minimize risk by applying sunscreen.

Studies show 90% of wrinkles are caused by excessive exposure to the sun, and only 10% by the natural aging process. If you have had repeated sunburns, examine your skin monthly. If you see a change in the size, shape or appearance of a mole, see your dermatologist.

TYPES OF SKIN

Each person's skin is different and if the skin is constantly abused, side effects such as blemishes, wrinkles, flakiness, roughness and a general lack of healthy color may appear. The skin requires a certain amount of care and attention on a daily basis to stay healthy and attractive. The thinnest skin occurs on eyelids, so be gentle on them when cleansing or applying makeup.

Although the structure of each person's skin is basically the same, the functioning of the various glands and the reactions of the skin to its environment can vary greatly. From a salon professional's point of view the surface of the skin falls into four basic types: dry, oily, normal and combination. It is important for you to be able to recognize these four types so that the proper cleansing and moisturizing regimen can be recommended for each client.

DRY SKIN

Dry skin is characterized by signs such as peeling and flaking. It chaps easily and has a general all-over taut feeling. Dry skin has fewer blemishes and is not prone to acne.

There are two types of dry skin: oil dry and moisture dry. Oil dry skin lacks sebaceous activity, while moisture dry skin lacks water. Although dry skin is often associated with more mature skin, it can be found on a younger person as well. Dry skin can be caused by many factors, including a systemic malfunction of the sebaceous glands, diet, hormones or a combination of these conditions. To keep your skin in its optimum condition, you should drink half your body weight in ounces of water per day.

A good treatment program is essential for dry skin to supply moisture, emollients and lubricants necessary for healthy, soft, smooth skin.

OILY SKIN

Oily skin usually has an all-over shiny look and/or a rough texture with blackheads and enlarged pores. The oily residue most often appears on the chin, nose, nasal-labial groove and forehead, which is commonly called the "T" zone. In a young person, oily skin is prone to acne, but the cause of acne or whiteheads cannot be attributed solely to oily skin. Any combination of conditions may be responsible, such as improper cleansing, hormonal imbalance, nervous problems, poor diet and even humid weather.

A good treatment program is very important for oily skin to keep it in an "acid-balanced" condition (pH 4.5 to 5.5). Maintaining the skin in an acid-balanced state aids in inhibiting the invasion of pathogenic bacteria that can contribute to skin infection. It also maintains the skin in its "natural" environment and, thus, causes less irritation to the skin than alkaline conditions.

NORMAL SKIN

Normal skin is very rare and quite beautiful. It is easily recognized because it has a fresh and healthy color, a firm, moist and smooth texture, freedom from blackheads and blemishes, and does not appear oily. This skin type requires a simple but consistent skin care routine to keep it in this condition. The treatment objective for normal skin is to maintain its natural, acid-balanced condition.

COMBINATION SKIN

The most common skin type is **combination skin.** It can be found on people of most any age and is recognized by the shiny "T" zone (forehead, nose, and chin) and the presence of a noticeable dryness in the cheek, jawline and hairline areas. Blackheads and enlarged pores are often evident on the nose and chin. Combination skin requires the most specialized skin regimen, as you are treating two totally different skin types at the same time—oily and dry. The treatment goal for this skin type is to stabilize the oily areas and lubricate the dry areas.

SKIN DISEASES AND DISORDERS

As a professional, you need to be familiar with skin disorders and diseases so that you can recognize any problems that would prevent you from performing a skin care service. Keep in mind that only a dermatologist or medical doctor should diagnose and treat skin diseases and disorders. **In this chapter certain conditions are accompanied by an asterisk (*), which indicates that skin care services may not be performed on the affected area.**

IMPORTANT VOCABULARY
Common terms related to the study of diseases and disorders and their definitions include:

- An **ALLERGY** is a sensitivity that may develop from contact with normally harmless substances. Symptoms of an allergy may include itching, redness, swelling and/or blisters.
- **INFLAMMATION** is an objective symptom (one you see) characterized by redness, pain, swelling and/or increased temperature.
- **CHRONIC** is a term used to identify conditions that are frequent and habitual.
- **ACUTE** is a term used to identify conditions that are brief and severe.
- A **CONTAGIOUS DISEASE** is communicable by contact. It is also known as an infectious or communicable disease.
- **SEASONAL DISEASE** is influenced by weather.
- **ETIOLOGY** is the study of cause of diseases.
- **PATHOLOGY** is the study of diseases.
- **PROGNOSIS** is a medical opinion of the future condition of illness.
- **OCCUPATIONAL DISORDERS** occur in certain types of employment. For example, salon professionals may be susceptible to **dermatitis venenata** (VEN-eh-nay-tah), sometimes referred to as contact dermatitis. Contact dermatitis is a condition in which the skin becomes red, sore or inflamed after direct contact with a substance. There are two kinds of contact dermatitis: irritant or allergic. Irritant contact dermatitis is the most common type. It is caused by contact with acids, alkaline materials such as soaps and detergents, solvents, or other chemicals such as hair dyes or perm solutions. The reaction usually looks like a burn and often shows as dry, red and rough skin. Allergic contact dermatitis is caused by exposure to substances or materials such as fragrances, cosmetics, soaps, hair dyes, perm solutions, nail polish or latex gloves to which a person has become extra sensitive or allergic and often causes a red, streaky, or patchy rash where the substance touched the skin. The allergic reaction is often delayed, with the rash appearing 24 - 48 hours after exposure. Hands that are immersed in water and shampoo many times a day are at high risk. Protective creams are available to provide a barrier for the skin. Infection control practices establish standards regarding protective gloves, goggles, surgical masks, etc., to assist in avoiding occupational disorders.

The **symptoms** or signs of a disease are divided into two classifications:
- Subjective – those you feel
- Objective – those you see

In other words, signs of a disorder or disease may be felt but nothing may be visible. Itching, burning, pain or symptoms that are felt are examples of **subjective symptoms**. Pimples or inflammation are **objective symptoms** because they are visible. In some cases, both objective and subjective symptoms may be present.

There are six signs of infection: pain, swelling, redness, local fever (heat), throbbing and discharge. Always avoid performing services on skin where symptoms indicate an infection may be present. Avoid direct contact with open wounds and/or tumors.

Tinea (TIN-ee-ah) is the medical term for ringworm. It is a contagious fungal disease characterized by a red circular patch of blisters, caused by a fungal vegetable parasite Tinea pedia (athlete's foot) is an example of tinea.

LESIONS

Diseases and disorders are often accompanied by skin **lesions**, which are any abnormal changes in the structure of an organ or tissue. There are three categories of lesions: primary, secondary and tertiary. As a salon professional, you need to recognize primary and secondary lesions.

PRIMARY SKIN LESIONS

Primary skin lesions include the following:

Macules are a discoloration appearing on the skin's surface. They are flat areas and, although they are usually rounded and distinct, they may be oval, irregular or have an outline that gradually fades into surrounding tissues.

Freckles, commonly found on the face, neck and chest, are considered macules. A lentigo, which appears larger and darker than a freckle, is also an example of a macule. The plural form of lentigo is lentigines.

Papules are hardened red elevations of the skin in which no fluid is present. These lesions normally vary in size from that of a pinhead to that of a pea. The actual shape and coloration of the lesions may vary. Consistency may vary from hard to soft. Papules may persist unchanged but they can sometimes proceed to other types of primary lesions. A large papule is known as a tubercle.

A *pimple* is an example of a papule.

Vesicles* are fluid-filled elevations in the skin caused by localized accumulation of fluids or blood just below the epidermis. Vesicles may develop from macules, papules or poison oak or ivy and are generally short-lived.

Herpes Simplex*, also known as fever blisters, is a contagious, chronic condition characterized by a single vesicle or a group of vesicles on a red, swollen base. It usually appears on the lips, nostrils or other parts of the face.

*Indicates that services may not be performed on the affected area.

Bulla* are lesions, like vesicles, but larger. Found above and below the skin, they contain a clear, watery fluid. They occur in cases of second degree burns.

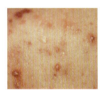

Pustules* are small elevations of skin similar to vesicles in size and shape, but containing pus. They appear whitish or yellowish in color and may be surrounded by a reddish inflammatory border. They may develop from vesicles or papules.

A *pimple with pus* is an example of a pustule

Wheals are a solid formation above the skin, often caused by an insect bite or allergic reaction. They are sharply defined and solid, rising above the skin (e.g., a mosquito bite). These lesions usually develop rapidly, disappear slowly and are accompanied by itching or tingling.

Hives*, also called urticaria (ur-ti-**KAR**-e-uh), are an example of wheal lesions.

Tumors* are solid masses in the skin. They are usually more than one centimeter in diameter. They may be soft or hard, depending upon their makeup, and may be fixed or freely movable. This classification often includes any new skin growths and any localized swelling, which may be elevated or deep. Skin tumors generally have a rounded shape.

A *nodule* is a small tumor.

A *cyst* (sist) is an abnormal membranous sac containing a gaseous, liquid or semi-solid substance.

SECONDARY SKIN LESIONS

Secondary skin lesions appear as a disease progresses into the later stages of development.

Scales are shedding, dead cells of the uppermost layer of the epidermis. The epidermis normally undergoes constant exfoliation (removal) of small, barely perceptible flakes of skin. When the formation of epidermal cells is rapid or the normal process of keratinization is altered, one sees abnormal exfoliation of the epidermis, which results in scales. They may be dry, such as psoriasis, or oily, such as dandruff.

Psoriasis* (soh-**RYE**-ah-sis) is round, dry patches of skin, covered with rough, silvery scales. It is chronic and not contagious. Service unless skin is inflamed or broken in the area to be serviced.

*Indicates that services may not be performed on the affected area.

Crusts* are dried masses that are the remains of an oozing sore. The crusty material may contain blood, pus, sebum, epithelial tissue and bacterial debris.

The *scab* on a sore is an example of a crust.

Excoriations* are mechanical abrasions to the epidermis or injuries to the epidermis. They appear bright to dark red, because of dried blood, and occur when an insect bite or a scab is scratched.

Scratches to the surface of the skin are considered excoriations.

Fissures* are cracks in the skin. They usually appear as cracks or lines that may go as deep as the underlying dermis. They may be dry or moist. These lesions often occur when skin loses its flexibility due to exposure to wind, cold, water, etc.

Chapped lips are one example of a fissure.

Scars are formations resulting from a lesion, which extend into the dermis or deeper, as part of the normal healing process. Scars are permanent; however, they generally become less noticeable with time. A scar is also called a cicatrix (**SIK**-uh-triks).
The size and shape of a scar are dependent upon the extent of the original injury. *Keloids* are thick scars.

Ulcers* are open lesions visible on the skin surface that may result in the loss of portions of the dermis and may be accompanied by pus.

HYPERTROPHIES (NEW GROWTH)
Hypertrophies are identified by an overgrowth or excess of skin.

Callus, sometimes called hyperkeratosis or keratoma, is a thickening of the epidermis, such as a corn, which occurs from pressure and friction applied to the skin.

Verruca* is a name given to a variety of warts. Warts are caused by a virus, can be contagious, and can spread all over the body. A dermatologist or medical doctor should be consulted for removal of warts. Warts are referred to as the most common tumor.

Skin tags are small elevated growths of skin, such as a small benign nodule, which can easily be removed by a physician.

*Indicates that services may not be performed on the affected area.

COSMETOLOGY FUNDAMENTALS

PIGMENTATION ABNORMALITIES

Pigmentation abnormalities describe conditions of too much color or too little color in a particular area of the skin.

MELANODERMA

Melanoderma is the term used to describe any **hyperpigmentation** caused by overactivity of the melanocytes in the epidermis. It can be triggered by overexposure to sunlight, overactivity of the pituitary gland, circulation of hormones, disease and drugs. An example of melanoderma is chloasma.

Chloasma (kloh-AZ-mah) **is a group of brownish macules (nonelevated spots) occurring in one place.** Chloasma is commonly called liver spots and often occurs on the hands and face.

Moles are small, brown pigmented spots that may be raised. Hair often grows through moles, but should not be removed, unless advised by a physician. If there is any change in appearance of a mole, seek medical advice. Melanotic sarcoma is a skin cancer that begins with a mole.

A naevus or nevus (NEE-vus) **is a birthmark or a congenital mole.** A birthmark may look like a stain on the face or other part of the body and is generally a reddish purple flat mark. The stain is caused by dilation of the small blood vessels in the skin.

LEUKODERMA

Leukoderma (loo-ko-DUR-mah) **describes hypopigmentation (lack of pigmentation) of the skin caused by a decrease in activity of melanocytes.** Leukoderma is occasionally the result of a congenital defect such as albinism, or can be acquired, as in vitiligo.

Albinism (al-bin-izm) **is a congenital failure of the skin to produce melanin pigment.** Persons with albinism have pink skin, white hair (it may sometimes be reddish) and pink eyes. They have a strong hypersensitivity to light and sun and their skin ages early. This skin should be protected from exposure to sunlight and ultraviolet lamps.

Vitiligo (vit-i-LYE-goh) **is characterized by oval or irregular patches of white skin that do not have normal pigment.** Vitiligo is usually seen on the face, hands and neck as patches of hypopigmentation that may enlarge slowly. These patches of skin must be protected from exposure to sunlight or ultraviolet lamps.

DISORDERS OF THE SEBACEOUS GLANDS

Comedones (KOM-e-donz), or blackheads, are masses of sebum (oil) trapped in the hair follicles. Comedones can be removed with proper extraction procedures.

Milia (MIL-ee-uh), or whiteheads, are caused by the accumulation of hardened sebum beneath the skin. This disorder can occur on any part of the face, neck and chest.

Acne (AK-nee) occurs most often on the face, back and chest and is a chronic, inflammatory disorder of the sebaceous glands. Acne can be found in two stages: acne simplex or acne vulgaris. People with vulgaris (serious) acne should seek medical attention.

Rosacea* (ro-ZA-sha), or acne rosacea, is a chronic inflammatory congestion of the cheeks and nose, observed as redness, with papules and sometimes pustules present. Advise clients to avoid excessive heat, spicy foods and caffeine. Facials may be done under physician's approval.

Asteatosis (as-tee-ah-TOH-sis) is a condition of dry, scaly skin with reduced sebum production.

Seborrhea (seb-oh-REE-ah) is a condition caused by excessive secretion of the sebaceous glands. Seborrhea is commonly associated with oily skin types.

Steatoma (stee-ah-TOH-mah), or sebaceous cyst or wen, is a subcutaneous tumor of the sebaceous gland, filled with sebum. This disorder usually appears on the scalp, neck or back and ranges in size from a pea to an orange.

Furuncles* (fu-RUN-kels), or boils, appear in the dermis and the epidermis and are caused by an acute bacterial infection. They are localized infections of hair follicles. Carbuncles* refers to a cluster of furuncles and are caused by an acute bacterial infection of several adjoining hair follicles.

DISORDERS OF THE SUDORIFEROUS GLANDS

Bromidrosis (broh-mih-DROH-sis) or osmidrosis is foul-smelling perspiration.

Anhidrosis (an-heye-DROH-sis) is a lack of perspiration caused by fever or disease and requires medical attention.

Hyperhidrosis (hy-per-hy-DROH-sis) is an over-production of perspiration caused by excessive heat or general body weakness and requires medical attention.

Miliaria rubra* (mil-ee-AY-re-ah ROOB-rah) or prickly heat is an acute eruption of small red vesicles with burning and itching of the skin caused by excessive heat.

*Indicates that services may not be performed on the affected area.

THE ABCDs OF SKIN CANCER

Listed below are guidelines for determining whether you should refer a client to a physician for further examination. Changes in any of these conditions require a referral to a physician for a medical opinion.

A **ASYMMETRY** – Asymmetrical, or inconsistent growths; refer to a physician.

B **BORDER** – Has a well-defined edge and does not "bleed", (meaning blend or fade into) the surrounding skin.

C **COLOR** – Consistent; does not vary within growth.

D **DIAMETER** – Should be no larger than an eraser head on a pencil.

OTHER INFLAMMATORY DISORDERS

Dermatitis* (dur-mah-TYE-tis) is an inflammatory disorder of the skin. The lesions come in various forms.

Eczema* (EK-sah-mah) is characterized by **dry or moist lesions with inflammation of the skin and requires medical attention**. Eczema may be chronic or acute and should be referred to a physician for treatment.

Impetigo* (im-peh-TIE-go) is a **highly contagious bacterial infection** that produces a honey-yellow, crusted lesion, usually on the face.

Folliculitis* (FO-lik-u-li-tis) is an infection in the hair follicles caused by bacteria, shaving or clothing irritation. It usually looks like red pimples with a hair in the center of each one.

Pseudofolliculitis barbae* (SOO-doh-fo-lik-u-li-tis bar-be) is the medical term for razor bumps or irritation following shaving.

Conjunctivitis* (kuhn-juhngk-tuh-VAHY-tis), referred to as pink eye, is an inflammation of the transparent membrane that lines the eyelid and eyeball; characterized by itching and redness; spreads easily.

Indicates that services may not be performed on the affected area.

15.2 SKIN CARE

Proper skin care is a combination of concerted efforts toward a good home-maintenance program, a well-balanced diet, proper intake of water, limited exposure to the sun, exercise, rest and professional skin care treatments and products.

Keeping skin in good condition requires a minimum of four steps:
1. Cleanse thoroughly with a product that does not rob or strip the skin of its natural conditioners.
2. Tone the skin with an astringent or freshener.
3. Moisturize the skin to make up for the unavoidable losses it sustains from aging and exposure to the environment.
4. Protect the skin from the damaging effects of sun exposure.

15

DID YOU KNOW

ONE CIGARETTE depletes the body of 15 mg to 25 mg of vitamin C. A deficiency of vitamin C in the body can contribute to cellular breakdown. Long term effects will speed up the aging and wrinkling process. Also, the ingestion of large amounts of caffeine, such as in coffee, tea or soft drinks, will affect not only the appearance but also the internal functioning of the skin. Research indicates that drinking a large amount of caffeine over a period of time will contribute to cellular aging.

The skin should be cleansed daily with an appropriate skin-cleaning product. Ordinary soaps are not recommended for cleaning since they are generally alkaline and can strip the skin of its protective acid mantle.

Using astringents, toners or refreshers (sometimes called tonic lotions or skin refiners) helps to further cleanse the skin while bringing it to a normal pH.

The third step is moisturizing, which helps to keep the skin smooth. Moisturizers in a product operate in several ways. Some products, called humectants, attract moisture. Other products create a barrier that helps keep moisture in.

It is important to remember that oily skin needs moisturizing (hydrating) as much as dry skin. Excessive oil in skin does not replace loss of moisture. In fact, proper moisturizing can actually reduce the oily appearance because it contributes to a better balance of oil and moisture in the skin. The fourth and final step, protecting, is one of great importance. The purpose of sunscreen is to protect the skin from the harmful UVA and UVB rays projected from the sun.

In addition to cleansing, toning, moisturizing and sun protection, getting regular professional facial services helps keep your clients' skin in optimum condition. Two of the steps generally performed in a facial include massage and facial masks.

MASSAGE

Massage dates back to the Greeks, who used it as a cure for ailments. Women had their bodies massaged with vegetable and animal oils to keep their skin soft. **Massage is a systematic, therapeutic method of manipulation of the body by rubbing, pinching, tapping, kneading or stroking with the hands, fingers or an instrument.**

Massage is an excellent method for providing a restful, relaxing skin care treatment to a client. Every muscle and nerve has a motor point. Applying pressure to motor points soothes and stimulates the nerves and muscles. (See illustration.) There are many additional benefits of massage:

1. Increases circulation of the blood supply to the skin, causing blood vessels to dilate
2. Contracts the muscle when the movement is firm and rapid
3. Stimulates the glandular activities of the skin
4. Strengthens weak muscle tissue; relieves pain
5. Softens and improves the texture and complexion of the skin
6. Calms and relaxes the client and can relieve emotional stress and body tension

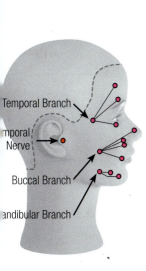

In most areas, salon professionals may massage the head, face, neck, shoulders, upper back, hands, arms and feet. For a complete body massage, many areas require that a client be referred to a licensed massage therapist. Refer to your area regulating agency for massage therapy licensure requirements.

COSMETOLOGY FUNDAMENTALS

THE FIVE BASIC MOVEMENTS OF MASSAGE

EFFLEURAGE (EF-loo-rahzh) **is a light, relaxing, smoothing, gentle stroking or circular movement (manipulation).** It is used on the face, neck and arms and is often used as the movement that begins and ends a massage treatment. This method is carried out with the pads of the fingertips or with the palms of the hands.

PETRISSAGE (PAY-tre-sahzh) **is a light or heavy kneading and rolling of the muscles.** It is used on the face, the arms, the shoulders and the upper back. Petrissage is probably the most important of the massage movements, as it deeply stimulates the muscles, nerves and skin glands and promotes the circulation of blood and lymph. It is done by kneading the muscles between the thumb and fingers or by pressing the palm of the hand firmly over the muscles, then grasping and squeezing with the heel of the hand and the fingers.

TAPOTEMENT (tah-POHT-mant), or percussion, **is a light tapping or slapping movement applied with the fingertips or partly flexed fingers.** The movement is usually carried out with the hands swinging freely from the wrist in a rapid motion. **Tapotement increases blood circulation, stimulates the nerves and promotes muscle contraction.** It should not be used when the client needs soothing. Hacking is a form of tapotement that is similar to a chopping movement with the edge of the hands used on the arms, back and shoulders.

FRICTION (FRIK-shun) **is a circular, or wringing movement with no gliding, usually carried out with the fingertips or palms of the hands.** Friction is used most often on the scalp, hands or with less pressure during a facial massage.

VIBRATION is a shaking movement in the arms of the salon professional while the fingertips or palms are touching the client. Vibration should only be used in facial massage for a few seconds in one location, as it is very stimulating to the skin.

The following points should be kept in mind during the massage:
- Massage should never be performed over an area exhibiting redness, swelling, pus, disease, bruises and/or broken or scraped skin.
- Avoid massage if client has high blood pressure, a heart condition or has had a stroke, since massage increases circulation and could present a risk for the client.
- Massage movements should be directed toward the origin of the muscles in order to avoid damage to muscle tissues
- When giving facial manipulations, an even tempo or rhythm is essential for the relaxation of the client. Do not remove the hands from the face once the manipulations have begun and, if it becomes necessary, feather the hands off the face and gently replace them on the skin with the same feather-like movements.

FACIAL MASKS

Facial masks (or packs) have many different benefits, which include hydration (adding moisture), tightening of the pores and reduction of excess oil. Facial masks can be used in conjunction with facial services or they can be offered as a separate service. Facial masks are either applied directly to the skin or over a layer of gauze.

Masks should always be applied to clean skin. If a facial is desired, the facial manipulations are usually given before the mask is applied.

TYPES OF FACIAL MASKS

- **Clay/mud** are usually recommended for normal or oily skin types.
- **Cream masks** are recommended for normal to dry skin.
- **Gel masks** are designed for a wide variety of purposes. Many contain botanicals and ingredients that are designed to calm and soothe sensitive skin.
- **Modeling masks** are mixed with water and applied in a thick consistency to the face. Within minutes these masks dry and harden to a rubber-like consistency, then can be pulled from the face in one piece. They not only deliver the benefits of the ingredients of which they are made, but also seal the skin, locking in moisture and creating a firm, taut feeling.
- **Paraffin (warm wax)** is heated and applied to the skin to rehydrate (moisturize) the skin's top layers. By coating the skin with warmth and blocking the skin's natural tendency to "breathe," the heat of a warm wax mask acts to draw oil and perspiration to the top layer of the skin. This mask is especially good for dry, wrinkled or dehydrated skin. It should be applied over a layer of gauze.

THE BENEFITS OF FACIAL MASKS

1. Increasing the firmness of the skin for a temporary period of time
2. Increasing the circulation of the blood in the areas treated
3. Absorbing and removing unwanted surface oil
4. Removing surface dirt
5. Absorbing and removing skin impurities
6. Softening and smoothing the skin
7. Relaxing and refreshing the client

SKIN CARE ESSENTIALS

As a salon professional, you will recommend the skin care treatments and products you will use during the service, as well as the products your client will take home. The following charts identify the products, implements and equipment you will use during a salon facial. Material Safety Data Sheets (MSDS) for all products used in the salon must be available.

SKIN CARE PRODUCTS

PRODUCT	FUNCTION
ANTISEPTIC	Aids in preventing the growth of bacteria on the skin
CLEANSING LOTION	Removes impurities from the skin
SKIN ASTRINGENT	Assists in cleansing skin and returns oily skin to a normal pH
TONER OR FRESHENER	Assists in cleaning skin and returns normal to dry skin to a normal pH
CHEMICAL EXFOLIANT	Removes dead skin cells by using enzymes and alphahydroxy acids
MANUAL EXFOLIANT	Removes dead skin cells by using a granular product manipulated on the skin; also called facial scrub
MASSAGE CREAM/OIL	Reduces friction and provides "slip" to the skin during massage
DRY SKIN MASKS	Add moisture to the skin
OILY SKIN MASKS	Absorb excess sebum and debris from the skin

SKIN CARE IMPLEMENTS/SUPPLIES

IMPLEMENTS/SUPPLIES	FUNCTION
SPATULAS	Remove product from containers
GLOVES	Protect hands
FAN BRUSH	Applies product on face or neck
CLEAN SHEETS, BLANKETS	Provide warmth and comfort to client
CLIENT ROBE/GOWN	Allows client to remove clothing to keep it clean
TOWEL	Cushions client's head; keeps hair protected; if wet and warm, removes mask product
COTTON PADS/SWABS	Remove product from face and neck
FACIAL TISSUE	Removes lipstick or debris from extractions; blots face after toning; disposable
HEADBAND OR HEAD COVERING	Protects hair from the face and keeps product out of the client's hair

SKIN CARE EQUIPMENT

EQUIPMENT	FUNCTION	CAUTIONS
MAGNIFYING LAMP	Provides thorough examination of skin's surface, using magnification and glarefree light; beneficial when analyzing the skin	Be aware of the electrical cord with floorstanding model
FACIAL STEAMER	Uses warm, humid mist to open follicles for cleansing; softens dead skin cells for easier removal; causes increased blood circulation by making the blood vessels expand; improves cell metabolism	Water level should be in compliance with the manufacturer's directions; average distance from client's face is 16-18" (40-45 cm); adjust ventilating systems to avoid interfering with the flow of steam
INFRARED LAMP	Provides a soothing heat that penetrates into the tissues of the body; relaxes the client, softens the skin to allow penetration of product and increases blood flow	Be aware of the electrical cord with floor-standing model; average distance from client is 30" (75 cm)
WOOD'S LAMP	Allows analysis of skin surface and deeper layers to aid in determining treatment by using deep ultraviolet light of the lamp; different colors will indicate various conditions	Do not allow the lamp to overheat; avoid direct contact between the lamp and skin; do not look directly at the bulb while it is being used
VACUUM	Creates mild suction; increases circulation to the surface; helpful in deep pore cleaning	Avoid use on skin with broken capillaries
HIGH FREQUENCY CURRENT	Creates current that is thermal, or heat producing, and germicidal	Do not use on clients who are pregnant or who have high blood pressure or heart problems

INFECTION CONTROL AND SAFETY

Infection control and safety are essential while performing skin care services in order to protect the health and well-being of you and your client.

1. Disinfect the chair, sink, table and counter area before and after every service with an approved broad-spectrum disinfectant.
2. Wash and sanitize your hands before and after every client.
3. Keep lids tightly closed on product jars to avoid spillage and contamination.
4. Remove all products from jars with a sanitized spatula.
5. Keep labels on all containers and store products in a cool place to protect shelf life.
6. Keep tools dry to avoid a short circuit when using electrical equipment.
7. Wear gloves during treatments, if required.

8. Discard any implements or supplies, such as protective hair coverings, that cannot be disinfected.
9. Use eyepads to protect and soothe the eyes when analyzing the skin or applying masks
10. Identify **contraindications**, which are conditions or factors that serve as reasons to withhold certain treatments. High blood pressure, heart problems, diabetes, pregnancy pacemaker or metal implants and/or medications are all examples of possible condition
11. Place used/soiled linens in a covered hamper.
12. Use clean linens with each new client.

SKIN CARE SERVICE ESSENTIALS

As with all professional services, consulting with your client prior to the actual service will ensure predictable results and will help you avoid any misunderstandings that may arise. As you review the four basic steps of the skin care service essentials, remember the importanc of active listening, critical thinking and analysis on the overall success of the service.

CONNECT
- Meet and greet the client with a firm handshake and a pleasant voice.
- Communicate to build rapport and develop a relationship with the client.
- Fill out skin care record form with client (sample shown below).

CONSULT

- Ask questions to discover client needs.
- Analyze client's face and complete appropriate sections of the skin evaluation form (sample shown on previous page).
- Assess the facts and thoroughly think through your recommendations after reading completed skin care record form.
- Explain your recommended solutions, the products that will be used and the price of the service. Think not only of today's service, but future services also.
- Gain feedback and approval from your client. Fill out the appropriate section(s) of the skin evaluation form to record your treatment plan.

CREATE

- Ensure client comfort during service.
- Stay focused on delivering the service to the best of your ability.
- Teach the client how to perform home skin care regimen.

COMPLETE

- Request satisfaction feedback from your client.
- Escort client to retail area and point out at least two products you used.
- Recommend products to maintain appearance and condition of your client's skin.
- Inform client that you keep these products in stock for purchase at all times.
- Invite your client to make a purchase.
- Ask your client for referrals for future services.
- Suggest a future appointment time and offer to prebook your client's next visit.
- Offer appreciation to your client for visiting the school or salon.
- Record recommended products on client record card for future visits.

WORKSHOP 01
BASIC FACIAL

The benefits the client can derive from receiving a professional facial service include relaxing muscles, soothing nerves, correcting minor skin problems, improving circulation and enhancing healthy skin. Properly given, a facial service is a relaxing and pampering experience.

Many of the more common skin problems a salon professional may encounter (for example, oily skin prone to blackheads or whiteheads or overly dry skin) can be improved with weekly facial services and the correct home-care regimen you will recommend. Remember, the salon professional does not treat skin disease. Skin problems of a serious nature should always be referred to a physician.

BASIC FACIAL PREPARATION

As with any professional service, it is important to have your area, products, implements and equipment in proper order prior to your client's arrival. Therefore, keep these points in mind:
- Disinfect facial service area
- Set up facial bed with clean blanket/sheet and arrange products
- Check equipment

BASIC FACIAL PROCEDURE

- Wash and sanitize hands*
- Drape client (cocoon wrap)
- Cleanse face
- Obtain cleansing cream
- Apply cleansing cream
- Remove cleansing cream
- Apply toner
- Place eyepads over client's eyes
- Analyze client's skin
- Apply exfoliant
- Remove exfoliant
- Apply toner
- Obtain massage cream
- Apply massage cream
- Perform massage movements
- Remove massage cream
- Apply toner
- Apply facial mask
- Allow mask to set
- Remove mask
- Apply toner
- Apply moisturizing cream

*Wear protective gloves if required by your regulatory agency.

DRAPING - COCOON WRAP

Drape cotton blanket over facial bed and position white cotton sheet over blanket. Lay one flat towel and one folded towel at the top of the bed for client's head. Have client lay on top of the sheet.

1. Fold one edge of blanket/sheet combination toward middle of bed
2. Repeat with the other edge, overlapping at center
3. Wrap the end of the blanket/sheet under the client's feet
4. Tuck towel over top of cocoon wrap

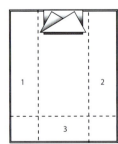 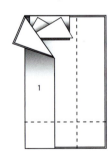  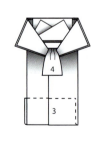

BASIC FACIAL

1-02 Wash and sanitize hands. Ask client to put on gown for the service, **drape client** and position head band or covering to secure hair off the face. **Cleanse the face.** Using cotton and eye makeup remover, perform downward and inward strokes to remove eye makeup. Remove lipstick with tissue, beginning from the outer corner to the center on both sides of the lips.

03 Obtain cleansing cream with a spatula and apply to both hands.

04 Apply cleansing cream over the face and neck, using both hands and starting at the chin. Slide to the end of the jaw, from the base of the nose to the temple, along side of the nose, up over bridge of nose, between brows, across forehead, across to temples. Use smooth, sweeping strokes. Work under the eyes toward the bridge of the nose and out over the eyelid using the ring finger.

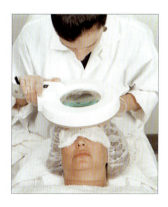

05 Remove cleansing cream using cotton pads and warm water. Start at the neck and follow the contour of the face, always working upward. Follow procedure until all cleansing cream has been removed.

06 Apply toner to skin surface with a piece of cotton. This restores pH and aids in cleansing.

ANALYZE
07 Place eyepads over client's eyes. Analyze client's skin using the magnifying lamp. Check for skin abrasions, excessive oil, flakiness or clogged pores. This will help you to determine skin type and to recommend additional services and retail products.

EXFOLIATE
08 Apply exfoliant product to the client's skin. If using a granular scrub, apply and massage in small circular movements. If using an alphahydroxy acid product, apply and let it stay on the skin for the given amount of time. If using an enzyme exfoliant, apply product and steam for approximately 10 minutes. Always follow manufacturer's directions.

COSMETOLOGY FUNDAMENTALS

MASSAGE

Massage techniques and manipulations are varied. The procedures listed here are considered a foundation that you can build on. **Obtain the massage cream** from the container with a spatula. **Apply massage cream** to the face and neck.

09 Remove exfoliant using hot towel or cotton pads. Release steam from the hot towel and test the temperature of the towel by holding the side of the towel that will not be placed on the client's skin against your own wrist or arm to evaluate the heat intensity prior to applying it to your client's face or body. **Apply toner** to close the pores.

10 Perform massage movements beginning at the forehead. Apply pressure to the forehead using a hand-over-hand movement and effleurage with the ring fingers. Cross the face, moving left to right and then right to left.

11 Slide the middle fingers of both hands over and under each other continuously, as you move across the forehead in half-circle movements.

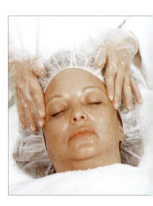

12 Apply slight pressure at the temples.

13 Perform tapotement around the eyes.

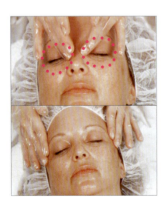

14-15 Circle the outside of the eyes with the ring finger using light pressure. Pause at the temples.

16 Massage the outer corners of the nose, slide fingers up either side of the nose and apply pressure into the eye sockets. Repeat three times.

17 Perform scissor movements on the nose by creating a V-pattern with the index finger and middle finger, starting at the base of the nose and sliding up to the hairline three times.

18 Lift upward slightly on the corners of the mouth three times on each side.

19 Massage in a small circular motion around the mouth three times.

20 Perform scissor movements on the mouth by creating a V-pattern with fingers on both hands and slide across the mouth.

21 Repeat the scissor movement across the chin.

22 Massage upward on the jawline in a circular movement with the thumb and index finger. Work upward to each earlobe.

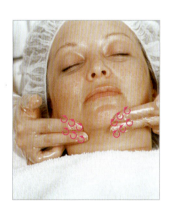

23 Massage neck in a small circular motion using both hands.

TIPS

- Maintain contact with your client using a consistent rhythm
- Use up-and-out motions to prevent damage to underlying muscle tissue

  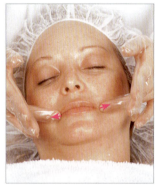 

24 Use a hand-over-hand effleurage movement to follow through with the neck movement and bring you back to the chin.

25-28 Working in a continuous movement up the face, perform scissor movements at the chin. Glide to the sides of mouth and apply lifting movements. Then continue to the sides of the nose and perform circular movements. Glide up the sides of the nose and apply light pressure at the eye sockets.

29 Perform effleurage on both sides of the face. Finish the massage treatment by performing a feathering-off movement. This is done by starting at the cheek area with the right hand, followed by the left. Repeat on opposite cheek.

30 Continue by crisscrossing hands over forehead to each temple. Pause and release.

31 Remove massage cream from the face and then **apply toner**.

TIPS

- Pressure of massage should be effective, but not severe
- Use caution around the eyes and eyelids to avoid stretching

ACIAL MASK
2 Apply a **facial mask** to the ntire face starting at the neck. se a brush and long strokes.

33-34 Allow **mask to set** on the face for approximately 5-10 minutes, then **remove mask** with a hot towel and cotton pads. **Apply toner** to the skin.

35 Apply a **moisturizing cream** over entire face and neck, using effleurage movements. Conclude with massage around the neck and shoulder area to relieve client of any lingering tension or pressure.

BASIC FACIAL COMPLETION

Perform after every facial service:
- Offer prebook visit to client; express appreciation for the client's visit.
- Recommend retail products for client.
- Throw away non-reusable materials used during the facial service, replace used towels with fresh towels and arrange all products and implements in proper order.
- Disinfect your facial service implements and facial bed.
- Wash your hands with liquid soap.

Many salons today are offering body treatments and spa services that cleanse, moisturize and pamper clients.

COSMETOLOGY FUNDAMENTALS

603

15.3 HAIR REMOVAL

Society and personal preferences have long dictated a person's need or desire for removing unwanted or superfluous hair. **This condition of unwanted or superfluous hair is referred to as hypertrichosis** (hi-per-tri-**KOH**-sis). It is up to you, as a salon professional, to recommend the best way to remove the unwanted hair or make it less visible.

There are two types of hair removal procedures: temporary and permanent. **Temporary** procedures include shaving, the use of chemical depilatories, tweezing, waxing, threading and sugaring. **Permanent** hair removal requires the use of electricity. Most regulating agencies will not license a salon professional to perform permanent hair removal services without additional specialized training. An overview of permanent hair removal techniques is included at the end of this section.

If your client wants hair to be less visible without having it removed, consider lightening the hair. You can use a prepared product designed to lighten hair on the face or arms, or you can mix one part oil lightener with two parts hydrogen peroxide. Apply mixture to the area to be lightened and monitor until hair has lightened to the desired shade (15 to 60 minutes, depending on the hair's color and texture.) Thoroughly rinse off lightener and cleanse area. Apply a moisturizing cream.

HAIR REMOVAL ESSENTIALS

To perform a professional hair removal service, you need a selection of products, implements and equipment. MSDS guidelines for all products used in the salon need to be available.

HAIR REMOVAL PRODUCTS

PRODUCT	FUNCTION
CLEANSING GEL	Removes dirt and oil
ANTISEPTIC	Prevents bacteria growth
WAX	Removes unwanted hair
WAX REMOVER	Cleans wax residue
SOOTHING LOTION	Calms the skin after waxing
POWDER (TALC)	Prevents wax from adhering to skin
CHEMICAL DEPILATORY	Removes unwanted hair (cream formula generally)

15

HAIR REMOVAL IMPLEMENTS/SUPPLIES

IMPLEMENT/SUPPLIES	FUNCTION
BROW BRUSH	Combs brow hair prior to shaping
TWEEZERS	Remove stray hairs
REMOVAL STRIPS	Aid in removing stray hair; applied over wax
WAX WARMER (POT)	Melts and holds wax
SPATULAS	Remove wax from container/warmer; spread the wax
GLOVES	Protect the hands
SHEET	Protects the facial bed
PLASTIC BAG	Holds garbage
HEADBAND	Holds hair out of the way
TISSUE	Aids in application of products

HAIR REMOVAL EQUIPMENT

EQUIPMENT	FUNCTION
FACIAL CHAIR	Holds client
HANDHELD MIRROR	Allows client to view results

INFECTION CONTROL AND SAFETY

Infection control and safety while performing hair removal services are essential in order to protect the health and well-being of you and your client.

1. Carefully read and follow manufacturers' instructions for products, implements, supplies and equipment.
2. Always test the temperature of heated wax before applying by checking temperature on your wrist.
3. Keep wax and/or chemical depilatories away from client's eyes and any other areas from which you do not wish to remove hair.
4. Do not use wax over moles, warts, irritated, abraded skin or sunburned skin, bruises or varicose veins.
5. Perform a patch test prior to performing a service.
6. Cleanse the skin prior to treatment.
7. Dispose of used wax after every client. Do not reuse wax.
8. Do not rewax sensitive skin or sensitive areas, such as eyebrows, within the same service time.
9. Use cold compresses or ice packs to soothe irritated skin.
10. Do not re-dip spatula; clean and disinfect cart and wax pot.
11. For 24 hours after waxing service, do not apply makeup following facial waxing or wear pantyhose following leg waxing.
12. Waxing vellus (also known as lanugo) hair is not recommended since it may cause the skin to lose its softness.

COSMETOLOGY FUNDAMENTALS

605

HAIR REMOVAL SERVICE ESSENTIALS

As with all professional services, consulting with your client prior to the actual service will ensure predictable results and will help you avoid any misunderstandings that may arise. As you review the four basic steps of the hair removal service essentials, remember the importance of active listening, critical thinking and analysis on the overall success of the service.

CONNECT
- Meet and greet the client with a firm handshake and a pleasant voice.
- Communicate to build rapport and develop a relationship with the client.
- Have client fill out hair removal record form.

CONSULT
- Ask questions to discover client needs.
- Analyze client's skin where hair will be removed.
- Assess the facts and thoroughly think through your recommendations after reading completed hair removal record form.
- Explain your recommended solutions, the products that will be used and the price of the service.
- Think not only of today's service, but future services also.
- Gain feedback and approval from your client.

CREATE
- Ensure client comfort during service.
- Stay focused on delivering the service to the best of your ability.

COMPLETE
- Request satisfaction feedback from your client.
- Ask your client for referrals for future services.
- Suggest a future appointment time for your client's next visit.
- Offer appreciation to your client and offer to prebook their next visit to the school or salon.
- Record recommended products on client record card for future visits.

TEMPORARY HAIR REMOVAL

Depending on the type of technique used, hair can grow back in a matter of hours or days, such as with shaving, or in several weeks, as with waxing.

SHAVING

The hair removal method most often used when unwanted hair covers large areas, such as women's legs, is **shaving.** Keep in mind that this service is usually performed by the client at home. Shaving can be performed using an electric shaver, clipper or razor. When using a razor, apply shaving cream before the service to make the skin softer and reduce the potential for skin irritations. Use moisturizing lotion or cream after the service to keep the skin soft and help eliminate dryness or flaking. As the hair grows back it may feel more coarse or thicker due to the blunt effect of the razor. Shaving unwanted hair at the nape hairline can be done with the clipper or razor. Be guided by your area's regulatory agency.

CHEMICAL DEPILATORIES

A **chemical depilatory** is a substance that dissolves the hair at skin level. Chemical depilatories are usually found in a cream, paste or powder form (which is designed to be mixed). The main ingredient of these products is a thioglycolic acid derivative, with an alkaline pH, that chemically softens and degrades the protein structure of the hair. An allergy test needs to be given to determine sensitivity to any depilatory product prior to use. A reaction, such as itching, burning or inflammation, is a negative indication to the use of the product. Always read and follow the manufacturer's instructions. To prepare for this hair removal service, assemble materials and prepare your workspace.

CHEMICAL DEPILATORY GUIDELINES

- **Wash and sanitize** hands.*
- **Drape client** after escorting to the hair removal service area.
- **Check patch test** area for reaction; if no signs are present, continue.
- **Cleanse** area to be treated.
- **Apply depilatory** with a spatula. Apply a thin, even coating. Avoid the mouth, eyes, and nose.
- **Start timing** (usually no more than 10 minutes). Keep room warm, since product works faster if the client's body is warm.
- **Wipe away depilatory** using a soft paper towel. After the manufacturer's recommended time, **reapply** if hair has not been removed.
- **Wash thoroughly** with a gentle soap and warm water. **Rinse.**
- **Apply moisturizer** to entire area. **Undrape and escort** client to reception area.
- **Offer prebook visit** to client.
- **Recommend retail products** for client.
- **Throw away non-reusable materials** used during the service. **Replace used towels** with fresh towels and **arrange all products and implements** in proper order.
- **Disinfect** your implements.
- Wash your hands with liquid soap.

Wear protective gloves if required by your regulatory agency.

TWEEZING

Tweezing is the hair removal method most commonly used to remove unwanted hairs from smaller areas, such as the eyebrows, chin or around the mouth.

EYEBROW GUIDELINES

While the shape of your client's eyebrows needs to be customized for facial features, follow these general guidelines to achieve a well-arched eyebrow.
- The brow should begin over the inside corner of the eye.
- The peak, or highest point of the arch, should occur over the outside of the iris of the eye.
- Then imagine a diagonal line from the outside of the nose that extends past the outside of the eye. This point is where the brow should end.

A good brow design creates a frame for the face and "opens" the eye. A person with excessive hair may benefit from waxing instead of tweezing since it is faster and less irritating.
- **Assemble materials** and **prepare workspace**.
- **Wash and sanitize hands**.
- **Cleanse area** to be tweezed.
- **Analyze your client's brows** using the guidelines above. Consider the client's overall appearance before you determine how thick or thin the eyebrows should be. Note that this is outlined in more detail in the makeup section of this chapter.
- **Brush the hairs up** with a brow brush. This will allow you to see the base of the hairs and to remove them in neat rows, rather than at random.
- **Hold the skin taut** with one hand by stretching it between the thumb and index finger. **Tweeze the hairs in the direction of the hair growth**, using quick movements.
- **Tweeze stray hairs** that appear below the brow. To create a more pronounced arch, tweeze in an upward direction from just inside the beginning of the brow to the area you determined should be the highest point of the arch. Continue tweezing, sloping gently downward, toward the outer edge of the brow. The points you choose to begin and end your arch and the degree of slope you create will determine how pronounced the arch will be.
- **Complete one brow**, then the other, making sure they match.
- **Apply astringent** to the area, then apply a soothing cream.
- **Offer prebook visit** in a 4-to-6 week period.
- Return to service area and **perform necessary infection control procedures**.

WAXING

Waxing is a procedure that is beneficial for temporarily removing hair from both large and small areas. Waxing, using either hot or cold wax, is a service in which the hair is physically removed from the follicle by applying the wax, allowing the hair to firmly adhere to the wax and, finally, pulling off the wax/hair. For clients who can't tolerate hot wax, which is outlined below, cold wax is an option. The application of cold wax is similar to a hot wax application, except that a thicker application of cold wax is used and strips are not used to remove the wax. Instead, the wax itself is pulled opposite the direction of the hair growth.

THREADING
Threading is an ancient method of hair removal that utilizes 100% cotton thread that is twisted and rolled along the surface of the skin.

SUGARING
Sugaring is a hair removal technique that utilizes a paste made primarily of sugar that is applied to the skin in a rolling motion.

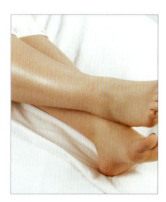

WORKSHOP 02
BASIC WAXING

Waxing is a quick, easy way to temporarily remove hair around the eyebrow area and on the legs. This procedure generally needs to be repeated every 4 to 6 weeks.

BASIC WAXING PREPARATION

As with any professional service, it is important to have your area, products, implements and equipment in proper order prior to your client's arrival. Before performing a basic eyebrow or leg wax, be sure to satisfy the following points:

- Disinfect service area
- Place protective covering on facial chair
- Pre-cut removal strips to be used
- Arrange pre-treatment cream/cleanser, powder, wax cleaner, soothing lotion, spatulas, tweezers, gloves and plastic bag
- Warm up wax at least 30 minutes before client arrives

BASIC WAXING PROCEDURE
This procedure applies to both eyebrow and leg waxing.

- Wash and sanitize hands*
- Drape client
- Examine area to be waxed
- Cleanse area to be waxed
- Apply powder on area to be waxed
- Test temperature of wax
- Obtain wax

- Apply wax at a 45° angle in direction of hair growth and discard spatula
- Apply removal strip
- Press down
- Pull skin taut
- Remove strip quickly in opposite direction

- Apply pressure immediately
- Apply antiseptic
- Repeat procedure
- Apply and remove wax cleanser
- Apply soothing lotion
- Tweeze
- Show client results

*Wear protective gloves if required by your regulatory agency.

COSMETOLOGY FUNDAMENTALS

EYEBROW WAX

01 Wash and sanitize hands. Drape client. Examine the area to be waxed. Clean area to be waxed with an antiseptic gel.

02 Apply powder on area to be waxed to create a barrier for the skin against the wax.

03 Test the temperature of the wax on your wrist. Obtain wax with clean spatula, apply wax at a 45° angle in the direction of the hair growth and discard spatula.

04 Apply the removal strip. Press down and pull skin taut holding the end of the strip in the direction of the hair growth.

05 Remove the strip quickly in the opposite direction of the hair growth. Do not pull upward.

06 Apply pressure immediately to minimize pain and redness. Apply an antiseptic if slight bleeding or irritation occurs. Repeat procedure for both eyes.

07 Apply and remove a wax cleanser.

08 Apply a soothing lotion with cotton.

9 Tweeze to remove any stray hairs not picked up by the wax.

10 Show your client the results. Undrape client and escort to reception area.

LEG WAX

01 Wash and sanitize hands. Drape client. Examine the area to be waxed for contraindications and problem areas, and continue if no signs are present. Cleanse area to be waxed with an antiseptic gel.

02 Apply powder on area to be waxed. Be sure to apply all over the leg.

03 Obtain wax with a clean spatula, **apply at a 45° angle in the direction of the hair growth and discard spatula.** Use sweeping motion when applying the wax. Keep in mind that wax should be applied in rows or sections, since you are covering a much larger area.

04 Apply the removal strip. Press down in the direction of the hair growth.

COSMETOLOGY FUNDAMENTALS

611

05-06 Pull skin taut and hold the end of the strip. **Remove the strip quickly in the opposite direction** of the hair growth. **Apply pressure immediately.** Work quickly so that the wax does not get cold and hard while on the leg. **Apply an antiseptic** if slight bleeding or irritation occurs.

07 Remove all the wax from each section before you **repeat procedure** on a new row or section. Once you've completed waxing the top area of both legs, have your client turn over and wax the back of both legs. When you've finished waxing the back of the legs, have your client turn back over. **Apply and remove wax cleanser.** Remove excess product with a towel. **Apply a soothing toner** with cotton. **Tweeze** stray hairs if necessary.

BASIC WAXING COMPLETION

Perform after every eyebrow or leg waxing service:
- Offer prebook visit to client.
- Recommend retail products for client.
- Dispose of non-reusable materials used during the waxing service, replace used towels with fresh towels and arrange all products and implements in proper order.
- Disinfect your waxing service implements, work area and facial bed.
- Wash your hands with liquid soap.

PERMANENT HAIR REMOVAL

Permanent hair removal, known as electrolysis, uses electric current to damage the cells of the papilla and disrupt hair growth. The goal is to damage enough papilla cells so that either a lighter, finer diameter hair grows back or, ideally, no hair grows from the follicle at all. Several treatments per follicle (exposure to current) are normally required before lasting results are achieved. This is not a one-time service, and many require multiple visits to obtain desired results. In most areas this method is performed by a licensed professional called an electrologist. An electrologist has advanced training specifically in the study of electrolysis or is a medical doctor.

The medical community recognizes three methods of permanent hair removal:
1. Galvanic electrolysis or multiple-needle process
2. Thermolysis or high frequency/short-wave method
3. Blend, a combination of galvanic and thermolysis

Each of these methods has advantages and disadvantages. Remember, advanced training is required to perform electrolysis in most areas.

GALVANIC METHOD

The galvanic electrolysis method destroys the hair by decomposing the papilla. In galvanic electrolysis, multiple wire needles or probes are inserted into the follicle. A low level of current passes into the needle and causes a chemical reaction in the cells of the papilla. The current is typically on from 30 seconds to 2.5 minutes. The instrument has multiple probes that are normally inserted with minimal discomfort and activated at one time; for this reason, galvanic electrolysis is sometimes called the multiple-needle process.

THERMOLYSIS METHOD

The thermolysis or high frequency/short-wave method involves inserting a single needle (probe) into the follicle. The current travels to the papilla for less than a second, resulting in a coagulation of the cells. The hair is immediately tweezed from the follicle. Because the time and intensity of the current are carefully controlled, preferably by an automatic timer, the client feels only a tiny "flash" of heat. Redness or a slight bump in the skin are normal reactions and disappear in two or three days. The wire used in thermolysis is substantially finer than the electrolysis probe, further reducing client discomfort.

BLEND METHOD

The **blend method** of hair removal is a combination of galvanic and thermolysis technology. A special instrument designed to combine galvanic current (for best results on resistant follicles) and high frequency current (for faster results) produce the blend. Highly trained electrologists may use this method if the other methods fail. The advantages and disadvantages are similar to those of the individually used methods. The importance of this method is that it offers a "last chance" to clients with excessive or resistant hair growth.

LASER HAIR REMOVAL

Laser hair removal treatments use wavelengths of light to penetrate and diminish or destroy hair bulbs. Depending on the local area regulations, this can be performed by licensed estheticians, medical professionals, or by technicians under a doctor's supervision. Laser hair removal systems emit a beam of light that passes through the skin to the hair follicle. The hair absorbs the light and transforms it into heat energy, which destroys the hair bulb. The benefit of laser is that it can treat hundreds of hair follicles simultaneously, generally making the process quicker than electrolysis.

Laser hair removal and photo-epilation light require training that is most often offered by the manufacturers of specialized equipment. Be guided by your regulatory agency's policies.

PHOTO-EPILATION OR PULSED LIGHT

Photo-epilation or pulsed light uses a similar principle as lasers, but this type of light is not considered to be a laser light. An intense pulsed light beam creates a burst of energy used to destroy hair bulbs with minimal scarring. Both lasers and pulsed light are a form of light beam. The difference between the two is that a laser is a constant beam of light and the pulsed is not constant. Both methods carry the risk of scarring, but there is much less chance of burning or scarring when using pulsed light since it is targeted at the skin in quick, short intervals. The benefit of this type of treatment is that large areas of the body such as the back or legs can be treated quickly.

COSMETOLOGY FUNDAMENTALS

15.4 MAKEUP

Makeup design and trends strongly relate to other fashion media, such as clothing and hair. This means that seasonal changes and trends from year to year follow swiftly, one after another. The concepts presented in this chapter are intended to give you the basic skills you'll need to perform makeup services in the salon. The designs you create for your clients in the salon will vary from person to person and will relate to current trends as well as the personal expression of your client. Remember that ideals of beauty vary from culture to culture and in different age groups. As your skill level increases, you may become more interested in other, more specific areas of makeup design. For example, designing makeup for photography, film and theater can be very challenging and rewarding.

Makeup design utilizes an artistic concept called chiaroscuro, an arrangement of light and dark parts, to visually alter the contours of the face. The basic premise of chiaroscuro is that lighter colors stand out and darker colors recede. By applying lighter and darker tones, you can change the apparent contours of the face. **Adding light or highlights will accentuate and emphasize areas or features that need to be "brought out." Darker tones are applied to shadow or contour areas and features you wish to diminish or minimize.** This understanding of the properties of darker and lighter colors allows you to visually alter the shape of the face.

FACIAL SHAPES

The well-proportioned oval face shape has long been considered the ideal or classic facial shape. Standards of beauty have certainly expanded during recent decades, but most corrective makeup and contouring are done to achieve the illusion of an oval face.

OVAL FACE
The generally balanced shape and regular features of the oval face will not require much in the way of "corrective" application. In most instances, **the oval shape represents the ideal, so creating the illusion of an oval face when working on other face shapes can be achieved with corrective makeup.**

ROUND FACE
Generally a fuller face, the round face, is characterized by a rounded hairline and chin line. Contouring can be used to slenderize the face, adding vertical emphasis and making it appear more oval.

OBLONG FACE (LONG FACE)
The oblong facial shape tends to be long and narrow. This face can be visually shortened by applying deeper tones under the chin and horizontally at the hairline. Horizontal lines should be emphasized whenever possible, in brow shape, cheek color and lip shape. Highlighting can be used to add visual width when possible.

PEAR-SHAPED FACE
A pear-shaped face has a narrow forehead and a wide jawline. Adding width to the forehead can be achieved with highlighting. Contour to reduce the width at the bottom of the face.

SQUARE FACE
The square face is usually characterized by a broad, straight forehead and hairline, with a broad jawline. The effect can be very angular and almost masculine. Contouring can be done to soften the angularity and reduce the width.

HEART-SHAPED FACE

The heart-shaped face is characterized by a wider forehead and a narrow jaw or chin line. Width across the forehead can be minimized by contouring while the jawline can be visually widened with highlighting.

DIAMOND-SHAPED FACE

Predominant width through the cheekbones is contrasted by narrow forehead and chin/jaw areas on the diamond-shaped face. Width through the cheekbones can be minimized with contouring and the jaw and forehead can be made to look wider with highlighting.

COLOR THEORY

The law of color is equally important in makeup design as it is in hair color design. Remember that all colors are comprised of the three primary colors: red, yellow and blue. Mixing two primaries in varying proportions creates the three secondary colors: green, orange and violet. Mixing primary and secondary colors in equal proportions creates tertiary colors. Colors opposite each other on the color wheel are called complementary colors. For instance, green is the complementary color of red. Complementary colors will neutralize each other when they are mixed together.

TERMS YOU SHOULD KNOW

HUE is another term for color
TINT is a hue with white added
SHADE is a hue with black added
VALUE is the lightness or darkness of a color
INTENSITY refers to the vibrancy of a color
TONE refers to the warmth or coolness of a color

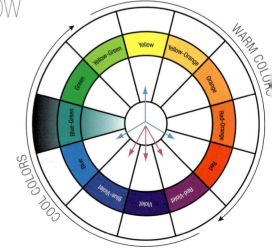

THE STUDY OF SKIN

COLOR SCHEMES

Monochromatic color schemes use the same color (with variations in value and intensity) throughout the face design. (See blue-green shading on color wheel illustration.)

Analogous color schemes use three colors that are adjacent to each other on the color wheel; often used for daytime face designs. (See pink arrows on color wheel illustration.)

Triadic color schemes use three colors located in a triangular position on the color wheel and are often used for more vibrant face designs. (See blue arrows on color wheel illustration.)

Complementary color schemes use colors that are across from each other on the color wheel in order to achieve the greatest amount of contrast and are often used to enhance eye color.

Warm and **Cool** are terms used to describe the tones found in both skin colors and cosmetic colors. Warm colors have red or yellow tones within them and cool colors have more blue tones within them.

Remember that dark colors seem to recede and diminish the appearance of features or areas, while lighter colors seem to advance, making features or areas appear larger or more prominent.

MAKEUP ESSENTIALS

To perform a professional makeup service, you will need the proper selection of products, implements and equipment. Makeup products are produced by many different manufacturers, are disposable and should be frequently replaced. MSDS guidelines for all products used in the salon should be easily available for your use. Makeup implements are hand-held tools, which should be disinfected or discarded after each use. Makeup equipment includes the furnishings and provisions necessary to provide a professional makeup service.

MAKEUP PRODUCTS

PRODUCT	FUNCTION
COTTON	Removes product
CLEANSER	Removes dirt, makeup and impurities
TONER	Purifies and restores pH
MOISTURIZER	Replenishes moisture/oil; protects skin
CONCEALER	Eliminates discolorations; reduces appearance of blemishes
FOUNDATION	Creates an even skin tone and uniform surface

PRODUCT	FUNCTION
BLUSH	Adds color or contour
EYE LINER	Accentuates and defines shape of eyes
EYE SHADOW	Accentuates shape and color of eye; contours
BROW PENCIL/POWDER	Fills in; corrects shape of eyebrow
MASCARA	Defines, lengthens and thickens the eyelashes
LIP LINER	Defines natural or corrected shape of the lips
LIPSTICK	Adds color and texture to the lips
TISSUE	Blots the skin; removes excess product
COTTON SWABS	Clean up; correct errors

MAKEUP IMPLEMENTS/SUPPLIES

IMPLEMENTS/SUPPLIES	FUNCTION
HEADBAND	Holds client's hair out of the way during application
TOWEL/MAKEUP DRAPE	Protects client's clothing
PALETTE	Holds desired amount of product(s)
SPATULAS	Remove product(s) from containers
LATEX SPONGES	Apply foundations and concealers; blending; clean up
TWEEZERS	Shape eyebrows; remove stray hairs
BRUSHES	Apply makeup; specific to needs
EYELASH CURLER	Curls and enhances lashes
MASCARA WANDS	Apply mascara
LASH SEPARATOR	Separates lashes after mascara application

MAKEUP EQUIPMENT

EQUIPMENT	FUNCTION
MIRROR	Allows artist to check balance; allows client to follow application
PROPER LIGHTING	Allows artist to work accurately and gauge results
MAKEUP CHAIR	Places client at proper height for makeup application/service

15

INFECTION CONTROL AND SAFETY

It is essential that you practice infection control and safety while performing makeup services so that you protect the health and well-being of your clients.

1. Wash and sanitize hands before and after every client.
2. Sanitize brushes after every client.
3. Use disposable applicators whenever possible and discard after use.
4. Avoid using products and makeup directly from containers. Use spatulas to place the desired amount of product on your makeup palette. If more product is needed, remember to use a fresh spatula.
5. Use a fresh drape on every client.
6. Sharpen all pencils before and after each use.
7. Remove product if you see signs of allergic reactions to cosmetic products, such as redness, swelling or inflammation.
8. Avoid excess pressure in and around the eye area.
9. Exercise extra precautions to avoid getting products or implements in the eyes.
10. Keep your fingernails well-groomed to avoid scratching your clients.

MAKEUP SERVICE ESSENTIALS

As with all professional services, communicating with your client prior to the actual service will ensure predictable results and will help you avoid any misunderstandings that may arise. As you review the four basic steps of the makeup service essentials, remember the importance of active listening, critical thinking and analysis of the overall success of the service.

CONNECT
- Meet the client and greet her with a firm handshake and a pleasant voice.
- Build rapport and develop a relationship with the client through communication.
- Assist client in filling out a makeup service record form.

CONSULT
- Ask questions; discover the purpose of the makeup application. Is it a special occasion or has the client come in for a makeup application lesson?
- Analyze your client's skin tone and skin type.
- Assess the facts found in the makeup service record form and in the answers to your questions; thoroughly think through your recommendations.

COSMETOLOGY FUNDAMENTALS

- Explain recommended face design and color selections.
- Identify products to be used and price for the service (if different from standard pricing).
- Gain feedback and approval from your client.

CREATE
- Ensure client comfort during service.
- Focus on and deliver the service that was agreed upon.
- If explanations are needed, be clear and precise.

COMPLETE
- Confirm that client is pleased with services rendered (satisfaction/feedback).
- Escort client to retail area and show at least two products used during service.
- Recommend products for future makeup applications.
- Invite client to make a purchase.
- Suggest a time for your client's next visit; schedule appointment if possible.
- Thank your client for visiting the school or salon.
- Record on client record card the products used and recommended.

MAKEUP TECHNIQUES AND PRODUCTS

Although makeup techniques and products can vary according to the occasion, the client's skin type and features, as well as the client's wishes, there are basic guidelines you can follow, which we'll outline in this section. To start, you'll want to keep the following points in mind before and/or during a makeup application:

- **Prepare the skin (cleanse, tone, moisturize and protect) before applying any cosmetics.** Proper skin care ensures smooth application and better product adherence.
- Facial hair removal and brow shaping are done prior to the application of makeup. Keep in mind that additional shaping and "filling in" of the brows may occur during the makeup service. Refer to the "Hair Removal" portion of this chapter for more information.
- Whenever appropriate, begin with light, sheer foundations that allow you to add if more coverage is required. A heavy, matte foundation will be more difficult to adjust as you work. Remember that foundation is meant to create an even base on the skin.
- Make use of the proper makeup brushes and applicators when applying cosmetics. Brushes are particularly helpful in that they provide more directional control and can be used effectively to blend colors and soften or smudge harder lines.

- Always apply makeup in appropriate lighting. Keep in mind the lighting in which the makeup will be seen and make adjustments according to the light in which you are working. Fluorescent lighting can be deceiving as it often accentuates any blue or green undertones and cancels out warmer tones. Since evening makeup tends to be more dramatic, you should compensate when working under salon lighting or daylight.
- Makeup design is about creating illusions. By using the principles of light and dark colors, you can highlight attractive features or areas and diminish those that are less attractive. Also, by making the best use of "shine" and "matte" products you can enhance or diminish appropriately. Careful blending between lights and darks, as well as shine and matte, will help you to create the most effective illusions.

BRUSHES

It is important to have a selection of makeup brushes available. Note that brush names may vary among manufacturers.

- **a.** Large powder brush (dome)
- **b.** Contoured brush
- **c.** Medium chisel brush
- **d.** Large blending brush
- **e.** Medium fluff brush
- **f.** Small fluff brush
- **g.** Small chisel brush
- **h.** Angle brush
- **i.** Detail angle brush
- **j.** Lip brush
- **k.** Large camouflage brush
- **l.** Eyelash separator
- **m.** Fan brush
- **n.** Latex sponge

MAKEUP CORRECTIONS/CONCEALER

Every makeup artist knows the necessity of correcting particular facial imperfections before applying foundation. After preparing the client's skin (cleansing, toning, moisturizing and protecting), you'll need to assess the skin for tone and value, as well as for specific problems. Problems such as under-eye circles (often with blue or purple undertones), broken capillaries and blemishes can and should be corrected. If they are not, they may stand out or detract from the completed makeup design.

Concealers are available in cream, pot and stick formulations. They are available in light, medium and dark "skin tones," generally with a yellowish base shade. With these tones, you may wish to match the foundation or go one shade lighter. You may also suggest products that offset the skin's natural undertones.

IF UNDERTONE IS:	USE:
Yellow	Violet Base
Red	Green Base
Green	Red Base
Blue/Purple	Yellow/Orange Base

To apply concealer to the eye area, form a half-moon shape that covers the inside edges of the top and bottom of the eye area. Also apply concealer to any darker or shadowed areas of the eye. You may apply with a camouflage brush, but blend with a latex sponge. Apply a minimal amount of pressure to this delicate area to help maintain the elasticity of the skin tissue and prevent wrinkling and creasing. Under the eye, blend toward the bridge of the nose.

To eliminate shadows or discolorations (such as broken capillaries) along the sides of the nose, use a camouflage brush to apply concealer to both sides of the nasal fold, in a triangular shape. Use a latex sponge to blend the concealer into the surrounding skin.

REMEMBER
Makeup applicators need to be discarded or disinfected after each use to follow infection control guidelines.

FOUNDATION

Foundation is used primarily for coverage and correction. Foundation can even out skin color and create a smoother skin texture, providing a good canvas on which to create a makeup design. Foundation is used to correct undesirable skin tones such as sallowness or redness. It also can conceal imperfections in the skin such as dilated blood vessels, freckles, birthmarks or blemishes. Today, many foundations also contain sunscreens, which can help protect skin from UV damage. Unless correction is required, match the foundation to the skin tone. **To test a foundation shade to determine if you have chosen the correct color, blend a small amount of foundation on the client's jawline.** The correct color will "disappear" into the client's skin. **Foundation may be considered the most important makeup product.**

Foundations are available in several forms. The liquid form offers coverage with a more natural appearance.

Cream foundation has a heavier consistency and is used for additional coverage. Cream foundations require more careful blending than liquid foundations.

Pancake or pan-stick foundations are used for very heavy coverage and are usually applied with water and a sponge. Grease-based foundations also offer very heavy coverage. Both types of "maximum coverage" foundations are used primarily for photography and theater. They are also used when major corrections are required, such as covering scars or large birthmarks.

In recent years, foundations have become available in a combination of makeup base and powder, which can be found in a compact form. This combination is sometimes called "one-step" or "dual finish" makeup because additional powder is not required. Coverage will vary from brand to brand, but is generally on the lighter side, for a more natural effect.

SKIN COLOR CLASSIFICATIONS

TONE	SKIN COLOR	TONE	SKIN COLOR
Light Creamy	Yellow to slightly peach; light	Olive	Yellowish-green; medium to dark
Golden	Yellow cast; light	Olive	Yellowish-green; medium to dark
Pink	Pink or blue to red; light to medium	Brown	Usually olive-toned; medium to dark with red or yellow undertones
Tan	Carmel-colored to brown; light to dark with red or yellow undertones	Ebony	Mahogany and/or blue undertones; dark to very dark

Foundation has other applications besides coverage and correction. It is often used to achieve the effects of facial contouring. Lighter shades of foundation are used to highlight a facial feature and darker shades of foundation are used to recess a facial feature. Foundati is also used to complete and correct the lip line.

To apply foundation, place approximately a dime-size amount of product onto your palette Use your fingertip or a cotton swab to transfer foundation from the palette. Apply to the face, starting in the "mask" area. The mask area is comprised of the center of the face, especially around the eyes. Measure approximately two-fingers' width around the eyes and near the nose. Then use a latex sponge to blend the product onto the face. Use a pat-and-roll or stippling technique to blend the foundation outward from the mask. Use very gentle pressure as you work. **If too much pressure is applied to the facial skin, broken capillaries can result.** Be sure to blend each section carefully before moving on. Foundation should blend and fade away toward the perimeters of the face, if the mask application is used. Thi application is used on relatively clear, blemish-free skin that does not require much color correction. **If a more traditional application is used (covering the entire face) or if two shades are used, foundation should blend into the hairline and to the neck, avoiding any lines of demarcation.**

CONTOURING AND HIGHLIGHTING

Contouring and highlighting can add the illusion of increased dimension to the face and, in some instances, appear to reshape the face. **In makeup application, highlighting the protruding bones can "bring out" these features, while shadowing of the cavities, or recessed areas, can add depth to the face. Contour** means to create an outline, especially of a curving or irregular figure or shape. Heightening the contrasts between lighter and darker tones can create more definition in the planes and surfaces of the face. Contour by using a darker shadow to give the appearance of a smaller or receding feature. For example a wider nose can appear thinner by applying darker tones to the sides of the nose. Highligh by using a lighter tint to create the appearance of a larger or more outstanding feature. Highlighting the receding areas of a weak chin can make the chin seem more prominent and well-proportioned with the rest of the face.

Many cosmetic products can be used to contour the face. The most common products com in powder, liquid and cream forms. Powders create a matte finish, while liquids and creams result in a "glowing" finish. Your client's skin type will help you to determine which type of product will work best for her. Oily skin types usually look best when powders are used. Dryer skin types can benefit from the moisturizing properties often found in liquid or crean formulations. Powders are applied with brushes. A small tapered brush and a shading brus are usually sufficient for all but theatrical contouring. Brushes or sponges may be used to apply liquid and cream contour products.

Remember that contouring needs to be done for subtle effect. Again keep in mind the lighting in which the clients will be seen (i.e., bright lighting may not be very flattering to the "cosmetic tricks" of highlighting and contouring). Also, products should be blended very well to achieve the most attractive effects.

EYES

The eyes, often called the windows to the soul, can be the most expressive feature of the face. Many first impressions are based on how well confidence and trust are communicated with the eyes. Since the eyes are such an attention-getting and important feature, you should be sure to use cosmetic artistry very wisely in this area.

The eye area can be divided into thirds. The three areas are the eyelid, the crease area and the brow bone. An eye that is in "perfect" or ideal proportions would have the following characteristics:
- The area between the base of the lashes and the crease line makes up one-third of the eye.
- The area between the crease line and the eyebrow makes up the remaining two-thirds.
- Well-spaced eyes have the width of one eye between them. "Close-set" eyes have a space of less than one eye between them. "Wide-set" eyes have a space greater than one eye.

EYEBROWS

Eyebrows "frame" the eyes and are very important to the balance of any face and makeup design. Refer to the hair removal portion of this chapter for complete procedures on waxing and tweezing.

Whether the brows are natural or have been shaped, it may be necessary to shade or fill in to create the most attractive and flattering shape. You can shade or fill in the brows using shadows (powder) or pencils.

GUIDELINES FOR SHAPING A WELL-ARCHED EYEBROW

- The brow should begin over the inside corner of the eye.
- The peak, or highest point of the arch, should occur over the outside of the iris of the eye.
- Then imagine a diagonal line from the outside of the nose that extends past the outside of the eye. This point is where the brow should end.

Variations on this basic shape will be appropriate for most face shapes. Keep the natural shape of the brow in mind, as it relates to the client's brow bone. Extreme changes in brow shape are appropriate for high fashion and theatrical looks.

You can use the shape of the eyebrows to offset imperfections of other facial features. For instance, if the eyes are set too close together, widen the distance between the brows to make the eyes seem more well-spaced. Wide-set eyes can be made to look closer together by extending the brows past the inside corners of the eyes. Straighter, more horizontal brows, with a minimal arch, will help diminish the illusion of length in a long face.

Keep these points in mind when filling in or shading brows:
- Work with sharp pencils and use small, hair-like strokes
- Use two colors to give you a more natural effect and allow you to match hair color more closely
- Make sure you've filled the brow evenly, leaving no sparse areas
- Use a brow brush to soften the edges of the eyebrow
- Strive for symmetry as you work on the other eyebrow

EYELINER

Eyeliner is used in makeup application to define and emphasize the shape and size of the eyes. Eyeliners come in liquid, pencil and powder formulas. Liquids and powders are usually applied with a brush. Pencil liners are applied to the eye using very short strokes. Eyeliner is usually applied at the lash line. Pencil liners can be applied inside the eyelid as well, but be sure not to cover the tear duct since this may cause injury. Keep in mind that harder lines, such as those achieved with liquid liner, may not be as flattering and are generally reserved for evening or specific fashion makeup designs.

EYE SHADOW

Eye shadows come in many forms, including creams, gel, powders and pencils or crayons. Shadows can be used to create a more contoured or exaggerated effect in areas such as the crease. They can also be used to highlight and accentuate areas such as the brow bone. Eye shadow design is often the focal point of a complete makeup design, so you should carefully analyze the client's lifestyle and personality, as well as the occasion for which the makeup is being designed. Blending is especially crucial in this area, since colors are often more intense. Again, it is important to apply very little pressure to the eye area to preserve and protect the delicate skin in this area.

MASCARA

Mascara defines, lengthens and thickens the eyelashes. The depth of color used may also serve to enhance and bring out the eye shadow color used. Mascara is available in liquid, cake and cream forms. It is applied with disposable mascara wands and is generally applied to the upper and lower lashes. Note that an eyelash curler may be used prior to the application of mascara to open up the eyes. Use a lash separator after applying mascara to avoid a clumpy look.

ARTIFICIAL LASHES

Artificial (false) lashes are not generally worn with day makeup, since they tend to create a more dramatic effect. The exception would be individuals who have lost their lashes or have particularly sparse lashes.

APPLICATION OF ARTIFICIAL STRIP LASHES

Quality, human hair lashes are the most natural looking. Brown or black will coordinate well enough to be worn with most hair colors. To apply artificial lashes, you will need an appropriate set of lashes, tweezers, scissors and lash adhesive. Follow these general steps to apply:

1. Begin by measuring the upper lash. Start midway between the inside corner of the eye and the curve where the iris begins and measure to the outside corner. If the lash is too long, trim it to fit.
2. Use your fingers to bend the lashes into a horseshoe shape to make them more flexible and easier to fit to the curve of the eyelid.
3. Apply a thin strip (small amount) of eyelash adhesive to the base of the artificial lashes and allow it to set for a few seconds.
4. Apply the lashes. Begin with the shorter, or inside, lashes and position them midway between the inside corner of the eye and the curve where the iris begins. Position the remaining lashes as close to the client's own lashes as possible. You may also work from the outside corner toward the inside corner, so long as the lashes have been accurately measured and trimmed.
5. Apply bottom lashes by using lash adhesive in the same manner as for the upper lashes. Place the lashes under the client's lower lashes, with shorter lashes toward the center of the eye and longer lashes toward the outside.

APPLICATION OF SEMI-PERMANENT INDIVIDUAL EYELASHES (EYE TABBING)
Although not done frequently, another method of applying false lashes is known as eye tabbing. Tabbing involves the application of individual, synthetic lashes to the client's own lashes. The application lasts approximately 6 to 8 weeks, with lashes falling off as the client's own lashes naturally fall out. Lower lashes will not last as long, since the oils in this area will cause the adhesive to break down.

FACIAL POWDER
Facial powders are primarily designed to "set" other makeup products so that they last longer without fading, streaking or rubbing off. They are applied after liquid or creme products, such as foundations or cream blushes. They are applied before powdered blushes or contour colors. The most common forms available are loose and pressed powders. Both forms can be found in translucent and tinted shades. **A colorless, translucent powder may be worn with any foundation shade since it is designed to allow the skin/foundation shade to show through without imparting any color.** Tinted powders should be used in coordination with matching foundations. They may also be worn successfully by women who do not wear foundation and want only the sheerest coverage. Application with a powder brush, or large dome brush, will yield lighter coverage. For heavier coverage, use a sponge or powder puff. Facial powder is generally applied before mascara.

BLUSH
Blush is used to add color to the face, especially to the cheek area. Without blush, the face may appear to be flat or dull, since foundation has evened out skin tone and reduced any natural "blush." Blush can also be used to enhance facial contouring. Blushes are available in liquid, cream, gel and powder forms. Cream and gel products are applied prior to the application of facial powder, usually with a small sponge. Powdered blush is applied after facial powder, usually with a brush. **Liquid cheek color products seem to be suitable for all skin types.** The fairness or darkness of your client's skin will determine the depth of the blush color you recommend. Blush should coordinate with the tones of the rest of the makeup application. Warm eye makeup and lip colors require warmer blush colors, while a cooler makeup design requires a cooler blush color.

Blush color is generally applied for a soft or subtle effect. Apply in a C-shaped motion from the temple to the cheekbone, being careful not to extend beyond the middle of the eye. If blush has been applied too heavily, soften the effect by applying translucent powder over it.

Like many other aspects of makeup design, blush application, particularly placement of color, will follow fashion trends. Be sure the application you choose is the most flattering to your client and not just the fad of the moment.

LIPS

Lips, like eyes, deserve special makeup considerations. Generally, a soft, natural look in lip color application is preferred, especially for daytime. **The mouth should not "stand out" above the other facial features.** Fashion trends may call for a stronger mouth at certain times, but overall the makeup design should remain proportionally balanced.

LIP LINER

Lip liner is applied to the outer edge of the lips to define the shape of the lips and to prevent lipstick from "bleeding" onto the skin around the mouth. It may also be used to visually correct imperfections in lip shape. Note that darker colors of lip liner and lip color are often chosen for evening to balance with more intense eye makeup design.

BRACE THE HAND UNDER THE CHIN TO STEADY THE APPLICATION.

LIP COLOR

The purpose of lip color is to complete the balance of color. It is usually the last cosmetic to be applied. Be cautious that the lip color you choose does not overpower the amount of color that you have applied to the cheeks and eyes. Lipstick and lip liner can correct the shape and size of a mouth to make it more proportionate with the rest of the facial features.

Lip color is available in a variety of forms, the most common of which is lipstick, contained in a cylindrical tube. It is best applied with a lip brush, which allows the contour of the mouth to be carefully followed or reshaped as needed.

Lip glosses tend to have less concentration of color than lipsticks. Glosses impart a shiny appearance and can also be used as highlighters over a lipstick shade. Glosses usually have moisturizing properties and are soothing for dry, chapped lips. They are popular with younger girls who want some color, but not as much as a lipstick.

Some lip products contain sunscreens to block out ultraviolet rays and prevent the lips from becoming chapped. As with all other makeup products, it is a good idea to look at the ingredients of lip color products, as well as the color, before making your selection.

TO PROPERLY APPLY MAKEUP TO THE LIPS, FOLLOW THESE BASIC GUIDELINES

1. Analyze the overall size of the mouth; check the proportions with the other facial features to determine if the mouth is too large or too small.
2. Apply foundation to the lips to block out the natural lip line so that you may create a new one if desired. Blocking out the natural lip color also allows for truer color from lip color products and prevents bleeding of color. Applying powder over the foundation will make lip color last longer.
3. Use a lip liner (pencil) or lip brush to line the lips. For general outlining, use a natural tone, two or three shades darker than the natural lip color or that matches the tone of the lipstick you have chosen.
4. Start lining the upper lip at the outside corners and work from either side toward the center or the "bow" of the lips. Then line the lower lip from the center toward either side. Note that this is the point at which you may need to 'correct' any imperfections in lip shape. See illustrations that follow.
5. When the lip liner is complete, fill in the shape using the appropriate shade of lip color. Use a sanitized lip brush and work to the edges of the lip shape, but not beyond the lip liner.

LIP SHAPES

An examination of the ideal mouth and lips would reveal:
- A frontal view in which the bottom lip is slightly fuller than the top, with a total shape and size that create balance and harmony with the rest of the facial features.
- A side view that shows an indentation above the upper lip and below the bottom lip. The top lip, the bottom lip and the chin should extend forward almost equally.

You can use the principles of contouring and highlighting, using darker and lighter colors, to make "corrections" on different lip shapes. Remember to keep corrections as subtle and natural as possible to avoid an overly "drawn-on" look. Foundation should be applied to the lips prior to corrective lining.

LIP SHAPES

Thin Lips

Use brighter, lighter colors to make them appear fuller. Increase the size of both the upper and lower lips by outlining them with a soft, curving line, just outside the natural lip line.

THIN LOWER LIP
Extend the curve of the lower lip to balance the shape of the mouth.

THIN UPPER LIP
Build up the curve of the upper lip to balance the shape of the mouth.

Full Lips

Use a pencil and outline just inside the natural lip line, and minimize fullness by choosing darker, more muted lip colors. Blend carefully within the "new" lip line.

Full Bottom Lip

If the bottom lip is a lot fuller than the top or the top lip is too thin or small, mute the lower lip with a deeper color and use a shade or two lighter for the upper lip. Be sure to use colors in the same color family. Line the lower lip to look smaller and leave the upper lip unlined or line it slightly outside the natural lip line.

Small Mouth

Build the outside edges of the upper and lower lips by lining slightly outside the natural lip line. Then extend the corners of the mouth outward.

Sharply Defined "Cupid's Bow"

As you line the upper lip, round off the sharp peaks and widen the curve of the upper lip.

Uneven or Crooked Lips

To create a more balanced shape, use lip liner to build up the areas that are not large enough or defined enough.

CORRECTIONS FOR FACIAL FEATURES

WIDE NOSE

To make a wide nose look narrower, apply a darker tone, or shader, along the sides of the nose and a thin line of highlighter down the center of the nose.

LONG NOSE
Visually shorten a long nose by contouring the tip of it.

PROMINENT CHIN
Make the chin visually recede by contouring the prominent area, blending underneath and onto the neck.

UNDEFINED CHEEKBONES
To give the cheekbones more dimension, apply highlighter over the very top of the cheekbone. Then contour the hollow under the cheekbone, where the cheekbones naturally indent. You may also use this technique to create a more dramatic emphasis for already well-defined cheekbone Avoid creating obvious stripes of contour in an effort to create the illusio

RECEDING CHIN
To "bring out" a chin that recedes or is weak, apply highlighter on and under the chin.

POINTED CHIN
Minimize the point of the chin by softening it with a contouring product or slightly darker foundation.

"DOUBLE" CHIN
Contour the heavier area to make it recede and appear slimmer.

BROAD OR SQUARE JAW
Contour along the jaw and through the sides of the face to minimize width. You may use a deeper foundation than on the rest of the face to help create balance between the upper and lower parts of the face.

HIGH OR BROAD FOREHEAD
Contour along the outside edges to narrow the forehead or along the top to visually shorten the appearance of a high forehead.

BROW DESIGN AND PLACEMENT OF LIGHTS AND DARKS

Brow design and the placement of lights and darks can visually alter the position of the eyes on the face. In this illustration, the eyes are the same distance apart in each of the three sets. Notice how, in the second set, **placing deeper tones toward the inside corners (or toward the nose), and extending the eyebrows beyond the inside corner of the eye make the eyes seem closer set than they are. Beginning the eyebrow farther out and using deeper tones toward the outside of the eyes** as illustrated in the third set, **create the illusion of wide-set eyes**. When following fashion trends, be sure that your makeup design is not accentuating less than perfect features.

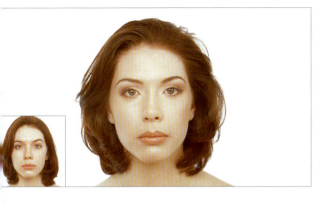

WORKSHOP 03
BASIC MAKEUP APPLICATION

Although different occasions call for different makeup applications, a daytime makeup application outlined here covers the general guidelines. Refer to the images in the preceding portion of this chapter for visual reference.

BASIC MAKEUP APPLICATION PREPARATION

Before you start your makeup application, it is important to have your area, products, implements and equipment in proper order prior to your client's arrival. Be sure to take care of the following points:

- Sanitize chair, station and brushes
- Set out brushes, applicators, spatulas and palette, cleaners, toners, moisturizers, cleansing pads, facial tissue, cape, headband, cotton pads, draping sheet or robe, towels, eyelash curler and assorted makeup

BASIC MAKEUP APPLICATION PROCEDURE

- Wash and sanitize hands
- Prepare client (drape, including headband, and position chair)
- Consult with client
- Cleanse, tone, moisturize and protect skin
- Analyze skin, face, brows, eyes and lips
- Groom brows if needed (brush and tweeze)
- Select appropriate foundation color
- Apply concealer as needed
- Apply foundation
- Shade brows (brush and fill in as needed)
- Check brows for symmetry
- Apply eyeliner
- Apply eyeshadow(s)
- Apply blush, if cream, liquid or gel
- Apply tinted or translucent powder
- Apply blush, if powder
- Apply mascara
- Apply lip liner
- Apply lip color
- Check coverage, balance accuracy
- Remove draping

BASIC MAKEUP APPLICATION COMPLETION

Perform after every makeup service:

- Offer prebook visit to client.
- Recommend retail products for client.
- Throw away non-reusable materials used during the makeup application service, replace used towels with fresh towels and arrange all products and implements in proper order.
- Disinfect your makeup service implements and makeup chair.
- Wash your hands with liquid soap.

EVENING MAKEUP APPLICATION

Although many of the actual step-by-step techniques remain the same for an evening makeup application, there are distinct differences. Generally, evening makeup designs are intended to be seen in softer, more indirect lighting than daytime makeup designs. Color is used more intensely and the overall effect is more dramatic. Here are some of the key changes that are made for an evening makeup application.

Darker eyeliner can be used for more depth of color. The harder edge is then blended slightly with a small detail brush.

More intense color is often used on the eyes. Color is sometimes applied to areas that are left more natural in a daytime design. Here a deep, coppery brown is applied with a dabbing motion, which results in more intense concentration of color.

e color is then worked up and ntoured into the crease and ghtly beyond for a dramatic ect. Note that there is no harsh e—the shadows should be very ll blended.

Color is more often "wrapped" around the eye for evening, bringing color and emphasis to the area below the eye.

Another application of eye liner, this time liquid, is used for more definition and drama. Note that mascara application is usually heavier for evening.

Darker colors can be used for a stronger, more defined mouth for evening. Stronger eye and lip colors may require stronger cheek color, so carefully check the balance of the face.

DARKER SKIN MAKEUP APPLICATION

Darker skin makeup applications require careful consideration. Foundations and concealers should be well chosen, as it is easy to go too light or too cool in your color choice. In general, these skin types can carry off more color than lighter skin colors without looking overly made up. Note that the application shown here is an example of an evening look.

Extra attention should be paid to color choices on deeper skin tones. Very often, unevenness of tone and depth will need to be corrected.

Yellow-based products are often appropriate for darker skin colors. Concealers and foundations that are too cool will look ashy or gray on these skin colors.

In this instance, a brow pencil is used to fill in and shape the brows. A pencil will create a stronger, more defined brow than a powder, particularly on this darker skin color.

Regardless of the pattern of application, note that richer, more intense colors can often be used on darker skin tones. Heavily pigmented skin can cause makeup colors to appear faded or washed out if they are too muted or sparingly applied. Keep the overall balance of color in mind as you design your makeup.

Cheek color needs to be in proportion with the rest of the color on the face. Again, remember that more color may need to be applied on darker skin tones in order to be effective. Here, blush is applied solely for color and to soften the look, not to contour the area.

Follow the basic guidelines for lip shaping. In this case, the lip line is redrawn just inside the natural lip line to subtly minimize the size of the mouth. The deeper tone used to line and fill the lips adds to the effect, while creating harmonious balance through the entire face.

BRIDAL MAKEUP APPLICATION

It's that once-in-a-lifetime occasion when a woman wants to look more beautiful than she has ever looked. Yet weddings and brides present special challenges to the professional makeup artist. The makeup application needs to last all day and/or evening with minimal upkeep. Many brides wear their hair up for their big day, and that can alter the appearance of the face shape. Brides usually wear white, ivory or other very light colors, which have the effect of draining color from faces with lighter skin tones.

One of the biggest challenges to the professional makeup artist is to create a makeup design that looks naturally beautiful to the naked eye and that can hold up to photography. Most women are photographed more on their wedding day than on any other day in their lives. Here are some specific points to consider when designing makeup for the bridal client:

- Make sure that skin is well prepared—exfoliated earlier if needed. The "canvas" should be as perfect as possible. Make sure skin is moisturized, but not oily. This precaution is especially important around the eyes. Preparation ensures that the makeup design will look good and helps the makeup to last longer.
- Ideally, the only touch-up products needed should be powder, lip liner and lipstick.
- Foundation should match and complement the bride's skin tone. Apply the least amount possible for a fresh, natural look. Use concealer on the inside corner of the eyes to hide imperfections.
- Remember that many types of photographic lighting have cool undertones and will bring out cool tones in the makeup design. Stay with a neutral-to-warmer palette.
- On oily skins, avoid face, cheek and eye products with orange or strong yellow undertones.
- These colors tend to oxidize more on oily skin and turn more yellow.
- Many gowns have lower-cut necklines. Be sure to powder the skin in the exposed areas so that light reflections in the face and the décolletage are similar.

- For longer-lasting cheek color, apply a cream blush (if skin is not oily), followed by an application of powder blush after the face has been powdered.
- Curl the lashes and use waterproof mascara.
- Eyes and brows should be accentuated with definition more than with color.
- Positioning white or very light highlights in the eye area will create a reflection of the dress, which is very effective.
- Brows tend to "disappear" in photographs, so make sure they are well groomed and defined. For a slightly more dramatic effect that will hold up to photos, use more styling on the outside edges.
- There is usually a bit of kissing going on at a wedding, so use good judgment in the design of your client's lip makeup. Be careful of overly glossy products that may smear and spoil the rest of the makeup.
- Use a long-lasting lip liner – products with silicone are excellent – and apply to the entire lip. Use a color about 2-3 shades darker than the natural lip color and that matches the tone of the lipstick color.
- An extra tip for "camera-ready" makeup: Be sure not to powder until after the eye makeup is complete. Then clean up under the eye using concealer on a latex sponge or small brush.

This chapter has set the foundation for you in the area of skin – skin theory, skin care, hair removal and makeup. The following images show you the multitude of inspirational and exciting possibilities open to you in makeup design.

  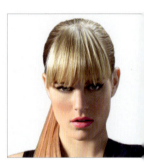

BEFORE   DAY   EVENING

15

BEFORE DAY EVENING

BEFORE DAY EVENING

BEFORE DAY EVENING

CONNECTING THEORY TO REAL-WORLD PRACTICE

THE STUDY OF SKIN	PERSONAL CONNECTION: IMPROVE YOURSELF	INDUSTRY CONNECTION: BECOME A PROFESSIONAL	CLIENT CONNECTION: SERVE THE GUEST
SKIN THEORY	Understand how the skin functions and the differences among skin types	Improve your salon skills by understanding the basics of dermatology	Help clients understand how their actions affect the health and appearance of their skin
SKIN CARE	Treat the skin in ways that encourage its healthy growth and appearance	Excel at facials that relax and remediate, as well as cleanse, tone and moisturize	Provide treatments that are individually suited to each client's specific skin type and characteristics
HAIR REMOVAL	Be aware of the methods of hair removal and the advantages and disadvantages of each	Recognize how licensure in electrolysis can be an expansion of one's professional options	Educate clients to make informed decisions from among the hair removal alternatives
MAKEUP	Apply makeup creatively and knowledgeably to achieve specific visual results	Expand your scope by creating day, evening, event and theatrical makeup designs	Transform your clients' appearance through the artistry of makeup design

IN OTHER WORDS

Your ability to apply the theory and techniques of professional skin care, hair removal and makeup application will enhance your clients' appearance and expand your career horizons.

LESSONS LEARNED

- The skin is the largest organ of the body and performs six specific functions.

- Cleansing, toning, moisturizing and protecting are the four basic steps of prop skin care.

- Salon hair removal services include temporary methods – shaving, depilatorie tweezing and waxing – and permanent methods, known as electrolysis, which use an electric current to inhibit hair growth.

- Makeup design and application combine principles of art and science to enha desirable features, balance uneven proportions and diminish facial flaws.

NDEX

dominal thrusts, 59
ductor muscles, 74
raded hair, 187
see also broken hair
celerator machine, 515
id-balanced shampoos, 121
id mantle, 180, 579-581
id waves, 127, 415
ne, 589
ute, 584
tive immunity, 49
ductor muscles, 74
vertising, 147, 162
ro-centric hair, 183
nails, 545
erent nerves, 81
DS (Acquired
    Immunodeficiency Syndrome),
    47-48
brushing, 561
forming, 352-354
    brush, 320
    guidelines, 353
    with round brush, 353-354
    scrunching layered form,
        352-353
kaline waves, 127, 414
binism, 184, 588
ergy, 584
ergic contact dermatitis, 584
opecia, 190
opecia areata, 193
opecia areata prematura, 191
opecia areata totalis, 193
opecia areata universalis, 193
-purpose comb, 202
ternating current, 91-92
ternation, 233
nines/quats, 126
nino acids, 113, 181
nmonium hydroxide, 127
nmonium thioglycolate
relaxer, 444, 466
np, ampere, 90
abolism, 64
agen, 181
alogous color schemes, 617
aphoresis, 99
atomy, 63
    circulatory system, 75-79
    digestive system, 84
    definition, 63
    endocrine system, 85

excretory system, 85
integumentary system, 86
muscular system, 70-75
nervous system, 79-83
reproductive system, 86
respiratory system, 85
skeletal system, 67-69
androgenetic alopecia, 190-191
    recognizing, 190
    treatment, 193
angles
    in sculpting, 289-291
angular artery, 78
anhidrosis, 589
antimicrobials, 133
antiseptic, 50, 51, 547,
    594, 604
anode, 98
anterior, 70
anthrax, 47
anti-dandruff shampoos, 122
areas of the head, 286-287
    apex, 287
applicator bottle, 433
apprentice, 146
arrector pili muscle, 180
arm, 69, 74
    and hand arteries, 78
    and hand nerves, 83
    wrist and hand bones, 69
aromatherapy, 212
aromatherapy, for the scalp,
    212-213
arteries, 76
    and veins of the face, head
        and neck, 78
    of the hand and arm, 78
    of the lower leg and foot, 78
artificial lashes, 627
artificial nail care, 562
    additional services, 564-574
    essentials, 562-563
    infection control and safety, 563
    nail tips, 564-567
    products, 562-563
    sculptured nails, 569-573
    tools/supplies, 563
artificial pigment, 488-489
asian hair, 183
asteatosis, 589
asymmetrical balance, 235
asymptomatic, 49
atomic number, 110
atoms, 111-112

attitudes, 37-38
auricularis, 72
    anterior muscle, 72
    posterior muscle, 72
    superior muscle, 72
auriculo temporal, 82
autonomic nervous system, 83
axons, 80

B

bacilli, 46
back strain, neck and, 29
    backbrushing and
        backcombing, 334, 369
    tips, 397
bacteria, 45
    growth of, 47
    movement of, 47
    nonpathogenic, 45
    pathogenic, 45
bactericidals, 53
bad breath, 25
balance, 235
    asymmetrical, 235
    symmetrical, 235
bargain buyer, 171
base coat, 548
base colors, 486
base control, 329-333
    for hairstyling, 330
    indentation, 329-331
    pincurls, 333
base retouch, 506
base size, 330, 421
base texturizing, 293
base-to-ends technique, 357
    see also curling
        iron techniques
basic facial, 597-603
    completion, 603
    preparation, 598
    procedure, 598
basic hair sculptures, 272-274
    combination form, 275
    gradation, 274
    graduated form, 273
    increase-layered form, 273
    solid form, 272
    square combination form, 292
    uniformly layered form, 274
basic makeup application,
    635-612
basic waxing, 609
battery, 92

Beau's lines, 545
belly, 71
benefits, job, 145-146
bicep, 74
bleeding and wounds, 58
blend method, 613
blood, 75-79
    cells, 76
    flow through the heart, 77
    plasma, 76
    platelets, 76
    vessels, 76-77
blood spill procedure, 56, 550
bloodborne pathogen, 48
    disinfection, 50
    standards, 54
blotting, 428, 451
blow dryer, 320, 336
blue nails, 543
blush, 628-629
bobby pin, 370
body language, 32-33
body shapes, 238-240
    average, 239
    entire body shape, 240
    short and sturdy, 239
    tall and lanky, 238
body systems, 66, 67-86
body-building conditioners, 125
bonding, 408-410
    strand by strand, 409
    weft, 408-409
bones, 67-69
bookend technique, 419
borrowing money, 156
braid, 376-377
brain, 65, 79-80
bricklay perm wrap, 423
bridal makeup application,
    639-640
broad spectrum disinfectants,
    53
broken hair, 187
bromidrosis, 589
bruised nails, 545
brush, or comb, 335
    disinfection procedure, 55-56
brushing and combing, 197-198
    removing tangles, 198
brushes, 320-321, 335
buccal, 82
buccinator, 73
building blocks of the human
    body, 63

building clientele, 147-148
bulla, 586
burns, 58-59
  chemical, 58
  heat or electrical, 59
bursitis, 31
business cards, 147
butyl parabens, 133
butylene glycol, 133
buyer types, 171-173
  identify, 171
  motivation, 171

C

callus, 587
candelilla waxes, 133
caninus, 73
canities, 188
canvas block, 389
capillaries, 75, 77
cap highlighting, 510
  (cap method)
capilli, 182
carbohydrates, 24
carbomer thickeners, 133
carbuncles, 589
cardiac muscle, 70
carnauba waxes, 133
Carpal Tunnel Syndrome, 30
carpals, 69
cascade, 398
catabolism, 64
catagen, 181
cataphoresis, 99
cathode, 98
caucasian hair, 183
celestial axis, 225
cells, 64
  form parts of the hair,
    180-181
  membrane, 64
central nervous system, 79-81
cervical, 69, 82, 83
  cutaneous, 82
  nerves, 82
  vertebrae, 68
cerebellum, 80
cerebrum, 80
cetyl alcohol, 133
chemical
  bonds, 112-115
  change, 109
chemical depilatory, 604, 607
chemical exfoliant, 594
chemical record card, 514
chemical relaxing, 441-468
  chemical phase, 447-448

consultation, 461-462
essentials, 461-462
hair analysis for, 444-446
infection control and
  safety, 459
physical phase, 449
product and application
  overview, 456-458, 462
relaxer application
  methods, 448
relaxer strengths, 443-444
techniques, 464-467
theory, 441-442, 451-452
types of relaxers, 443-444
chemical services
  draping for, 435, 460
chemical texturizing, 411-468
chemistry, 107-136
  conditioners, 123, 124-126
  of cosmetics, 118-119
  curl reformation, 128
  hair color, 129-132, 489-502
  ingredients, 132-134
  inorganic, 110
  organic, 110
  perms, 126-127
  product information, 132
  relaxers, 127-128
  rinses, 124
  of shampoos, 119-123
chicken pox, 47
chignon, 399
children as clients, 302
chin strap, 388
chloasma, 588
choking, 59
chronic, 584
circuit, see closed path, 93
circuit breaker, 95
circulatory system, 66, 75-79
  cardiovascular, 75-76
  lymph-vascular, 75, 79
citric acid, 134
clavicle, 69
clay mask, 593
clean sheets, 594
cleansing gel, 604
cleansing lotion, 594
client
  designer relationship,
    148-149
client robe/gown, 594
clientele, 147-148
  building, 147-148
clip, 514
clipper-over-comb
  technique, 298

clippers, 278, 284-285
clockwise movement,
  of hair, 326-327
closed path, 93
closing the sale, 170-171
cloth cape, 306, 389
cloth towels, 433
clothing, 28, 255-256
coarse hair, 183
cocci, 46
cocoon wrap, 598
cold waves, 414
color
  complementary, 476
  in design, 232
  laws of, 472-473
  in makeup, 616-617
  primary, 472, 616
  secondary, 473, 616
  tertiary, 473-474
  theory, 471-482
  warm and cool, 475- 476
  wheel, 474-476
color brush, 513
color stain remover, 513
comb
  control, 298
  disinfection of, 55
  electrode, 98
  types, 285, 322-323, 335
combination equipment, 96
combination form sculpture,
  275-277
combination skin, 583-584
comedones, 589
common carotid arteries, 78
communication,
  effective, 32-36
  environment, 260
  professional appearance, 265
  nonverbal, 32-33
  and technical skills, 32
  time, 257
  two-way, 34-36
  verbal, 33-36
compensation, 161
compliance, 155
components of a curl, 329
compound dyes, 132, 502
concave lines, 287
concave profile, 249
concealers, 622
concentrates, 497
conditioners, 123-126, 491
conduction, 103
conductor, 89, 90
conical rollers, 336

conjunctivitis, 590
connective tissue, 65
consultation, 259
  four C's, 258-259
consumerism, 139
contact dermatitis, 584
contagious disease, 584
contaminated, 56
contour tips, 27
contouring, and highlighting,
  624-625
contraindications, 596
convection, 103
convex lines, 287
convex profile, 249
corporation, 153
corrugations, 544
corrugator, 72
cortex, 180, 183
cosmetology, 22
cosmetic spatula, 549
cotton balls, 547
cotton pads/swabs, 594
cotton roll, 514
cotton strips, 433
counterclockwise movement,
  of hair, 326-327
cover letter, 142
cowlick, 302
CPR (Cardiopulmonary
  Resuscitation), 96
cranium, bones of, 67-68
cream masks, 593
crest area, 272
crimping irons, 322
croquignole, 414, 416
cross-checking, 292
crown, 286
crusts, 587
curl segment, 399
curl reformation, 128, 454
  consult, 461-462
  essentials, 456-458
  infection control and safety,
    459-461
  service, 460
  theory, 454-456
curling iron techniques, 357-
  358
curly hair considerations, 304
current, electric, 89, 91-93
cushion brush, 321
cushion end paper
  technique, 420
custom wrapping patterns, 424
  partial perms, 418, 426
  perimeter perms, 425

644   INDEX

iggyback, 425
icle, 180, 539
ream or oil, 548
n hair, 180, 183
of the nail, 539
ail care, 553-554
ipper, 549
usher, 548
emover cream, 547
ved shapes, 327
indrical rollers, 336
toplasm, 64

ndruff, 189
description, 189
shampoos, 122
treatment, 102
rk colors, 617
rker skin makeup application,
637-639
rts, 393
& C red no. 7 calcium
ake, 133
colorization,
degrees of, 498
ltoid, 74
mi-permanent colors,
494, 522
ndrite, 80
nsity, of hair, 254, 432, 445
pressor septi, 72
rmatitis, 590
rmatitis venenata, 584
rmatology, 577
rmis, 578, 579
sign decisions
adaptability, 236-251
clothing, 255-256
communication, 258-261
composition, 258-266
hair, 251-255
ifestyle, 256-257
personality, 260-263
sign elements, 221
sign line, 292
sign principles, 232
tailing, of hairstyle, 334
velopers, 129, 131, 500-501
agonal lines, 224
ator, 70
amond facial shape, 246, 248
makeup for, 616
aphragm, 85
ffusers, 336
gestive system, 66
gital nerve, 83

dimethicones, 126
diplococci, 46
direct application, 101, 102
direct current (DC), 91
direct method, 100
direction, of hair, 319-320
directional distribution, 289
disinfection, 53-56
    of brush or comb, 55
    definition of, 50
    guidelines and procedures,
        55-56
    in infection control, 53-54
    level of infection control, 57
    precautions, 56
disinfectants, 53
displays, in retailing, 174-176
distribution
    of hair, 288-289
    and molding, 324-325
distributor sales consultant, 155
disulfide bond, 115
double bagging, 56
double chin, 633
    makeup for, 633
double-process blond,
    498-499
    completion, 530
    preparation, 529
    procedure, 529-530
    retouch, 530-531
double-prong clips, 336
drabbers, 497
dramatic style, 256
draping, 195-214
    for chemical services, 435,
        460, 517, 598
    essentials, 202
    for hair design services, 338
    infection control and
        safety, 203
    procedure, 205-207
    theory, 195-196
dry scalp treatment, 102, 201
dry skin, 583
    characteristics, 583
    masks, 594
    treatment, 102

E

ear, muscles of, 72
ecology, 44
eczema, 590
efficacy, 50
efferent nerves, 81
effleurage, 592
elasticity, of hair, 123, 431,

445
electric clippers, 278
electric current, 89, 91
    effects of, 97
    electrochemical effects, 97
electric heater, 549
electric nail services, 561
electricity
    in cosmetology, 97-106
    and electric current, 89
    principles, 89
    safety, 94-96
    vocabulary, 89
electrons, 111
electrode, 98
electrotherapy, 89, 97-106
elements, 110-112
elliptical shape, 179-180
emery board, 548
emotional buyer, 171
emulsifiers, 120, 133
emulsions, 119
end bonds, 113
    see also peptide bonds
end paper techniques, 419-420
end papers, 433
end texturizing, 294
ends technique, 358
    see also curling
        iron techniques
ends-to-base technique, 358
    see also curling iron
        techniques
endocrine system, 66, 85
environment, in design
    decisions, 260
enzymes, 84
EPA (Environmental Protection
    Agency), 53
epicranium, 71
epidermis, 578
epithelial tissue, 65
eponychium, 539
esophagus, 84
essential oils, 201
ergonomics, 29-31
ethics, 40-41
    professional code of, 41
ethmoid bone, 68
etiology, 541
eumelanin, 184, 483
evening makeup application,
    636-637
excretion, 577, 580
excretory system, 66, 85
excoriations, 587
exercise, 23

exfoliate, in facials, 600
expenses, and income, 158-160
extensor, 74
external carotid artery (ECA), 78
external maxillary, 78
extreme porosity, 488
eye injury, 60
eye shadow, 618, 626
eyelashes, artificial, 627-628
eyeliner, 626
eyebrow, 608
    makeup, 625-626
    waxing, 609-611
eyes, 65
    muscles, 72

F

face
    head and neck nerves, 81-82
    structure, 242
facial
    basic, 597
    completion, 603
    equipment, 595
    masks, 593
    preparation, 598
    procedure, 598-603
    shapes, 243-247
    skeleton, 68
facial powders, 628
facial steamer, 595
fall, 399
fan brush, 594
Faradic Current, 100
fat, 24
fatty alcohols, 126
favus, 48
FDA (Food and Drug
    Administration), 132,
    193, 490, 564
feet, 27
filing, nails, 566, 569, 572
fillers, 364, 496-497
fill-ins, of acrylic nails, 573
financial statement, 152
finger bowl, 549
finger, and shear position, 291
finger styling, 354
fingerwaves, 340-341
    completion, 351
    preparation, 350
    procedure, 351
finishing products, 135
first aid, 58-60
    bleeding and wounds, 58
    burns, 58
    choking, 59

COSMETOLOGY FUNDAMENTALS

645

cream, 338
eye injury, 60
fainting, 59
fixed rent, 157
flat bones, 67
flat, volume and indentation
pincurls, 344-345
flagella, 47
flexor, 74
floor plan, 155-156
fluorescent light, 104
foil/thermal strips, 513
follicle, 179
folliculitis, 590
forehead, high or broad
makeup for, 633
form
in hair design, 222, 316-317
in sculpting, 272-277
foundation, 27, 623-624
fragilitis crinium, 187
franchise, 153
free edge, 539
freeform painting, 509
french manicure, 560
frequency, 92
friction
in combing and brushing, 187
in massage, 199, 592
fringe, 287
fringe and nape variations, 303
frontalis muscle, 71
frontal artery, 78
frontal bone, 67
fungicidals, 54
furuncles, 589
furrows, 544
fuse, 95

G

Galvanic Current, 98-99
electrotherapy, 98
galvanic electrolysis, 613
gasses, 109
gastrointestinal infections, 47
gamine style, 256
gel
for hair, 306, 323, 336
nails, 574
general circulation, 77
general disinfectant, 547
general electrification, 101
general infection, 49
general orientation
program, 146
general shock, 96
genes, 184
glands
types of, 86

glass container, 549
glass or plastic bowl, 513
glasses, 250-251
selecting styles, 250-251
gloves, 27
glycerin, 133
glyceryl monostearate, 133
goals, 140, 150
good samaritan laws, 58
graduated form sculpture, 273,
290, 317
gradation, sculpture, 274
grammar, in communication,
33-34
gray hair, 484
greater auricular nerve, 82
greater occipital nerve, 82
greeting, the client, 34
gross anatomy, 63
grounding wire, 95
growth patterns, in hair,
255, 302
guest appearances, 148

H

habits, 39-40
hair, 113
care, 185
cells, 179-181
and climate, 187
and clothing, 195
density, 185, 254, 432
and design composition, 217
and design decisions, 216
disorders, 189
evaluation, 185-187
elasticity, 186
growth, 180-182
and lifestyle, 256
loss, 189-194
and personality, 260-263
porosity, 186, 431, 445,
487-488
pressing, 354
shape, 225
structure and behavior, 182
test for strength, 186
texture, 185, 461
theory, 179
treatments, 189
hair additions, 403
bonding, strand by strand,
409-410
bonding, wefts, 408-409
drawing board, 403
hackle, 403
methods, 403-410
off-the-scalp braiding,
403-404

on-the-scalp braiding,
404-405
track and sew, 406
hair care, and image, 26
hair color, 129
changing existing, 488-489
chemistry, 489-490
considerations, 487-488
identifying existing, 482
intensity of, 481
level of, 479
theory, 471
hair coloring, 469-536
application, 505-506
cap highlighting, 510
client consultation, 519-520
double-process blond,
498-499
draping for, 517
essentials, 511-515
equipment, 514-515
retouch, 506
lowlighting, 507
retouch, 511
infection control and safety,
515-516
oxidative color: darker result,
525-526
retouch, 526
oxidative color: lighter result,
526-528
guidelines, 526
retouch, 528
predispostion (skin patch) test,
516-517
problems and solutions,
531-533
products, 512-513
promoting and retailing,
521-522
record card/release form, 521
removal techniques, 534-535
semi-permanent color,
491-492
retouch, 534
strand test, 518-519
surface painting, 509, 512
temporary color,
490-491, 523
tint back, 533-534
tools/supplies, 513-514
hair bulb, 179-180
hair fiber, 179
hairpins, 370, 388
hair pressing, 354-355
hair removal, 604-613
consultation, 606
equipment, 605
essentials, 604-605

infection control and safety,
605
permanent, 612-613
products, 604
temporary, 606-612
tools/supplies, 605
hair root, 179
hair sculpting, 269-310
basic forms, 272-274
consultation, 307-308
essentials, 305-307
equipment, 307
form, 270
fundamentals, 269
infection control and
safety, 307
procedures, 286-292
products, 306
station, 307
structure, 271
texture, 270-271
theory, 269
tools/supplies, 306
hairpieces, 398-400
see also wigs
hair design, 311-380
base control-indentation, 331
base controls, 329-331
base size, 330
client consultation, 339-340
components of a curl, 329
direction, 319-320
distribution and molding,
324-325
essentials, 335-337
equipment, 337
finishing, 333-335
form, 316-317
infection control and
safety, 337-338
movement, 325
partings, 328
parts of a pincurl, 341
primary considerations, 315
products, 323
sectioning, 367
shapes, 325-327, 332
texture, 318-319
theory, 313-340
tool position, 332
tools/supplies, 335-336
half-off base pincurl, 343
halitosis, 25
hand lotion, 548
hand muscles, 74
hand, and nail examination,
541-542
hand nerves, 83
hand washing, 51

ndbook, for salon, 160
nds, 27
nds, and wrists, 30-31
ad lice, 48, 189
ad band or covering, 599
ad position, for hair
 sculpting, 287
alth, body and mind, 23-31
alth risks, of chemicals, 136
art, 65, 75-76
art facial shape, 247
 makeup for, 616
at burns, 59
at energy, 103
at rays, 71
at waves, 415
ated lamps, 515
ating effects, 97
nna, 132, 502
redity, and hair, 182
rpes Simplex, 585
rtz rating, 91
h frequency current, 103
h frequency machine, 595
ing, 161
tology, 63
V (Human Immunodeficiency
 Virus), 47-48
es, 586
lding spray, 388
neycomb ringworm, 48, 189
oded dryer, 96
rizontal lines, 288
t brush/comb, 336
t oil manicure, 561
man Hepatitis B (HBV), 47
man relations, 36-41
merus, 69
draulic chair, 307, 337,
 389, 514
dration, 577
drochloric acids, 84
drogen, 111
drogen bond, 114
drogen peroxide, 129
giene, 25
oid, 68
perhidrosis, 589
perpigmentation, 588
pertrophy, 587
ponychium, 539

age, 26
clothing, 28
feet, 27
hands, 27

hair care, 26
posture, 28
skin care and makeup, 26
immunity, 49
inactive bacteria, 47
income, expenses and, 158-160
incandescent light, 104
increase-layered form
 sculpture, 273
indentation pincurls, 345
infection, 48-49
infection control, 50
inferior labial, 78
inferioris, 70
inflammation, 584
infraorbital, 82
infrared lamp, 434, 458, 595
infrared light, 105
infratrochelar nerve, 82
ingredients,
 for conditioners, 126
ingrown nails, 544
inorganic chemistry, 110
insertion, of muscle, 71
instant conditioners, 125
insulator, 89
insurance, 157-158
 types of, 157-158
insurance agent, 154
integumentary system, 66, 86
intensifiers, 497
intensity, of hair color, 481, 616
internal carotid artery, 78
intestines, 65
inventory, and product control,
 162-163
invisible light, 105
IRS, 158
irritant contact dermatitis, 584
isopropyl lanolate, 133
itch mite, 189

J

jaw, broad or square, 633
 makeup for, 633
jawline, and makeup, 614-616
J and L color ring, 388
job, 140-147
 benefits, 145-146
 interviews, 142-144
 search, 140-141
jugular veins, 78

K

keratin, 113, 181
keratinization, 181
kidneys, 65

kilowatt, 91
koilonychia, 544

L

labels, on disinfectants, 53-54
lamp, 549
lancets, 57
lanolin, 133
lanthionization, 128
large figure, hairstyle, 240
large intestine, 84
large-tooth comb, 334
laser hair removal, 613
latissimus dorsi, 73
Lauramide DEA, 133
law of color, 472
lawyer, 155
lease, 157
left atrium, 75
left auricle, 77
left ventricle, 75
Leg,
 leg, ankle and foot bones, 69
 leg and foot muscles, 75
 arteries of the lower leg
 and foot, 78
 nerves of the lower leg
 and foot, 83
lesions, of the skin, 283,
 585-587
lesser occipital, 82
leuconychia, 545
leukoderma, 588
level, of hair color, 482
levator palpebrae, 72
lifestyle, 256-257
 family, 257
 hobbies, 257
 job/career, 257
 money investment, 257
 skills, 257
 time, 257
lifter, 335
light rays, 103
light therapy, 103-106
 fluorescent light, 104
 incandescent light, 104
 infrared light, 105
 invisible light, 105
 ultraviolet light, 105
light-cured gels, 574
lighteners, 130-131, 498
 degrees of decolorization, 498
 off-the-scalp, 131
 on-the-scalp, 130-131
line of demarcation, 491
liquid dry shampoos, 122

liquid polish, 548
liquid soap, 51, 119
liquid sterilant, 57
liquid tissue, 65
liquids, 109, 119
line, 223
 in sculpting, 283
 in hair design, 224
lips, 27
 makeup for, 630-631
liver, 65, 85
load, 89
local infection, 49
local shock, 96
location, of salon, 154
logarithmic, 116
logical buyer, 171
long bones, 67
long hair, 210
 form, 362-363
 fundamentals, 310
 procedures, 379
 and shampooing, 204
 styling, 28
long nerve fibers, 80
long nose, 632
 makeup for, 632
long wavelengths, 104
lowlighting, 507
lunula, 543
lungs, 65, 85
lymph, 79
lymph nodes, 79
lymphatic system, 79
lymph-vascular system, 79

M

machine-made wigs, 387
macules, 585
magnesium aluminum
 silicate, 134
magnifying lamp, 595
makeup, 26-27
 application, 635-639
 basic, 635
 bridal, 639-640
 evening, 636-637
 ethnic, 637-639
 basics, 27
 color theory, 616
 consultation, 619-620
 essentials, 619-620
 for facial shapes, 614-616
 infection control and
 safety, 619
 techniques and products,
 620-634

theory, 614
making change, 164
Malassezia, 189
male manicure, 556
male-pattern baldness, 192
malpractice insurance, 157
mandible, 68
mandibular branch, 82
manicure, 552
  completion, 555
  consultation, 551
  equipment, 549
  essentials, 547-549
  infection control and safety, 550
  preparation, 552
  procedure, 552
  products, 547-548
  tools/supplies, 548-549
mantle, 539
market need, 154
mascara, 627
massage, 67
  basic movements of, 592
  facial, 68
  optional, neck and
    shoulder, 208
  scalp, 198-199
  scalp, basic, 206
masseter, 73
Master Sketcher comb, 285
marcel technique, 358
  see also curling
    iron techniques
material safety data sheet
  (MSDS), 53, 60
matter, 109-115
matting, of hair, 188
maxillae, 68
maxillary branch, 82
measles,
measuring device, 513
measuring tape, for wigs, 389
mechanical, or magnetic,
  effects, 97
mechanical equipment, 96
medicated rinses, 124
medicated shampoos, 122
medium hair, 182
medulla, 180
medulla oblongata, 80
melanin, 184
  in the hair, 184
  in the skin, 184
melanocytes, 184
melanoderma, 588
melanonychia, 544
melanosomes, 184
mending fiber (nails), 549

mentalis, 73
merchandise, pricing, 175
metabolism, 64
metacarpals, 69
metalic salt, 132
  test for, 436
metalic dyes, 502
methylisothiazolinone, 133
microbes, 45, 50, 51
microbiology, 45-49
  bacteria, 45
  growth, 47
  movement, 47
  external parasites, 48
  immunity, 49
  infection, 48-49
  viruses, 47-48
microscopic anatomy, 63
milia, 589
miliaria rubra, 590
milliampere, 90
mitosis, 578
mixed nerves, 81
modacrylic wig fibers, 386, 394
moisturizers, 635
moisturizing agent, 201
moisturizing conditioners, 125
molding hair, 322, 324
molecules, 112
moles, 588
monilethrix, 188
monofilaments, 386
motivation, to buy, 171-172
motor nerves, 81
mousse, 135, 306, 336, 491
MSDS, 53
mumps, 47
muscles, 70-75
  ear, 72
  eye and nose, 72
  hand, 74
  leg and foot, 75
  mastication, 73
  mouth, 72-73
  neck and back, 73
  scalp, 71
  shoulder, chest and arm, 74
muscular system, 66, 70-75
muscular tissue, 65
myology, 70

N

naevus, 588
nail, 539-574
  bed, 539
  body, 539
  conditions, 545-546
  diseases, 542-543

  disorders, 543-545
  external parasites, 48,
    546, 573
  groove, 539
  growth, 540
  matrix, 539
  root, 539
  shapes, 547
  structure of, 539
  theory of, 539-546
  wall, 539
nail art, 561
nail bleach, 548
nail brush, 549
nail and cuticle scissors, 549
nail repair, with silk, 560-561
nail service cushion, 549
nail service stool, 549
nail service table, 549
nail strengthener, 548
nail technician, 546
nail tips, 564
  completion, 567
  preparation, 565
  procedure, 564-566
nail tips, with acrylic
  overlay, 567
  completion, 569
  preparation, 567
  procedure, 567-569
nameplate, 91, 92-93
nape, in sculpting, 287
nape, and fringe variations, 303
nasal, 68
natural-bristle hair brush, 202
natural distribution, 288
natural fall, 271
natural hair color, 485
natural nail care, 546
natural parts, 302
natural style, 255
neck
  and back strain prevention, 29
  bones, 68
  muscles of, 73
  types of, 241
neck strip, 196, 306
needle and thread, 388
nephrons, 85
nerve impulses, 80
nerve terminal, 80
nerve tissue, 65
nerves, 80-83
  arm and hand, 83
  face, head and neck, 81-82
  and massage, 83
  types of, 81
nervous system, 66, 79-83

  autonomic, 83
  central, 79-80
  subsystems of, 79
  peripheral, 80-81
networking, 147
neurology, 79
neutral colors, 231, 251-252
neutralizing, 428, 451
  in perms, 426
  in relaxers, 451, 454
  shampoo, 451, 456
neutrons, 111
nevus, 588
nodules, 188
non-aerosol hairspray, 337
nonflammable liquid
  shampoo, 388
nonoxidative colors, 129
  semi-permanent, 129,
    491-492
  temporary, 129, 490-491
nonpathogenic bacteria, 45
nonverbal communication, 32
normal hair loss, 190
normal projection, 271
normal skin, 583
nose
  corrective makeup for,
    631, 632
notching, 295
nucleus, of cell, 64
nutrition, 24

O

objective symptoms, of the skin
  585
oblong facial shape, 245
  makeup for, 615
oblong and spiral bricklay, 423
occipital artery, 78
occipital bone, 67, 286
occipitalis muscle, 71
occipito-frontalis, 71
Occupational Safety and
  Health Administration (OSHA), 5
off-base pincurls, 343
off-base tool position, 330-333
off-the-scalp braiding, 403-404
off-the-scalp lighteners, 499
ohm, 89, 91
oil lighteners, 130
oily skin, 583
  masks, 594
oleic acid, 133
on-base pincurls, 342
on-base tool position, 422
on-the-scalp braiding, 377, 40
on-the-scalp lighteners, 499

top of the fingers, 280
ychatrophia, 543
ychauxis, 545
ychia, 543
ychocryptosis, 544
ychogryposis, 544
ycholysis, 543
ychomycosis, 542
ychophagy, 546
ychoptosis, 543
en circuit, 93
erating expense, 158-159
hthalamic branch, 82
ponens, 74
ngewood stick, 548
al hygiene, 25
icularis oculi, 72
icularis oris, 72
ganic chemistry, 110
gans, 65
entation, of the salon, 146
gin, of muscle, 71
67
HA (Occupational Safety and
Health Administration), 53
eology, 67
tlining, in sculpting, 300
al facial shape, 244
makeup for, 614
al shape nail, 547
ercomb techniques, 298
clipper-over-comb
technique, 298
comb control, 298-299
shear-over-comb
technique, 298
erdirected base control, 330
erdirected tool position, 330
erload, 93
erloading, 93-94
nership, 151-166
ypes of, 153
see also salon business
dative color: darker result,
525-526
completion, 526
preparation, 525
procedure, 525-526
etouch, 526
dative color: lighter result,
526-528
guidelines, 526
etouch, 528
dative colors, 493
demi-permanent, 129, 494
permanent, 129, 494-495
dation, 129, 501
ygen, 76-77

oxygenated, 77

P
palm down, 280
palm-to-palm, 280
palm up, 280
pancake, or pan-stick,
foundations, 623
panthenol, 133
papilla, 179
papules, 585
paraffin wax, 593
parietal artery, 78
parasites, 48
paronychia, 542
partial perms, 426
parting, 287-288, 328
for sculpting, 287-288
for hairstyling, 328
partnership, 153
passive immunity, 49
pathogenic bacteria, 45, 51
pear facial shape, 246
makeup for, 615
pectoralis, 74
pediculosis capitis, 48, 189
pedicure, 556-560
bath or tub, 557
chair, 557
completion, 560
equipment, 557
essentials, 556-557
foot rest, 557
preparation, 557
procedure, 558-560
table, 557
tools/supplies, 557
pelvic tilt, 29
peptide bonds, 113
performance review, 151
pericardium, 75
perimeter, of the hairline, 287
perimeter perming, 425
perionychium, 539
peripheral nervous system,
80-81
peristalsis, 84
perm bib, 433
permanent color removal, 535
permanent hair colors, 129,
494-495
permanent hair removal, 604,
612-613
blend method, 613
galvanic electrolysis
method, 613
thermolysis method, 613

perming, 413-441
base size, 421
blotting, 428
chemical phase, 426-431
chemistry of, 126-127
client consultation, 437-438
croquignole, 416
custom wrapping
patterns, 424
draping for, 435
end paper techniques,
419-420
ergonomic tips, 426
essentials, 432-434
hair analysis for, 431-432
history, 413-415
infection control and safety,
434-435
neutralizing, 428
new technology, 415
perm solution, 427, 429-431
perm tools, 417-418
perm procedure overview,
438-439
perming patterns, 423
physical phase, 415-426
preliminary test curls, 436
problems and solutions,
439-441
rinsing, 428
scalp analysis, 435
spiral, 416-417
test curl, 436
test for metallic salt, 436
theory, 413
tool position, 421-422
perpendicular distribution, 288
personal appearance, 142
personal ethics, 41
personal hygiene, 25
personal qualities, 143-144
personality, 36-37
in hair design, 260-263
petrissage, 199
pH, 116
adjusters, 134
level, 116
meter, 117, 134
paper, 117, 134
pencil, 117, 134
ranges, 134
scale, 116-117
value, 117
phalanges, 69
pharynx, 84
phenoxyethanol, 133
pheomelanin, 184, 483
philosophy, policies and

procedures, of salon, 160-161
phoresis, 99
physical change, of matter, 109
physiology, 63
picks, 336, 420
piggyback perms, 425
pigmentation
problems, 546
of the skin, 581-582
pincurls, 341-345
base controls, 342-343
base shapes, 342
components of, 341
flat, 344
indentation, 345
types of, 343-345
volume, 344
pityriasis, 189
plain shampoos, 121
plastic applicator bottle, 513
plastic cap, 202
plastic client cape, 306, 338
plastic sectioning clips, 433
plasma, 76
platysma, 73
pledglets, 547
podiatrist, 27
points, lines and angles,
223-225
in sculpting, 223-225
point of origin, 324
polish remover, 547
polypeptide molecules, 84
polysorbates, 133
pomade, 306, 337
pons, 80
porcelain bowl, 389
porosity, 123, 445, 487-488
posterior auricular artery, 78
posterior auricular nerve, 82
posterior dilator noris, 72
postpartum alopecia, 193
potential hydrogen, 116
posture, 28
powder dry shampoos, 122
powders, 119,
facial, 628
prebooking, 148
predisposition test, 516-517
pressing comb, 321
pressing and curling,
354-355, 360
pressing oil, 337
pricing, of salon services, 162
primary hairstyling
considerations, 315-320
direction, 319-320
form, 316-318

COSMETOLOGY FUNDAMENTALS
649

movement, *319-320*

texture, *318-319*

primary skin lesions, 585-586

primitive hair germ, 179

prism, 104

procerus, 72

product information, 132-136

product liability insurance, 157-158

professional appearance, 265

professional ethics, 41

professional products, 168-169

professional relationships, 146-151

profit, or gain, 172

progression, in hair design, 234

projection, of hair, 271

prominent chin, 632

makeup for, *632*

promotional displays, 175

promotional literature, 148

proper lighting, 618

property insurance, 157

proportion, 219

body shapes, *237-240*

face, *242-248*

profile, *249*

special considerations, *250-251*

standard, *237*

protective apron, 514

protective cape, 514

protective gloves, 27, 433, 514

protective skin cream, 433

protein, 24, 112-115

protons, 111

protoplasm, 64

pseudofolliculitis barbae, 590

pseudomonacidals, 53

psoriasis, 586

pterygium, 545

public hygiene, 25

pulmonary artery, 77

punctuality, 143

pustules, 586

Q

quadratus labii superioris, 72

quaternium-15, 133

R

rabies, 47

radial, artery 78

radial nerve, 83

radiation, 103

radius, 69

rake comb, 335

razor, 278, 282, 306

dispenser, *284*

etching, *296*

how to hold, *282-283*

inserting blade, *283*

parts, *282*

removing blade, *283*

rotation, *296*

safety tips, *283*

RDA (Recommended Dietary Allowances), 24

receding chin, 632

makeup for, *632*

receptionist duties, 163-166

record card, 173

for chemical services, *438, 461*

for hair coloring service, *514*

for nail services, *551*

for skin care, *596*

rectangle pattern, 423

rectangle perm wrap, 423

completion, *439*

preparation, *438*

procedure, *439*

referrals, 147

reflex action, 81

relaxer retouch, 442

relaxers

chemistry of, *127-128*

see also chemical relaxing completion, *467*

preparation, *463-464*

procedure, *464-467*

rental agreements, 157

repetition, in design, 233

reproductive system, 66, 86

requirements of a salon, 154

resistance, 91

respiratory system, 66, 85

rest and relaxation, 23

resumés, 141-142

retail display guidelines, 175

retailing, 166-176

knowledge and confidence, *168*

prescribing, *167*

selling, *166-168*

retouch color, 506

retouch relaxer, 442, 448

richter scale, 116

ringed hair, 188

ringworm, 48, 189, 542

rinses, 123-124, 201

risorius, 73

rollable color/product table, 514

rollers, 321, 336, 346

in curvature shapes, *347*

diameter, *346*

in straight shapes, *346-347*

romantic style, 255

root

hair, *179*

nail, *539*

sheath, *179*

rosacea, 589

round brushes, 320

round facial shape, 244

makeup for, *615*

S

salary structure, 161

salivary glands, 84

salon business

job search, *140-146*

ownership, *151-166*

professional relationships, *146-151*

retailing, *166-175*

salon industry, *139-140*

salon products

and pH ranges, *134-135*

salt bond, 114

sanitation, 50, 51-53

saprophytes, 45

scales, 586

scalp conditions, 189

scalp massage, 195

completion, *212*

essentials, *200-202*

manipulations, *199*

preparation, *210*

procedure, *210-212*

theory, *198-199*

scalp muscles, 71

scalp toner, 201

scalp treatment, 102

scapula, 69

scars, 587

scheduling appointments, 166

scrunching layered form, 354

sculpting positions, 280

sculpting comb, 285

sculpting lotion, 306

sculptured nails

completion, *572*

preparation, *570*

procedure, *570-572*

seasonal disease, 584

sebaceous gland, 180, 580-581

sebum, 180, 580

seborrhea, 589

secondary skin lesions, 586-587

sectioning clips, 433, 457

sectioning, for sculpting,

286-287

sectioning, in hair design, 325, 367

selling, 166-167

semi-permanent colors, 129, 491, 493, 494

semi-permanent hair coloring, 524

sensation, 577

sensory nerves, 81

series wiring, 93

serratus anterior, 74

shampooing

bowl, *202, 307, 337, 434, 458, 515*

chair, *202*

essentials, *200-202*

preparation, *204*

procedure, *204-210*

theory, *196-197*

shampoos, 119-120

how they work, *123*

the role of water in, *120-12*

types of, *121-123*

shears, 277, 278

how to hold, *279, 280*

parts of, *279*

shear-over-comb, 298

shifted distribution, 288

shock, 96

short circuit, 93-94

short wave lengths, 104

shoulders, 31

hair designs for, *241-242*

side bonds, 114-115

silica, 134

Sinusoidal Current, 100, 103

skeletal system, 66, 67-69

skin, 65, 577

color classifications, *623*

composition of, *578-582*

disorders and diseases, *584-590*

function of, *577*

pigmentation, *581-582*

types, *582-584*

skin care, 26, 590

consultation, *597*

essentials, *593-595*

masks, *593*

massage, *591-593*

skin patch test, 516-517

skin tags, 587

skip waves, 345

skull, 67

slide cutting, 296

slithering, 296

small intestine, 84

mall organisms, 45
mall pox, 47
oapless shampoos, 121
oaps, 119
ocial security, 158
odium hydroxide relaxer,
  128, 443
odium lauryl sulfate, 134
ole proprietorship, 153
olid form sculpture, 272
olids, 109
olutions, 118
olvents, 133
oace requirements,
  for the salon, 155-156
oatula, 457, 594, 605
oeed dry, 548
oherical spores, 47
PF, 582
ohenoid, 68
oinal cord, 79, 80
oiral perm method, 413
oiral technique, 416-417
  curling irons, 358
oirilla, 46
olit ends, 187
oray bottle, 306, 433
oray gel, 337
quare facial shape, 245, 248
  makeup for, 615
quare form sculpture,
  277, 289
aphylococci, 46
earic acid, 133
erilization, 50, 56-57
ernocleido mastoideus, 73
ernum, 69
omach, 65, 84
raight profile, 249
raight shapes, in
  hair design, 325
raightening, or flat, irons,
  321, 336, 359
rand test, 460, 518-519
ratum corneum, 579
ratum germinativum, 578
ratum gransulosum, 579
ratum lucidum, 579
ratum spinosum, 579
reptococci, 46
riated muscles, 70
ructure, 271
  in sculpting, 271
ructure graphic, 271
ubborn buyer, 171
yling lotion, 337, 456
ibcutaneous, 578, 581
ibjective symptoms, 585

suction, 595
sudoriferous glands, 580
sulfur, 110
sunlight, 105
supercilia, 182
superficial temporal, 78
superior labial, 78
superior vena cava, 77
superioris, 70
supinator, 74
supraorbital, 82
surface painting, 512
surfactants, 120-121
suspensions, 118
switch, 399
symmetrical balance, 235
systemic circulation, 77
systemic infection, 49

T

tail comb, 322-323, 335, 514
talcum powder, 513
taper shears, 277, 280
  parts of, 281
tapotement, 199, 592
taxes, 158
teamwork, 40
telephone techniques, 164-166
telogen, 181
telogen effluvium, 193
temporal bones, 67
temporal nerve, 82
temporalis muscle, 73
temporary colors, 129, 490-
  491, 523
temporary hair removal,
  606-609
tendonitis, 30
Tesla Current, 101-102
  uses for in cosmetology, 102
test curl, 428
tetanus, 46, 47
texture .
  in nature, 228, 445
  of hair, 254
  in sculpting, 270, 271
  in hair design, 229, 318-319
texturizing, 293
  considerations, 293
  types of, 294-297
thermal design
  infection control and
    safety, 339
  procedure, 349-351, 360
  theory, 313-315
thermal equipment, 96
thermal irons, 355-356
  considerations, 359

  how to hold, 356
  manipulations, 356-357
  techniques, 357-358
thermal reconditioning, 452-
  454
thickeners, 133
thioglycolic acid, 127, 414
thorax, 69
three-sectioning
  of the face, 243
three-strand overbraid, 376
three-strand underbraid, 377
thrombocytes, 76
timer, 434, 458, 515
tinea capitis, 48, 189
tint back, 533-534
tips, nail, 564-569
  with acrylic overlay, 567-569
  completion, 567, 569
  preparation, 564, 567
  procedure, 564-566,
    567-569
tissues, 65
tocopherol, 133
tone, 474
  identifying, in hair color,
    485-487
  of voice, 33
toners, 496
tool position, 330
  half-off base, 330, 331,
    332, 422
  off base, 330, 331, 332, 422
  on base, 330, 331, 332, 422
  overdirected, 330
  underdirected, 330, 331,
    332, 422
toupee, 399, 400-402
  completed styles, 402
  establishing front hairline, 402
  measuring, 401
tourniquet, 58
towel, 196, 202, 433, 514, 594
track and sew hair additions,
  406-408
  sewing methods, 406-408
  tracking, 406
traction or traumatic
  alopecia, 193
transfer clients, 166
transverse artery, 78
trapezius muscles, 73
tricep, 74
trichology, 179
triethanolamine, 134
trifacial nerve, 81
trimmer, 300, 306
trisodium edetate, 133

tumors, 586
turbinal bone, 68
tweezers, 605, 618
tweezing, 634
two-way communication, 34-36

U

ulcers, 587
ulna bone, 69
ulnar, artery 78
ulnar nerve, 83
ultrasonic cleaner, 55
ultraviolet light (UV), 105-106
unactivated hair texture,
  228, 254
underdirected base control,
  330, 331, 332, 343, 422
Underwriter's Laboratory
  designation (UL), 91
undulating irons, 322, 359
uniformly layered form
  sculpture, 274, 317
universal precautions, 49
upper back muscles, 73
ureter, 85

V

vagus nerve, 76
van der Waal's Forces, 114, 115
variable rent, 157
varicose veins, 77
vegetable dyes, 132, 502
veins, 75-78
ventilation, 25, 52-53
verbal communication, 33-36
verruca, 587
vertical lines, 224, 288
vesicles, 585
vibration, 199, 592
vinegar rinses, 124
villi, 84
virgin darker technique, 505
virgin lighter technique, 506
virgin sodium hydroxide
  relaxer, 465
  completion, 467
  preparation, 463-464
  procedure; 465
virgin thio relaxer, 466
  completion, 467
  preparation, 463-464
  procedure, 466
viricidals, 53
viruses, 47-48
visible light, 104-106
volt, 89, 90
volume base control, 329-333
volume pincurls, 344

voluntary muscles, 70
vomer, 68

W
walk-in clients, 166
warm and cool colors, 475
water, 118
  purification, 121
  and shampoo, 120-121
watt, 89, 91
wave clamp, 336
wavelengths, 104
waxing, 609
  basic waxing, 609-612
weaving and slicing, 507-508
wen, 589
wet disinfectant container, 55
wet hair service, 204-207
  shampooing, 204-207
wet hair design, 323
  fingerwaves, 340-341
  overview, 349
  pincurls, 341-345
  rollers, 346-348
  skip waves, 345
  techniques, 350
wheals, 586
white blood cells (WBC), 76
white light, 104
whiteheads, 589
whorl, 303
wide-tooth comb, 514
wiglet, 398

wigs, 383-398
  blocking, 392-393
  cleaning and conditioning,
    394-396
  coloring, 396
  colors, 386
  composition, 386
  construction, 387
  customizing, 393
  essentials, 388-389
  infection control and
    safety, 389
  history, 383-385
  measurement and fitting,
    390-391
  putting on a wig, 391-392
  sculpting, 397
  setting and finishing, 398
  stretching or shrinking cap
    wigs, 393-394
Wood's lamp, 595
workers' compensation, 158
W-2 form, 158

Z
zygomatic, 68, 82
  bones, 68
  nerves, 82
zygomaticus muscle, 73